Woodsmith

VOLUME 33

2200 Grand Avenue
Des Moines, IA 50312
www.Woodsmith.com

Woodsmith

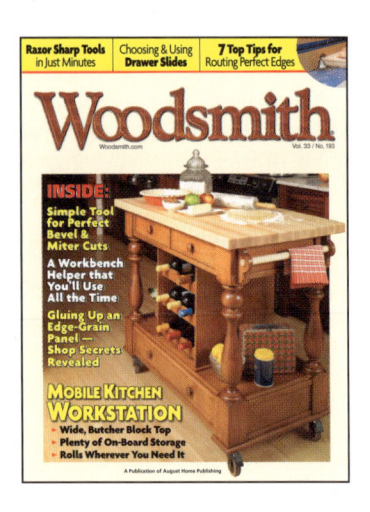

ISSUE NUMBER 193
February/March 2011

Projects

Cottage-Style Storage Cabinet 16
Bathroom storage has never looked better or been more practical.

Craft Center............ 22
The expansive worksurface and abundant storage make this project a crafter's dream.

Kitchen Workstation 32
This handsome workstation will transform your kitchen and become the center of attention.

Departments

Tips & Techniques 4
Metal Drawer Slides 8
Bench Grippers 10
Digital Angle Gauges....... 12
Perfect Edge Profiles 14
Shop Notebook........... 30
Edge-grain Top 40
Diamond Plate Sharpening .. 44
Spraying Water-Based Finish. 46
Table Top Edges........... 48
Q & A................. 50
Sources 51

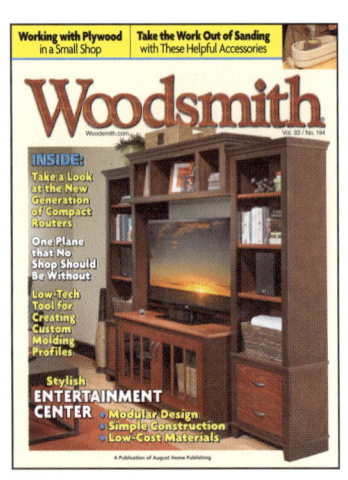

ISSUE NUMBER 194
April/May 2011

Projects

Marking Gauge 14
Work on an interesting project that you'll use every day in your shop.

Sliding-Door Wall Shelf..... 18
Simple, knock-down construction guarantees this practical project will go together in a flash.

Contoured Keepsake Box.... 22
This lidded box lets you pull out all the stops on a project with a manageable size.

Entertainment Center....... 30
Classic details, no-fuss joinery, and low-cost materials come together in a great project.

Departments

Tips & Techniques 4
Sanding Profiles & Contours.. 8
Compact Routers 10
Hardware Installation Jigs... 12
Shop Notebook........... 28
Plywood on the Table Saw .. 42
Shoulder Planes 44
Using Paste Wax 46
Scratch Stock 48
Q & A................. 50
Sources 51

ISSUE NUMBER 195
June/July 2011

Projects

Countertop Wine Rack 18
This stylish countertop wine rack features classic woodworking and custom details.

Classic Four Poster Bed......24
Inexpensive materials and simple construction make this bed an easy build with a timeless look.

Step-Back Cupboard 30
Fine proportions, a beadboard back, and a raised panel door tie everything together.

Departments

Tips & Techniques 4
7 High-Tech Hinges......... 8
Benchtop Router Tables 10
Wolfcraft Drill Guide....... 12
Perfect-Fitting Box Joints ... 14
Shop Notebook........... 32
Tips for Buying Lumber 44
Working with Milk Paint.... 46
The Versatile Chamfer...... 48
Q & A................. 50
Sources 51

VOLUME 33
THE YEAR AT A GLANCE

ISSUE NUMBER 196
August/September 2011

Projects

Curved-Handle Serving Tray 18
Round up some of those special scraps you've been saving and tackle this weekend project.

Veneered Credenza 22
The retro style of this project is a great opportunity to try something different.

Curio Cabinet 34
If you're a collector, this is a project you won't want to pass up.

Departments
Tips & Techniques 4
Cabinet Lighting 8
Hand Drills 10
Tapering Jig 12
Veneering Large Panels 14
Shop Notebook 32
Building Better Drawers . . . 42
Perfect Band Saw Cuts 44
Finishing Poplar 46
Construction Goals 48
Q & A 50
Sources 51

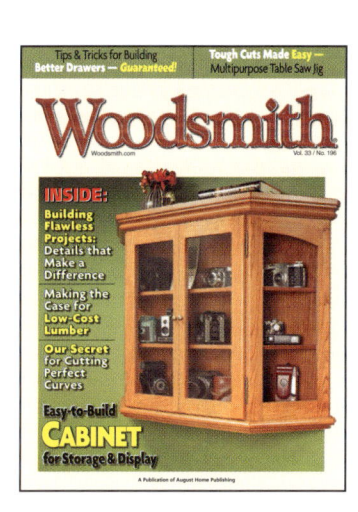

ISSUE NUMBER 197
October/November 2011

Projects

3 Small Gift Projects 16
Eye-catching looks and unique techniques combine for gifts you'll be proud to give.

Folding Table 24
This stylish, Craftsman-style table will double in size with next to no effort.

Jewelry Chest 34
Build a beautiful chest with versatile storage, a truly unique design, and a few new techniques.

Departments
Tips & Techniques 4
Mahogany 8
Air Compressors 10
5 Handy Tool Holders 12
Cutting Small Parts 14
Shop Notebook 32
Router Table Secrets 44
Using Water-Based Dye 46
Making Curved Parts 48
Q & A 50
Sources 51

ISSUE NUMBER 198
December/January 2012

Projects

Classic Entry Bench 16
Craft a lasting bench with a casual look and traditional mortise and tenon joinery.

Craftsman-Style Lamp 22
Stained glass panels set in solid-wood frames give this lamp an unbeatable style.

Cherry Armoire 30
With loads of storage, simple construction, and a modern look, this armoire has everything.

Departments
Tips & Techniques 4
Clean Cuts Every Time 8
5 Top Hand Tools 10
The Versatile Fast Joint Jig . . 12
Tips for Tight Dovetails . . . 14
Shop Notebook 28
Plans to Perfect Projects 42
Fast, Foolproof Finishing . . . 46
Face Frame Secrets 48
Sources 51

Woodsmith

Please contact us to find out about other Woodsmith products and services:

By Phone: 1-800-444-7527
By Mail: 2200 Grand Avenue, Des Moines IA 50312
By Email: woodsmith@woodsmith.com
Or Visit Our Web-Site: www.Woodsmith.com

Copyright 2012 August Home Publishing Co.

Razor Sharp Tools in Just Minutes | **Choosing & Using Drawer Slides** | **7 Top Tips for Routing Perfect Edges**

Woodsmith

Woodsmith.com

Vol. 33 / No. 193

INSIDE:

Simple Tool for Perfect Bevel & Miter Cuts

A Workbench Helper that You'll Use All the Time

Gluing Up an Edge-Grain Panel — Shop Secrets Revealed

MOBILE KITCHEN WORKSTATION

- Wide, Butcher Block Top
- Plenty of On-Board Storage
- Rolls Wherever You Need It

A Publication of August Home Publishing

looking inside

Table of Contents

from our readers
Tips & Techniques 4

all about
Metal Drawer Slides 8
Learn why metal slides provide a handy, versatile option for installing drawers.

tools of the trade
Bench Grippers 10
You're guaranteed to find a load of uses for these new benchtop accessories.

jigs and fixtures
Digital Angle Gauges 12
These easy-to-use, inexpensive gadgets make precise tool setups a snap.

techniques from our shop
Perfect Edge Profiles 14
Here are the tips and techniques you need to rout crisp edge profiles at the router table.

tips from our shop
Shop Notebook 30

woodworking technique
Edge-Grain Top 40
Take an in-depth, step-by-step look at assembling this woodworking standard.

working with tools
Diamond Plate Sharpening 44
You'd be hard pressed to find a faster sharpening method. We'll tell you why.

finishing room
Spraying Water-Based Finish 46
The combination of water-based finish and an HVLP spray system is hard to beat.

details of craftsmanship
Table Top Edges 48
We'll show you how to complement a design by choosing the right edge profile.

in the mailbox
Q & A 50

hardware and supplies
Sources 51

Cottage-Style Cabinet page 16

Craft Center page 22

projects

weekend project
Cottage-Style Storage Cabinet . . 16
Bathroom storage has never looked better — or been more practical. But the best thing about this project is that straightforward construction gets the job done in a flash.

designer series project
Craft Center 22   DESIGNER'S NOTEBOOK
The expansive worksurface and abundant storage make this project a gift from crafter's heaven. However, you'll find that all the woodworking is very down to earth.

heirloom project
Kitchen Workstation 32   DESIGNER'S NOTEBOOK
Which is the top draw — the versatility that will turn this project into the hub of activity in your kitchen, or the handsome appearance that will make it the center of attention?

Kitchen Workstation page 32

editor's note
Sawdust

Storage. No matter how much you have, it never seems like enough. That's why we decided to devote the three projects in this issue to overcoming storage challenges. Each one is designed to address storage problems in a different room of the house.

Kitchens and bathrooms are notorious for being short on storage. So that's where we started. For the kitchen, we designed a roll-around work cart. In addition to an ample worksurface, it provides plenty of on-board storage in the three drawers and an open storage bay for cookware or kitchen appliances. As an option, you can add a combination wine rack and shelf unit. And if you take a look at the photo on the cover, you'll see that this project is as attractive as it is functional.

Moving on to the bathroom, we're featuring a small storage cabinet. Its compact footprint allows it to fit in just about any bathroom. But inside there's plenty of room for towels, bathroom tissue, soap, or any of the dozens of items that always seem to accumulate in the bathroom.

The last project in this issue is one that can be used in a number of locations. It's a craft center that serves as a place to work on your craft projects and doubles as a multi-purpose storage unit as well. Individual "cubbies" provide room for books, supplies, and anything else you wish to store. Doors and drawers help to organize and conceal your items.

If you don't have a need for the large worksurface that the craft center offers, you can build the two end units alone and stack them to use as a combination bookcase and storage cabinet. It's a versatile project that can be used in a living room, basement, den, or craft room.

Terry

This symbol lets you know there's more information online at Woodsmith.com. There you'll see step-by-step videos, technique and project animation, bonus cutting diagrams, and a lot more.

from our readers

Tips & Techniques

Miter Saw Dust Collection

My miter saw sees a lot of use. Consequently the amount of sawdust it creates is overwhelming and it goes everywhere. To help get some control over this problem, I built the sliding dust port you see in the photo above.

The key component in this system is the large dust port. It's mounted to a plywood frame that slides in grooves in the surrounding frame's rails. This way, you can move the port to catch the sawdust when mitering.

The drawings show how it's all put together. The assembly is designed to bolt or clamp to the back of the miter saw station. It can be modified to suit your particular setup.

I started the construction by making the outside support frame. Grooves in the top and bottom pieces house a plywood dust port frame, as shown in details 'a' and 'c.' After assembling the frame, you can make the plywood frame to fit the dust port.

With the frame assembled, you can attach the large dust port to the plywood using a set of rabbeted cleats (main drawing and detail 'a'). Now you can fasten the assembly to the station and get to work.

Tim Kelley
Newport News, Virginia

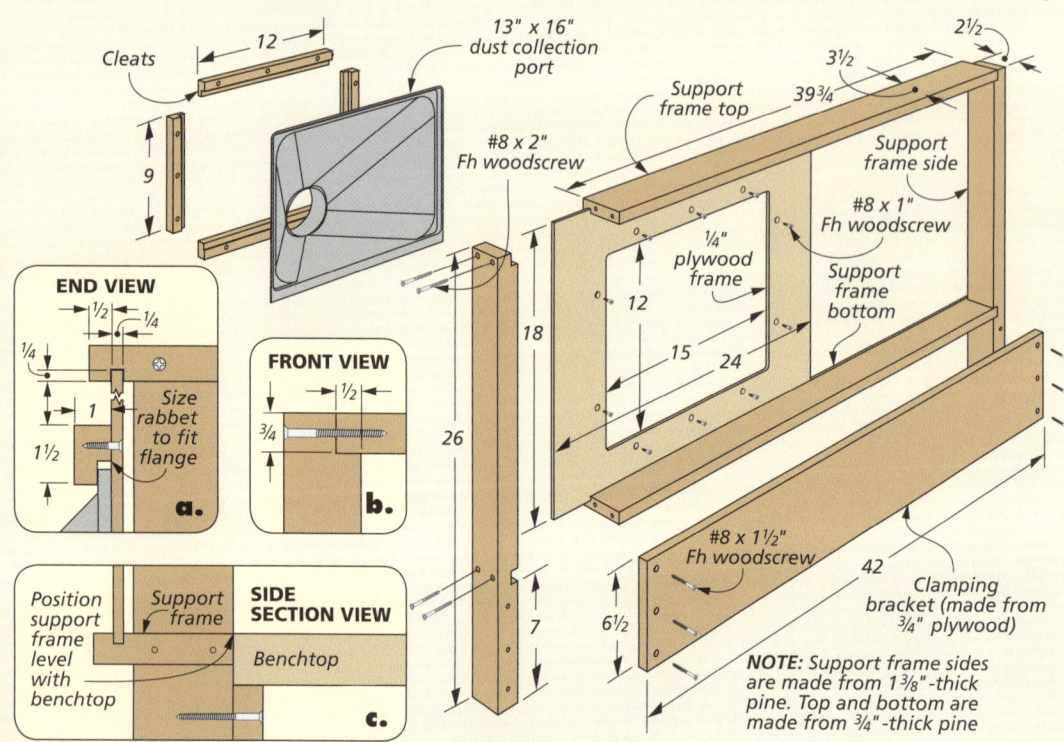

Point Storage

I could never find a good place to store my painter's points so they ended up scattered on the workbench. The little hook you see in the photo above solves the problem and is easy to make.

Bend a 1"-wide piece of aluminum bar to form a short hook. Drill a small hang hole at the other end. Just slip the bar through a hole in the side of each point to stack and store them (photo at right).

Ted Baca
Greeley, Colorado

Sled Stop

A crosscut sled on the table saw makes accurate crosscuts a breeze. But one of the downsides is steering clear of the blade as it exits the back of the sled. Instead of building an elaborate blade guard, I use a much simpler solution — a stop block.

As you can see below, I clamp a wood block along the back edge of the table saw. It's positioned to keep the bulk of the blade from exiting the back of the sled at the completion of the cut. A simple and safe solution.

Bill Wells
Olympia, Washington

SUBMIT YOUR TIPS ONLINE

If you have an original shop tip, we would like to hear from you and consider publishing your tip in one or more of our publications. Go to:

Woodsmith.com
Click on the link,
"SUBMIT A TIP"

You'll be able to tell us all about your tip and upload your photos and drawings. You can also mail your tips to *"Woodsmith Tips"* at the editorial address shown at right. We will pay up to $200 if we publish your tip.

FREE TIPS BY EMAIL

Now you can have the best, time-saving secrets, solutions, and techniques sent directly to your email inbox. Just go to
Woodsmith.com
and click on
"Sign Up for Free E-Tips."
You'll receive one of our favorite tips each week.

Woodsmith.
No. 193   February/March 2011

PUBLISHER Donald B. Peschke

EDITOR Terry J. Strohman
MANAGING EDITOR Vincent Ancona
SENIOR EDITOR Ted Raife
ASSOCIATE EDITOR Dennis Perkins
ASSISTANT EDITOR Carol Beronich
CONTRIBUTING EDITORS Bryan Nelson, Phil Huber, Randall A. Maxey, James Bruton

EXECUTIVE ART DIRECTOR Todd Lambirth
SENIOR ILLUSTRATORS David Kreyling, Harlan V. Clark, Peter J. Larson, David Kallemyn
SENIOR GRAPHIC DESIGNER Bob Zimmerman
GRAPHIC DESIGNER Shelley Cronin
GRAPHIC DESIGN INTERN Megan Leafgreen
CONTRIBUTING ILLUSTRATORS Dirk Ver Steeg, Peter J. Larson, David Kallemyn, Erich Lage

CREATIVE DIRECTOR Ted Kralicek
SENIOR PROJECT DESIGNERS Ken Munkel, Kent Welsh, Chris Fitch, Jim Downing
PROJECT DESIGNER/BUILDER John Doyle
SHOP CRAFTSMEN Steve Curtis, Steve Johnson
SENIOR PHOTOGRAPHERS Crayola England, Dennis Kennedy
ASSOCIATE STYLE DIRECTOR Rebecca Cunningham
SENIOR ELECTRONIC IMAGE SPECIALIST Allan Ruhnke
PRODUCTION ASSISTANT Minniette Johnson
VIDEO EDITOR/DIRECTOR Mark Hayes, Nate Gruca

Woodsmith® (ISSN 0164-4114) is published bimonthly by August Home Publishing Company, 2200 Grand Ave, Des Moines, IA 50312.
Woodsmith® is a registered trademark of August Home Publishing.
Copyright© 2011 August Home Publishing Company. All rights reserved.
Subscriptions: Single copy: $4.95.
Canadian Subscriptions: Canada Post Agreement No. 40038201. Send change of address information to PO Box 881, Station Main, Markham, ON L3P 8M6. Canada BN 84597 5473 RT
Periodicals Postage Paid at Des Moines, IA and at additional offices.
Postmaster: Send change of address to *Woodsmith*, Box 37106, Boone, IA 50037-0106.

WoodsmithCustomerService.com

ONLINE SUBSCRIBER SERVICES
- **VIEW** your account information
- **RENEW** your subscription
- **CHECK** on a subscription payment
- **PAY** your bill
- **CHANGE** your mailing or e-mail address
- **VIEW/RENEW** your gift subscriptions
- **TELL US** if you've missed an issue

CUSTOMER SERVICE   Phone: 800-333-5075

SUBSCRIPTIONS
Customer Service
P.O. Box 842
Des Moines, IA 50304-9961
subscriptions@augusthome.com

EDITORIAL
Woodsmith Magazine
2200 Grand Avenue
Des Moines, IA 50312
woodsmith@woodsmith.com

AUGUST HOME PUBLISHING COMPANY   Printed in China

more tips from our readers

Tool Handles

I have a number of unhandled turning tools. Instead of making a handle for each one, I built the one you see in the drawing below. It consists of a drill chuck mounted on the end of a wood dowel with a threaded rod. The great thing is, this handle is useful for other shop tasks, as well.

It starts with a length of hardwood dowel. Then you need to find a length of threaded rod that fits the threads in your drill chuck. I used epoxy to secure the rod into a deep hold drilled in the end of the dowel. A nylon washer helps keep the chuck secure yet easy to remove if needed.

To use the handle, you can simply insert the tool in the chuck and tighten it. It not only works for lathe tools but for drill bits and countersink bits, too. And you can use a smaller chuck to make a pin vise for holding small objects.

Ken Kennedy
Santa Maria, California

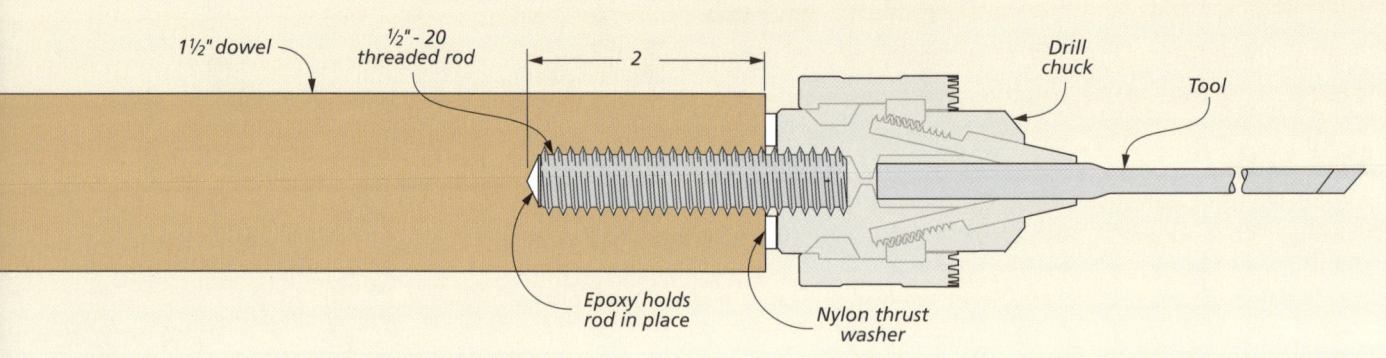

1½" dowel • ½"-20 threaded rod • 2 • Drill chuck • Tool • Epoxy holds rod in place • Nylon thrust washer

Joint Thin Strips

Sometimes it's necessary to joint the the edge of a thin strip to remove saw marks or shave off some width. But this can be a challenge on the jointer. So I made the jig you see in the photo at left. This jig not only protects my hands, but keeps the workpiece square to the fence, too.

To make the jig, I cut a groove in the edge of a "carrier" board. The groove should be sized to hold the thin strip firmly in the jig. Then I attached a cleat on the back of the board. This keeps the thin strip in place as you run it across the jointer.

To use the jig, keep the face of the carrier board flat to the fence while jointing the thin strip.

Rick Melpignano
Bellingham, Massachusetts

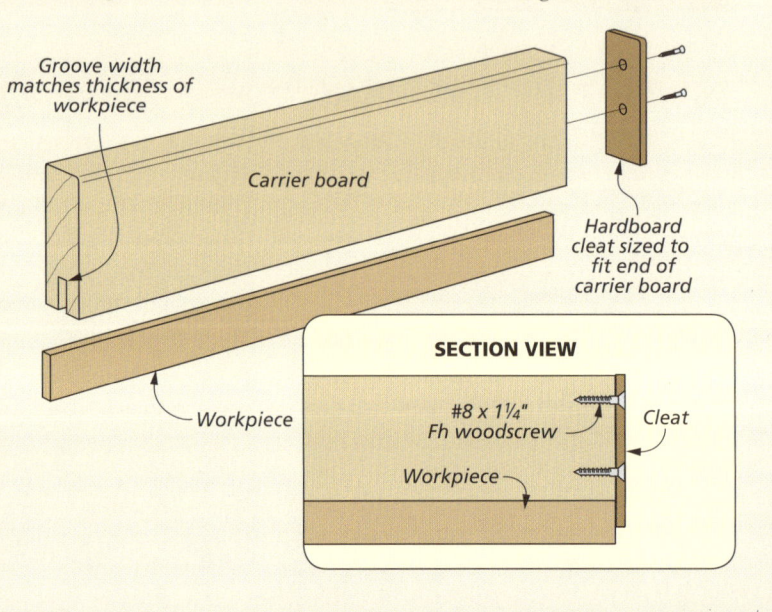

Groove width matches thickness of workpiece • Carrier board • Hardboard cleat sized to fit end of carrier board • Workpiece

SECTION VIEW
#8 x 1¼" Fh woodscrew • Cleat • Workpiece

Woodsmith

Sand on a Scroll Saw

I use my scroll saw for sanding the edges of small pieces. Although sanding strips designed for scroll saws can be purchased, they tend to be expensive. Instead, I make my own. They're easy to make.

Start by bending two 8d finish nails or pieces of 10-gauge wire into open hooks. Next, create a loop on each end of a strip of cloth-backed sandpaper by folding the ends over. Fasten the loose ends with hot-melt glue.

Making your own sanding strips has a few advantages. Like I mentioned, they're easy and inexpensive to make. The strip can be made either single or double-sided. Plus, you can use any grit sandpaper and make the strip in custom widths to suit the task at hand. Just use light tension when installing it on the saw.

Ed Schumann
Poughkeepsie, New York

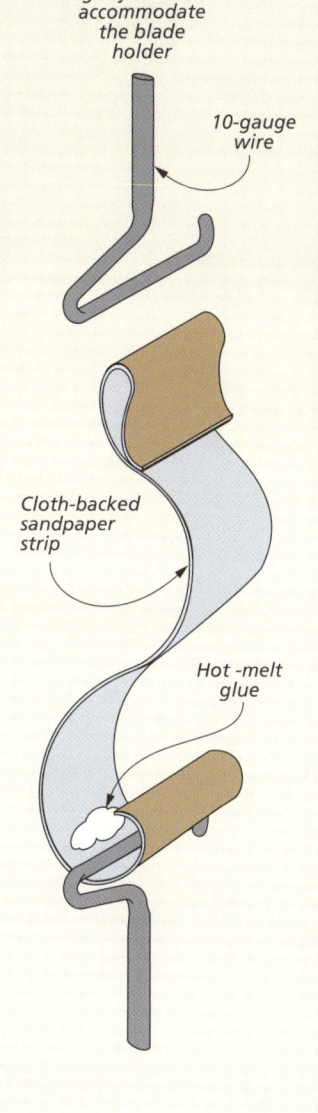

NOTE: Ends may be flattened slightly to better accommodate the blade holder

10-gauge wire

Cloth-backed sandpaper strip

Hot-melt glue

WIN THIS BOSCH IMPACTOR

That's right, send us your favorite shop tips. If your tip or technique is selected as the featured reader's tip, you'll win a *Bosch* impact driver just like the one shown here. To submit your tip or technique, just go online to *woodsmith.com* and click on the link, "SUBMIT A TIP." You can submit your tip and upload your photos for consideration.

The Winner!

Congratulations to Tim Kelley, winner of the *Bosch Impactor* driver. To find out how you could win a *Bosch* driver, check out the information on the left.

Quick Tips

PREFINISH PLYWOOD

When I'm using plywood to build a project I always apply a couple coats of finish to the uncut panel before I cut it into pieces. There are a number of reasons why this makes it easier to work with.

The best thing is I don't have to worry about getting finish into tight corners of the finished project. Another benefit is the finish seals the veneer so there's less tear out when I cut it. And there's less hassle during glue-ups. The finish allows any glue squeezeout to just wipe right off for clean joint lines.

I apply the finish with the plywood flat on a worksurface. This way, I don't have to worry about drips and runs.

John Bailie
Houston, Texas

EASY GLUE DISPENSING

I buy the large bottles of wood glue to save some money in the shop. But pouring glue from the large bottles to the smaller dispensers is difficult and messy.

I found the solution at a local restaurant supply store. I bought a plastic pump like the kind you see on the large ketchup bottles in restaurants. Now I just pump the glue into the smaller bottle without any drips or mess.

Chris Riley
Thunder Bay, Ontario

RUST PROOFING

Keeping tools rust-free can be a challenge, but I use a trick my grandfather taught me.

I keep a block of refined camphor in each of my tool boxes to keep the rust away. You can find these blocks on the internet at *Amazon.com*. Be sure to look for pure or refined camphor. Camphor gum is not as reliable.

Kevin Ruud
Las Vegas, Nevada

all about metal Drawer Slides

Bottom-mount slide
Rail and track separated
Side-mount slide
Center-mount slide

These modern marvels take the hassle out of installing drawers.

Fitting drawers to a case in the traditional "wood-to-wood" way has always been a challenge. And even when a drawer is fit perfectly, there's no guarantee that it will operate smoothly over the long term. The combination of wood movement and wear can easily undo a lot of careful work.

The introduction of metal drawer slides changed things. Drawer slides make fitting and installing drawers easier, they'll open and close with less effort, and slides offer long-term reliability. For many heavy-duty, high-use, or general utility applications, they're a real blessing.

MANY CHOICES. Today there are many types of slides available that are each designed to meet different needs. The trick is choosing the right one for a particular project. This really isn't all that difficult. For use in furniture, you can generally narrow the decision to a choice between several basic styles. Then it's just a matter of deciding on a few specifics.

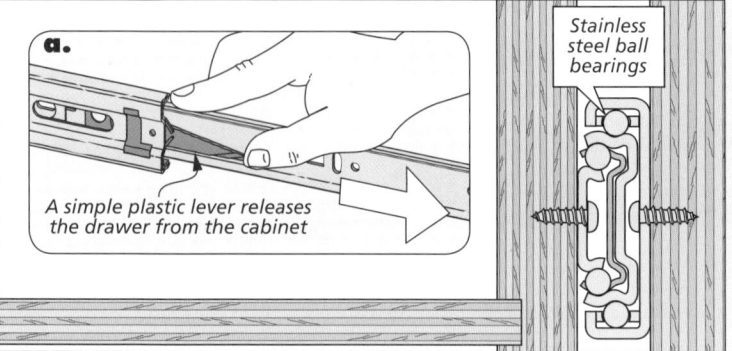

THE BASICS. In our shop, we always choose ball-bearing type slides for our projects, as shown above. This type offers an effortless slide and is very durable.

A simple plastic lever releases the drawer from the cabinet

Stainless steel ball bearings

The slide consists of two or three nesting sections. The single section is always attached to the drawer while the remaining assembly is attached to the case (see the box on the opposite page). The sections nest together compactly when the drawer is closed and then telescope out when the drawer is opened. The drawer and case parts can be separated for

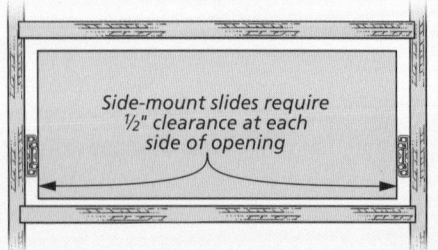

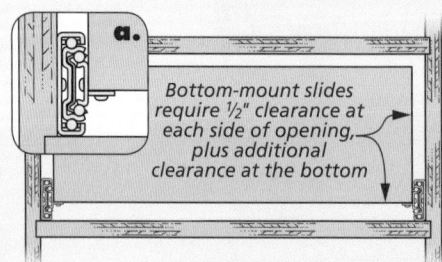

Side-mount slides require 1/2" clearance at each side of opening

Bottom-mount slides require 1/2" clearance at each side of opening, plus additional clearance at the bottom

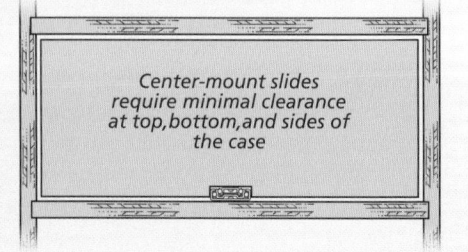

Center-mount slides require minimal clearance at top, bottom, and sides of the case

8   Woodsmith   No. 193

installation of the slide or removal of the drawer (upper detail drawings, opposite page).

MOUNTING STYLES. A major distinction in slide types is how and where the slides mount to the drawer and case. The drawings across the bottom of the opposite page illustrate the differences.

Side mount slides are the most commonly used type. The drawer part of the slide is mounted to the drawer side, usually near the mid point or lower. This type of slide requires a standard ½" clearance between the drawer and case at each side. So you sacrifice 1" of usable space. This dimensioning has to be taken into account when building the drawer.

Bottom-mount slides are similar to side-mount slides with one difference. Mounting tabs are incorporated into the drawer part of the slide that allow you to fasten it to the bottom edge of the drawer side. The advantage is that positioning this part is easier and the mount is more solid. However, this arrangement requires approximately an extra ⅝" top-to-bottom clearance in addition to the ½" required at each side.

A center-mount slide is installed beneath the drawer. (Only one slide is used). The drawer part is fastened to the drawer bottom or a cleat, while the case section is mounted at the center of the drawer opening. The benefit is that the slide is hidden and only minimal side clearance and top-to-bottom clearance is needed. A drawback is that they don't provide near the support of two slides mounted to the sides of the drawer. They're recommended only for light-duty applications.

LOAD CAPACITY. This leads us to the next subject. All metal slides carry a load rating. This is the combined weight (the drawer and its contents) the slides can handle when the drawer is opened.

Good quality side-mount slides start at a rating of 75 lbs. Slides with ratings of 100 lbs., 200 lbs., and up are available. However, a 75 to 100 lb. rating is more than adequate for most furniture and cabinetry. As I mentioned, center-mount slides have a significantly lower load rating — 25 to 35 lbs.

ACCESS. Another feature that you'll want to consider is the amount of drawer extension the slides allow. The range is shown in the photo above.

On the low end of the cost scale you have ¾-extension slides. This type allows the drawer to be pulled out of the case about ¾ of its depth. So access to the back of the drawer may be inconvenient. (Note that center-mount slides are only available in ¾-extension.)

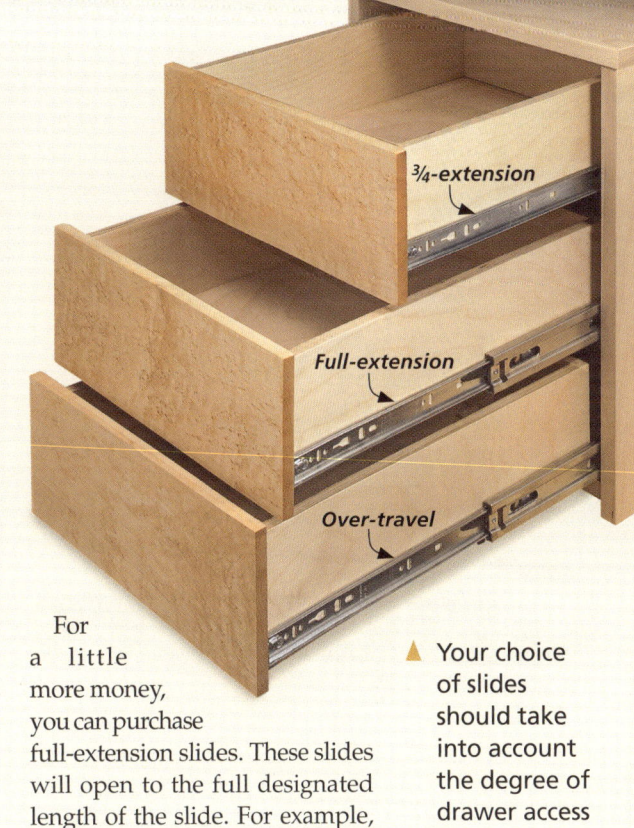

For a little more money, you can purchase full-extension slides. These slides will open to the full designated length of the slide. For example, an 18"-long slide will extend 18".

In some instances, an even greater degree of extension is welcomed — such as when a drawer is beneath an overhanging top. Here, you may want to use over-travel slides. This type is designed to extend about 1" beyond the overall length of the slide.

You probably won't want to use metal slides on every drawer project. But it's nice knowing that when you do decide to use them, there's almost certainly a slide that will meet the need. **W**

▲ Your choice of slides should take into account the degree of drawer access needed.

¾-extension

Full-extension

Over-travel

Easy Installation: Drawer Slide Mounting Aids

Metal slides work great on cabinets with face frames — with one minor catch. When installing the case part of the slide, you need a way to bridge the offset between the face frame and the case side. Wood spacers are one option. But slide manufacturers offer some handy, ready-made solutions that are worth a look.

The photos at right show inexpensive, easy-to-install plastic spacers that can be used to fill the gap. Once positioned in the case, the slide is screwed to the spacer.

The photo at left shows another strategy — an adjustable bracket that fits over the end of the slide and mounts to the back of the case.

▼ This mounting bracket fastens to the case back.

► These handy mounting spacers come in a variety of thicknesses.

tools of the trade

working with Bench Grippers

Find out how these handy accessories make everyday shop tasks go a little more smoothly.

When using a router or orbital sander on a flat workpiece at the bench, I've always relied on a router mat. It cushions the workpiece and keeps it from sliding around on my bench.

Within the last few years, though, there's been a new challenger to the trusty router mat — bench grippers. These rubber-padded blocks serve the same purpose as a router mat, but with some important additional features and benefits.

SHOP BENEFITS

Rockler gets the credit for developing the first commercial gripper — the *Bench Cookie*. These hockey puck-like disks are just round blocks of plastic with a layer of high-friction rubber on each side. (In fact, *Rockler* used actual hockey pucks in an early prototype.)

The textured rubber pads on each side of the disk tenaciously grip the workpiece and the worksurface to keep everything steady as you use your power tools. An added benefit is that they also elevate the workpiece to provide clearance when edge-routing.

BENCH COOKIES PLUS. *Rockler* followed up on the success of their original gripper design with the *Bench Cookie Plus*. The key difference is the addition of a threaded insert on one side of the gripper. This allows you to add a "riser" to elevate the cookie off your workbench (see main photo above).

The risers are available in two different heights and simply screw into the insert in the center of the gripper. They are sized to fit into ¾"-dia. dog holes, and the longer riser also features a molded stop, as shown in the photo below.

For some situations, the added height of the risers really comes in handy. For example, I use them during glue-ups when I need extra clearance to slip large bar clamps under an assembly.

MORE VARIETY. Imitation is the sincerest form of flattery. And since the *Bench Cookie's* introduction, a

Rockler Bench Cookie Cones

Rockler Bench Cookie Risers

Rockler Bench Cookies Plus

Woodworker's Supply Wolf Bench Paws

Peachtree Woodworking Loc-Blocks

couple of other companies have quickly followed suit with similar products. You can see the *Wolf Bench Paws* and *Loc-Blocks* at the bottom of the opposite page. Aside from their shape, these grippers perform the same basic function as the *Bench Cookies*. However, the *Loc-Blocks* can be fastened together to provide a wider gripping surface.

FINISHING HELPERS. Besides gripping and elevating a workpiece, these handy accessories can help you out with another shop task — applying a finish. *Rockler* recently introduced their *Bench Cookie Cones* shown in the left margin on the opposite page. The cone snaps in place over a *Bench Cookie*, providing the same function as the popular "painter's points." They allow air to circulate under the finished workpiece without marring the finish. This allows you to apply finish to all areas of the project. This means you don't have to wait for one side to dry before turning it over to finish the other side.

The *Wolf Bench Paws* perform this small task, as well. As you can see in the photo below, short dowels (included) can be sharpened with a pencil sharpener to be used as painter's points. The dowels fit a hole molded into the face of the *Wolf Bench Paw*.

STORAGE. Any time I buy little accessories like these grippers, I'm stuck with figuring out where to store them. For the *Rockler Bench Cookies*, the solution is easy. *Rockler* makes an inexpensive rack designed especially for them. The rack is designed to sit on your benchtop or can be wall-mounted. I installed my rack on pegboard (photo above).

Wherever you store the grippers, you'll want to be able to grab them quickly for sanding or routing a workpiece. And in the middle of a glueup, you don't need to spend time looking for them.

MAINTENANCE. When you look at these grippers, you get the impression there's nothing much that can go wrong with them. They're made of durable plastic and rubber material that can put up with a lot of abuse. While that's true, sawdust can quickly make them lose their grip.

The solution is easy. Whenever I see the rubber material getting dusty and dirty and losing its effectiveness, I simply grab a damp rag and wipe them off. That's it. They'll be as good as new following this quick cleaning.

SHOP-MADE GRIPPERS. I'll admit that before all these commercial versions of grippers came along, I was making my own from scrap pieces of MDF and old router mats or shelf liner material. You can see how in the box below. If you've got some spare time, you can make a bunch to have on hand wherever you need them.

HANDY HELPERS. Whether you make your own or spend a few dollars on commercial grippers (Sources, page 51), you'll find yourself reaching for them often. They're so simple in concept yet you'll wonder how you ever got along without them. W

▲ Storing *Bench Cookies* is easy in this handy rack.

▲ Bench grippers hold assemblies steady even against the force of power tools.

▲ Using bench grippers to elevate a project for finishing is just one way to use this accessory. *Woodworker's Supply* includes dowels with their *Wolf Bench Paws* to use as painter's points.

Shop Tip: Shop-Made

Making your own bench grippers in the shop only takes a few minutes. And it can save you a little money.

To make your own, you can cut small pieces from MDF. Then attach router matting to both sides with hot glue or rubber cement.

jigs & fixtures

versatile
Digital Angle Gauges

Stop leaning over your table saw and squinting in an effort to set the blade angle. Try one of these handy gauges instead.

For as long as man has been cutting wood, he's also struggled to find a reliable way to cut precise angles. Power tools made the cutting easier, but didn't really improve accuracy. The blade tilt scales on most table saws are notoriously inaccurate and hard to read. And while a protractor works well for layout work, it can be difficult to use when setting up tools.

Fortunately, there's a 21st century tool that should find a home in just about every workshop. A digital angle gauge can take the hassle out of setting up your saw for cutting any angle.

THE DIGITAL ADVANTAGE. I recently tried out three different models. The first was the *Wixey Digital Angle Gauge*. This one was first on the market. I also looked at the *Beall Tool Company's Tilt Box* and the *Angle Cube* from *iGaging*. You can find out where to get them all in Sources on page 51.

I found that digital angle gauges offer an inexpensive and accurate method of measuring any angle you'll use in the woodshop. By using one, you can quickly dial in the right setup angle for your saw every time. And that translates to perfectly cut project parts.

▲ Calibrate the device by setting it on the saw table and pressing the "zero" button.

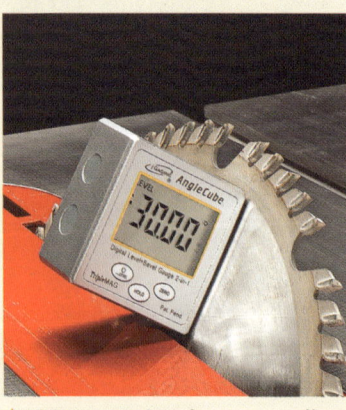

▲ Magnets in the case allow you to attach it to the blade for an instant readout.

12   Woodsmith   No. 193

EASY TO USE. Best of all, using a digital angle gauge couldn't be easier. As you can see in the photos at the bottom of the opposite page, you start by placing it on the tool's flat surface (usually the table of your saw) and calibrate the display simply by pushing a button.

Then all you need to do is place the gauge on the blade (all the gauges have magnets to hold firmly at any angle) and crank in the angle you need. An LCD display gives you a readout while you move the blade.

HOW THEY WORK. The gauges rely on gravity for measuring the difference in two angles, so it doesn't matter if your saw is sitting on an uneven floor. But the gauge must be upright in use. You can't lay the gauges flat on their backs to set the angle for a miter gauge. For that, take a look at the digital protractor in the box below.

ACCURACY & RELIABILITY. I admit that before trying out these gauges, my primary concern was whether they're accurate enough to rely on in everyday use. All three passed the test with flying colors. Each gauge is accurate to within 0.1° (one-tenth of a degree). And that's plenty accurate for any woodworking task.

As a test, I set up my table saw to cut 45°, 30°, and 22.5° angles to make four, six, and eight-sided boxes. Every one came out with gap-free joints on the first try.

But the best testament to their accuracy is probably the fact that both of our shop craftsmen, Steve Curtis and Steve Johnson, keep an angle gauge by their table saws. They each have over thirty years of woodworking experience and neither of them is fond of "bells & whistles" gadgets. They both like the accuracy and ease of use.

Each of the gauges worked equally well. I liked the *Wixey's* display best. But on the downside, it uses a watch-style battery that runs out quickly. The *Tilt Box* and *Angle Cube* both take a longer-lasting 9-volt battery.

The gauges are all available for under $40. At that price, it's hard to resist picking one up.

▲ Keeping the fence of your jointer square is a breeze with an angle gauge.

▲ Setting a miter saw blade for an accurate bevel cut has never been easier.

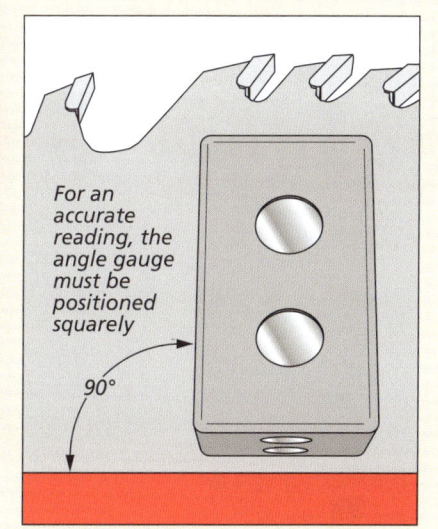

For an accurate reading, the angle gauge must be positioned squarely

90°

Worth a Look: Wixey Digital Protractor

Once you get used to using an easy-to-read, digital setup tool at the table saw, you'll want the same reliability and convenience for other uses. When it comes to setting miter angles, or a drill press for example, a digital protractor is just the ticket.

Wixey built the same ease-of-use into the protractor as they introduced in the angle gauge. This device works in any position, however, making it perfect for setting up a miter saw or miter gauge.

You're not limited to tool setups either. You can take the protractor anywhere you need to measure an angle.

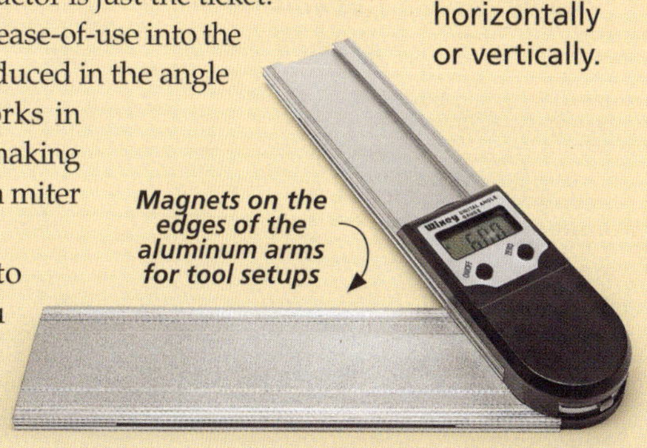

▲ The long arms on the digital protractor make short work of setting any angle on your miter gauge or miter saw.

▼ The digital protractor can be used horizontally or vertically.

Magnets on the edges of the aluminum arms for tool setups

techniques from our shop

7 tips for Routing Perfect Edge Profiles

Woodworking can be pretty flexible. There's usually more than one tool and technique you can use to perform a particular task. But, there are some woodworking operations that can best be accomplished in a particular way. Adding a decorative edge profile to a glued-up panel falls into this category. Routing the profile is the number one option for this task.

Assuming the size of the panel allows it, I always rout edge profiles at the router table. The setup is easier and the large surface of the table provides good support for the panel. And although the operation may seem pretty foolproof, there are always a few tips and techniques that can be used to help produce a smooth, crisp, attractive profile.

1 Flatter is Better

The router table provides a large, stable bearing surface. But in order to realize the full benefit it offers, the table has to be smooth, flat, and "catch-free."

If the table isn't flat, you may have trouble routing a consistent, full-depth profile along an entire edge. A table with a very minor "hump" is workable, but it's difficult to get good results with a concave surface. The center of the panel will ride up as it passes over the bit and you may not be able to press it flat against the table. So make sure the table is flat.

If you use an insert in the table, it should be perfectly flush with the surrounding surface. This will eliminate the chance of the panel catching, bumping, or dipping as it passes over the edge of the insert, resulting in a "hiccup" in the profile. Then check for rough spots, protruding screws, or other irregularities that might mar the surface of the panel.

▼ You'll get much better results when the table is flat and smooth.

2 Use the Fence

Most profile bits have a bearing on the top that will guide the cut along an edge. Although using the bearing for this purpose simplifies the setup, I prefer to use the router table fence to guide the panel across the bit.

A bearing-guided bit will follow any irregularities in the panel edge and you may not get a smooth, consistent profile. You'll also find that cuts made using only the bearing tend to produce a rougher, "chattery" surface.

The fence provides a long, stable guide surface that's completely independent of the spinning bit. Just make sure that both your fence and the edges of the panel are good and straight.

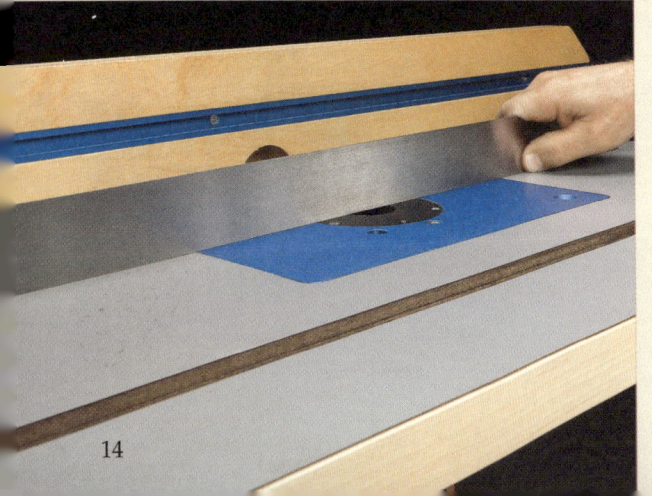

3 Multiple Passes

When routing all but the very smallest profiles, it works best to make multiple, light passes. Taking light cuts will minimize chipping, leave a much smoother surface, and it's easier on the bit and the router. The depth and number of passes is determined by the size and shape of the profile you're routing and the type of wood. However, always make the final pass a very light "skim" cut, removing only fine shavings.

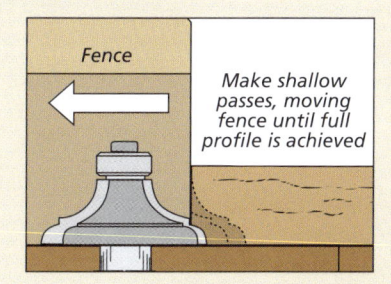

Make shallow passes, moving fence until full profile is achieved

There are two techniques for taking multiple passes — you can raise the height of the bit between cuts, or move the fence back, exposing more of the bit. I prefer the latter approach.

For starters, it's easier to move the fence than to change the bit height. And once the bit height is set and tested, you're assured of an accurate depth-of-cut.

4 Correct Order

When routing across end grain, you'll always experience some degree of chipout as the bit exits the cut. So if you're going to rout a profile on all four edges of a panel, always start by routing across one end-grain edge. This way, the following long grain pass will rout away any problems.

If you plan to rout a profile on three edges of a panel (for example the bathroom cabinet on page 16), plan your first end cut so that you can next rotate the panel counter-clockwise to rout the long edge. Follow this with the final end cut. To avoid chipout on the second end, use a backer board.

▲ *Always make your first pass across one of the end-grain edges.*

5 Consistent Depth

It can be a challenge to rout a profile to a consistent depth along all the edges. This is especially true at the corners. And adjoining profiles that don't match up can be particularly noticeable.

The cause is inconsistent downward pressure when feeding the panel across the bit.

It's common to hold back on the force at both beginning and end of the cut. A simple solution is to take another pass applying firm pressure from end to end.

You can avoid this problem entirely by using a featherboard to help press the panel flat to the table, as shown at left.

▲ *A featherboard will help ensure the profile is cut to a consistent depth all around.*

6 Feed Rate

Finding the perfect feed rate is always tricky. If you move the panel too fast, you may get chipout or a rough cut — too slow and you'll burn the edge.

A natural inclination is to slow down as you approach the end of a cut. This is especially problematic on end grain. Your goal is to avoid chipout, but the unintended result is burning. The solution is to use the initial passes to find a feed that minimizes both problems. Then try to be consistent.

◀ *A feed rate that's too slow leads to burning on the end grain.*

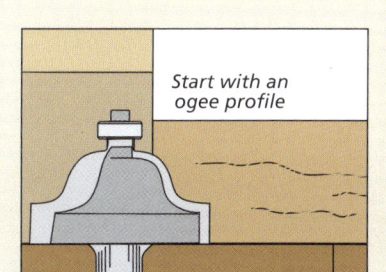

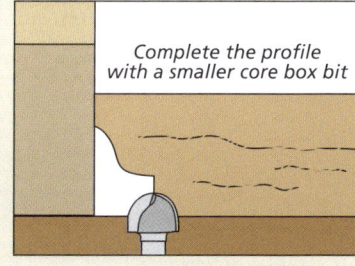

Start with an ogee profile

Complete the profile with a smaller core box bit

7 Complex Profiles

Some profiles require cuts made with two different bits. In this case, routing the larger or outer profile first establishes a "baseline" to guide you when routing the second profile. **W**

Weekend Project

cottage-style Storage Cabinet

If your need is practical storage in a small package, this simple, eye-catching cabinet will fill the bill.

In many homes, convenient bathroom storage is always in short supply. The list of grooming necessities is long and most of these items need to be kept within easy reach, yet preferably out of sight. And of course, there's the issue of limited floor space.

Let me offer a solution — the compact, attractive cabinet you see at left. For starters, you'll find abundant hidden storage behind the two lower doors. In addition, it provides more accessible space in the upper compartment and on top. And all this comes with a very small footprint.

In addition to this practicality, it's easy to see that style hasn't been ignored. The frame and panel construction, bun feet, and simple molding profiles combine for a look that complements just about any decor. And a durable painted finish in your choice of color adds to the appeal.

For me, the clincher is that this project involves woodworking at its best. There's nothing tricky here — straightforward joinery and techniques make the work go quickly. You'll be in and out of the shop in two shakes.

There may be one catch. When the cabinet is done, you might not want to hide it in the bathroom. But there's nothing wrong with that.

CONSTRUCTION DETAILS

OVERALL DIMENSIONS: 12"D x 26"W x 38½"H

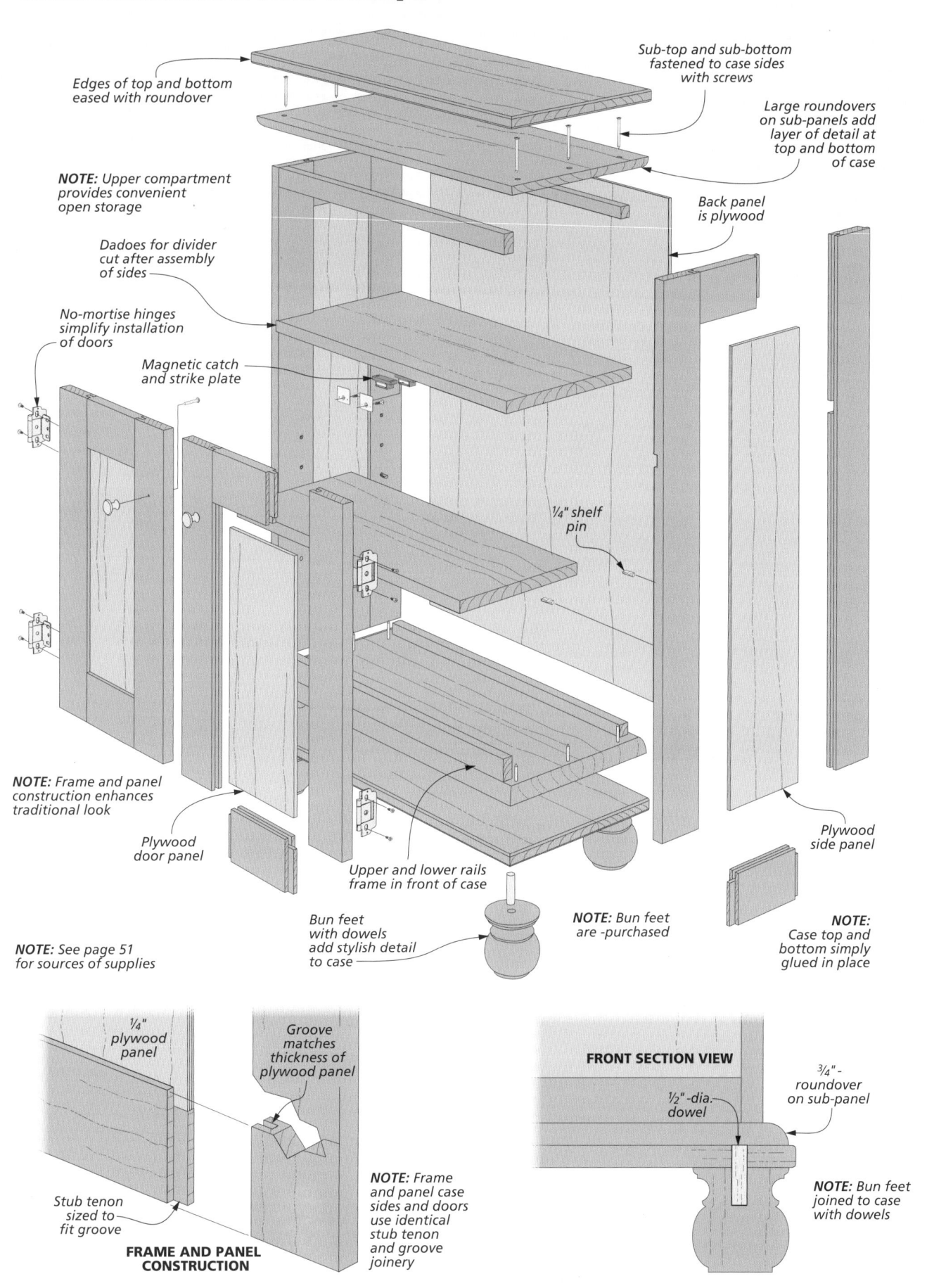

- Edges of top and bottom eased with roundover
- Sub-top and sub-bottom fastened to case sides with screws
- Large roundovers on sub-panels add layer of detail at top and bottom of case
- **NOTE:** Upper compartment provides convenient open storage
- Dadoes for divider cut after assembly of sides
- Back panel is plywood
- No-mortise hinges simplify installation of doors
- Magnetic catch and strike plate
- ¼" shelf pin
- **NOTE:** Frame and panel construction enhances traditional look
- Plywood door panel
- Upper and lower rails frame in front of case
- Plywood side panel
- Bun feet with dowels add stylish detail to case
- **NOTE:** Bun feet are -purchased
- **NOTE:** Case top and bottom simply glued in place
- **NOTE:** See page 51 for sources of supplies

¼" plywood panel

Groove matches thickness of plywood panel

Stub tenon sized to fit groove

FRAME AND PANEL CONSTRUCTION

NOTE: Frame and panel case sides and doors use identical stub tenon and groove joinery

FRONT SECTION VIEW

- ½"-dia. dowel
- ¾"- roundover on sub-panel
- **NOTE:** Bun feet joined to case with dowels

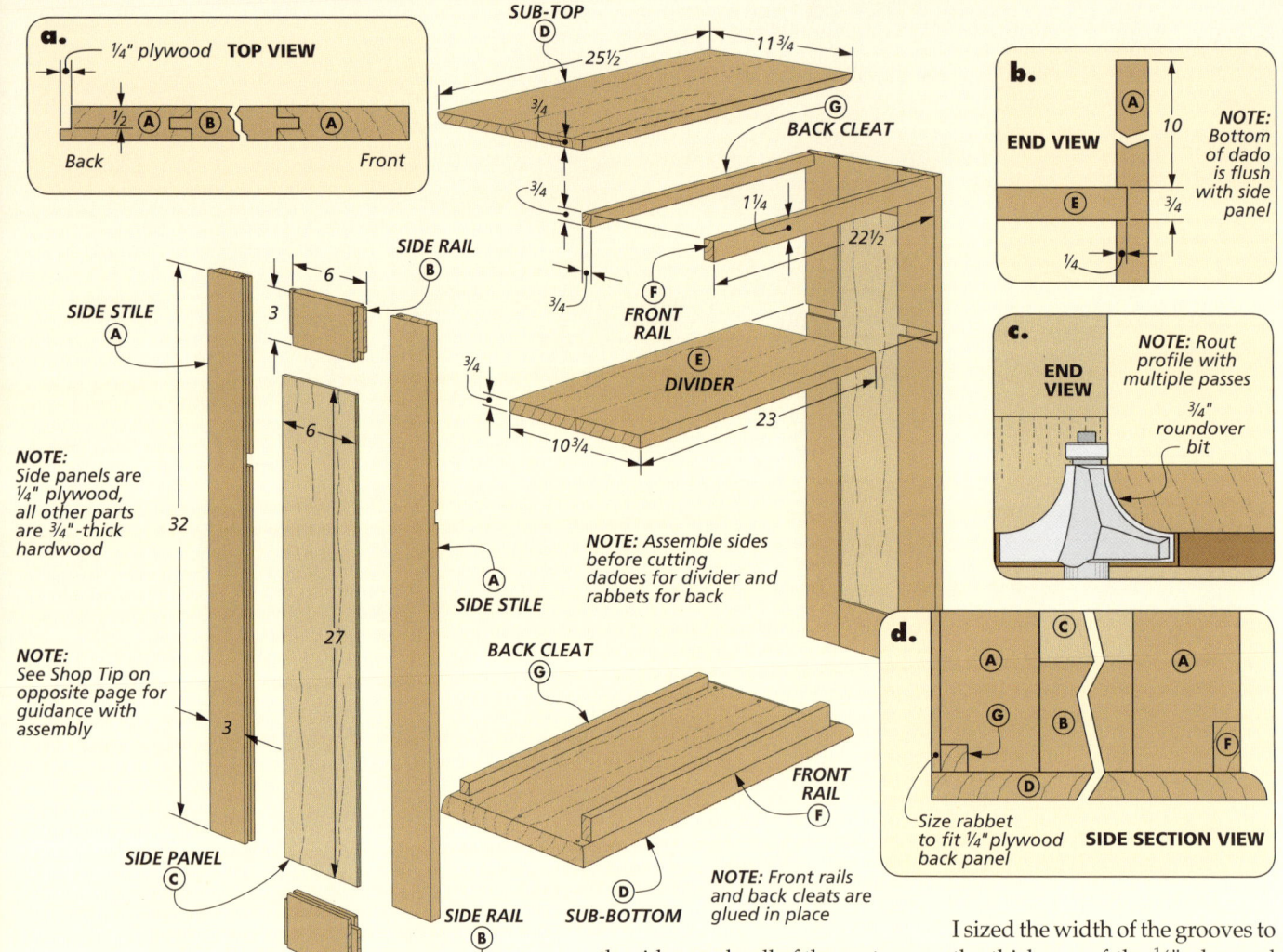

start the CASE

Building a basic framework for the case is your starting point. This consists of two frame and panel sides, a sub-top and sub-bottom, a divider, and pairs of rails and cleats, as shown above. Except for the side panels, all of the parts are solid wood (poplar).

THE SIDES. I began by assembling the two frame and panel sides. They're constructed with sturdy stub tenon and groove joinery as shown in detail 'a.'

THE JOINERY. The joinery technique I used is illustrated below. After cutting the stiles and rails to size, you'll cut ½"-deep, centered grooves in all the pieces. I sized the width of the grooves to the thickness of the ¼" plywood used for the panels. Two passes across a standard blade in the table saw will get the job done.

Next, I switched to a ¾"-wide dado blade buried in an auxiliary rip fence to cut the stub tenons on the rails. Sneak up on a good fit by adjusting the rip fence and the height of the blade.

With the joinery completed, you can cut plywood panels to

How-To: Make the Sides

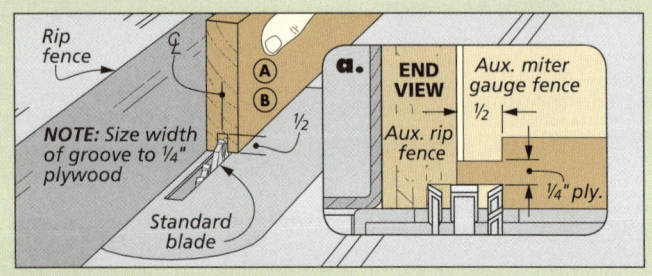

Grooves, then Tenons. Cut centered grooves by flipping the pieces end-for-end between passes. I used a dado blade buried in an auxiliary fence to cut the tenons.

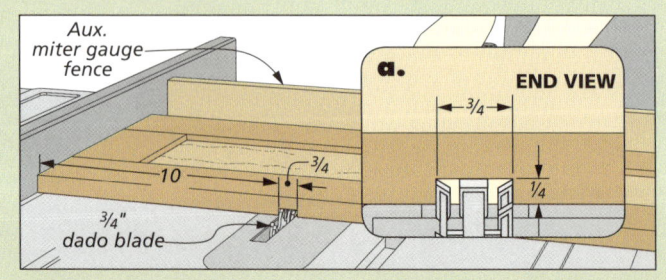

Dadoes. Use the rip fence to accurately position the dadoes in the side assemblies. Set the blade height so the bottoms of the dadoes end up flush with the face of the panels.

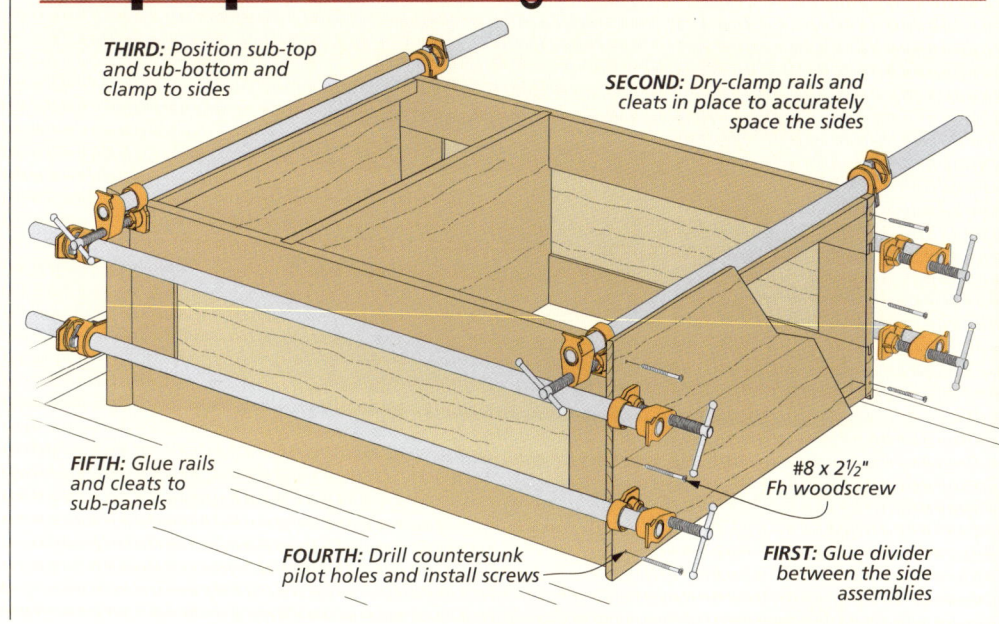

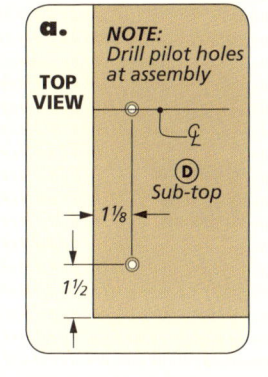

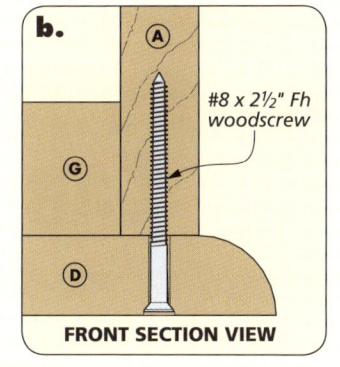

size and assemble the sides. For added strength, I glued the panels into their grooves.

DADOES & RABBETS. When the clamps come off, gather up the two side assemblies and head back to the table saw. Now, the sides need dadoes to hold the divider and rabbets for the back.

The How-To drawings on this and the opposite page show how I made both cuts. I tackled the dadoes for the dividers first (detail 'b,' opposite page). When the divider is installed, you want it to butt snug against the plywood side panels. This means that the bottoms of the dadoes should be flush with the inside face of the panels. A depth of ¼" worked for me, but if your plywood (and groove) is undersized, you'll need to cut the dadoes a bit deeper.

Don't be concerned if you score the panels lightly. This will be covered by the end of the divider.

With the dadoes completed, I set up the saw to cut the rabbets for the back panel. All you need to do is bury the blade in an auxiliary rip fence, as shown below.

SUB-TOP, SUB-BOTTOM & DIVIDER. The next task is to make the sub-top, sub-bottom, and the divider that connect the two sides. I'll just cover a few highlights of this.

All the panels are glued up from ¾"-thick stock. The sub-panels are identical and sized larger than the footprint of the case. The front and sides are rounded over (detail 'c,' opposite page). The panels are fastened to the top and bottom edges of the sides with screws. This makes assembling the case easy while adding a layer of detail at the top and bottom of the case.

The width of the divider is sized to fit flush with the front edges of the sides and flush to the shoulder of the rabbets at the back. And note that if your side dadoes are deeper than ¼", you'll have to compensate by making the divider a little longer. The goal is an inside measurement of 22½".

RAILS & CLEATS. With the sub-top, sub-bottom, and divider ready to go, all that's needed before assembly are the front rails and the back cleats. The front rails simply "frame in" the front of the case at the top and bottom. They fit between the sides flush with the front edges. The narrower back cleats are installed flush with the shoulders of the rabbets to complete the pocket for the back panel (detail 'd,' opposite).

ASSEMBLY. Once the rails and cleats are made, you can start putting the pieces together. The drawings above offer guidance.

First, I glued and clamped the divider between the sides, making certain this assembly was square. Then I installed the sub-top and sub-bottom with the rails and cleats clamped in place to act as spacers. Be sure the overhangs are even and the case is square before drilling the countersunk pilot holes and installing the screws (details 'a' and 'b'). Finally, you can glue the front rails and back cleats to the panels.

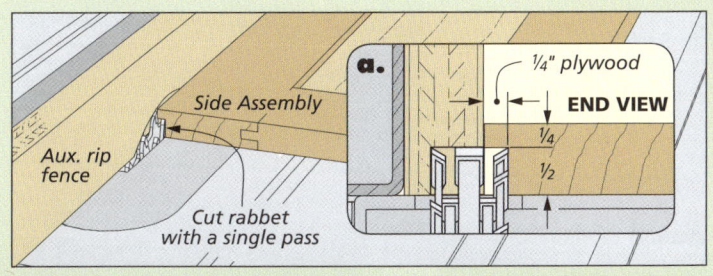

Shop Tip: Assembling the Case

THIRD: Position sub-top and sub-bottom and clamp to sides

SECOND: Dry-clamp rails and cleats in place to accurately space the sides

FIFTH: Glue rails and cleats to sub-panels

FOURTH: Drill countersunk pilot holes and install screws

FIRST: Glue divider between the side assemblies

#8 x 2½" Fh woodscrew

a. TOP VIEW
NOTE: Drill pilot holes at assembly
1⅛
1½
Sub-top

b. FRONT SECTION VIEW
A
#8 x 2½" Fh woodscrew
G
D

Rabbets. You can use the same ¾"-wide dado blade to cut the deep rabbets for the back panel. Just clamp an auxiliary rip fence in place and then bury the blade by raising it to final height.

Side Assembly
Aux. rip fence
Cut rabbet with a single pass

a. END VIEW
¼" plywood
¼
½

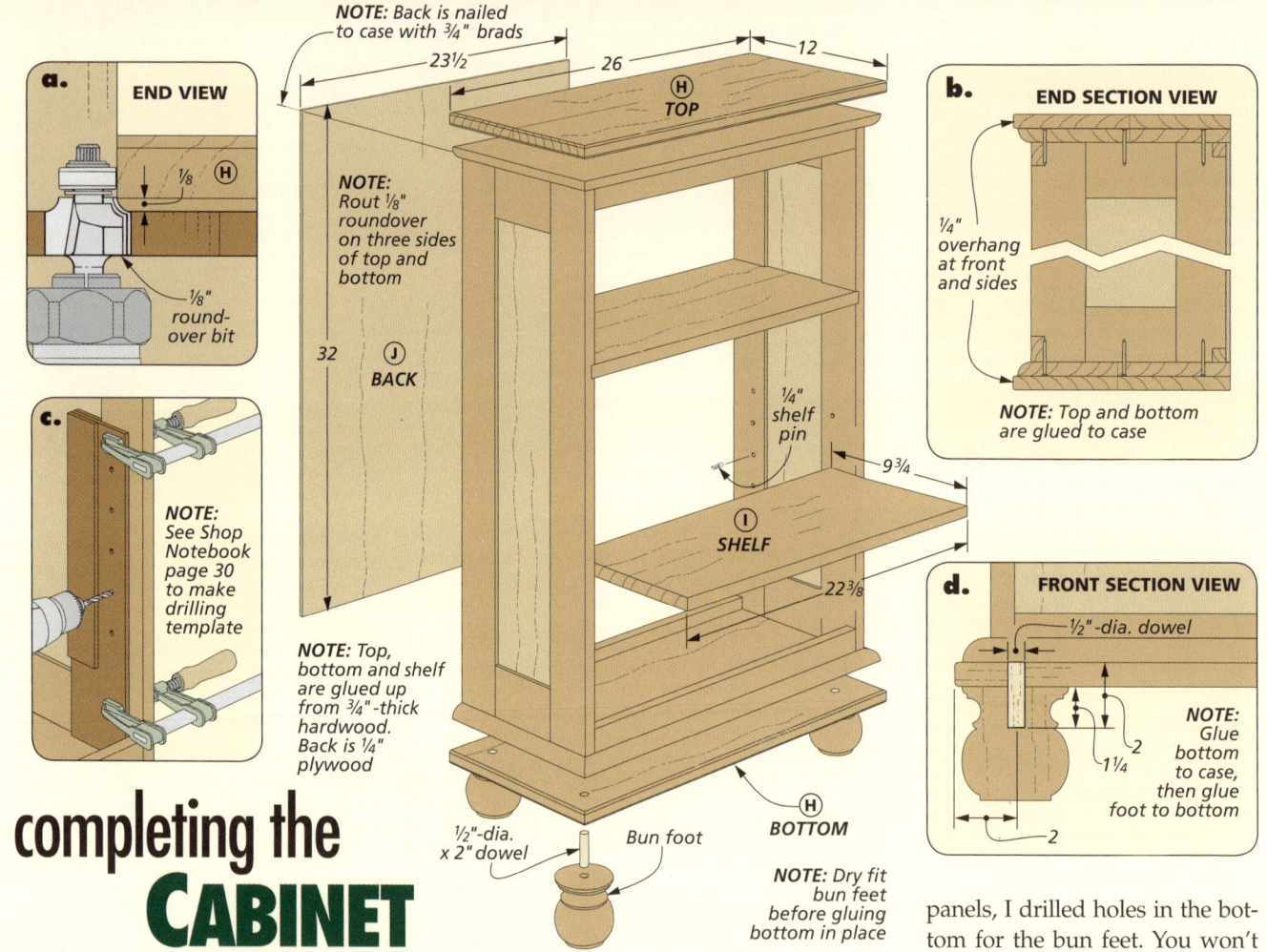

completing the CABINET

a. END VIEW — 1/8" H, 1/8" round-over bit

NOTE: Back is nailed to case with 3/4" brads

23 1/2 26 12
H TOP

NOTE: Rout 1/8" roundover on three sides of top and bottom

b. END SECTION VIEW — 1/4" overhang at front and sides
NOTE: Top and bottom are glued to case

32 **J BACK**

1/4" shelf pin

9 3/4
I SHELF

22 3/8

c. **NOTE:** See Shop Notebook page 30 to make drilling template

NOTE: Top, bottom and shelf are glued up from 3/4"-thick hardwood. Back is 1/4" plywood

d. FRONT SECTION VIEW — 1/2"-dia. dowel, 2, 1 1/4, 2
NOTE: Glue bottom to case, then glue foot to bottom

1/2"-dia. x 2" dowel   Bun foot   **H BOTTOM**

NOTE: Dry fit bun feet before gluing bottom in place

The addition of a few more items will flesh out the case. A top and bottom panel, a set of bun feet, a shelf, and the back come first. Then you can complete the job by building and installing a pair of frame and panel doors.

TOP & BOTTOM. Making the identical top and bottom panels is quick work. Start by gluing up two oversize panels from 3/4"-thick stock. When the glue is dry, you can clean them up and trim them to final size.

Next comes a short stop at the router table. Here, I softened the front and side edges of the panels with a 1/8" roundover (detail 'a').

BUN FEET. The top is ready to go. However, before I installed both panels, I drilled holes in the bottom for the bun feet. You won't attach them until after the bottom is installed. You'll simply find it's easier to get this out of the way before the bottom is attached.

The feet are attached with sections of 1/2"-diameter dowel, as in detail 'd.' The procedure I used to locate and drill the dowel holes in the feet and bottom is illustrated in the How-To box below. Once the holes are drilled, you can cut

How-To: Attach the Bun Feet

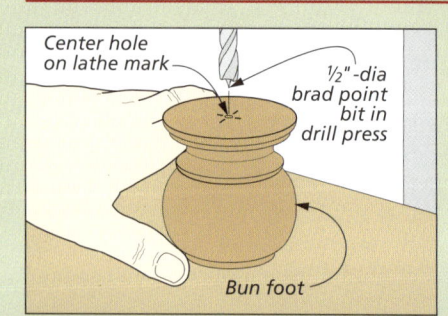

Center hole on lathe mark — 1/2"-dia brad point bit in drill press — Bun foot

NOTE: Set combination square to mark line from each edge — 2, 2

NOTE: Drill through holes — Mark center-point with awl — 1/2"-dia. brad point bit

Centered Holes. You can use the dimple left by the lathe center to locate the dowel hole in the top of each bun foot.

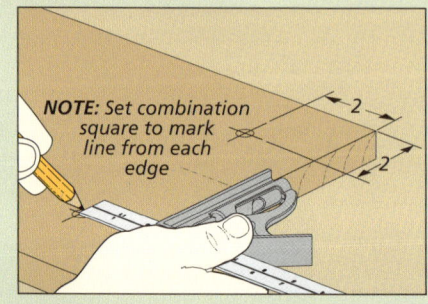

Bottom Layout. Find the centerpoints for the holes in the bottom by marking two lines with a combination square.

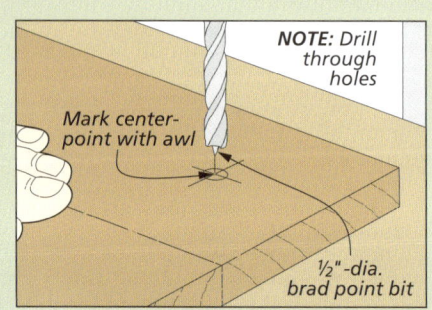

Bottom Holes. A dimple made with an awl helps position the bit when drilling the through holes in the bottom.

the dowels to length and then glue the dowels into the feet only.

Now the top and bottom can be glued to the case. The orientation of the panels can be seen in detail 'b' on the opposite page — flush at the back with an even overhang on the front and sides. And when the clamps come off, you can finish installing the feet.

THE SHELF. Before adding the plywood back to the cabinet, you'll want to complete the shelf and drill a series of holes for the shelf pins. Making the shelf is just a matter of gluing up a panel and then cutting it to final size.

For the shelf to sit level, the ¼"-diameter holes for the pins need to be located and aligned accurately. To accomplish this, I used a simple drilling template to index the holes (detail 'c,' opposite). You'll find more information on the this in Shop Notebook on page 30.

THE DOORS. Once the back is cut to size and tacked in place (detail 'b,' opposite), you can start on the two frame and panel doors. This should be familiar. The stub tenon and groove joinery is identical to that used on the case sides.

First you'll cut two sets of rails and stiles to size from ¾"-thick stock. The two doors are sized to allow a generous ⅛" clearance at the top, bottom, and sides.

You know the routine from here. First, cut centered grooves in all the pieces sized to the plywood you'll use for the panels. Next, a dado blade in the table saw will take care of the stub tenons. After cutting the panels to size, the doors can be assembled.

HARDWARE. No-mortise hinges make installing the doors go quickly. The only trick is positioning and aligning the doors correctly in the case opening. Double-sided tape and shims are the key. You'll find more details on the technique I used in Shop Notebook on page 31.

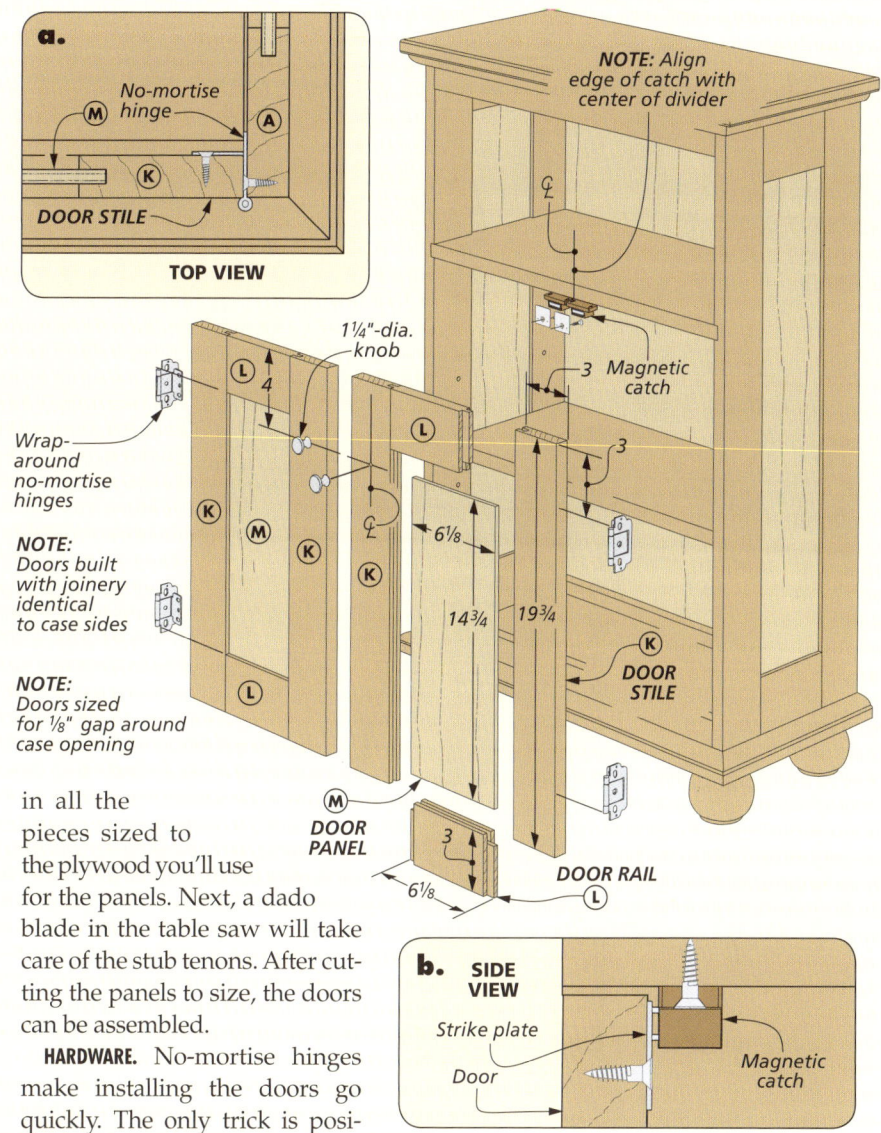

Finally, adding a pair of knobs and a pair of magnetic catches wraps up the job. And after a thorough sanding, you have a date with a paint brush.

Materials, Supplies & Cutting Diagram

A	Side Stiles (4)	¾ x 3 - 32	**H**	Top/Bottom (2)	¾ x 12 - 26
B	Side Rails (4)	¾ x 3 - 6	**I**	Shelf (1)	¾ x 9¾ - 22⅜
C	Side Panels (2)	¼ ply. - 6 x 27	**J**	Back (1)	¼ ply. - 23½ x 32
D	Sub-Top/Btm. (2)	¾ x 11¾ - 25½	**K**	Door Stiles (4)	¾ x 3 - 19¾
E	Divider (1)	¾ x 10¾ - 23	**L**	Door Rails (4)	¾ x 3 - 6⅛
F	Front Rails (2)	¾ x 1¼ - 22½	**M**	Door Panels (2)	¼ ply. x 6⅛ - 14¾
G	Back Cleats (2)	¾ x ¾ - 22½			

- (4) Bun Feet (3⅜" dia.)
- (4) 2" x ½"-dia. Dowels
- (12) #8 x 2½" Fh Woodscrews
- (4) ¼" Shelf Pins
- (2 pr.) No-mortise Hinges
- (2) 1¼"-dia. Knobs
- (2) Magnetic Catches
- (24) ¾" Brads

¾" x 6½" - 96" Poplar (Two boards @ 4.3 Bd. Ft. each)

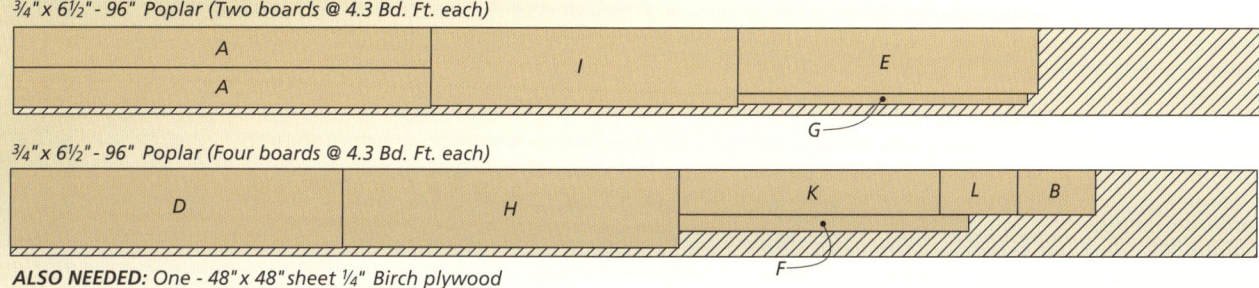

¾" x 6½" - 96" Poplar (Four boards @ 4.3 Bd. Ft. each)

ALSO NEEDED: One - 48"x 48" sheet ¼" Birch plywood

Designer Series Project

modular
Craft Center

With a large worksurface and lots of handy storage, this work center is sure to please even the most demanding hobbyist.

Having a dedicated space for all your hobbies means more time doing what you enjoy instead of hunting around for supplies or clearing space to work. This all-in-one craft center fills the bill.

The design includes two shelf units that support a waist-high tabletop for easy access to the work area. Ample space in the shelf units means you can store all your tools and supplies in one place, so they're right at hand. Plus, I included options for the top to suit your specific needs. Speaking of options, you can also stack the shelf units to make a tall storage cabinet. You'll find more information about building stacked shelves on page 29.

As a woodworker, you'll appreciate the finer points of the construction. Tongue and dado joinery means the shelf units are strong and sturdy. And all the joinery is the same size, so there's only one setup on the table saw. And the top is just as easy. It's made from a sheet of plywood with a replaceable top.

CONSTRUCTION DETAILS

OVERALL DIMENSIONS: 60"L x 39"W x 38"H

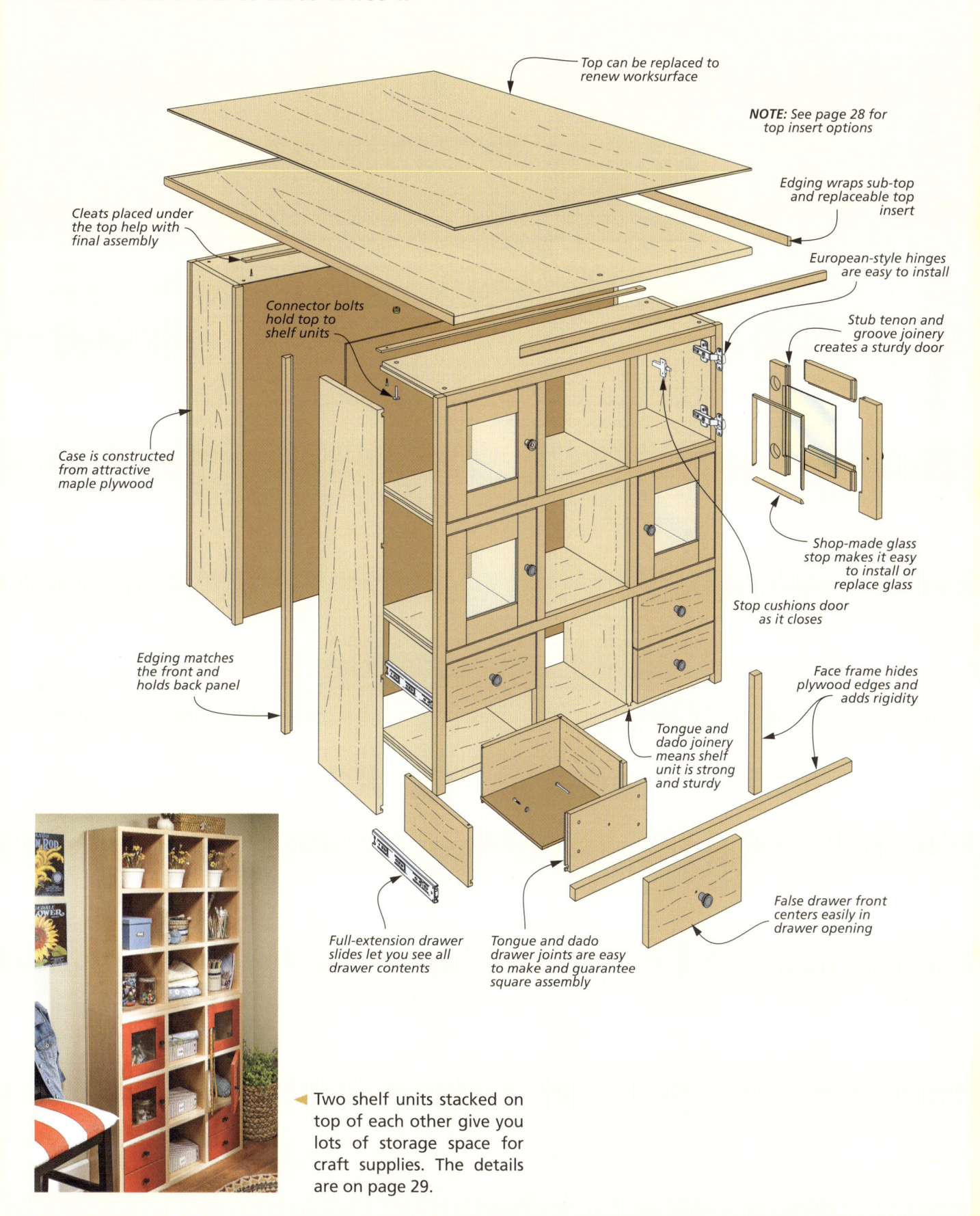

Top can be replaced to renew worksurface

NOTE: See page 28 for top insert options

Edging wraps sub-top and replaceable top insert

Cleats placed under the top help with final assembly

European-style hinges are easy to install

Connector bolts hold top to shelf units

Stub tenon and groove joinery creates a sturdy door

Case is constructed from attractive maple plywood

Shop-made glass stop makes it easy to install or replace glass

Stop cushions door as it closes

Edging matches the front and holds back panel

Face frame hides plywood edges and adds rigidity

Tongue and dado joinery means shelf unit is strong and sturdy

Full-extension drawer slides let you see all drawer contents

Tongue and dado drawer joints are easy to make and guarantee square assembly

False drawer front centers easily in drawer opening

◀ Two shelf units stacked on top of each other give you lots of storage space for craft supplies. The details are on page 29.

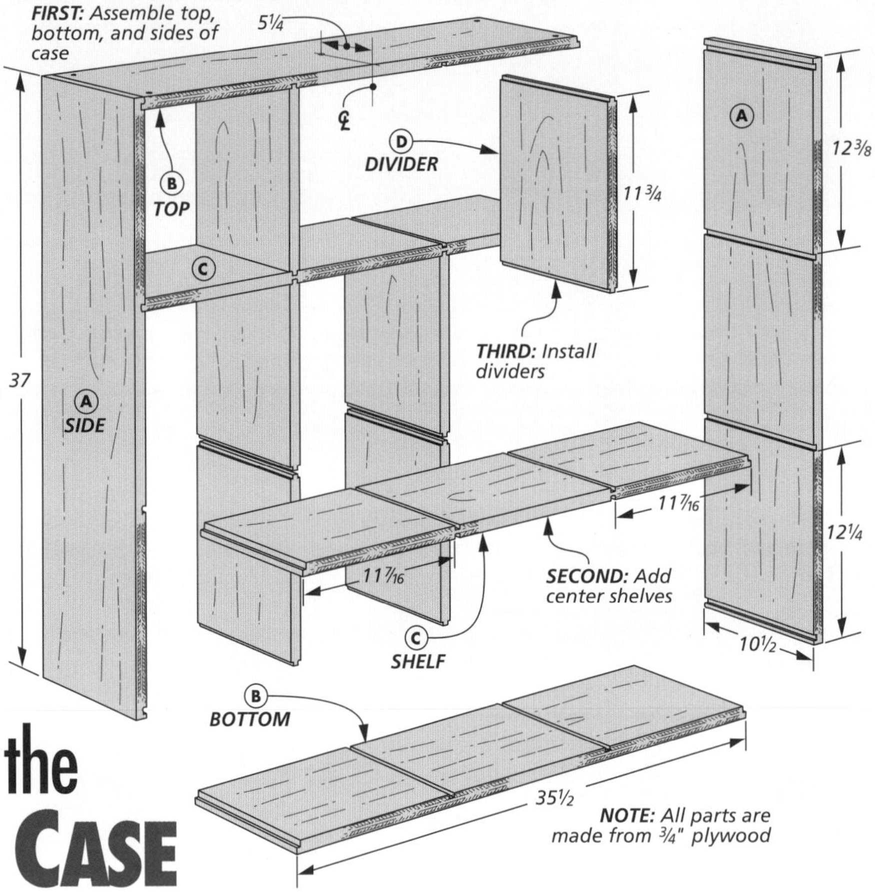
FIRST: Assemble top, bottom, and sides of case
5¼
℄
D DIVIDER
B TOP
C
11¾
THIRD: Install dividers
A
12⅜
37
A SIDE
11⁷⁄₁₆
12¼
11⁷⁄₁₆
SECOND: Add center shelves
C SHELF
10½
B BOTTOM
35½
NOTE: All parts are made from ¾" plywood

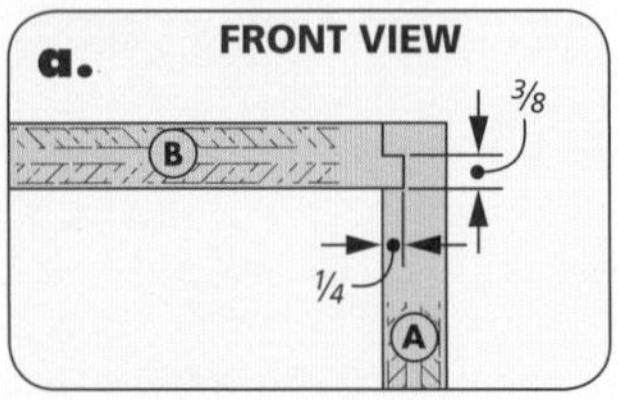
a. FRONT VIEW
B
⅜
¼
A

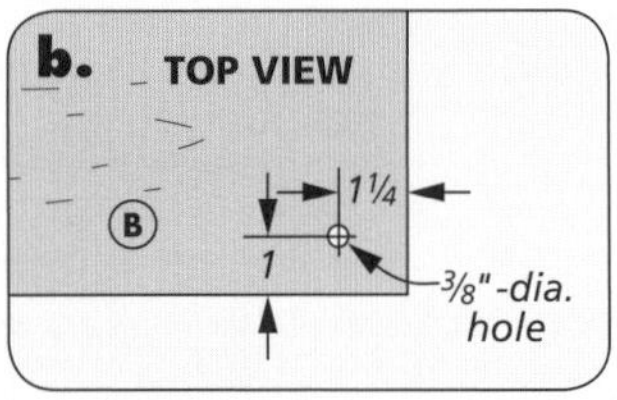
b. TOP VIEW
B
1¼
1
⅜"-dia. hole

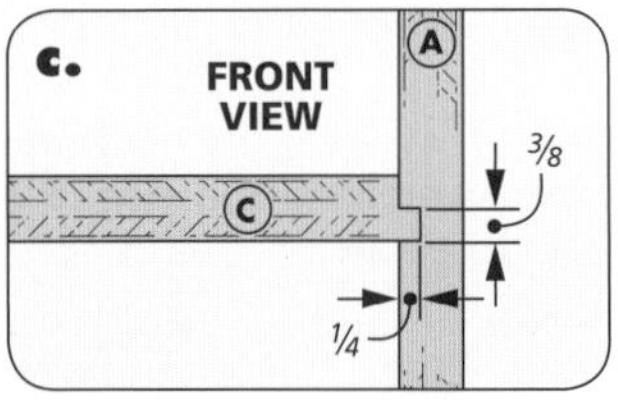
c. FRONT VIEW
A
⅜
C
¼

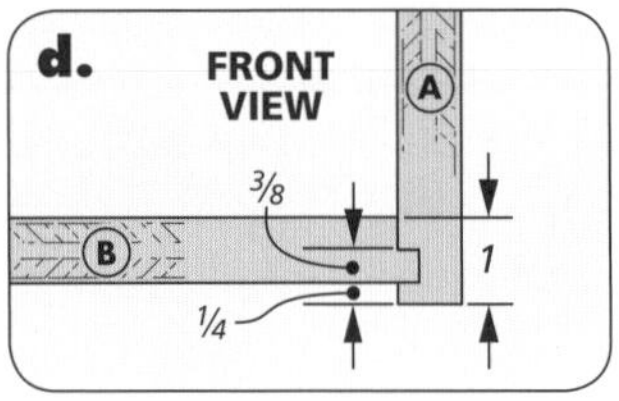
d. FRONT VIEW
A
⅜
B
1
¼

build the CASE

Each shelf unit is a square plywood case with shelves and dividers that create cubby holes for handy storage. The entire case is built using basic tongue and dado joinery for easy assembly.

CUT TO SIZE. To get started, cut the plywood to size for the case sides, top, bottom, shelves, and dividers. Next, I drilled the mounting holes in the top because it's easier to measure for placement before the joinery is cut (detail 'b').

JOINERY. Tongue and dado joinery is a reliable way to join plywood workpieces. You can make all the cuts on the table saw. The result is maximum gluing area without a lot of complicated measuring and fitting. This makes for sturdy construction that's easy to assemble. Another plus with this project is that all the tongues and dadoes are sized the same, so there's a minimum amount of setup. For precise locations of each dado, take a look at the main drawing and detail 'c.'

ASSEMBLE THE CASE. I found it easier to assemble and square up the sides, top and bottom, without the center shelves in place. Once the glue is dry, you can slide the shelves in and add the dividers. A thin layer of glue spread in the dadoes is all you need to secure them in place.

BACK. The hardboard back of the case serves two purposes. First, it

How-To: Make the Case & Back Edging

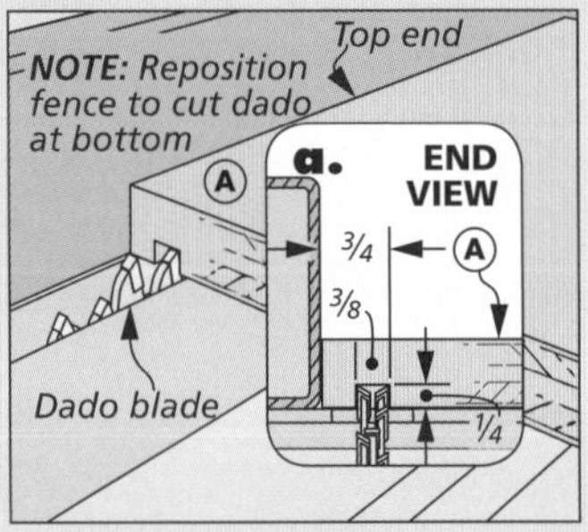
Top end
NOTE: Reposition fence to cut dado at bottom
A
a. END VIEW
¾
A
⅜
¼
Dado blade

Sides. *Cut dadoes in the sides to hold the tongues in the top and bottom of the case.*

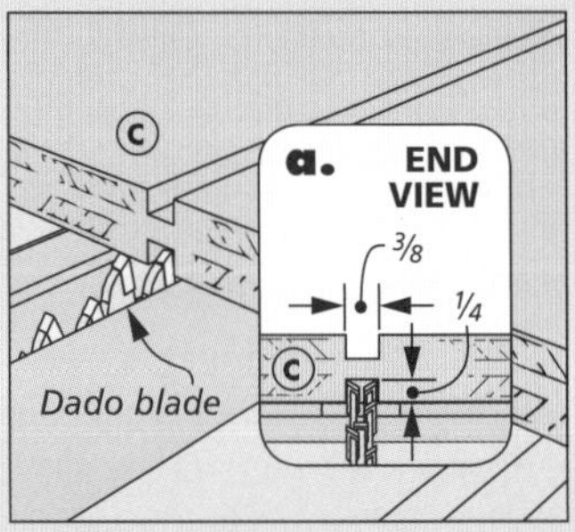
C
a. END VIEW
⅜
¼
C
Dado blade

Shelves. *The shelves have dadoes on both sides to hold the dividers in place.*

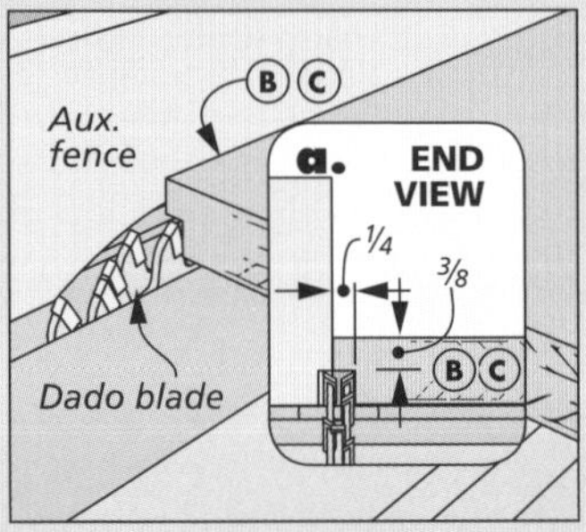
B C
Aux. fence
a. END VIEW
¼
⅜
B C
Dado blade

Shelf Tongues. *Use a dado blade buried in an auxiliary fence to form the tongues.*

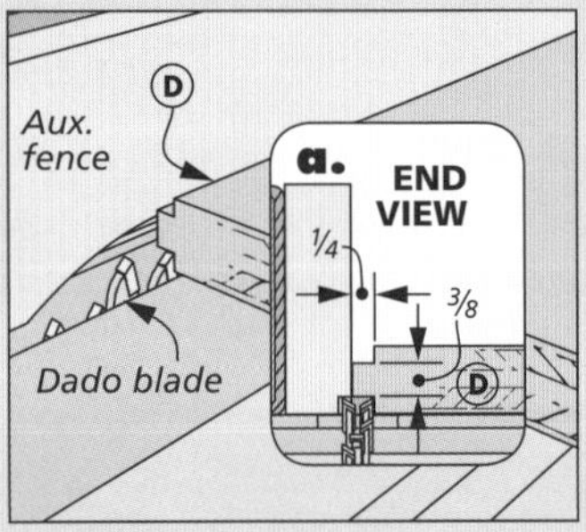
D
Aux. fence
a. END VIEW
¼
⅜
D
Dado blade

Dividers. *Each divider has a centered tongue cut to fit in the dadoes in the shelves.*

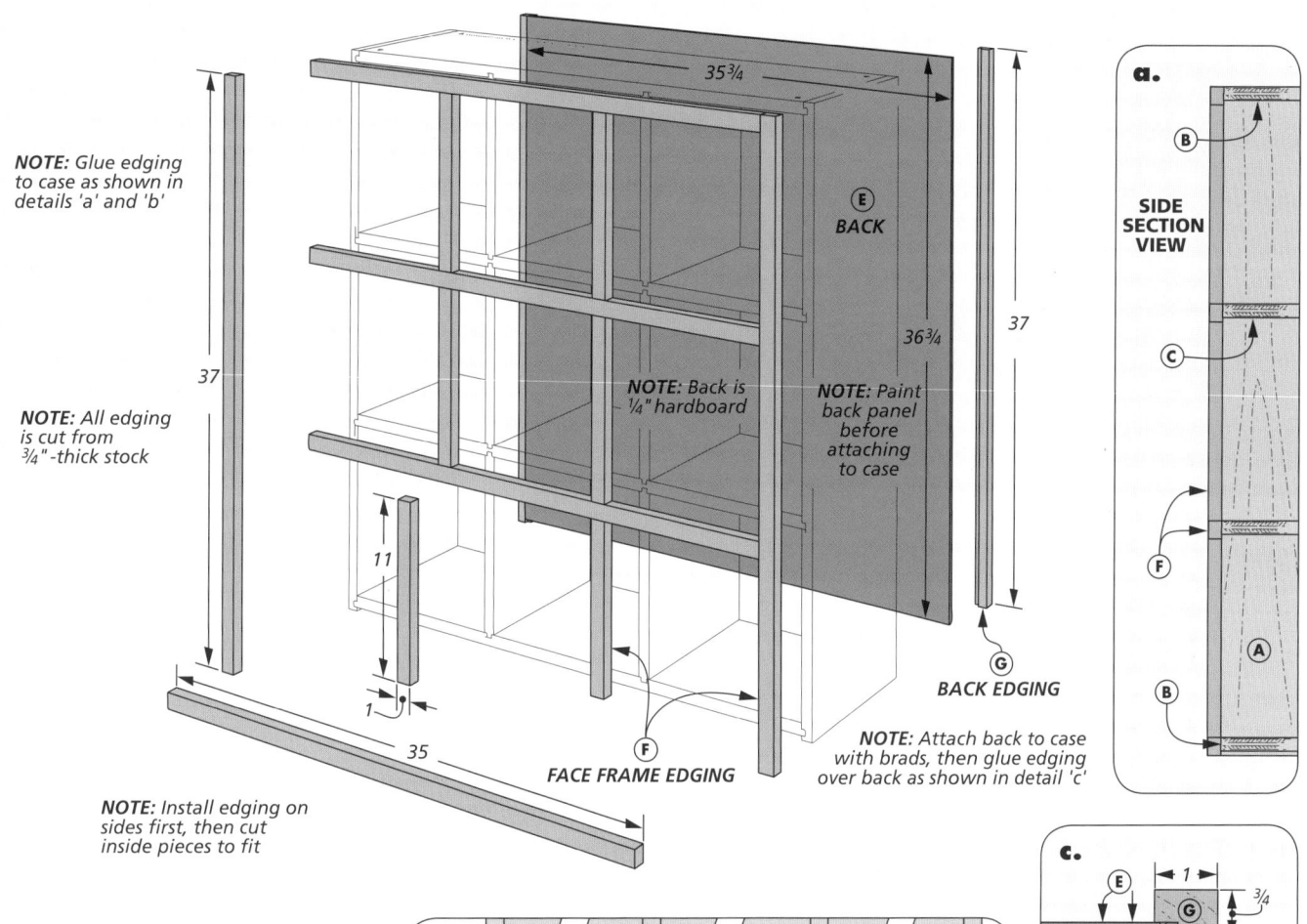

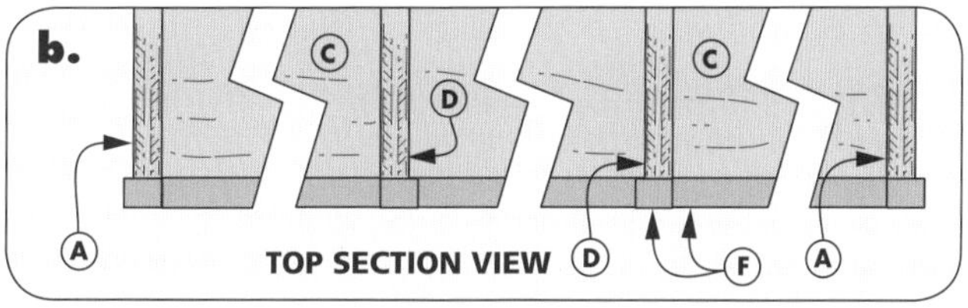

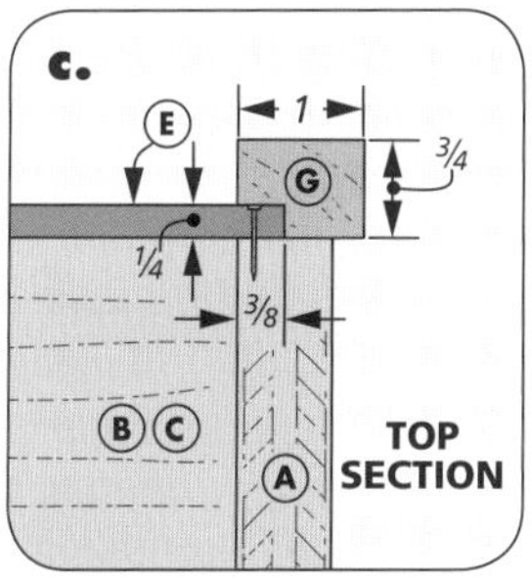

helps stiffen the entire cabinet assembly. Second, it keeps items contained within the cubbies. The back is mounted flush with the top and bottom of the case and inset 3/8" on the sides. You just need to cut the back to size, paint both sides, and attach it to the case with brads (detail 'c').

EDGING. To complete the case, I added edging to the front and back. This not only adds additional stiffness to the case, but also covers the plywood edges, giving the case a finished look. All of the edging is the same width and thickness, so I ripped it all at the same time. Then cut each piece to length as you progress with the assembly.

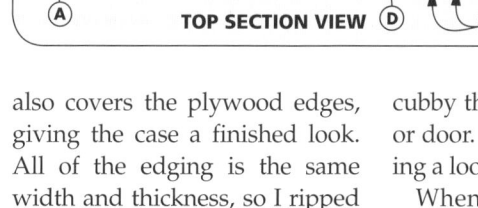

I started on the front with the outside edges first. The corners are simple butt joints, so no miters are necessary. Just be sure to attach these pieces flush with the inside edge of the cubbies.

The remaining edging can then be cut to fit, starting with the horizontal pieces. You'll need to leave room for the doors and drawers that you'll add later, so glue the horizontal strips flush with the top of each shelf, as shown in detail 'a.' Then add the vertical strips to complete the front. I glued the edging flush with the sides of each cubby that would hold a drawer or door. See what I mean by taking a look at detail 'b.'

When installing the edging pieces, you can clamp them by using a caul along the length of the edging and a clamp at each end. This holds the edging flat.

The edging on the rear of the case helps to secure the back panel. It also completes the look of the case by matching the front edges. You'll notice that the edging stands 1/4" proud of the case. A rabbet that fits over the edge of the back panel makes it all possible. (For details on making the rabbet, see the drawing at left.)

Complete the case by gluing and clamping the edging to the case back, as shown in detail 'c.' While the glue dries, you can start on the doors and drawers.

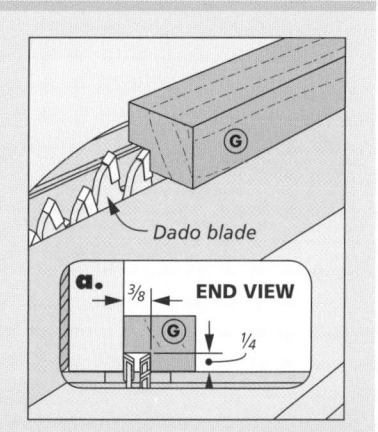

Back Edging. Cut a rabbet in the back edging pieces to fit around the case back.

build the DOORS

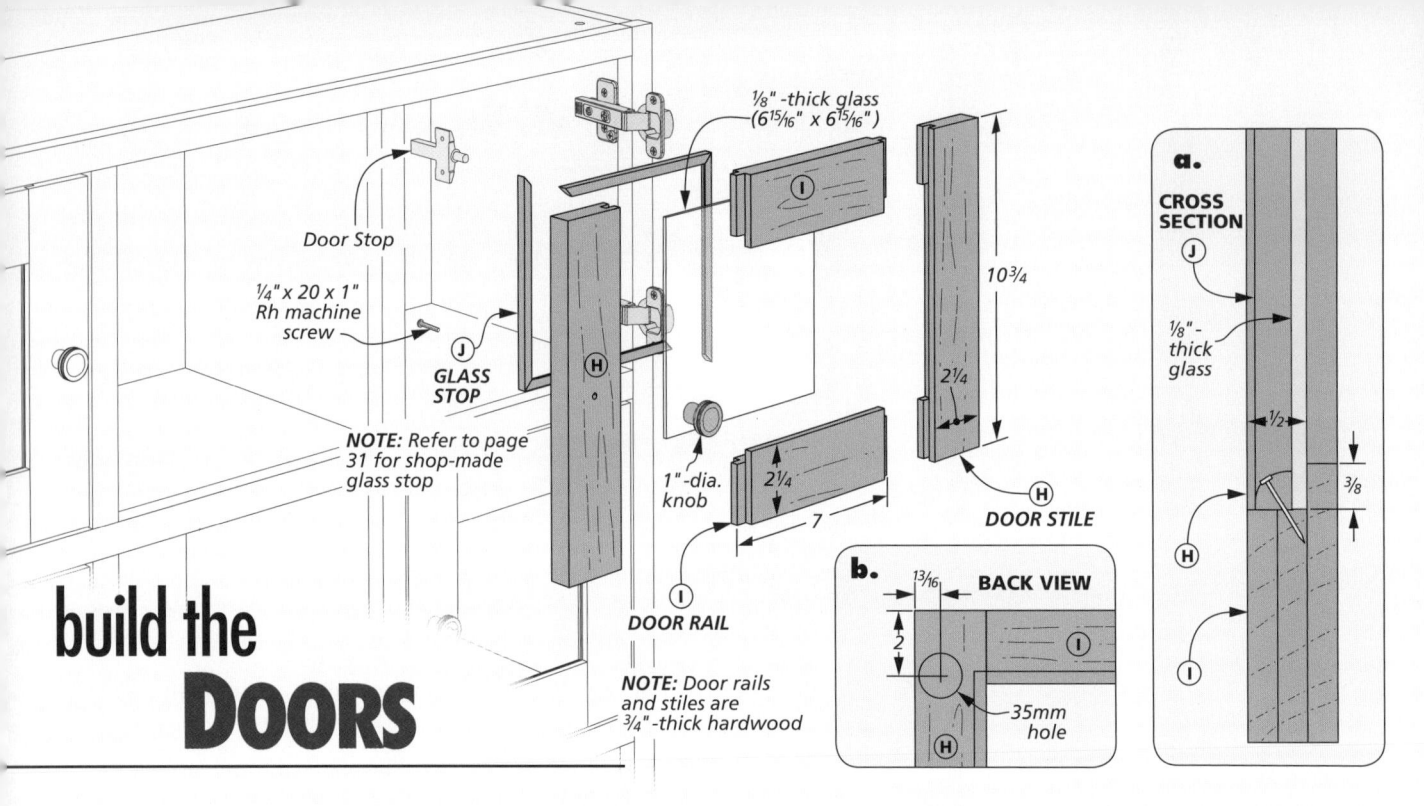

With the case complete, I added the doors and drawers. They're optional, but do help keep your supplies organized. Both the doors and drawers are installed flush with the front of the case for a clean, contemporary look. I chose full-extension slides for the drawers so they can be pulled out far enough to see the entire contents. European-style hinges on the doors are easy to install and easy to adjust too.

DOORS. The doors are constructed with stub tenons and grooves. Shop-made quarter round holds the glass panel in place.

After you cut the door pieces to final size, you can go ahead and cut the grooves in the rails and stiles. Match the stub tenons on the rails to the grooves. The details are shown in the box below.

Now that the joinery is complete, assemble each door and rout a rabbet on the back side of the opening, as shown in the right drawing below. A chisel will help you square up the corners.

QUARTER ROUND. The glass panel is held in place with narrow pieces of quarter round. I routed the quarter round on an extra-wide blank and cut the molding free. You'll find more information in Shop Notebook on page 31.

DOOR ASSEMBLY. Once again, I painted the parts before assembly. This way you won't need to mask off the glass. After the paint is dry, install the glass in the door and tack the quarter round in place (detail 'a').

HINGES AND KNOBS. Before you move on to the drawers, go ahead and mount the doors to the case and add the door stops. I used a small nylon knob on each door. You can find more information about the hardware for this project in Sources on page 51.

How-To: Create a Glass Panel Door

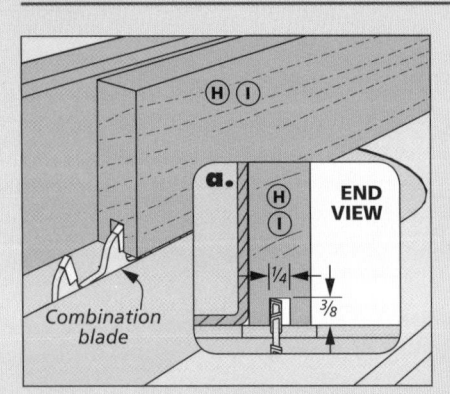

Groove. Using a single saw blade, cut one side of the groove and then flip the workpiece for a dead-center groove.

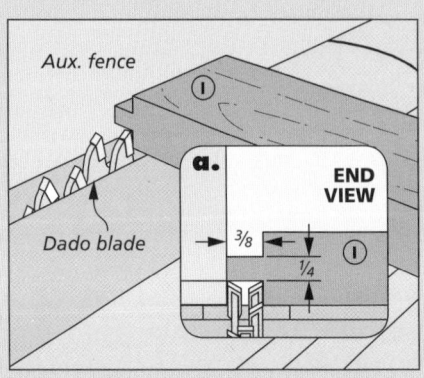

Stub Tenon. With an auxiliary fence on the rip fence, raise the blade to sneak up on a snug fit for the stub tenon.

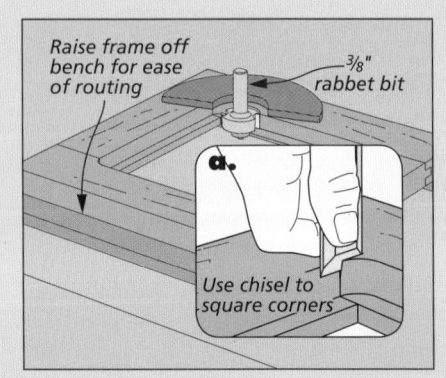

Rabbeted Opening. A rabbeting bit creates a pocket for the glass panel. Use a chisel to clean up the corners.

add the DRAWERS

The drawers are assembled with tongue and dado joinery, just like the case. To hide the side-mounted drawer slides, I added a false front to each of the drawers. The drawers are mounted flush with the case to match the doors.

DRAWERS. You can start the drawers by cutting the sides, fronts, and backs to size. Then drill oversize holes in each drawer front for the screws that hold the false front in place, as shown in the main drawing above. This will allow you to center the false front in the case opening and then tighten the screws for a perfectly aligned fit.

Your next step is to cut the joinery for the drawers, as shown in detail 'a.' There's more information about this in the box below. Finally, cut the groove for the drawer bottoms in each piece. After completing the joinery, cut the drawer bottoms to size and paint them.

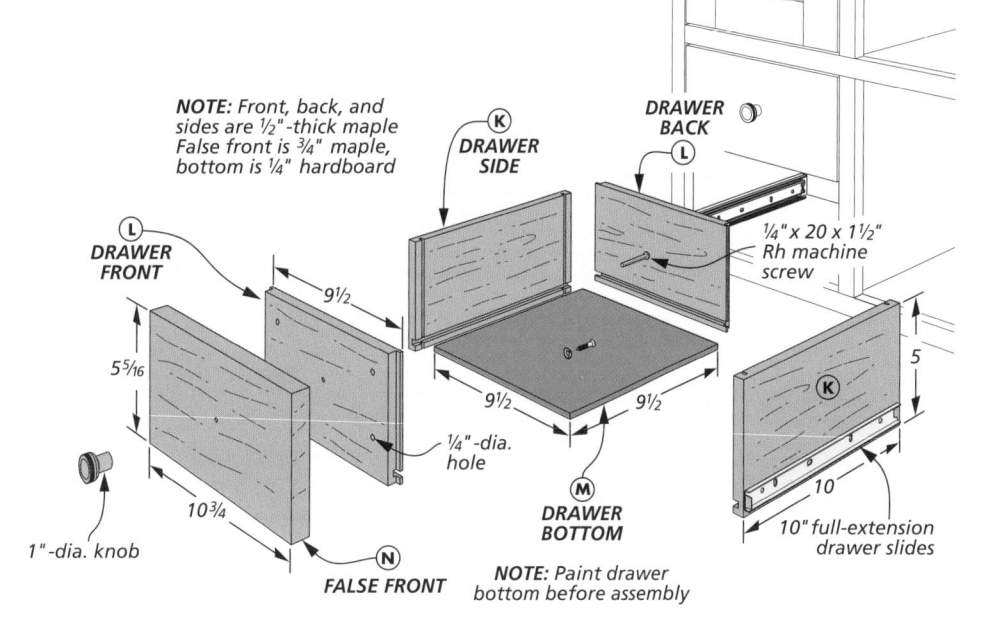

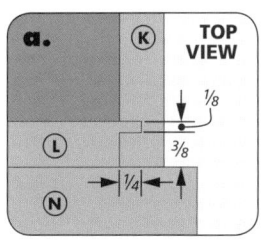

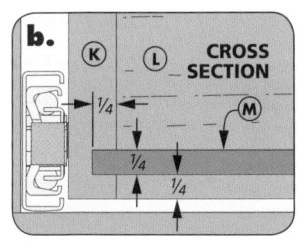

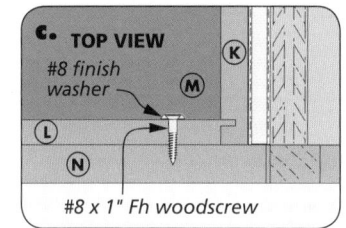

When the paint is dry, you're ready to assemble and install the drawers. I found it better to wait until the drawers are installed in the case before adding the false fronts.

DRAWER SLIDES. The two-part slides are the next step in installing the drawers. You can see how they fit in detail 'b.' It's easiest to attach the slide to the cabinet first. Be sure to mount the drawer slides flush with the inside face of the edging, as shown in detail 'c.' This will allow for the false front to fully seat inside the case. Next, align and attach the other part of the slide to the drawer.

FALSE FRONT. The false front is attached with screws and finish washers, as shown in detail 'c.' Just cut the workpiece to size, paint it, and attach it to the drawer. When the front is installed, you can drill a hole for the knob and attach it.

Drawer Joinery

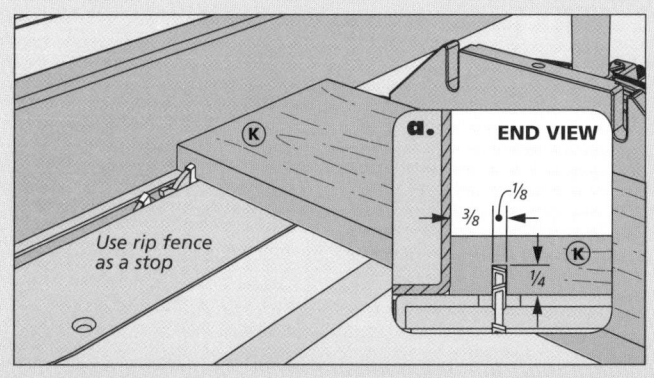

Cut the Dadoes. Use a standard saw blade to cut the dadoes in the drawer sides. Use the rip fence as a stop and the miter gauge to feed the stock across the blade.

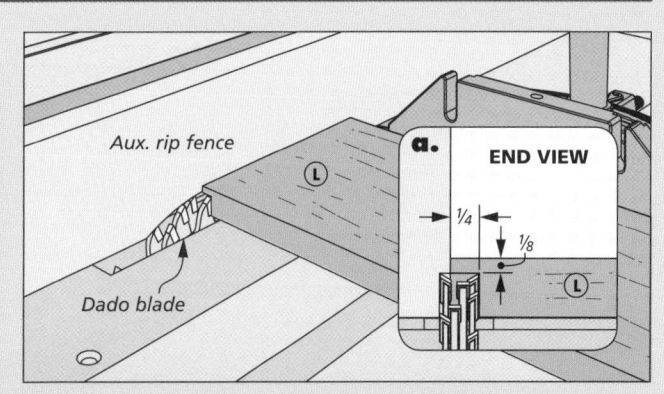

Tongues. Bury a dado blade in an auxiliary fence to cut the tongues on the ends of the drawer fronts and backs. Sneak up on a perfect fit by adjusting the blade height.

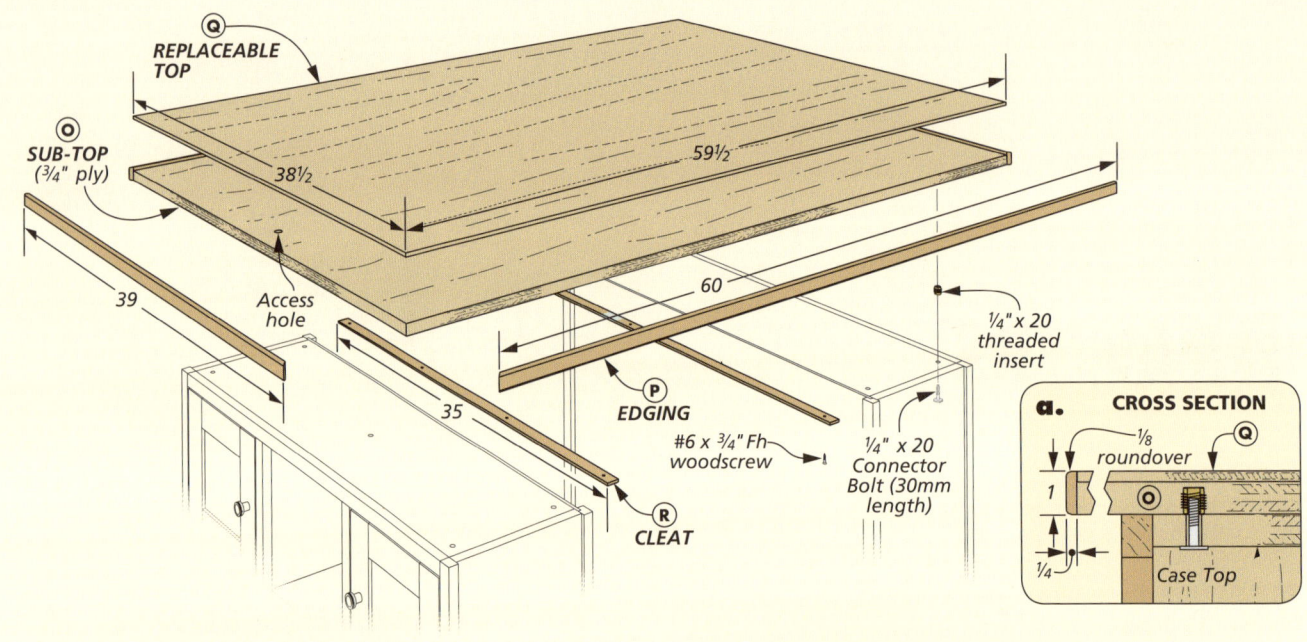

adding the TOP

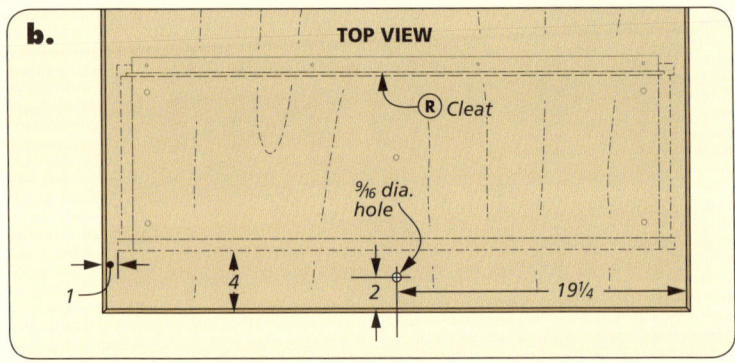

Assembling and installing the top will complete the craft table. The base for the top is cut from ¾" plywood. Then this panel is wrapped with 1"-wide edging. A replaceable top panel fills in the recess created by the edging. I used ¼" plywood for the top panel, but glass, melamine, or hardboard are all good choices. The top is fastened to the two cases with connector bolts and threaded inserts (detail 'a').

I started by cutting the plywood sub-top to size. Once this is done, you can drill holes for the inserts. You'll also want to drill a larger through hole near one edge of the base (detail 'b'). This hole can be used to remove the top panel, if it becomes scared or dirty and needs to be replaced.

EDGING. Detail 'a' shows the edging I applied to the top. To make the ¼"-thick edging, I resawed blanks from ¾"-thick stock. Then after planing the blanks to final thickness, I routed a roundover on two edges. Finally, miter the edging to fit and glue it to the sub-top, flush with the bottom face.

CLEATS. Next, you'll need to add a pair of cleats to the underside of the top, as shown in detail 'b.' These cleats will help you align the top and the two shelf units when you assemble the table.

FINAL ASSEMBLY. With the top complete, all that remains is to attach it to the two shelf units. Then you can cut and fit a replaceable top in the recess. I used double-sided tape to hold it. No matter what type of panel you choose, you'll have a large, sturdy worksurface for your craft of choice. **W**

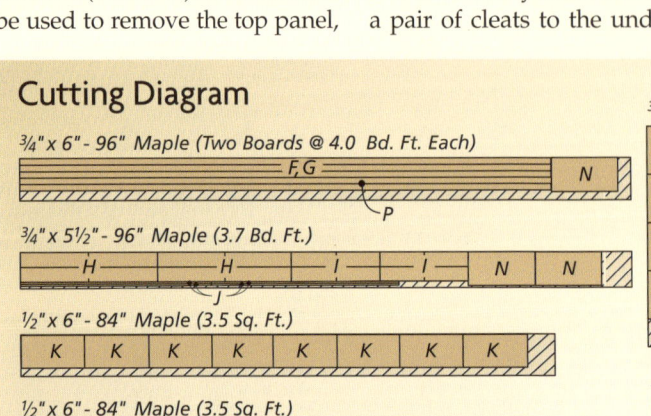

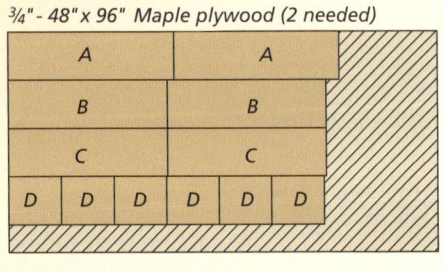

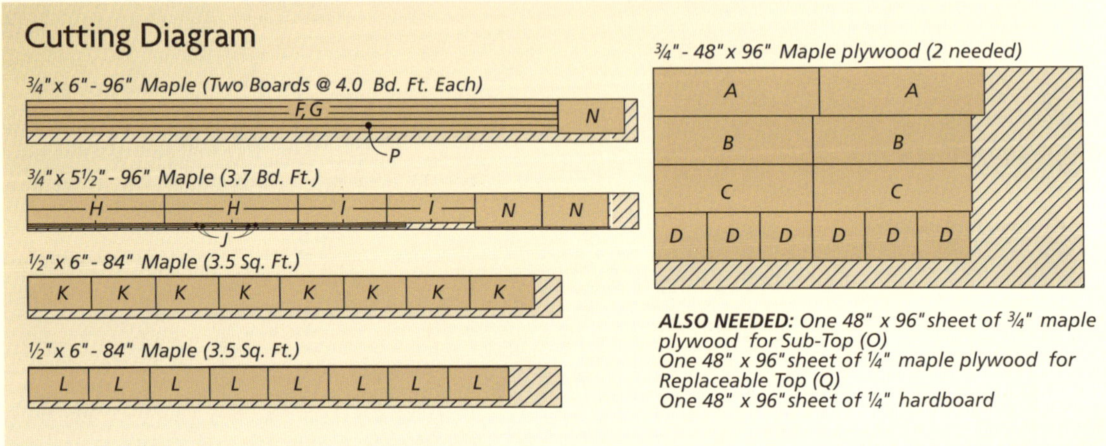

DESIGNER'S NOTEBOOK

Stacking it Up

If you just need extra storage space without the worksurface, you can stack two shelf units to make a tall storage case, as shown in the drawing on the right. You'll save valuable floor space too.

To stack the shelf units, drill holes in the top of the lower unit and install threaded inserts in the bottom of the upper unit. To connect the two units, you'll need to use 40mm-long connector bolts (see detail drawing below).

Should you decide at a later time to use the shelf units as a base for a worksurface, the two shelf units can be separated just by removing the connector bolts. For the present, you have a handy storage unit.

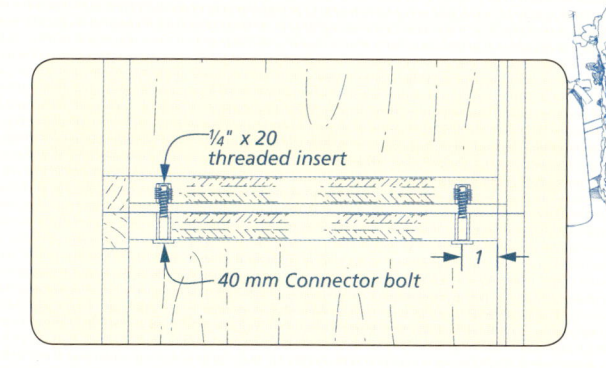

Materials & Supplies

A Sides (4)	3/4 ply. - 10 1/2 x 37	**P** Top Edging (1)	1/4 x 1 - 200 (rgh.)
B Tops/Bottoms (4)	3/4 ply. - 10 1/2 x 35 1/2	**Q** Replaceable Top (1)	1/4 ply. - 38 1/2 x 59 1/2
C Center Shelves (4)	3/4 ply. - 10 1/2 x 35 1/2	**R** Cleats (2)	1/4 hdbd. - 1 x 35
D Dividers (12)	3/4 ply. - 10 1/2 x 11 3/4		
E Back Panels (2)	1/4 hdbd. - 35 3/4 x 36 3/4		
F Back Edging (4)	3/4 x 1 - 37		
G Face Frame Edging (2)	3/4 x 1 - 580 (rgh.)		
H Door Stiles (8)	3/4 x 2 1/4 - 10 3/4		
I Door Rails (8)	3/4 x 2 1/4 - 7		
J Glass Stop (2)	1/4 x 1/4 x 230 (rgh.)		
K Drawer Sides (8)	1/2 x 5 x 10		
L Drawer Fronts/Backs (8)	1/2 x 5 x 9 1/2		
M Drawer Bottom (4)	1/4 hdbd. - 9 1/2 x 9 1/2		
N False Drawer Front (4)	3/4 x 5 5/16 - 10 3/4		
O Sub-Top (1)	3/4 ply. - 38 1/2 x 59 1/2		

- 3/4" Brads
- (4 pr.) 120° Inset European-Style Hinges
- (8) 1"-dia. Knobs
- (4 pr.) 10" Full-Extension Drawer Slides
- (16) #8 x 1" Fh Woodscrews and Finish Washers
- (4) 6 5/16" x 6 5/16" Glass Panels (1/8" thick)
- (10) 1/4"-20 Threaded Inserts
- (10) 1/4"-20 Connector Bolts (30mm length)
- (4) Door Stops
- (8) #6 x 3/4" Fh Woodscrews
- (4) 1/4" x 1" Rh Machine Screws
- (4) 1/4" x 1 1/2" Rh Machine Screws

1/4" x 20 threaded insert
40 mm Connector bolt

Woodsmith.com   Woodsmith   29

tips from our shop

SHOP NOTEBOOK

Shelf Pin Template

Drilling the shelf pin holes in the storage cabinet on page 16 is pretty easy. The only challenge is spacing each set of holes identically so the shelf will rest solidly on the shelf pins. To do this, I made a simple template.

As you can see in the drawing at left, the template is nothing more than a piece of ¼" plywood with a row of holes drilled 2" apart. The template is sandwiched between a pair of plywood cleats. The cleats allow you to register the template against the inside edge of the side stiles.

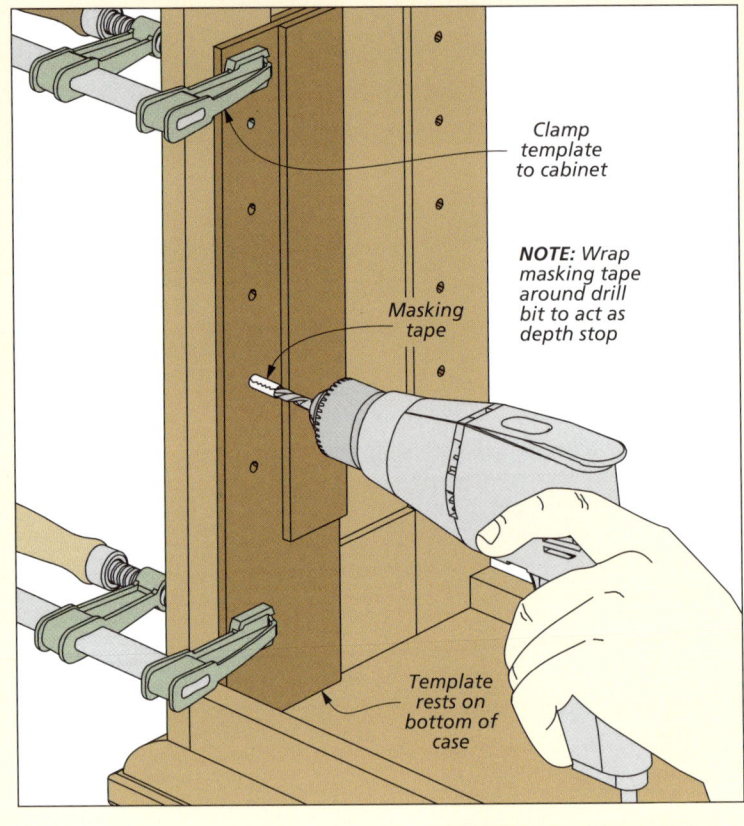

To drill the shelf pin holes, rest the template on the bottom of the cabinet with the cleat against the edge of the stile, as shown in the drawing above.

DRILL THE HOLES. Using the holes in the template as a guide, drill the shelf pin holes. (A piece of masking tape attached to the drill bit can serve as a depth stop.) Then, to drill the holes at the back of the case, simply flip the template around and repeat the process.

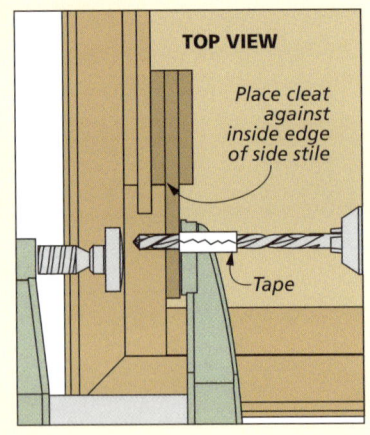

Chamfering a Dowel

The towel holders for the kitchen workstation on page 32 are nothing more than 1"-dia. dowels, cut to length. To ease the edges of the ends of the holders and give them a more finished appearance, I chamfered the ends at the router table. The trick to this is to create a "channel" to hold the dowel while routing the chamfer.

I started by installing a chamfer bit in the router and raising it so the top of the cutting edge was ⅛" above the surface of the table. Then I clamped a scrap piece to the table to hold the dowel against the fence, as shown in the drawing at left.

To chamfer the end of the dowel, simply feed it into the bit until the end contacts the bearing. Then rotate the dowel (toward the fence) to create the chamfer. Once you've routed the entire end, just slide the dowel back away from the router bit.

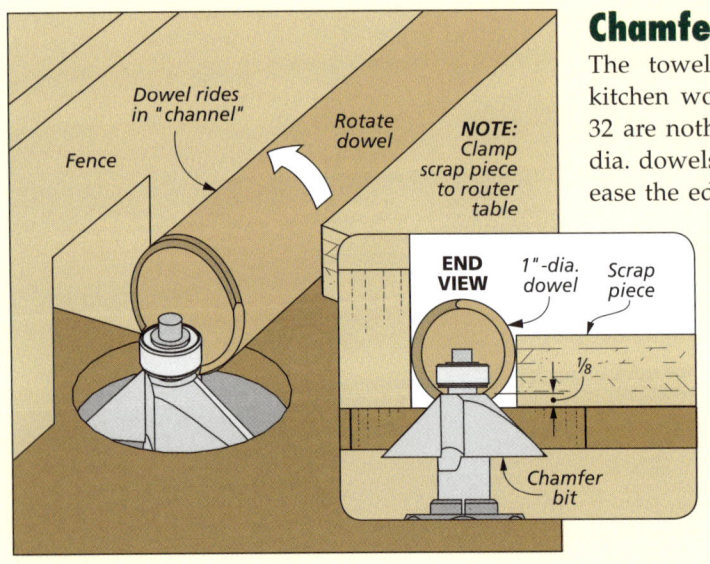

Leg Notches

To cut the leg notches in the plywood case tops and bottoms of the kitchen workstation, I used the table saw. In order to support the workpiece, I added a tall auxiliary fence to my miter gauge. And to keep the spacing of the cuts consistent, I taped a scrap block to my rip fence and used it as a stop, as shown in the drawing at right.

I cut each notch in two passes, standing the workpiece on edge to make the first cut and then standing the workpiece on end to complete the notch.

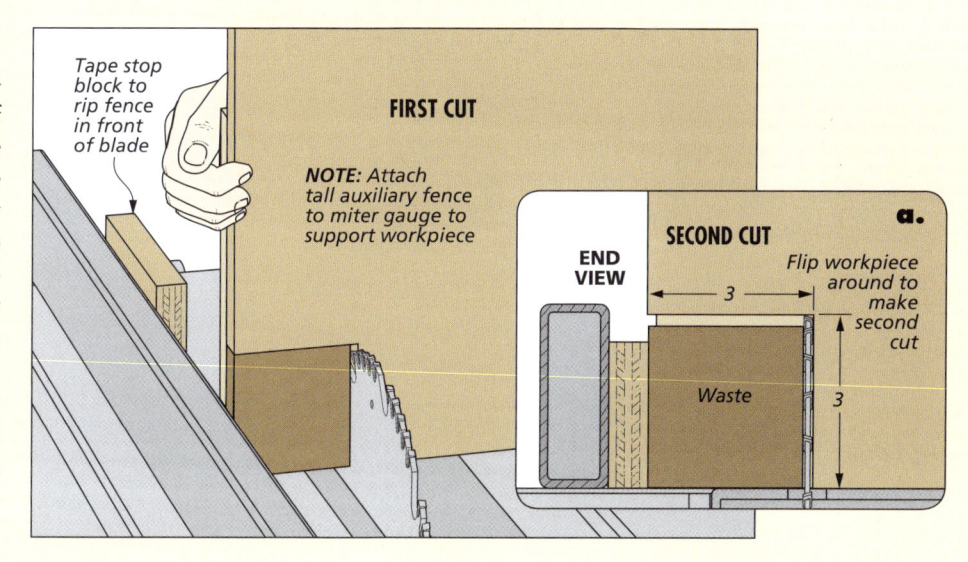

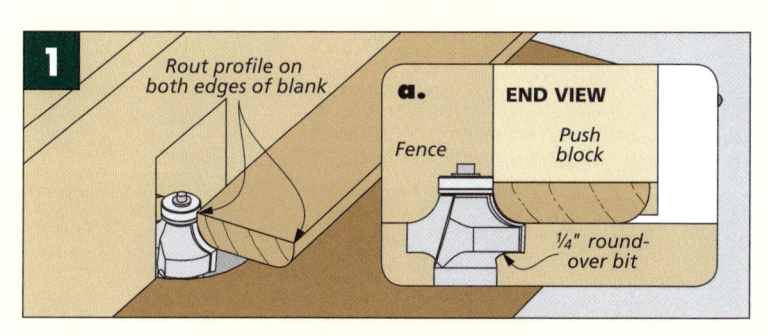

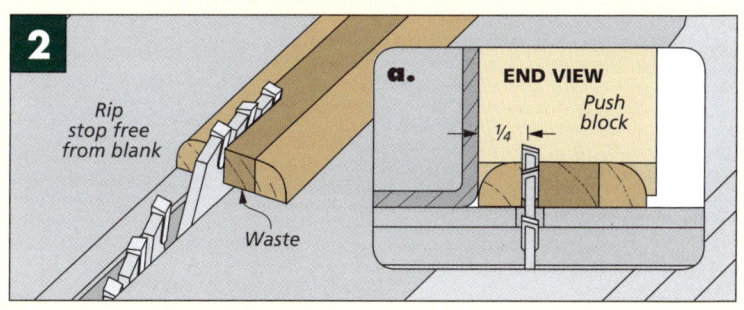

Glass Stop

The glass panels in the doors of the craft table on page 22 are held in place with quarter-round stop. To make this glass stop, I began by planing a wide blank to final thickness ($\frac{1}{4}$"). Once this was done, I routed a roundover on both edges of the blank, as you see in Figure 1 at left.

To complete the glass stop, I simply ripped it free from both edges of the blank at the table saw (Figure 2). A push block helps to safely guide the workpiece past the blade. All that's left after this is to miter the pieces to length and install them into the door frames.

No-Mortise Hinges

The doors of the storage cabinet are installed with wrap-around, no-mortise hinges. I installed the hinges to the doors first. (They simply wrap around the edge and back of each door and are screwed directly in place.)

To locate the hinges on the sides of the cabinet, I placed a piece of double-sided tape on each hinge (Figure 1). Then I pressed the door against the side of the cabinet, using an $\frac{1}{8}$"-thick shim to provide clearance, as shown in Figure 2.

With the hinges taped in place, I carefully opened the door and used the hinge as a template to drill the screw holes (Figure 3). Then it's just a matter of removing the tape and screwing the hinges to the sides of cabinet.

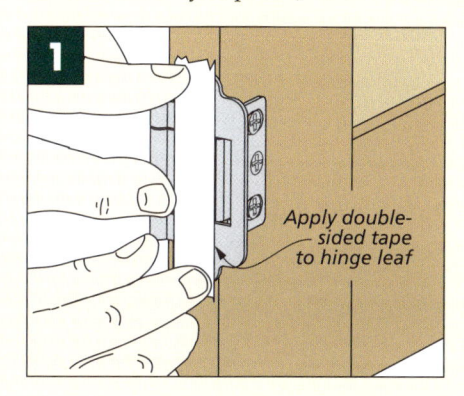

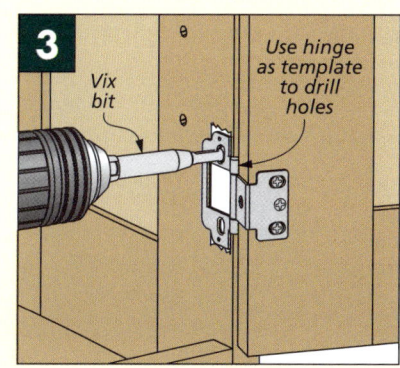

Heirloom Project

Kitchen Workstation

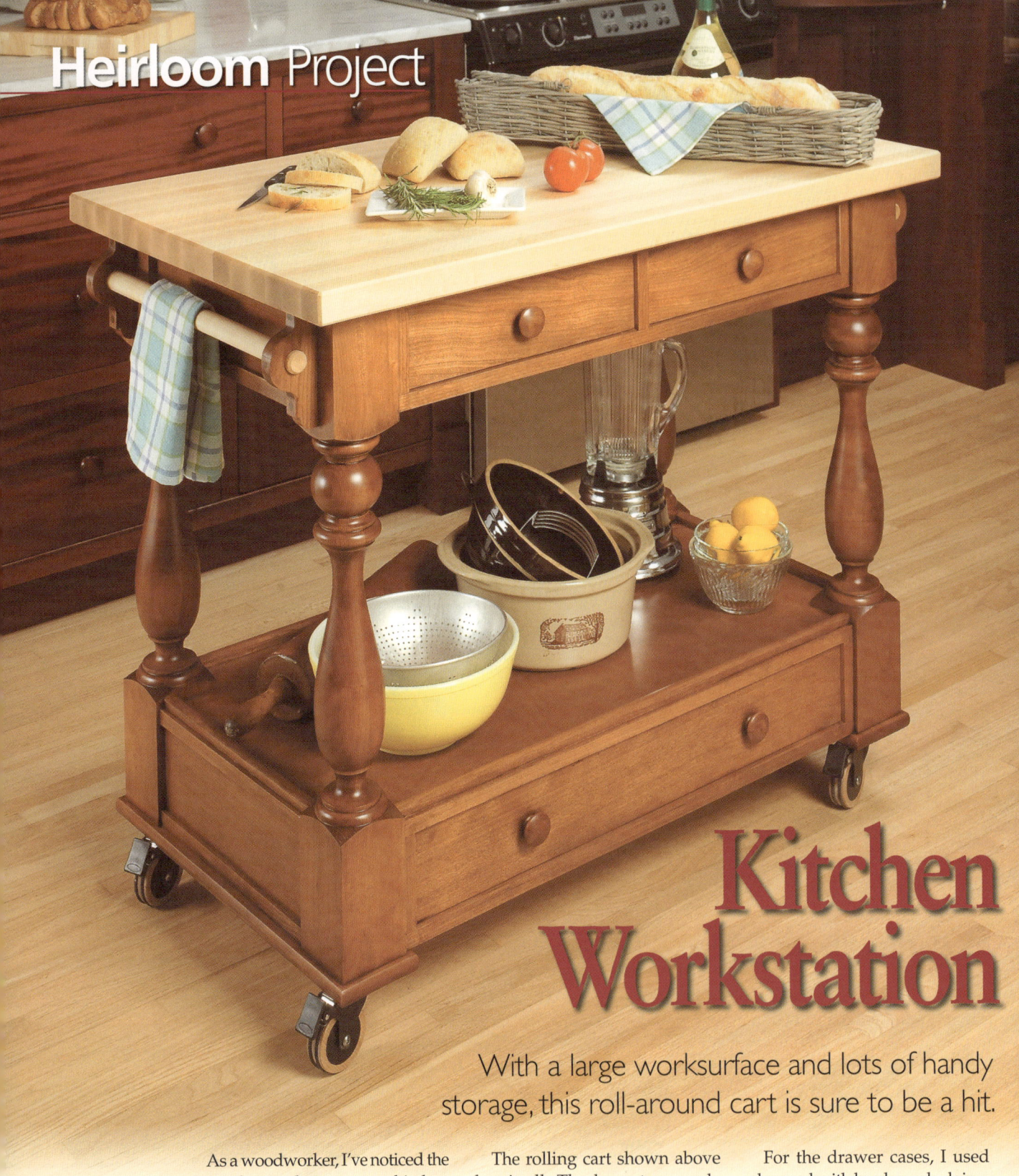

With a large worksurface and lots of handy storage, this roll-around cart is sure to be a hit.

As a woodworker, I've noticed the similarities between my kitchen and my workshop. After all, both are used for preparing the individual pieces of a project. Each place requires tools, storage, and plenty of worksurfaces. So having a roll-around cart makes as much sense in the kitchen as it does in the shop. It helps make kitchen projects a little easier to tackle.

The rolling cart shown above has it all. The large top, made from glued-up, edge-grain maple, provides a durable and attractive worksurface. With three drawers and a large space under the top, the cart is also a great place to store a few often-used kitchen items. Full-extension drawer slides help take advantage of every square inch of the drawer space.

For the drawer cases, I used plywood with hardwood edging. The turned cherry legs came from an on-line supplier, but you can easily turn your own if you have a lathe. You can even customize the space between the upper and lower cases. I decided to add a small wine rack (see the photo on the opposite page and Designer's Notebook on page 39).

32   Woodsmith   No. 193

CONSTRUCTION DETAILS

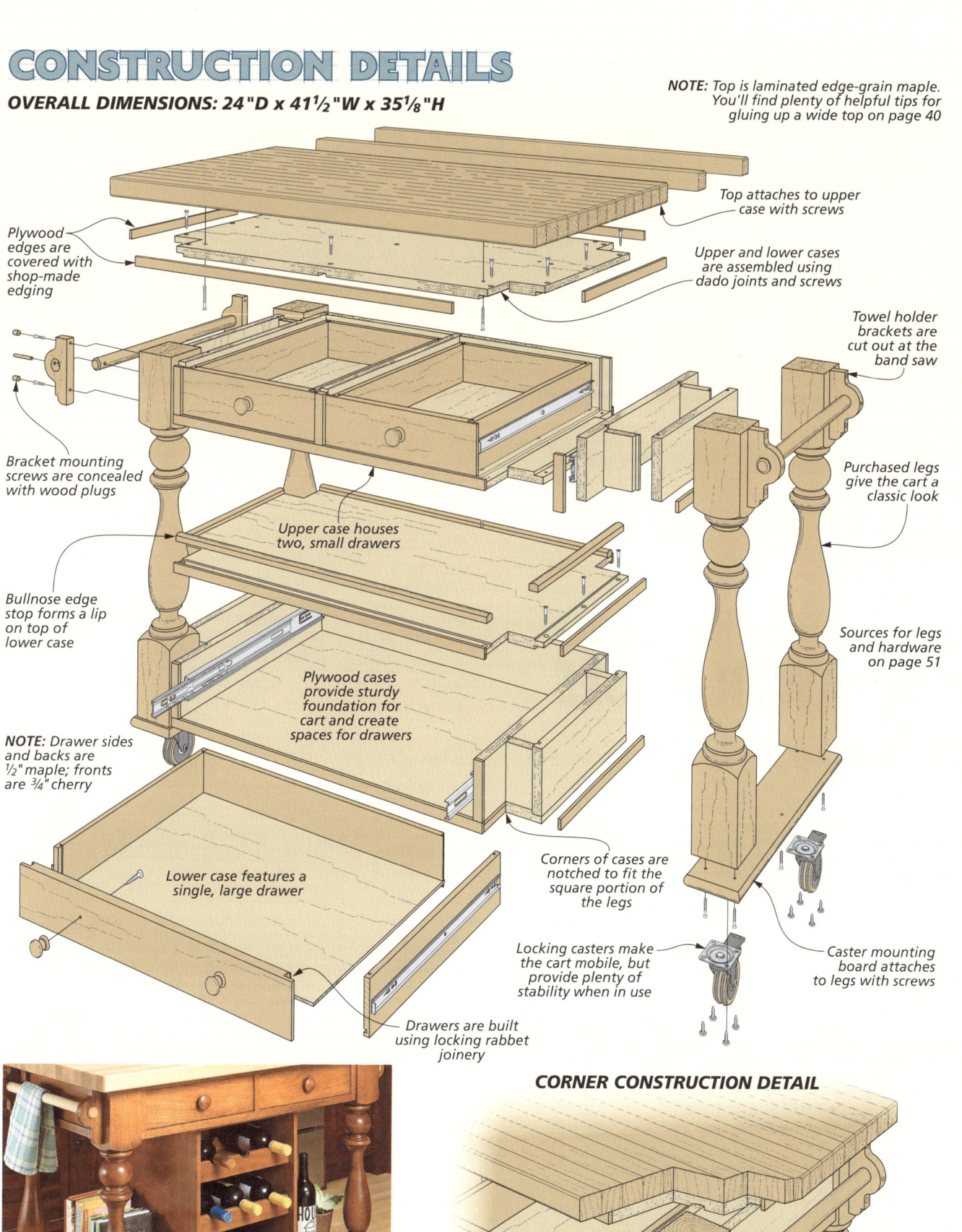

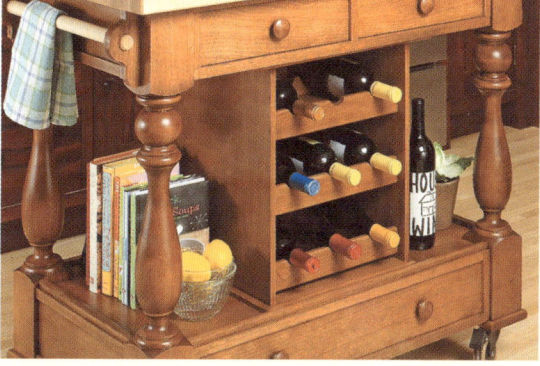

OVERALL DIMENSIONS: 24"D x 41½"W x 35⅛"H

NOTE: Top is laminated edge-grain maple. You'll find plenty of helpful tips for gluing up a wide top on page 40

- Plywood edges are covered with shop-made edging
- Top attaches to upper case with screws
- Upper and lower cases are assembled using dado joints and screws
- Towel holder brackets are cut out at the band saw
- Bracket mounting screws are concealed with wood plugs
- Purchased legs give the cart a classic look
- Upper case houses two, small drawers
- Bullnose edge stop forms a lip on top of lower case
- Sources for legs and hardware on page 51
- Plywood cases provide sturdy foundation for cart and create spaces for drawers
- **NOTE:** Drawer sides and backs are ½" maple; fronts are ¾" cherry
- Lower case features a single, large drawer
- Corners of cases are notched to fit the square portion of the legs
- Locking casters make the cart mobile, but provide plenty of stability when in use
- Caster mounting board attaches to legs with screws
- Drawers are built using locking rabbet joinery

▲ The kitchen cart is the perfect place for a small wine rack. The details for building the wine rack can be found on page 39.

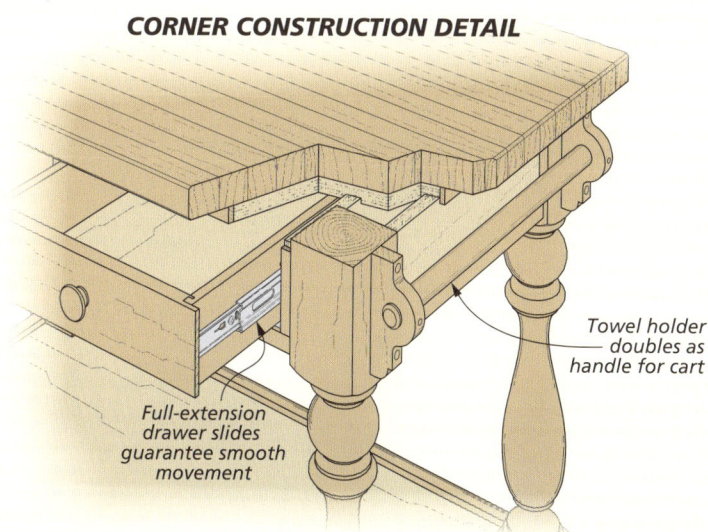

CORNER CONSTRUCTION DETAIL

- Towel holder doubles as handle for cart
- Full-extension drawer slides guarantee smooth movement

Woodsmith.com　　Woodsmith　　33

making the DRAWER CASES

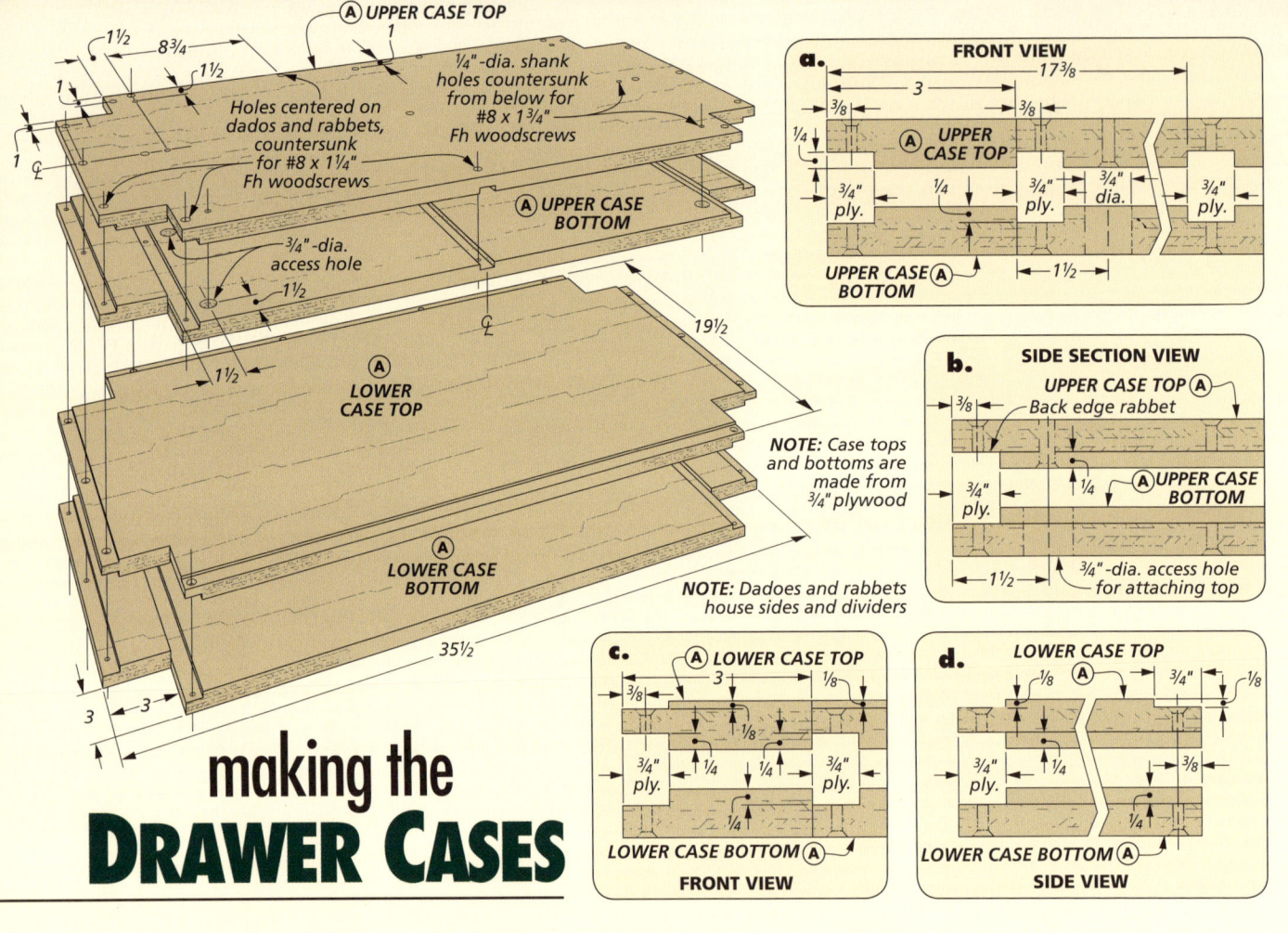

The upper and lower cases are at the heart of this project. In addition to housing the drawers, they provide the foundation for attaching the legs, top, and the casters. So assembling the pair of cases is the first priority. The lower case is a little taller than the upper one, but they're built using the same techniques. If you build them together you can avoid repeating saw setups. Just be sure to make careful layout marks to keep the pieces properly oriented.

THE TOPS & BOTTOMS. I started by cutting the plywood tops and bottoms to final size. Each set requires a different combination of dadoes and rabbets to hold the sides and dividers, with opposite faces being mirror images of each other. So an accurate alignment is only possible if the workpieces and the joinery cuts are square.

Next, I cut the notches in the corners of all four pieces. Turn to page 31 to find a safe and reliable technique for making these cuts using the table saw.

To cut the joinery, I installed a stack dado blade matching the thickness of the plywood. The details above show you where the dadoes and rabbets are located and the box at left demonstrates how to make the cuts. Finish up by cutting the shallower rabbets on the top face of the lower case. These rabbets will hold a bullnose edge stop you'll add later.

At this point, you can drill the countersunk screw holes at the locations shown in the main drawing. Note that one set of holes is for fastening the sides and another set is used to attach the top. The large-diameter holes in the bottom of the upper case provide access to the screws when adding the top.

How-To: Cut Dadoes & Rabbets

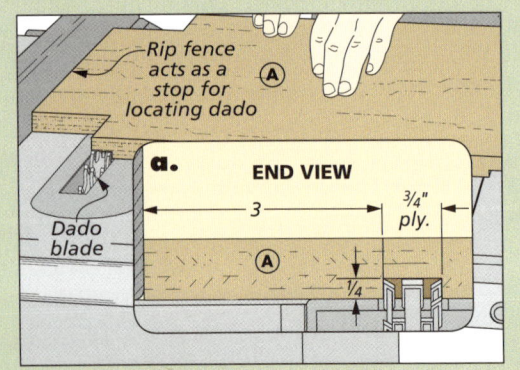

Dado for the Sides. Using the rip fence as a guide for cutting the dadoes for the sides guarantees perfect placement.

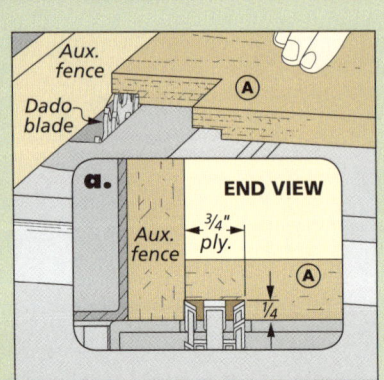

Rabbets on the Ends. Adding an auxiliary fence makes cutting the rabbets on the ends a breeze.

SIDES & DIVIDERS. After cutting a plywood blank for the sides, divider, ends, and back to width, cut each piece to final length. You can also cut the fillers that fit between the sides and ends.

I installed a dado blade and used the miter gauge to cut a centered dado in the back of the upper case. This dado houses the divider. While you're at it, cut the rabbets on the ends of both back pieces.

Now change the width of the dado blade to ¼" and cut the dadoes in the sides. These dadoes fit the tongues on the fillers.

You'll also need to cut dadoes in the ends. The box below shows the technique for this and for making the tongues on the fillers, as well.

DRY FIT. It's a good idea to take a few minutes and dry fit the assembly to make sure everything is square and the joints have a snug fit. You can also drill pilot holes in the sides, ends, dividers, and fillers.

ASSEMBLY. Once you're happy with the fit, take everything apart again and get ready to move on to the final assembly. Start by adding glue and screwing in the upright pieces from the bottom first. This way, you can position and fasten the drawer slides before attaching the top. (You'd be hard pressed to reach inside the case later and screw them in place accurately.)

I've found the easiest way to add drawer slides is to make a spacer block to support the slide while driving the screws. This simple technique not only guarantees uniform positioning of the slides, but it also makes sure they're installed level.

All that remains is to add the case tops. Using screws makes this a pretty stress-free process.

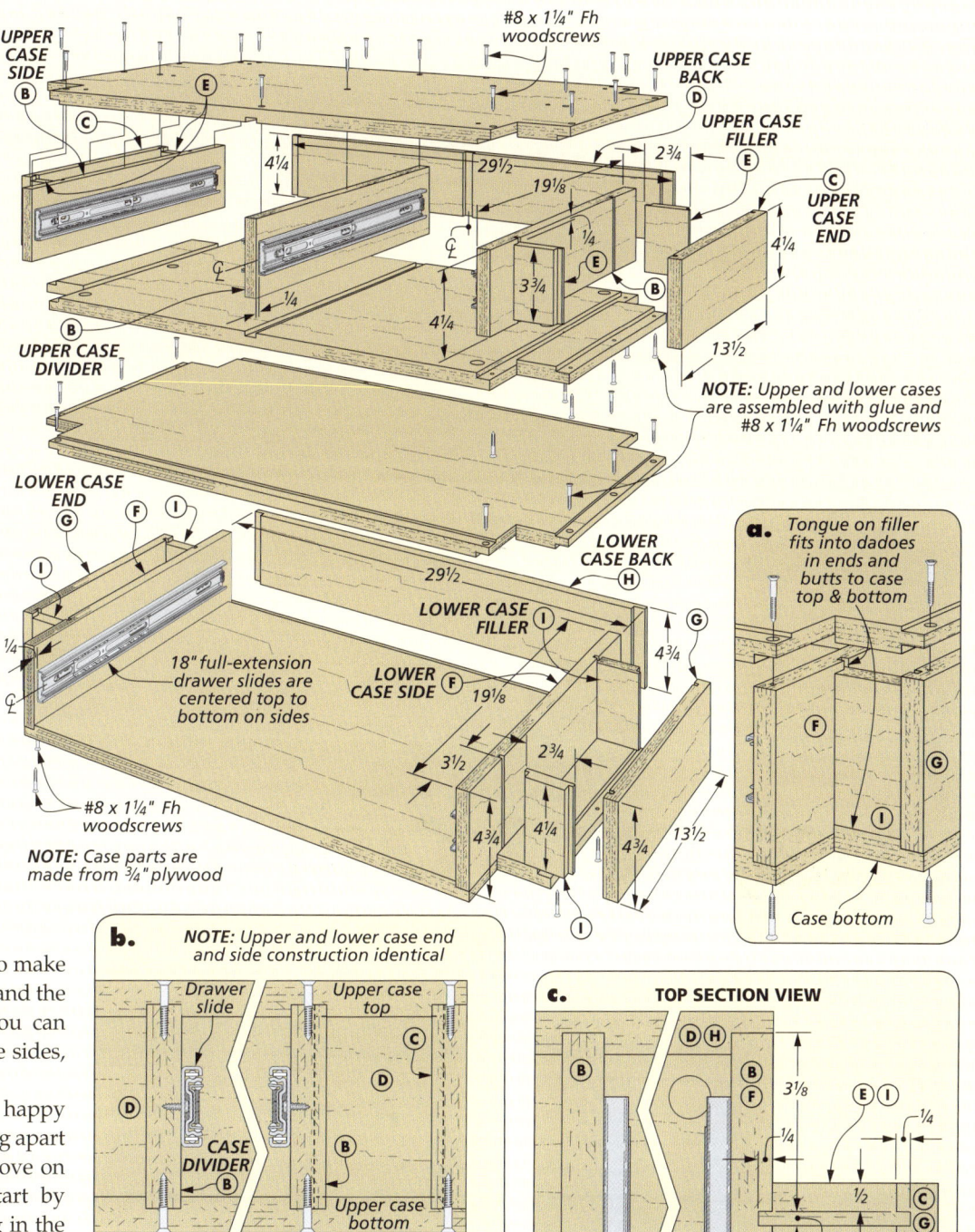

How-To: Cut End Assembly

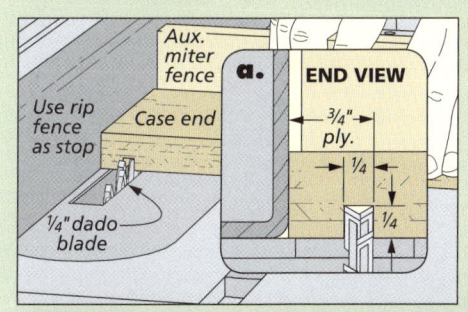

Dado the Ends. Using an auxiliary fence on the miter gauge, cut the narrow dado on both ends of the end pieces.

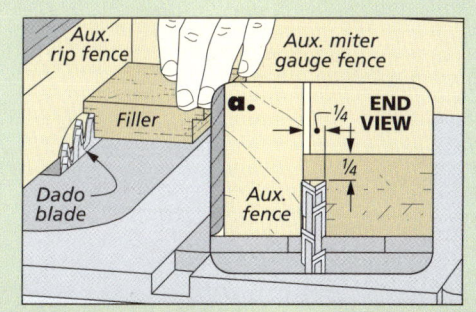

Rabbet the Fillers. When cutting the tongues, sneak up on the depth of cut to achieve a snug fit in the dadoes.

Woodsmith.com   Woodsmith   35

adding the
LEGS, TRIM & CASTERS

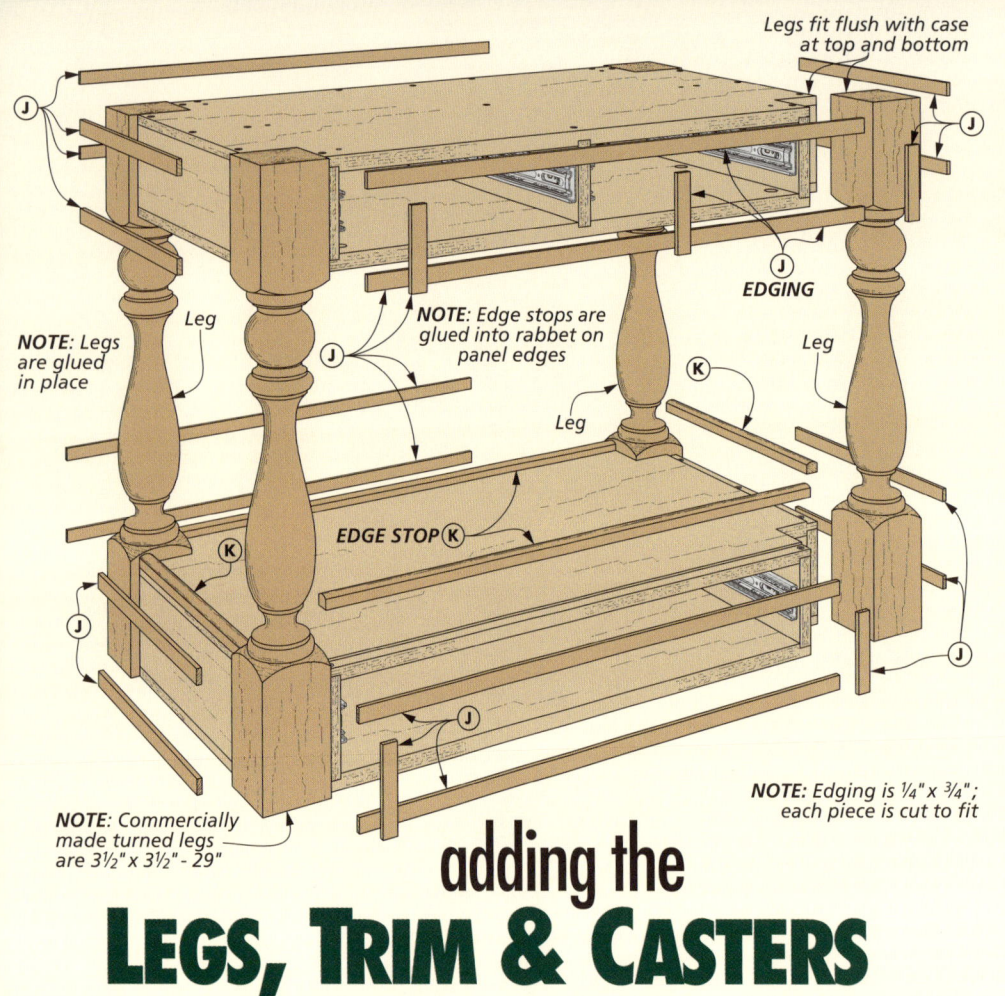

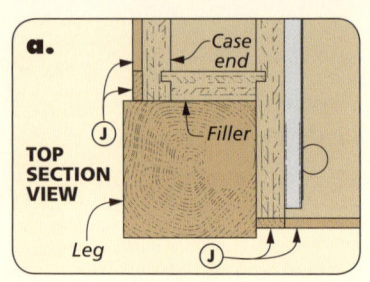

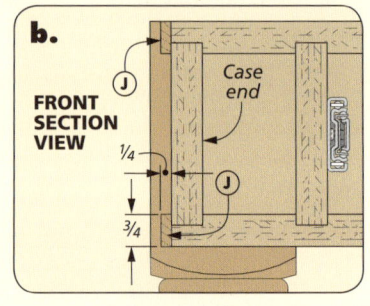

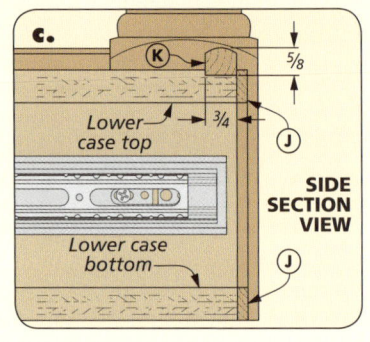

With the upper and lower cases complete, the cart starts to take shape pretty quickly. This is where the legs come in. As I said earlier, I purchased the legs from an on-line supplier. Gluing them in place is the next order of business. After that, you'll add a few other details to wrap up the lower part of the cart. Then you can make a towel holder for each end of the cart. Finally, I added some casters that complement the look of the project. (See sources on page 51 for details.)

ATTACHING THE LEGS. It's a good idea to make sure the edges of the legs are square before you attach them to the cases. Then it's just a matter of gluing them in the notches in both cases. The large glue surface ensures a strong joint.

I started by dry fitting the legs on one end and clamping them in position. Then I checked the fit in the case on the opposite end to make sure the legs were parallel. Once you're happy with the fit, simply add glue and clamps. Be sure to keep the top and bottom ends of the legs flush with the cases throughout the assembly.

HARDWOOD EDGING. At this point, you're ready to cover the plywood edges with some shop-made, hardwood edging. I started by planing a wide blank to match the thickness of the plywood. Then, simply rip the edging to just over $1/4$" thick. Finish up by planing it to final thickness.

To make sure you get a gap-free fit on the edging, it helps to cut and fit each piece individually. Blue painter's tape works well as a clamp to hold the edging in place while the glue dries.

How-To: Make Bullnose Edge Stop

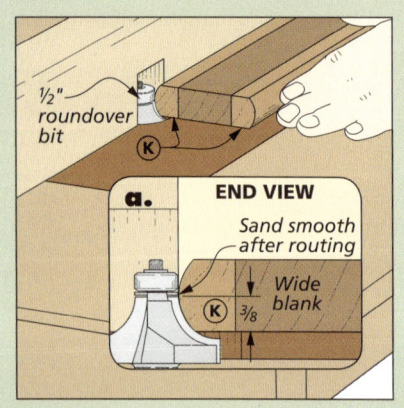

Routing the Bullnose Profile. Use a roundover bit to rout the profile on both edges of a wide blank.

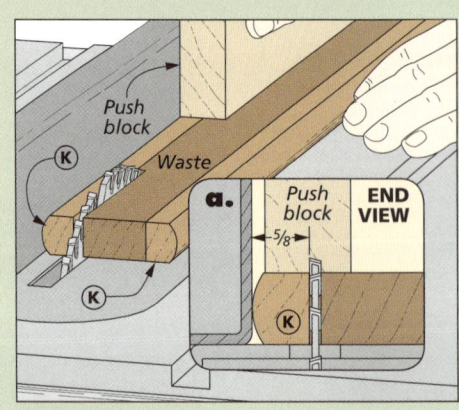

Ripping the Strips. Set the rip fence on the table saw to match the height of the edging and use a push block to rip the strips.

EDGE STOP. I added a bullnose edge stop on the top of the lower case. This helps keep anything you store there from sliding off. Once again, it's a simple process to make the bullnose stop. The box at the bottom of the opposite page walks you through it. Glue the edge stop in place in the rabbets you cut in the top.

TOWEL HOLDERS. The towel holders on each end of the cart serve double duty as convenient handles for moving the cart. You can make the brackets using the pattern in the right margin. After attaching them to the case, add a dowel towel rack. The box below shows how to go about it.

I added a small chamfer to the ends of the towel holder. (See Shop Notebook on page 30.) Detail 'a' shows how the dowel plugs cover the screw holes. You can also see how I used a dowel to pin the towel rack in place.

ADDING THE CASTERS. I chose wood casters with rubber "tires" for the kitchen cart. To attach the casters, you'll first need to add a mounting board. As you can see in the main drawing and in detail 'c,' I routed the same bullnose profile I used for the edge stop on all edges of the mounting boards. Attach the mounting boards to the underside of the lower case with screws, then attach the casters.

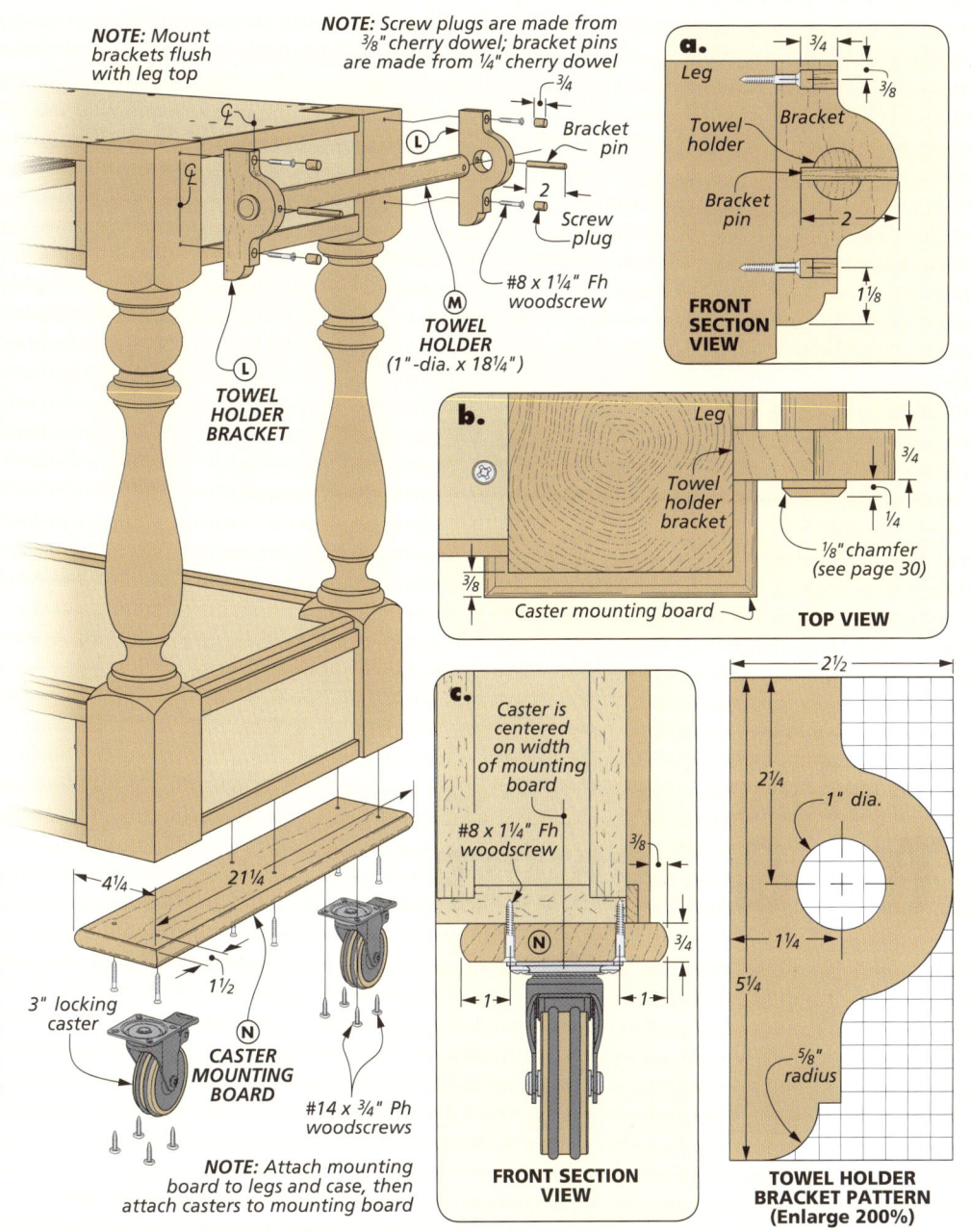

Shape the Towel Holder Brackets

Cutting Out the Bracket. Cut the brackets to shape at the band saw and then sand them smooth.

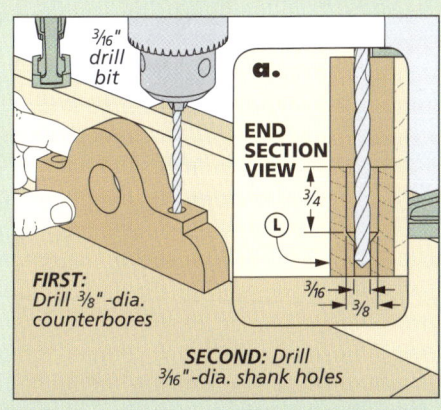

Drill the Holes. After drilling the hole for the towel holder in the bracket, drill the counterbores and the shank holes.

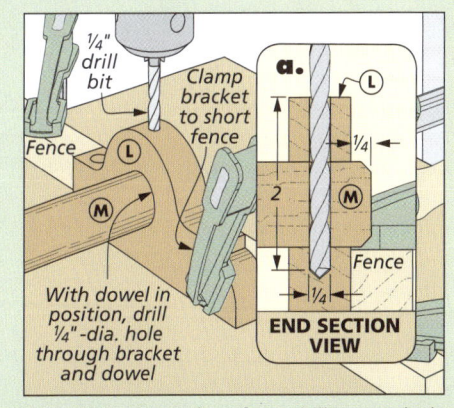

Pin the Dowel. After drilling a hole through the bracket into the dowel, use a 1/4"-dia. dowel to secure the towel holder.

Woodsmith.com   Woodsmith   37

building the
TOP & DRAWERS

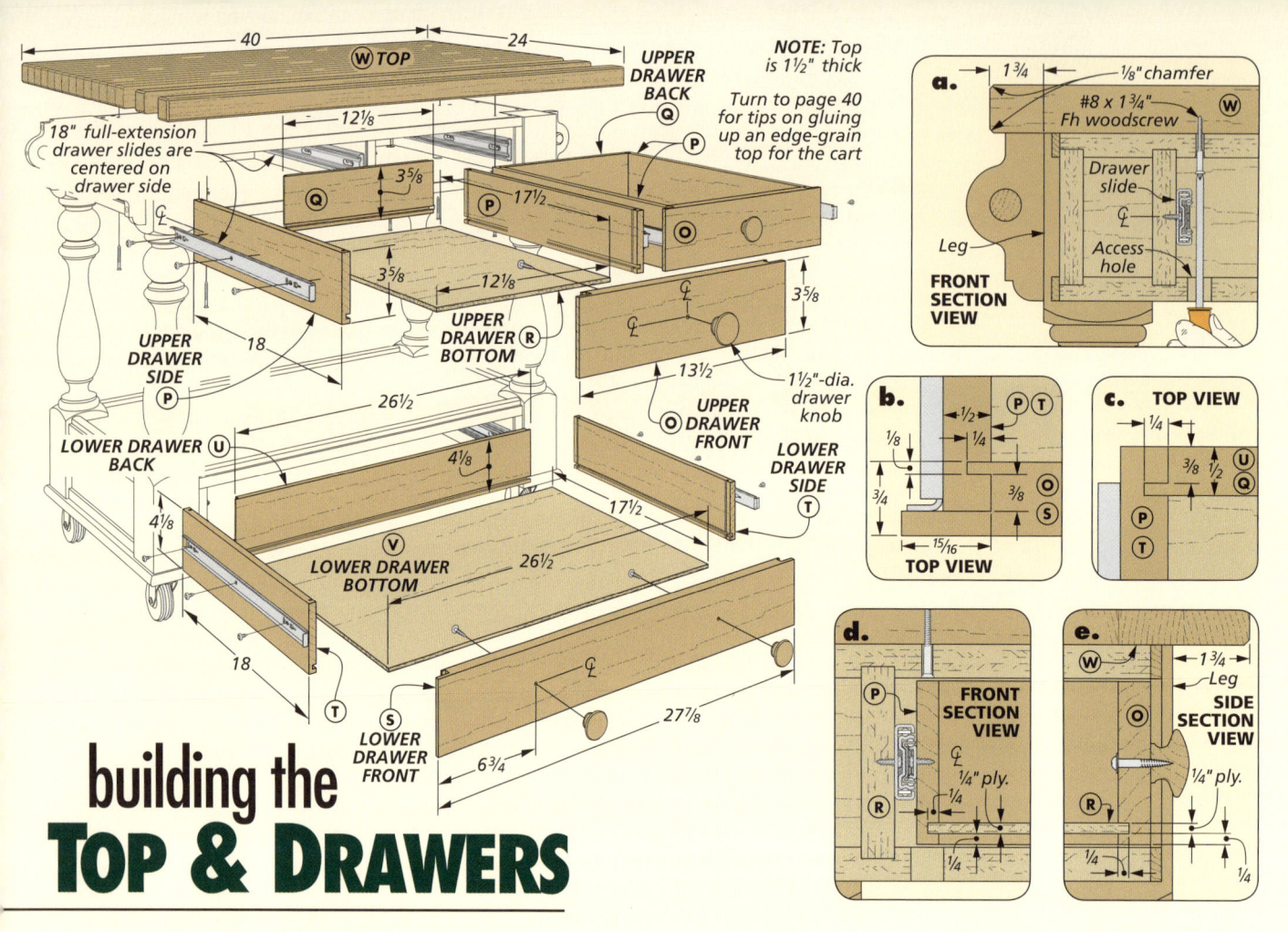

The kitchen cart wouldn't be complete without a few drawers. After all, you can never have enough storage space. I completed the cart with a glued-up, hardwood top.

DRAWERS. The two drawers in the upper unit are shorter than the bottom drawer, but all three are made using locking rabbet joinery on the fronts and tongue and dado joints for attaching the backs. They also feature wide fronts to conceal the drawers slides. It's a good idea to make them all at the same time.

LOCKING RABBETS. I used 1/2"-thick maple for the drawer sides and backs, and 3/4"-thick cherry for the fronts. After cutting all the parts to final size, you can start on the joinery (details 'b' & 'c'). The box below shows you how to cut the locking rabbet joints for the drawer fronts.

After completing the fronts, you can move on to cut the dadoes in the sides. Once again, use the miter gauge. Attach an auxiliary rip fence to cut the tongues on the drawer backs. Finally, cut a groove near the bottom edge of all the pieces to hold the drawer bottom (detail 'd,' & 'e').

I used 1/4" plywood for the drawer bottoms. I simply cut them to final size at the table saw.

Now you can assemble the drawers using glue and a few clamps. After the glue dries, lay out the locations for the drawer knobs and drill the holes. Then install the knobs with screws. Finally, just attach the drawer slides and install the drawers in the case.

THE TOP. The top is glued up from edge-grain strips of maple. You'll find some tips for a successful glue-up procedure in the article on page 40. When you've completed the top, attach it to the case using screws. An oil finish for the top and stain and lacquer for the cart completes the project. **W**

How-To: Cut a Locking Rabbet Joint

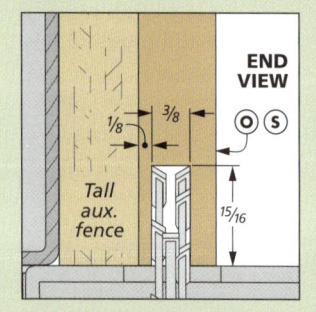

Drawer Fronts. With the drawer front held vertically, cut the off-center groove.

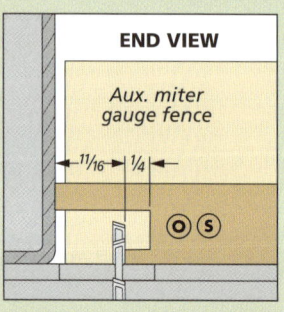

Tongue. Using an auxiliary fence on the miter gauge, cut the tongue to length.

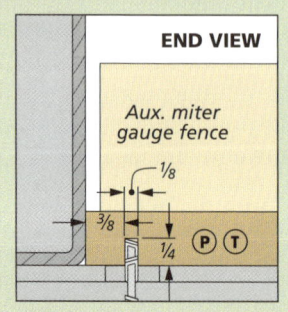

Sides. Use the rip fence as a stop for cutting the dadoes in the drawer sides.

FRONT VIEW

BACK VIEW

DESIGNER'S NOTEBOOK

For detailed plans of the optional wine rack, visit our website at Woodsmith.com

One way to take advantage of the space under the top of the cart is to add a handy wine rack. The design shown above also features a couple of extra storage shelves on the back side. If you're interested in building the wine cabinet to add to your cart, you can find the details on our website at Woodsmith.com.

Materials, Supplies & Cutting Diagram

A	Case Tops/Bottoms (4)	¾ ply. - 19½ x 35½
B	Upper Case Sides/Divider (3)	¾ ply. - 4¼ x 19⅛
C	Upper Case Ends (2)	¾ ply. - 4¼ x 13½
D	Upper Case Back (1)	¾ ply. - 4¼ x 29½
E	Upper Case Fillers (4)	¾ ply. - 3¾ x 2¾
F	Lower Case Sides (2)	¾ ply. - 4¾ x 19⅛
G	Lower Case Ends (2)	¾ ply. - 4¾ x 13½
H	Lower Case Back (1)	¾ ply. - 4¾ x 29½
I	Lower Case Fillers (4)	¾ ply. - 4¼ x 2¾
J	Edging (1)	¼ x ¾ - 30 ft. rgh.
K	Edge Stop (1)	⅝ x ¾ - 96 rgh.
L	Towel Holder Brackets (4)	¾ x 2½ - 5¼
M	Towel Holders (2)	1"-dia. x 18¼
N	Caster Mounting Boards (2)	¾ x 4¼ - 21¼
O	Upper Drawer Fronts (2)	¾ x 3⅝ - 13½
P	Upper Drawer Sides (4)	½ x 3⅝ - 18
Q	Upper Drawer Backs (2)	½ x 3⅝ - 12⅛
R	Upper Drawer Bottoms (2)	¼ ply. - 17½ x 12⅛
S	Lower Drawer Front (1)	¾ x 4⅛ - 27⅞
T	Lower Drawer Sides (2)	½ x 4⅛ - 18
U	Lower Drawer Back (1)	½ x 4⅛ - 26½
V	Lower Drawer Bottom (1)	¼ ply. - 17½ x 26½
W	Top (1)	1½ x 24 - 40

- (4) 3" Locking Casters
- (3 pr.) 18" Full-Extension Drawer Slides
- (4) 1½"-dia. Drawer Knobs
- (86) #8 x 1¼" Fh Woodscrews
- (16) #14 x ¾" Ph Sheet Metal Screws
- (6) #8 x 1¾" Fh Woodscrews
- (1) ¼"-dia. x 12" Cherry Dowel
- (1) ⅜"-dia. x 12" Cherry Dowel
- (2) 1"-dia. x 36" Maple Dowels
- (4) 3½" x 3½" - 29" Turned Legs

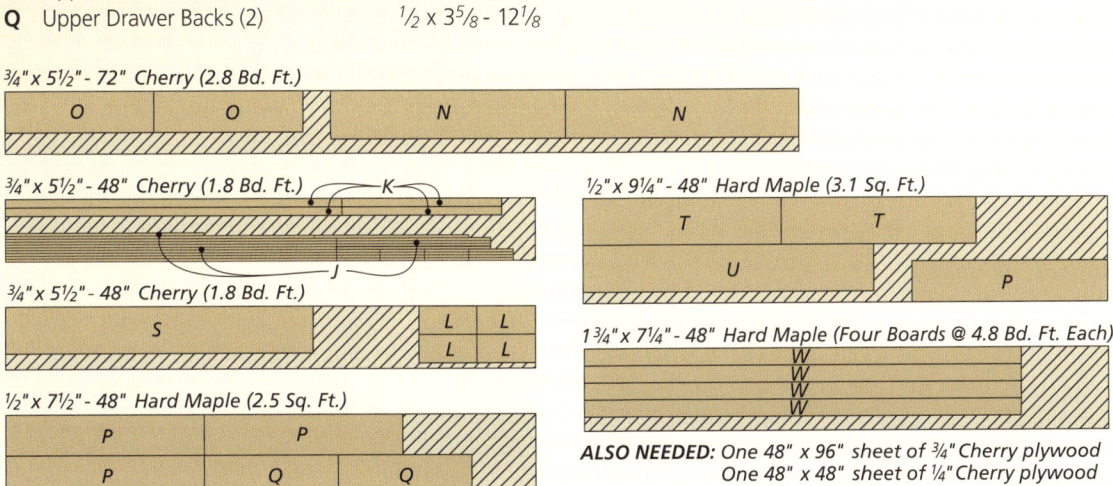

¾" x 5½" - 72" Cherry (2.8 Bd. Ft.)

¾" x 5½" - 48" Cherry (1.8 Bd. Ft.)

½" x 9¼" - 48" Hard Maple (3.1 Sq. Ft.)

¾" x 5½" - 48" Cherry (1.8 Bd. Ft.)

½" x 7½" - 48" Hard Maple (2.5 Sq. Ft.)

1¾" x 7¼" - 48" Hard Maple (Four Boards @ 4.8 Bd. Ft. Each)

ALSO NEEDED: One 48" x 96" sheet of ¾" Cherry plywood
One 48" x 48" sheet of ¼" Cherry plywood

woodworking technique

making an
Edge-Grain Top

Gluing up a wide lamination for a worksurface might seem like a daunting task, but it's just a matter of taking it in stages.

A solid-wood top made from glued-up hardwood strips is both attractive and very functional. It shows off the straight grain and is less prone to cupping or splitting than a single, wide piece, even when it gets wet. So it's no surprise that it's a popular choice for kitchen worksurfaces.

The inset photo above shows an edge-grain top as the worksurface on the kitchen cart. (That project starts on page 32.) This is the perfect application for an edge-grain lamination.

CHALLENGES. But if you've ever struggled to glue up a solid top, chances are you've probably encountered a few problems along the way. For instance, the lumber in my shop seldom stays perfectly flat and straight. Nor does it all have a pleasant, uniform color. So unless I pay careful attention and take steps to solve these problems, the finished product won't look as good as the photo above.

However, if you break the process down into a few simple operations, you'll get predictable results every time. It starts with choosing the right wood and milling it properly. Then, you need to take the time to work out the best color and grain match by arranging the individual workpieces.

Finally, the key to a good assembly is to glue up the top in sections. This not only keeps the size of the individual glueups more manageable, but it also allows you to take advantage of your planer to smooth the face of each section. Then you only have two or three joints to worry about in the final assembly. But it all begins with a trip to the lumberyard.

START WITH THE RIGHT STOCK. There's no doubt that maple is the first choice for a laminated top. It's hard, fairly stable, and has very attractive edge grain. Ash is another option, offering slightly better stability if not as tight a

Woodsmith

grain pattern. Of course, you can use these techniques with any wood. In fact, I've made some very nice-looking tops for shop projects using inexpensive, "two-by," construction lumber.

WHAT TO LOOK FOR. No matter what species you choose, there are a few rules of thumb to keep in mind as you pick through the stock to select the individual boards.

First, find flatsawn boards. Ripping them into strips and flipping them on edge will expose the straight, edge-grain pattern. You don't want quartersawn lumber for this kind of assembly.

Straight-grain stock with consistent ring spacing and uniform color will result in the best-looking top. (You can check the end grain of the boards to see how closely the rings are spaced.) I try to avoid boards containing contrasting sapwood and heartwood.

THICKER IS BETTER. I usually choose 1¾"-thick stock for an edge-grain glueup. It not only makes a great-looking top, but it also tends to be a little more stable after you cut it. You can use ¾"-thick stock, of course, but the narrower strips will give a different look to the top (and double the number of strips you'll need to glue up).

PREPARING THE STOCK. Planing the stock before ripping it into strips makes the whole process easier. In most cases, the face of the board will become the glued-up edge joint in the finished product. So getting both faces as flat as possible is a great way to start.

Before you begin, check the knives in your planer. If possible, install a fresh (or recently sharpened) set. This can nearly eliminate further jointing work.

Keep the workpieces extra long while planing (about 6") and cut them to final length later. This makes it possible to cut off snipe. Snipe will result in gaps in the ends of a glued-up section.

Finally, before you begin running boards through the planer, check the grain direction on the edge of each one. The point here is to identify which end to put into the planer so the blades cut "downhill." The photo above and the drawings below show you what I mean. By taking the time to identify the correct feed direction, you can avoid tearout in the planer. And since the planed face will eventually be a joint, this prevents gaps and unsightly voids in the joints on the finished top.

PLANING. Now you can start planing the workpieces. The key here is to take light passes. I plane both faces so each ends up flat and ready for gluing. In order to avoid tearout, you'll need to feed the opposite end of the board into the planer as you flip it over to plane the opposite face.

JOINT ONE EDGE. Now you can prepare the workpieces for ripping. And for that, I move to the jointer. Once again, pay attention to the grain direction as you pass the boards over the jointer (as in the drawing below). When you're done, it's time to head over to the table saw to rip the workpieces.

▲ Check the edge of a workpiece to spot the grain direction before planing.

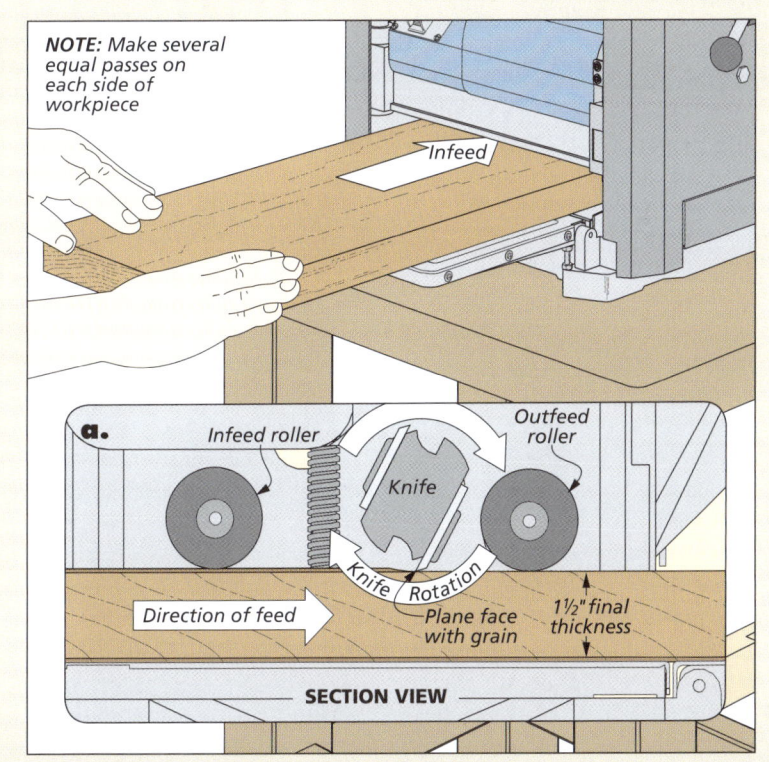

Planing the Faces. After determining the grain direction on each workpiece, run them through the planer. You'll want to take light cuts and remove just enough stock to flatten both faces.

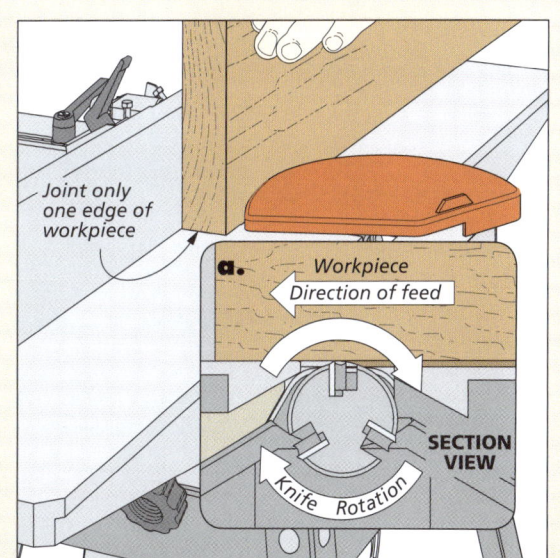

Jointing the Edges. The jointer provides a perfectly straight, reference edge. Check the grain direction on the face of each workpiece to avoid tearout.

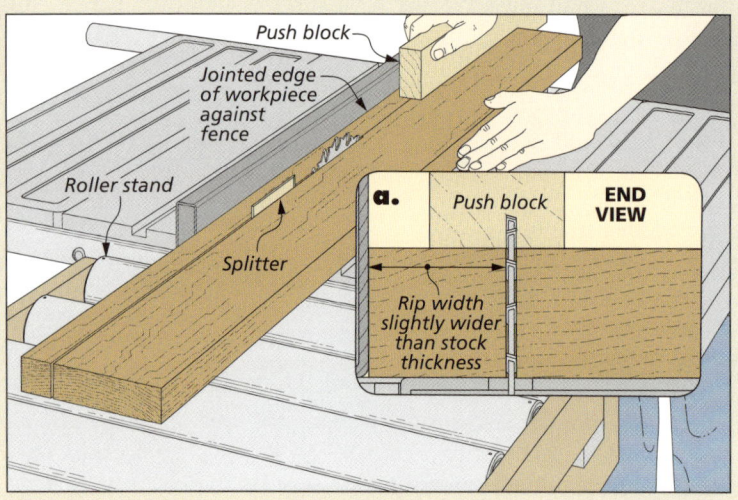

Ripping. After installing a rip blade and setting up good outfeed support for your table saw, rip the strips extra wide. This allows you to run them through the planer to clean up the saw marks on the edges.

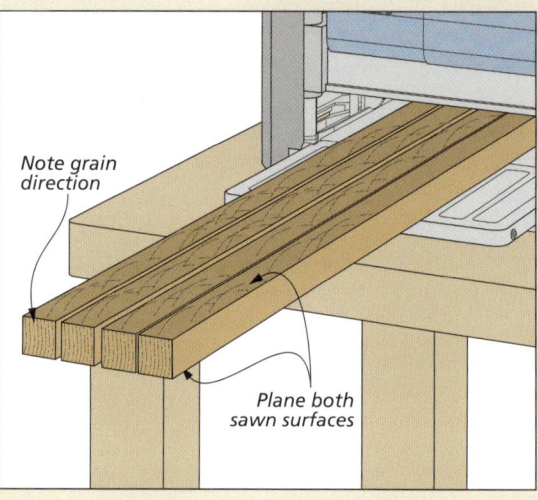

Planing the Strips. Plane both freshly sawn surfaces to remove all the saw marks. Take shallow cuts with each pass to help prevent tearout.

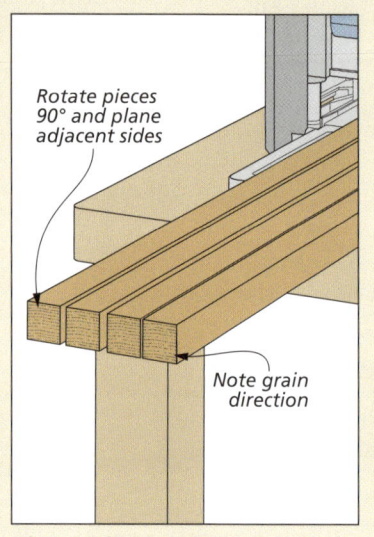

Plane Adjacent Faces. Rotate the blanks and plane both adjacent surfaces to square the pieces.

RIPPING, PLANING & ASSEMBLING

It may seem like you spent a lot of time selecting and preparing the stock. But by taking the time to do it properly, you've made the rest of the process easier. Now you're ready to start ripping the wide boards and assembling the top.

SET UP THE TABLE SAW. Ripping thick hardwood stock can be a challenge. But there are a couple of things you can do to guarantee safe and smooth sailing.

RIP BLADE. For a quick rip cut in thin stock, a combination blade is fine. But when you set out to rip lots of thick hardwood, you need to install a good rip blade. A thin-kerf blade can also be a big help in an underpowered saw.

Now is the time to make sure the blade is square to the table and the fence is parallel to the blade. It's also a good idea to give the stock a final inspection before you begin ripping the wide blanks. Check to be sure each piece sits flat on the table saw without rocking. Any rocking can cause dangerous kickback.

Another concern is the stock pinching the blade during the cut. To avoid this, make sure the splitter is installed on your saw. Finally, use a push block to feed the stock and a roller stand or table for outfeed support, as shown in the left drawing above.

RIPPING. With your saw tuned up and outfeed support in place, you're ready to start ripping the strips. Two things to keep in mind here are to hold the stock tight against the fence and to maintain a consistent feed rate. The feed rate will be dictated by your saw. Cutting 1¾"-thick maple can be a real test. Feed the stock too fast and the saw bogs down, too slow and the stock burns.

Set the rip fence to cut the strips slightly wider than the thickness of the stock. This way, you can clean up the edges in the planer and finish at the desired thickness.

PLANING. A couple passes through the planer will clean up both faces. Making a final pass on the adjacent faces will square up the blanks and offer you more flexibility when assembling the top. When I've finished planing, I like to let the stock rest for a couple days to allow it to stabilize.

LAYOUT & DRY ASSEMBLY. Now that you have a supply of strips planed and ready to assemble, it's time to put them together for the best look. I like to do the layout on a sheet of MDF on my bench. The flat surface of the MDF helps highlight any imperfections in the surfaces of the workpieces. Now is the time to spot them, not when you're clamping the glued-up sections. You may need to make another pass through the planer.

It helps to be patient when working on the arrangement. While the goal is for each piece to be perfectly square and flat, the wood seldom cooperates. In reality, there will usually be

Rip Blade

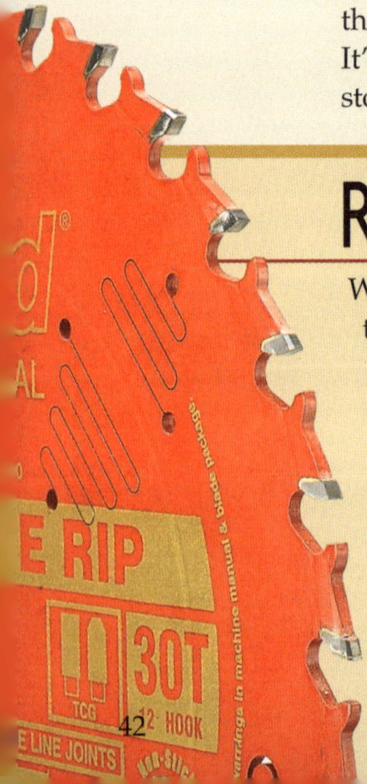

When it comes to ripping thick hardwood stock, a good rip blade is a must. You want a blade with about 24-30 teeth so there aren't too many in the stock at a time. Any more can cause burning. And a rip blade's deep gullets keep the chips clear.

some small bows. You can compensate for these by alternating the direction as shown in Figure 1, at right. I worked with four strips at a time. You don't want to have to pull any big gaps together with the clamps. When you've put together a grouping you're happy with, mark the faces (Figure 2).

GLUING UP THE SECTIONS. Turn one edge of each piece face up and apply a bead of glue to one surface of each joint. Use a brush or plastic spreader to even out a thin coat. A "rub joint" technique helps to coat both glue surfaces. (Simply rub the glued surface against the opposite piece until you get an even coat on both.)

It's a good idea to have your clamps laid out and opened to the rough size of the assembly. This way, you can simply put them in place and tighten them up. You can use your favorite bar, pipe, or parallel-jaw clamps (Figure 4).

CLEANING UP. After the glue dries, scrape the squeezeout from both surfaces as shown in Figure 5. A belt sander can also be handy for cleaning up stubborn glue and preparing the sections for the planer. (If you run hardened glue squeezeout through your planer, it can nick the blades.) When you're done, plane both surfaces smooth. Of course, you'll need to plane all the sections to an equal thickness for the final assembly.

FINAL ASSEMBLY. After planing the individual sections, assembling them is a breeze. If any of the sections want to slide out of position, simply use a clamp on the joints to hold them in place.

SANDING & FINISHING. The final appearance of the top depends on a good sanding job. You need to be careful not to sand dips or depressions into the surface. One way to avoid this is to use plenty of pencil marks and a straightedge to gauge your progress.

Now just square up the ends using a circular saw or crosscut sled on the table saw. Add an oil finish and you have the perfect kitchen worksurface. **W**

How-To: Glue Up the Top

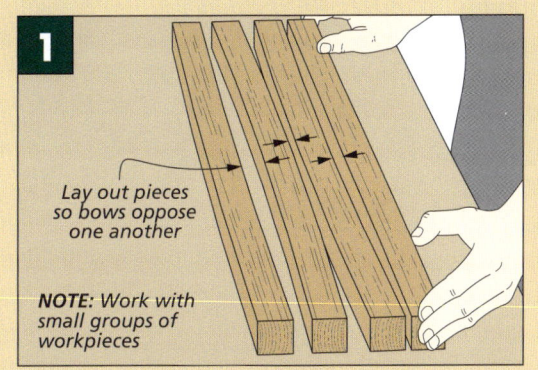

1 Lay out pieces so bows oppose one another. NOTE: Work with small groups of workpieces

Color and Grain Matching. Lay out the pieces for the best appearance. If the stock is bowed, arrange the bowed faces opposite each other.

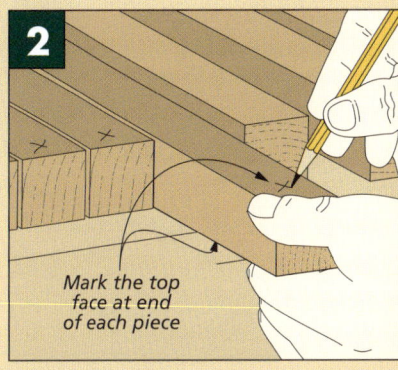

2 Mark the top face at end of each piece

Marking. When you have the best arrangement for each group, mark the top face of each piece.

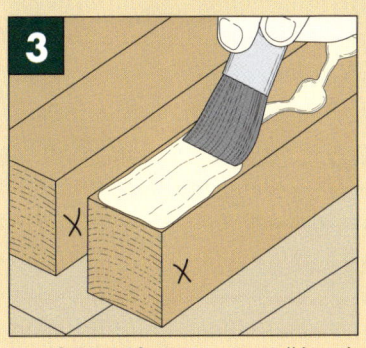

3 **Applying Glue.** Use a small brush to spread an even coat of glue on one face of each joint.

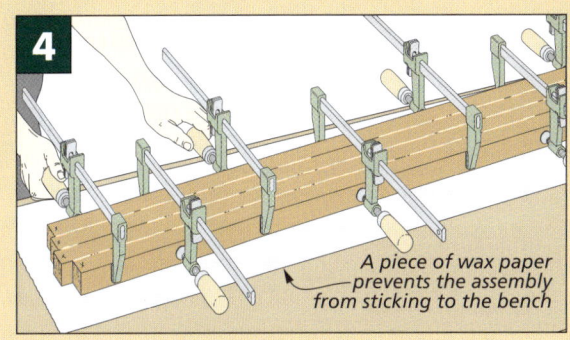

4 A piece of wax paper prevents the assembly from sticking to the bench

Glue Up the Sections. By working in narrow sections, you have plenty of time to keep each joint flat. This helps minimize planing later.

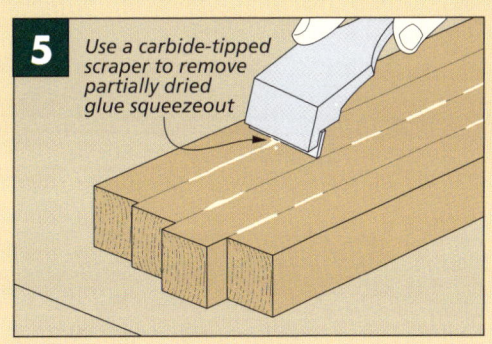

5 Use a carbide-tipped scraper to remove partially dried glue squeezeout

Scrape the Squeezeout. Use a scraper to remove the beads of partially dried glue from both surfaces of each section.

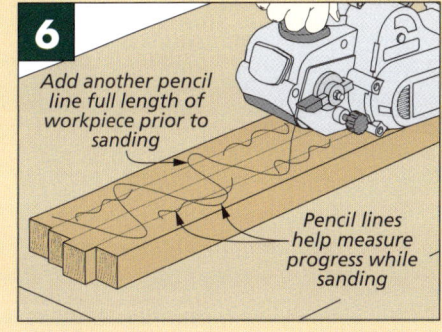

6 Add another pencil line full length of workpiece prior to sanding. Pencil lines help measure progress while sanding

Sanding. If a section slipped in the clamps or otherwise doesn't come out flat, a belt sander can help flatten one face.

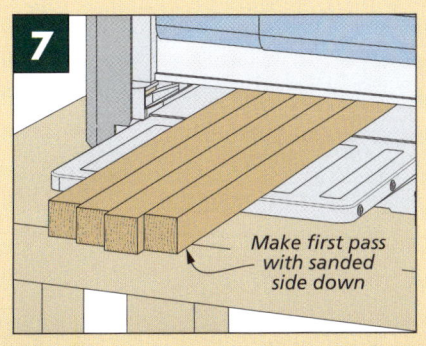

7 Make first pass with sanded side down

Planing. Once the glue is removed, run each section through the planer until they're all the same thickness.

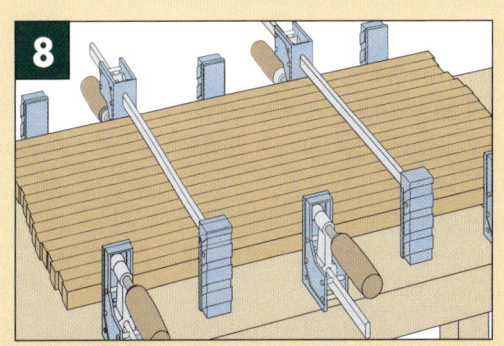

8 **Final Glueup.** At this point, you only have three joint lines to worry about as you assemble all the narrower sections.

working with tools

sharpening with
Diamond Plates

It's tough to beat the convenience of sharpening with diamonds, and a couple new products make it almost irresistable.

▼ You can find a diamond sharpening option for just about any situation.

Ask a dozen woodworkers what's the "best" way to sharpen edge tools and you'll get a dozen different answers. But compared to the other options, diamond plates offer some advantages.

WHY DIAMONDS? First, diamonds sharpen steel faster than other abrasives. This is due to the hardness of the diamond crystal.

Another advantage is the ease of using diamond plates. You don't need to soak or prepare them in any way. You can use them dry or with a lubricant. There's also very little maintenance required. There's no need to worry about flattening a diamond plate like you would a waterstone or oilstone. The plates stay perfectly flat during normal use. In fact, they're ideal for flattening your other types of abrasive stones.

Finally, it's the only sharpening medium available to the home woodworker that's hard enough to sharpen carbide. This makes diamonds the go-to tool for touching up router bits (photo in upper right corner of opposite page).

HOW THEY'RE MADE. Most waterstones and oilstones are solid blocks of abrasive. But diamond plates are made by bonding a thin layer of diamond particles to a steel plate, as shown in the photos at left.

EZE-Lap super-fine

EZE-Lap fine

EZE-Lap Super fine

DMT DiaSharp Extra-extra fine

DMT DuoSharp Fine/Extra fine

Single-grit plates

Combination plate has different grits on each side

44 Woodsmith No. 193

The two main manufacturers of diamond plates — *DMT* and *EZE-Lap* — each offer an assortment of plate sizes in a range of "grits." (See page 51 for sources.)

TECHNIQUES. You can use your favorite sharpening jig on the diamond plates just like you would any other sharpening stone. The thing to remember is to keep the pressure light. Diamonds cut very aggressively, so a few minutes work on a stone is done in a few seconds on a diamond plate. You might want to blacken the edge of your tool with a marker before you start. This helps keep track of your progress as you sharpen.

DRY OR WET. You can use the plates dry, but I find the best results come by using water and a drop of dishwashing liquid to lubricate the plate. When you're done, simply clean off the plate with a brush and dry it with a paper towel. This is to prevent the metal particles from rusting.

One odd thing about diamond plates is that it takes a little use to break them in. Don't be surprised if a new plate leaves more scratches than you expect. After continued use, the sharpest points will wear down and the finish will gradually look more even.

WHAT'S NEW? Although diamond plates from *DMT* and *EZE-Lap* have been available for several years, until recently they've suffered from one shortcoming. You could only sharpen to the equivalent of 1200 grit with diamonds.

While that might be acceptable for some tools, if you're looking for a super-sharp edge for your chisels or plane irons, it's not quite enough. I always needed to finish by honing the bevel on a waterstone.

DMT's addition of an extra-extra fine plate makes it possible to assemble a complete diamond sharpening system. This 3-micron grit plate hones like an 8000-grit waterstone for a razor's edge. The box below helps compare this and other sharpening media.

CATCH THE WAVE. Sharpening carving gouges presents a special challenge. Another new product from *DMT*, known as the *Wave* (photo at left) offers a simple, but innovative solution. The *Wave* is simply a thin steel plate rolled to form both convex and concave surfaces. The diamonds in the surface allow you to find the right diameter for sharpening any gouge.

Once you give diamond sharpening a try, chances are you'll find a place for a few of these handy tools in your shop. **W**

◄ Diamond paddles are useful for touching up carbide-tipped router bits.

▼ A micro-bevel honed on the extra-extra fine plate rivals an edge honed on a waterstone.

Micro-bevel

► Slide the gouge on the surface to find the correct diameter.

Convex surface *Concave surface*

▲ *DMT*'s aptly named *Wave* excels at sharpening the curved edge on most gouges.

Grading the Grit: Apples & Oranges?

Comparing "grit" between different types of sharpening media can be difficult. Some comparisons are at best, approximations. And the designation of "coarse" and "fine" can mean completely different things in different systems.

Rather than rely solely on these labels, it's helpful to look at the size of the particles in each abrading medium, measured in microns (one millionth of a meter). This chart gives you a better idea of how the different sizes compare.

Abrasive Particle Sizes

Sandpaper	Waterstone	Oilstone	DMT Diamond	Micron
P100	220	Coarse India	Extra-extra Coarse	125
P150				100
P220		Medium India	Extra Coarse	68
P320		Washita	Coarse	46
P600			Fine	25
P1000	1000	Soft Arkansas		18
P1500				13
P2000	6000	Hard Arkansas	Extra Fine	10
	8000		Extra-extra Fine	3

finishing room

spraying
Water-Based Finish

This unbeatable finishing combination guarantees top-notch results with an absolute minimum of time and effort.

▼ This HVLP turbine system has everything you need in a portable package.

Spraying is a very efficient way to apply a finish. You can complete the job in a fraction of the time needed with other methods and the quality is usually hard to beat. The obvious drawbacks are the equipment expense and the need for a suitable space for spraying volatile finishes. Not many of us have a dedicated spray booth. However with the introduction of lower-cost HVLP (High Volume Low Pressure) spraying systems and user-friendly water-based finishes, spray finishing is now much more accessible.

THE RIGHT COMBINATION. HVLP systems are designed to minimize the amount of finish dispersed into the air as overspray and bounceback. Due to the lower air pressure needed, most of the finish lands on the surface of your project and stays put. Combine this with the fact that water-based finishes are nearly odorless, non-flammable, dry quickly, and are less toxic, and you have a very desirable combination for use in small-shop finishing.

THE EQUIPMENT. There are two types of HVLP systems (photos at left). An integrated system uses a turbine to provide a large volume of air at low pressure (about 10 lbs.). You use a large-diameter air hose and a gun compatible with the HVLP turbine.

A second option is to use an HVLP conversion gun along with a standard air compressor. This type works at a slightly higher pressure — 25 to 30 lbs., but you'll get equally good results. A conversion gun looks much like a standard, gravity feed spray gun with the same controls. If you already own an air compressor, this is a good way to go.

BASIC SAFETY. Although water-based finishes are fairly benign, you'll still want to take some basic precautions. Your spray area should be well ventilated and free from dust. And then always wear a respirator.

STIR, STRAIN, & THIN. The photos across the top of the next page show how to prepare the finish for spraying. Start by stirring it to an even consistency. Next comes straining. This will prevent small clumps of finish from clogging the gun or spoiling the film.

Finally, I like to thin my finish slightly. Water-based finishes have a high solid content and are relatively thick compared to other finishes. So to get better atomization, it helps to add a little water.

▼ If you already own an air compressor, a good option is an HVLP conversion gun.

Most water-based finishes can be thinned up to 20% without affecting the curing characteristics.

RAISED GRAIN? Water-based finish will raise the grain of the wood. There are several strategies for dealing with this problem. One is to pre-raise the grain by dampening the wood. Then you can sand it smooth prior to finishing.

A different tack is to use a sealer such as shellac. I like this approach because it has the added advantage of imparting a pleasant color to the wood. Finally, you can simply allow the first coat of finish to act as a sanding sealer. Spray on a light coat, let it raise the grain, then sand it smooth.

First, stir the finish to an even consistency

Second, strain to remove any clumps

Third, thin about 10% with water

▲ Preparing the finish for spraying is a simple, three-step process.

SPRAY TECHNIQUE

Now you're about ready to start spraying your project. I'll just offer a few basic tips to help get you off on the right foot.

ADJUSTMENTS. First, you need to adjust the spray pattern. A gun will spray a "fan" perpendicular to the fins on the air cap. The cap can be rotated to any angle depending on the orientation of the surface being sprayed.

The upper drawing below, shows the ideal fan pattern for most surfaces — an oval shape with a length that matches the optimum spraying distance of 6" to 8". A longer spray pattern will produce coverage that's too light, a condensed pattern too heavy. You can test the spray pattern on a piece cardboard.

LIGHT COATS. You'll get better results with several thin coats rather than one thick coat. You want to spray on a wet coat, but not one that looks thick and puddled. You shouldn't see a milky opaqueness to the film. Too little finish will leave a surface that appears dull and rough.

Don't worry if the wet film develops a slight "orange peel" texture. It will disappear as the finish dries.

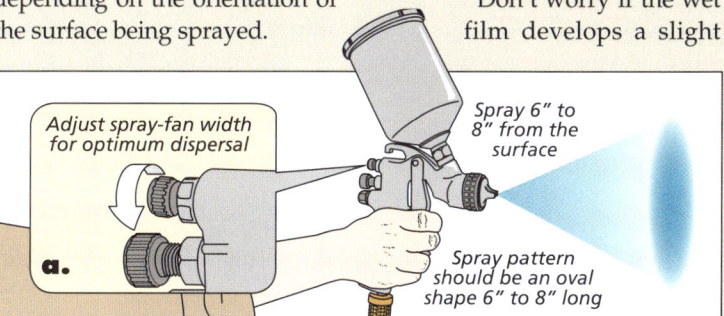

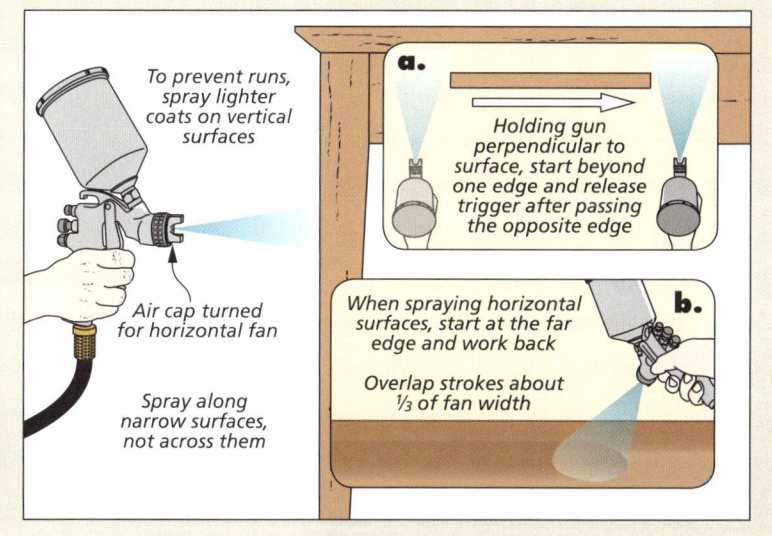

HORIZONTAL. When spraying a horizontal surface, start at the far edge and work back toward yourself. Use back and forth passes, overlapping each stroke about 1/3 of the fan width. For consistent coverage, always keep the gun perpendicular to the surface, as shown below. As I mentioned, the tip should be about 6" to 8" from the surface. Start spraying beyond the edge and move slowly and steadily across the surface, releasing the trigger only when you've passed over the opposite edge.

VERTICAL. Water-based finishes have a tendency to run on vertical surfaces. The solution is to spray lighter coats. You do this by moving the gun at a faster pace.

FINAL TIPS. I like to spray from the inside out. Inside surfaces are easier to access before the exposed areas are sprayed. And if needed, the project can be tipped or turned to get at hard-to-reach spots. When spraying in tight areas, trigger on and off quickly and try to keep the gun moving.

Spray along narrow surfaces like table and chair legs, not across them (lower left drawing). Square edges can be sprayed diagonally along their length so that both adjacent edges are coated simultaneously. This helps prevent thick buildup of finish along the edge.

Once you're accustomed to spraying water-based finish, you might not want to go back to your past finishing ways. The ease, speed, and quality make it an awfully appealing option.

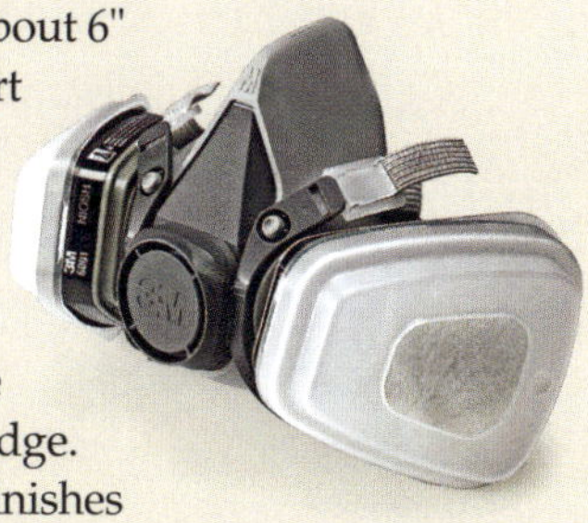

▲ You should always wear a respirator when spraying any type of finish.

Adjust spray-fan width for optimum dispersal
Spray 6" to 8" from the surface
Spray pattern should be an oval shape 6" to 8" long

To prevent runs, spray lighter coats on vertical surfaces
Air cap turned for horizontal fan
Spray along narrow surfaces, not across them

a. *Holding gun perpendicular to surface, start beyond one edge and release trigger after passing the opposite edge*

b. *When spraying horizontal surfaces, start at the far edge and work back. Overlap strokes about 1/3 of fan width*

details of craftsmanship

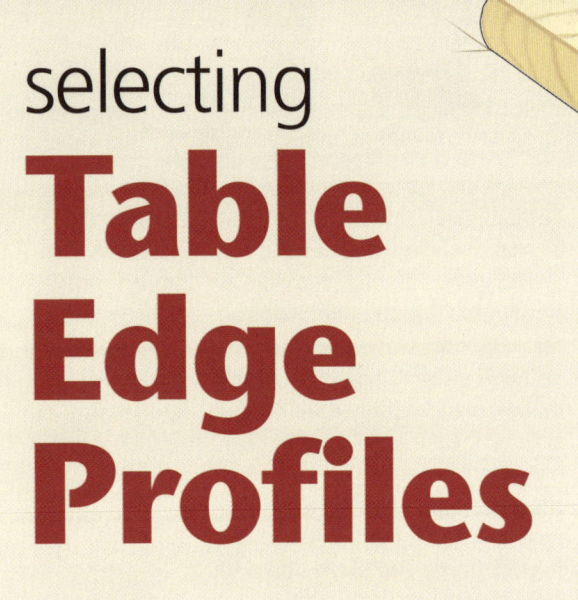

selecting Table Edge Profiles

Try one of these time-tested profiles to dress up your next table project.

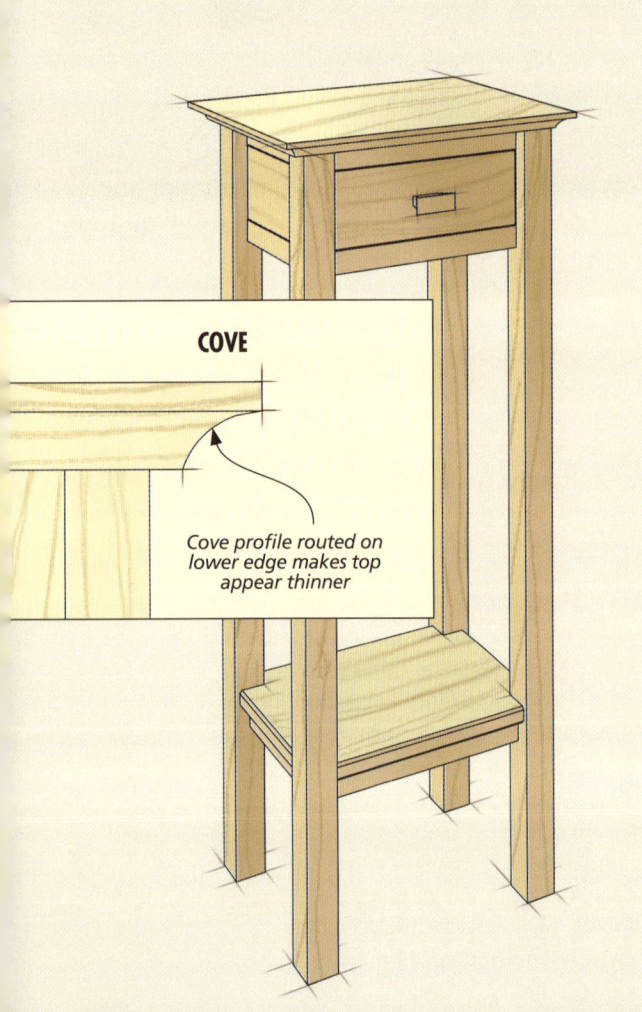

BULLNOSE

Upper and lower edges are eased with a roundover bit

COVE

Cove profile routed on lower edge makes top appear thinner

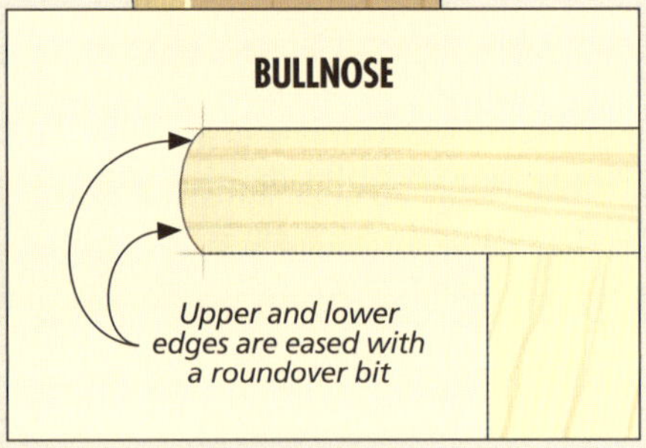

One of the first things people notice about a table is the top. So besides selecting the best-looking wood, a great way to draw attention to the top is to add the right edge treatment. With the right choice, the edge profile helps complement the style of the table.

COMFORT FACTOR. While you might think that an edge profile is purely decorative, there's a little more to it than that. Softening the edge of a tabletop serves a practical purpose, as well.

On dining tables and side tables, a profile eliminates the sharp edge that can be uncomfortable for your hands and arms to rub against. And for any type of table, a profile protects the corners from damage.

SIMPLE PROFILES. Since the top of a project is so prominent (and can be large), it's tempting to choose a complex profile created by an expensive "table edge" router bit. But usually, a better option is to select a smaller, simpler profile — one that blends well with the overall design instead of attracting too much attention.

The five profiles shown on these pages are the ones I turn to most often to create comfortable and attractive edges. Best of all, each one can be made with just a common, inexpensive router bit or a simple cut at the table saw. You can find step-by-step instructions for creating all of these profiles and several others at our website, Woodsmith.com.

BULLNOSE

Perhaps the most common profile I use is the bullnose shown in the main drawing above. This rounded detail spans the entire edge of the tabletop. It's easy to change the look of a bullnose by varying the curve from a gentle radius on the edge to a complete half circle. And all it takes is a roundover bit.

Versatility is the main reason I like this profile. It looks just as good on traditional projects as it does on contemporary pieces. In the example shown here, the table has a lot of straight lines, so the subtle curve provided by the bullnose offers a good contrast without being a distraction.

COVE

Normally, you think of creating a profile on the upper edge of a tabletop where it will be most visible. So the cove profile shown on the accent table on the opposite page may seem out of place. Here, the main job of the cove is to create a particular visual effect.

Routing a profile on the lower edge with a cove bit makes the top appear thinner when viewed from above. And it helps draw your eye along the narrow frame of the table. The simple, crisp curve works well on this Asian-inspired, contemporary table.

THUMBNAIL

Sometimes the form and function of a table edge profile work together. The drop-leaf table shown at upper right is a good example. The outer edge of the table features a classic variation of a roundover called a thumbnail profile. It's at home on traditional as well as country-style projects. The rounded portion of the profile softens the edge, while the short shoulder creates a shadow line to add extra interest.

A thumbnail profile also serves double duty by forming one half of a rule joint. The thumbnail is routed on the straight edges of the main section of the top. The opposite profile (a cove) is routed on the mating edges of the folding leaves. The result is a practical and attractive connection between the moving parts of the top.

BEVEL

An edge profile often helps define the style of a project. And this is the case with the wide bevel profile used on the Craftsman-style sofa table below. Wide chamfers and bevels are hallmarks of this style of furniture. Here again, the profile is shaped on the lower edge. The bevel complements the taper cut at the bottom of the thick legs to help make the table appear lighter. A wide bevel profile like this can be shaped at the table saw.

OGEE

An ornate, traditional project, such as the example shown at the lower right, calls for an edge profile with the same degree of detail. The timeless ogee profile serves this purpose well. It can be used in combination with applied moldings to create a complex, built-up appearance. However, the simple shape lends itself for use with many styles.

If you keep these ideas in mind, the result is sure to be a top that's attractive and complements the style of the piece. **W**

THUMBNAIL
Shoulder on roundover adds another level of detail
Small roundover on lower edge softens corner

Woodsmith GO ONLINE EXTRAS
To download a detailed article on how to create edge profiles, visit our website at Woodsmith.com

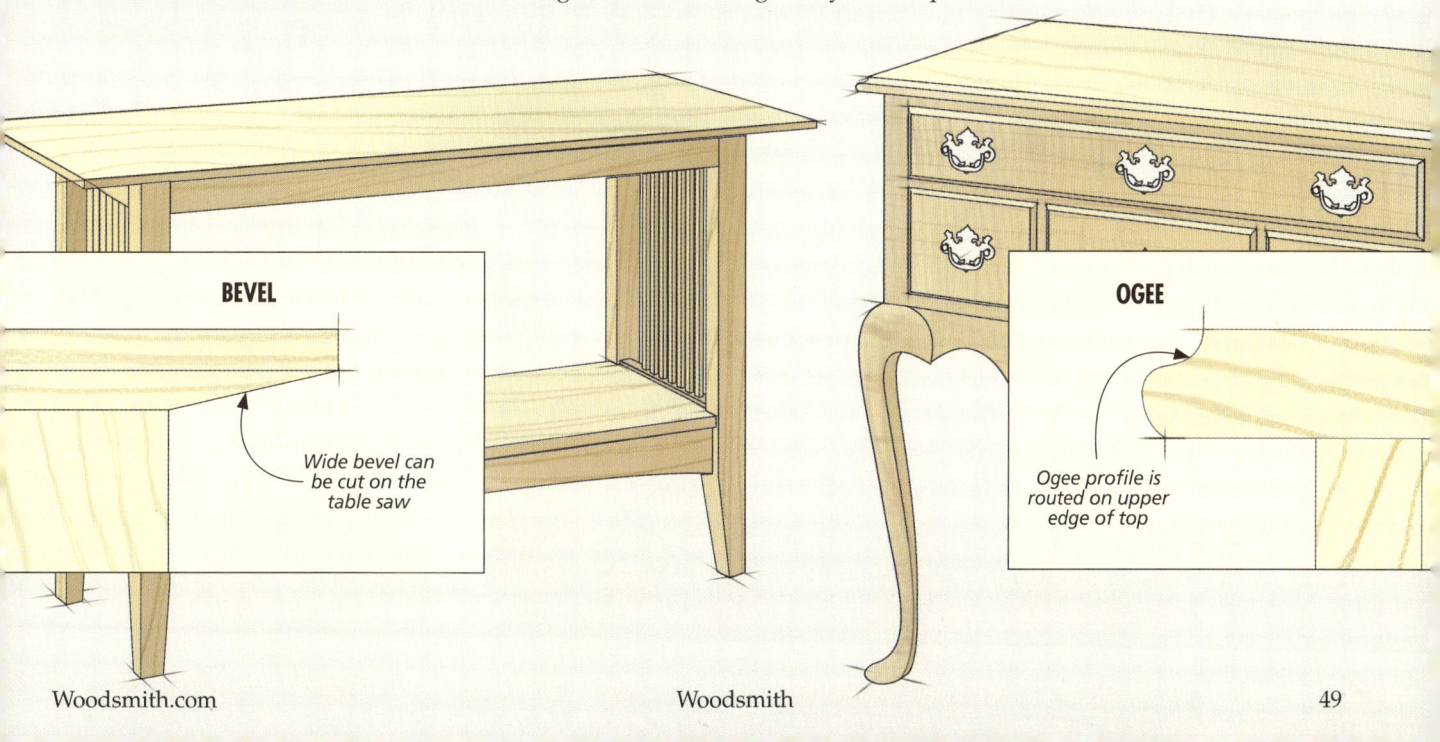

BEVEL
Wide bevel can be cut on the table saw

OGEE
Ogee profile is routed on upper edge of top

in the mailbox

Questions & Answers

Drum Sanders

Q I've been thinking about purchasing a drum sander, but since I already have a planer, I wonder how much use I'd get out of the sander. Does it make sense to own both tools?

Randy Caswell
Bloomington, Indiana

A Years ago, you'd typically find drum (or thickness) sanders only in large, commercial shops. But with the advent of smaller, more affordable models, the drum sander has become a more common tool in home shops as well.

If you have room in your shop — and your budget — a drum sander can be a valuable tool, even if you already own a planer. And although these two tools share some similarities, they actually perform very different functions.

The planer is really a stock preparation tool. It's great for dressing rough lumber, or quickly turning thick boards into thinner ones. But the surface left behind by a planer is often rippled with mill marks from the planer knives.

On the other hand, a drum sander is more of a "finishing" tool. Although it can be used to reduce stock thickness to a minor degree, it's not ideally suited for this task — it simply can't remove material as quickly as a planer.

However, a drum sander will leave a smooth surface that requires minimal hand sanding before applying a finish. That's why I'll often run my workpieces through a drum sander after planing them to thickness, simply to remove the mill marks.

FIGURED WOOD. But the advantages of a drum sander go beyond the surface that it leaves. Drum sanders are great when you're working with figured woods, such as curly or bird's-eye maple. A drum sander won't tear out the grain of these woods the way a planer does.

THIN STOCK. Drum sanders are also excellent for sanding thin stock and veneers. Most planers can only plane down to a thickness of 1/8". And even if you attach the workpiece to a carrier board, the striking action of the planer knives can cause the workpiece to crack or break. But drum sanders can easily handle material as thin as 1/32" and as short as 3".

LARGE PANELS. Although the construction of drum sanders varies between makers, most units made for home shop use have an open-end design (see photo).

▲ The open-end design of some drum sanders allows you to sand wide panels by turning the workpiece around between passes.

This allows you to sand large, glued-up panels that are nearly twice as wide as the sanding drum by simply turning the panel around and making another pass.

Although I wouldn't go so far as to classify the drum sander as a "must-have" shop tool, it's definitely a useful addition to any woodworking shop. **W**

Do you have any questions for us?

If you have a question related to woodworking techniques, tools, finishing, hardware, or accessories, we'd like to hear from you.

Just write down your question and mail it to us: Woodsmith Q&A, 2200 Grand Avenue, Des Moines, Iowa 50312. Or you can email us the question at: woodsmith@woodsmith.com.

Please include your name, address, and daytime telephone number in case we have questions.

hardware & supplies
Sources

DRAWER SLIDES
Metal drawer slides, like those shown on page 8, are available at most hardware stores and home centers. The spacers and rear mounting brackets came from *Lee Valley* and *Rockler*.

BENCH GRIPPERS
When it comes to bench grippers, you have a number of choices. *Rockler* sells the original *Bench Cookies* and *Bench Cookies Plus*, as well as the risers, storage rack, and cones.

The *Wolf Paw* grippers are available from *Woodworker's Supply* and the *Loc-Blocks* are sold through *Peachtree Woodworking*. Contact information for these companies is listed in the margin at right.

DIGITAL ANGLE GAUGES
A digital angle gauge is a simple way to increase the accuracy of your woodworking. The gauges shown in the article on page 12 are available from a number of the sources shown at right.

STORAGE CABINET
The hardware used to build the cottage storage cabinet on page 16 came from *Rockler*. This includes the knobs (26244), shelf pins (22773), magnetic catches (26559), and no-mortise hinges (49393). The bun feet (303-BF.SM) are from *Classic Designs by Matthew Burak*. The paint used on the cabinet is *Benjamin Moore's* "Monroe Bisque."

CRAFT CENTER
The craft center on page 22 requires quite a few hardware items. The threaded inserts (00N11.13), connector bolts (00N16.30), hinges (00B15.24), door stops (00B17.34) and drawer slides (02K42.10) all came from *Lee Valley*. The knobs used on the doors and drawers are from *Reid Supply* (ESP-285).

The painted portions of the craft center were painted with *Benjamin Moore's* "Raspberry Truffle." The unpainted parts were simply finished with a couple coats of lacquer.

KITCHEN WORKSTATION
In addition to some screws and washers, there are a few other items you'll need to build the kitchen workstation on page 32. The turned legs (505-29T.CH) were purchased from *Classic Designs by Matthew Burak*. The knobs (02G11.21) and drawer slides (02K42.18) came from *Lee Valley*. And we turned to *Rockler* for the casters (35377).

The cherry portions of the cart were stained with a mix of three parts *Zar* cherry stain and one part *WoodKote Jel'd Stain* (cherry). After spraying on a coat of lacquer, we applied a coat of *General Finishes' Gel Stain* (*Java*) as a glaze. Then the whole project was given a couple more coats of lacquer.

DIAMOND PLATES
Long-lasting diamond plates are a practical option compared to other sharpening methods. They're available from several of the sources listed at right.

Online Customer Service
Click on *Magazine Customer Service* at **Woodsmith.com**
- Access your account status
- Change your mailing or email address
- Pay your bill
- Renew your subscription
- Tell us if you've missed an issue
- Find out if your payment has been received

MAIL ORDER SOURCES

Project supplies may be ordered from the following companies:

Woodsmith Store
800-444-7527
Bench Cookies, Drawer Slides, Storage Cabinet Hardware, Wixey Gauges

Rockler
800-279-4441
rockler.com
Bench Cookies, Casters, Drawer Slides, Storage Cabinet Hardware, Wixey Gauges

Amazon
amazon.com
Digital Angle Gauges, DMT Diamond Plates, Drawer Slides

Classic Designs by Matthew Burak
800-748-3480
tablelegs.com
Bun Feet, Turned Legs

EZE-Lap
800-843-4815
eze-lap.com
EZE-Lap Diamond Plates

Lee Valley
800-871-8158
leevalley.com
Craft Center Hardware, Drawer Slides

Peachtree Woodworking
888-512-9069
ptreeusa.com
Loc-Blocks

Reid Supply
800-253-0421
reidsupply.com
Craft Center Knobs

Woodcraft
800-225-1153
woodcraft.com
DMT Diamond Plates, Wixey Gauges

Woodworker's Supply
800-645-9292
woodworker.com
Wolf Bench Paws

Woodsmith®

NEW! Volume 31

- Sturdy, spiral-bound hardcover
- Six complete issues with reference index
- An entire year of project plans, tips and techniques for your shop — all at your fingertips

Item #WV31 *Woodsmith* Hardbound Volume 31 .... $29⁹⁵

Go to Woodsmith.com
or Call 1-800-444-7527 Today to Order Yours!

looking inside
Final Details

Cottage-Style Cabinet. The compact size of this simple storage cabinet allows it to be tucked away in a corner. But it's attractive enough that you may want it front and center. Complete plans begin on page 16.

Craft Center. The large top on this craft table offers plenty of room for you to spread out your work. And you're sure to appreciate the storage "cubbies" at each end. You'll find step-by-step plans on page 22.

Kitchen Workstation. When it's not being used for food preparation, this handsome cart can double as a serving buffet. An optional wine rack adds to the versatility of this project. Take a look at the plans starting on page 32.

Working with Plywood in a Small Shop

Take the Work Out of Sanding with These Helpful Accessories

Woodsmith

Woodsmith.com

Vol. 33 / No. 194

INSIDE:

Take a Look at the New Generation of Compact Routers

One Plane that No Shop Should Be Without

Low-Tech Tool for Creating Custom Molding Profiles

Stylish ENTERTAINMENT CENTER
- Modular Design
- Simple Construction
- Low-Cost Materials

A Publication of August Home Publishing

looking inside

Table of Contents

from our readers
Tips & Techniques 4

all about
Sanding Profiles & Contours 8
Take a look at a few handy accessories that take the drudgery out of sanding curves.

tools of the trade
Compact Routers 10
These mighty routers offer a surprising range of features in an easy-to-handle package.

jigs & fixtures
Hardware Installation Jigs 12
Here's a quick and accurate way to add knobs and pulls to your projects.

tips from our shop
Shop Notebook 28

woodworking technique
Plywood on the Table Saw 42
Learn the secret to cutting perfectly sized project parts from full sheets of plywood.

working with tools
Shoulder Planes 44
Find out why his classic plane is one of the most valuable hand tools in the shop.

finishing room
Using Paste Wax 46
This easy-to-use product offers a great way to protect and enhance the look of your projects.

details of craftsmanship
Scratch Stock 48
Create custom beads and other molding profiles with this traditional shop-made tool.

in the mailbox
Q & A 50

hardware and supplies
Sources 51

Marking Gauge page 14

Wall Shelf page 18

Keepsake Box page 22

projects

shop project
Marking Gauge 14
Here's your chance to work on an interesting project that you'll also be able to put to use in your shop nearly every day.

weekend project
Sliding-Door Wall Shelf 18
Simple, knock-down construction and a clean, uncluttered look guarantee this practical project will go together in a flash.

designer series project
Contoured Keepsake Box 22
Building this attractive lidded box will give you a chance to pull out all the stops. The small size keeps it all manageable.

heirloom project
Entertainment Center 30
Don't let the large size fool you. Classic details, no-fuss joinery, and low-cost materials come together in a great-looking project.

Entertainment Center page 30

editor's note
Sawdust

A while back, I was talking to a woodworker who had built half a dozen keepsake boxes from a plan in *Woodsmith* No. 185. The workmanship was excellent and the completed boxes looked beautiful — which is no small achievement considering that the construction of these boxes is fairly exacting. Yet, when I asked him what he thought he might build next, he replied that he was a little intimidated to try bigger projects; so he would probably just stick to something small, like the boxes he had already made.

This got me thinking about a couple of the projects in this issue. We have a small, bevel-sided box as well as an entertainment center that takes up an entire wall. Going strictly by size, it would be easy to say that the entertainment center is the more difficult project of the two. But the truth is that each project presents its own set of challenges. The box requires careful fitting of miter joints, veneering, inlaying, and some beveling and routing to create the graceful final shape. It calls for a good deal of patience and careful attention to detail.

On the other hand, the entertainment center seems daunting because of its sheer size. However, it's made in four separate sections, so you can work on it one piece at a time. And each section is really just a plywood case with a few moldings added, along with some door, drawers, and shelves. As far as techniques go, it's all pretty standard stuff. The real challenge comes in working with large plywood pieces and keeping everything square.

The point I'm trying to make is that you shouldn't let the physical size of a project deter you from attempting to build it. If you have the skills to build small projects, you have what it takes to successfully build larger pieces.

Terry

This symbol lets you know there's more information online at www.Woodsmith.com. There you'll see step-by-step videos, technique and project animation, bonus cutting diagrams, and a lot more.

from our readers

Tips & Techniques

Vertical Drilling Jig

Occasionally, I have a project that calls for drilling into the edge of a workpiece. Balancing a workpiece on edge while I try to line up the drill bit is a chore. So I made this jig that holds the workpiece in place and centers it under the drill bit as well.

As you can see in the photo, the jig fits the drill press table. I installed it with a couple of threaded inserts and knobs in the sub-base. The base moves forward or backward on a pair of runners to locate the workpiece under the bit.

The runners are cut from hardboard and waxed for easier movement. Then I added carriage bolts and knobs to keep the base secure on the sub-base.

The front fence holds a screw clamp that secures the workpiece to the back fence. I also added a pair of V-blocks to hold round objects in place. These blocks can be taped in place so they're removable for drilling a square workpiece.

With this jig, I can align workpieces that need edge drilling faster and with near perfect accuracy. And this means less time setting up and more working.

John Lucas
Baxter, Tennessee

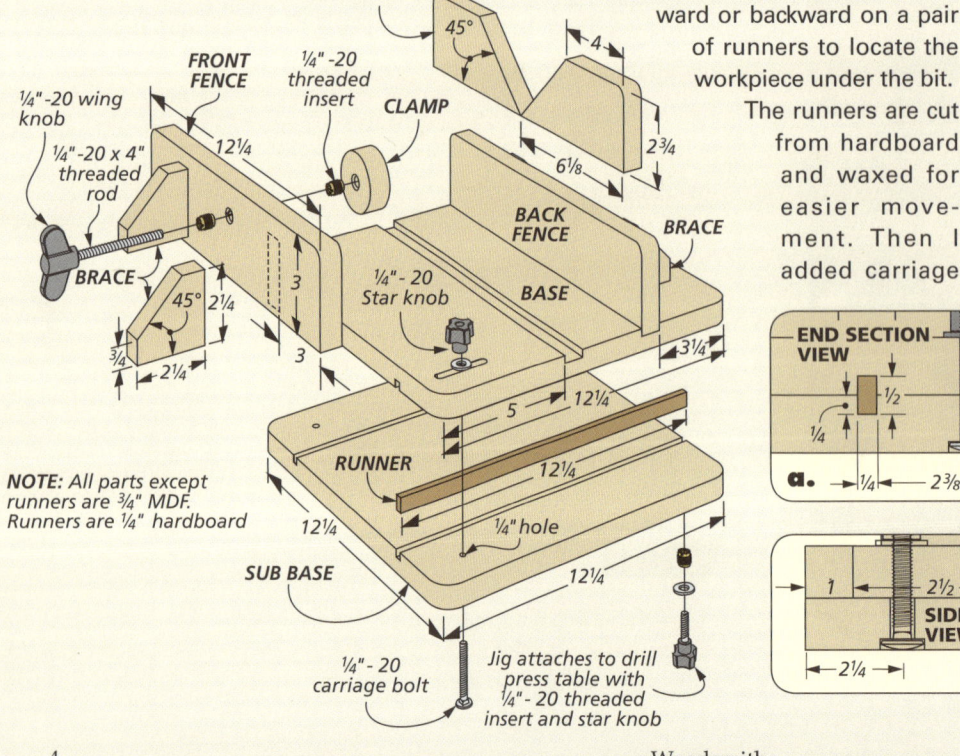

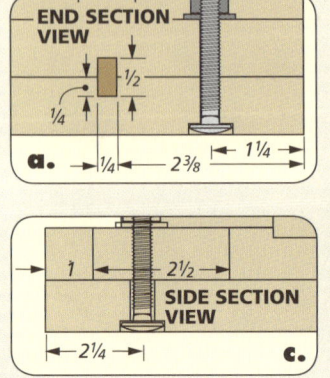

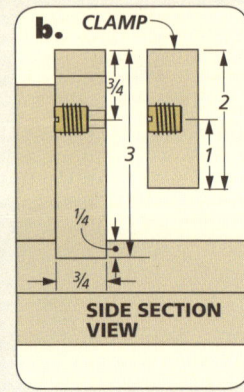

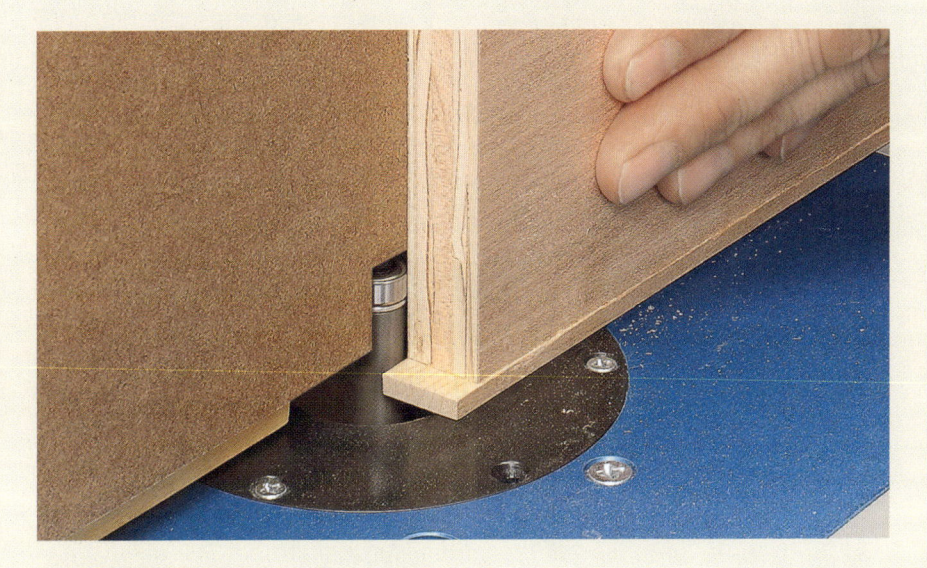

Flush Trim Router Fence

I needed a tall router table fence for flush trimming plywood edging. But I also wanted the fence to be easy to attach and secure. So I built the auxiliary fence you see in the drawing below.

The fence slips over my existing router table fence, so it's quick and simple to attach without using clamps or fasteners. But the secret behind this fence is that the front face of the fence is about 3/8" shy of resting on the table. This gives me room to slide the edging under the face of the fence (photo).

To build the fence, I just glued all the layers shown in the drawing together after I cut a small opening on one face for the router bit.

Al Krum
Huntington Beach, California

Woodsmith
No. 194   April/May 2011

PUBLISHER Donald B. Peschke

EDITOR Terry J. Strohman
MANAGING EDITOR Vincent Ancona
SENIOR EDITOR Ted Raife
ASSOCIATE EDITOR Dennis Perkins
ASSISTANT EDITOR Carol Beronich
CONTRIBUTING EDITORS Bryan Nelson, Phil Huber, Randall A. Maxey, James Bruton

EXECUTIVE ART DIRECTOR Todd Lambirth
SENIOR ILLUSTRATORS David Kreyling, Harlan V. Clark, David Kallemyn
SENIOR GRAPHIC DESIGNER Bob Zimmerman
GRAPHIC DESIGNER Shelley Cronin
GRAPHIC DESIGN INTERN Megan Hann
CONTRIBUTING ILLUSTRATORS Dirk Ver Steeg, Peter J. Larson, Erich Lage

CREATIVE DIRECTOR Ted Kralicek
SENIOR PROJECT DESIGNERS Ken Munkel, Kent Welsh, Chris Fitch, Jim Downing
PROJECT DESIGNER/BUILDER John Doyle
SHOP CRAFTSMEN Steve Curtis, Steve Johnson
SENIOR PHOTOGRAPHERS Crayola England, Dennis Kennedy
ASSOCIATE STYLE DIRECTOR Rebecca Cunningham
SENIOR ELECTRONIC IMAGE SPECIALIST Allan Ruhnke
PRODUCTION ASSISTANT Minniette Johnson
VIDEO EDITOR/DIRECTOR Mark Hayes, Nate Gruca

Woodsmith® (ISSN 0164-4114) is published bimonthly by August Home Publishing Company, 2200 Grand Ave, Des Moines, IA 50312.
Woodsmith® is a registered trademark of August Home Publishing.
Copyright© 2011 August Home Publishing Company. All rights reserved.
Subscriptions: Single copy: $4.95.
Canadian Subscriptions: Canada Post Agreement No. 40038201. Send change of address information to PO Box 881, Station Main, Markham, ON L3P 8M6.
Canada BN 84597 5473 RT
Periodicals Postage Paid at Des Moines, IA and at additional offices.
Postmaster: Send change of address to Woodsmith, Box 37106, Boone, IA 50037-0106.

WoodsmithCustomerService.com

ONLINE SUBSCRIBER SERVICES
- **VIEW** your account information
- **RENEW** your subscription
- **CHECK** on a subscription payment
- **PAY** your bill
- **CHANGE** your mailing or e-mail address
- **VIEW/RENEW** your gift subscriptions
- **TELL US** if you've missed an issue

CUSTOMER SERVICE   Phone: 800-333-5075

SUBSCRIPTIONS
Customer Service
P.O. Box 842
Des Moines, IA 50304-9961
subscriptions@augusthome.com

EDITORIAL
Woodsmith Magazine
2200 Grand Avenue
Des Moines, IA 50312
woodsmith@augusthome.com

AUGUST HOME PUBLISHING COMPANY   Printed in China

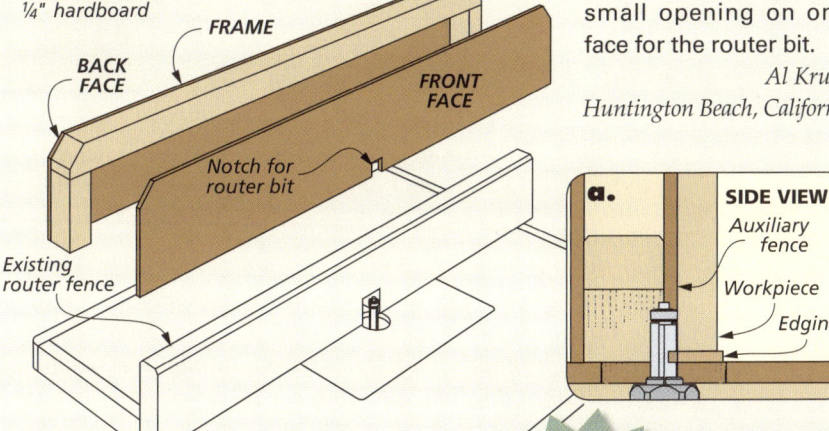

SUBMIT YOUR TIPS ONLINE

If you have an original shop tip, we would like to hear from you and consider publishing your tip in one or more of our publications. Go to:

Woodsmith.com
Click on the link,
"SUBMIT A TIP"

You'll be able to tell us all about your tip and upload your photos and drawings. You can also mail your tips to *"Woodsmith Tips"* at the editorial address shown at right. We will pay up to $200 if we publish your tip.

FREE TIPS BY EMAIL

Now you can have the best, time-saving secrets, solutions, and techniques sent directly to your email inbox. Just go to **Woodsmith.com** and click on **"Sign Up for Free E-Tips."** You'll receive one of our favorite tips each week.

more tips from our readers

Band Saw Support

When I have a large workpiece to cut on the band saw, it's always a challenge to balance it on the small table. I could build a larger table for my band saw, but that would take a lot of valuable space in my shop. So I built a support for the table top that slides out of the way when not in use.

The table extension is built from a couple pieces of pipe, brackets, and a row of ball bearing rollers attached to a wood block (main photo). The pipes move back and forth through the brackets, so I can retract the extension when I don't need it (inset).

To build the support, I glued three narrow strips of plywood together to make the block to hold the rollers as you can see in the drawing below. Then I attached the rollers to the block. When the block was complete, I made the brackets and bolted them to the saw. Then I determined where to drill the holes for the pipe that holds the assembly by leveling the rollers with the table. Finally I added caps to the ends of each pipe.

Now when I need to cut an extra-long workpiece on the band saw, I don't have to hunt around the shop for an extension table. I just pull out the attached support and go to work.

Karl Mueller
Fairport, New York

▲ The band saw support slides back out of the way when it's not in use, saving valuable floor space in your shop.

NOTE: Brackets are mounted in existing threaded holes on band saw table

Band saw table

½" galvanized threaded pipe

1" ball bearing rollers

#8 x ¾" Ph screws

¼" washer

¼"-28 x 2" bolt (to fit existing holes in band saw table)

BRACKET ROLLER BLOCK

NOTE: Bracket and bearing block made from glued-up layers of ¾" plywood

½" end cap

2¼

17

1½

Bracket

Band saw table

3

¼"-28 x 2" bolt

2

⅞"-dia. hole

NOTE: Hole location is determined by individual band saw configuration

6 Woodsmith No. 194

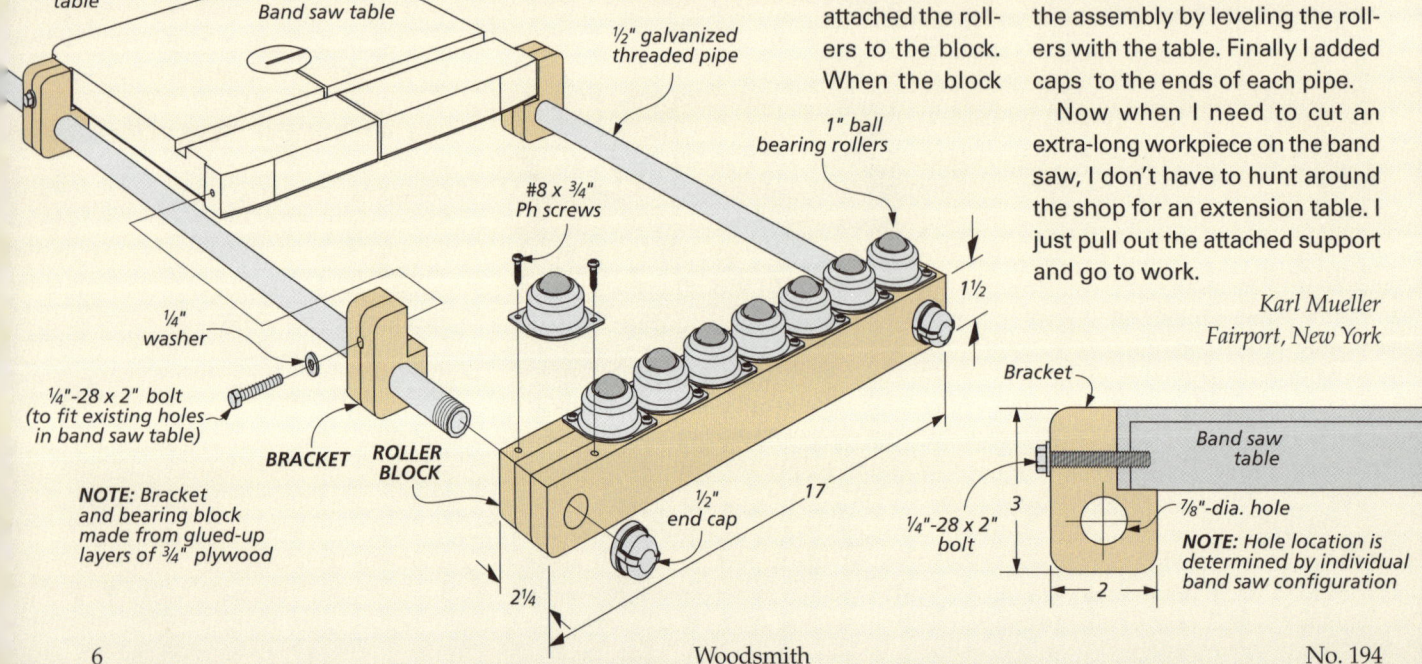

Aluminum Square

I build a lot of small boxes and drawers. The tools made for squaring up an assembly are usually too big to fit in these boxes, so I've found a better solution. It's a small piece of aluminum angle.

As you can see in the right photo, I cut a piece of the aluminum to fit the height of the box I was gluing. I have several for boxes of different heights.

The 90° angle on extruded aluminum is very accurate, so you won't have any worries about squaring a project. You can even clamp the aluminum to the corners of the box to hold the joint while the glue dries. This saves a few steps when squaring and gluing up small projects.

Now when I have a box or drawer to glue up, I have a variety of squares to guarantee good results.

Allen Bushman
Goleta, California

A Third Hand

I found a "third hand" to hold a router bit above the collet while I use my two hands to tighten the collet. As you can see in the left photo, it's a rare-earth magnet.

Once I have the bit raised to the proper position, I snap a magnet next to the bit. The magnet holds the bit in position while I tighten the collet. When the bit is secured, I remove the magnet and my bit is properly placed.

Charles Mak
Calgary, Alberta

Win This BOSCH IMPACTOR

That's right, send us your favorite shop tips. If your tip or technique is selected as the featured reader's tip, you'll win a *Bosch* impact driver just like the one shown here. To submit your tip or technique, just go online to *woodsmith.com* and click on the link, "SUBMIT A TIP." You can submit your tip and upload your photos for consideration.

The Winner!

Congratulations to Karl Mueller, winner of the *Bosch Impactor* driver. To find out how you could win a *Bosch* driver, check out the information on the left.

Quick Tips

CLEANING DIAMOND STONES

Diamond sharpening stones are expensive, so when it's time to clean the buildup from a stone, I need to use something that won't damage it, but still works effectively.

That's why I use a fingernail brush. These brushes are inexpensive, readily available, and do a great job of restoring the stones to like-new condition.

Donald Henderson
Orleans, Ontario

FINISHING SUPPORTS

If I want to raise a project for finishing, I use plastic banding protectors instead of buying painter's points. Banding protectors wrap around the edge of sheet goods to keep the edges from being crushed by the banding straps during shipping. Standing on edge, these protectors make great painter's points. Best of all, if you ask at your local lumberyard, you'll probably get them for free.

Bart Lessner
Oregon, Wisconsin

CLEAN SANDING BELTS

I looked for a long time for a way to remove built-up glue and pitch on my sanding belts. It was especially bad on my thickness sander, which uses expensive belts. I finally discovered a remedy almost by accident.

I just use water and a soft brush. These belts are usually cloth-backed, so soaking them in warm water won't damage the belt. And since most glue is water soluble, the belts come clean with just a little scrubbing.

Now I can use the belts on my thickness sander much longer and save myself some money for other projects.

Edwin Hackleman
Omaha, Nebraska

all about
sanding
Profiles & Contours

If you thought you could only power sand flat surfaces, take a look at these products that make short work of curves and contours.

I have to confess, I've been spoiled by my random-orbit sander. It's taken most of the drudgery out of smoothing the rough surfaces of my woodworking projects. The problem is, a random-orbit sander isn't much help when it comes to project parts that aren't flat.

In those cases, it usually means breaking out the sandpaper sheets and limbering up the elbows for some good old-fashioned hand sanding. And for me, the very thought of hand sanding more than just a few touch-ups makes me want to run and hide.

That's why I'm constantly on the lookout for products that can help me avoid the jobs I don't like. I'm happy to share a few of my profile sanding solutions with you.

IT STARTS WITH A DRILL. As you can see in the photo of the assorted sanding aids at left, they all have either a spindle (or a collar that fits a spindle). That's because they all get their power from a hand drill, a drill press, or in one extreme example, an angle grinder.

Of course, this shouldn't come as a surprise. Hand drills and drill presses offer plenty of torque, and the speed is often easily adjustable to suit the task at hand. If you've ever installed a sanding drum on your drill press, then you've seen how useful the idea can be. These different tools simply build on that concept and offer a few options for a bit more flexibility.

A SANDER FOR EVERY TASK. Each of these accessories relies on high-quality, cloth-backed abrasives. In Sources on page 51, you'll find that we purchased most of these

▼ Flapwheels and sanding mops excel at shaping and smoothing contoured parts.

Drill press sanding mop
Hand drill sanding mop
Angle grinder flap disc
Finish flapwheels
1" Flapwheel

8   Woodsmith   No. 194

sanding accessories from *Klingspor's Woodworking Shop*. They offer a wide assortment of specialized abrasive products.

SANDING MOPS. One of the first products to consider is the sanding mop. You can use it on just about any surface. As you can see in the main photo on the opposite page, the mop consists of several individual cloth-backed abrasive strips. By stacking the strips on a mandrel, you can build them up to whatever thickness you need.

After tightening up the mandrel and installing it in a drill press, it's a good idea to "break in" the abrasives on a scrap of hardwood. This helps soften the edges and makes the mop perform better.

The other type of mop, shown in the photo on the opposite page, works best in a hand drill. The thin "fingers" can reach into the hardest-to-sand nooks and crannies to leave a smooth surface.

FLAPWHEELS. Another very useful class of sanding accessories is the flapwheel. It's easy to see how they get their name. You can see a couple different kinds in the photo on the opposite page.

The first type of flapwheel is simply tightly packed swatches of stiff, cloth-backed abrasive fixed to a spindle. These provide a very aggressive cut. They're great for hogging out a lot of stock and can be very useful for sculpting, or cleaning up coarse carvings.

The second type are the "finish" flapwheels. These wheels also rely on swatches of abrasive cloth, but between each one is a section of non-woven abrasive pad. The combination of the two types of abrasives results in a noticeably less aggressive cut from the cloth, followed by a smoothing action provided by the pads.

They're perfect for cleaning up irregular shapes, like the bowl shown above. As with the regular flapwheels, the finish wheels are available in different diameters to suit any project and can be used in a hand drill or drill press.

ANGLE GRINDER FLAP DISC. For really aggressive shaping, an angle grinder flap disc might be just the ticket. As you can see in the photo below, this disc makes short work of shaping a chair seat or just about any task where lots of stock needs to be removed. With zirconia alumina abrasive on a phenolic resin backing plate, the discs last a long time.

SMALL SCALE. At the other end of the spectrum are abrasive brushes for the *Dremel* rotary tool, shown in the box below. They provide a gentle touch for delicate work.

No matter what the project, one of these handy accessories is sure to help you get the job done. **W**

▲ The finish flapwheel on a hand drill is a lifesaver for removing the burn marks left on the inside of this routed bowl.

▲ It only took about ten minutes to shape the rough profile of a chair seat using the angle grinder and a coarse sanding disc. With the shape roughed in, a mop on a hand drill can finish the job.

Dremel Abrasive Brush

When you need to smooth out the fine, detailed work of a carving or even an intricate molding detail, the *Dremel Abrasive Brush* is what you need. As you can tell from the photo, it looks like a flap sander, but the flexible strips are actually rubber impregnated with coarse, medium, or fine abrasive. They can get into the tightest spots.

Woodsmith.com   Woodsmith   9

tools of the trade

multi-base
Compact Routers

Packing more features into small routers proves that bigger isn't always better.

The trend in power tools usually runs uphill to bigger and more powerful models. So it's a little ironic that the latest thing in routers has taken the opposite course.

From laminate trimmer to trim router to palm router, the popularity of small-bodied routers has soared with woodworkers. In fact, they're among the hottest-selling tools today. As a result, several major tool manufacturers have developed new, small routers. The new multi-base router kits jointly developed by *Porter-Cable* and *DeWalt* continue the evolution of these handy tools.

WHY A COMPACT? Since buying a palm router, I can honestly say it sees more action than my full-sized routers. The reason is simple. It's quicker and more convenient to set up and use than a big router. And I find that the lower power is rarely an issue. Although these routers won't accept ½"-shank bits, you'll find just about every profile you need is available in a ¼" shank.

WHAT'S NEW? The *Porter-Cable 450PK* and *DeWalt 611PK* kits are nearly identical. Both have a 1¼-hp motor with soft start and electronic feedback to keep the RPMs up under load. (The *DeWalt 611* even includes a variable-speed control motor.) They've also added a very well-designed plunge base — a first for this class of router. These features take them to the next level of performance.

▼ *DeWalt* and *Porter-Cable* offer compact routers with all the features of their larger counterparts.

- Handy and durable tool bag
- DEWALT DWP611PK
- Switch with dust cover
- Variable speed
- Ergonomic handles
- Solid bases with positive cam-lock levers
- Clear bases
- PORTER-CABLE 450PK
- Plunge lock lever
- Plunge base accepts standard guide bushings

10 Woodsmith No. 194

This new breed is simply called a compact router. And frankly, this is the name that makes the most sense. These are full-featured routers, capable of handling most of your common routing tasks.

DEPTH ADJUSTMENT & LOCK. The *Porter-Cable* and *DeWalt* routers feature a cam lock with an adjustable clip that you can set by tightening a hex screw. After releasing the lock, adjusting the bit depth is pretty straightforward. On the fixed base, simply turn the adjustment ring (right photo, below). After installing a bit and zeroing out the depth on the fine-adjustment ring shown in the inset photo, you can dial in a precise depth of cut.

When in the plunge base, the plunge-lock lever offers smooth movement (right photo at the bottom of the opposite page). The left photo below shows how the depth adjustment relies on a standard turret-style stop. You can even make micro-adjustments by turning the knurled knob on the depth stop rod. The rod has a cursor on the scale to keep track of even minor changes in bit depth.

GUIDE BUSHINGS. Another thing I like about these routers is the fact that the bases accept standard-size guide bushings. These routers are great for pattern and inlay work, so I believe this is a must-have feature. Too many other compact routers ignore this application. You won't need to buy an after-market base plate or special adaptor to take advantage of this handy capability.

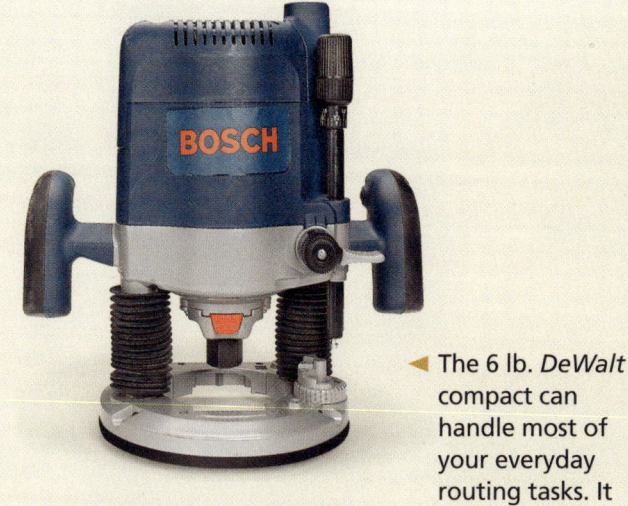

CLEAR BASE. When it comes to intricate work, I really want a clear base. It makes it easier to see your layout marks if you're routing something like a hinge mortise. Both routers have clear, polycarbonate bases. And the *DeWalt* includes a pair of LEDs that light up the work nicely for great visibility even in tight, dusty spaces.

SWAPPING BASES. If you've ever fought with the too-tight fit of most multi-base routers, then you're sure to appreciate how easy it is to swap bases on these models. Both have quick-release tabs on the motor that allow you to remove it with ease. The right photo below shows a tab on the *Porter-Cable*. To insert the motor in either base, all you need to do is line up a single pin in the base with a groove in the motor and slide it in place. This is the best design for changing bases I've seen on any router, large or small.

SPINDLE LOCK. Since the motor is so easy to remove, a spindle lock button makes single-wrench bit changes a breeze. The center photo below shows what I mean.

CONVENIENT BAG. A canvas bag easily holds everything. These bags are a big improvement over molded plastic cases.

BOTTOM LINE. *DeWalt* and *Porter-Cable* have done an amazing job designing these routers. From the ergonomic grips to the smooth travel of the plunge base, you can immediately tell that you're holding a high-quality tool.

The $190 price tag may be enough to put off some woodworkers. But to me, they're well worth the cost. My only gripe is that I wish a dust collection port and edge guide were included. They're available separately.

With a larger router mounted in a table, a compact might be all you need for the hand-held applications in your shop.

◀ The 6 lb. *DeWalt* compact can handle most of your everyday routing tasks. It might save you the trouble of getting out a full-sized router, like this 13 lb. *Bosch* model.

▲ A turret depth stop is handy for routing multiple passes to achieve a deeper cut.

▲ The handy spindle lock button enables you to make single-wrench bit changes.

▲ The quick-release tabs make for easy base changes. A fine-adjustment dial (inset) allows super-accurate depth adjustment.

jigs & fixtures

hardware
Installation Jigs

Accuracy is key when you're adding the hardware to your project. You'll find these handy templates can be a big help.

▼ Large jigs like the *Euro Handle-It* and *Rockler JIG-IT* allow repeatable installation for drawer pulls.

When I arrive at the point where I can install knobs or pulls on my completed project, I know I'm in the home stretch. But I find laying out and drilling the holes a little tedious. So I rely on a template to help me accurately place the hardware. Of course, you can make your own template for each project you build. But there are several manufactured jigs that are easy and accurate to use.

These handy jigs have pre-drilled holes precisely spaced for any drawer or door pull, whether it's sized in metric or imperial measurements. They all have some type of measuring, centering, and marking system on the jig. All you have to do is mark the centerline for the hardware, match it to the jig and reference line, then mark the holes for drilling.

EASY USE. The *JIG-IT* by *Rockler* is one template that's easy to use for drawer or doors. The template mounts to a T-track and has a stop block at one end, as shown in the above photo. The jig

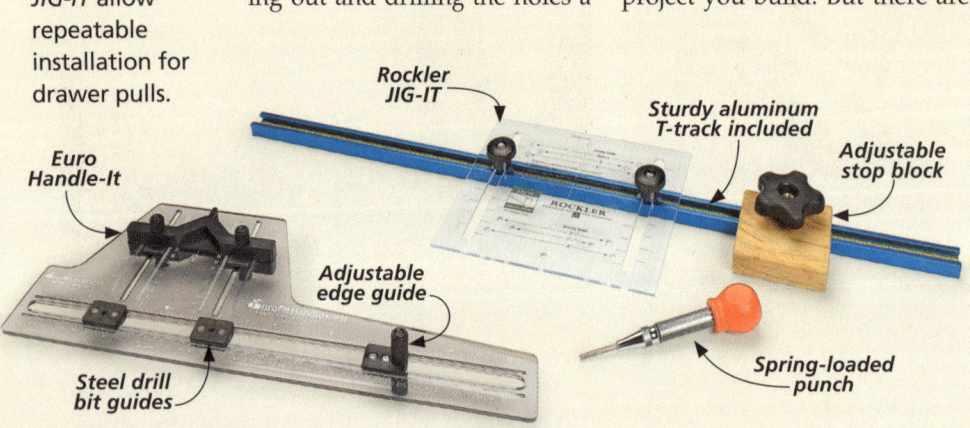

- Euro Handle-It
- Steel drill bit guides
- Adjustable edge guide
- Rockler JIG-IT
- Sturdy aluminum T-track included
- Adjustable stop block
- Spring-loaded punch

12   Woodsmith   No. 194

also slides up and down on the T-track so you can position the pulls and knobs vertically, too (left photo below). All you need to do is place it against the top edge of the drawer, adjust the template to the drawer front and tighten down the stop block on one side. Once the stop is set, the setup is repeatable on as many drawers or doors as you have.

The jig includes a spring-loaded center punch to mark for hole placement (right photo below). After removing the jig, you can drill the holes. The pre-drilled holes in the jig match the spacing of most common drawer pulls. And a centered hole is used for knobs. There's also a self-adhesive measuring tape included that you can install on the T-track to help with measuring and centering.

The *Rockler* jig is definitely an adequate jig, but if you're installing long pulls or double handles then you might want to consider the *Euro Handle-It*.

EURO HANDLE-IT. The *Euro Handle-It* has a few added features that makes it more versatile. As you can see in the photos above, this jig also includes a stop for repeatable setups. What makes this jig different is that the centering holes can be positioned anywhere along the jig, so you can drill holes up to 24" apart for extra long handles. The centering holes also adjust vertically on the jig so you can center holes on a drawer as tall as 12".

The jig is made of polycarbonate and features hardened steel guide bushings for use with a standard 3/16"-dia. drill bit. That's another advantage to this jig. You can drill the holes with the jig in place, which saves a step later.

If you're installing two handles on the same drawer front, you won't need to reset the *Euro* jig. It has a fence on both faces of the jig so you can set it once, mark one side, and then flip the jig for the opposite side (top photo). Plus the jig has imperial and metric markings for all types of pulls.

The sliding fence also has a "V" notch. This lets you place handles at 45° to the edge (right photo).

Either of these jigs is great to have in the shop, especially if you have a project with a lot of doors or drawers or you build a lot of cabinets. But if you just need to install a few pulls or knobs, then check out the simple and inexpensive jig in the box below. **W**

FIRST: Set the horizontal and vertical hole locations on one side, then drill holes

SECOND: Flip the jig and drill the opposite side

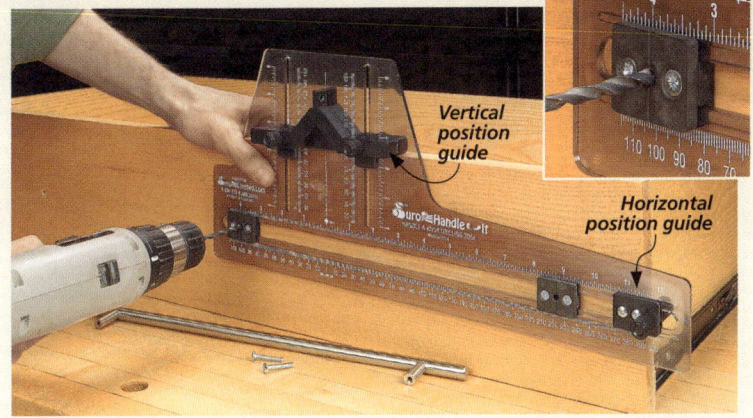

Vertical position guide

Horizontal position guide

◀ The *Euro Handle-It* accommodates a range of pulls, and the steel bushings (inset) make drilling an easy, one-step operation.

▲ The *Euro Handle-It* also lets you drill holes for pulls at 45°.

▲ To use the *Rockler JIG-IT*, first adjust the vertical position of the template.

▲ Next align the template with the centerline and use a punch to mark the holes.

No-Frills Jig

The *PerfectMount for Drawers* is an inexpensive, easy-to-use jig for installing pulls. This $6 jig simply registers off the top edge of any drawer to mark placement of most common size pulls or knobs. There are multiple, pre-drilled holes for most drawer heights.

Shop Project

rosewood Marking Gauge

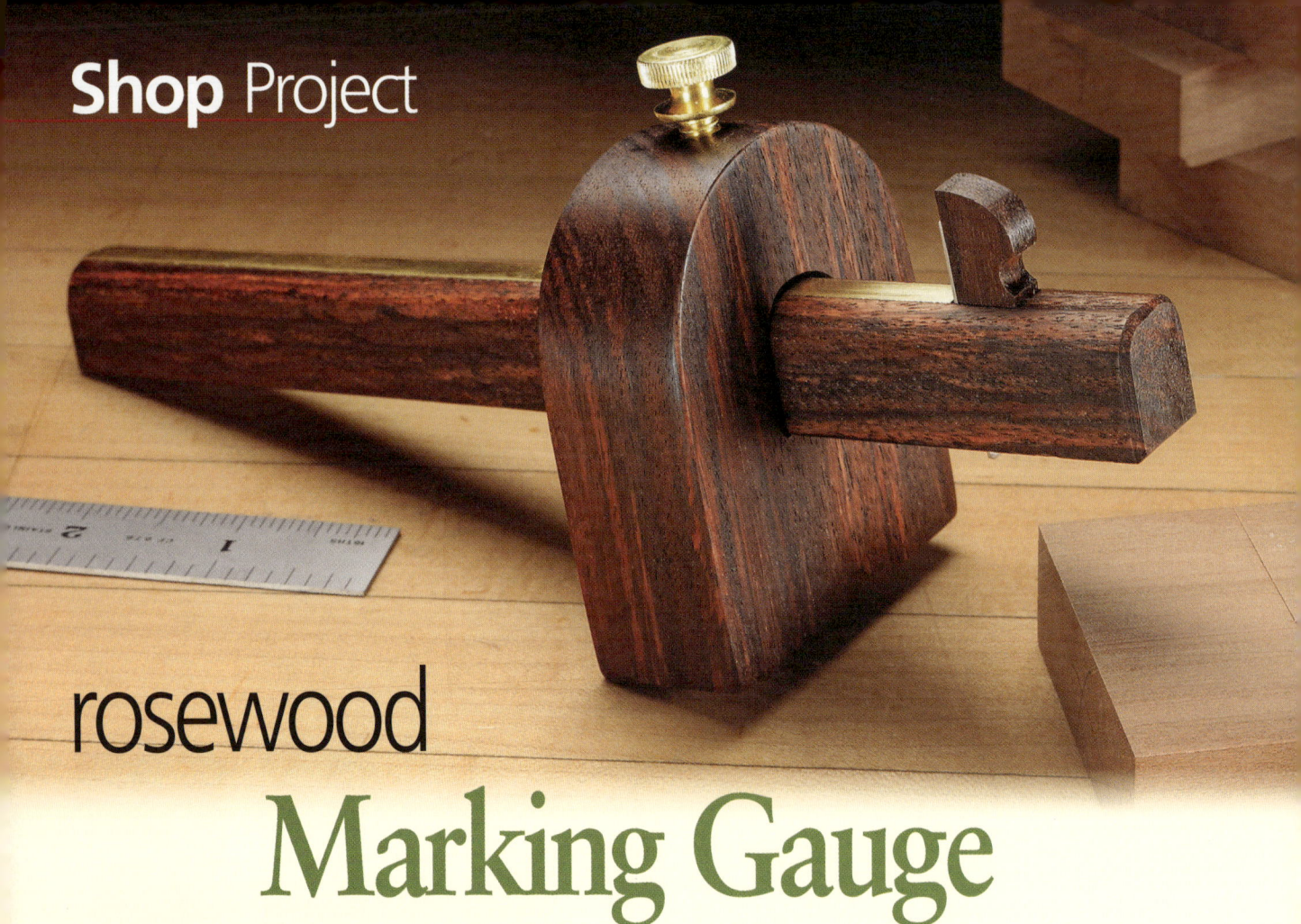

▲ This rosewood marking gauge might become one of your most-used tools for laying out mortises, tenons, and a variety of other joinery.

Materials & Supplies

A Beam (1)   ¾ x ¹¹⁄₁₆ - 8½
B Fence (1)   1 x 2¼ - 2¾
C Wedge (1)   ¼ x ⅜ - 1⅜

- ¹⁄₁₆" x ¼" - 12" Brass Strip
- ¼"- 20 x 1" Brass Knurled Knob
- Hacksaw Blade

An heirloom-quality marking gauge is not only a functional and attractive tool, but a pleasure to use when laying out joinery.

Making your own hand tools is a great way to personalize your shop. This marking gauge is a tool that's sure to see lots of action. The beauty of rosewood, a traditional tool wood, is hard to deny. But any special piece of hardwood will work just fine.

The marking gauge is a classic design consisting simply of a beam and fence. On the beam, a thin brass strip acts as a wear plate and a small wedge holds the shop-made blade in place.

START WITH THE BEAM. Completing the beam first allows you to use the finished profile to lay out the shape of the opening in the fence more accurately.

I started by cutting the stock for the beam to final thickness and width. But I left the blank extra long for stability during subsequent operations. You need the extra length to leave the ends square as you rout the roundovers on the top edges of the blank and the groove for the brass.

I made layout marks on the blank showing the final length as well as the centerline of the top edge. Finally, I drilled a ¼"-dia. hole for the through mortise. The top drawing on the opposite page shows you what it looks like.

SHAPING THE BEAM. With the blank marked, you're ready to start shaping it into a beam. Head to the router table and install a ¼" roundover bit. Set the fence so the workpiece will just touch the bearing on the bit and rout the profile on the top edges. As I mentioned earlier, you'll need to

14   Woodsmith   No. 194

leave the last inch or two at each end of the blank square.

Using the layout marks on the blank as a reference, rout the roundover profile on the upper edges of the blank, as shown in the left drawing below.

ROUT A GROOVE. After shaping the top of the beam, the next step is to rout a shallow groove for the brass strip. For this, I installed a ⅛"-dia. straight bit. By using an undersized bit, you can rout the groove in multiple passes and sneak up on the right width for a perfect fit for the brass. I raised the bit above the table so the height of the bit was equal to the thickness of the brass strip.

For this cut, set the fence so the bit is slightly off-center on the blank. Then, mark the start and stop locations for the cut on both ends of the blank. After making the first pass, flip the blank end-for-end and repeat. The right drawing below shows how this keeps the groove centered.

Check the size of the groove with the brass strip. Move the fence and rout the blank again, until you have a good fit.

CUT THE MORTISE. Next, you need to complete the through mortise that holds the blade and wedge. You can use a chisel to square up the ¼"-dia. hole you drilled earlier. You'll also need to taper the front edge of the mortise slightly (side section view, above). This taper helps make a tight fit for the wedge you'll add later.

BRASS WEAR STRIP. At this point, you're ready to cut a thin strip of brass to fit in the groove. Then you can spread a thin coat of cyanoacrylate (super glue) in the bottom of the groove and press in the brass strip. Finally, remove the square ends by cutting the beam to final length.

FIRST: Cut the beam blank to thickness and width, leaving it extra long

SECOND: Mark centerline and final length on blank and drill ¼"-dia. hole 1" from end

THIRD: Rout the ¼" roundover on both upper edges

FOURTH: Use a ⅛" straight bit to rout the shallow, centered groove for the brass wear strip (box below)

FIFTH: Use chisel to complete the through mortise for blade and wedge; then install brass wear strip

SIXTH: Cut beam to final length

▲ The combination of rosewood and brass makes for a beautiful and long-lasting tool.

How-To: Rout the Beam

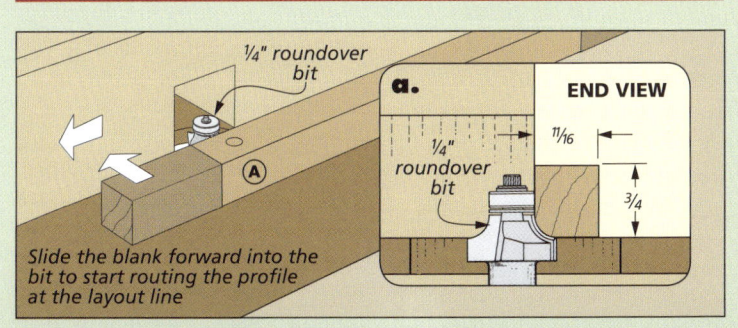

Routing the Top Edges. Lay out the final length of the beam on the blank. Then you can use the marks as guides for where to start and stop routing the roundover profile on the upper edges of the beam.

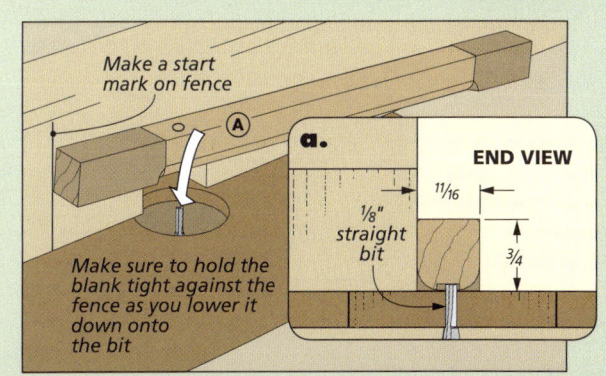

A Centered Groove. With the fence set so the bit is slightly off center, rout the shallow groove. Then flip the blank and repeat to form a centered groove.

shaping the FENCE

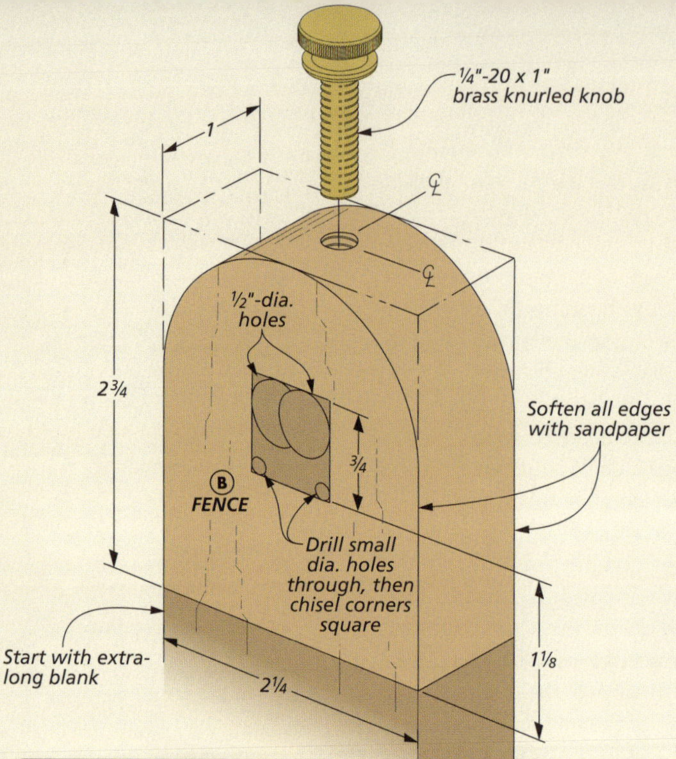

With the beam completed, you can appreciate the beautiful contrast of rosewood and brass. As you move on to making the fence, you'll further show off this look by adding a brass knob to lock the fence in position.

THE FENCE. The fence is simply a matching block of hardwood with a hole in the face to fit the beam and another hole on the top, tapped to accept a brass knob. When tightened, the knob locks the position of the fence.

Start by cutting a blank to width, but leave it extra long. I used a simple circle-cutting jig to cut the round top at the band saw. (You can find out how to build and use the jig in Shop Notebook on page 28).

Now you can sand the arc smooth by placing the blank in a vise and using a "strap" of sandpaper, as shown in the margin photo. In spite of its density, rosewood sands very easily and you can have a polished surface with just a few minutes of effort.

When you're done sanding the arc on the top of the fence, go ahead and cut the fence blank to final length at the table saw.

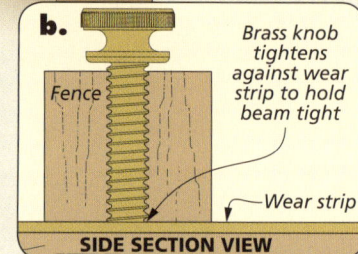

SHAPE THE HOLE. The next step is to cut the holes in the fence that will allow you to shape an opening that matches the profile of the beam. To get started, I marked the lower edge of the opening on the face of the fence. Then, I laid the fence flat on my workbench and held the beam in position and traced the outline (detail 'a'). By using this mark, you can zero in on a good fit for the beam.

Since the round profile on the top of the beam was created using a ¼" roundover bit, you can easily match the shape by drilling ½"-dia. holes in the fence blank (drawings below). Remember to

▲ Fold a piece of sandpaper in half to sand the curve.

How-To: Shape the Beam Opening

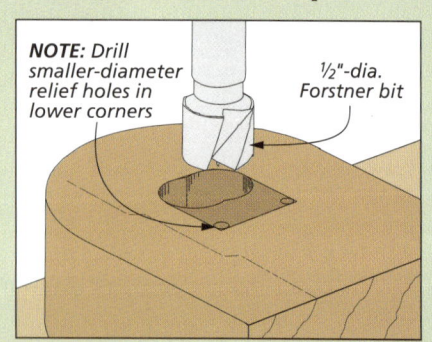

Drill. Using a drill bit that matches the radius of the beam profile, drill two holes at the top of the opening.

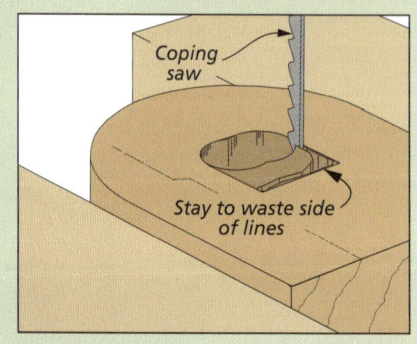

Saw. A coping saw is the perfect tool for making the inside cuts that further shape the opening for the beam.

Chisel. A sharp chisel makes short work of cleaning up the edges and fine-tuning the final fit of the opening.

16 Woodsmith No. 194

drill the holes just inside the layout marks for a good fit. You can widen them, if necessary, in the final fitting of the beam.

Finish the bottom portion of the hole by drilling starter holes for a coping saw blade. Now you can connect the upper and lower holes using a coping saw. A small chisel works well for smoothing the sides of the opening.

Test fit the beam in the opening and continue to pare the sides until you have a good fit. (The beam shouldn't be too tight, and should slide easily in the fence.)

TAP THE TOP. A nice, brass knurled knob locks the fence in position. With most woods, you'd need to drill a large hole and install a threaded insert to provide threads for the knob. But since rosewood is very dense, you can simply drill a hole and tap a ¼"-20 thread for the brass knob.

To make the marking gauge comfortable to use, I softened all the edges with a light sanding.

MAKE A BLADE. The business end of the marking gauge is a shop-made blade. I've often been frustrated by marking gauges that rely on a pin to score the surface of the wood. Too often, they tear the wood instead of cutting it. So for this gauge, I decided to make a rounded-edge blade that will slice cleanly and make a highly visible layout mark by cleanly cutting the wood fibers.

I didn't have to look far for the perfect material for the blade. An old hacksaw blade is ideal. The box below walks you through the steps of turning the old blade into the perfect, custom-shaped blade for your marking gauge.

WEDGE. A wedge holds the blade. I cut a blank and shaped it as in the pattern above. Fit the blade and wedge as shown in detail 'a.'

Now all it takes is a coat or two of oil to add the perfect finish to the marking gauge. **W**

▶ The completed wedge and blade will provide years of service.

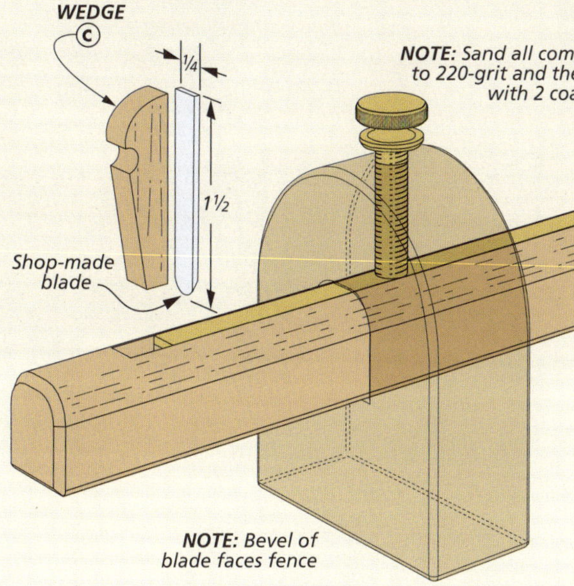

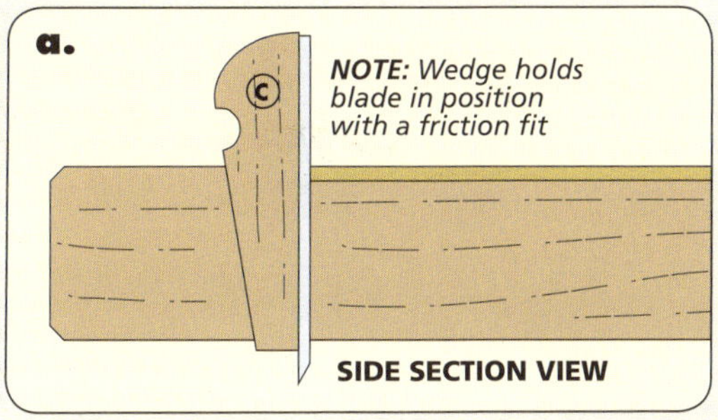

NOTE: Sand all components to 220-grit and then finish with 2 coats of oil

NOTE: Bevel of blade faces fence

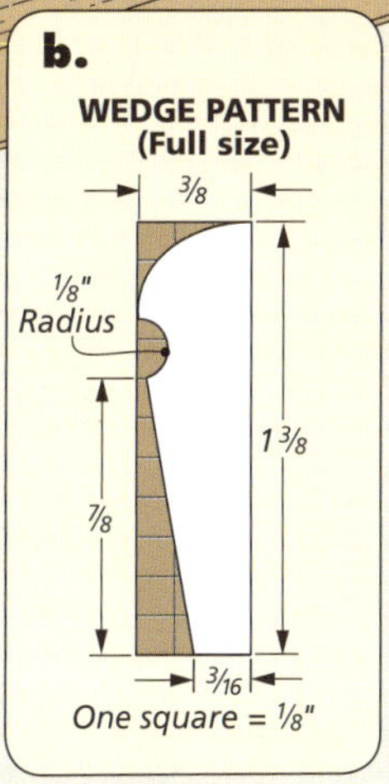

b. WEDGE PATTERN (Full size)
One square = ⅛"

a. SIDE SECTION VIEW
NOTE: Wedge holds blade in position with a friction fit

Woodsmith GO ONLINE EXTRAS
For more on using a marking gauge, visit our website at Woodsmith.com

▲ Fine-tune the fit of the wedge using sandpaper.

Making a Marking Gauge Blade

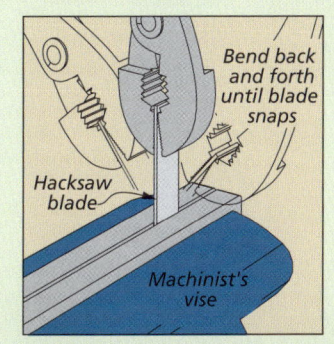

Length. With the hacksaw blade in a machinist's vise, snap a piece to length.

Width. Use a pair of pliers to bend the blade across its length and snap it to final width.

Profile. A grinder makes short work of adding a rounded end to the small blade.

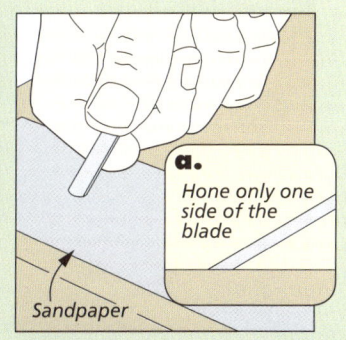

Hone. Hone the rounded bevel with different grits of sandpaper glued to a flat surface.

a. Hone only one side of the blade

Weekend Project

sliding door Wall Shelf

A sleek design with lots of handy storage makes this project a great home accent.

Anytime I can add storage space to my home that doesn't take up valuable floor space, I consider it a bonus. That's why I like this shelf. It hangs on the wall, so I can place it over a desk or buffet. And that gives me more room to stash books or other items.

As you can see in the photos, this shelf has sliding glass doors that add to the overall design. The frosted-glass doors slide in a track and give you a place to conceal the clutter.

You'd think that building a sturdy wall shelf would require a lot of complicated joinery. But that's not the case. I assembled the shelf using *Minifix* fasteners. The two-part fasteners, shown in the photo on the opposite page, draw the workpieces together and hold them firmly. This means you can simply cut the pieces to size and not worry about cutting a lot of complicated joinery to assemble the project.

▲ Frosted glass sliding doors conceal stored items on the bottom shelf. The doors ride smoothly in plastic tracks.

BUILD THE SIDES

What gives this wall shelf its classic look are the tapers on the sides. In addition, each shelf has a rail across the back to add support and enhance the overall look. So I started by making the two sides for the shelf.

HOLES. Once the sides are cut to overall width and length, you can drill the stopped holes for the *Minifix* fasteners, as shown in detail 'b.' If you take a look at the photo at right, you'll see that the connector pin has a flange about midway. The flange needs to seat against the surface of the workpiece in order for the fastener to work properly.

To drill the holes, you'll need an 8mm bit. I'll talk more about the installation of these fasteners later. For now, just follow the layout for the holes in detail 'a.'

TAPERS. At this point, I taped the two sides together so I could shape them identically. You can start by laying out the tapers at each end. Then cut the tapers at the band saw. Finally, use a sanding block to clean up any saw marks on the tapers and to gently round the corners at the ends. I've shown the step-by-step drawings in the How-to box below.

BULLNOSE. Once the sides are shaped, you can separate the two workpieces and take them over to the router table to create the bullnose on the top, bottom, and front edges. You'll need to use a ½" roundover bit buried in the table, as shown in detail 'c.' Rout one side of the edge, then flip the workpiece over and rout the other side. Finally you can smooth the profile with sandpaper to remove the center ridge.

▲ The *Minifix* fasteners have two parts — a connector pin and a cam.

How-To: Shape the Sides

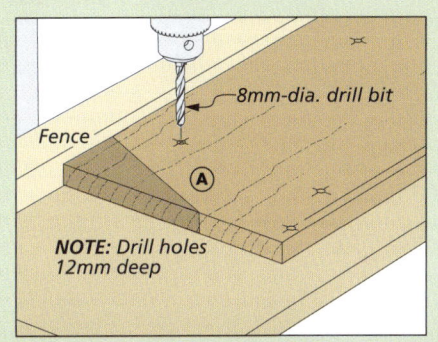

Drill. Once you have the holes marked according to detail 'a' above, you can drill the stopped holes in the sides.

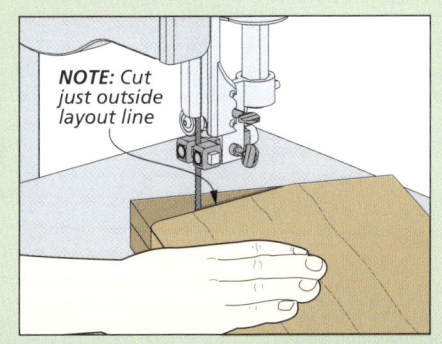

Cut Tapers. Join the two sides together with double-sided tape, mark the tapers, and then cut them at the band saw.

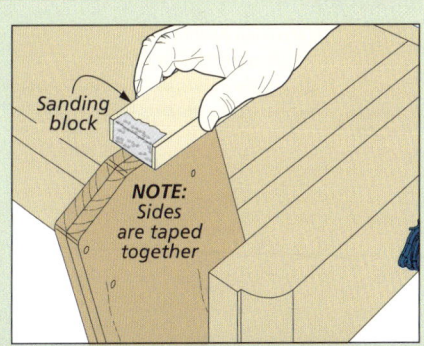

Sand Corners. With the two shelf sides still taped together, sand the tapers and gently round the corners.

Woodsmith.com

complete the SHELVES

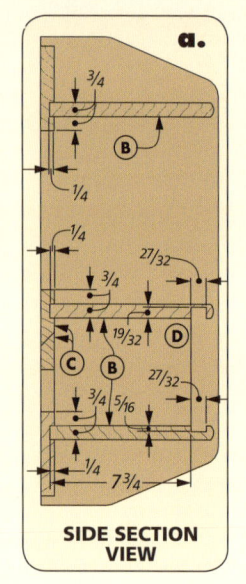

All three shelves are identical except for the placement of the dadoes and grooves. They're stabilized by rails attached to the back. The center rail is eventually cut into two parts to create a pair of interlocking cleats.

GROOVES. Your first task is to cut the shelves to size. Then you can drill the holes for the fasteners. It's important that the holes are placed exactly 34mm from the end of the shelf, so that the fasteners will seat properly (box below).

Now you can take the center and bottom shelf to the table saw to cut the grooves for the door tracks. If you take a look at the box at the bottom of the opposite page, you'll see that each groove is a different depth. They're also wider than the standard dado blade, so you'll need to make two passes on the saw. This is shown in details 'a' and 'b' of the same drawing.

DADOES. The center divider is held in a pair of stopped dadoes. To make these, I used a handheld router guided by a clamped-on fence (box, opposite page).

BULLNOSE. When the grooves and dadoes are complete, you can take the shelves over to the router table to form the bullnose profile on the front of each shelf.

TRACKS. Your final step for the shelves is to install the tracks in the grooves. The track is designed to snap in place, but I also added epoxy.

RAILS. Once the shelves are complete, you can turn your attention to the rails. The three rails start off the same. After they're cut to size, you can drill holes for the cams in the ends of the upper and lower rails (detail 'b'). Then you can cut the grooves.

When the grooves are finished, take the center rail to make the cleat. It's ripped on the table saw to form matching bevels. The top section is glued and screwed to the center shelf. The lower part of the cleat is attached securely to the wall to hold the shelf.

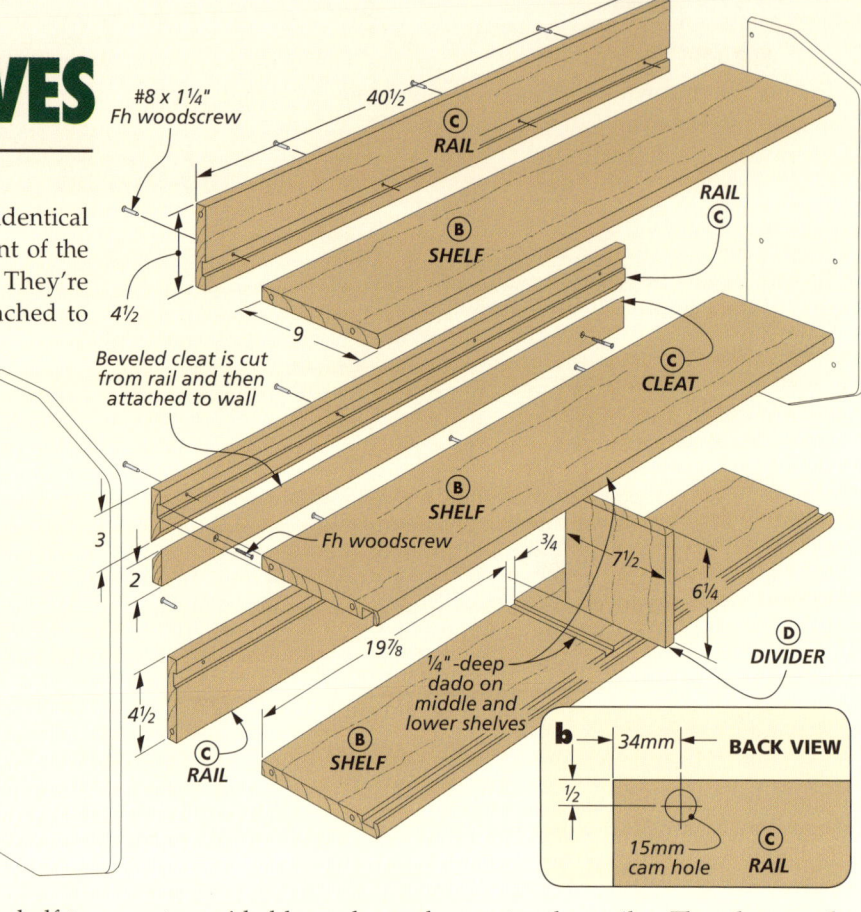

▲ The top track for the glass is taller to make installing and removing the glass easy.

How-To: Join the Shelves

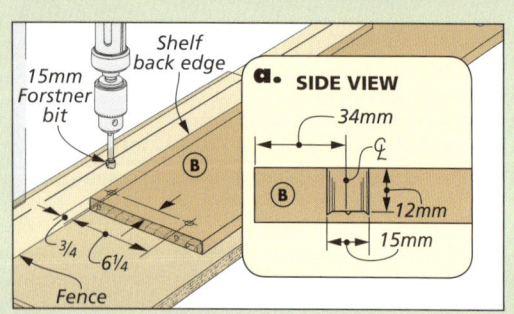

Shelf Holes. The stopped holes for the cams are drilled in the bottom of each shelf. You'll need to use a metric rule for some layout tasks.

Pin Holes. The holes for the connector pins are drilled using a jig shown on page 28.

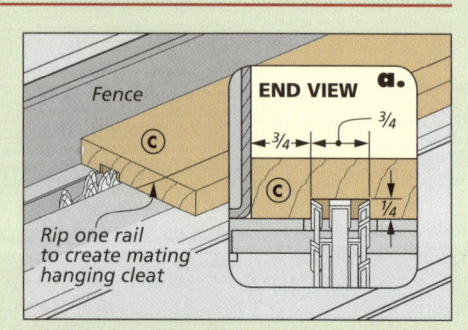

Rail Grooves. The groove on each rail holds the back edge of each shelf. They should be sized to fit the shelf thickness.

SHELF DIVIDER. The last part to make is the shelf divider. I added a divider to the enclosed shelf for added organization.

GLASS. You'll also need to purchase two pieces of frosted glass for the sliding doors. Your local glass shop should be able to cut, frost it, and add the depressions that form the pulls.

ASSEMBLY

With the workpieces ready, it's time to assemble the wall shelf. The key here is to understand how the fasteners work.

FASTENERS. As you can see in detail 'b,' the *Minifix* fastener has two parts. The ribbed end of the connector pin slides into the hole in the side of the wall shelf. The flange on the pin should fit tight against the side. The metal end of the pin slides into the hole in the end of the shelf or rail, as shown in detail 'b.' You'll be able to see the end of the pin in the hole for the cam you drilled on the face of the shelf or rail. The cam should be inserted as shown in detail 'a.' Then all you need to do is turn the case with a Phillips screwdriver to pull everything tight.

After mastering the fasteners, you can assemble the shelf. I glued and screwed each shelf to a it's rail and then attached the sides to the shelves and rails, adding the center divider in the process.

All that's left is to apply the finish (Sources on page 51), insert the doors, and find the perfect spot to hang your new wall shelf. **W**

FIRST: Glue and screw shelves and rails together

SECOND: Install divider in dadoes

Lower cleat is cut ¼" shorter to ease mounting shelf to wall

THIRD: Attach both sides to shelves and rails

¾" x 2" finger pull ground into glass door

FOURTH: Slide glass panels in place

a. Align small arrow with hole for pin

Turn cam in direction of large arrow to pull joint together

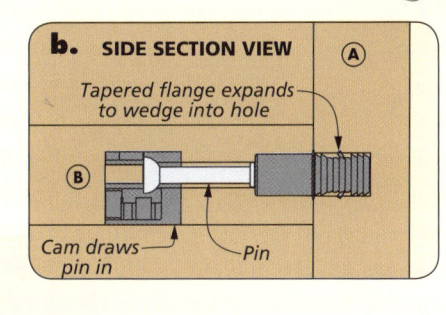

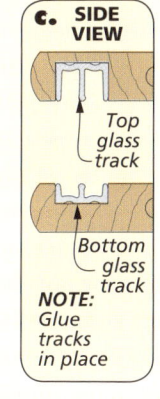

b. SIDE SECTION VIEW
Tapered flange expands to wedge into hole
Cam draws pin in — Pin

c. SIDE VIEW
Top glass track
Bottom glass track
NOTE: Glue tracks in place

Materials, Supplies & Cutting Diagram

- **A** Sides (2) — ¾ x 9¾ - 25
- **B** Shelves (3) — ¾ x 9 - 40½
- **C** Rails/Cleat (3) — ¾ x 4½ - 40½
- **D** Shelf Divider (1) — ¾ x 7½ - 6¼

- (16) ¾" *MiniFix* Fasteners
- (1) 48" Sliding Door Track
- (2) ¼" x 6³⁄₁₆" - 20½" Glass Doors
- (12) #8 x 1¼" Fh Woodscrews

¾" x 10" - 96" Cherry (6.7 Bd.Ft.)
¾" x 10" - 96" Cherry (6.7 Bd.Ft.)
¾" x 10" - 96" Cherry (6.7 Bd.Ft.)

Fitting Glass Track

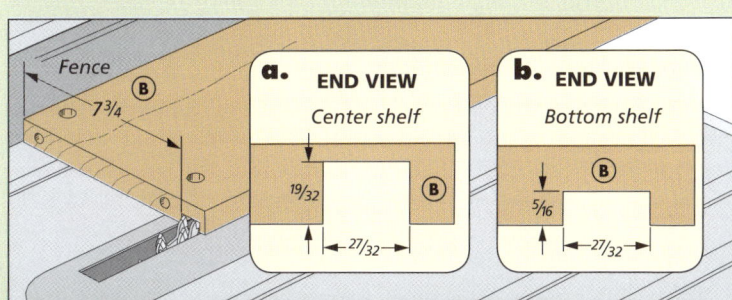

a. END VIEW Center shelf
b. END VIEW Bottom shelf

a. FRONT SECTION VIEW

Glass Track. The grooves for the glass track in the bottom and center shelf are cut the same width.

The groove in the center shelf is deeper to hold the upper track (details 'a' and 'b').

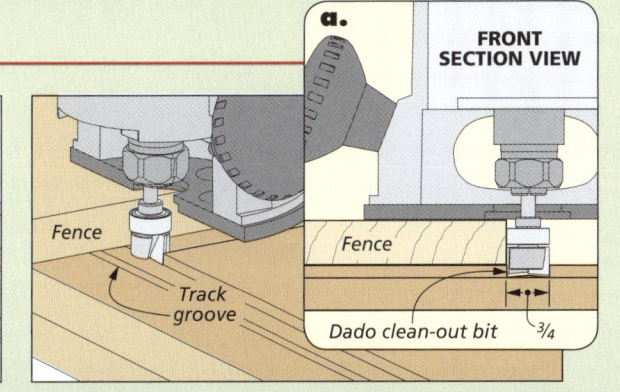

Stopped Dado. The shelf divider sits in a pair of stopped dadoes centered in the bottom and center shelf. Start routing in the existing track groove.

Designer Series Project

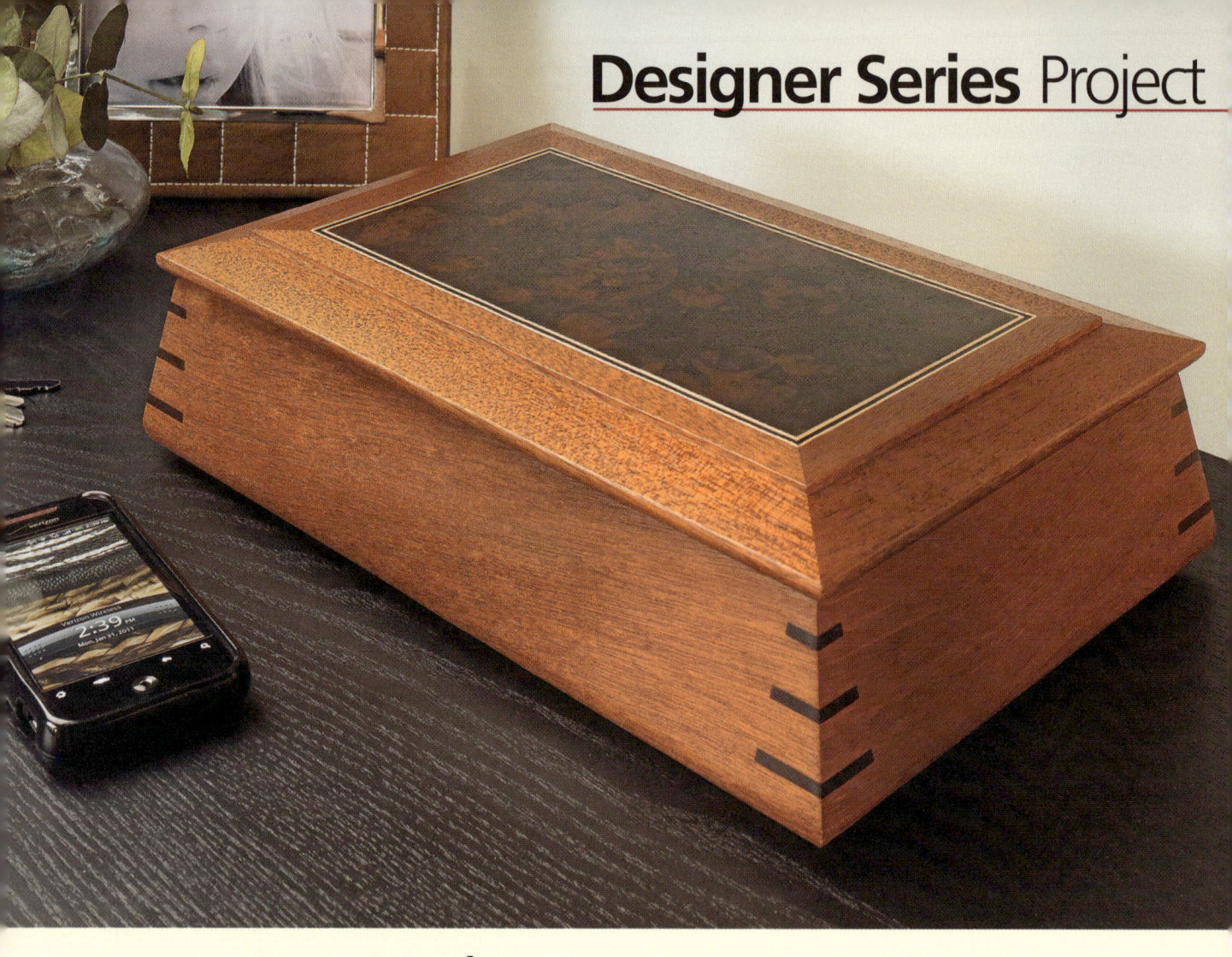

contoured
Keepsake Box

Great-looking veneer and hardwood plus a few interesting woodworking techniques add up to a memorable project.

A keepsake box is something that just about everyone appreciates. And an elegant design like the one shown above is suitable for any occasion. On top of that, you can enjoy trying out a few interesting woodworking techniques that go into making the box.

Splined miters and contoured sides are the focal points of the basic box. The hinged lid not only has an interesting profile, but it features a veneered center panel trimmed with thin, inlaid banding. I used an easy and reliable method to veneer the panel without using an expensive vacuum press or any special tools.

The best thing about this project is that you can find most of the material you'll need to build it in the scrap bin. Any hardwood will do just fine. (I chose mahogany.) You can change the look of the box by choosing matching material for the splines, or use a contrasting wood, like I did. And since it only requires a small piece of veneer, you can look for an interesting piece without spending a fortune.

It's hard to imagine a better way to spend your shop time.

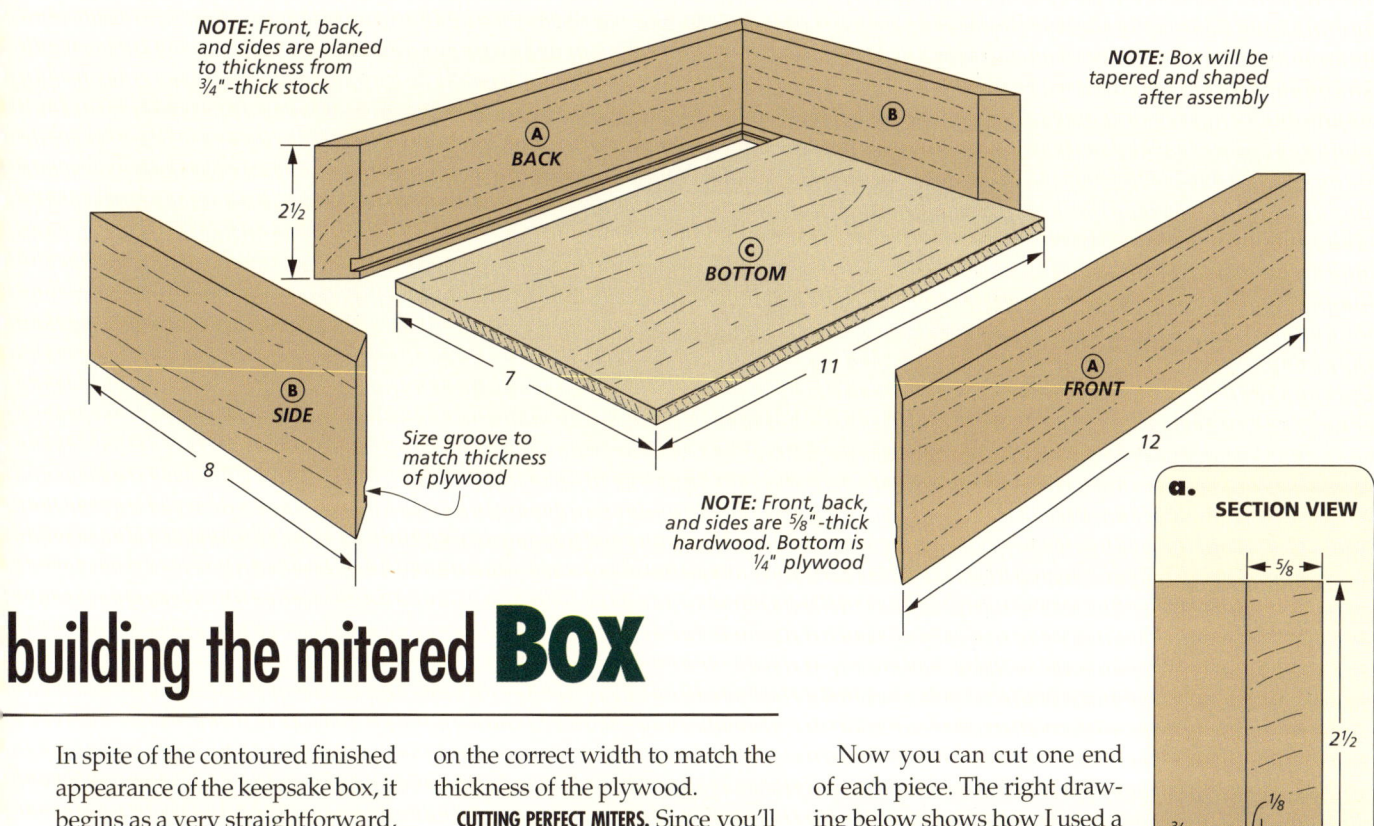

building the mitered BOX

NOTE: Front, back, and sides are planed to thickness from ¾"-thick stock

NOTE: Box will be tapered and shaped after assembly

Size groove to match thickness of plywood

NOTE: Front, back, and sides are ⅝"-thick hardwood. Bottom is ¼" plywood

In spite of the contoured finished appearance of the keepsake box, it begins as a very straightforward, rectangular assembly. Later, you'll add splines in the corners and taper the outside.

MILL THE STOCK. The front, back, and sides of the box are all ⅝" thick. So I started by planing some ¾"-thick stock to this thickness. Then I cut the pieces to final width and rough length.

GROOVE. The box below shows how I used a standard blade to cut the groove for the bottom. By moving the rip fence slightly between passes you can sneak up on the correct width to match the thickness of the plywood.

CUTTING PERFECT MITERS. Since you'll shape the sides of the box, it's very important that the miter joints are as close to perfect as possible.

You can start by tilting the saw blade 45°. Here, you'll want to take the time to set this angle accurately. Then attach an auxiliary fence to the miter gauge. The auxiliary fence backs up the cut, and stops it from tearing out on the back side. I also attached adhesive-backed sandpaper to the fence to prevent the workpiece from slipping during the cut.

Now you can cut one end of each piece. The right drawing below shows how I used a stop block to keep the length of opposite sides exactly the same. This step is critical to assembling tight miter joints.

ASSEMBLY. To assemble the box, lay out all four pieces against a straightedge with their inside faces down and tape across each joint. Then, cut the plywood bottom and dry fit the assembly. Finally, add glue to the miters, insert the bottom in the groove, and bring the pieces together, taping the final corner.

How-To: Prepare the Front, Back & Sides

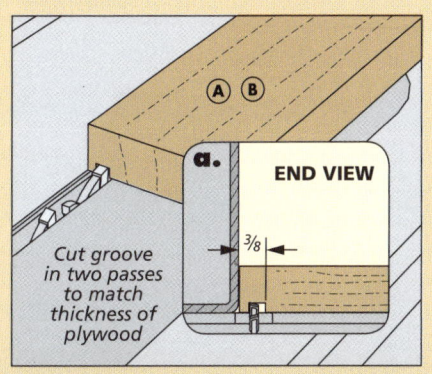

Groove. First, cut the upper edge of the groove. Then bump the rip fence in to sneak up on a good fit for the bottom.

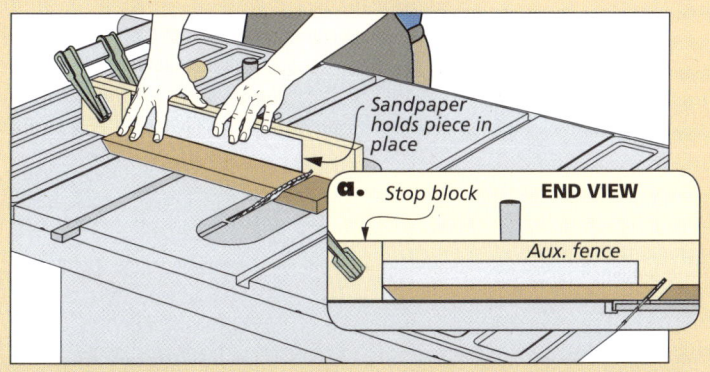

Miter to Length. With an auxiliary fence on the miter gauge and the blade set to 45°, start by cutting one end of each workpiece. Then set up a stop block to cut the opposite end to final length.

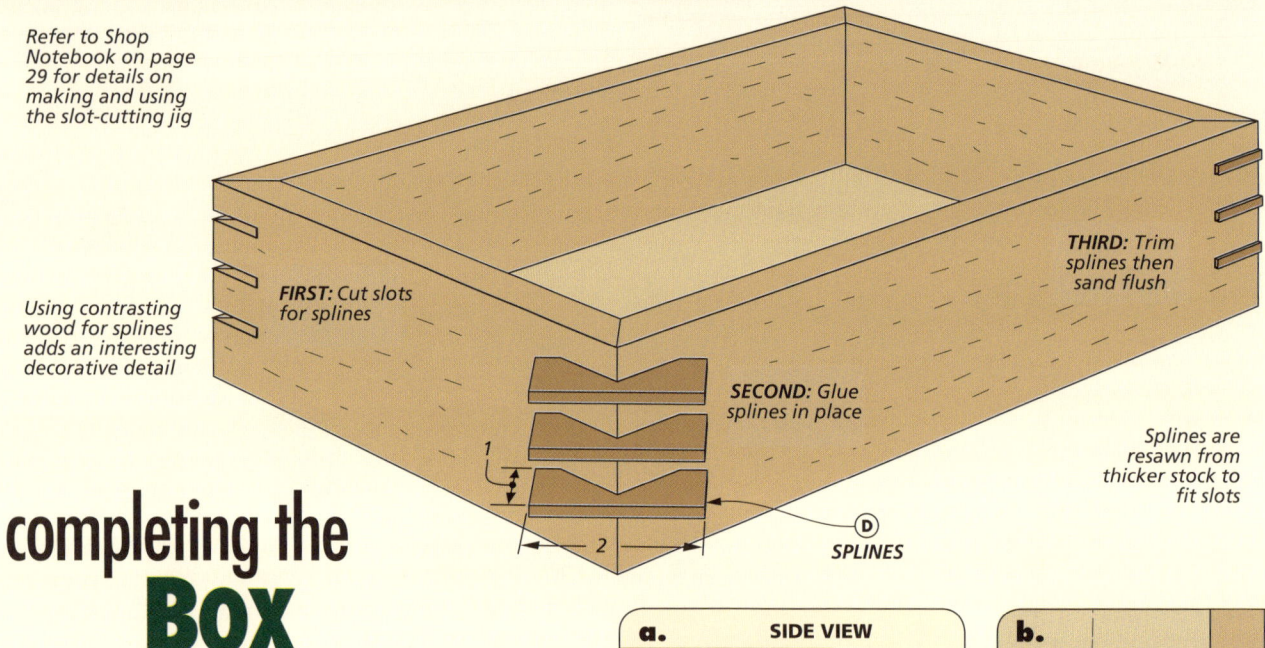

Refer to Shop Notebook on page 29 for details on making and using the slot-cutting jig

Using contrasting wood for splines adds an interesting decorative detail

FIRST: Cut slots for splines

SECOND: Glue splines in place

THIRD: Trim splines then sand flush

Splines are resawn from thicker stock to fit slots

D SPLINES

completing the BOX

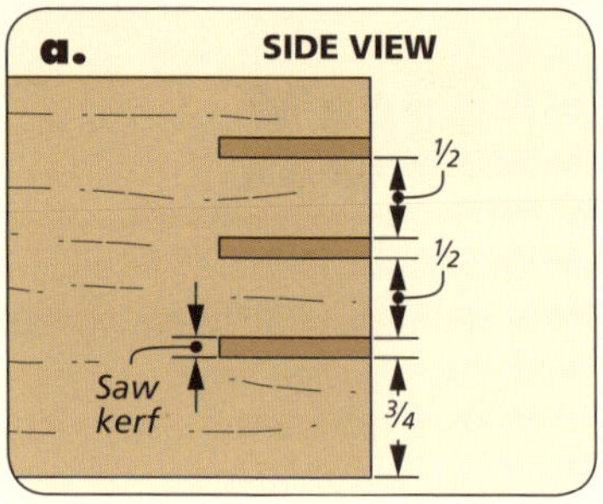

a. SIDE VIEW — Saw kerf, 1/2, 1/2, 3/4

b. TOP VIEW — 11/16

▲ The corner block makes it possible to clamp the splines in position.

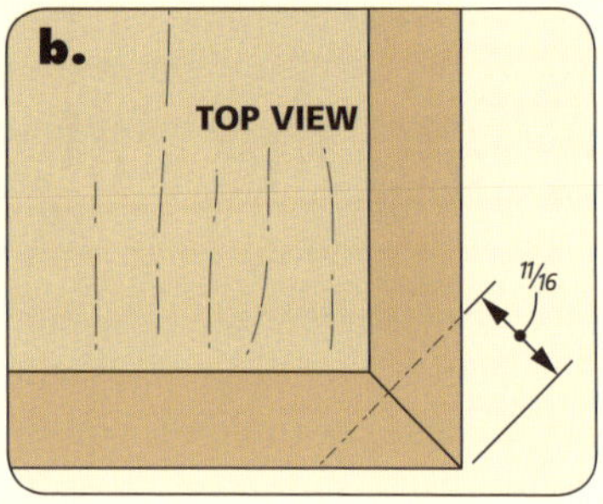

With the box assembled, the next order of business is to cut slots in the corners and add the splines. As you can see in the box below, I use a simple, shop-made jig to hold the box at the proper angle to cut the slots. You can find the plans for making the jig on page 29.

CUT THE SLOTS. Using the jig is a reliable way to accurately cut the slots. But there are a couple of things to set up first.

Start by setting the blade height to cut through the jig to the correct depth on the corners. You can see what I mean in detail 'b' above. Make test cuts through the jig and measure the blade height to get it set properly. Since the jig rides against the rip fence, all you need to do is set the fence to the correct spacing for each slot. Detail 'a' shows the positions of the slots.

MAKE THE SPLINES. The center drawing below shows an easy way to cut splines from a piece of contrasting stock. (I used walnut.) Plane or sand the splines for a snug fit. They should not be so tight they need to be pounded in place. After applying glue, I used a piece of scrap with beveled edges as a clamping aid, as you see in the margin photo at left.

A flush-cutting saw makes short work of trimming waste from the splines. Then, a little sanding is all it takes to smooth out the sides of the box. And since subsequent

How-To: Create Slots & Splines

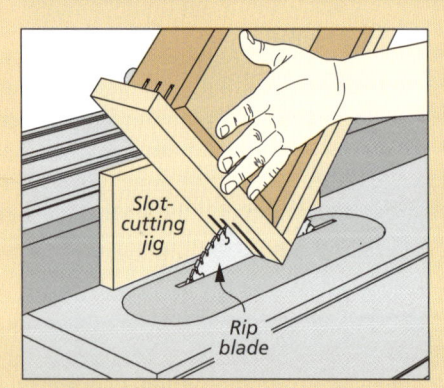

Cutting the Spline Slots. Hold the box firmly in position in the jig as you cut the slots for the splines.

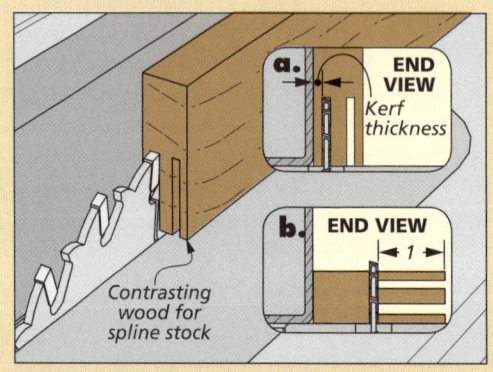

(Slot-cutting jig, Rip blade)

Ripping Spline Stock. Set the rip fence and cut (detail 'a'), then flip the workpiece over and repeat. Cut the splines free as in detail 'b.'

a. END VIEW — Kerf thickness
b. END VIEW — 1
Contrasting wood for spline stock

Trimming. Using a flush-cutting saw, carefully trim the waste to avoid breaking off the splines.

Flush-cutting saw

NOTE: Secure box in vise to trim splines

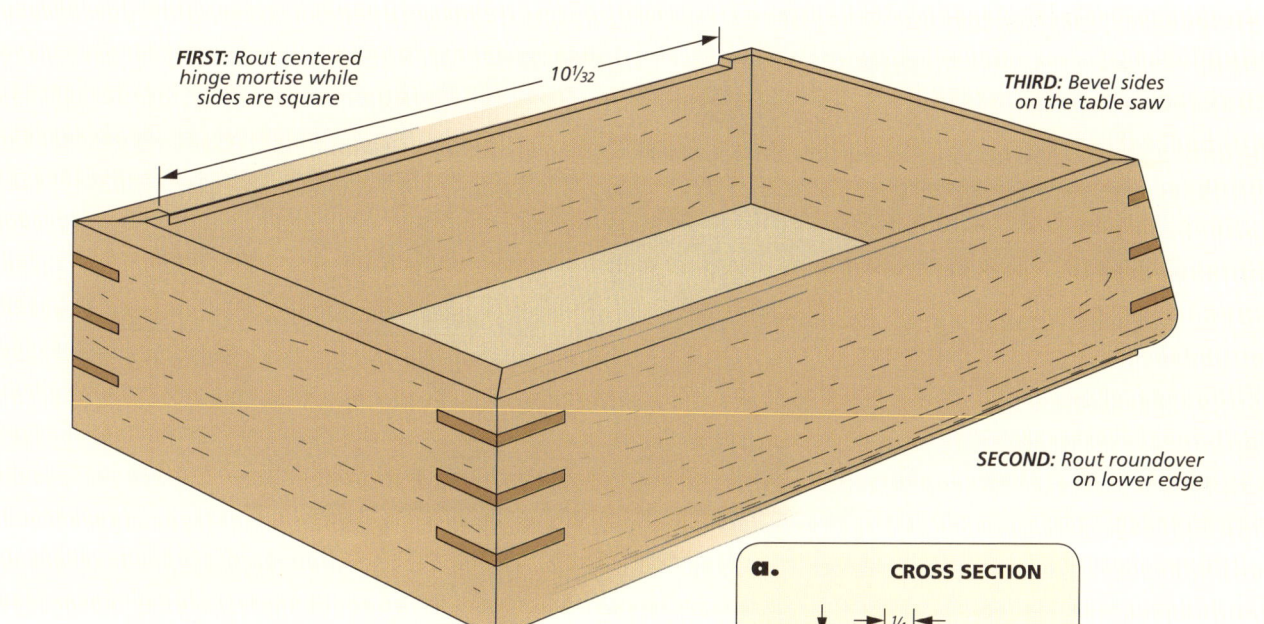

operations rely on the sides riding against the fence on the table saw and router table, having the sides flat is important for getting consistent, even cuts.

HINGE MORTISE. The lid is connected to the box with a continuous (piano) hinge. To get a good fit for the lid, the hinge needs to be mortised into the back edge of the box. The depth of the mortise equals the full thickness of the hinge. (The lid isn't mortised.)

The edge of the box is too narrow to support the router during this cut. And there's a risk of tearout if you try this on the router table. I came up with an easier plan to rout the mortise.

I simply sandwiched the back of the box between a couple of support blocks. With the blocks taped in place, there's plenty of surface area to safely rout away most of the waste for the hinge mortise (left drawing, below). Then I squared up the ends of the mortise with a chisel.

ROUTING THE BOTTOM EDGES. Next, I used a roundover bit to add a visual detail to the lower edge of the box. The center drawing below shows how this profile creates a small foot on the base.

BEVELING THE SIDES. The beveled sides provide a very distinctive look for the box. The bevel also gives the illusion that the splines are each a different size. You can safely make this bevel cut by installing a rip blade and tilting the blade 11°. The right drawing below has the details.

It's not unusual to get a little bit of burning here, so be sure to use a sharp, clean blade. Finish up with a good sanding.

Shape the Box

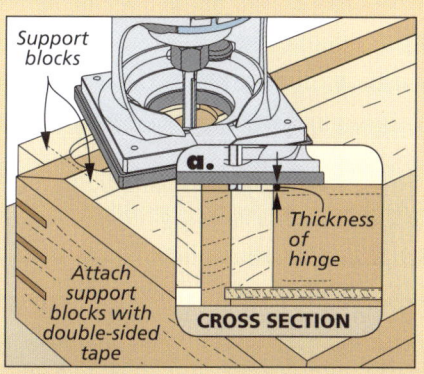

Hinge Mortise. By taping support blocks to both sides of the back, routing the hinge mortise is a breeze.

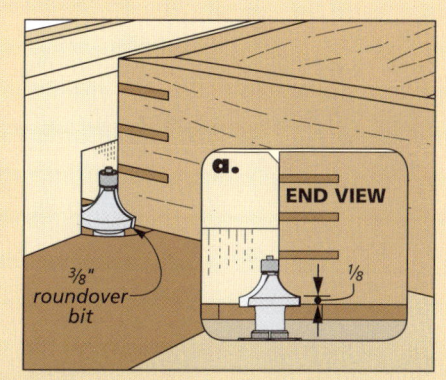

Rout. Using a roundover bit, rout the bottom edges. By making multiple, shallow passes you'll get a clean profile.

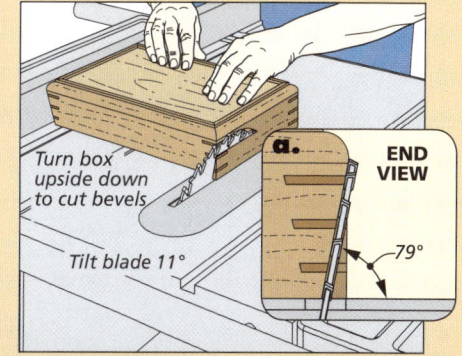

Beveling the Sides. With the box upside-down on the table saw, sight down the edge to set the fence.

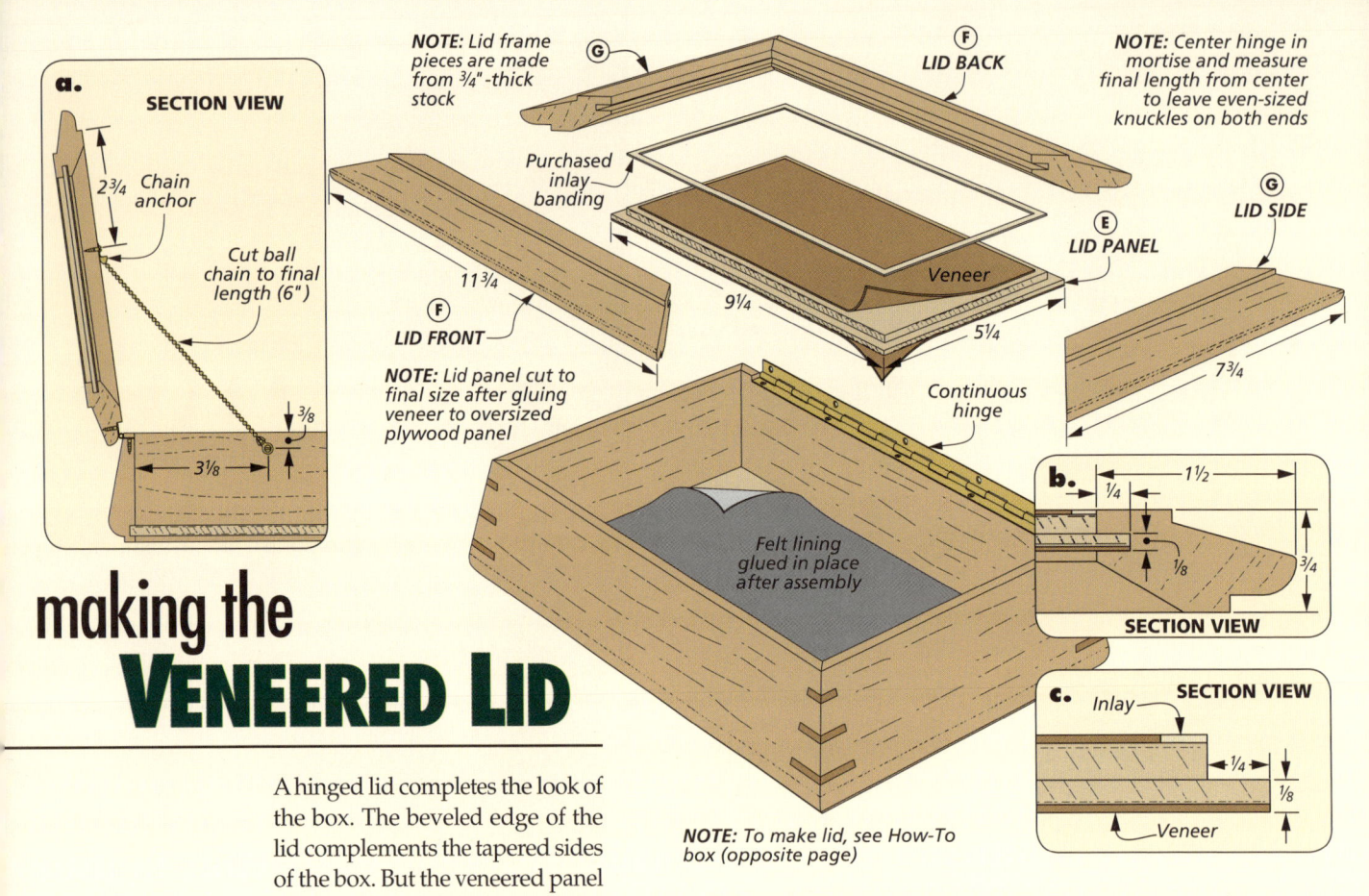

making the VENEERED LID

A hinged lid completes the look of the box. The beveled edge of the lid complements the tapered sides of the box. But the veneered panel and inlaid border really make the box stand out.

START WITH THE PANEL. After finding a special piece of figured veneer, I prepared a slightly oversize plywood panel to use as a substrate. Since this is a very small panel, you can glue the veneer to the substrate using only clamps and some cauls. The cauls are just a couple of ¾"-thick flat panels slightly larger than the lid panel.

I applied glue and attached veneer to both sides of the panel. Next, I sandwiched the panel between two cauls with waxed paper in between to prevent the panel from sticking to the cauls. Then, just place several clamps around the assembly.

For this kind of glueup, I like to let the panel stay under clamping pressure longer than normal to ensure a good bond. So after letting the glue set up overnight, you can remove it from the clamps and cauls and trim it to final size.

RABBET & RECESS. As you can see in detail 'c' above, you'll need to rabbet the edges of the panel to fit into the frame. In addition, you'll also need to cut a very shallow recess for the inlay banding. Then glue the banding in place in the shallow groove. The box below shows all three operations.

How-To: Create the Veneered Lid & Inlay

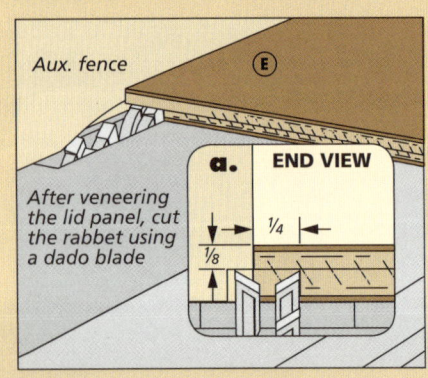

Rabbet. With an auxiliary fence installed, bury the dado blade and cut the rabbet on the outside edges of the panel.

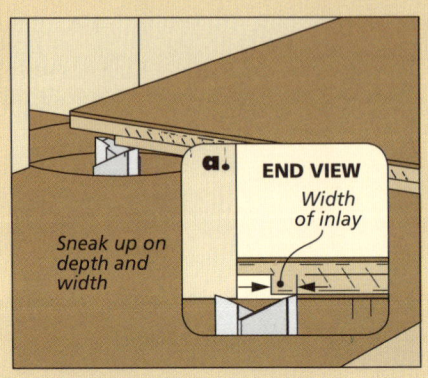

Rout Channel for Inlay. Using a straight bit, rout the very shallow channel to hold the narrow inlay banding.

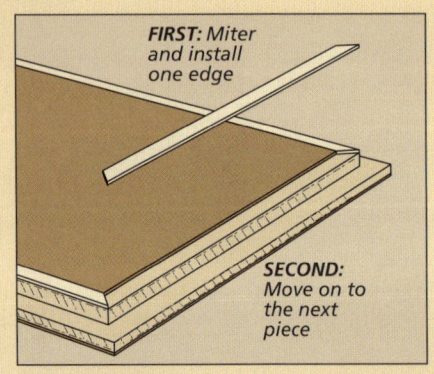

Install the Inlay. Fit each piece of inlay one at a time, mitering the corners with a sharp chisel or plane iron.

LID FRAME. To hold the veneered panel, I made a mitered frame. Of course, it will become the lid of the box, but you'll go through the same sort of process as you would for making a picture frame. The step-by-step instructions at right break down what looks to be a complicated task into easier, single cuts.

After selecting the stock and milling it to final size, head over to the table saw and cut a groove to fit the tongue on the panel. Then tilt the saw blade 30° and cut the bevel on the lower inside edge, as shown in Step 2.

ASSEMBLY. At this point, you can miter the frame pieces using the same techniques as before. Then, install the panel and assemble the frame. The remaining steps to create the profile are completed after assembly.

COMPLETING THE PROFILE. Now, cut the shallow notch shown in Step 3 to create the shoulder of the "raised panel" profile. The final bevel cut (Step 4) should just meet the edge of the notch, as shown in the detail.

In the final two steps, you'll rout a shallow rabbet on the underside of the frame and round over the edge, as well. The rabbet you rout in Step 5 creates a lip for the lid to rest on the upper edge of the box. After completing the rabbet, install a roundover bit and rout the profile to soften the appearance of the lid (Step 6).

FINAL DETAILS. By now, you've got a good fit for the lid. There are just a few final details to complete.

After cutting the hinge to length with a hacksaw, I used double-sided tape to hold it in position while installing the screws. Now you can apply your favorite finish to the box before you install the chain and anchors, as you see in detail 'a' on the opposite page. Finally, glue a felt lining in the bottom of the box.

The result of your effort is sure to gain a prominent spot in the home and a lot of admiration from your friends and family.

How-To: Make the Lid Frame

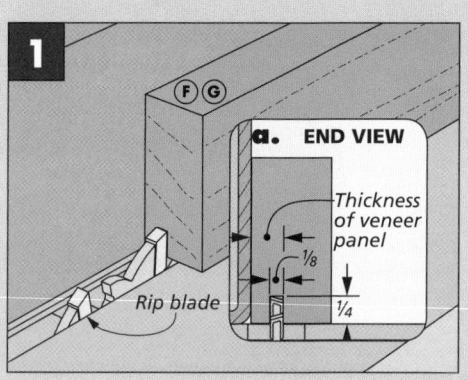

1 Groove. With a rip blade installed, cut the shallow groove that will hold the veneered top panel in the frame.

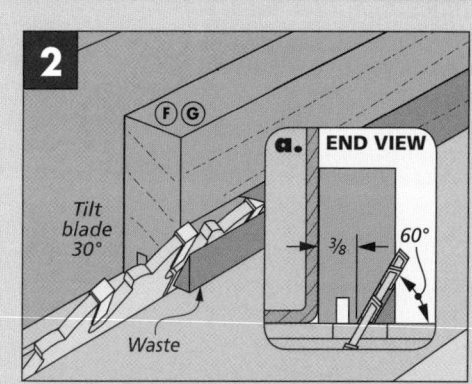

2 Inside Bevel. The next step is to tilt the blade 30° and cut the bevel on the inside edge of each of the frame pieces.

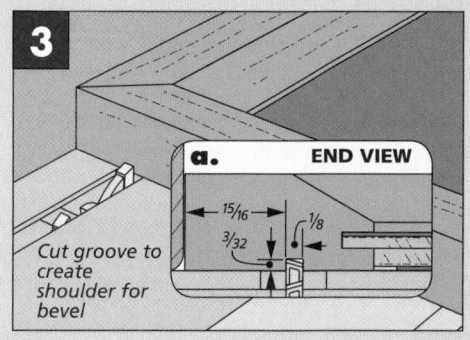

3 Shoulder. After assembling the frame, cut a very shallow groove that will define the border of the frame's top.

4 Outside Bevel. As you did earlier on the box sides, carefully sight the edge of the saw blade to meet the shoulder.

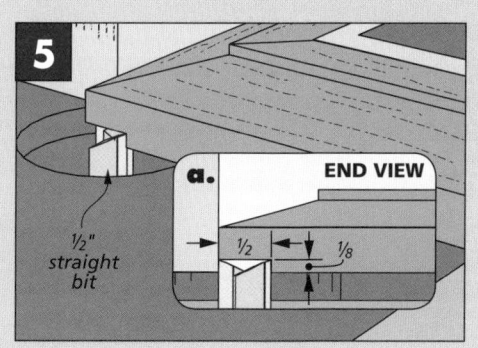

5 Rout the Lip. With a straight bit installed in the router table, rout the rabbets to form the bottom lip of the lid.

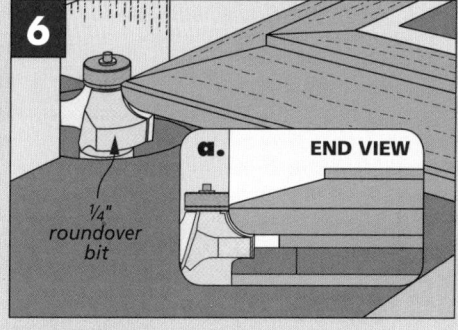

6 Round Over the Edge. Complete the profile of the frame by adding the roundover to soften the look of the lower edge.

Materials & Supplies and Cutting Diagram

A	Front/Back (2)	5/8 x 2 1/2 - 12
B	Sides (2)	5/8 x 2 1/2 - 8
C	Bottom (1)	1/4 ply. - 7 x 11
D	Splines (12)	1/8 x 1 - 2
E	Lid Panel (1)	1/4 ply. - 5 1/4 x 9 1/4
F	Lid Front/Back (2)	3/4 x 1 1/2 - 11 3/4
G	Lid Sides (2)	3/4 x 1 1/2 - 7 3/4

- (1) 16mm x 780mm Continuous Brass Hinge
- (10) #1 x 3/8" Fh Brass Woodscrews
- (1) #3 Ball Chain
- (2) #3 Chain End Anchors
- (2) #4 x 3/8" Rh Brass Screws
- (1) 6 3/4" x 10 3/4" Felt
- (2) 6" x 12" Veneer
- (1) 36" Inlay Banding

1/4" Birch plywood 12" x 48"

3/4" x 5" - 48" Mahogany (1.7 Bd. Ft.)

ALSO NEEDED: Contrasting wood for splines

tips from our shop

SHOP NOTEBOOK

Circle-Cutting Jig

To get a smooth curve on the top of the marking gauge fence (page 14), I made a circle-cutting jig for my band saw (see photo). The jig is just a ½" plywood base with a hardwood runner glued to the bottom to fit in the miter gauge slot of the band saw. A rabbeted cleat glued to the edge of the base acts as a stop.

To set up the jig, place the runner in the miter gauge slot of your band saw and cut a kerf in the base. Then measure over 1⅛" from the end of the kerf and, using a small finish nail as drill bit, drill a pivot hole (Figure 1).

Next, to create the pivot pin, drive a nail into the blank (centered on the width) and then snip the head off, as in Figure 2.

To use the jig, slip the pivot pin into the hole. Then turn on the band saw, slide the jig forward, and rotate the blank to cut an arc on one end (Figure 3).

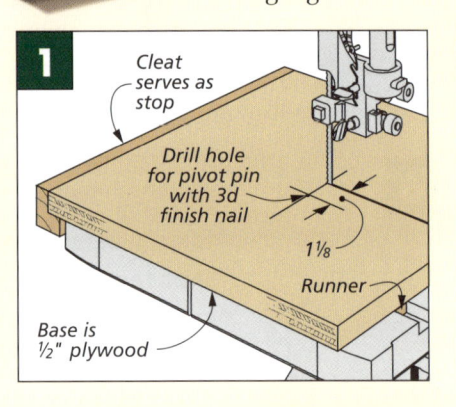

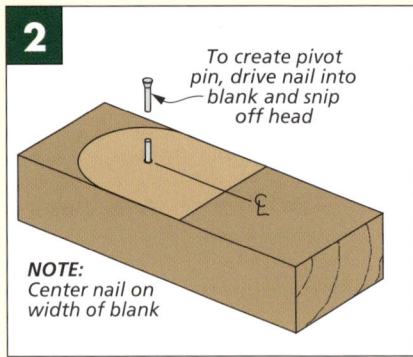

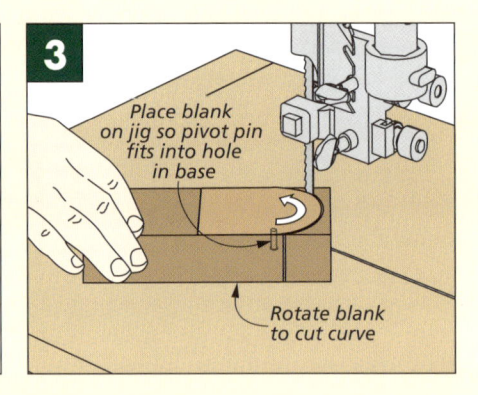

Drilling Jig

The wall shelf on page 18 is assembled with *Minifix* knockdown fasteners. In order for these fasteners to fit together, you have to accurately drill the holes for both parts of the fastener. The holes for the cams are drilled on the drill press. But the crossholes for the connector pins are drilled in the end of the workpiece. In order to locate these holes accurately and drill them straight, I made a drilling jig.

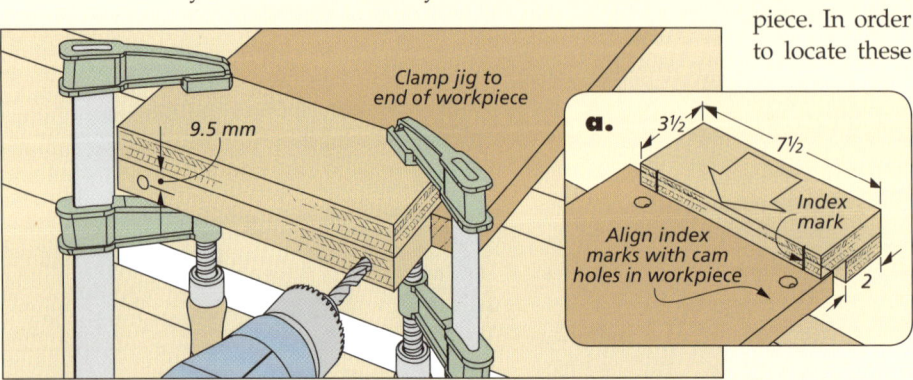

The jig is glued up from two pieces of plywood. A pair of guide holes are drilled through one piece. The second piece is a fence that registers the jig. The guide holes are carefully laid out to match the spacing of the cam holes. Their location is also marked on the edge of the fence (detail 'a').

To use the jig, simply clamp it to the end of the workpiece, lining up the index marks with the cam holes. Then you can use a handheld drill to drill the crossholes for the connector pins.

28   Woodsmith   No. 194

Making Large Cutouts

In order to accommodate the various cords, wires, and cables, the entertainment center on page 30 has a number of cutouts for clearance. There are cutouts at the back of the slide-out trays and the back of the center divider. There's also a large cutout in the back panel of the main cabinet to allow for ventilation.

DRILL HOLES. Although the size of these cutouts varies, I used the same general procedure to make all of them. Using the back panel as an example, start by drilling a 2"-dia. hole at each corner of the cutout, as in Figure 1.

CUT WASTE. Next, using a jig saw, I cut away the interior waste of the cutout, as shown in Figure 2. (For the cutouts in the trays and center divider, you can use a band saw to cut away the waste.) The key here is to cut close to the layout line, but remain on the waste side.

TRIM FLUSH. Finally, to smooth out the rough-cut edge, I used a router and a straightedge guide. I simply clamped a straight piece of hardboard along the layout line. Then using a pattern bit, I trimmed the waste flush, like you see in Figure 3. The result is a cutout with straight, smooth edges and nicely radiused corners.

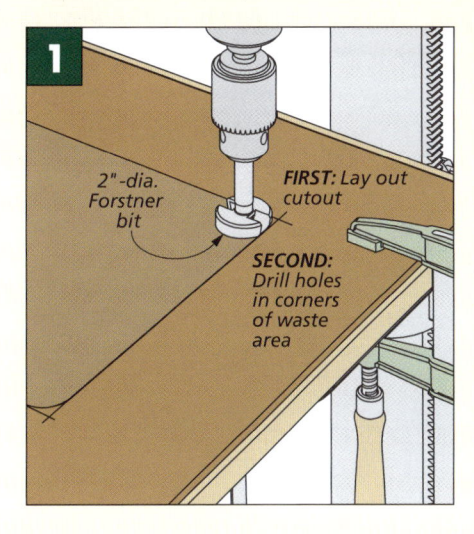

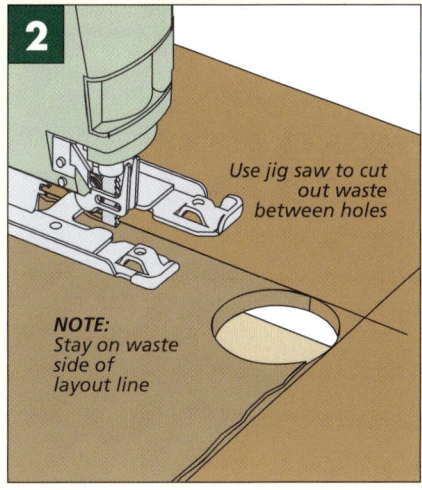

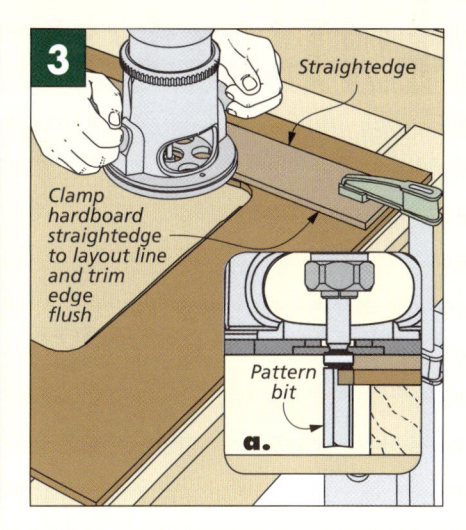

Splined Miters

To strengthen the miter joints in the corners of the box on page 22, I added splines. The splines create additional gluing surface and help prevent the miter joints from opening up over time.

The hardwood splines are glued into slots cut across the miter joints. The easiest way to cut these slots is at the table saw. But the trick is to hold the box at a 45° angle while cutting the slots. To do this, I made a simple jig like the one shown at right. The jig is just a short fence with a couple of supports that cradle the box at the proper angle.

As you can see in the lower right drawing, the jig rides against the rip fence of your table saw. This way, you can use the rip fence to position the slots on the box. After you set the rip fence for the first (bottom) slot, simply rotate the box to cut identical slots on all four corners before moving on to the next (middle) slot.

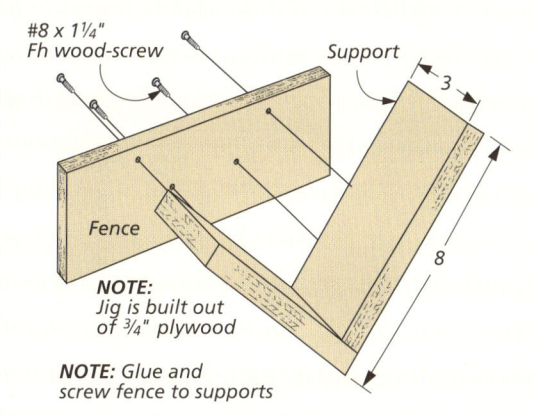

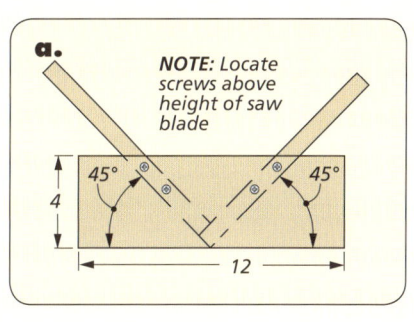

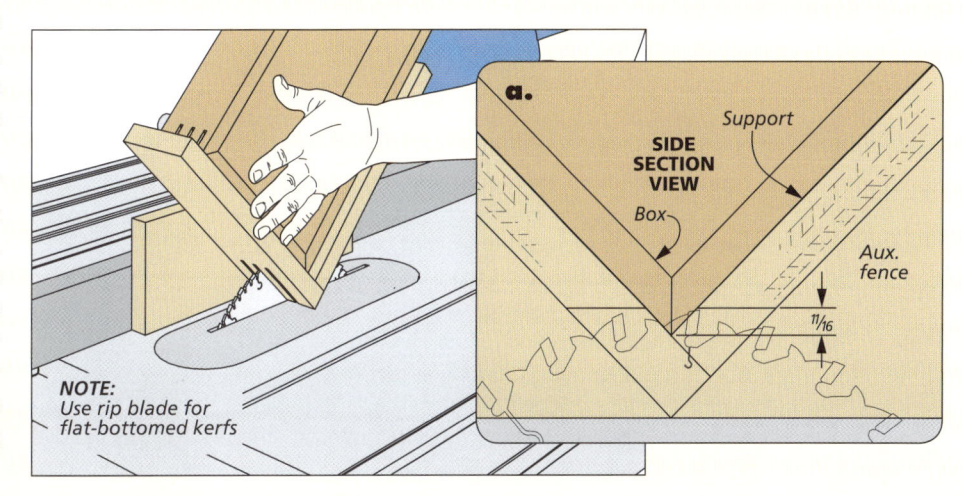

Heirloom Project

contemporary Entertainment Center

Where do I start — abundant storage, low cost, a stylish look, simple construction? I guess that about says it all.

Just the thought of building a large, full-featured entertainment center is enough to scare off many woodworkers — too much work and cost for a limited amount of shop time. But creating space for a large-screen TV and the multitude of electronic necessities that go with it doesn't have to be an expensive, drawn-out endeavor. The solution is to couple time and cost-conscious modular construction with a lean, contemporary look. As you can see at right, this combination really hits the mark.

The full version comes with loads of storage — more than enough to hold all the gadgets you'll ever accumulate. The center cabinet will accommodate a 50" TV with room to spare. Behind the glass doors below, you'll find convenient pull-out storage for all the extras. Flanking the center cabinet are two tower cabinets with both drawers and open storage. And if this isn't enough, a bridge connects the towers to round out the storage and balance the appearance.

To streamline the construction, all the large case panels are cut from economical birch plywood. Poplar face frames assembled with pocket screws finish off the case fronts. Finally, easy-to-make moldings, divided-light doors, and a dark, two-tone finish add just the right amount of simple, sophisticated detail. And I should mention, if your needs and ambition are more modest, consider building just the center cabinet as a stand-alone piece.

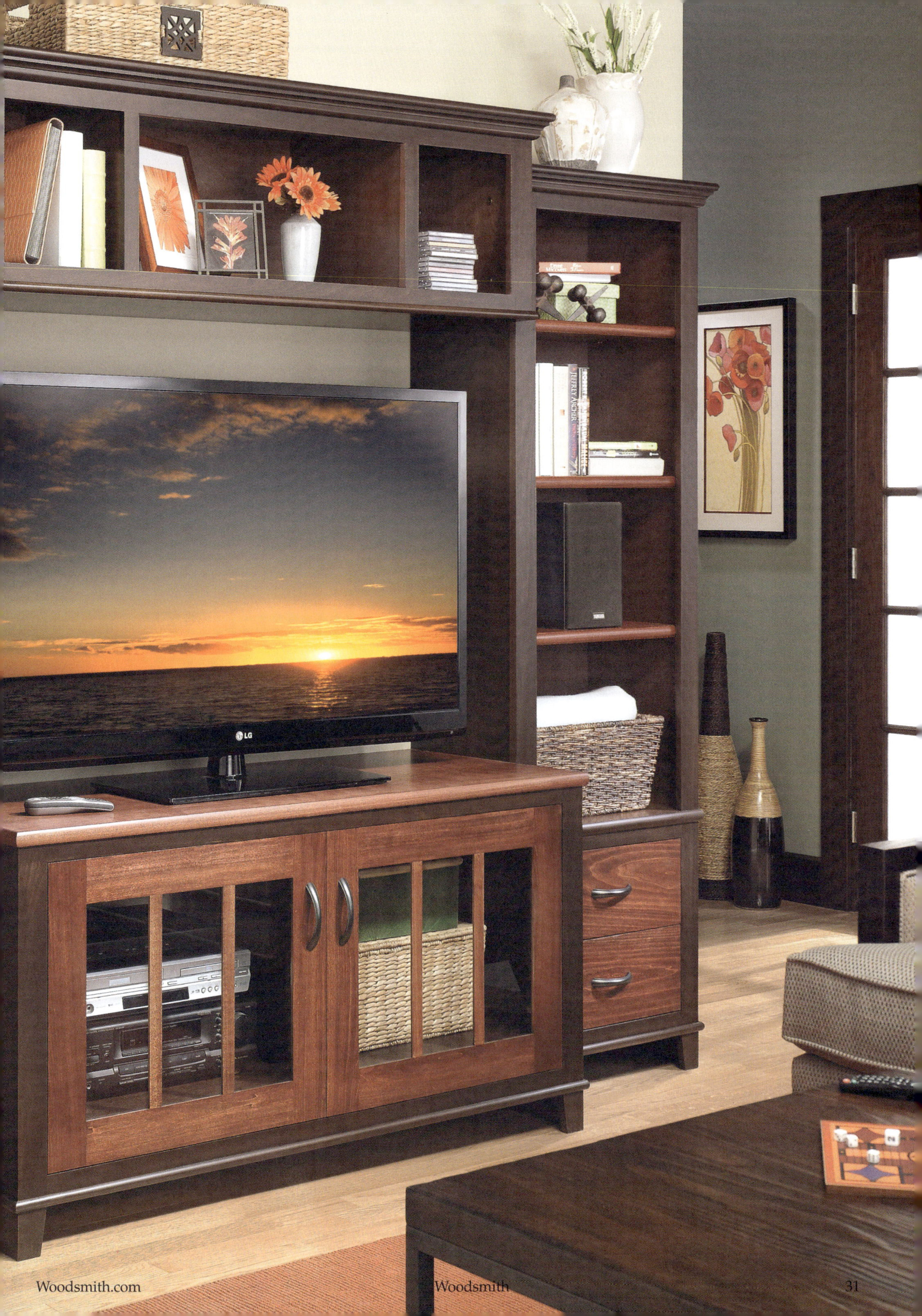

CONSTRUCTION DETAILS

OVERALL DIMENSIONS: $98\frac{3}{4}$"L x $22\frac{3}{8}$"D x $80\frac{3}{4}$"H
CENTER CABINET ONLY: $52\frac{3}{4}$"L x $22\frac{3}{8}$"D x 28"H

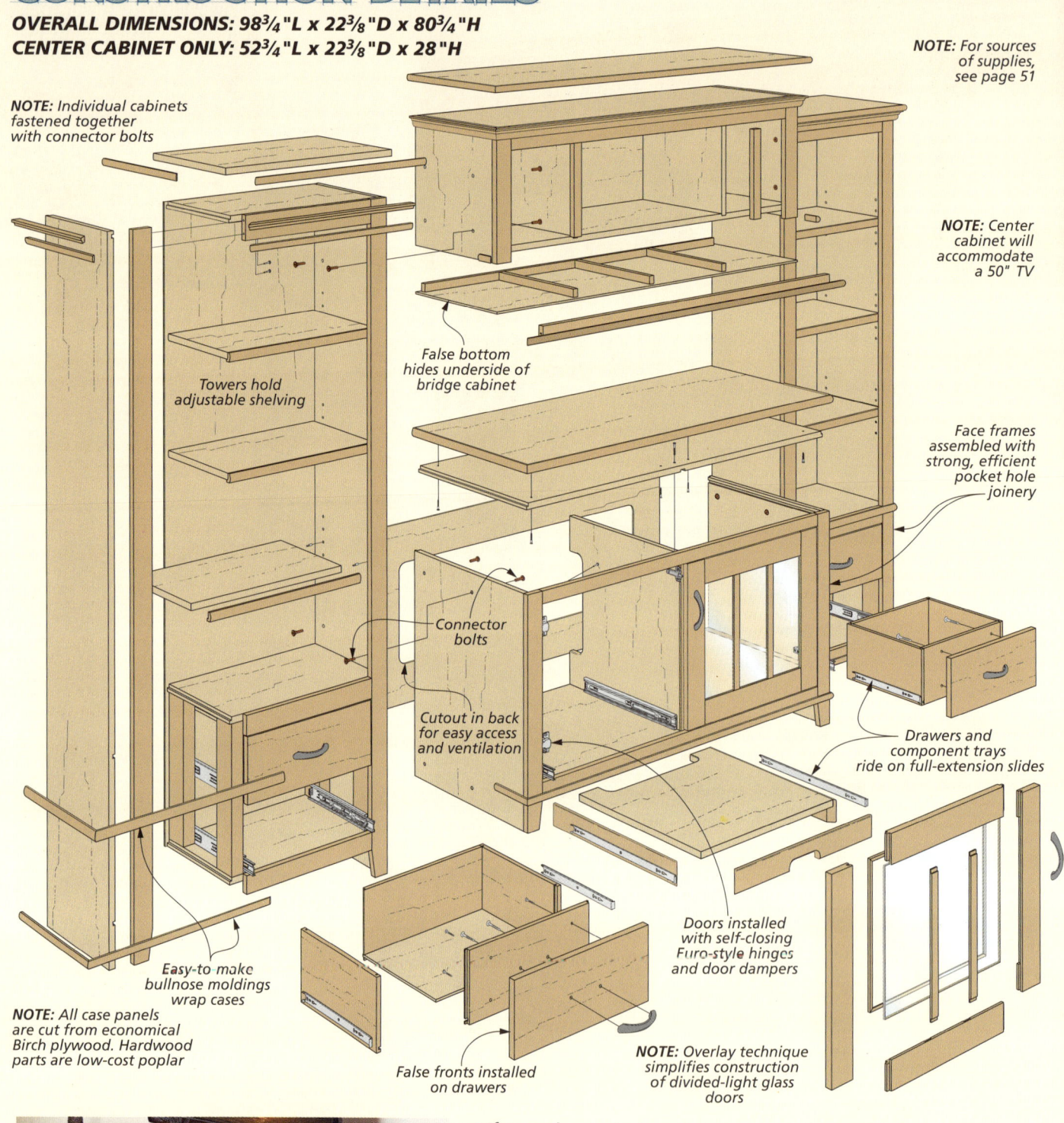

NOTE: For sources of supplies, see page 51

NOTE: Individual cabinets fastened together with connector bolts

NOTE: Center cabinet will accommodate a 50" TV

Towers hold adjustable shelving

False bottom hides underside of bridge cabinet

Face frames assembled with strong, efficient pocket hole joinery

Connector bolts

Cutout in back for easy access and ventilation

Drawers and component trays ride on full-extension slides

Easy-to-make bullnose moldings wrap cases

NOTE: All case panels are cut from economical Birch plywood. Hardwood parts are low-cost poplar.

False fronts installed on drawers

Doors installed with self-closing Euro-style hinges and door dampers

NOTE: Overlay technique simplifies construction of divided-light glass doors

◀ If space is limited, build the center cabinet alone to serve your needs.

SIDE SECTION VIEW

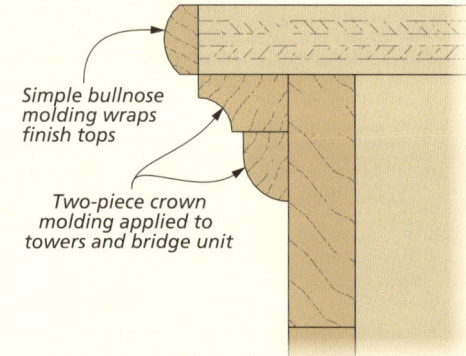

Simple bullnose molding wraps finish tops

Two-piece crown molding applied to towers and bridge unit

Materials, Supplies & Cutting Diagram

Center Cabinet

A	Case Sides (2)	3/4 ply. - 21 1/4 x 27 1/4
B	Case Top/Bottom (2)	3/4 ply. - 21 x 51
C	Case Divider (1)	3/4 ply. - 20 3/4 x 21 3/4
D	Divider Edging (1)	1/4 x 3/4 - 21 3/4
E	Face Frame Stiles (2)	3/4 x 2 1/4 - 27 1/4
F	Face Frame Top Rail (1)	3/4 x 1 1/2 - 47 1/2
G	Face Frame Bottom Rail (1)	3/4 x 2 - 47 1/2
H	Finish Top (1)	3/4 ply. - 22 x 52
I	Finish Top Molding (1)	1 x 3/8 - 100 rgh.
J	Base Molding (1)	3/4 x 3/8 - 100 rgh.
K	Case Back (1)	1/4 ply. - 22 3/4 x 51 1/2
L	Component Tray Tops (2)	3/4 ply. - 19 3/4 x 20 5/8
M	Component Tray Front Rails (2)	3/4 x 2 1/2 - 21 1/8
N	Component Tray Side Rails (4)	3/4 x 2 1/2 - 20
O	Tray Spacers (2)	1 3/4 x 2 3/4 - 21
P	Door Stiles (4)	3/4 x 3 - 20 1/4
Q	Door Rails (4)	3/4 x 3 - 18 5/16
R	Door Muntin (2)	1/4 x 1 - 15
S	Glass Stop (2)	5/16 x 5/16 - 72 rgh.

Tower Cabinets

T	Case Sides (4)	3/4 ply. - 13 1/4 x 76 1/4
U	Case Tops/Bottoms/Dividers (6)	3/4 ply. - 13 x 21
V	Face Frame Stiles (4)	3/4 x 2 1/4 - 76 1/4
W	Face Frame Top Rails (2)	3/4 x 2 3/4 - 17 1/2
X	Face Frame Middle Rails (2)	3/4 x 2 1/4 - 17 1/2
Y	Face Frame Bottom Rails (2)	3/4 x 2 - 17 1/2
Z	Drawer Guide Spacers (8)	1 1/2 x 3 - 16 1/2
AA	Finish Tops (2)	3/4 ply. - 15 x 23
BB	Finish Top Molding (1)	3/4 x 3/8 - 84 rgh.
CC	Tower Backs (2)	1/4 ply. - 21 1/2 x 71 3/4
DD	Shelf Panels (6)	3/4 ply. - 12 3/8 x 20 3/8
EE	Shelf Edging (6)	1 x 3/4 - 20 3/8
FF	Drawer Sides (8)	1/2 x 7 - 12 3/4
GG	Drawer Fronts/Backs (8)	1/2 x 7 - 16
HH	Drawer Bottoms (4)	1/4 ply. - 12 1/4 x 16
II	Drawer False Fronts (4)	3/4 x 7 5/16 - 17 1/4

Bridge Cabinet

JJ	Case Sides (2)	3/4 ply. - 15 1/4 x 15 3/4
KK	Case Top/Bottom (2)	3/4 ply. - 15 x 51
LL	Case Dividers (2)	3/4 ply. - 15 x 13 3/4
MM	Face Frame Stiles (2)	3/4 x 2 1/4 - 15 3/4
NN	Face Frame Top Rail (1)	3/4 x 2 3/4 - 47 1/2
OO	Face Frame Bottom Rail (1)	3/4 x 1 3/4 - 47 1/2
PP	Face Frame Dividers (2)	3/4 x 1 1/4 - 11 1/4
QQ	False Bottom Fillers (1)	3/4 x 1 - 96 rgh.
RR	False Bottom Panel (1)	1/4 ply. - 16 x 52
SS	Finish Top (1)	3/4 ply. - 17 x 54
TT	Finish Top Molding (1)	3/4 x 3/8 - 96 rgh.
UU	Bridge Back (1)	1/4 ply. - 15 3/4 x 51 1/2
VV	Crown Cove Molding (1)	5/8 x 1 - 180 rgh.
WW	Crown Roundover Molding (1)	1/2 x 3/4 - 180 rgh.
XX	Bridge Lower Bullnose (1)	3/4 x 3/8 - 90 rgh.
YY	Tower Middle Molding (1)	1 x 3/8 - 80 rgh.
ZZ	Tower Base Molding (1)	3/4 x 3/8 - 80 rgh.

- (2 pr.) 20" Full-Extension Drawer Slides
- (4 pr.) 12" Full-Extension Drawer Slides
- (2 pr.) Full-Inset Face Frame Euro-style Hinges
- (2) 18 1/4" x 14 15/16" Glass Panels (1/8" thick)
- (6) Pulls w/1 1/2" Screws
- (2) *Blu-Motion* Door Dampers
- (16) 30mm Connector Bolts
- (16) Connector Bolt Caps
- (24) Shelf Support Pins
- (40) 1 1/4" Pocket Screws
- (8) #8 x 1 1/4" Fh Woodscrews
- (6) #8 x 2" Fh Woodscrews
- (16) #8 x 1" Fh Woodscrews
- (16) #8 Finish Washers
- 1" Brads

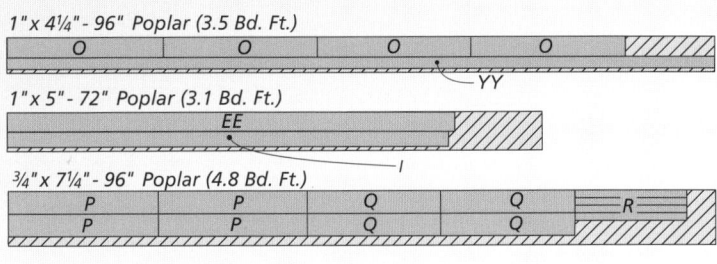

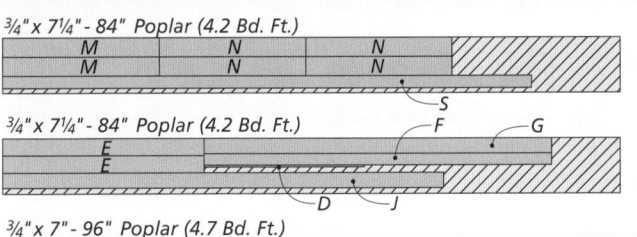

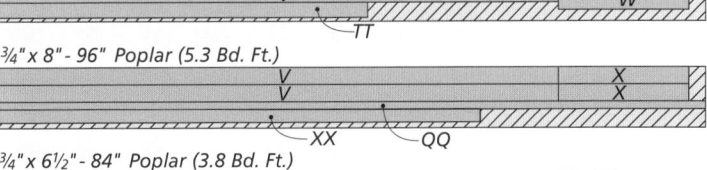

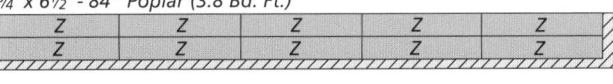

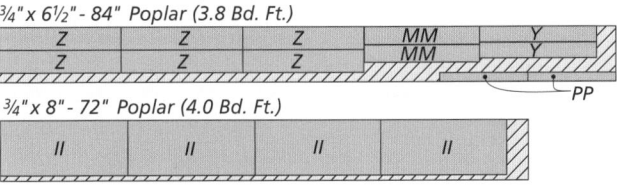

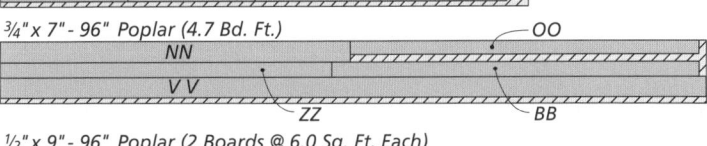

1" x 4 1/4" - 96" Poplar (3.5 Bd. Ft.)
1" x 5" - 72" Poplar (3.1 Bd. Ft.)
3/4" x 7 1/4" - 96" Poplar (4.8 Bd. Ft.)
3/4" x 7 1/4" - 84" Poplar (4.2 Bd. Ft.)
3/4" x 7 1/4" - 84" Poplar (4.2 Bd. Ft.)
3/4" x 7" - 96" Poplar (4.7 Bd. Ft.)
3/4" x 8" - 96" Poplar (5.3 Bd. Ft.)
3/4" x 6 1/2" - 84" Poplar (3.8 Bd. Ft.)
3/4" x 6 1/2" - 84" Poplar (3.8 Bd. Ft.)
3/4" x 8" - 72" Poplar (4.0 Bd. Ft.)
3/4" x 7" - 96" Poplar (4.7 Bd. Ft.)
1/2" x 9" - 96" Poplar (2 Boards @ 6.0 Sq. Ft. Each)
1/2" x 7 1/4" - 60" Poplar (3.0 Sq. Ft.)

ALSO NEEDED: *Five 48" x 96" sheets of 3/4" Birch plywood*
Three 48" x 96" sheets of 1/4" Birch plywood

constructing the CENTER CASE

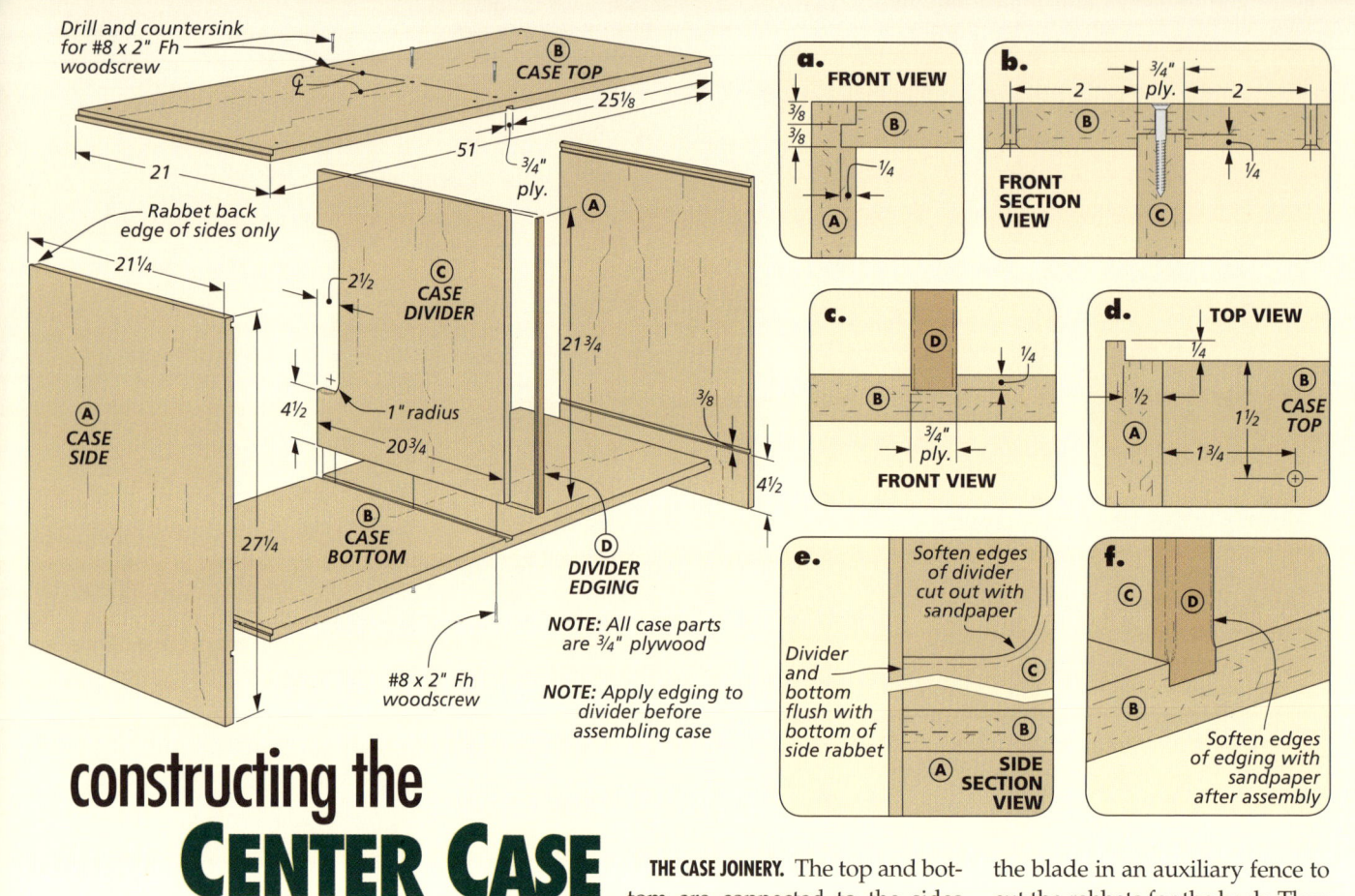

For me, the most logical way to attack a large, modular project like this is from the inside out and the ground up. So I started with the lower center cabinet.

The first step is to cut the two side panels, the top and bottom, and the vertical divider to finished size from ¾" plywood. Be sure to note that these parts are three different widths.

THE CASE JOINERY. The top and bottom are connected to the sides with tongue and dado joints as in detail 'a.' The divider fits into full-width dadoes cut into the top and bottom (detail 'c'). Rabbets in the sides hold the ¼" plywood back (detail 'd'). So next, I switched to a ⅜"-wide dado blade in the table saw to start work on cutting this joinery. The How-To box below provides guidance.

First, I cut a pair of ¼"-deep dadoes in each side. Next, I buried the blade in an auxiliary fence to cut the rabbets for the back. Then I used this same setup to cut the tongues on the ends of the top and bottom. You'll finish up at the table saw by cutting centered dadoes in the top and bottom sized to the ¾" plywood.

ODDS & ENDS. Before the case can be assembled, there are a few details to take care of. The front edge of the divider won't be covered by the face frame so a piece of edging is needed (detail 'f').

How-To: Case Joinery

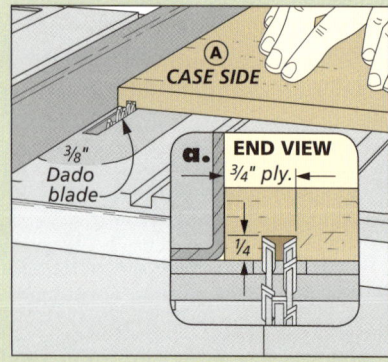

Side Dadoes. With a ⅜" dado blade installed, use the rip fence to accurately position the dadoes in the case sides.

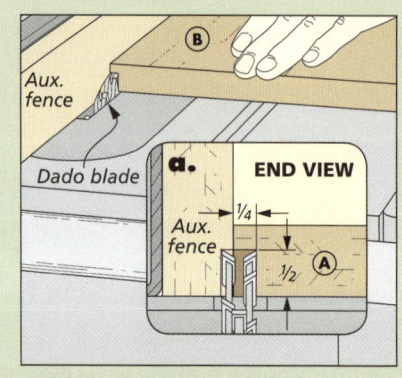

Rabbets. To cut the rabbets for the back panel, raise the dado blade into an auxiliary rip fence.

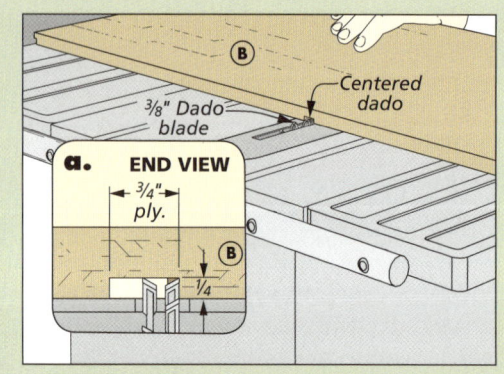

Centered Dadoes. You can sneak up on the width and also center the dadoes in the top and bottom by flipping them between passes.

And as you can see in the main drawing, I formed a wiring cutout along the back edge of the divider. Last of all, I drilled countersunk screw holes from the inside of the top for attaching the finish top.

ASSEMBLY. You can make assembly of the case easier by using woodscrews along with glue to hold the divider (detail 'b,' opposite). You want all the case panels to be flush across the front.

FACE FRAME. The case is now ready for the face frame. The pocket hole joinery I used to build it made the job go quickly (detail 'a'). The box below covers the basics of this handy technique. And before assembly, you'll need to bevel the ends of the stiles (detail 'a').

THE FINISH TOP. With the face frame glued on, the exterior of the case is trimmed out by adding a finish top and a bullnose base molding. The finish top is a plywood panel wrapped on three sides with a 1"-wide bullnose. The panel fits flush with the outside of the case while the molding laps over to hide the seam (detail 'c').

There's an easy way to size this part for an exact match to the case. Simply attach a rough size blank then trim it flush with a router.

MOLDINGS. How you proceed next depends on whether you plan to build the tower and bridge cabinets. If the answer is yes, you'll want to hold off on installing the top and the base bullnose. It will be easier to fit all the moldings accurately with the cabinets fastened together.

If you're building just the center cabinet, you can add the moldings now. The box below shows how to shape them at the router table. Then miter the pieces and glue them in place (details 'b' and 'c').

BACK PANEL. I saved adding the back for last. This panel is sized to fit between the sides and lap over the case top and bottom (details 'c' and 'd'). It features a large cutout for ventilation and wiring access. Check out page 29 for help with this task. And when the cutout is completed, the back can be tacked in place.

Pocket Holes & Moldings

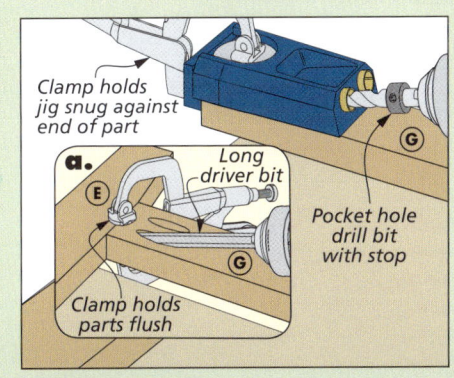

Drill & Drive. A jig allows you to drill the pocket holes easily and accurately. Clamp the pieces together to drive the screws.

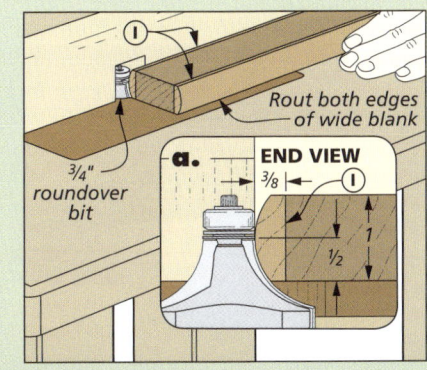

Top Bullnose. I made the bullnose molding for the top with two passes across a 3/4" roundover bit.

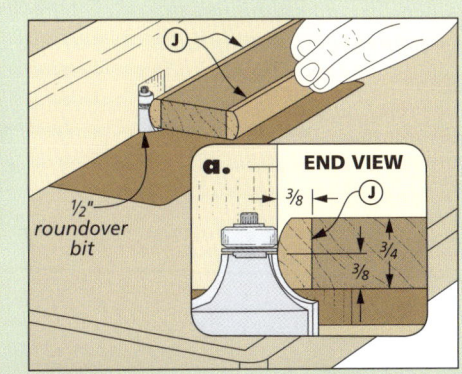

Base Bullnose. Use the same technique to make the base bullnose. Then rip the moldings free at the table saw.

Woodsmith.com   Woodsmith   35

adding the TRAYS & DOORS

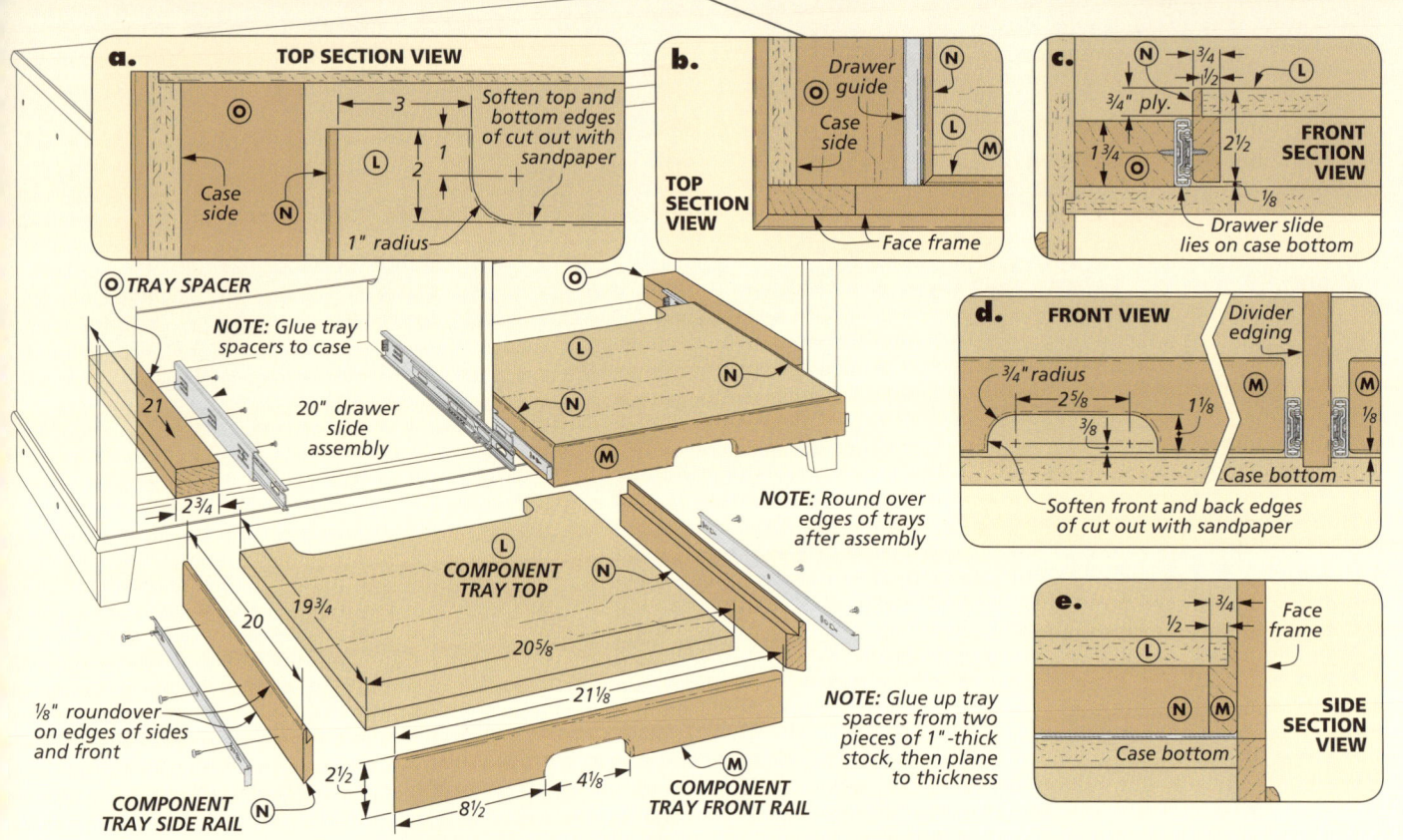

To complete the center cabinet, you'll first add a pair of sliding component trays and finally, two divided-light doors. The trays make wiring the components much easier while the glass doors allow use of remote controls.

TRAYS. The identical trays are essentially short platforms that travel on metal drawer slides. They're made by wrapping three edges of a plywood top with hardwood rails, as shown above.

I started by cutting the tray tops to final size. Then to create a recess for excess wire, I formed a cutout across the back edges (detail 'a').

RAILS. The tray rails are rabbeted to capture the tops, as in detail 'c.' So after cutting blanks to width and rough length, I set up the table saw to cut the rabbets (How-To box below). When this is completed, you can fit the rails around the tops, mitering the front corners (main drawing).

FINGER PULLS. Before gluing the rails to the tray panels, I laid out and shaped a pull centered on each front rail (detail 'd'). And then, after the clamps come off the trays, you'll want to soften the edges of the rails with a 1/8" roundover (How-To box).

INSTALLATION. To install the trays, you'll need to add a spacer along each side of the case, as in details

How-To: Platform Details

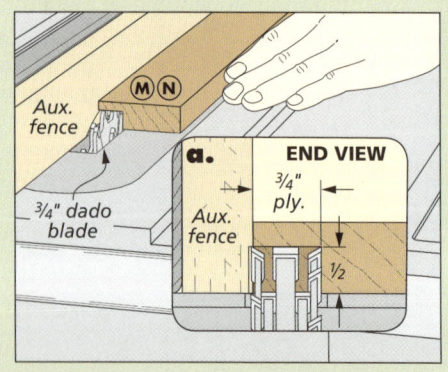

Rail Rabbets. I buried a wide dado blade in an auxiliary rip fence to cut rabbets in the platform rails with several passes.

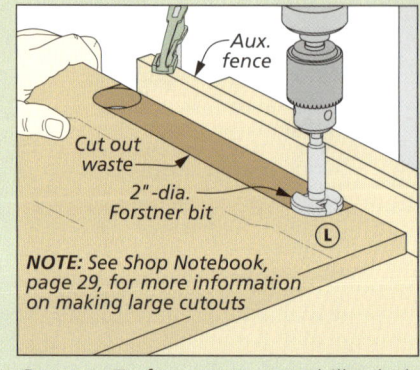

Cutout. To form a cutout, drill a hole at each end, remove the waste at the band saw, and then smooth the cut.

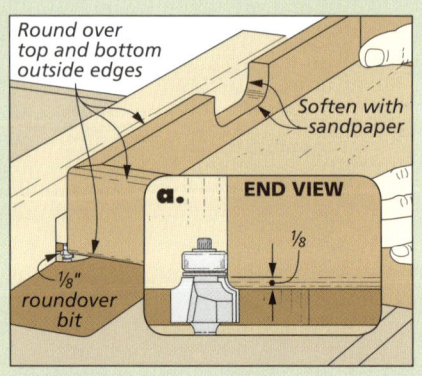

Ease Edges. After assembly, I rounded all the edges of the tray rails at the router table. Use sandpaper on the finger pulls.

'b' and 'c' on the opposite page. And when you install the slides, allow ⅛" clearance between the tray and the bottom of the case (detail 'c,' opposite page).

DOORS

The divided-light design of the doors adds a nice touch and isn't hard to accomplish. The thin dividing bars (muntins) simply overlay a single panel of glass.

FRAMES. The How-To box at right gives you a step-by-step guide to the construction of the doors. You'll start by putting together frames using stub tenon and groove joinery. I allowed ⅛" of clearance at the edges and between the two doors.

RABBETS. Once the frames are assembled, the next step is to form a pocket for the glass. This is done by routing away the inside shoulder of the grooves to create rabbets. A hand-held router and a rabbeting bit will do the job.

MUNTINS. Now you're ready to fit the muntins. Detail 'a' and the lower right drawing show how this works. The ends of the muntins are rabbeted to fit shallow "mortises" chiseled into the inside face of the frame recess.

When rabbeting the muntins, shoot for a snug shoulder-to-shoulder fit between the frame rails. Next, you can use the muntins to mark the mortises.

Sneak up on the depth of each mortise until the muntin sits flush with the outside face of the rails. Then glue them in place.

STOP. It's best to wait until after the finish is applied to install the glass, but you can make and fit the ⁵⁄₁₆" quarter-round stop now (detail 'b'). I planed a wide blank to thickness, routed the profile on both edges, and ripped the finished pieces free. Once in hand, the stop can be mitered to fit.

EURO-STYLE HINGES. European-style adjustable hinges make installing the doors a snap (detail 'c'). Then a pair of door dampers added to the case divider and a pull on each door will wrap things up.

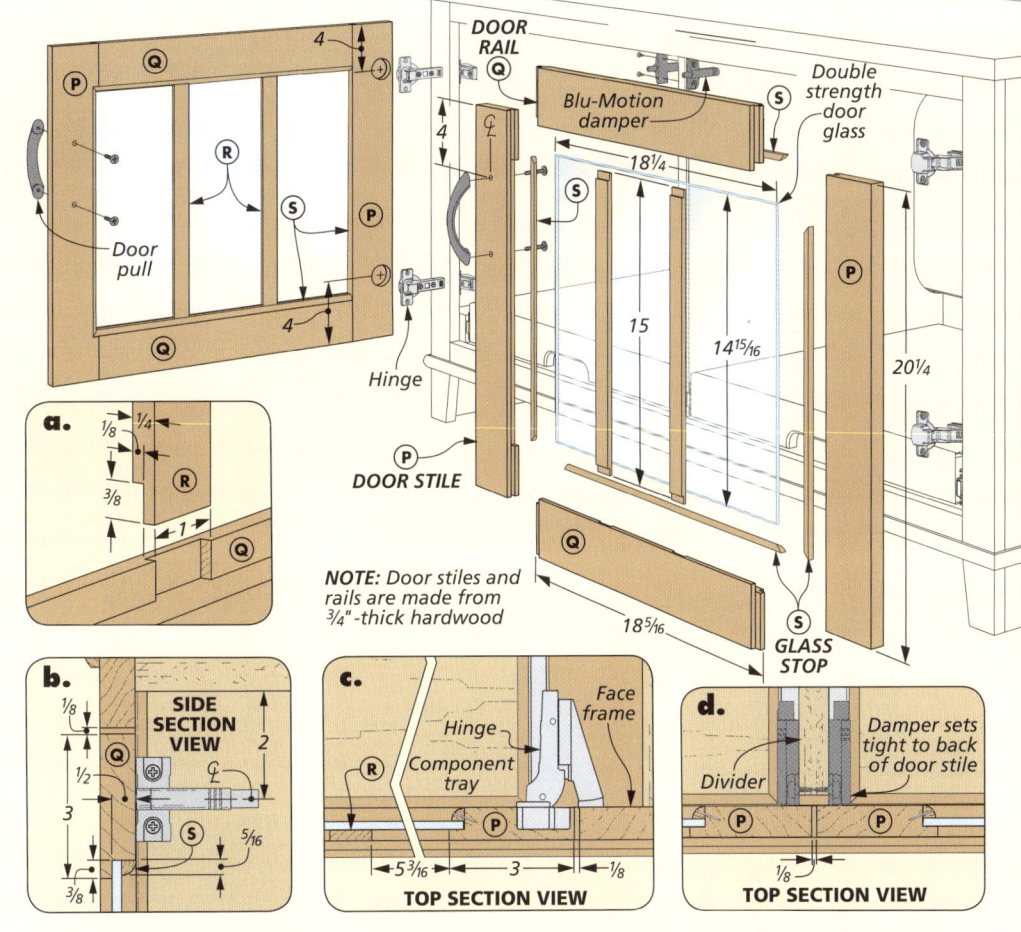

How-To: Door Frame & Muntins

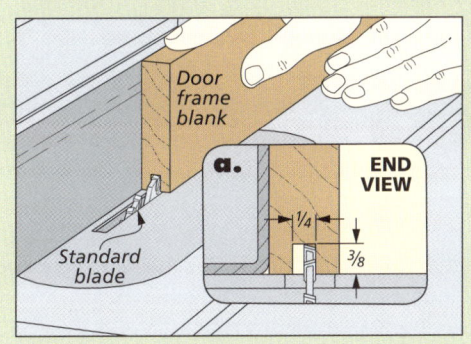

Grooves. Start by cutting centered grooves in the rails and stiles. Make two passes, flipping the pieces end-for-end in between.

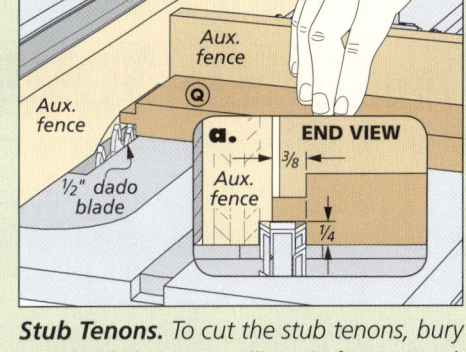

Stub Tenons. To cut the stub tenons, bury a dado blade in an auxiliary rip fence. Sneak up on a snug fit to the grooves.

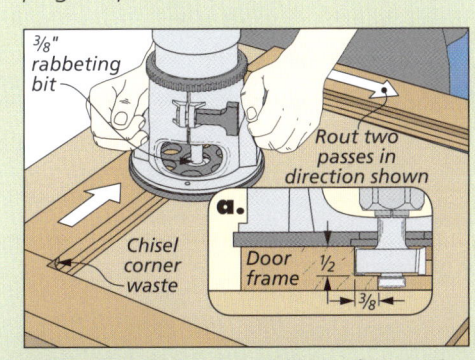

Glass Recess. Form rabbets by routing away the inside shoulders of the grooves. Square up the corners with a chisel.

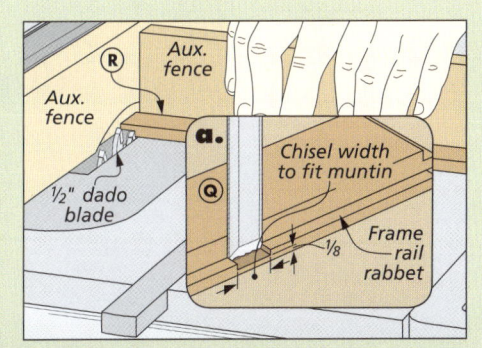

Muntins. Adding the muntins is a two-step process. First rabbet the ends, then chisel mortises into the frame recess.

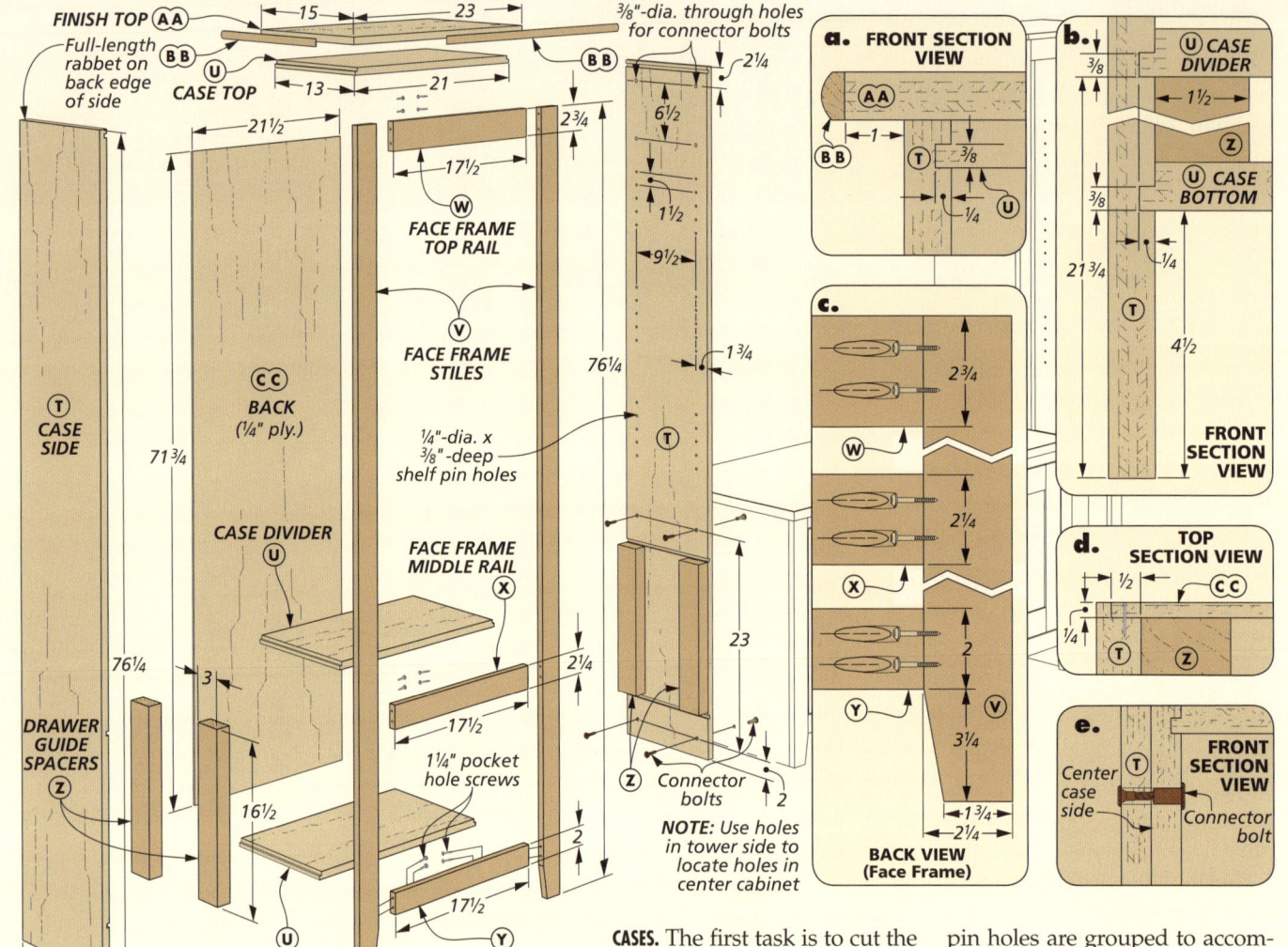

building the TOWERS

With the center cabinet completed, next in line are the two, mirror-image tower cabinets that flank it. Beyond size and shape, much of the case construction is very similar. Then once the bridge is built, you'll add the simple moldings that tie everything together.

CASES. The first task is to cut the sides, tops, bottoms, and dividers to size. Note that the tops, bottoms, and dividers are narrower.

Now, you'll revisit the joinery used to assemble the center cabinet. Start by laying out and cutting three, ⅜"-wide dadoes in each side (details 'a' and 'b'). Then follow up with rabbets for the back panel, as shown in detail 'd.'

GROUPED HOLES. The sides are completed by drilling two types of holes — first for shelf pins, then for connector bolts. The shelf pin holes are grouped to accommodate three shelves. The Shop Tip below shows how to drill the holes quickly and accurately with the aid of a template.

Detail 'e' shows how connector bolts are used to fasten the towers to the center cabinet and the bridge. You'll need to drill a set of holes at the top and bottom of each tower's inner side.

TONGUES. All you need to do to the tops, bottoms, and dividers is cut tongues on the ends to fit the dadoes in the sides. Once this is taken care of, you can get out the glue and clamps.

FACE FRAME. The face frame comes next. Again, the procedure will be familiar. I cut the rails and stiles to size, beveled the bottom edges of the stiles, and then assembled the frames with pocket screws, as shown in detail 'c.' You'll want to position the middle and lower rail carefully. When the face frame is glued to the case, their upper edges should be flush with the case divider and bottom.

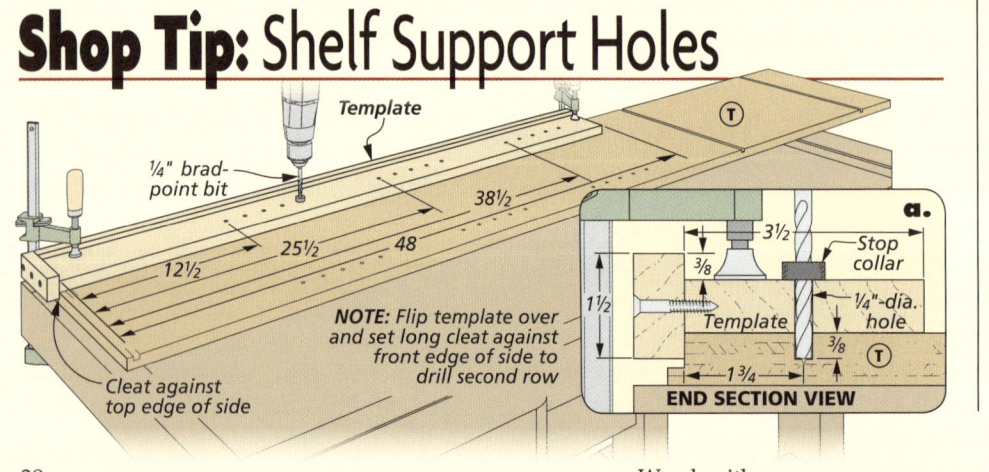

Shop Tip: Shelf Support Holes

FINISH TOP. With the face frame in place, the finish top can be added. It's made up of a plywood panel with bullnose edging. It overhangs the case at the front and the outer side only (detail 'a,' opposite). So be sure to note which case goes on which side.

When making the tops, it works best to miter and glue the edging to the panels before routing the bullnose profile at the router table. Once they're ready to go, the tops can be glued to the case.

DRAWER SPACERS & BACKS. Two more quick tasks and the case will be ready for shelves and drawers. First, I glued up some spacers to hold the drawer slides and installed them along the sides of the cases, as shown in the main drawing and detail 'd' on the opposite page. Finally, I cut the plywood back to size and glued and tacked it to the case.

SHELVES. The shelves are simply plywood panels with a bullnose edging applied. As you can see in detail 'a,' the 1"-wide edging wraps under the panel to add stiffness. The How-To box at right shows how to make the rabbeted edging. After it's glued in place, the bullnose profile is routed.

DRAWERS. Adding two drawers to each case will complete this stage. This is a straightforward job. You'll assemble the drawer boxes using tongue and dado joinery, install them in the case with metal slides, and then add false fronts. The drawings above and in the How-to box cover all the important details.

FRONTS. The false fronts should sit flush with the face frame. So when installing the drawer boxes set them back ¾". I attached the false fronts with screws and finish washers through oversized holes (detail 'd'). This allows you to adjust the fronts for an even ⅛" gap all around and in between. You can use shims and double-sided tape to temporarily position the fronts on the boxes. Once the fronts are permanently attached, you can add the pulls.

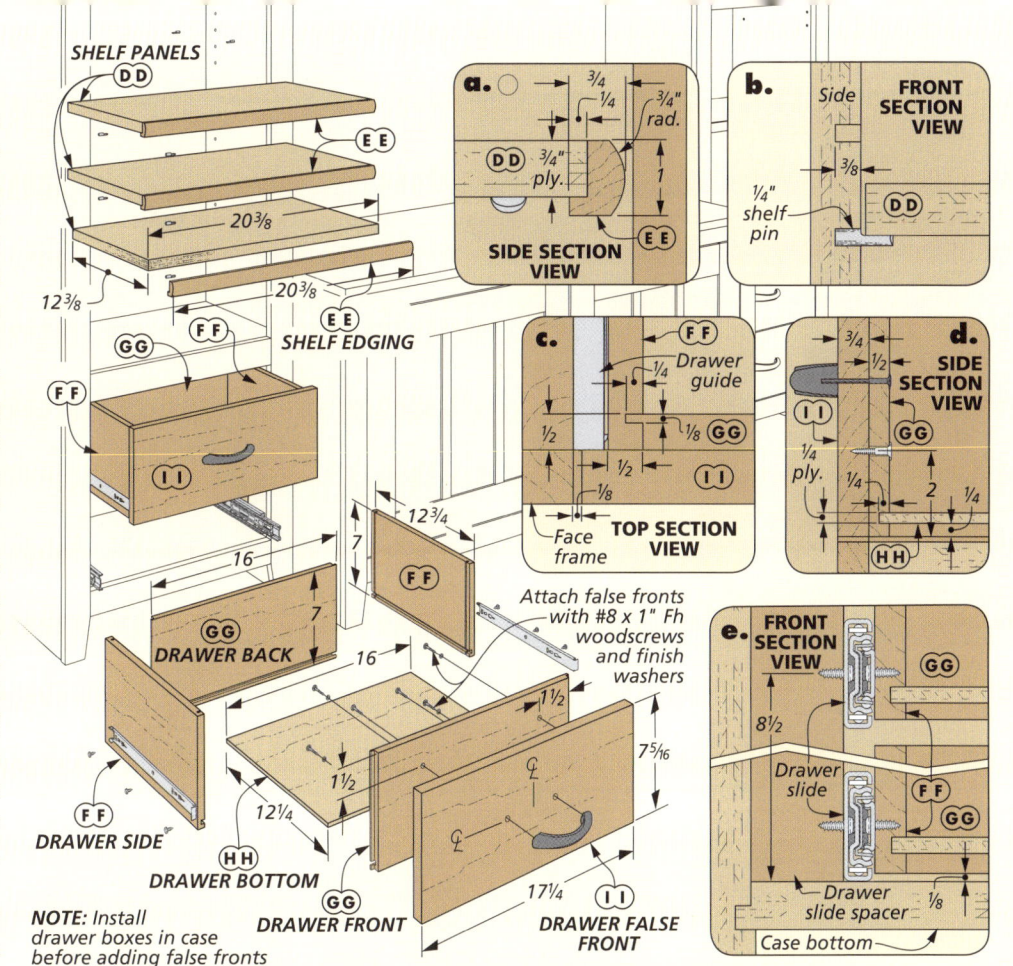

How-To: Shelf Edging & Drawer Joints

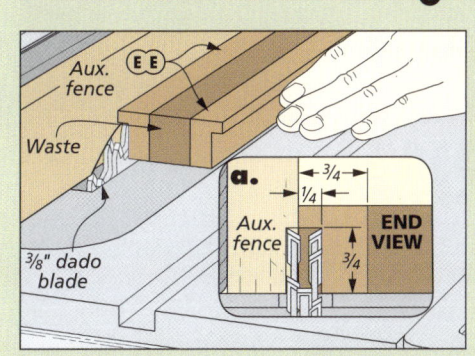

Rabbeted Edging. Start by cutting a rabbet in both edges of a wide blank. Then rip the edging pieces to finished width.

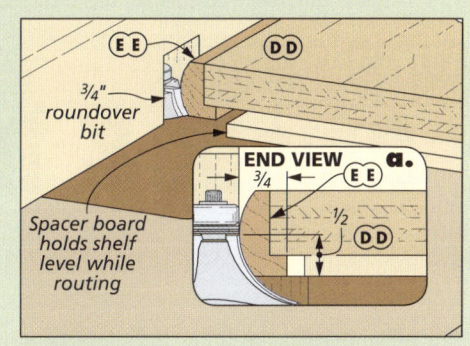

Rout Bullnose. I used a spacer to support the shelf panel when routing the lower section of the bullnose profile.

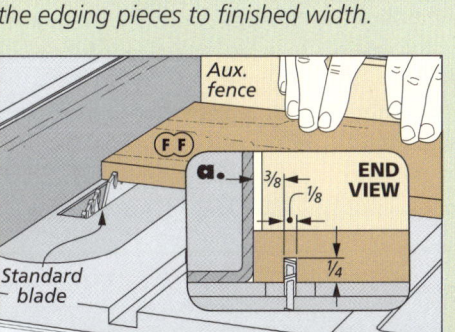

Drawer Side Dadoes. All it takes is a single pass across a standard saw blade to create the dadoes in the drawer sides.

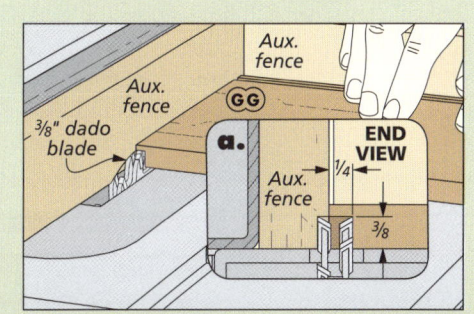

The Tongues. Switch to a dado blade to form the mating tongues on the ends of the drawer fronts and backs.

Woodsmith.com · Woodsmith · 39

completing the
BRIDGE & TRIM

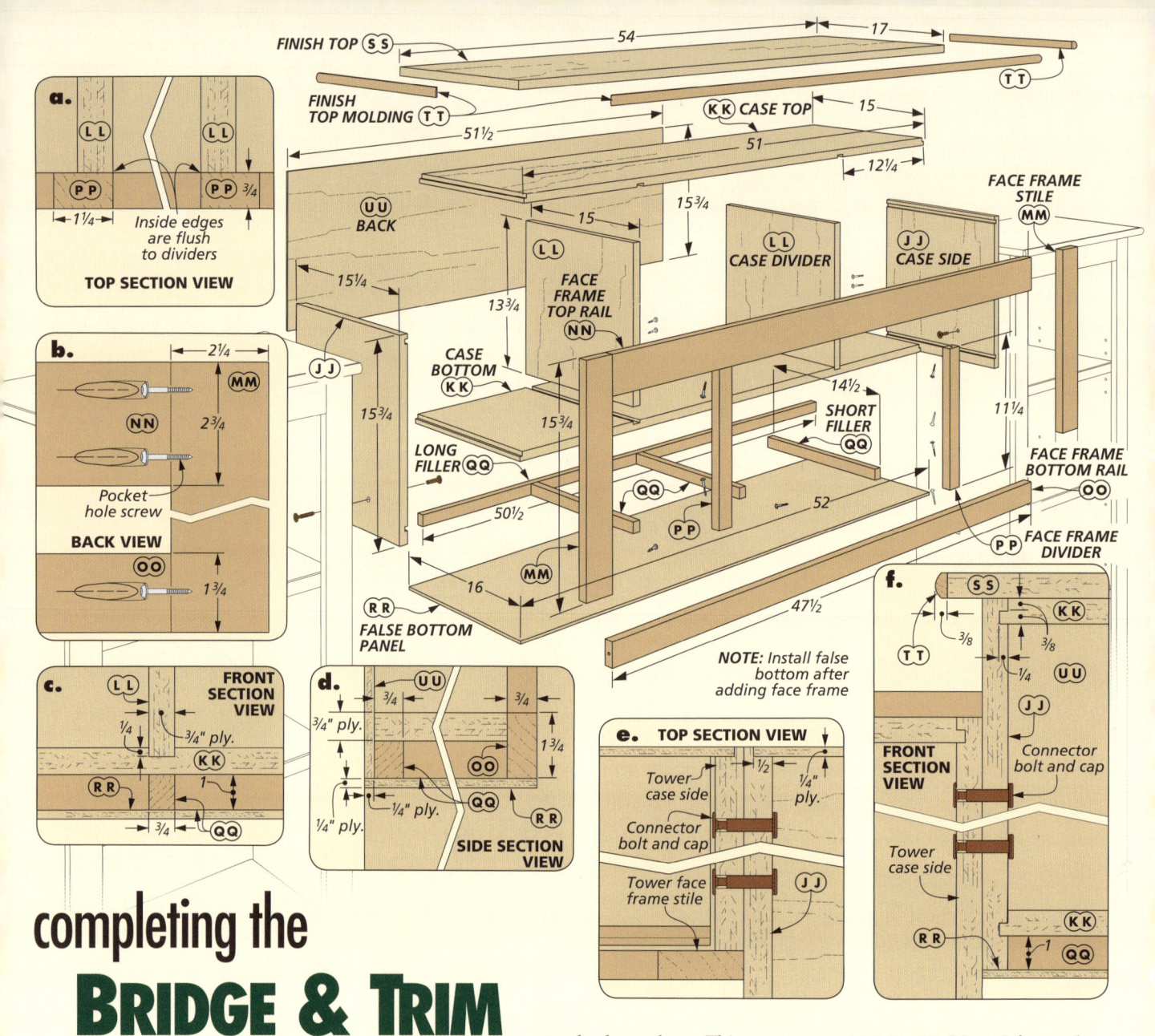

Building the bridge cabinet that connects the towers will draw the major construction to a close. In general, the casework simply repeats what's come before. However, I did include a false bottom to hide the underside of the case. And with the bridge completed, you'll bring all the cabinets together to add the moldings.

THE RIGHT SIZE. The first thing to do is note how the cabinet is sized and how it fits to the other cabinets. The cabinet's width should be an exact match to that of the center cabinet below. And as you see in the drawing on the opposite page, the bridge is slightly deeper than the tower units and extends above them. This creates a pleasing "stepped" effect.

SAME ROUTINE. You know the routine well by now. After cutting the two sides, the top and bottom, and the two vertical dividers to finished size, you'll switch to a dado blade to cut the joinery. This mirrors the center cabinet — tongue and dado at the sides and full-width dadoes for the dividers. Don't forget the rabbets in the sides for the back panel.

FACE FRAME. Once all the joinery is completed and the case is assembled, you can build and install the face frame (detail 'b'). Detail 'a' shows you how the narrow divider stiles should fit on the case — flush with the inside edges of the case dividers.

FALSE BOTTOM. Next, I focused on adding the ¼" plywood false bottom. This panel is sized to match the footprint of the case. It's simply glued to the case and a set of fillers (detail 'd'). Bullnose molding wrapping the bottom of the case will hide the panel's edges.

I installed a long filler along the back edge of the case and then added three front-to-back fillers through the middle (details 'c' and 'd'). With the fillers in place, the false bottom panel can be cut to size and glued on. Just make sure it fits flush at the edges.

FINISH TOP. The cabinet is capped with a finish top similar to those on the towers. The only difference is that it overhangs on both sides (detail 'f').

After the top is glued to the case, the back can be fit and tacked on.

ALL TOGETHER. Before adding the moldings, it's a good idea to fasten the cabinets together. This will give you a real picture of how the moldings need to fit.

First I connected the towers to the center cabinet. Then I used 36"-long plywood spacers to support the bridge while completing the job (details 'e' and 'f,' opposite). You can use the holes in the tower sides to drill corresponding holes in the center and bridge cabinets.

THE MOLDINGS. Now for the moldings. The drawings at right show the molding profiles and how they're positioned. I'll start at the top and work down.

I made a two-piece crown molding to fit below the finish tops of the towers and bridge. The How-To box at right shows how to shape the cove and roundover moldings at the router table. Then you just miter pieces to fit and glue them in place as shown.

As I mentioned, the bottom of the bridge is wrapped with a ¾"-wide bullnose (detail 'b'). You'll find details on making this molding on page 35. The front corners are mitered. The back ends of the side pieces fit against the towers.

The finish top of the center cabinet gets a similar treatment. Only here, I used a 1"-wide bullnose. Again, you can turn to page 35 for more information.

An identical 1" bullnose separates the upper and lower sections of the towers. It's positioned flush with the upper edge of the face frame middle rail and butts to the center cabinet (detail 'd').

The final molding is a band of ¾"-wide bullnose that's mitered around the center cabinet and towers. You want it to fit flush with the lower edge of the face frame rails, as in detail 'e.'

That's it. A little sanding and the project will be ready for the attractive dark finish. You'll find more on this on page 51. Then it's out of the shop and into the family room. The move is up to you. **W**

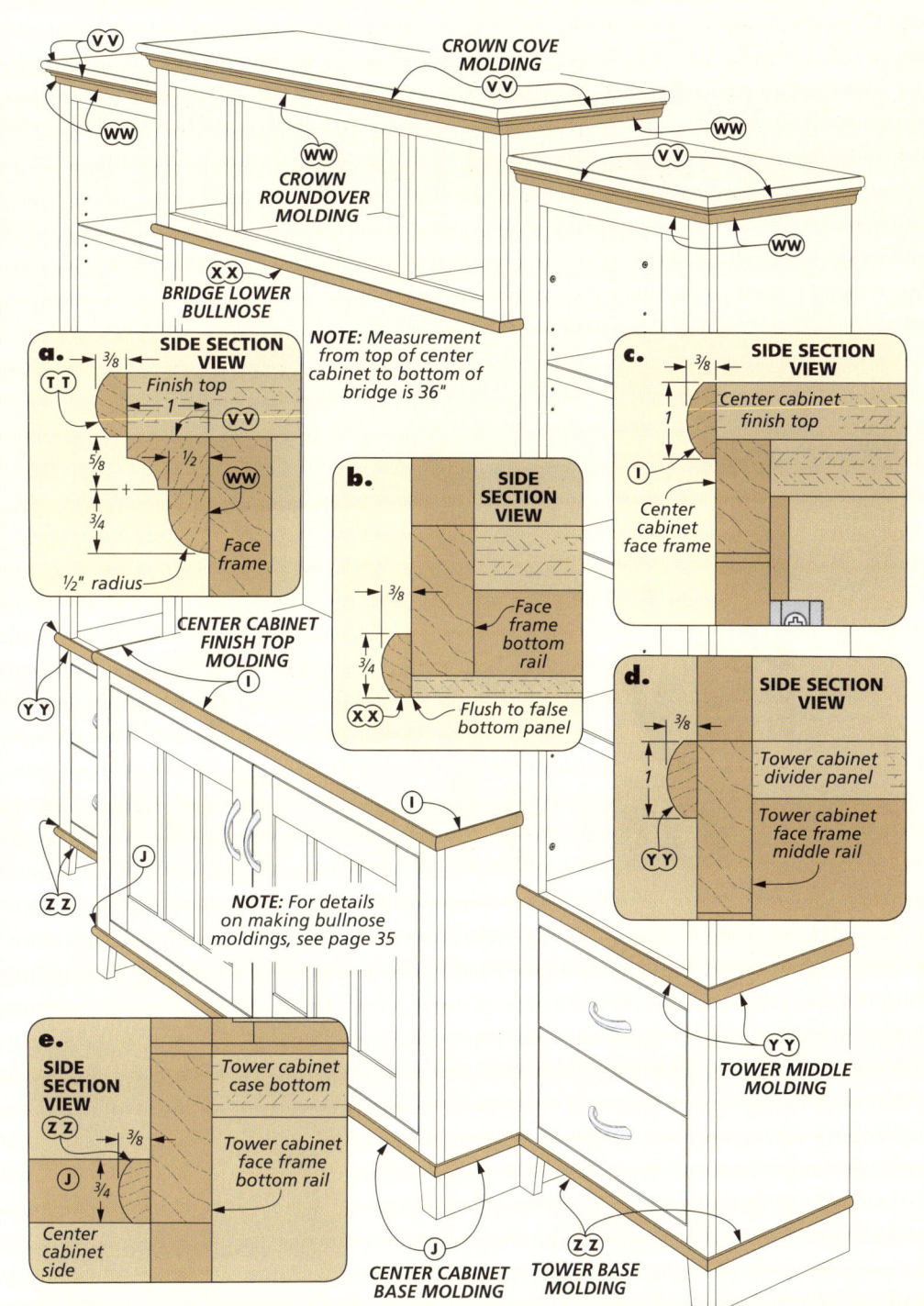

How-To: Two-Piece Crown Molding

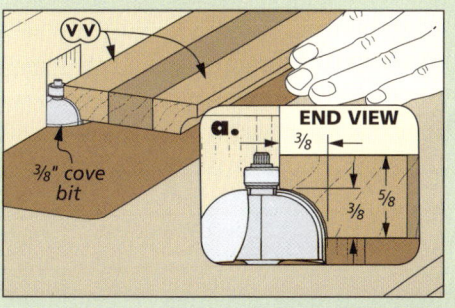

The Cove. To make the upper piece of the crown, rout a ⅜" cove on both edges of a wide blank. Then rip the pieces free.

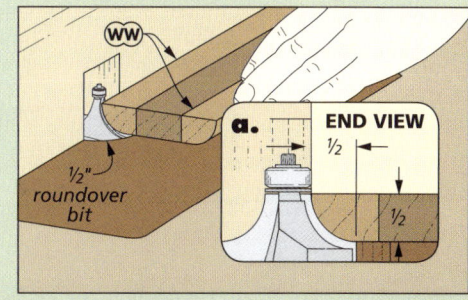

The Roundover. Use the same technique to shape the lower roundover molding on a blank planed to ½" thick.

woodworking technique

perfect Plywood Panels on the Table Saw

With the right setup and a well-thought-out approach, it's a breeze to go from full sheets to crisp, accurately sized panels.

▼ A 60-tooth carbide blade and a zero-clearance insert will yield smooth, chip-free cuts.

The table saw and plywood are certainly two of the most important woodworking innovations of all time. I can't imagine working without either. And although the two may not seem like a good match, the table saw is always my first choice when the task is breaking down full sheets of plywood into accurately sized panels for a project. The media center on page 30 presented this challenge. It's all in how you plan for the job. I'll offer my simple approach.

THE BEST SETUP. The first step is to make sure your saw setup is up to snuff. This starts with the right blade. A 60-tooth triple chip or crosscut blade will produce clean cuts with minimal chipping. Installing a zero-clearance insert as shown below, will guarantee even better results.

Next comes outfeed support. When cutting large panels, stable outfeed support covering both sides of the blade is a must (main photo). And if necessary, don't hesitate to position support to the left side of the saw.

ROUGH SIZE. Now you're staring at a 4' x 8' sheet wondering how to proceed. You want to begin by breaking the sheet down into manageable, rough-sized pieces. Then you can cut these rough-sized pieces to finished size.

TWO HALVES. I like to start by ripping the sheet into approximate halves, as in the photo above. (The exact width may depend on the finished widths required.) You'll find that the resulting half sheets are much easier to handle.

The factory edges on a sheet of plywood are usually straight enough to be used as a guide for cutting. But they're generally not clean enough to be used as a finished edge. You'll always want to trim a factory edge during final sizing of a panel. So always allow extra width for this trim cut.

The goal is to end with a straight, clean cut on each piece. This edge will be used to begin cutting the pieces to final size. So take care and maintain good control when making the cuts (Shop Tip, opposite page).

ROUGH LENGTH. If the project calls for wide panels (the center cabinet of the media center), you next face the task of crosscutting the half sheets to rough length. There are a couple of ways to get this done. Whenever possible, I use the rip fence as a guide to crosscut wide panels. Although a half sheet of plywood can be a bit unwieldy, the end of the panel riding against the rip fence will provide a stable guide edge.

You'll need adequate outfeed and side support to hold and catch both pieces. The trick is to keep the end snug to the fence while feeding the panel. You'll need to push the trapped piece completely through the blade, so position yourself with one hand on each side of the blade.

GUIDE CLEAT. If the saw's rip capacity won't let you make the cuts using the fence, you can work around this by using a cleat to guide the cut. The cleat is clamped to the underside of the panel and positioned to run along the edge of the saw's left extension wing, as in the upper right photo.

ROUGH TO FINAL SIZE

Once the sheet or sheets are broken down into the rough sizes that are needed, cutting them to finished size follows a straightforward sequence.

The first step is to rip the pieces to finished width. You should have one clean, straight "long" edge on each piece. The factory edge will always be trimmed away (upper left photo below). So the opposite edge should serve as your reference edge. If this edge isn't cut clean and straight, you'll want to re-cut it before going further.

Set the rip fence to the desired finished width and with the good edge against the fence, run the panel through the blade. To make the smoothest, cleanest cut, always try to feed the panel steadily without pausing. A jerky, inconsistent feed can create a scored or burned edge. Think ahead to position your hands and body to allow for a steady, controlled push.

CROSSCUT TO LENGTH. The final step is to crosscut the pieces to finished length. Again, this is not a "one technique fits all" situation.

To ensure clean edges and a square panel, I always make a finish cut on both ends. The first cut simply trims and squares one end. This is followed by a square cut to finished length.

One of the easiest and most accurate ways to cut the panels to length is to use a crosscut sled, as shown below. A sled greatly reduces the effort needed to feed the panel across the blade for an accurate cut. When multiple identical pieces are needed, a stop block can be clamped to the sled for the final squaring cut. (I avoid using the miter gauge. It provides poor support and control.)

A sled may not accommodate wide panels. Here, you have a couple of options. One is to use a square factory edge referenced against the rip fence to guide the panel. If a panel is not too long in relation to its width (no more than 2 to 1), it can be safely cut to length in this way. Again, this can be a good way to accurately size identical multiple pieces.

Panels too large for either a sled or the rip fence can be cut to final length using the cleat method mentioned previously and shown above. Make sure the edge of the table is parallel to the blade and the cleat is attached squarely.

The lesson here is that when building a large plywood project, starting with square, accurately sized panels makes everything else easier. And the table saw is the place to get this done. **W**

▲ A straight-edge running along the extension wing of the saw allows an accurate crosscut on a wide panel.

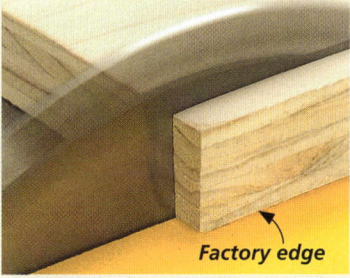

▲ When rough-cutting panels, be sure to allow for trimming of the factory edge.

Factory edge

▲ A large, sturdy sled makes crosscutting large panels to accurate, final length easy. All you have to do is hold the workpiece against the fence and push the sled through the blade.

Shop Tip: Hold-Down

A simple hold-down will help control large panels of plywood on the table saw. Just clamp a long cleat to the rip fence to trap the panel.

Woodsmith.com   Woodsmith   43

working with tools

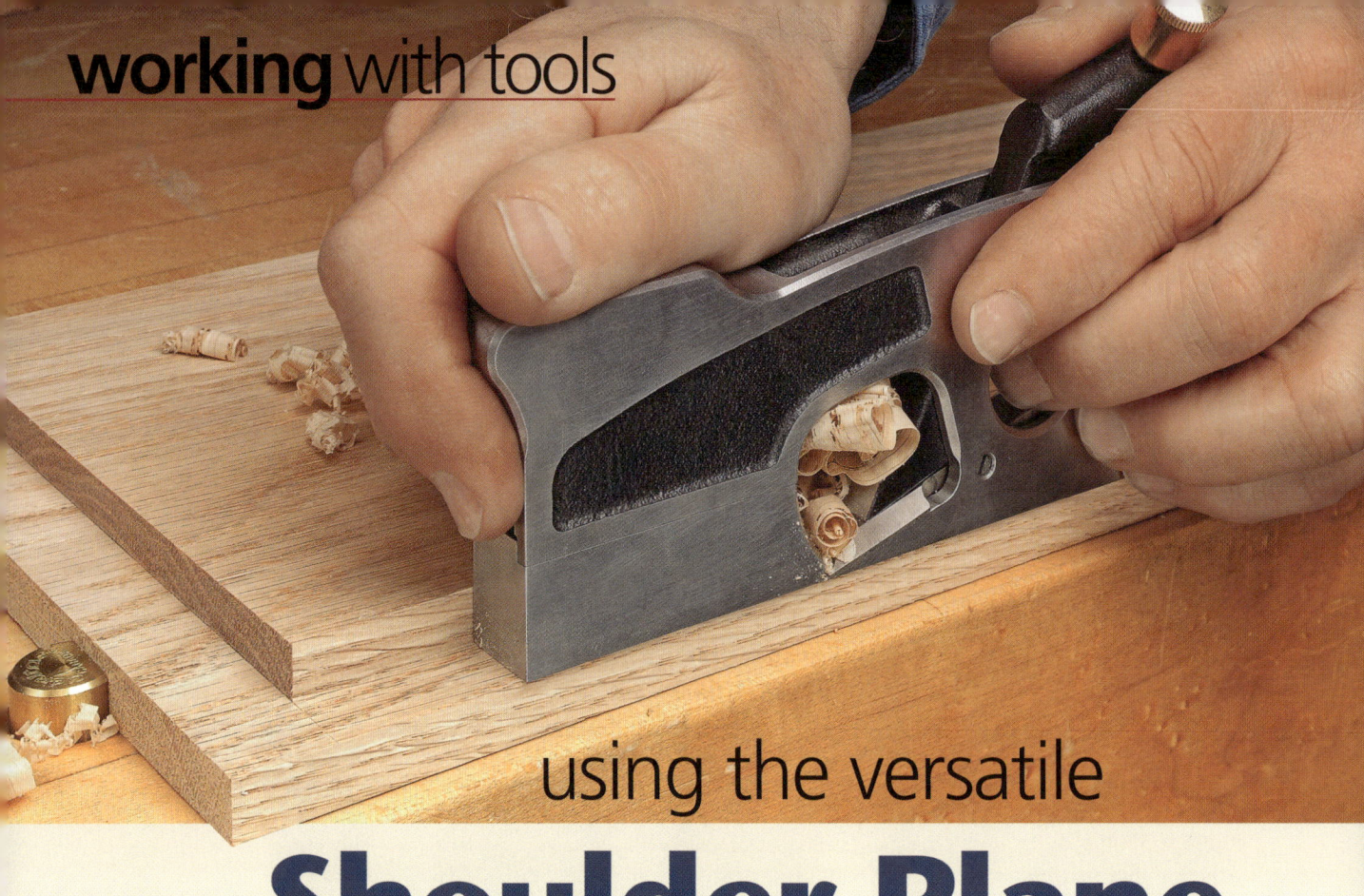

using the versatile
Shoulder Plane

Once you add this handy plane to your tool chest, you're sure to find one hundred and one ways to put it to work.

▼ Shoulder planes are available in a variety of sizes and styles.

Before modern technology took much of the manual labor out of woodworking, hand planes were manufactured in an amazing array of sizes, shapes, and styles. There was a plane for every task — from smoothing boards to shaping moldings to forming joints. Many of the more specialized planes that were once "standard issue" are now obsolete. However, there are a few of these lesser-known planes that still deserve a place in the shop. One of these is the shoulder plane.

WHY A SHOULDER PLANE? Most planes derive their name from their function. A jointer is used for edge jointing, a smoother for smoothing surfaces. So what does a shoulder plane do? Specifically, the name refers to the use of this plane to square up or trim the shoulders of tenons and other joints. But as you'll see, the uses for a shoulder plane go way beyond this single task.

HOW IT WORKS. Although the design of shoulder planes can vary quite a bit, as you can see in the lower left photo, they all share one notable feature. The cutting edge on the iron of a shoulder plane extends across the entire width of the plane's sole. This allows you to cut right up to a square edge or into a corner as is necessary when trimming a tenon shoulder. But it also opens up many other possibilities as well. I think of my shoulder plane as an all-purpose, joinery-tuning tool.

SHOULDER OR RABBET? The distinction between a shoulder and a rabbet plane is a bit blurry. Like a shoulder plane, a rabbet plane is set up to cut edge-to-edge. The difference is that a rabbet plane is designed specifically to cut rabbets — often having a fence, depth stop, and scoring nickers for making cuts across the grain.

Another difference is that a shoulder plane has a lower cutting angle. This feature allows it to cut end grain or across the grain smoothly and with less effort.

In practical terms, a rabbet plane and a shoulder plane can handle a lot of the same tasks.

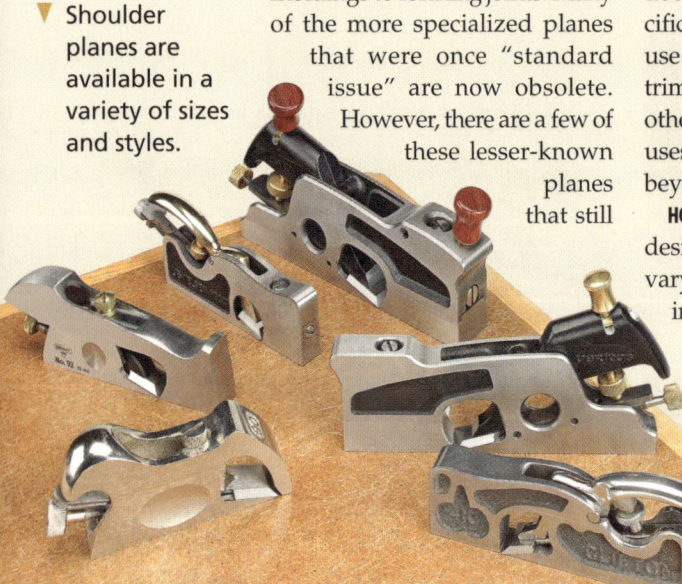

But all-in-all, a shoulder plane is the more versatile of the two.

WHICH SIZE? Shoulder planes can vary in width from ½" to 1½". You'll find that a size in the mid-range — ¾" to 1" will be the most useful and handle the widest range of tasks. The larger sizes of shoulder planes can be pretty bulky for fine work.

PLANE SETUP. Today's adjustable shoulder planes are much more user-friendly than past types. However, to get the best results, you need a basic grasp of the proper setup. The upper right drawings illustrate these points.

Since a shoulder plane cuts over the full width of the sole, the cutting edge should be honed perfectly straight across and square to its sides. Most shoulder planes allow only limited lateral adjustment of the iron. If the cutting edge isn't square, you won't be able to set it parallel to the throat.

You'll find that the iron of a shoulder plane is actually slightly wider than the sole. When the iron is installed it should extend a hair beyond both sides of the plane. This allows the plane to cut more effectively into a square corner.

As I mentioned, the cutting edge also needs to be parallel to the throat. If it's not, you won't get a consistent, full-width cut. You can simply eyeball this setting or make test cuts to check it.

Finally, many shoulder planes have an adjustable throat. Since the plane is generally employed for light-duty trimming, you'll be taking fine cuts. Here, a narrow throat is desirable. You'll get a cleaner cut with less tearout.

TECHNIQUE. Using a shoulder plane will come pretty naturally. You'll develop your own feel and form with your particular plane. As with any hand plane, one of the keys is firm control. Since the plane is generally used for light trim work, this isn't difficult.

The smallest shoulder planes often work best as "one-handed" tools — like a block plane. With the larger sizes, a two-handed grip will give you better control. In most instances, I push the plane through the cut. But a shoulder plane also lends itself to a pull cut when this is more practical.

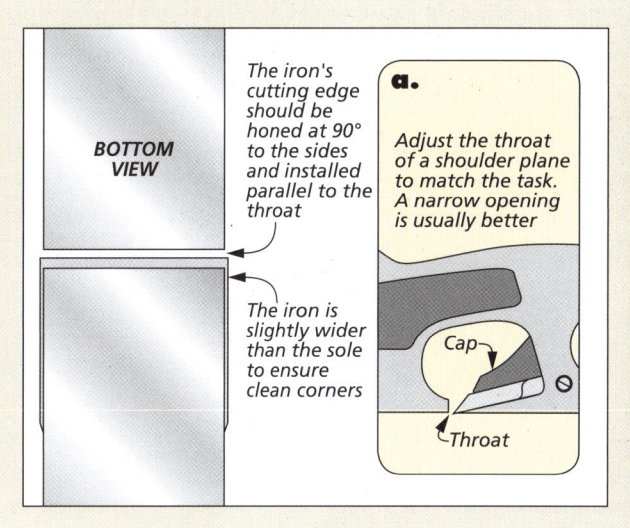

MANY TASKS. So where do you put a shoulder plane to work? The photos below and the main photo on the opposite page illustrate a sampling of the tasks a shoulder plane can handle — from trimming shoulders to smoothing rabbets to shaping contours. Once a shoulder plane finds a home in your shop, it's guaranteed to become a trusted and well-used problem solver. **W**

BOTTOM VIEW

The iron's cutting edge should be honed at 90° to the sides and installed parallel to the throat

The iron is slightly wider than the sole to ensure clean corners

a. Adjust the throat of a shoulder plane to match the task. A narrow opening is usually better

Cap
Throat

Shoulders. Set the iron for a very light cut when trimming the end grain of a tenon shoulder.

Cheeks. A shoulder plane leaves a smooth surface when used "cross-grain" on the cheeks of a tenon.

Tongues. A few quick passes is all it takes to fit the tongue on this back board to the groove in the mating piece.

Dadoes. A narrow shoulder plane is perfect for adjusting the depth or flattening the bottom of a dado.

Raised Panels. The bevel cuts on a raised panel can be smoothed more efficiently than sanding.

Shaping Contours. A shoulder plane can sometimes reach places even a block plane can't go, allowing you to refine contours.

finishing room

understanding & using
Paste Wax

Don't overlook this valuable "tool." You might find that paste wax provides a simple answer to some of your finishing challenges.

For many woodworkers, the benefits of paste wax are a bit of a mystery. The questions of when, why, what, and how surrounding the use of wax just don't get much discussion. But honestly, wax is too versatile and valuable a tool to be overlooked. The real clincher is that paste wax is very easy to use. And with finishing, that's a big advantage. All it takes is a basic understanding.

WHY USE WAX? In terms of durability, wax is near the bottom of the finish scale. It won't form a hard, scratch-resistant film and is generally not very moisture or heat resistant. For these reasons, wax has limited use as a stand-alone finish. The real advantage to wax can be measured elsewhere.

The main purpose of paste wax is to create a first line of defense, not for the wood, but to the finish you've so carefully applied. And although the wax film may not hold up well long term, unlike the finish, it can easily be renewed and the original luster restored.

Wax can also be used to enhance the appearance of a finish — old or new. On a new finish, wax will create a consistent sheen. Or, wax can be used to add a higher gloss than the finish alone provides.

RENEW. An old finish that begins to look dull and distressed can be revived with a coat of wax. The wax will renew the sheen. If the piece has been waxed previously, the old wax may need to be stripped before a new coat is applied. Wax doesn't adhere well to itself, so to get good results, you may need a clean surface. A mild solvent such as naphtha or mineral spirits works well to remove the old wax.

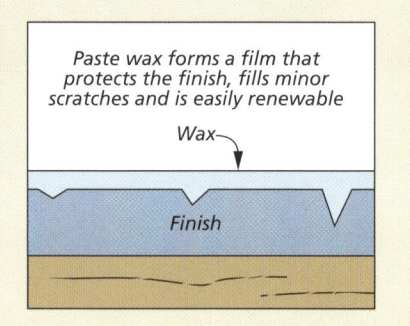

TINTED. Although most waxes are essentially clear, tinted varieties are also available. Tinted wax can be applied as a glaze to add color or produce an antiqued effect. These waxes are also the best choice for open-grained woods

▼ Commercial paste waxes are blends of different types of wax.

Paste wax forms a film that protects the finish, fills minor scratches and is easily renewable

Carnauba wax

Beeswax

Paraffin

46   Woodsmith   No. 194

such as walnut, mahogany, or oak where a clear wax might leave noticeable white residue in the pores. Tinted wax is also useful for hiding shallow scratches in a finish, as shown at right.

ABOUT WAX. Most packaged waxes are blends of several different types of wax. A solvent is added to reduce the wax to a soft, creamy form that's easy to apply. The different types of wax in the blends offer varying properties of hardness, moisture resistance and heat resistance.

Waxes can come from three general sources — animals, plants, and petroleum. Beeswax is the only animal wax commonly found in blends. It has a relatively low melting point and when rubbed out leaves a soft film with a low sheen. However, its high cost limits its use.

Carnauba and candelilla wax come from plants. Although it may not say so on the can, these are the types most blends are based on. Both form a hard film, can be buffed to a high gloss, and are relatively heat resistant.

A third class of wax is refined from petroleum — paraffin being the most familiar type. The fact that paraffin is inexpensive, soft, and clear makes it a common component of many blends.

At the high end of the cost scale is a group of petroleum-derived waxes referred to as micro-crystalline. These offer very good water resistance and are also very clear. The high cost of this type is a drawback, but when protection is a priority, it can be worth it.

CHOOSING A WAX. There are a number of high-quality furniture waxes that will give good results — *Renaissance, Briwax, Liberon, Mylands*, to name several. Look for a soft consistency that will be easy to apply and buff out. You want to avoid the thicker waxes that are formulated to create a very hard film (floor waxes).

APPLYING WAX. There's a right way to apply paste wax. Fortunately, it's not hard to master. The goal is to apply a light, thin coat. This makes removing the excess and buffing the remaining film to an even sheen much easier.

PAD ON. The process is shown below. The key is a simple applicator that allows you to "pad on" a light coat of wax. The applicator is made from a section of porous cloth — cheesecloth or t-shirt cloth works well. As you rub the pad over the surface, a controlled amount of wax will be released through the pad.

LET IT DRY. Before beginning the buffing process, the wax needs time to dry and harden. As the solvent evaporates, the wax will lose its wet, glossy appearance. Catching the wax at the right time is the trick. It should be hard enough to stick to the surface but not too hard to buff out. Different brands have different drying times — 10 to 15 minutes is the general range.

BUFF IT OUT. When the wax has hardened properly, you can begin the two-in-one buffing step. You'll use a clean, soft cloth to rub off the excess wax and buff the film to a nice sheen.

Plenty of elbow grease is the key at this stage. I rub the surface vigorously with a circular motion. As the cloth picks up wax, flip it to expose a fresh surface. You'll notice an immediate change — dull and streaky to slick and glossy (right photo below and main photo opposite). That's a pretty good payoff for a small amount of effort. **W**

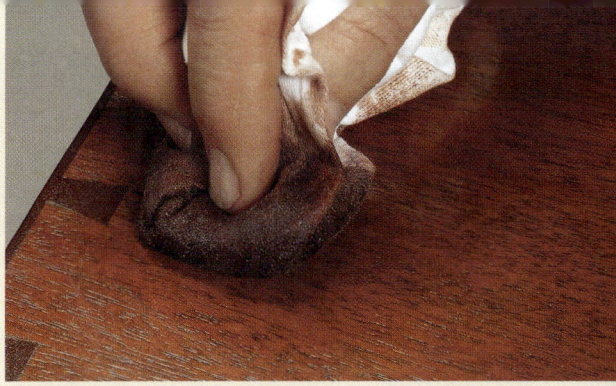

▲ Tinted wax will hide small scratches in the finish.

How-To: Apply Paste Wax

A Wax Pad. *To make a wax applicator, place a dollop of wax in the center of a cloth and then gather up the edges.*

A Thin Coat. *Squeeze the pad while rubbing in a circular motion to apply a light, wet coat of wax.*

Buff. *After the wax has dried, rub vigorously with a soft cloth to remove the excess and buff the remaining thin film.*

details of craftsmanship

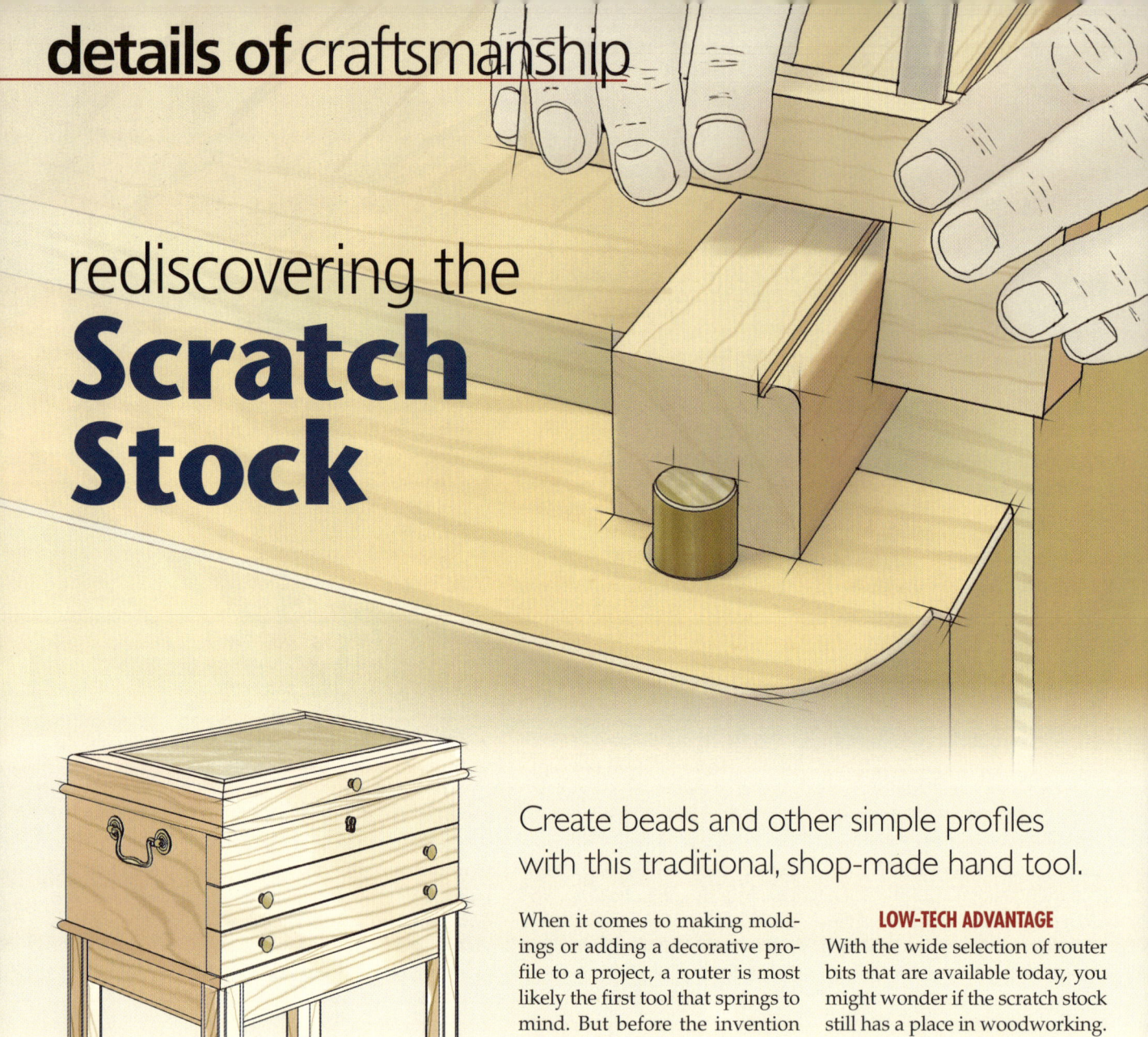

rediscovering the
Scratch Stock

Create beads and other simple profiles with this traditional, shop-made hand tool.

When it comes to making moldings or adding a decorative profile to a project, a router is most likely the first tool that springs to mind. But before the invention of the electric router, a common method for creating beads, flutes, and other simple profiles was to use a scratch stock.

A scratch stock is about as basic a woodworking tool as you can imagine. Essentially, it's nothing more than a small, L-shaped block of wood that holds a thin, steel cutter. The end of the cutter is shaped to match the profile you wish to make.

The scratch stock is used by scraping the cutter over the surface of the wood, similar to how you use a card scraper. By making repeated passes, the cutter "scratches" the profile into the wood. While it may sound a bit crude, a scratch stock actually works surprisingly well.

LOW-TECH ADVANTAGE

With the wide selection of router bits that are available today, you might wonder if the scratch stock still has a place in woodworking. But there are a few good reasons why this tool remains useful.

For starters, scratch stock cutters can be ground to just about any profile you desire. So you can create profiles for which router bits don't even exist. This is especially useful if you're trying to duplicate a profile for a period reproduction or repair a damaged section of molding on an antique.

Second, a scratch stock can be more cost effective than purchasing a router bit, especially if you just need a few feet of molding. Rather than buy a router bit that you may never use again, you can make a scratch stock cutter in half an hour or so.

And third, a scratch stock can even be used on round or curved

Creating the delicate beads on the legs of this stand is a task that is ideally suited to a scratch stock

workpieces that you may not be able to shape with a router.

MAKING A SCRATCH STOCK. Because a scratch stock is such a simple tool, it's usually shop-made. (You'll find details for making a scratch stock at Woodsmith.com.)

Typically, the handle, or "stock," is an L-shaped block of wood that's either cut into two pieces or slit down the center to hold the cutter. Beveling or rounding the bottom edge of the stock will create the necessary clearance to allow you to change the angle of the cutter as needed.

The cutter can be made out of a thin piece of tool or spring steel. Old cabinet scrapers or old handsaws make an excellent source for scratch stock cutters. You can even make cutters from worn-out band saw or hacksaw blades.

You can file or grind the profile on the end of the cutter. I usually start by scribing the profile on the face of the steel and then removing the waste with a set of needle files. Most simple profiles can be shaped in just a few minutes. Then the cutter is clamped in the body of the scratch stock by tightening a couple of wood screws (see drawing in upper right).

WOOD SELECTION. The type of wood you select for your project can affect the quality of the profile when using a scratch stock. A scratch stock works best in even, straight-grained hardwoods like walnut, mahogany, and cherry. It doesn't work as well in softwoods. (Softwood fibers tends to tear and compress.)

USING A SCRATCH STOCK. There's nothing very difficult about using a scratch stock, but it does take a little practice. Creating the profile is essentially a matter of holding the scratch stock against your workpiece and dragging it across the surface. The short leg of the "L" acts as a fence by riding against the edge of the workpiece, as shown in the lower left drawing.

PUSH OR PULL. You can either push or pull the scratch stock, but I find it easier to work in short sections, rather than trying to make each pass along the entire length of the workpiece. You'll also have to experiment with the cutting angle by tilting the scratch stock toward you or away from you to get the best cutting action.

For the first few passes, you'll want to make sure that you're holding the scratch stock tight against the edge of the workpiece. But as the profile starts to take shape, the cutter will "track" in its own path and become easier to control.

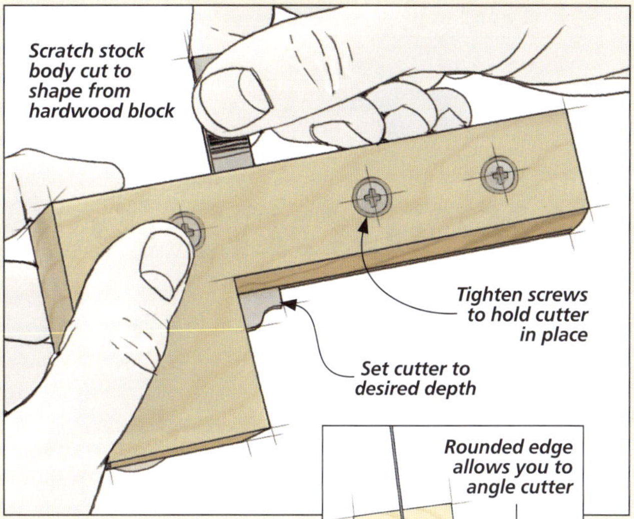

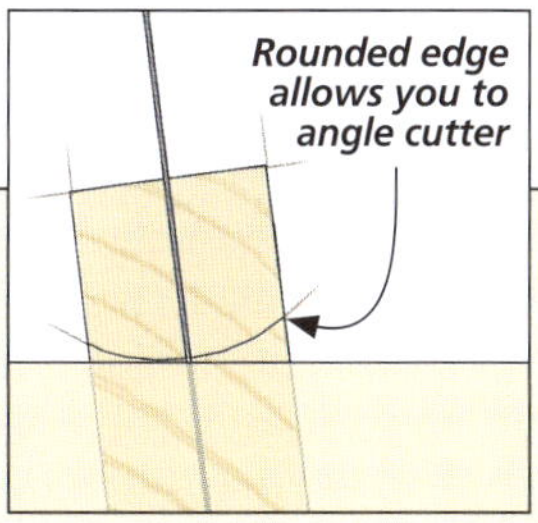

Since there's no depth stop on a scratch stock, you'll have to pay attention to how deep you're cutting and stop when you reach the desired depth of the profile.

One final note. Don't expect a scratch stock to create a profile as sharp and consistent-looking as a router bit. Like many hand tool methods, your results will likely have some minor variations. But these will be subtle enough that they won't detract from the overall appearance of the project. And if anything, they'll give the project a handcrafted look.

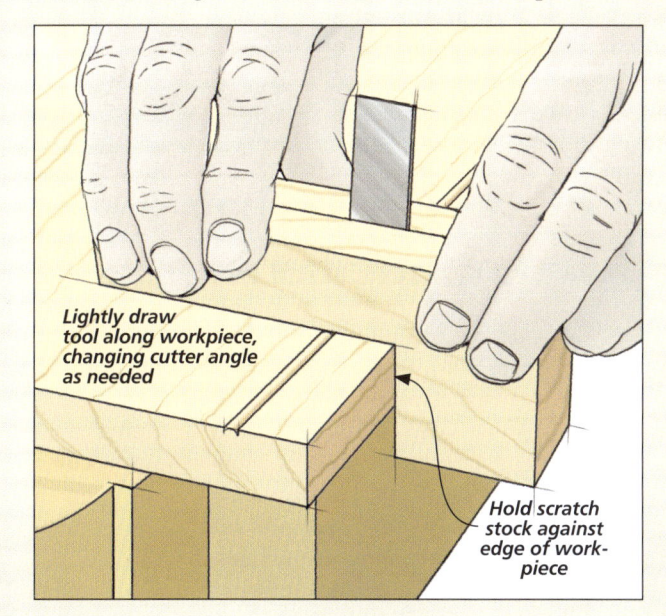

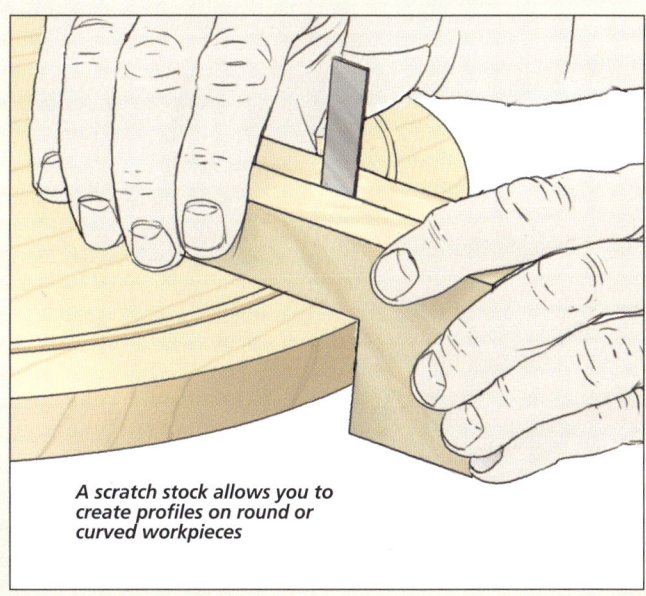

in the mailbox

Questions & Answers

Using an Auxiliary Rip Fence

Q *I've noticed that whenever you show a rabbet being cut on the table saw, you talk about "burying" the dado blade in an auxiliary fence. What's the purpose of the auxiliary fence?*

Charles Jarman
El Cajon, California

A There are several benefits to using an auxiliary fence with a dado blade to cut rabbets. These include more consistent results, easy adjustability, and improved safety. To understand why, let's take a closer look.

A rabbet is cut on the edge (or end) of a board. At first glance, it might seem logical to simply set up your dado blade to match the desired width of the rabbet and then place the rip fence right next to the blade so it's almost touching it.

But there are a couple of problems with this method. For one, the only way to change the width of the rabbet is to readjust the width of your dado blade.

More importantly, with the rip fence right next to the blade, you run the risk of the blade striking the fence. This can not only damage your rip fence, but your blade as well.

So why not just move the rip fence over so that the workpiece is between the fence and the dado blade? While this allows you to make adjustments to the width of the dado, it also creates some new issues.

For starters, if the workpiece isn't held tightly against the fence during the entire cut, you can end up with a rabbet that's wider than it should be.

Second, if you need to cut identical rabbets on workpieces of different widths, you'll have to reposition the rip fence.

AUXILIARY FENCE. Clamping an auxiliary fence of plywood or MDF to your rip fence solves these problems. As you can see in the drawing at left, the auxiliary fence covers part of the blade.

By installing an extra-wide dado blade in your saw, you can control the width of the rabbet by simply moving the rip fence over as needed. And you're guaranteed that all the rabbets you cut will be a consistent width.

Finally, this method is safer as well, since it allows you to keep your hands well away from the dado blade. **W**

▲ An auxiliary fence clamped to your rip fence increases safety and accuracy when cutting a rabbet on the edge of a workpiece.

END VIEW

Dado blade is buried in auxiliary fence

Do you have any questions for us?

If you have a question related to woodworking techniques, tools, finishing, hardware, or accessories, we'd like to hear from you.

Just write down your question and mail it to us: Woodsmith Q&A, 2200 Grand Avenue, Des Moines, Iowa 50312. Or you can email us the question at: woodsmith@woodsmith.com.

Please include your full name, address, and daytime telephone number in case we have questions.

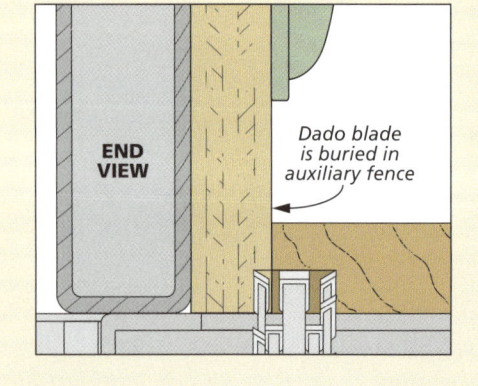

hardware & supplies Sources

SANDING ACCESSORIES
The flap sanders, sanding mops, and discs shown in the article on page 8 came from *Klingspor's Woodworking Shop*. They have a large assortment of sandpaper and sanding accessories. The *Dremel Abrasive Brush* is available wherever *Dremel* tools and accessories are sold.

COMPACT ROUTERS
Both of the routers featured on page 10 are new models that were just released this year. They are available from woodworking dealers that carry *DeWalt* and *Porter-Cable* tools.

HARDWARE JIGS
Any of the jigs shown on page 12 will make installing door and drawer pulls or knobs a lot easier. The *Drawer Pull JIG-IT* is available from *Rockler* (37268). The *Euro Handle-It* (EUR-005) and the *Perfect Mount for Drawers* (BH14810) are both sold through *Klingspor's Woodworking Shop*.

MARKING GAUGE
The marking gauge on page 14 requires just a couple of small hardware items. We purchased the knurled brass knob (70003) from *Rockler*. The brass stock used for the wear strip can be found at most hardware stores or home centers.

WALL SHELF
To build the bookshelf on page 18, you'll need some *Minifix* fasteners (22161) and a plastic sliding door track (10007). We purchased both of these items from *Rockler*. For the frosted glass doors, we went to a local glass shop.

The bookshelf was stained with a mix of three parts *Zar* cherry stain and one part *WoodKote Jel'd Stain* (cherry). Then it was finished with two coats of spray lacquer.

KEEPSAKE BOX
All of the hardware used for the contoured-side box on page 22 is available from *Lee Valley*. This includes the hinge (00D52.16), hinge screws (91Z01.02X), ball chain (00G40.01), chain end anchors (00G42.15), and brass chain screws (91Y04.02X). The felt used to line the box can be purchased at a fabric store.

To finish the box, we wiped on a coat of *General Finishes' Seal-a-Cell* and then sprayed on two coats of lacquer.

ENTERTAINMENT CENTER
Nearly all of the hardware for the entertainment center on page 30 was purchased from *Lee Valley*. This includes the drawer slides (02K42.20 and 02K42.12), hinges (00B15.34), door dampers (00B17.32), pulls (02W40.54), connector bolts (00N16.30), and bolt caps (00N20.12). The antique brass shelf pins (22765) are available from *Rockler*.

We used two different stain colors (both from *General Finishes*) on this project. The doors, drawer fronts, shelves, and top of the base cabinet were stained with *Georgian Cherry*. The rest of the project was stained with *Java*. Once the stain was dry, everything was sprayed with two coats of lacquer.

Online Customer Service
Click on *Magazine Customer Service* at
www.woodsmith.com
- Access your account status
- Change your mailing or email address
- Pay your bill
- Renew your subscription
- Tell us if you've missed an issue
- Find out if your payment has been received

MAIL ORDER SOURCES

Project supplies may be ordered from the following companies:

Woodsmith Store
800-444-7527
*Drawer Pull JIG-IT
Paste Waxes, Shelf Pins*

Rockler
800-279-4441
rockler.com
*Compact Routers,
Drawer Pull JIG-IT,
Knurled Brass Knob,
Minifix Fasteners,
Paste Waxes, Shelf Pins,
Sliding Door Track*

Amazon
amazon.com
Compact Routers

Highland Woodworking
800-241-6748
highlandwoodworking.com
*Compact Routers,
Paste Waxes,
Shoulder Planes*

Klingspor's Woodworking Shop
800-228-0000
woodworkingshop.com
*Euro Handle-It Jig,
Flap Sanders,
Perfect Mount for Drawers,
Sanding Discs & Mops*

Lee Valley
800-871-8158
leevalley.com
*Ball Chain & Anchors,
Brass Hinge & Screws,
Connector Bolts & Caps,
Door Dampers,
Drawer Slides, Hinges, Paste
Waxes, Pulls,
Shoulder Planes*

Lie-Nielsen
800-327-2520
lie-nielsen.com
Shoulder Planes

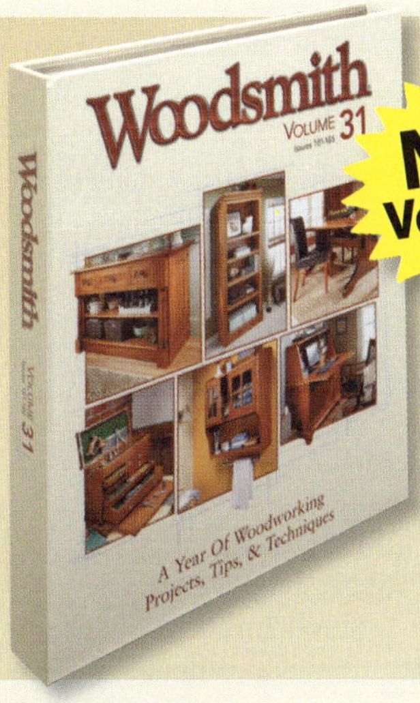

Woodsmith®

NEW! Volume 31

- Sturdy, spiral-bound hardcover
- Six complete issues with reference index
- An entire year of project plans, tips and techniques for your shop — all at your fingertips

→ Item #WV31 *Woodsmith* Hardbound Volume 31 .... $29⁹⁵

Go to Woodsmith.com
or Call 1-800-444-7527 Today to Order Yours!

looking inside
Final Details

▲ *Wall Shelf.* Sporting clean, simple lines and sliding glass doors, this wall shelf is versatile enough to use in just about any room of the house. To learn how to make it, turn to page 18.

▲ *Marking Gauge.* A combination of rosewood and brass give this marking gauge a classic look. But this project isn't just for show — it's also a practical and useful shop tool. Turn to page 14 to see just how it's made.

▲ *Keepsake Box.* The splined mite and contoured sides give this b a distinctive look. And the veneer lid adds the crowning touch. Step-b step instructions for making the b begin on page 22.

◀ *Entertainment Center.* With plenty o storage space for books, CDs, DVDs and electronic components, thi entertainment center brings every thing together in one place. Complet plans start on page 30.

- Steps to Better Box Joints
- Tips for Buying Top-Quality Lumber
- Drill Perfect Holes Without a Drill Press

Woodsmith

Woodsmith.com

Vol. 33 / No. 195

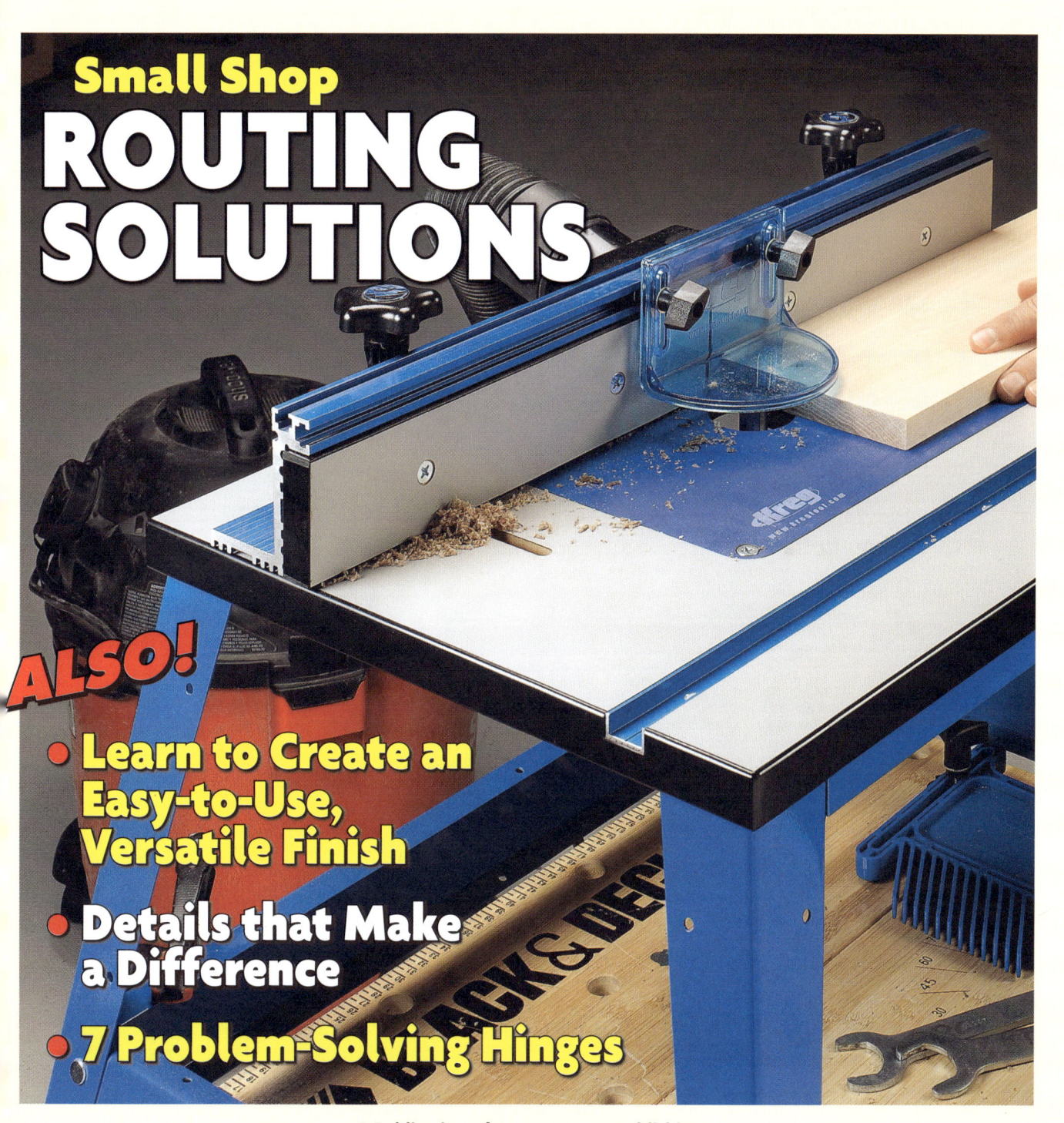

Small Shop ROUTING SOLUTIONS

ALSO!
- Learn to Create an Easy-to-Use, Versatile Finish
- Details that Make a Difference
- 7 Problem-Solving Hinges

A Publication of August Home Publishing

looking inside

Table of Contents

from our readers
Tips & Techniques 4

all about
7 High-Tech Hinges 8
These hinges solve challenging hardware problems on almost any project.

tools of the trade
Benchtop Router Tables 10
A compact package doesn't mean sacrificing full-size routing capabilities.

jigs and fixtures
Wolfcraft Drill Guide 12
Inexpensive and easy-to-use, this drill guide makes drilling straight, square holes a snap.

woodworking technique
Perfect-Fitting Box Joints 14
Create tight-fitting box joints with a simple table saw jig and step-by-step instructions.

tips from our shop
Shop Notebook 32

woodworking essentials
Tips for Buying Lumber 44
Learn the ins and outs of getting the most for your money when buying lumber online.

finishing room
Working with Milk Paint 46
This unique finish might be the solution to creating a one-of-a-kind project.

details of craftsmanship
The Versatile Chamfer 48
Simple to create but complex in its uses, here's what you need to know about chamfers.

in the mailbox
Q & A 50

hardware and supplies
Sources 51

Wine Rack page 18

Four Poster Bed page 24

projects

weekend project

Countertop Wine Rack......18 DESIGNER'S NOTEBOOK

Looking for a small project with a ton of style? This countertop wine rack features classic woodworking and custom details.

designer series project

Classic Four Poster Bed......24

Inexpensive materials and simple construction make this bed an easy build. The details and finish give it a timeless look.

heirloom project

Step-Back Cupboard..........34

This cupboard features some great design elements that tie everything together: fine proportions, a beadboard back, a raised panel door, and traditional hardware.

Step-Back Cupboard page 34

Woodsmith.com

editor's note
Sawdust

There are times when I wish things wouldn't change so fast. Instead of struggling with a sheet of plywood, I'd still be able to easily carry it from the truck to my shop. And then to cut it to size, I'd be able to accurately set the rip fence — without having to search for my reading glasses just so I could zero-in on a setting.

A couple of the projects in this issue take me back to a slower-paced, less changing time. The four poster bed (page 24) is a classic design that will always look great, no matter what's changing around you. And on page 34, you'll find a step-back cupboard that, at least for me, brings back memories of simpler days.

But things never seem to stay in one place. Change is inevitable, and so it is around here, too. Terry Strohman, the Editorial Media Director for *Woodsmith* and *ShopNotes* magazines has moved on to assume that role for *Cuisine at home* (another publication here at August Home). He's going to do a great job there, but I wanted to thank him for the past 20+ years of hard work and guidance in making *Woodsmith* and *ShopNotes* two of the best woodworking publications available today.

As part of the change, Vince Ancona will take over the day-to-day tasks associated with managing *ShopNotes* (my old job), in addition to *Woodsmith*. Vince spent a number of years on *ShopNotes*, so he's well-suited for the job. Finally, I've picked up the responsibilities of editor for both magazines. It's a change that I'm finding has a host of great opportunities, and new challenges, as well.

We'll still continue to provide you with original tips and techniques, great projects, and detailed instructions to help make you a better woodworker and get more out of the time you spend in your shop. But I'd also like to hear what you think we should be doing or any changes you feel we need to be making. Drop me a note at bgnelson@augusthome.com and let me know.

Bryan

This symbol lets you know there's more information online at www.Woodsmith.com. There you'll see step-by-step videos, technique and project animation, bonus cutting diagrams, and a lot more.

from our readers
Tips & Techniques

Sharpening a Skewed Blade

I have a couple of tools with skewed blades. I find it a difficult task to sharpen these tools with a standard honing jig. So I built the jig you see in the photo above. This jig holds the blade at the proper angle to the sharpening surface so I can hone a perfect edge identically every time I use it.

As you can see in the drawing at left, the jig consists of a block with a fence and a stop to position the tool. Acrylic attached to the bottom of the block allows it to glide over a base that holds a strip of sandpaper for sharpening. Since the jig is built to fit a specific chisel, plane iron, or turning tool, you may need to adjust the size or angle to your needs.

I chose MDF to make the base. It's smooth and flat, so it makes the perfect base for sharpening. The mitered block is made from hardwood. The bevel on top of the block is cut to match the bevel on the blade, as shown in Figure 1 below. The next step is to cut a wide dado so that the block straddles the base (Figure 2). Figure 3 shows you how to cut an angled kerf in the top of the block to match the skew of the blade. Finally, you can cut two pieces of hardboard for a fence and a stop then glue them in place.

To finish off the block, I added two glides on each end of the block. The glides are made from acrylic and are glued in place.

When the jig is complete, you can clamp it to a worksurface to start sharpening. I cut several extra bases so I can use different grit sandpaper for a progressively finer hone on the blade.

Ted Raife
Des Moines, Iowa

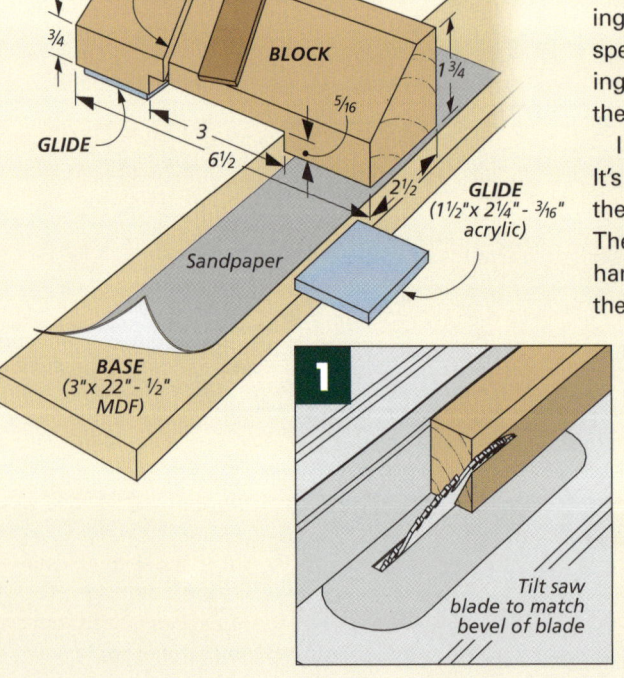

NOTE: Fence and stop are made from (5/8" x 3 1/2" - 1/8" hardboard)

FENCE
STOP
Kerf
BLOCK
3/4
5/16
1 3/4
GLIDE
3
6 1/2
2 1/2
GLIDE (1 1/2" x 2 1/4" - 3/16" acrylic)
Sandpaper
BASE (3" x 22" - 1/2" MDF)

1 Tilt saw blade to match bevel of blade

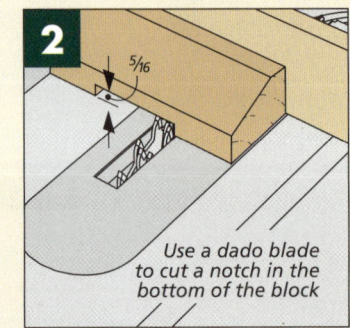

2 Use a dado blade to cut a notch in the bottom of the block (5/16)

3 Cut an angled kerf in the beveled top to match the skew angle of the tool

Quick Insert Leveling

Leveling a shop-made insert plate on your table saw can be a time-consuming process. But I found a quick and easy way to tackle this chore using a hot-melt glue gun and some paste wax.

I start by applying a coat of paste wax on the tabs that support the plate. After the glue is heated in the gun, squeeze a dab of glue onto each tab where they meet the insert, as shown in Step 1. Then press the plate into the opening until it's flush with the table. I use a straightedge, like the level shown in Step 2. The paste wax prevents the glue from sticking to the tabs. But it sticks to the insert plate to keep it level. In just a few seconds I have a flush insert plate that I can use over and over.

Jordan Shatsoff
Waltham, Massachusetts

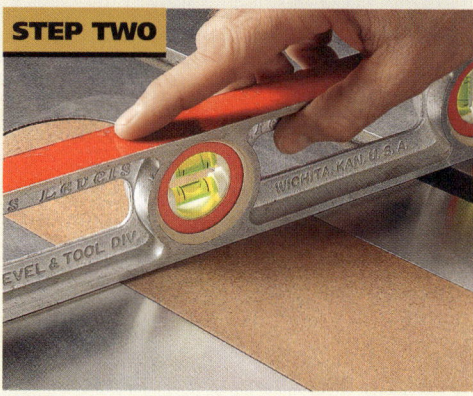

Handy Tool Storage

Single hooks on a pegboard take up too much space for my extensive collection of screwdrivers and other small hand tools.

A compact solution for storing a lot of tools is a section of ammunition belt, like the one you see in the photo. These belts can be purchased in most sporting goods stores.

Larry King
Clanton, Alabama

SUBMIT YOUR TIPS ONLINE

If you have an original shop tip, we would like to hear from you and consider publishing your tip in one or more of our publications. Go to:

Woodsmith.com
Click on the link,
"SUBMIT A TIP"

You'll be able to tell us all about your tip and upload your photos and drawings. You can also mail your tips to *"Woodsmith Tips"* at the editorial address shown at right. We will pay up to $200 if we publish your tip.

FREE TIPS BY EMAIL

Now you can have the best, time-saving secrets, solutions, and techniques sent directly to your email inbox. Just go to **Woodsmith.com** and click on **Woodsmith Tips**
You'll receive one of our favorite tips each week.

Woodsmith

No. 195   June/July 2011

PUBLISHER Donald B. Peschke

EDITOR Bryan Nelson
MANAGING EDITOR Vincent Ancona
SENIOR EDITOR Ted Raife
ASSOCIATE EDITOR Dennis Perkins
ASSISTANT EDITOR Carol Beronich
CONTRIBUTING EDITORS Phil Huber, Randall A. Maxey, James Bruton

EXECUTIVE ART DIRECTOR Todd Lambirth
SENIOR ILLUSTRATORS David Kreyling, Harlan V. Clark, David Kallemyn
SENIOR GRAPHIC DESIGNER Bob Zimmerman
GRAPHIC DESIGNER Shelley Cronin
CONTRIBUTING ILLUSTRATORS Dirk Ver Steeg, Peter J. Larson, Erich Lage

CREATIVE DIRECTOR Ted Kralicek
SENIOR PROJECT DESIGNERS Ken Munkel, Kent Welsh, Chris Fitch, Jim Downing
PROJECT DESIGNER/BUILDER John Doyle
SHOP CRAFTSMEN Steve Curtis, Steve Johnson
SENIOR PHOTOGRAPHERS Crayola England, Dennis Kennedy
ASSOCIATE STYLE DIRECTOR Rebecca Cunningham
SENIOR ELECTRONIC IMAGE SPECIALIST Allan Ruhnke
PRODUCTION ASSISTANT Minniette Johnson
VIDEO EDITOR/DIRECTOR Mark Hayes, Nate Gruca

Woodsmith® (ISSN 0164-4114) is published bimonthly by August Home Publishing Company, 2200 Grand Ave, Des Moines, IA 50312.
Woodsmith® is a registered trademark of August Home Publishing.
Copyright© 2011 August Home Publishing Company. All rights reserved.
Subscriptions: Single copy: $4.95.
Canadian Subscriptions: Canada Post Agreement No. 40038201. Send change of address information to PO Box 881, Station Main, Markham, ON L3P 8M6.
Canada BN 84597 5473 RT
Periodicals Postage Paid at Des Moines, IA, and at additional offices.
Postmaster: Send change of address to Woodsmith, Box 37106, Boone, IA 50037-0106.

WoodsmithCustomerService.com

ONLINE SUBSCRIBER SERVICES
- **VIEW** your account information
- **RENEW** your subscription
- **CHECK** on a subscription payment
- **PAY** your bill
- **CHANGE** your mailing or e-mail address
- **VIEW/RENEW** your gift subscriptions
- **TELL US** if you've missed an issue

CUSTOMER SERVICE   Phone: 800-333-5075

SUBSCRIPTIONS
Customer Service
P.O. Box 842
Des Moines, IA 50304-9961
subscriptions@augusthome.com

EDITORIAL
Woodsmith Magazine
2200 Grand Avenue
Des Moines, IA 50312
woodsmith@woodsmith.com

AUGUST HOME PUBLISHING COMPANY   Printed in China

more tips from our readers

Dowel Maker

Odd-sized dowels and dowels of specialty wood species are often hard to come by. You can buy a dowel maker to make your own but the high price is often hard to justify for a small shop. I came up with the dowel maker you see in the right photo. It is nothing more than a section of angle iron with a series of holes drilled in the center. The rim of each hole makes a sharp cutting edge that removes material from the sides of an octagonal blank to make a round dowel (left photo).

I drilled the holes in the center of the angle iron with the corner resting in a v-block. A twist bit creates a sharp cutting edge. Then I flipped the angle iron over and clamped it to a drill press table.

To make the dowel, I first beveled the corners of a square peg. Then I chucked the blank in the drill press. With the drill off, I pushed it through the round hole in the angle iron. I find the drill press gives me the leverage I need to drive the blank through.

Bruce Sibbett
San Bernardino, California

CD Storage Bin

For years, I've stored surplus hardware in glass jars. These jars work great — until you drop one. That's why I switched to the plastic storage bins that writable compact disks come in.

The large plastic containers are light and can be easily screwed to the underside of cabinets. Plus they come apart much quicker than ordinary glass jars. Another advantage is the opening. A jar usually has a narrow mouth. But the large opening in the CD containers gives easy access to the contents without dumping it out.

Mike Sonnenberg
Lexington, Kentucky

Level a Miter Saw

Leveling a miter saw to an adjoining workbench can be a frustrating job. I found an easy way using leg levelers under a saw platform.

As you can see in the drawing, I built a simple frame that sits on a saw stand. Then I mounted levelers upside down on the frame and drilled holes in the stand so I could adjust their height. Finally, I bolted the miter saw to the platform and placed it on the frame. Counterbores drilled in the underside of the platform line up with each leveler and secure the platform in place. Now it's an easy task to level the miter saw.

Robert Dixon
East Falmouth, Massachusetts

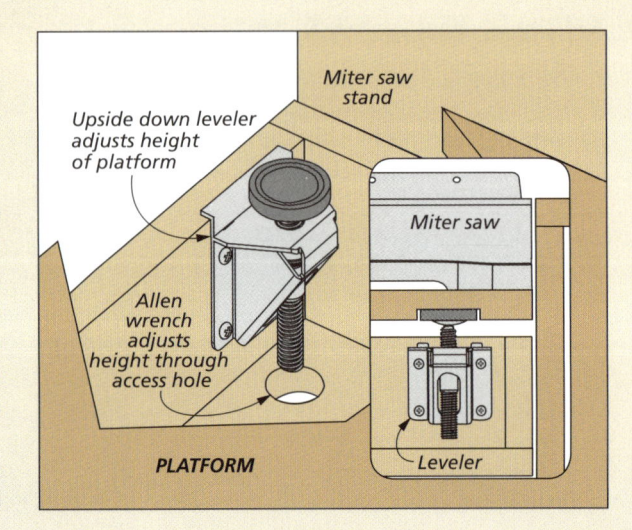

Wedges

Cutting a compound miter on splayed legs is an easy task if you have a compound miter saw. But it can be a hassle on a table saw to tilt the saw blade and angle the miter gauge correctly. Plus, drilling out the mortises becomes even more time-consuming.

To make the task easier, I use a pair of hardwood wedges. The wedges are used with a sled to make a compound miter cut at the ends. Then you can use them at the drill press for the mortises. With these wedges, compound miters are much easier to work with.

Gregory Habas
Georgetown, Texas

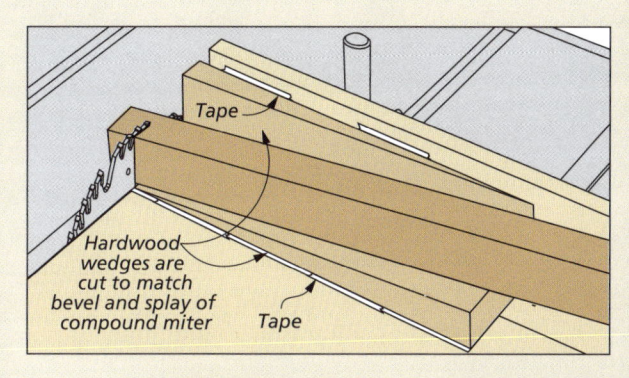

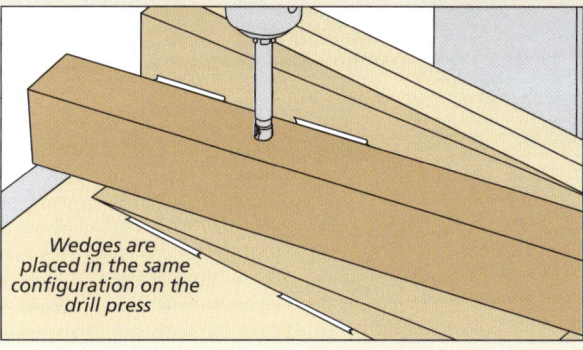

Hardwood wedges are cut to match bevel and splay of compound miter

Wedges are placed in the same configuration on the drill press

Delicate Parts Clamp

Finding a clamp for small or delicate parts is always a challenge. The typical clamp is either too cumbersome or has too much force for fragile workpieces.

I found the answer in a clothespin. As you can see in the photo, I took spring clothespins and sanded the ends back for greater control. The ends can be sanded to any shape you need, including a point for clamping models.

The small spring that holds the clothespin together provides just enough clamping power for the job.

Alexander Bove
Chestnut Hill, Massachusetts

Win This Bosch Impact Driver

That's right, send us your favorite shop tips. If your tip or technique is selected as the featured reader's tip, you'll win a *Bosch* impact driver just like the one shown here. To submit your tip or technique, just go online to woodsmith.com and click on the link, "SUBMIT A TIP." You can submit your tip and upload your photos for consideration.

The Winner!

Congratulations to Robert Dixon, winner of the *Bosch* impact driver. To find out how you could win this driver, check out the information on the left.

Quick Tips

HANDY MIRROR

I use a ceiling-mounted air cleaner in my shop with a remote to turn it off and on. The only problem is I need to be in the direct line of sight with the switch in order for the remote to work. Sometimes that's just not possible. But a strategically placed mirror is a big help.

I mounted a small mirror to the shop ceiling so I could see the switch in it. Now I just aim the remote at the mirror and the signal bounces off it and turns the air cleaner on.

John Kaner
Anchorage, Alaska

FOAM SANDER

You can buy contoured sanding blocks for sanding odd shapes. But these are expensive. I found foam water "noodles" to be an inexpensive alternative.

Water noodles are a child's pool toy that can be purchased at most discount stores for a few dollars. They're made from foam and you can easily cut them into any shape you desire for sanding profiles and curves.

Charles Mak
Calgary, Alberta

PREVENT BLISTERS

When I use a screwdriver for an extended period, I always end up with blisters on my hands and my grip seems to wane over time.

I found the answer in an oven mitt with a silicone cover. The mitt protects my hand and the silicone helps strengthen my hold on the slippery tool handle.

Ellis Biderson
Huntington Beach, California

all about

7 high-tech Hinges

Blumotion Soft Close
Lid-Stay Torsion
Euro-Style Lipped Door
No-Mortise Concealed
Hold-Up
Compact Face Frame
Adjustable Fall Door

Take a look at a few engineered hinges that solve some vexing installation challenges.

For many years, a hinge was just a hinge. There were different styles, sizes, and shapes, but they all worked pretty much the same way — two leaves pivoted around a pin. However, when it comes to some of the high-tech hinges available today, that simple description doesn't really apply. Here's a selection of hinges that offer something extra. You'll find source information on page 51.

1 Fall Door Hinge

This clever hinge takes the hassle out of accurately installing a 90° fall door on a desk or cabinet. To mount the two-piece hinge, all you have to do is bore a pair of 35mm holes. Then once installed, the hinge allows easy lateral, height, and gap adjustment to achieve a perfect fit between the door and the cabinet.

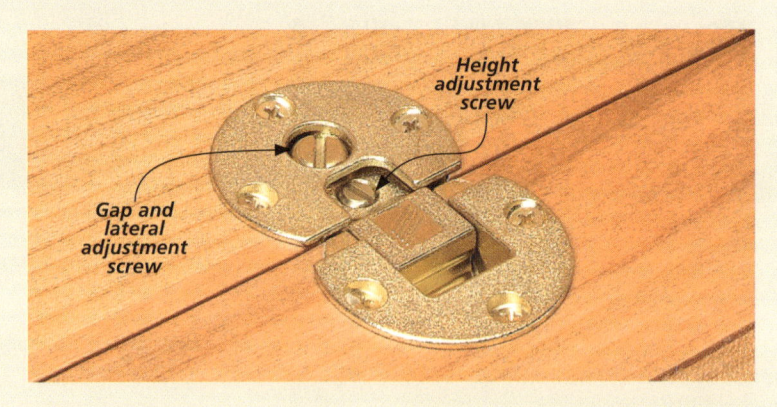

Height adjustment screw
Gap and lateral adjustment screw

2 Compact Face Frame

If you don't like the bulky, two-piece design of most Euro-style hinges, try this one-piece compact style. This hinge offers easy installation, three-way adjustability, snap closing, and comes in several overlay widths.

Hinge features one-piece construction

3 Lid-Stay Torsion Hinge

Installing a set of these heavy-duty lid hinges on a toy or blanket chest will kill two birds with one stone. They'll fill the role of both hinge and lid stay.

The trick here is that built-in torsion resistance allows the hinges to support a heavy chest lid safely in any open position. At the same time, the lid will open and close smoothly with minimal effort. This same type of function is seen on laptop computers.

To accommodate lids of different sizes and weights, the hinges are available in a range of torque capacities. The supplier offers a formula for figuring your needs.

Hinge mounts over ¾"-thick stock

8   Woodsmith   No. 195

4 No-Mortise Concealed Hinge

One drawback to using concealed Euro-style hinges is the need to drill large, accurately positioned cup holes on the inside face of the door. The concealed hinge shown above offers similar features along with the advantage of quick and easy, surface-mount installation. This versatile hinge can accommodate both inset and overlay installations, opens a full 90°, and has a spring action hold-open and snap-closing feature. An added bonus is that it's less expensive than most concealed hinges.

5 Hold-Up Hinge

From the look of the hinge shown at right, you would think it has to perform a pretty specialized task. And you would be right. This hinge is designed to make getting at the contents of an overhead bin a bit more convenient. When you lift the drop-down door to horizontal, a built-in lock automatically engages to hold it open at 75°. To close the door, all you do is lift it slightly to disengage the locking mechanism.

6 Lipped Door Hinge

Doors that are rabbeted to lap over a face frame have been a mainstay of all types of cabinetry for years. It's a pretty foolproof way to fit a door. But until recently, there was no Euro-style hinge to handle this common application. Fortunately, that void has been filled by this new lipped door hinge.

7 Blumotion Soft Close

When you first observe a *Blumotion* hinge closing a door, you'd swear there was magic involved. All you have to do is start the door on its way. When almost closed (at about 25°), the hinge takes over and slowly, gently, and quietly completes the job. They're available for numerous installation types.

tools of the trade

benchtop Router Tables

You don't need to sacrifice features or accuracy to save space. Benchtop router tables offer plenty of both in compact packages.

▼ The open base *Kreg* benchtop router table stores easily.

A router table is one of those "must-have" tools for any serious woodworking shop. But in a small shop, a large table can take up too much space to be a viable option. Fortunately, there are several portable benchtop alternatives. They make it possible to have a fully functional router table without sacrificing key features.

JOBSITE PORTABILITY. For years manufacturers designed benchtop tables with two different types of woodworkers in mind. Many early models seemed to cater to the needs of the finish carpenter and cabinet installer. These users need portability and durability. And they need a table rugged enough to be tossed in the back of a pickup and set up quickly.

SMALL SHOP SENSIBILITY. The other group is the growing number of home-shop woodworkers. This group looks for the accuracy of full-sized tables. These tables include features like split fences, dust collection, easier height adjustment and a few other features many carpenters consider "bells and whistles."

Now, most manufacturers incorporate the best ideas from both types of users into the benchtop tables you'll find today. And frankly, it's a win for everyone.

Today's router tables can easily be stored under a workbench or counter in the shop, as in the photo at left. The modern designs also offer accurate but easy-to-use fences and other features. Either way, these tables make a lot of sense, especially if you don't use your router table every day.

TWO TYPES

Current benchtop router tables can be divided into two types — open base or cabinet style. I picked one of each kind to try out. The open-based *Kreg Benchtop Precision* table (main photo) and the *Benchdog ProTop Contractor* cabinet-style table (right photo) are great representatives of the two types.

SIMILARITIES. In spite of their differences, both tables satisfy the major requirements of a portable router table. They easily clamp to a benchtop or worktable and they accommodate most common routers. Plus, they're easy to store, as shown in the lower left photo on the opposite page.

These tables share a number of common design ideas and features. For example, both offer large (16" x 24") tables made from laminate-covered MDF. Both also feature adjustable fences with dust ports and T-track to hold accessories (photos below).

They also rely on phenolic mounting plates rather than directly attaching the router to the tabletop. Finally, both manufacturers provide rubber feet to minimize vibration. In short, you can't go wrong with either table. (Refer to Sources on page 51.)

A SECOND TABLE? Even if you have a full-sized router table, there are times when a second one can be a useful addition. Especially when you have to deal with tricky set-ups like cope and stick bits, template routing using both flush trim and pattern bits, and creating multi-bit molding profiles. In these situations, having two tables for the different setups is a big time saver.

Of course, if you prefer a quick and easy shop-made solution for your routing needs, the box below points you toward the plans for a simple alternative. **W**

▲ Miter slot allows accurate routing of end grain and dadoes with a miter gauge

▲ Split-face fence provides opening for dust collection

▲ Door helps keep the noise down

▲ Rubber feet minimize vibration

▲ A small, cabinet-style table can handle just about any routing task.

▲ A fence-mounted dust port is the norm on most tables with quick hook-up to your shop vacuum or dust collector.

▲ T-track incorporated into the fence allows you to install bit guards or other accessories, like featherboards or auxiliary fences.

Build Your Own: Benchtop Router Table

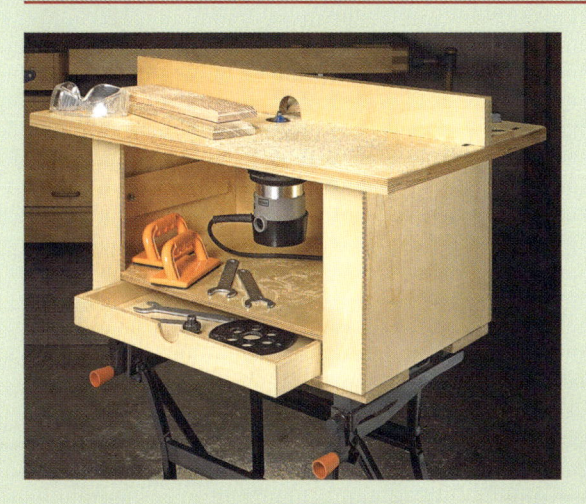

Convinced you need a benchtop router table but don't want to spend a lot? Here's a shop-made alternative that will serve you well for years without breaking the bank. The table features a simple fence that's easy to adjust and locks down tight for precise, accurate cuts every time. On top of that, there's a handy storage drawer for your bits and accessories.

Best of all, it's easy to build. And by using ½" plywood, you can also keep the weight down, which can be a big plus when it's time to stow it away. You can set it up on your workbench or mount it on a portable worktable, as shown in the photo. You'll find the detailed plan and step-by-step instructions for building the table online at Woodsmith.com.

Woodsmith GO ONLINE EXTRAS
To download plans for this benchtop router table, visit our website at Woodsmith.com.

jigs & fixtures

Wolfcraft
Drill Guide

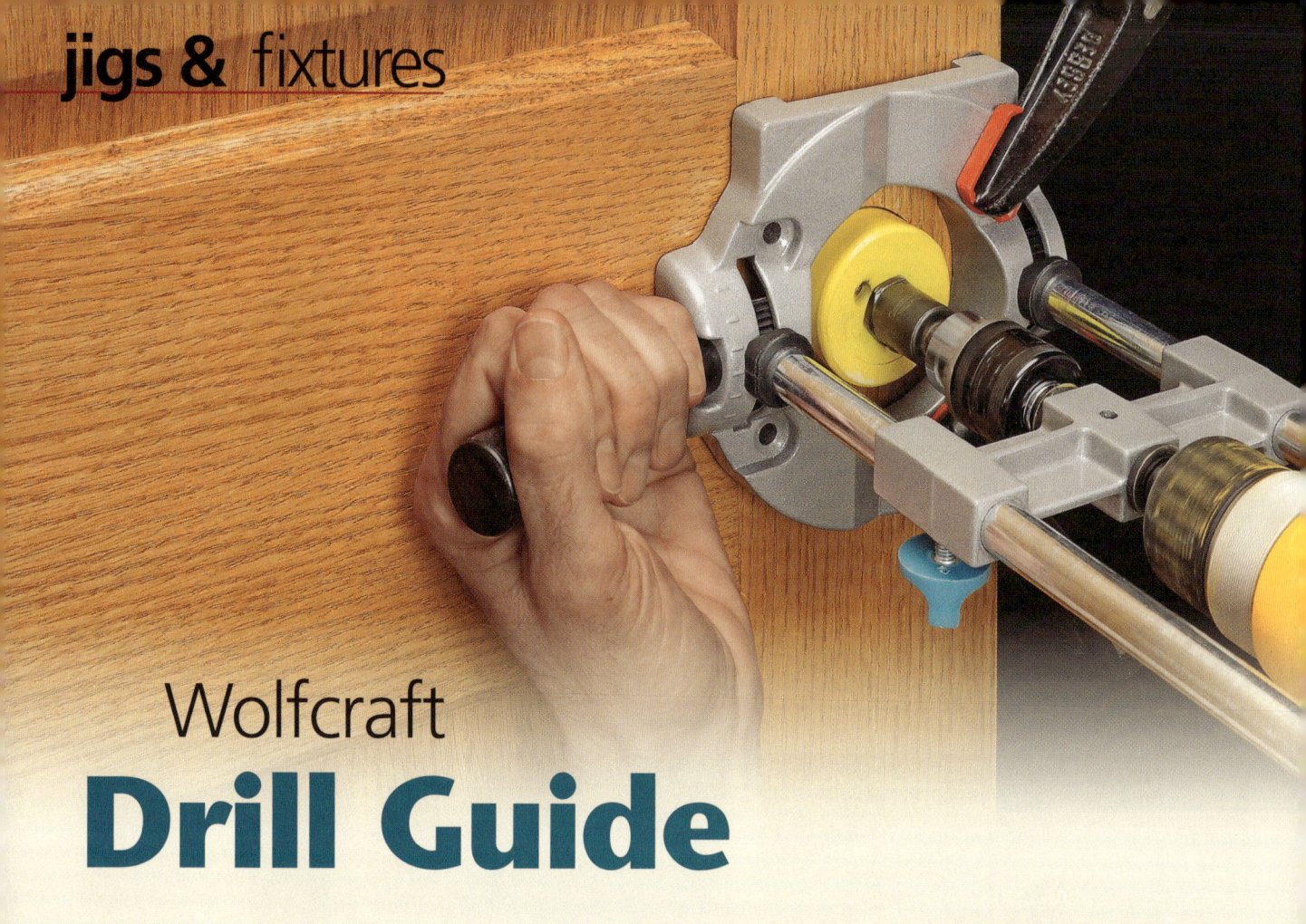

Bring drill press accuracy to your hand-held drill with this inexpensive and easy-to-use accessory.

▼ The *Wolfcraft* drill guide mounts in the chuck of any hand-held drill.

- Cross guide with ⅜" chuck
- Guide rods and springs
- Lock knob
- Handle
- Depth stop
- Base

When it comes to drilling holes for a project, a drill press is usually my first choice. But sometimes, a hand-held drill is more convenient and practical — particularly if you're dealing with large workpieces that exceed the capacity of your drill press.

The challenge with using a hand drill, however, is drilling straight, square holes (especially deep ones). Fortunately, there's a simple, low-cost solution. A drill guide, like the one shown above, makes drilling straight holes by hand just about foolproof.

A drill guide is nothing more than a jig that mounts to the end of your drill and guides it in a straight path. Think of it as a set of training wheels for your drill.

There are several makes of drill guides on the market, but they all work on the same principle. The one shown here is my

▲ An adjustable depth stop allows you to drill holes to a predetermined depth.

favorite and is made by *Wolfcraft* (see page 51 for sources). It sells for around $25. This same guide is also sold through *Sears* under the *Craftsman* label.

As you can see in the photo at left, the design of the *Wolfcraft* guide is really pretty simple. The jig consists of a pair of guide rods mounted to a round base.

A drill chuck mounted in a cross guide slides on these two rods.

To use the jig, you simply attach your drill to the shaft of the chuck. Then insert a drill bit in the chuck jaws. (You can use any type of bit with the guide, up to 2⅞" in diameter.) A pair of coil springs helps to support the drill over your workpiece until you apply downward pressure, much in the same way that the springs on a plunge router work.

A detachable handle allows you to hold the guide in place during use. And a removeable depth stop is included for drilling holes to a precise depth. (You'll need to remove the springs to use the depth stop.)

APPLICATIONS

There are a number of situations where I find a drill guide invaluable. For starters, it's really handy if you have to drill holes in a workpiece that's too large to take to a drill press. A good example is drilling dog holes in the top of a workbench. The drill guide makes it easy to start the hole without worrying about the drill bit slipping and marring your project. And it also guarantees that your holes will be straight.

EDGE DRILLING. A drill guide can also be used to center holes on the edge of a workpiece. As you can see in the photo above, a wide, shallow notch is cast into the base of the guide. Rotating the base until the corners of the notch contact the sides of the workpiece automatically centers the drill bit on the edge. This is useful for drilling out mortises or drilling holes for dowel joints.

ROUND STOCK. Another feature common to most drill guides is a V-notch, also cast in the base. This allows you to drill centered crossholes in dowels or pipe, as shown in the lower left photo.

ANGLED HOLES. Drilling angled holes is always a bit of a challenge, even on a drill press. Trying to hold the workpiece steady on the tilted table of the drill press is difficult at best. But the *Wolfcraft* guide makes drilling angled holes quite simple.

As you can see in the photo at right, the base pivots on the end of the guide rods. All you have to do is loosen the knobs at the top end of the rods and pivot the base to the proper angle. A scale cast into the base helps you with setting the angle. Since the guide holds the drill at the desired angle, your workpiece remains flat on the workbench (center photo below).

If you don't own a drill press, the *Wolfcraft* drill guide is the next best thing. But even if you have a drill press, I'm willing to bet that you'll find plenty of uses for this jig. It's the kind of tool that doesn't take up much space or cost a lot of money, but can be a real lifesaver when the occasion calls for it. It's definitely a tool worth having in your shop. **W**

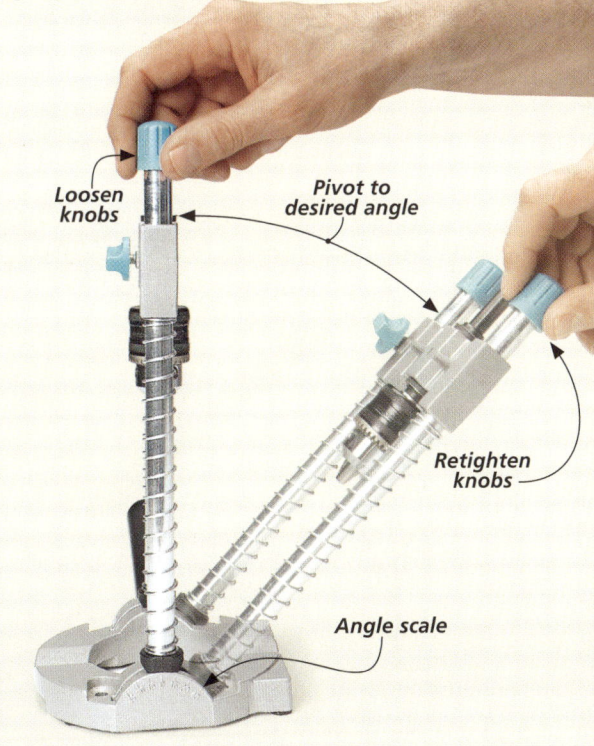

▲ A shallow notch on the underside of the base (inset photo) allows you to automatically center the bit on the edge of a workpiece by simply rotating the base of the guide.

▼ To drill angled holes, simply loosen the rods and pivot the base.

▲ A V-notch in the base of the guide allows you to drill centered holes in dowels.

▲ The pivoting base of the drill guide makes drilling angled holes a snap.

Loosen knobs
Pivot to desired angle
Retighten knobs
Angle scale

woodworking technique

perfect-fitting Box Joints

All it takes to make this super-strong joint is a simple shop-made jig, a dado blade, and a table saw.

I often turn to box joints when I need an effective and attractive way to join the corners of a case or box. This joint has interlocking pins that create extra glue surface to assure a strong, long-lasting joint. And the contrasting grain patterns really make a project stand out.

If there's one thing I like best about this joint, it's that I can cut it entirely on the table saw.

The series of slots are cut with a dado blade or special box joint blade, to create equally spaced pins that fit snugly in slots on the adjacent workpiece. The cuts go pretty fast when you use a simple, shop-made jig.

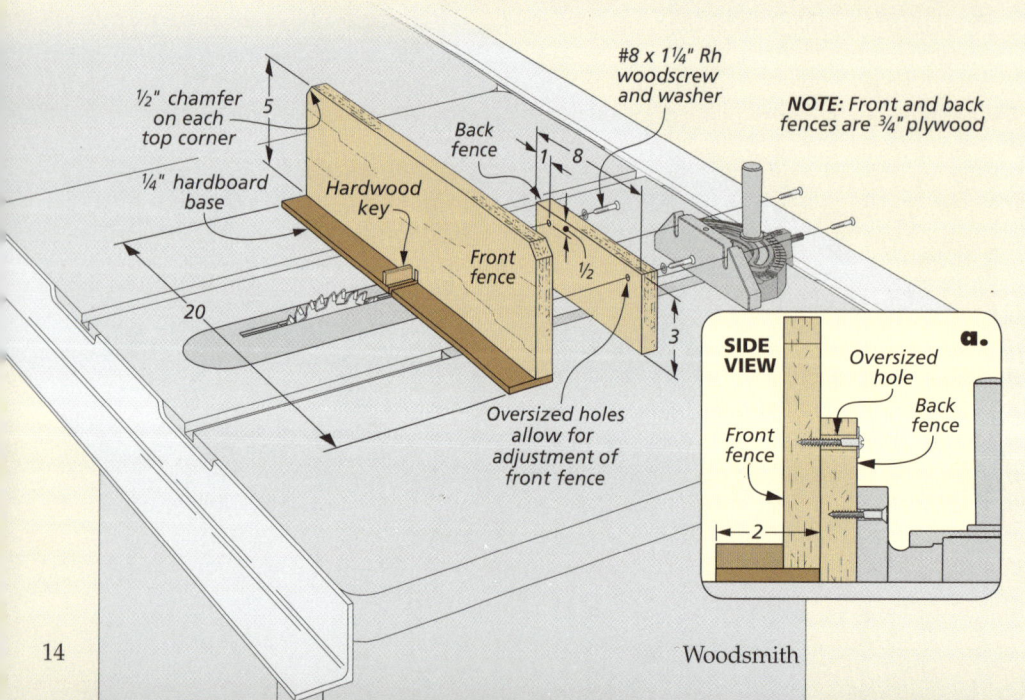

A SIMPLE JIG

In order for the box joints to look good and, more importantly, fit properly, you'll need to space the pins on each workpiece precisely. And the best way to do that is with a box joint jig.

If you take a look at the drawing on the left, you'll see that the jig consists of two fences attached to your saw's miter gauge. The rear fence is simply screwed firmly to the miter gauge. And the front fence is attached with screws through two over-sized holes, so you can easily make adjustments to dial in a good fit.

14   Woodsmith   No. 195

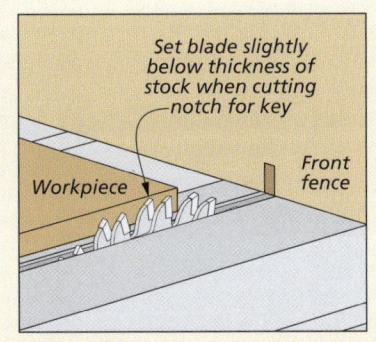

Key Notch. Set the blade just below the thickness of your workpiece when you cut the notch.

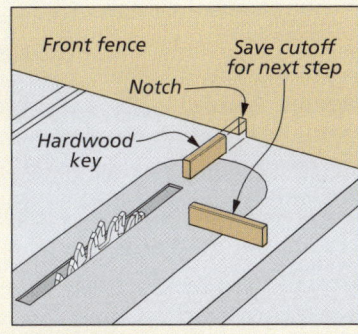

Cutting a Key. Size the hardwood key to fit in the notch made by the dado blade in the front fence.

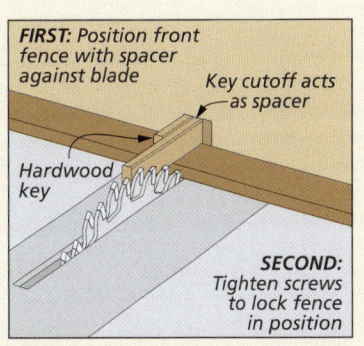

Space the Key. The key cutoff should fit snugly against the saw teeth during setup.

The front fence is your guide for cutting the workpieces. It has a key sized to match the width of the dado blade. The key is positioned the same distance from the blade as the width of the blade to create a pin between each cut. This setup guarantees that the pins align with the slots in the mating piece. The fence backs up the cut. And a sled attached to the bottom of the front fence ensures that the workpiece is level.

BUILD THE JIG. I chose Baltic birch plywood for both fences because it's flat and stable, and it takes screws well. Once you've cut the workpieces to fit your saw, drill the oversized holes in the back fence (detail 'a', opposite page).

SET UP THE JIG. Completing the jig is really a combination of construction and setup. So your next step is to choose the dado blade you'll use to cut the slots. For the wine rack on page 18, you'll need a ¼" dado blade. For slots with perfectly flat and square bottoms, you can purchase a box joint blade set, like the one shown in the box on the right. But any dado blade will get the job done.

To make a notch for the key, raise the blade to just under the thickness of the workpiece (½" for the wine rack). You'll readjust the height later when you cut the box joints. With the front fence not yet attached to the back fence, cut a notch roughly centered on the front fence (upper left drawing). You can simply hold the front fence against the back fence to make this notch.

With the notch cut, you can turn your attention to making the hardwood key. The key registers the workpiece as you make a series of cuts along the end to create the pins and slots. I cut an extra-long blank so I could use a piece of it to set the spacing between the key and the saw blade later. Size the key to fit the notch in the fence. It should fit snugly, but not too tight. When you're sure of the fit, cut it to length and glue it in the slot in the front fence. Save the remaining piece of the key for the final setup steps.

BASE. With the key seated in the notch, you can glue the base to the bottom of the front fence. This base provides a flat surface for the workpiece to rest on while you make the box joints on the saw.

SET THE SPACING. To finish the setup, you'll need to space the key the correct distance from the blade. This is where the remaining length of the key comes into play. Place the cutoff portion of the key against the teeth of the saw blade and slide the fence over until the fixed key butts against it (right drawing, above). Again, this should fit snugly, but not tight against the saw blade. When the key is the proper distance from the dado blade, you can drive the screws into the front fence.

With the jig built and the setup completed, you can move on to make a test cut first, and then cut the final box joints in your project. I think you'll find the work goes pretty fast once you have the jig set up and ready to use.

Worth a Look: Box Joint Blade

If you're looking for precise setups for common box joint sizes, then the *Freud Box Joint Cutter Set* is what you want.

The teeth are brazed to the blade off center so this set can cut precise slots at ¼" or ⅜", as shown in the drawing below. Plus the blade tips are ground to give you flat-bottom slots every time.

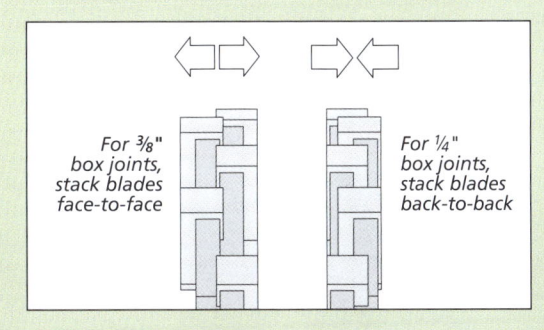

For ⅜" box joints, stack blades face-to-face

For ¼" box joints, stack blades back-to-back

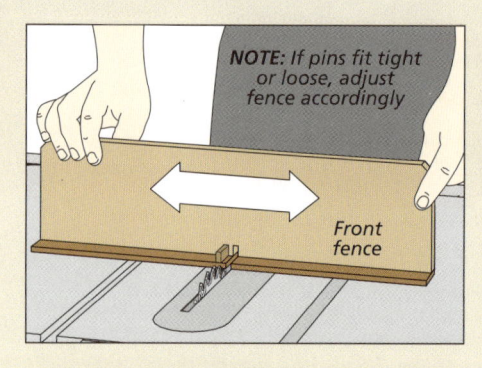

NOTE: If pins fit tight or loose, adjust fence accordingly

Front fence

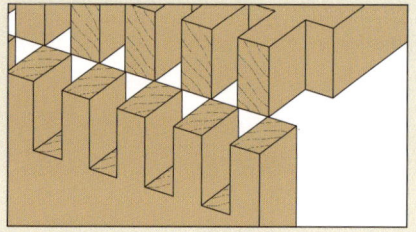

Key

END VIEW

NOTE: If pins are too long or short, adjust height of blade

Too Tight. If you find the joint requires too much force, or won't go together at all, move the key toward the blade.

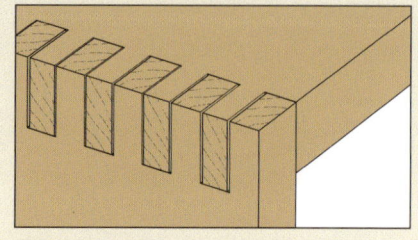

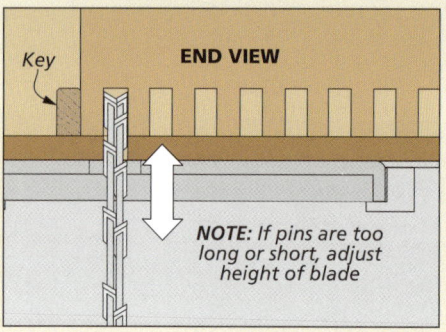

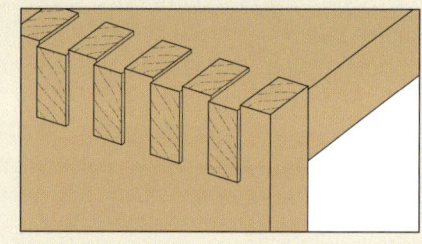

Long Pins. If the pins protrude too far (more than 1/32"), you'll need to lower the blade to correct this.

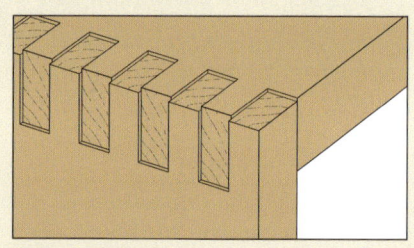

Too Loose. If there are noticeable gaps between the pins, adjust the fence to move the key away from the blade.

Short Pins. Short pins are the result of the blade being too low. Simply raise the blade to correct the problem.

Now you're ready to put your jig to the test by making the box joints. After some test cuts, you'll be on the way to the glueup.

LABEL THE WORKPIECES. Before you start cutting, you'll want to label each end and the top and bottom of the workpieces. This will help you keep the workpieces in the proper order while you're making the box joints.

TEST CUT. With joinery this exact, it's always a good idea to make a couple test cuts. I started the process with test pieces milled to the same thickness and width as my project pieces. When you're ready to make your first cut, raise the saw blade to 1/32" over the thickness of the workpiece. I did this so that the pins were just a little long. Then I can sand the ends of the pins after the glue up and remove any glue squeezeout. (Remember to take the thickness of the sled into account when you're setting the blade height.)

There are a couple things to note as you make your first cut. Make sure you hold the workpiece tight against the fence at all times. And make sure the end of the workpiece is seated flat

STEP ONE
First Cut. Maintain a firm grip to keep the workpiece in position against the fence and tight against the key.

STEP TWO
Cut & Repeat. As you move the workpiece after each cut, make sure the bottom edge stays flat on the sled.

STEP THREE
Cut the Mating Piece. Flip the workpiece around to act as a spacer to cut the initial notch in the mating piece.

STEP FOUR
Complete Second Workpiece. Continue across the second workpiece until all the slots are cut.

STEP FIVE
Trim to Fit. If needed, trim the workpieces so that each one ends with a full pin or notch for a more finished look.

Jig ensures evenly spaced pins for a perfect fit

against the sled. This consistency ensures that all the pins and slots will be identical in size.

CUT. To make the box joints, you'll cut a series of pins and slots along the end of the workpiece. The first slot is cut with the edge of the workpiece against the key, as shown in Step 1 at the bottom of the opposite page. When that slot is cut, fit it over the key and make the next cut. Then continue across the workpiece until all the slots are cut (Step 2).

ADJOINING SIDE. When the slots are cut in one workpiece, flip the workpiece around and use the first pin as a spacer to start the mating workpiece (Step 3). Continue cutting slots until you've reached the end of the second workpiece.

TEST FIT. When all the pins are cut, you can check the fit of the test joint. You should be able to insert the pins in the slots with gentle hand pressure. If you have trouble with the fit, take a look at the drawings at the top of the opposite page for some tips. A joint that's too loose won't hold well and could come apart. Likewise, a joint that fits too tight could cause the wood to split at the slots once the glue is added.

TRIM THE EDGES. Even though the pins and slots are the same size, each one may be just a hair smaller or larger than you intended. When this happens, you'll find you have an odd-sized pin or slot at one edge of the piece. In order to keep the case even, you can trim the edges of the workpieces so that a full pin or slot remains, as shown in Step 5 on the opposite page.

For tips on gluing and assembling box joint jigs, take a look at the box on the right. When assembly is done, you can sand the ends of the pins flush with the case and remove any glue squeezeout.

Box joints are an attractive option to join case or box corners. And I think you'll find they'll stand up to heavy loads and a lifetime of use, too. **W**

How-To: Gluing it Up

All the painstaking setup and test cuts you've gone through will finally pay off when it's time for assembly. Box joints that are cut properly square up easily. But you'll still need to work quickly once you apply the glue. You can use a slow-setting glue like liquid hide glue or *Tightbond III* to give you a little more open time during the glueup.

GLUE. The advantage of box joints is the large amount of gluing surface the interlocking pins and slots create. So it only takes a small amount of glue to create a solid joint. In fact, you don't need to put glue on every surface. I like to use a brush to apply a small amount of glue to the top of each pin, as shown in the top right photo.

As you assemble the joint, the glue will spread to other surfaces. And you will get some glue squeezeout. I place masking tape next to the pins (top photo). This will trap any squeezeout on the inside corners where it's tough to remove. When the glue has skinned over, pull the tape off and the glue will come with it (bottom photo).

CLAMPING. Clamping box joints is a little different than clamping other types of joinery. Since the pins are slightly long, you won't be able to apply clamps directly to the corners of the case. So when you're ready to apply the clamps, you'll find clamping blocks come in handy. Take a look at the center photo to see how I used blocks to clamp the case. You can see that the blocks give you the ability to apply pressure to close the joint in both directions without touching the pins.

▶ With its longer open time, *Titebond III* is excellent for gluing box joints.

▲ By applying glue only to the top of each pin, a strong long-grain to long-grain joint is created at each pin and slot.

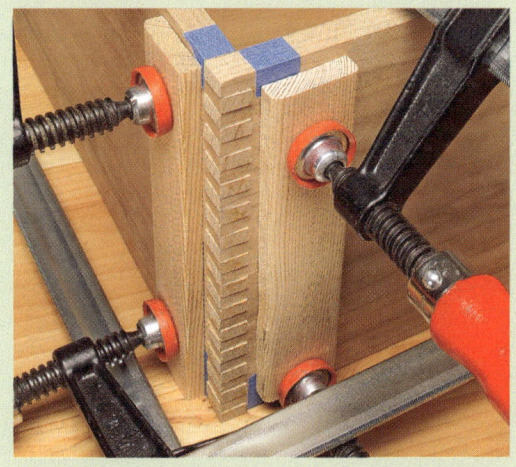

▲ Clamping blocks distribute the force of the clamps evenly, without interfering with the proud-standing pins.

▲ After the glue has set, removing the tape reveals a clean joint, with no cleanup required.

Weekend Project

space-saving Wine Rack

Traditional construction and modern accents combine to create style and practicality in one small package.

A wine rack is a great addition to any kitchen or dining room. But if you don't have space for a large wine rack, then I think you'll like this one. This rack takes the concept of a basic wine crate and pumps up the style. It sits on a countertop or buffet so it's always ready when company arrives.

Just because the rack is compact doesn't mean I cut back on the details. The case is assembled with box joints, which make any project look impressive. Plus, I added contrasting feet and edging on the face of the rack.

From a woodworking point of view, this project will give you a chance to hone your skills. And if you're new to making box joints, I've included some helpful hints in a separate article on page 14.

I've also included design options with this project. If a low-profile rack would better suit your space, check out the Designer's Notebook on page 23.

box joint CASE

The wine rack is built by constructing a case and then adding a series of dividers and shelves. Later, you'll add edging and feet to complete the rack. The biggest challenge is cutting the box joints. But before you can start on the box joints, you'll need to size your workpieces.

PANELS. I glued up panels for the sides, top, and bottom. Starting with an extra-wide and extra-long blank, square up the ends and cut the four pieces to identical length. Later you can trim the extra width to even up the case. I used the simple table saw jig shown on page 14 to cut the box joints. You can see how it's done in the box below.

DADOES. When you've completed the box joints, go ahead and cut the dadoes for the dividers and shelves you'll add later. The top and bottom each have two dadoes, but the sides only have one. It's a good idea to mark each piece before you cut them, so you won't get the workpieces confused when you start the glueup.

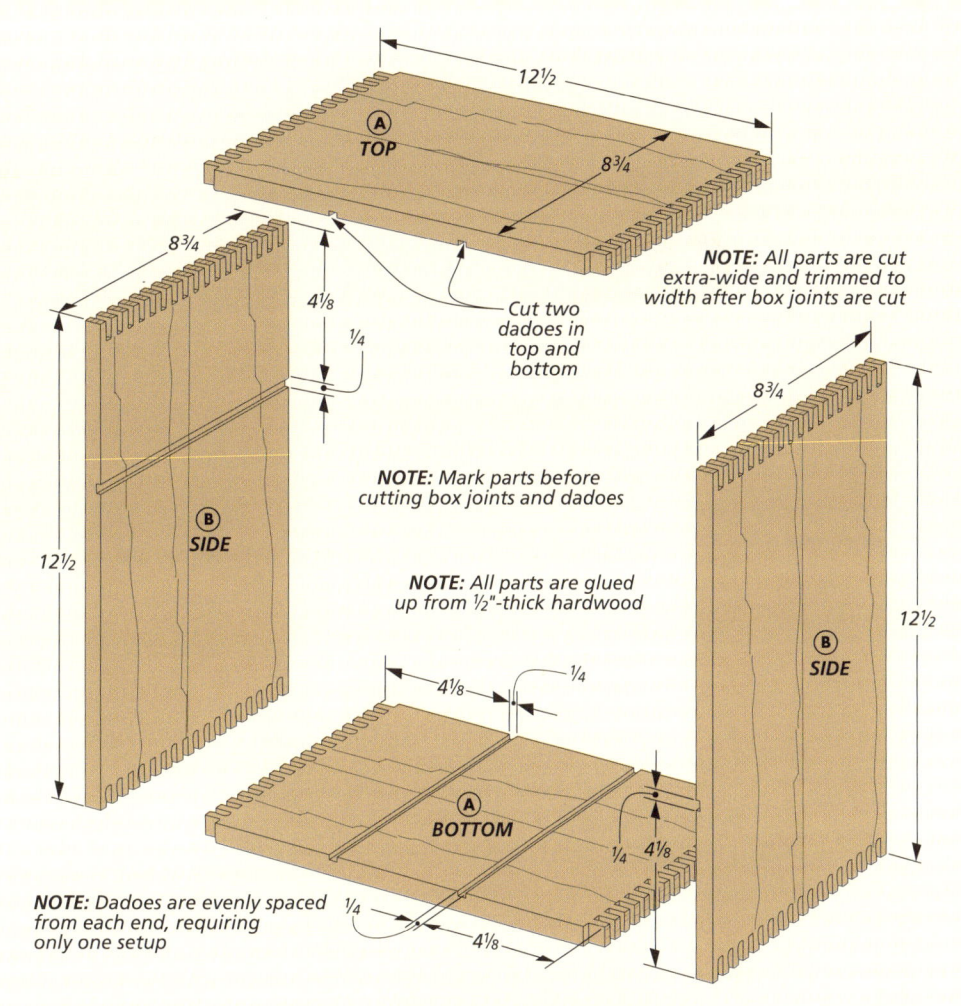

GLUE UP. You can glue up the case before adding the shelves and dividers. This way, you'll have an easier time squaring up the case without extra workpieces in the way. But before you add any glue to the joints, dry assemble the case. After testing the fit, you can add the glue.

◀ For a step-by-step article on cutting perfect-fitting box joints, see page 14.

NOTE: All parts are cut extra-wide and trimmed to width after box joints are cut

NOTE: Mark parts before cutting box joints and dadoes

NOTE: All parts are glued up from ½"-thick hardwood

NOTE: Dadoes are evenly spaced from each end, requiring only one setup

How-To: Cut the Case Joinery

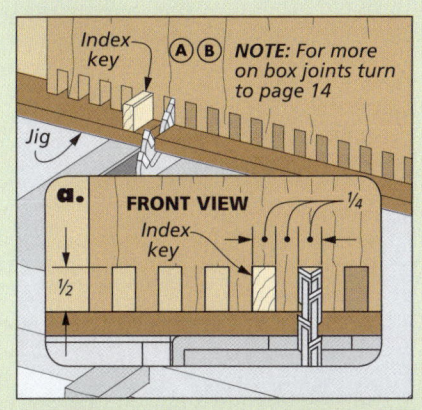

Cut Slots. The secret to perfect box joints is having the key, dado blade, and space between sized identically.

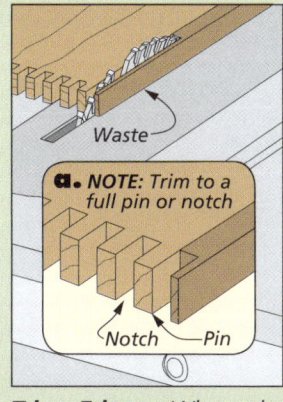

Trim Edges. When the box joints are cut, trim the edges to final width.

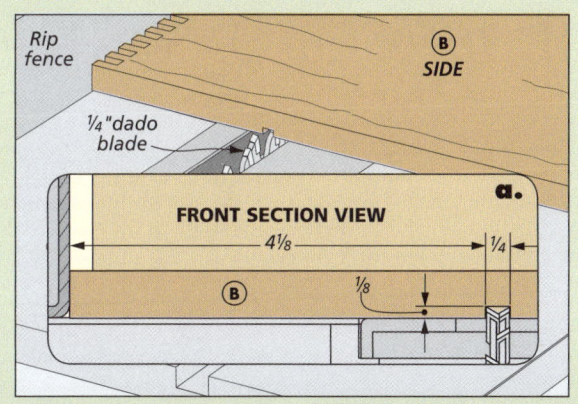

Dadoes. You can use the same dado blade to cut the dadoes in the case sides, top, and bottom. The dadoes are equally spaced so only one set up is needed.

woodsmith.com   Woodsmith   19

complete the CASE

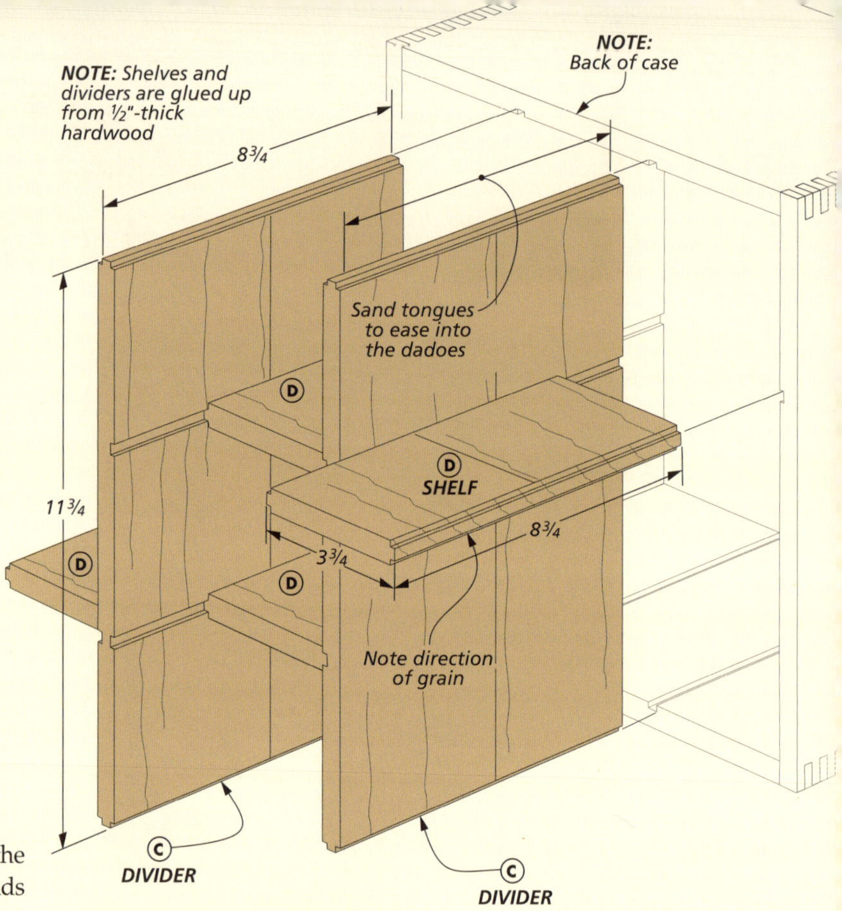

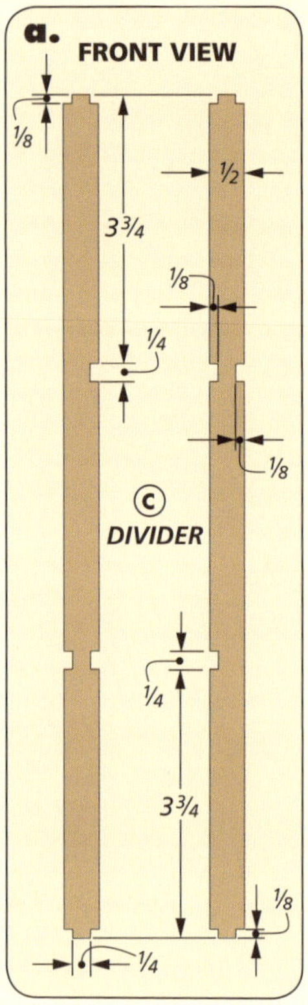

The inside of the rack is organized into sections with dividers and shelves. These create separate spaces to store bottles and glasses. A stop at the back of each shelf helps keep items contained.

DIVIDERS. To build the dividers, I glued up panels and cut them to final length and width. Then I cut dadoes in the dividers to hold the shelves (box below). Here again all the dadoes are located the same distance from the ends of the dividers, so you can use one setup to make all the cuts (detail 'a'). Finally, you can cut the tongues on the ends of the dividers to match the dadoes in the case. This is shown in the center drawing in the box below.

SHELVES. The shelves are also cut from glued up panels (note grain direction in main drawing). Once they're cut to size, you can cut centered tongues to fit the dadoes (detail 'c').

ASSEMBLY. The dividers and shelves slide into the dadoes from the back of the case. To make this easier, I lightly sanded the tongues, as shown in the right drawing below. Keep checking the fit as you sand them and then glue them in the dadoes. Apply the glue sparingly to the back of the dadoes. As you slide the pieces in from the back, the glue will spread to cover the tongues and you'll get less squeezeout. While the glue dries on the case, you can get started making the edging for the front of the rack.

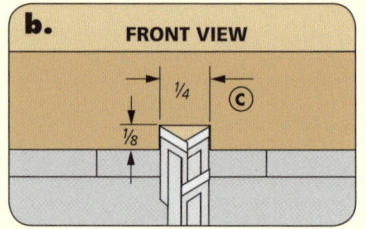

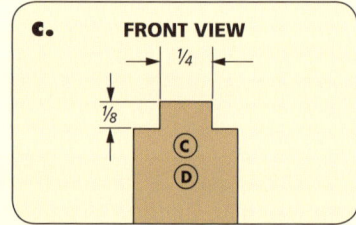

How-To: Cut Dadoes & Tongues

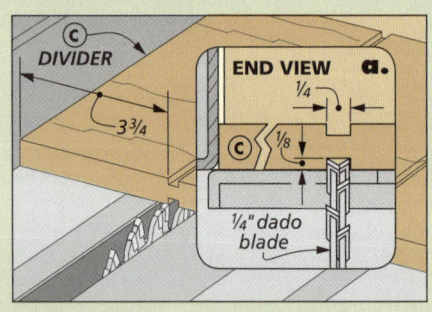

Divider Dadoes. The two dividers have a series of dadoes that hold the shelves in place on the rack (detail 'a').

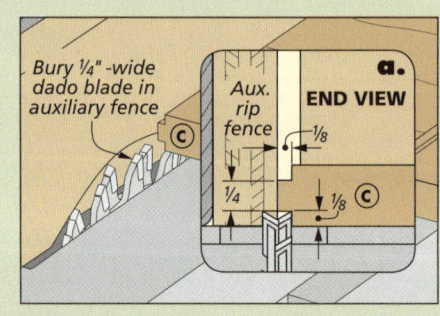

Tongues. Each end of the shelves and dividers are held in place with tongues cut to match the dadoes on the case.

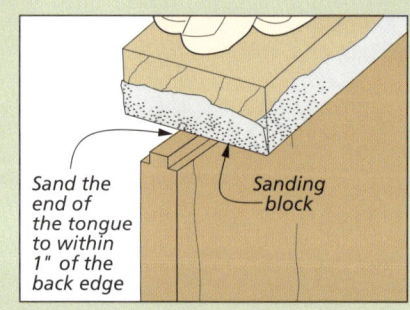

Ease the Tongues. Lightly sand the ends to within 1" of the back edge of the tongue, for an easier fit.

EDGING. The edging on the face of the case serves two purposes. First it provides visual appeal through the contrasting wood. And second, the edging covers the tongue and dado joints where the shelves and dividers join.

As you can see in the box at the bottom of the page, I ripped the edging from a wide board. Once the edging is cut, it's centered on the front edges of the case. At first, getting it aligned exactly looked like it was going to be a challenge. So to solve the problem, I used a couple shop-made guides to help me glue the edging in place.

GUIDES. If you take a look at the right drawing in the box below, you'll see the guides are nothing more than blocks of wood with a rabbeted edge. I left a 1/8" lip on the guides to center them over the edge of the case. Then I inserted the edging between the guides so that it was perfectly centered on the edge.

ATTACH EDGING. To attach the edging, I worked from the outer edges of the case to the inside. I glued the outside vertical edging first. Then I cut the remaining edging to fit, following the step-by-step process shown in the main drawing at right.

With the edging attached, there are just a couple details to add before the project is complete.

STOPS. There are stops at the back of each shelf to keep stored items contained on the shelves. These stops are just strips of hardwood with a small roundover on the top edges.

Cut the stops to length to fit the openings. Then lightly round over the top edges with sandpaper. Finally, glue the stops in place flush with the back edge of each shelf, as shown in detail 'b'.

There's just one final thing to take care of on the case. And that's to add the contrasting feet. You'll find more about the details for this on the next page.

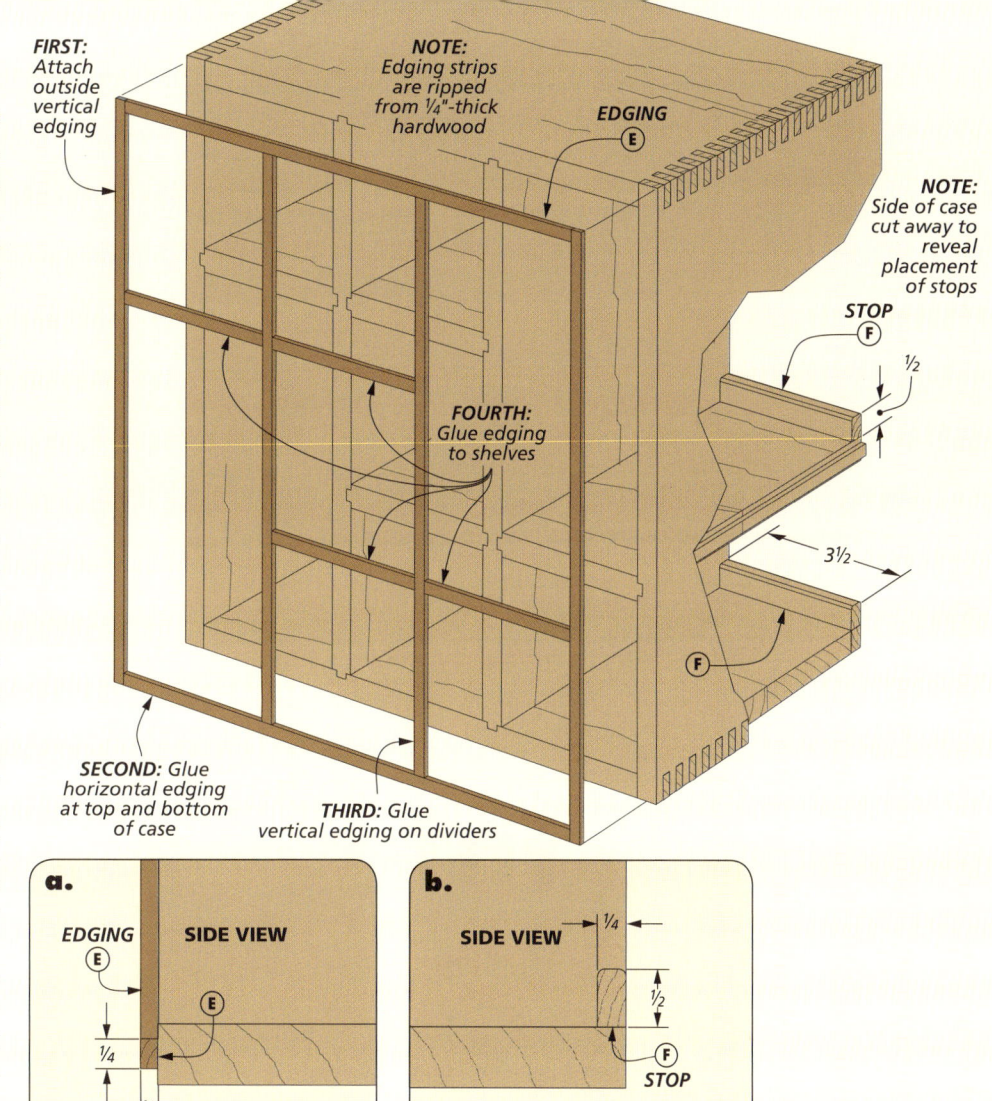

Making & Adding the Edging

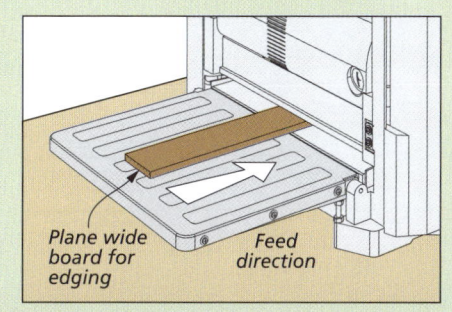

Plane Edging. Plane an extra-wide board to 1/4" thickness before cutting it into strips for the edging.

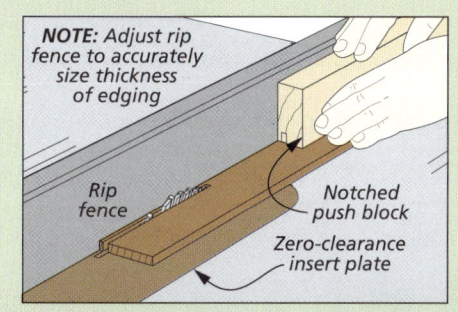

Rip Edging. Adjust the rip fence to the thickness of the edging and rip the individual strips free.

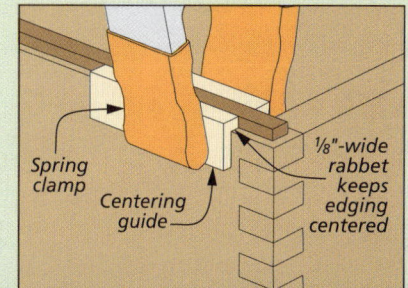

Center Edging. Clamp two guides on either side of the edge and insert the edging in between to center it.

contrasting FEET

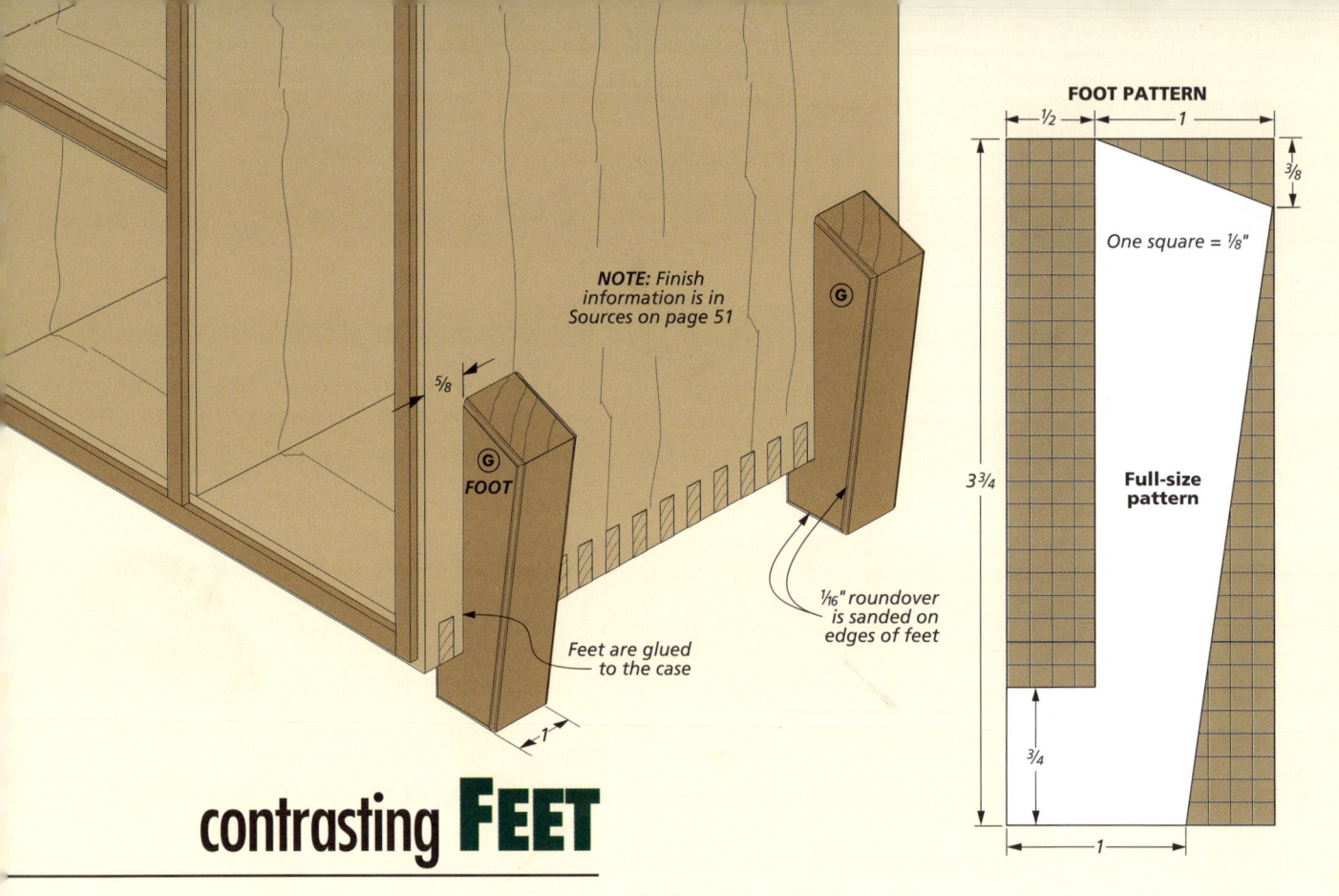

The feet on the wine rack are another interesting detail of this project. Made with contrasting wood, they really make the rack stand out from the ordinary. And the tapers on the feet make them even more striking.

SHAPE THE FEET. Shaping the feet is pretty straightforward. But to make them easier to cut, you can use the the full-size pattern in the upper right corner.

To make the feet, I started with a couple of extra-long blanks. I found it easier to work with a blank long enough to make two feet. Start shaping the feet by cutting a wide dado to form a notch that wraps around the case (left drawing, below).

Your next step is to cut the tapers on each foot. I did this on the band saw (center drawing below). Then you can sand to the line to remove the blade marks. I taped the feet together to sand them, so they were identical. Take a minute to sand a 1/16" roundover on the feet. When the feet are done you can glue them to the case.

GLUE FEET. I used a simple spacer to position the feet from the edge accurately. It's a scrap piece with a 5/8"-wide rabbet cut in the edge. As you can see in the right drawing below, I placed the spacer on the edge of the case and aligned the foot for the glueup.

Once the feet are in place, all that's left is to add the finish. There's more about the finish in Sources on page 51. Then to complete the set, you can fill the rack with your favorite wines and special serving glasses. **W**

How-To: Shape the Feet

Cut a Notch. A 3/4" dado blade makes short work of the notch in the foot blank. Use the template as a cutting guide.

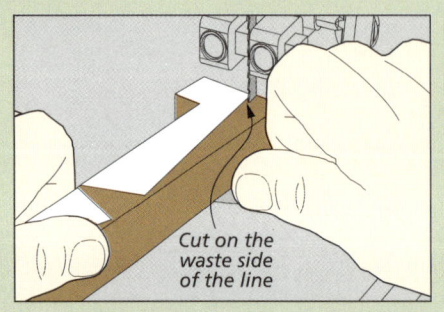

Shape the Feet. Cut the tapers on the top and side of the foot at the band saw. Clean up the saw marks with sandpaper.

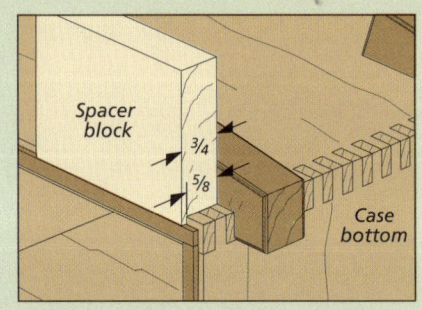

Position Feet. Position the feet 5/8" from the front and back of the case. A simple spacer helps with this task.

DESIGNER'S NOTEBOOK

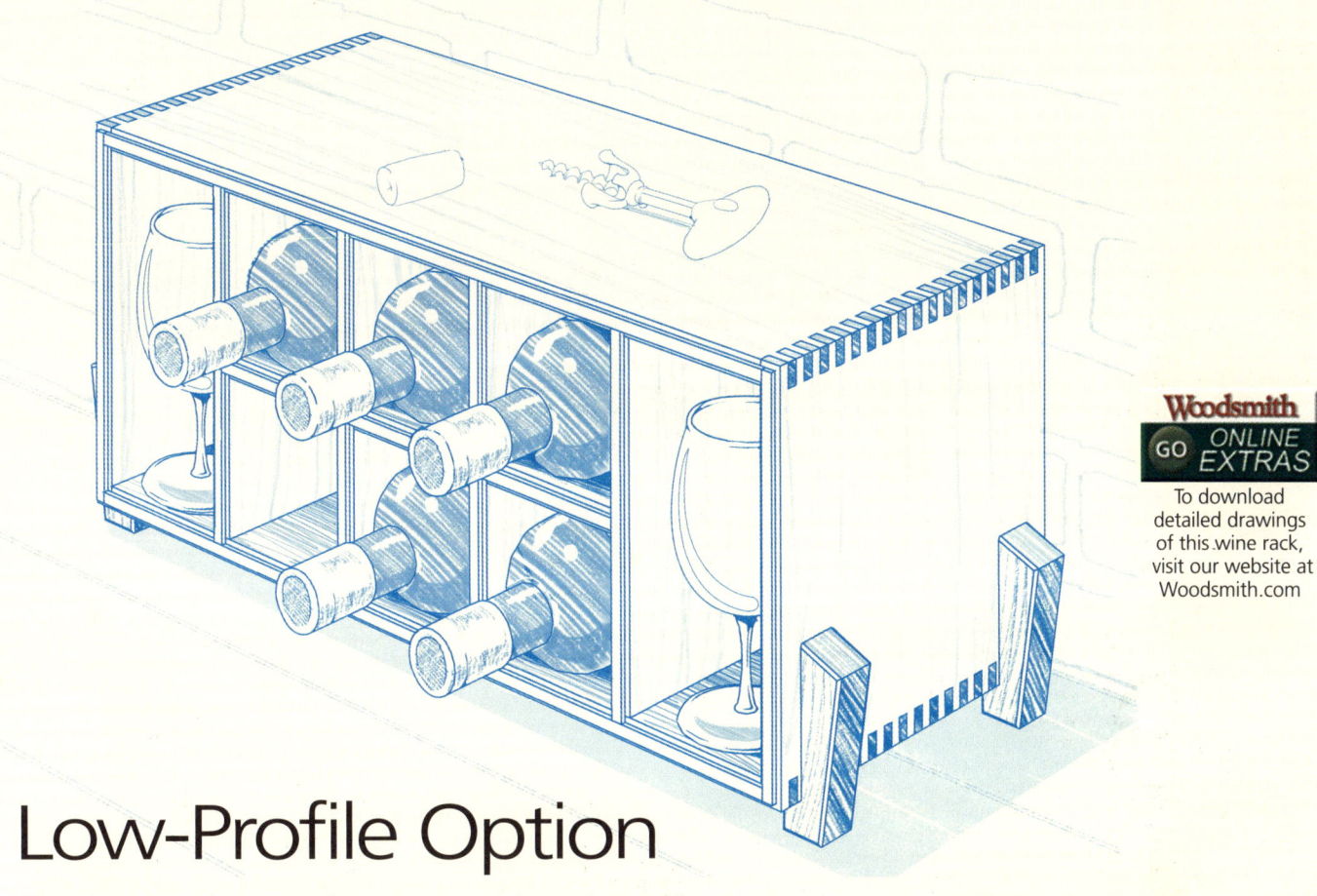

Low-Profile Option

If you have a wider space for a countertop wine rack, then take a look at the modified version shown above. It has room for up to six bottles and several glasses, but it sits lower than the rack in the main article, so it may be a better fit for your space.

For this one, I used the same joinery and details as the square rack. While it's a simple task to modify the plans for this longer rack, our designers have done all the work for you. You'll find the complete drawings for this rack on our website at Woodsmith.com.

Woodsmith GO ONLINE EXTRAS
To download detailed drawings of this wine rack, visit our website at Woodsmith.com

Materials, Supplies & Cutting Diagram

A	Top/Bottom (2)	1/2 x 8 3/4 - 12 1/2	E Edging (1)	1/4 x 1/8 - 84 (rgh.)
B	Sides (2)	1/2 x 8 3/4 - 12 1/2	F Stops (7)	1/4 x 1/2 - 3 1/2
C	Dividers (2)	1/2 x 8 3/4 - 11 3/4	G Feet (4)	1 x 1 1/2 - 3 3/4
D	Shelves (4)	1/2 x 8 3/4 - 3 3/4		

1/2" x 5" - 96" Cherry (Two Boards @ 3.3 Sq. Ft. Each)

1" x 3 1/2" - 24" Wenge (.7 Bd. Ft.)

Designer Series Project

modern
Four Poster Bed

Combine your woodworking skills, straightforward construction, and elegant styling to create a restful retreat for years to come.

At some point, just about every woodworker is called upon to build a bed. Whether it's for yourself, one of your children, or a guest bedroom, finding the right design can be a struggle.

The bed shown in the photo above offers a timeless solution. From the tall tapered posts to the frame-and-panel headboard and footboard, these classic design elements make this bed a showpiece that's at home in just about any bedroom decor.

In addition to the style considerations, you'll appreciate the ease of construction and attention to the overall structure. Since the bed will be moved at some point, you can't use permanent joinery to attach the headboard and footboard to the rails.

Fortunately, modern knockdown hardware makes it possible to accommodate almost any design. I've chosen some very common hardware and assembly ideas for this bed. But there are still plenty of woodworking challenges to keep you busy.

CONSTRUCTION DETAILS

OVERALL DIMENSIONS: 87¾"L x 67"W x 80"H (Queen Size)

CANOPY DETAIL

Canopy rails fit over dowel in end of post

NOTE: Using inexpensive poplar keeps down project cost

Canopy rails fit on posts for easy assembly and removal

Tapers on posts are cut using a table saw sled (refer to page 32)

Posts are glued up from three layers of hardwood

NOTE: Bed is sized for a queen-size mattress

NOTE: Find sources for hardware and finish on page 51

Posts are tapered on inside faces only

Two-piece caps make assembly easy

Cleats on side rails support bed slats

Hardwood bed slats support box spring and mattress

Mortise formed in lamination prior to glueup

Headboard and footboard made up of hardwood frame with plywood panels

Wide caps strengthen rail

BED RAIL FASTENER DETAIL

Stub tenon and groove joinery used for frame and panel assembly

Rails are joined with strong and secure hardware that is easy to disassemble

RAIL CAP DETAIL

Two-piece rail is notched to wrap around dado in posts

Woodsmith.com

Woodsmith

25

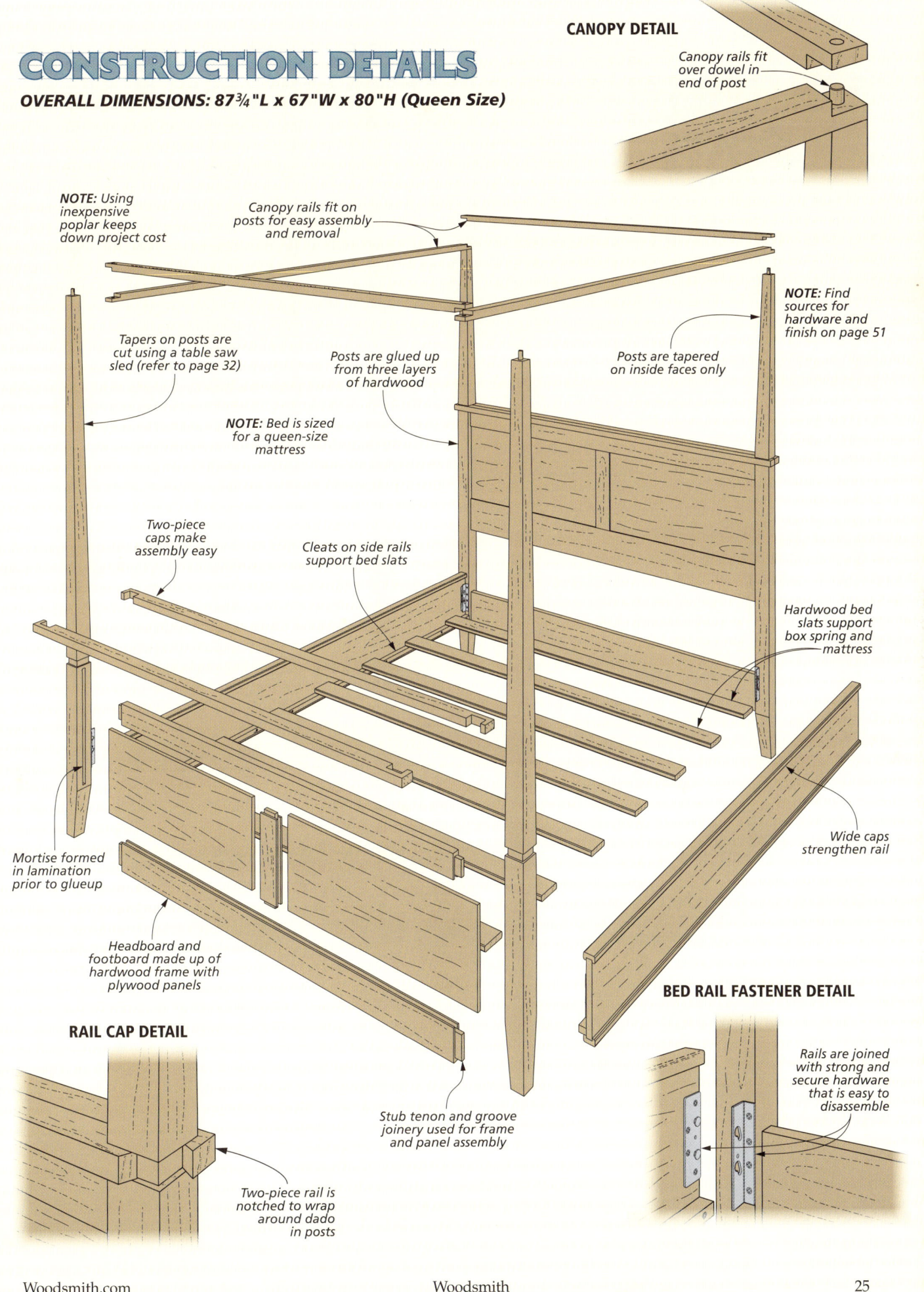

making the POSTS

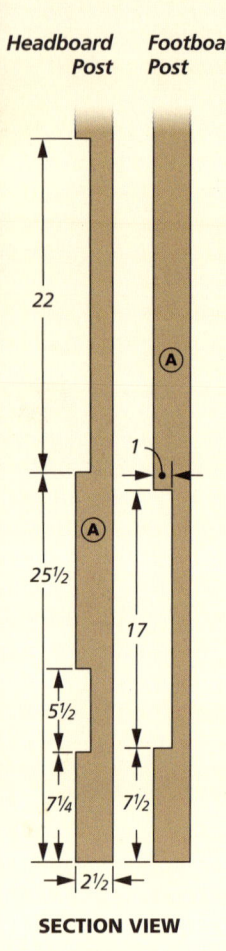

The tapered posts are not only the focal point for the bed, but all the joinery for the headboard and footboard depends on them as well. So they're the first parts to get under way.

If you take a look at the drawings, you can see how I laminated three strips of hardwood to create a blank for each post. Each lamination consists of two 1"-thick outer layers and a notched inner layer. The pieces are ripped to width but left a little long. You'll trim them to final length later.

The inner layer is planed to match the thickness of the plywood you'll use for the headboard and footboard panels. When you glue up the leg blanks, the notches in this layer form mortises that secure the rails and panels.

START WITH THE INSIDE. As you can see in the margin drawing, the inner layers for the headboard and footboard posts are different. The location of the notches accommodates the different configuration of the headboard and

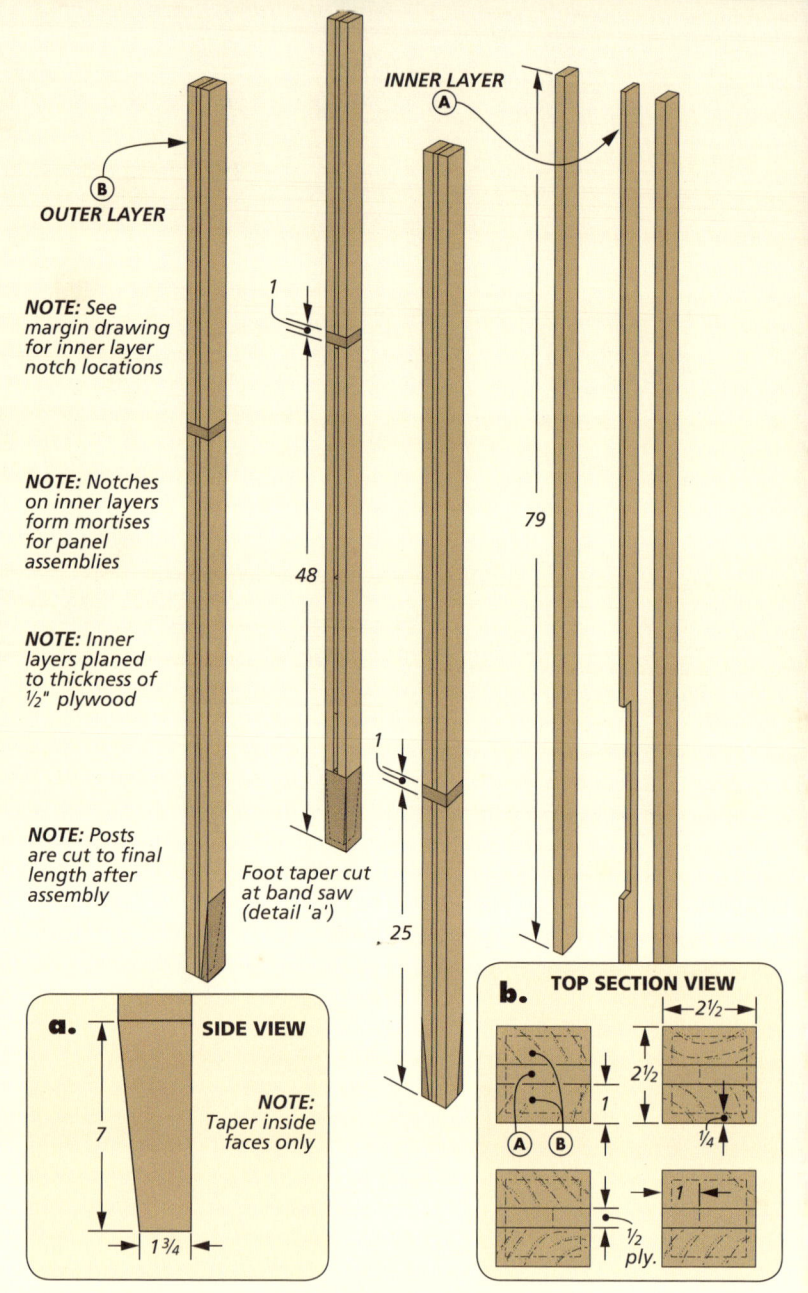

Shop Tip: Glue Layout

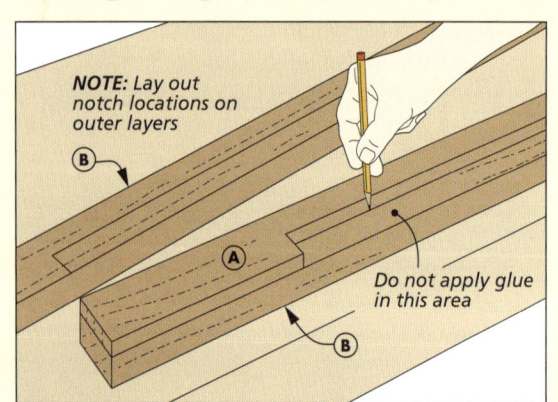

Marking the "No-Glue" Zone. After cutting the notches in the inner layers that form the mortises, trace their outline on the outer pieces.

How-To: Notches & Holes

Gang Cut. Tape each pair of inner layers together to cut the notches that form mortises.

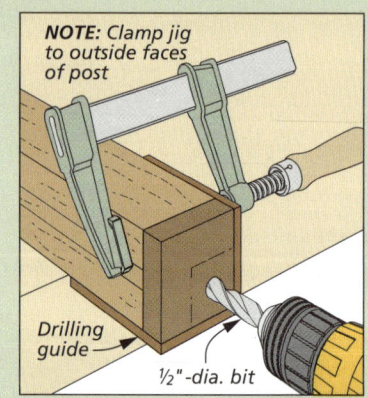

Drilling a Centered Hole. A simple drilling guide registers against the post sides.

footboard assemblies. I started by laying out these notches then clamping each pair together to cut the notches with a dado blade (box on the opposite page.)

MARK BEFORE GLUING. You can also find a shop tip on the opposite page showing how I marked the position of the notches on the outer layers before applying glue. This step helps prevent glue from being applied to the mortises when you assemble the three layers. Finally, spread glue on the pieces and add clamps. Keeping the layers even while you apply the clamps makes it easier to smooth the faces later.

When the glue dries, make a light pass at the jointer. Before cutting the blanks to final length, be sure to measure from the ends of the mortises so each post in the pair will match the other.

LAYOUT. Before you go any further, it's a good idea to do a little layout work. I started by marking the ends of the tapers on the top of each post (right drawing). Then go ahead and mark the center for the dowel that holds the canopy rails in place.

DRILL THE TOPS. After that, you're ready to drill the dowel holes in the top of each post, as you see in detail 'a.' I made a simple drilling guide (right drawing, opposite page). It registers on the outside faces of the posts to locate and guide the bit as you drill.

CUT THE DADOES. Each post has a dado cut on all four faces. This holds the caps on the headboard and footboard. Cutting these is simply a matter of installing a dado blade in the table saw and setting the rip fence as a stop. Then you can use the miter gauge to cut perfect dadoes in the posts, as in the box below. Just be aware when laying them out that the dadoes on the headboard posts are in a different location than those on the footboard posts.

LONG TAPERS. At this point, all that remains is to cut the tapers on the four posts, as you can see in the drawing at right. For this, I built a long tapering jig (refer to Shop Notebook on page 32). The only trick here is making sure to cut the tapers on the *inside* face of each post. And note that the wraparound dado serves as the starting point for the tapers.

TAPERING THE FOOT. Each post also has a small taper on the lower end to form a decorative foot, as shown in detail 'a' on the opposite page. These short tapers can be cut easily on the band saw.

CLEANUP WORK. Now is the time to clean up the four faces of each post. A combination of hand planing and a little sanding takes care of this task.

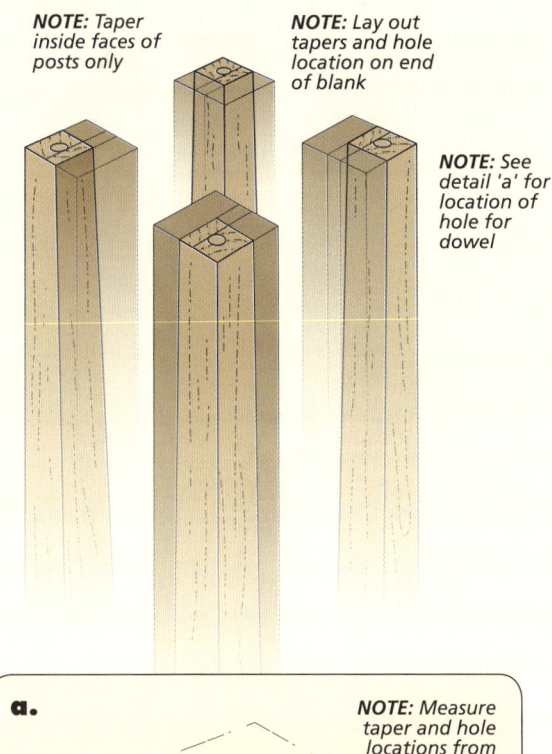

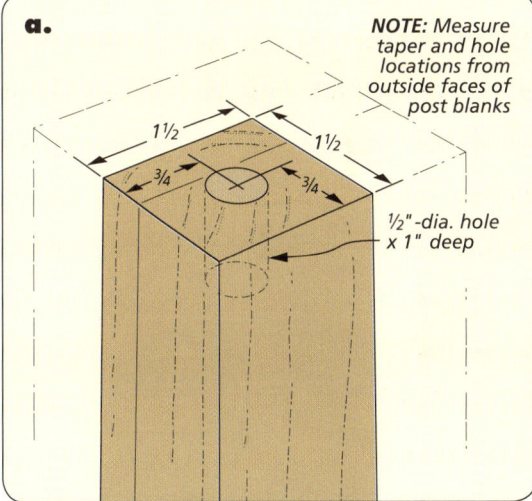

NOTE: Taper inside faces of posts only

NOTE: Lay out tapers and hole location on end of blank

NOTE: See detail 'a' for location of hole for dowel

a.

NOTE: Measure taper and hole locations from outside faces of post blanks

1½   1½
¾   ¾
½"-dia. hole x 1" deep

Dadoes & Tapers

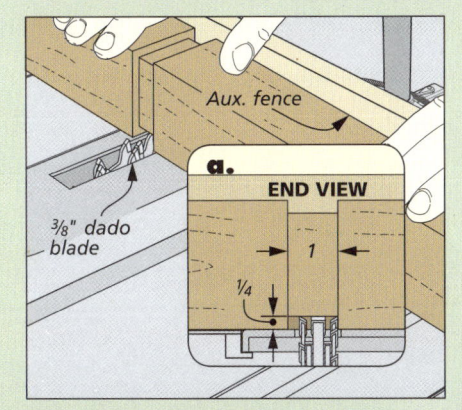

Dadoes for Caps. Use the rip fence as a stop to accurately locate the wraparound dadoes for the caps you'll make later.

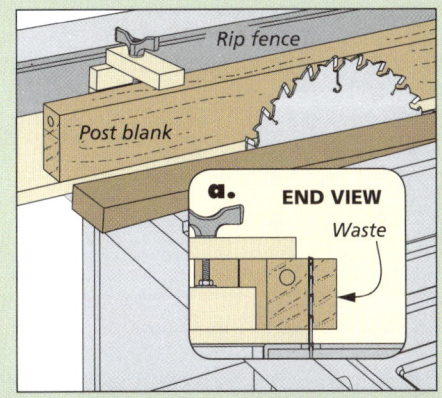

Aux. fence
⅜" dado blade
END VIEW
1
¼

Cutting Long Tapers. Use a taper sled (page 32) and a sharp rip blade to cut the first of the long tapers on the posts.

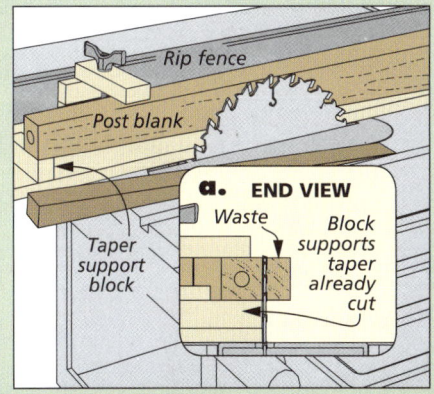

Rip fence
Post blank
END VIEW
Waste

Second Taper. To cut the adjacent taper, you'll need to place a support block under the end of the post.

Rip fence
Post blank
Taper support block
END VIEW
Waste
Block supports taper already cut

creating the PANELS

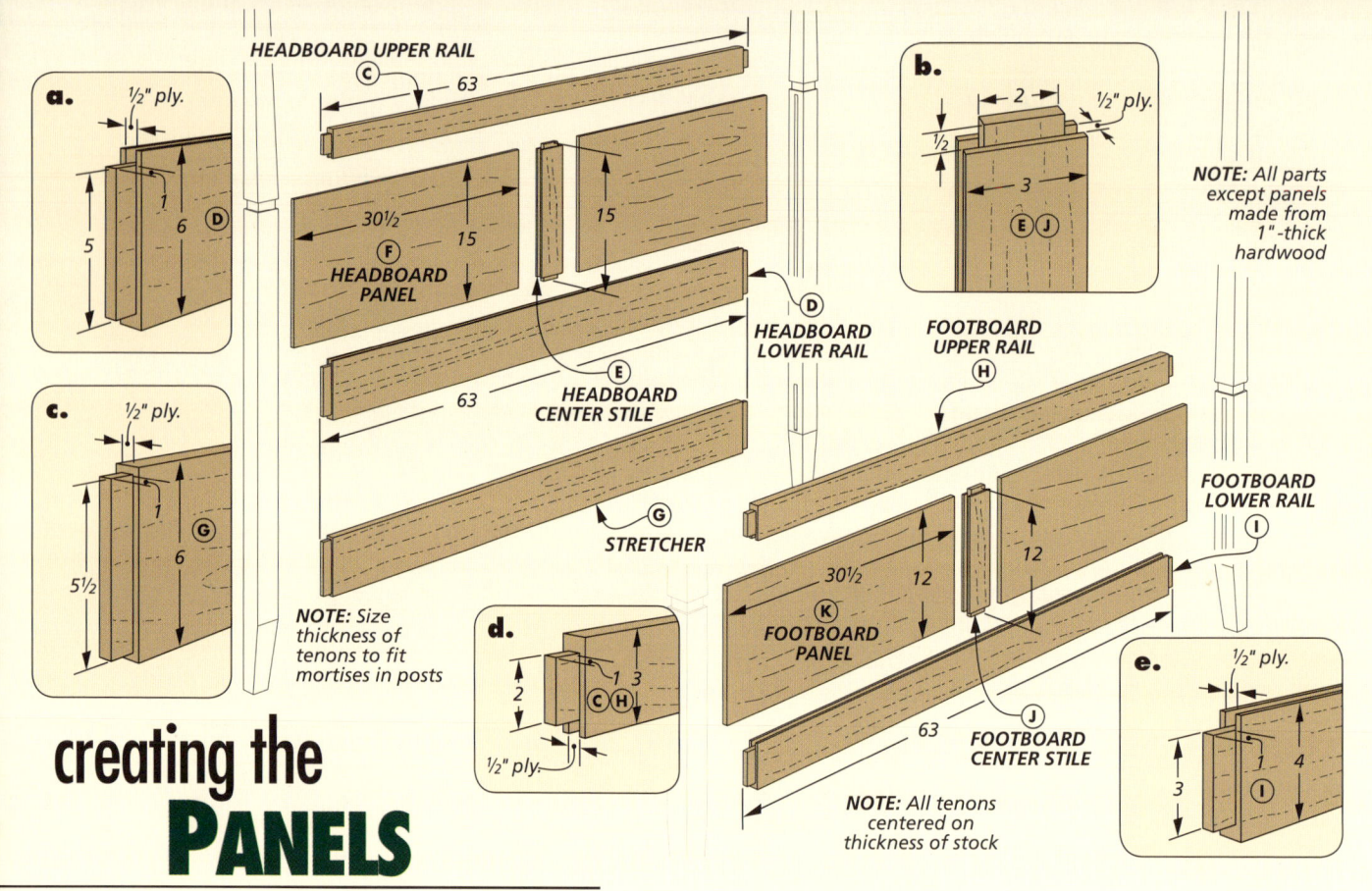

The completed posts form the main supports for the headboard and footboard panel assemblies. Both units consist of a pair of plywood panels and a center stile trapped between a grooved upper and lower rail. After gluing the assemblies to the posts, you'll add a two-piece cap that wraps around the posts. For added strength, the headboard also an additional stretcher near the bottom of the posts.

MAKING PANELS. The building procedure for both of the assemblies is similar. The joinery is the same, so you can use one setup for everything. The only difference is the overall size of the panels.

RAILS & CENTER STILE. I started by cutting the four rails and stretcher to final length and width. The center stile is cut to final width but leave it a little long for now. Then you can concentrate on the joinery (see the box below).

GROOVES. The first step is to install a ⅜" dado blade and cut centered grooves in the rails to hold the panels, as in details 'a,' 'd,' and 'e' above. Next, cut the grooves on both edges of the center stile as shown in detail 'b.'

TENONS. At this point, you're ready to cut the tenons on each piece. Once again, I turned to the table saw and the dado blade for this. You can start by installing an auxiliary fence on the miter gauge to help prevent tearout as you cut the tenons. I like to use the rip fence as a stop, measuring from the fence to the outside edge of the dado blade. Set the blade height by sneaking up on a good

How-To: Make a Groove & Tenon

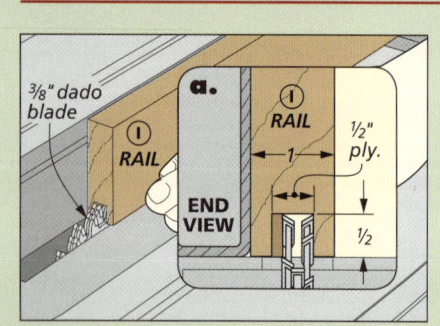

Centered Groove. Use a ⅜"-wide dado blade to cut a centered groove. Flip the workpiece between passes.

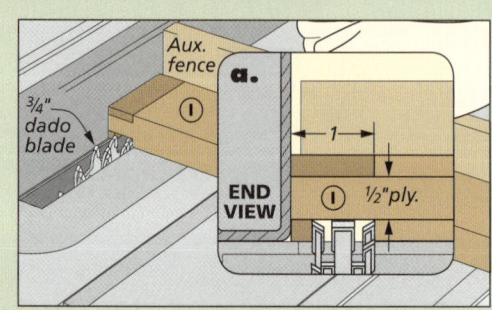

Tenon Length & Thickness. Use the rip fence as a stop to establish the tenon length. Sneak up on the thickness by raising the blade.

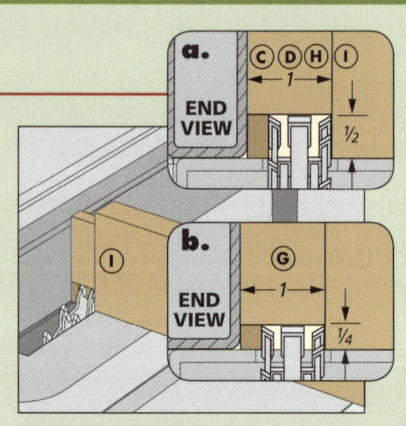

Two Shoulders. Without moving the rip fence, adjust the blade height to cut the edge shoulders.

fit for the grooves you cut earlier. Now you can cut foolproof tenons and be assured they're all exactly the same length and a snug fit. Take some time to study the details on the opposite page for the differing tenon dimensions on each of the pieces.

PANELS. A pair of plywood panels fill the frames. All you need to do is cut them to final size before gluing things up. And now is a good time to cut the stile to length and cut the stub tenons.

ASSEMBLY. Assembling the headboard isn't too difficult, but there are several pieces to get in place before applying the clamps. Dry-assembling first then taking things in stages during glueup makes the process go smoother.

Start by gluing up the rail and panel assemblies. When the glue dries, you can glue each assembly into the posts. Just remember to install the stretcher between the headboard posts while gluing the panel assembly in place.

ADDING THE CAPS. When the glue dries, you're ready to add the two-piece caps. The drawing above and detail 'a' show how each half of the cap is notched to fit into the dadoes you made in the posts earlier. For a less visible joint line, I ripped both pieces from the same board.

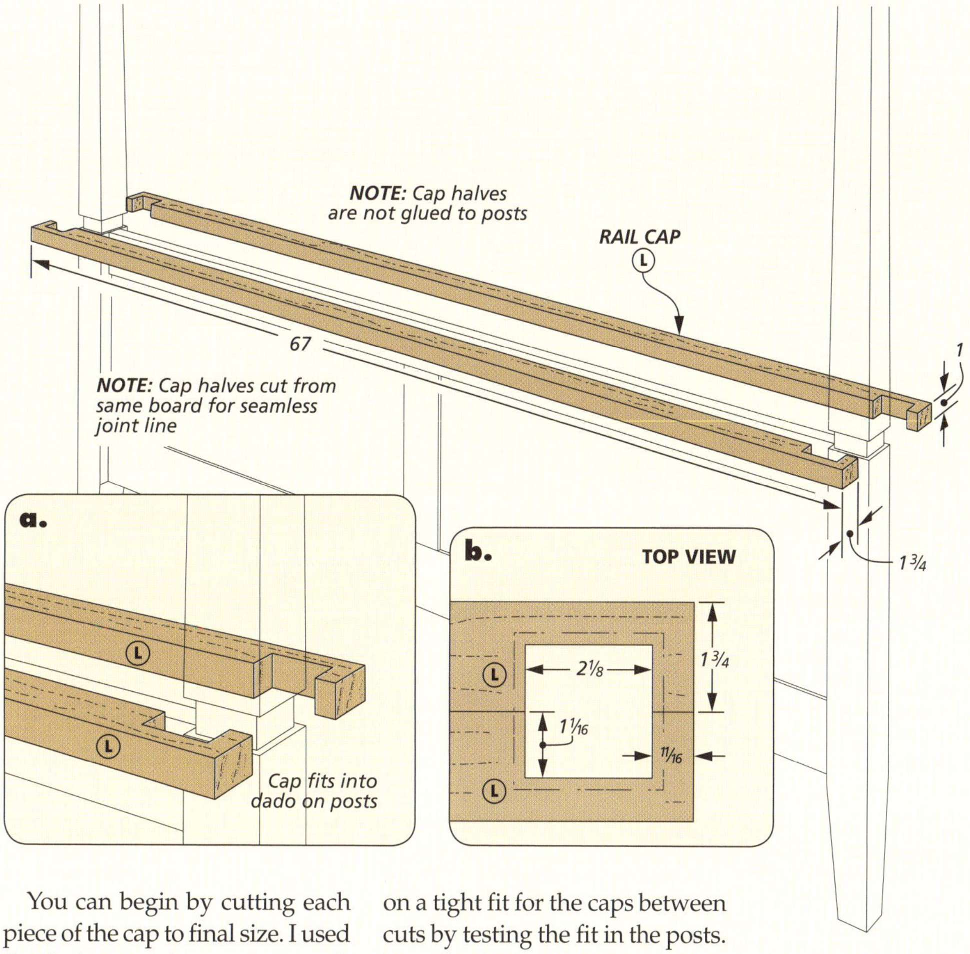

You can begin by cutting each piece of the cap to final size. I used the dadoes on the posts to mark the location of the notches. (Make sure the piece is centered before making the marks.)

The box below shows how I went back to the table saw and used a dado blade to cut the notches. I also taped the pieces together to make sure the notches were perfect mirror images of each other. As before, make sure to attach an auxiliary fence on the miter gauge to prevent tearout on the back side of the cuts. Sneak up on a tight fit for the caps between cuts by testing the fit in the posts. I made the notches extra deep and wide to make them easier to fit around the posts and allow for expansion and contraction.

FINAL ASSEMBLY. The right drawing below shows how to clamp everything together. The cap halves are glued together around the posts and onto the upper rail of the headboard and footboard panels. Short clamps work great for clamping the halves together while longer clamps hold them tight to the upper rail.

NOTE: Cap halves are not glued to posts
RAIL CAP L
67
NOTE: Cap halves cut from same board for seamless joint line
1
1 3/4

a. Cap fits into dado on posts

b. TOP VIEW
2 1/8
1 3/4
1 1/16
11/16

Two-Piece Caps

Rip fence
NOTE: Use double-sided tape to hold cap halves together
a. END VIEW
11/16 2 1/8 1 1/16

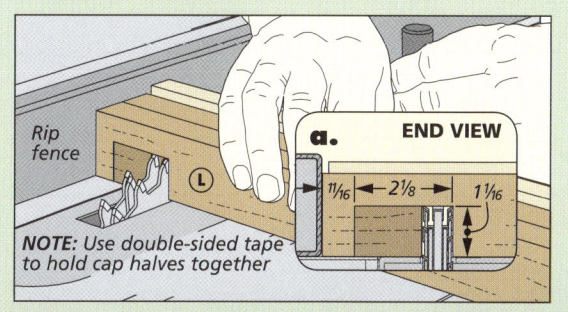

Identical Twins. Clamp the two blanks for the cap rail to the auxiliary miter gauge fence. Use the rip fence to gauge the inside face of the notches.

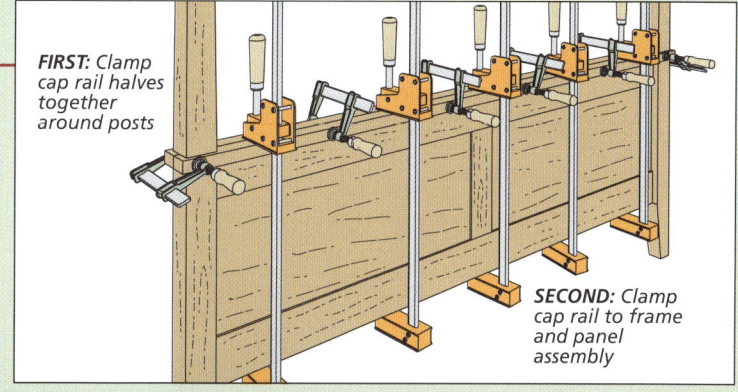

FIRST: Clamp cap rail halves together around posts
SECOND: Clamp cap rail to frame and panel assembly

Multiple Clamps. Apply glue to the inside edges of each cap half. Clamp the pieces around the dadoes in the posts and to the panel rail while clamping them to each other. No glue is needed in the dadoes.

bed & canopy RAILS

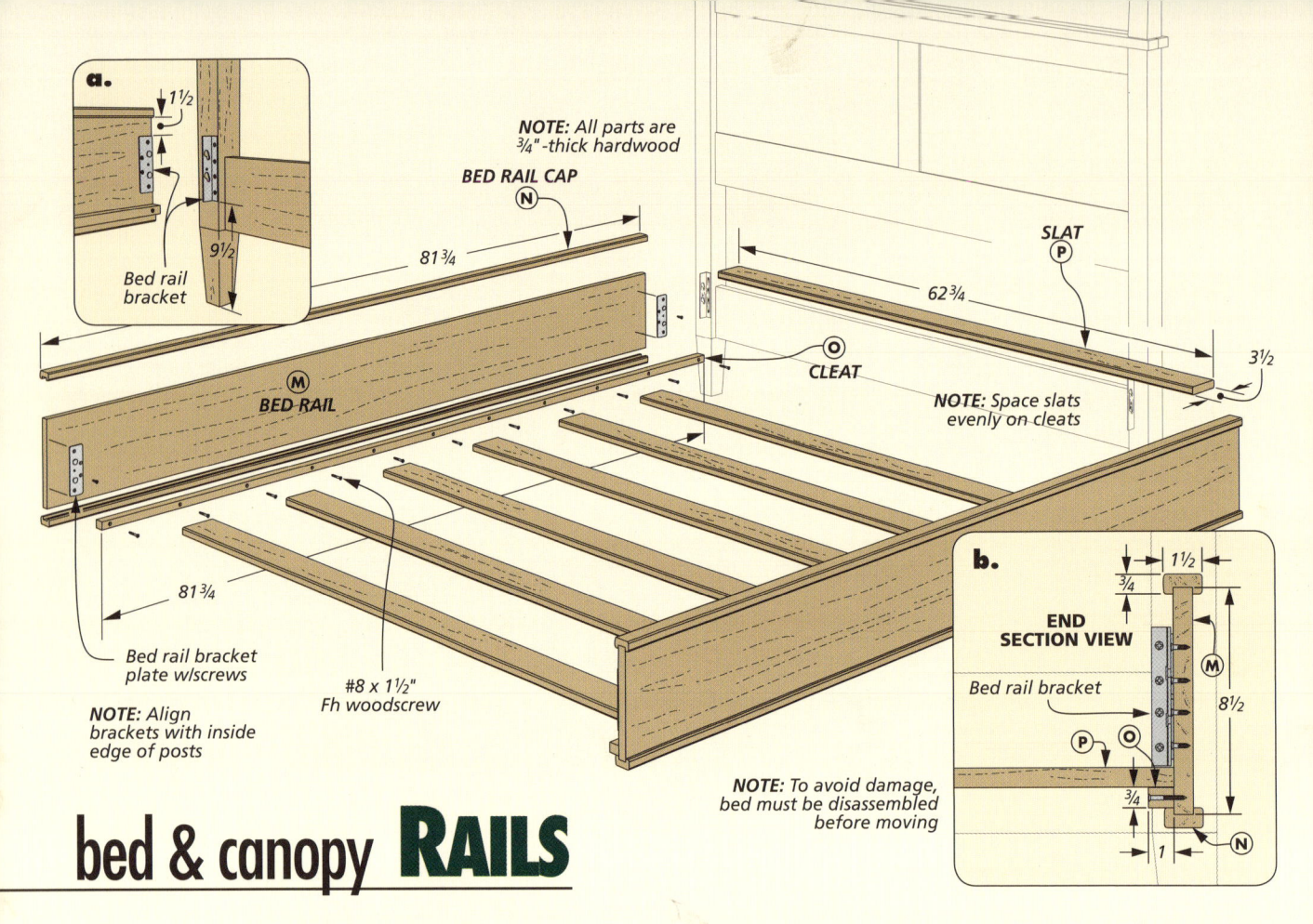

To tie the headboard and footboard together, a pair of bed rails are needed. To give them plenty of strength (like an I-beam), I added caps to the top and bottom edges. After you finish the bed rails and add slats to support the mattress and box spring, the last task is to install a set of canopy rails around the top of the posts.

BED RAILS. You can get busy on the bed rails by selecting a couple of wide, straight-grained boards and cutting them to final size. As you can see in detail 'b,' I also added a pair of caps to each rail. The box below shows how I cut the long grooves and routed roundovers on the corners. After that, you can glue and clamp the caps to the rails.

SUPPORT CLEATS. Detail 'b' also shows the placement of a cleat on each bed rail. The cleat supports the set of slats that hold the box spring and mattress. After you cut both cleats to size, use glue and screws to attach them to the inside of the bed rails.

ADD THE HARDWARE. Now you're ready to attach the bed rail brackets in the corners and assemble the frame. Detail 'a' shows how the pieces fit together. The key here is to make sure the components are installed at exactly the same height on the posts. Spacer blocks will help you locate the parts to ensure level rails.

How-To: Bed Rail Caps & Canopy Rail Ends

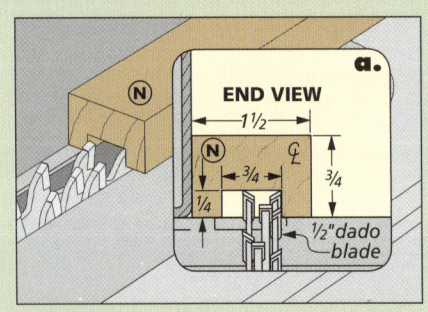

Centered Groove. Use a ½" dado blade to cut a centered groove in the rail caps, flipping the workpiece for each pass.

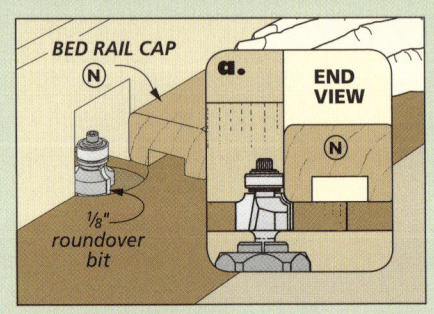

Rout Roundovers. To ease the edges of the rail caps for looks and comfort, make a quick pass at the router table.

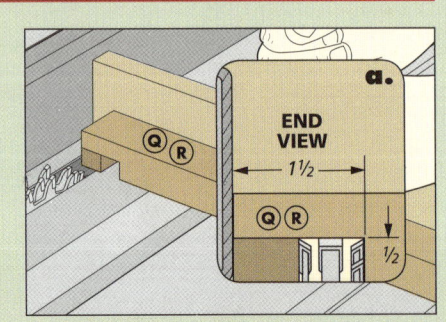

Half-Lap Joinery. Use the rip fence as a stop and make several passes over a dado blade on the canopy rail ends.

30   Woodsmith   No. 195

When everything is in place, test the fit by attaching the bed rails to the headboard and footboard.

SLATS. Finally, you can cut the seven slats that fit between the bed rails. But before you do, it's a good idea to square up the frame and measure the actual distance between the bed rails to make sure the slats slide in easily.

ADDING THE CANOPY RAILS. With the frame set up, the last bit of construction is the set of four canopy rails. These are fit with half-lap joints and secured with a dowel at the top of each post.

I started by installing a short dowel in the hole at the top of each post. Then, after taking a length measurement from the outside face of each pair of posts, I cut the rails to final size. Detail 'a' above shows you the dimensions for the half-lap joinery at the ends.

The holes at the ends of each canopy rail slip over the dowels to lock them in position. (Don't bother gluing them so they can be removed to install curtains.) Some careful layout work is in order to locate the center of each hole. Once the holes are drilled you can place the rails in place.

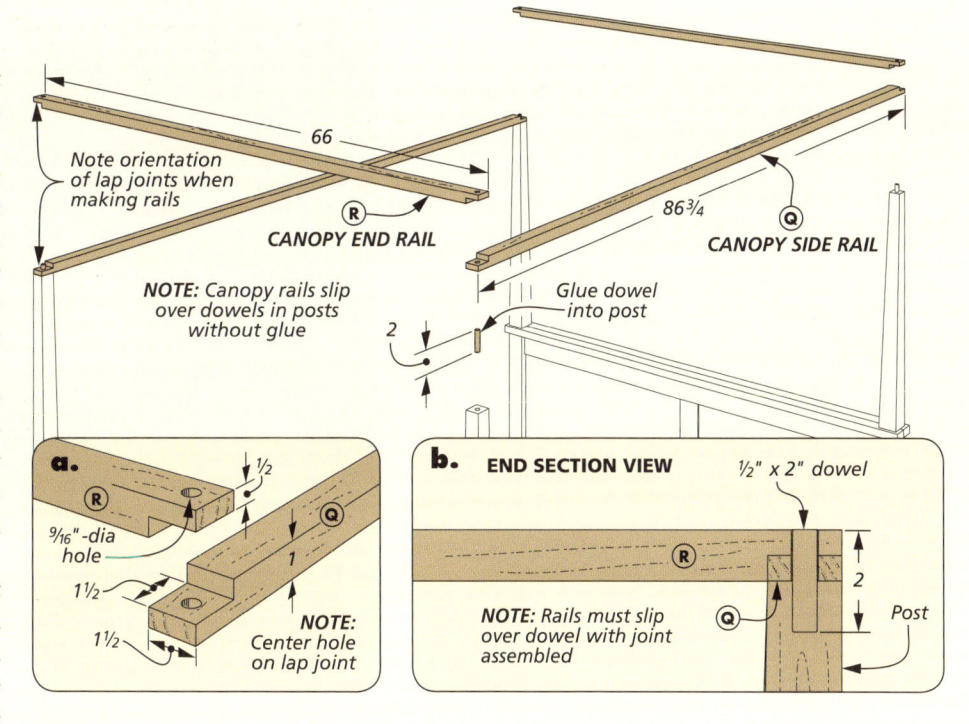

ADD A FINISH. One of the best things about a knock-down bed is that it's easy to finish. I wiped on a couple coats of gel stain and followed up with a couple coats of lacquer. You can find out more in Sources on page 51.

Before nightfall, you can carry the pieces into the bedroom and assemble the bed. Add a decorative curtain and then lie down to relax on this heirloom piece. **W**

Materials, Supplies & Cutting Diagram

A	Inner Layers (4)	1/2 x 2 1/2 - 79
B	Outer Layers (8)	1 x 2 1/2 - 79
C	Headboard Upper Rail (1)	1 x 3 - 63
D	Headboard Lower Rail (1)	1 x 6 - 63
E	Headboard Center Stile (1)	1 x 3 - 15
F	Headboard Panels (2)	1/2 ply. - 15 x 30 1/2
G	Headboard Stretcher (1)	1 x 6 - 63
H	Footboard Upper Rail (1)	1 x 3 - 63
I	Footboard Lower Rail (1)	1 x 4 - 63
J	Footboard Center Stile (1)	1 x 3 - 12
K	Footboard Panels (2)	1/2 ply. - 12 x 30 1/2
L	Caps (4)	1 x 1 3/4 - 67
M	Bed Rails (2)	3/4 x 8 1/2 - 81 3/4
N	Bed Rail Caps (4)	3/4 x 1 1/2 - 81 3/4
O	Cleats (2)	3/4 x 1 - 81 3/4
P	Slats (7)	3/4 x 3 1/2 - 62 3/4
Q	Canopy Side Rails (2)	1 x 1 1/2 - 86 3/4
R	Canopy End Rails (2)	1 x 1 1/2 - 66

- (1 Set) Surface-Mounted Bed Rail Brackets w/Screws
- (4) 1/2"-dia. x 2" Dowel
- (22) #8 x 1 1/2" Fh Woodscrews

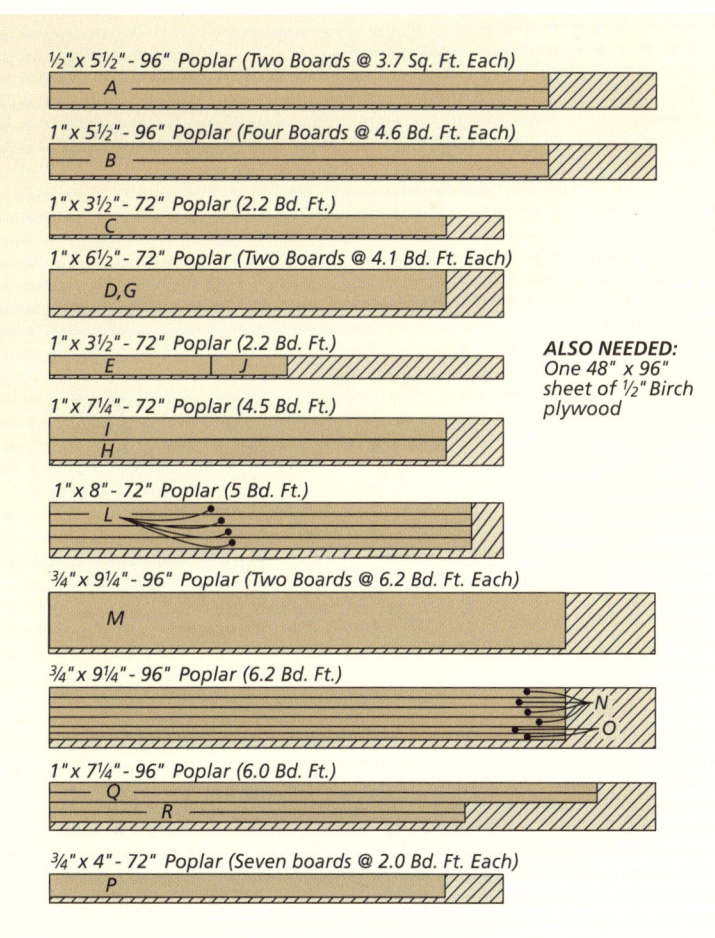

ALSO NEEDED: One 48" x 96" sheet of 1/2" Birch plywood

tips from our shop

SHOP NOTEBOOK

Taper Sled

When it came to tapering the posts for the bed on page 24, I faced a couple of challenges. One was the sheer length of the posts. And the other was the fact that the posts for the headboard and the footboard have different length tapers. To solve both of these issues, I made the taper sled you see in the photo at right and drawings below. The sled supports the entire length of the post and is adjustable for the two lengths of tapers.

BUILDING THE SLED. The sled consists of a ½" plywood base, an end stop, and a pair of hold-downs. As you can see in the drawing below and detail 'a,' the hold-downs are made up of a two-piece stop and a clamp block. They're attached to the base with a carriage bolt, hex nut, plastic wing knob, and a pair of washers.

If you take a look at the drawing in the margin at left, you'll notice that there are two holes in the base for attaching the rear hold-down. This is because the position of the hold-down changes in between cutting the headboard posts and the footboard posts.

To use the sled, position the rip fence so the edge of the base butts up against the saw blade. Then place the first leg in the sled and tighten down the hold-downs.

CUT THE TAPERS. To avoid bogging down the motor on my table saw, I cut each taper in two passes, raising the blade in between. After cutting the first taper, you'll need to add a block under the end of the leg to support it while cutting the second taper.

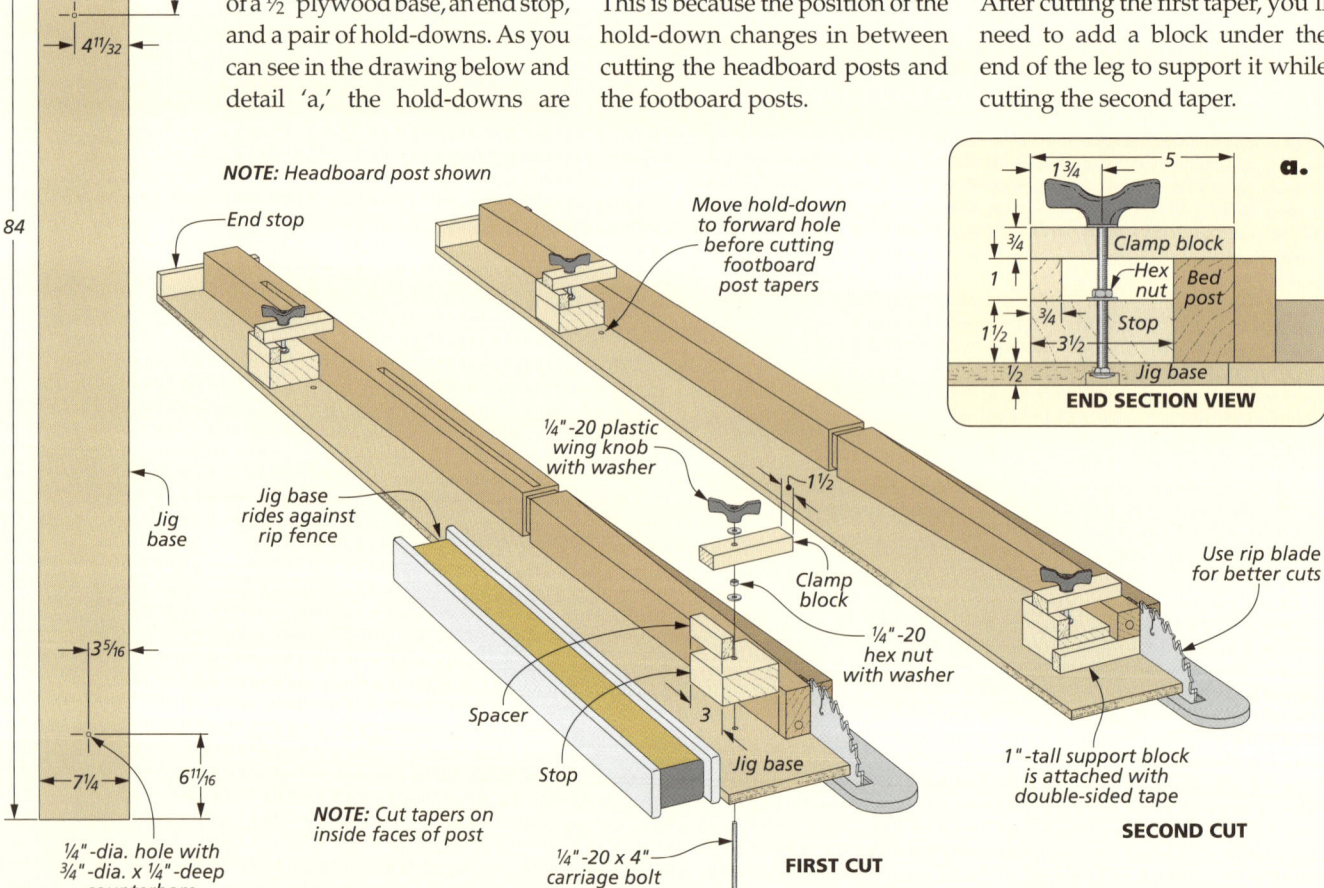

Beveled Feet

One of the distinctive features of the step-back cupboard on page 34 are the beveled feet. On the front of the cupboard, these feet are incorporated into the face frame stiles. But on the sides and back, they're made by cutting out a large notch in the ends of the sides and the back rail. I made these cutouts using a jig saw and a router.

CUT. To begin, you can cut out the bulk of the waste with a jig saw, as shown in Figure 1. The key here is to remain just shy of the layout line. I made the two end cuts first, followed by the longer cut across the width.

SMOOTH. To clean up the saw marks left by the jig saw, I used a router and a flush trim bit (Figure 2). Here, I clamped a board on the underside of the workpiece, along the layout line of the cutout. This gives the bearing of the flush trim bit something to ride against. You can use the same technique for the angled sides of the cutout. Lastly, you can square up the corners with a chisel.

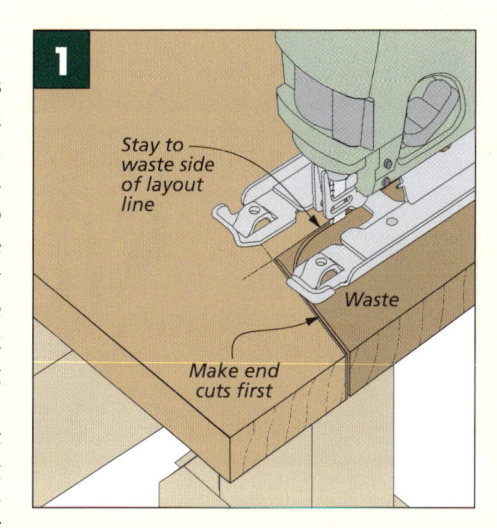

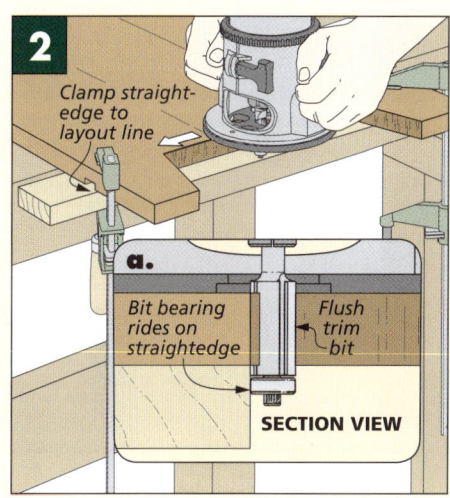

Cut Nail Technique

To add to the rustic look of the step-back cupboard, I used cut nails and brads. But the tapered shape of these nails can act like a wedge, sometimes splitting the wood. This is particularly the case when nailing near the end of a board (Figure 1).

To minimize splitting, I took a couple of precautions. First, I drilled a pilot hole for each nail. And second, I made sure to orient the nails so the heads run parallel with the grain (Figure 2).

▲ Cut nails are tapered for better holding power.

Stopped Chamfers

The upper stiles of the step-back cupboard feature stopped chamfers. For the best appearance, you'll want to make sure that the chamfers start and stop at the same points on each stile.

To do this, I marked the ends of the chamfers on the stiles. (Note: The distance from the end of the chamfer to the end of the stile is different at the top and bottom. So you'll need to lay out right and left stiles.) Next, I marked the centerline of the chamfer bit on the fence of my router table.

To rout the chamfers, simply pivot the stile into the rotating bit so that the layout line on the workpiece lines up with the line on the fence (Figure 1). When you reach the end of the chamfer, pivot the workpiece away from the fence (Figure 2).

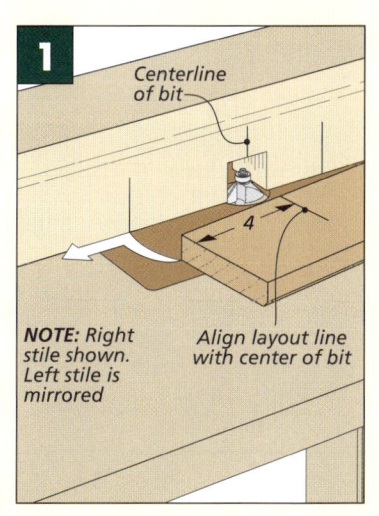

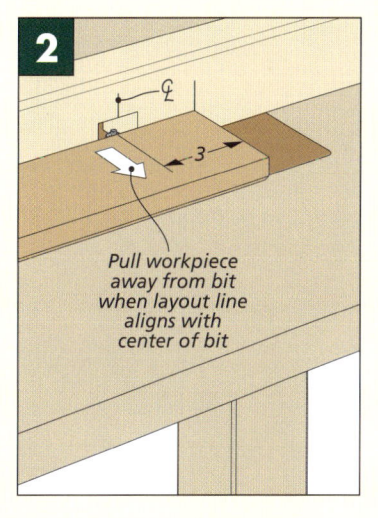

The router bit leaves the ends of the chamfers asymmetrical. So I sanded the chamfer ends to even them up (photo in margin). **W**

▲ A dowel wrapped with sandpaper can be used to smooth out the end of each chamfer.

Heirloom Project

rustic Step-Back Cupboard

The classic design of this practical project is matched by its traditional construction.

Simple "farmhouse" furniture has an unpretentious charm that's very attractive in these complicated times. This classic step-back cupboard hits the mark square on. As you can clearly see, the ornamentation is simple and subtle — nothing the least bit fussy. And the practicality is unmistakable. The deep lower section and the open upper section offer abundant storage and display options.

However, despite its humble design, I think you'll be pleasantly surprised by the interesting woodworking involved. The all solid-wood construction is definitely old-school. A beadboard back, "sawtooth" shelf supports, and a mortise and tenon raised panel door — it's all here. I even used inexpensive, knotty red alder lumber, exposed square nails, and an "aged" finish to add authenticity. My guess is that you'll be sorry to see this project end.

▲ A recessed shelf in the lower section of the cupboard creates versatile, two-tier storage for all sorts of household items.

CONSTRUCTION DETAILS

OVERALL DIMENSIONS: 19¼"D x 30 5/16"W x 76¾"H

NOTE: Construction is all solid wood

Beadboards used for cornice shelf

Beaded back boards installed with floating ship-lap joints

Square nails reinforce case joinery

NOTE: Cornice added to case as an assembly

Adjustable shelf cleats

"Sawtooth" shelf supports

Stopped chamfer routed on inner edge of stile

Door built with haunched mortise and tenon joinery

Raised panel shaped on table saw

Simple chamfered molding

Lower shelf supported by fixed cleats

Traditional cabinet latch

H-style surface-mounted hinges

Stepped sides glued up with easy two-stage technique

NOTE: Traditional sawtooth supports and cleats allow adjustment of upper shelves

NOTE: See page 51 for finishing information

NOTE: Cupboard is built from economical red alder lumber

▲ Square cut nails and an "aged" finish add to the rustic look of the cupboard.

SIDE SECTION VIEW

"Sawtooth" shelf supports

Shelf

Adjustable shelf cleats fit into bevel notches

FRONT SECTION VIEW

Cornice cap

Beadboard shelf provides additional display space

Cornice base

Rake trim fits into angled grooves in cornice base and cap

Woodsmith.com

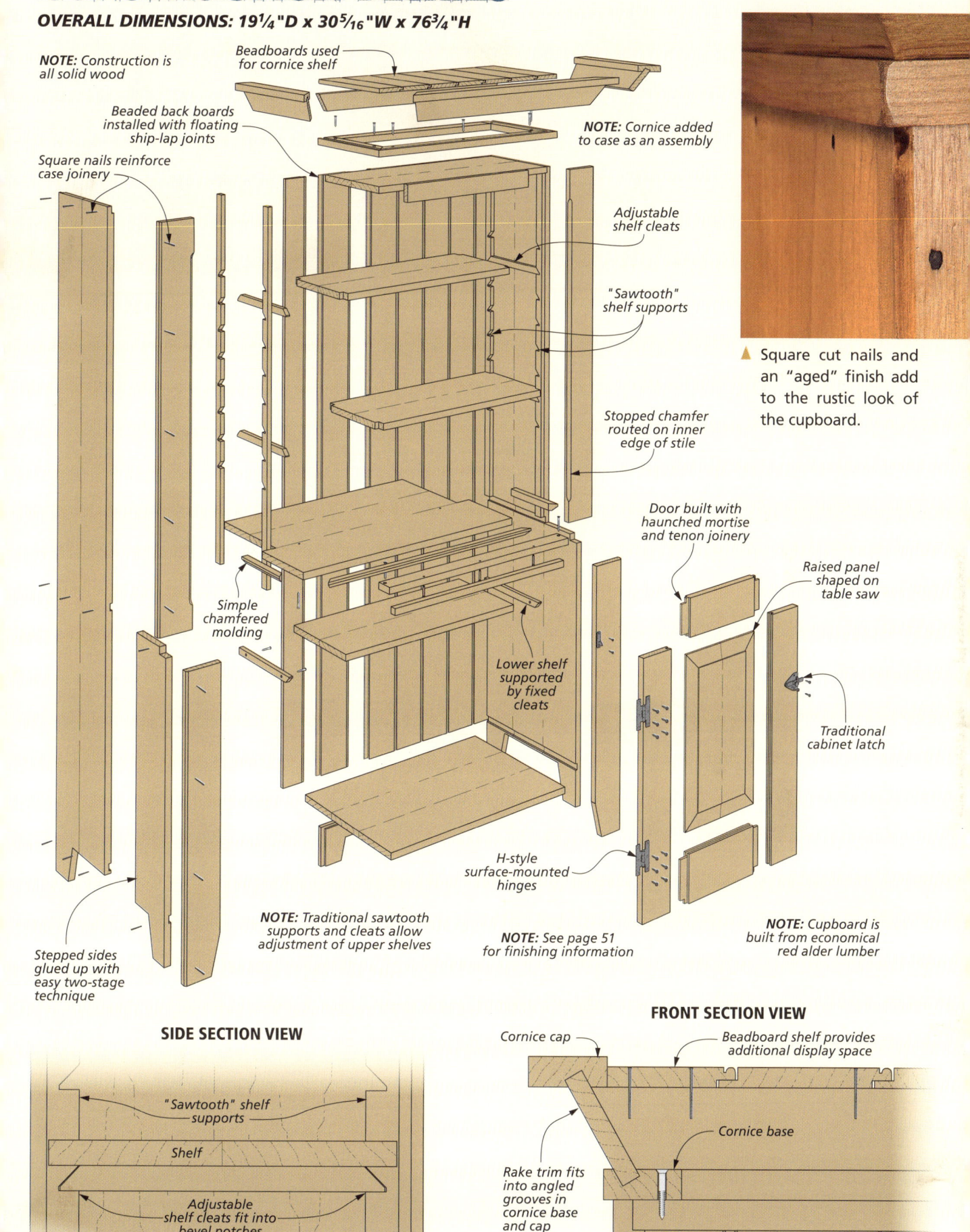

Woodsmith

35

building the CASE

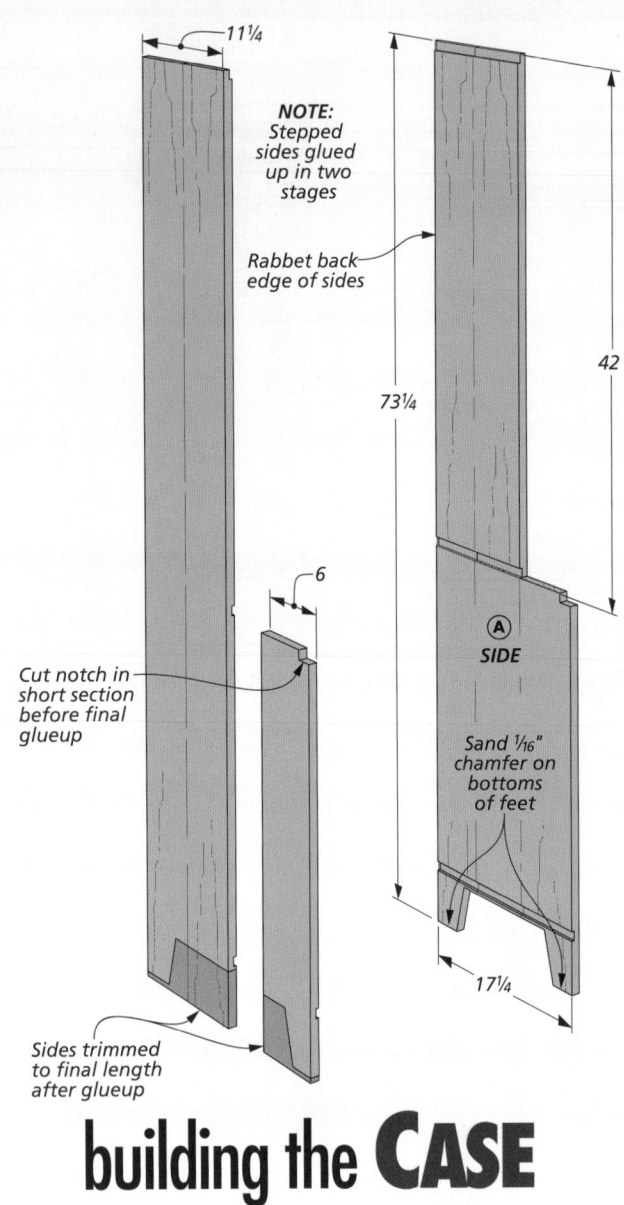

The only real challenge to building the case is creating the "stepped" sides. But this is a lot easier than you might think. The trick is to make extra-long tall and short sections for each side. Then after squaring up the top end of each side section, you just glue them together in the proper alignment and trim the side to final length.

TWO SECTIONS. I started by gluing up oversized panels for the tall sections. I cut the narrower short sections to width from a single board, but depending on your lumber, you may have to glue these up as well. Once the clamps come off, trim them to final width and square up the top ends.

NOTCHES. The How-To box below shows the next couple of steps. First, before gluing up the two sections, you need to cut a notch in the front upper corner of each short section (detail 'c'). These notches hold the divider rail that ties the two sides together and anchors the divider. A dado blade will handle the job.

GLUEUP. With the notches cut, you're ready to glue the tall and short sections together. To be certain the alignment was accurate, I measured down from the top of

How-To: Glue Up the Sides

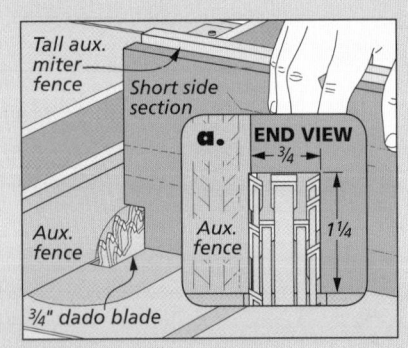

Divider Rail Notches. Bury a dado blade in an auxiliary rip fence to cut a notch in the short sections.

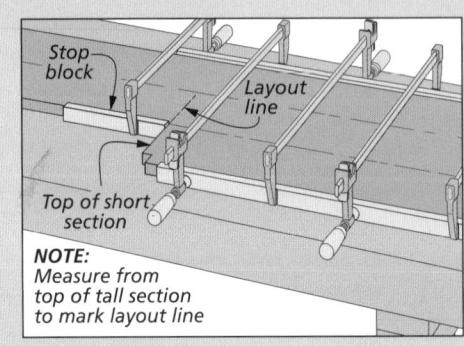

Final Glueup. A stop block clamped to the tall section ensures proper alignment of the top end of the short section.

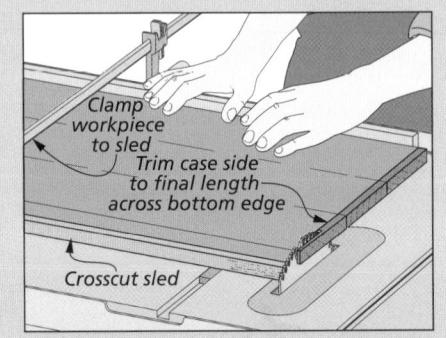

Finished Length. With the two sections glued together, cut the side to length by trimming the bottom.

36   Woodsmith   No. 195

each tall panel and then clamped a stop block at my mark. Then you can apply glue and clamps, making sure the short panel is snug to the stop block.

FINAL LENGTH. When the clamps are back in the rack, cut the sides to final length by trimming the bottoms. I used my crosscut sled on the table saw. A circular saw guided by a straightedge is another good option.

JOINERY. Cutting the joinery for the top, divider, and bottom comes next. The top fits into rabbets in the sides while the divider and bottom are held in dadoes. You'll also need to cut a rabbet along the back edge of each side to hold the back. A look at the How-To box below and the details on the opposite page will fill you in on the specifics.

FEET. The final step is to cut out the beveled feet (detail 'd,' opposite page). You'll note that the front foot is narrower than the back foot. Adding the face frame stiles will make up this difference. After laying out the profile, I removed the waste with a jig saw, and then smoothed the cuts with a router and straightedge. (For more on this, turn to page 33.)

THE PANELS. Now you can get to work on the top, divider, and bottom panels. The top and bottom are straightforward. I simply glued up oversized panels and then trimmed them to final size.

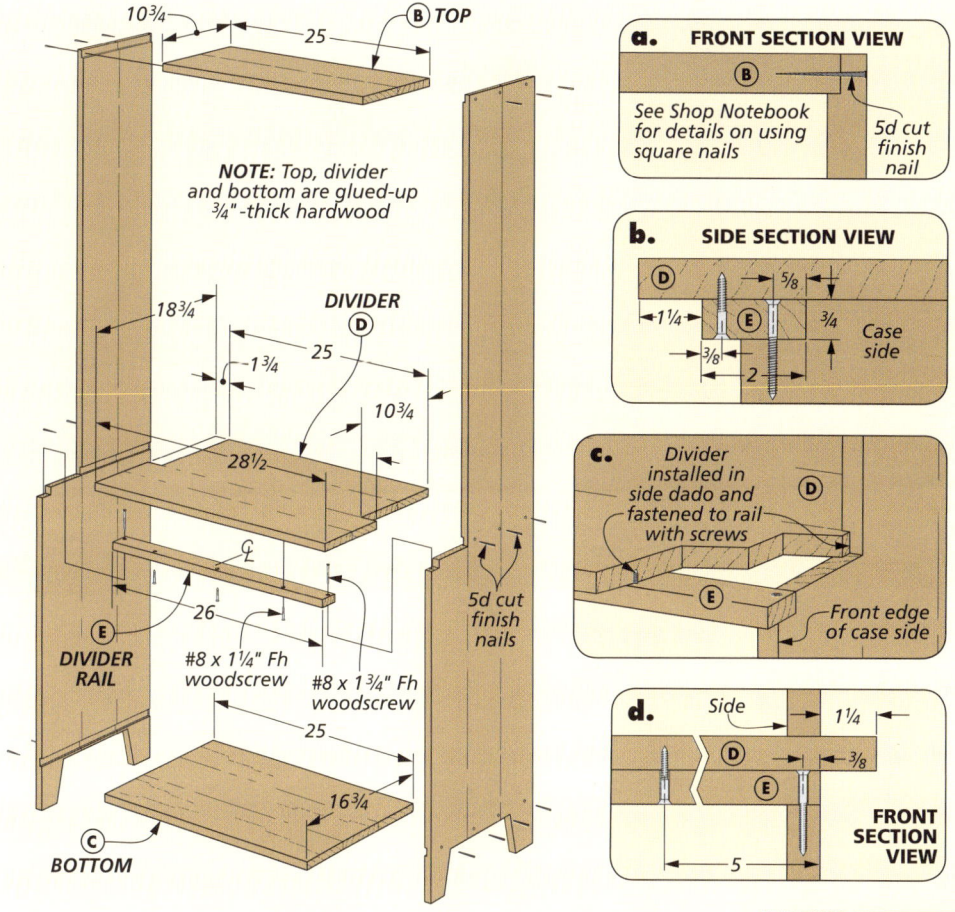

The divider is different. As you can see above, the front section overhangs both sides of the case. Like the sides, you can easily create the offsets by gluing up the panel from pre-sized sections.

ASSEMBLY. After cutting the divider rail to size and drilling holes for the screws, you can begin the assembly. To get started, I set one case side across sawhorses, spread glue in the top rabbet and bottom dado, and inserted those panels.

The bottom is set flush to the front of the sides. After adding the second side, I clamped up the case before installing the divider rail. Finally, spread glue in the front portion of the middle dadoes and slide the divider into place.

I let the glue dry and then removed the clamps before driving the nails and installing the screws through the rail. You'll find a primer on using square nails in Shop Notebook (page 33).

▲ For details on cleaning up the jig saw cuts, turn to page 33.

Rabbets & Dadoes

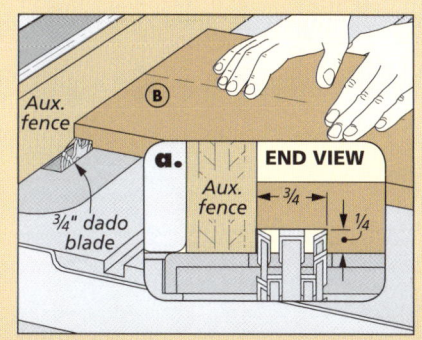

Top Rabbets. *You'll want to have extra support to the left of the saw when rabbeting the tops of the sides.*

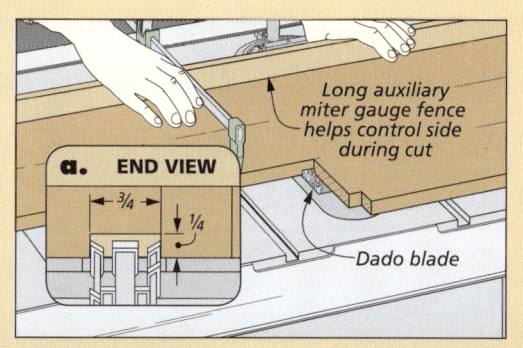

Divider Dadoes. *I clamped the side to a long auxiliary miter gauge fence when cutting the dadoes for the divider.*

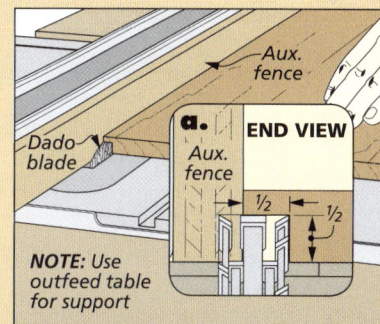

Back Rabbets. *Bury the dado blade in an auxiliary rip fence to cut the deep rabbets that hold the back boards.*

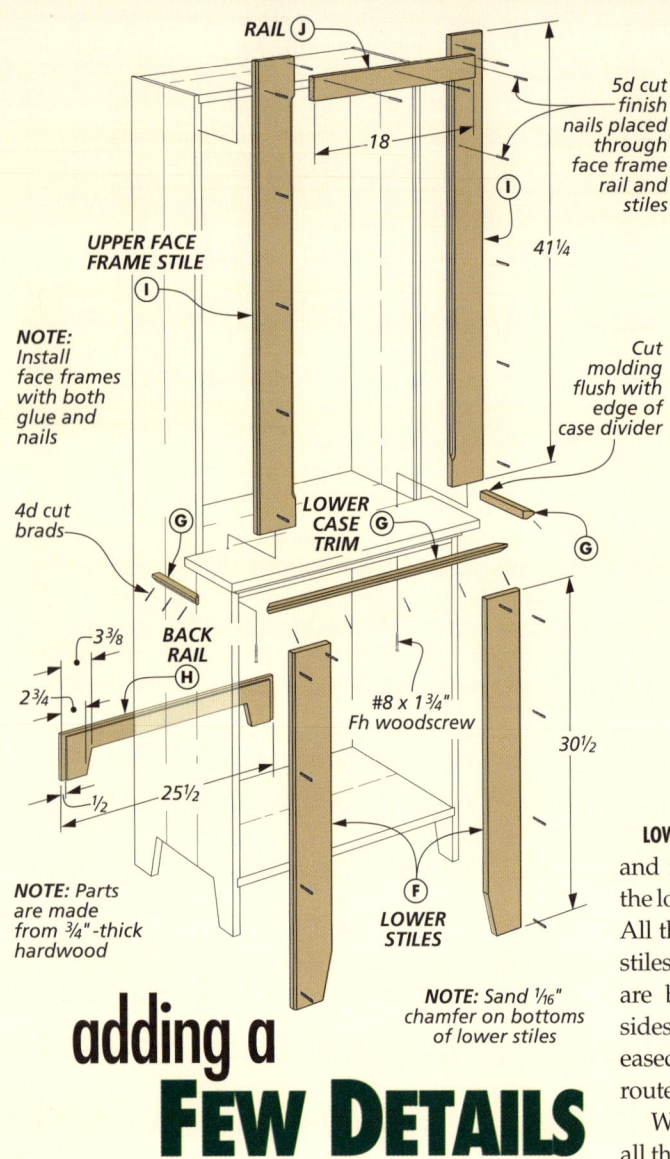

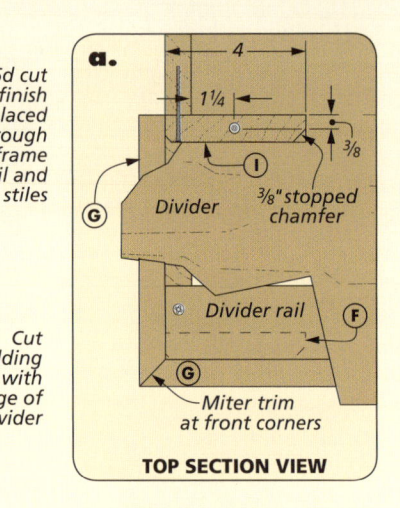

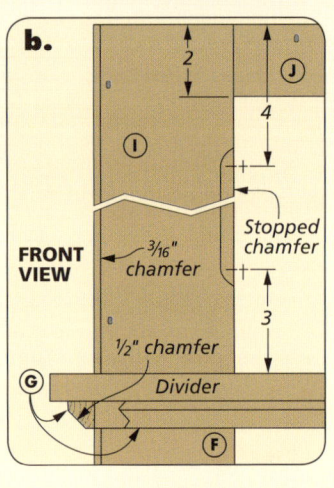

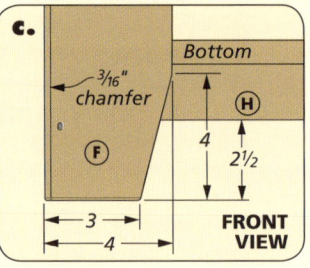

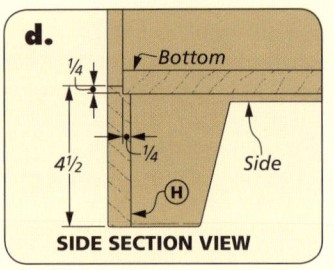

adding a FEW DETAILS

Now you can begin to add some of the important exterior and interior details. The face frames and a bit of molding come first, followed by the shelving.

LOWER STILES. I started by fitting and installing the face frame to the lower section of the cupboard. All this consists of are two, wide stiles. The lower ends of the stiles are beveled to match the case sides. And the outside edges are eased with a small chamfer at the router table (detail 'c').

With the stiles cut to size and all the details completed, you can glue them to the case. And again, I added square nails.

TRIM. To dress up the case and beef up the ends of the divider, I made some chamfered molding to install beneath the divider. The box below shows how to make the trim on the table saw. Then I mitered pieces to wrap the front and sides. The back ends of the side pieces are cut flush with the divider (details 'a' and 'b').

BACK RAIL. To finish up the lower section of the cupboard, I installed a rail across the back. The ends and top edge of this piece are rabbeted so that it will fit between the sides and lap over the bottom panel, as shown in the How-To box below. The rail is shaped to mirror the foot profile of the front and sides. Once ready, it can be glued in place.

How-To: Make the Molding & Back Rail

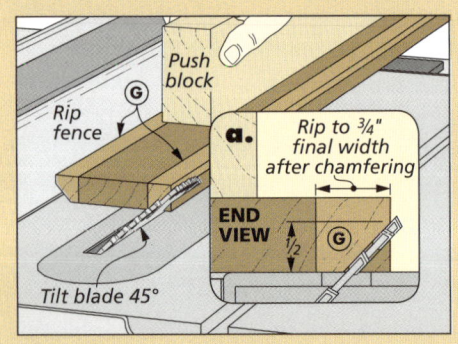

Chamfered Molding. Cut a 45° chamfer on both edges of a wide blank, and then rip the finished molding free.

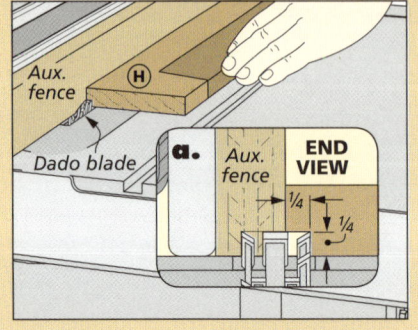

Top Edge. I used a dado blade buried in an auxiliary rip fence to cut a rabbet along the top edge of the back rail.

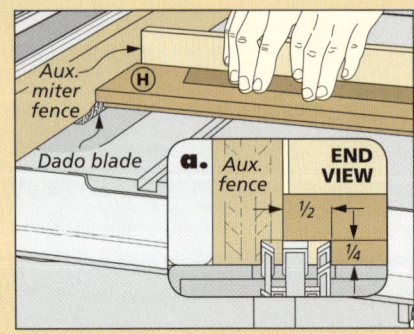

End Rabbets. After adjusting the rip fence, use the miter gauge to rabbet the ends of the back rail.

38   Woodsmith   No. 195

UPPER FACE FRAME. Now comes the upper face frame. It's made up of two, wide stiles and an upper rail. The stiles feature a narrow chamfer on the outer edge and a wider, stopped chamfer on the inner edge. There's no joinery to factor in. The upper rail is merely cut to fit between the stiles.

After cutting the stiles to width and length, you can take them to the router table for the chamfers. First, I routed the outer chamfers, then I reset the height of the bit for the stopped chamfers. Note that the chamfers stop 4" from the top but only 3" from the bottom. Marks on the stiles and fence will show you where to start and stop the cuts, as explained on page 33 of Shop Notebook.

When the stiles are completed, they can be glued and nailed to the case. In addition, I pinned the lower ends with screws installed through the divider. With both stiles in place, the upper rail can be added to the case.

THE SHELVES

The upper section of the case holds two adjustable shelves while the lower section has one fixed shelf. The lower shelf is simply supported by a pair of cleats screwed to the case sides.

SAWTOOTH SUPPORTS. The traditional support system I used for the adjustable shelves is a little more interesting. These shelves are also supported by cleats. But here the cleats are installed between pairs of notched "sawtooth" supports (main drawing and detail 'a'). To adjust the height of a shelf, you simply use a different set of notches.

The box below shows how to make the supports. To ensure that the beveled notches were aligned, I ganged the strips with masking tape before making the cuts.

When the supports are completed, glue one into each corner of the case. The rear supports should be flush with the shoulders of the rabbets in the sides, as shown in detail 'a.'

CLEATS. Now you can make cleats to fit between the supports as well as a pair for the lower shelf. I cut the upper cleats to a length slightly less than the spread of the notches and then beveled both ends. You want an easy fit between the supports. The lower cleats are simply cut to size, beveled on one end, and then fastened with screws.

SHELVES. The three shelves are the same overall size. However, the two upper shelves need to be notched to fit around the supports. After cutting the shelves to size, a dado blade will handle the notches (detail 'c').

Sawtooth Shelf Supports

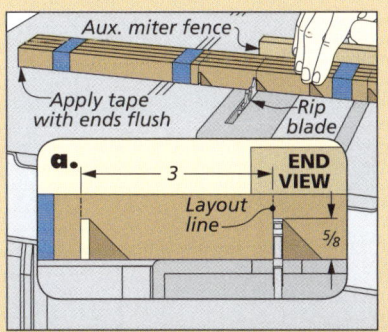

Square Cuts. Lay out the notches, then use a rip blade to begin removing the waste with square cuts.

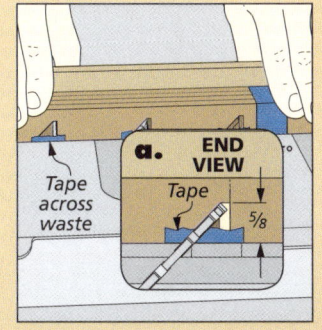

Bevel Cuts. Masking tape will control the waste pieces during the bevel cuts.

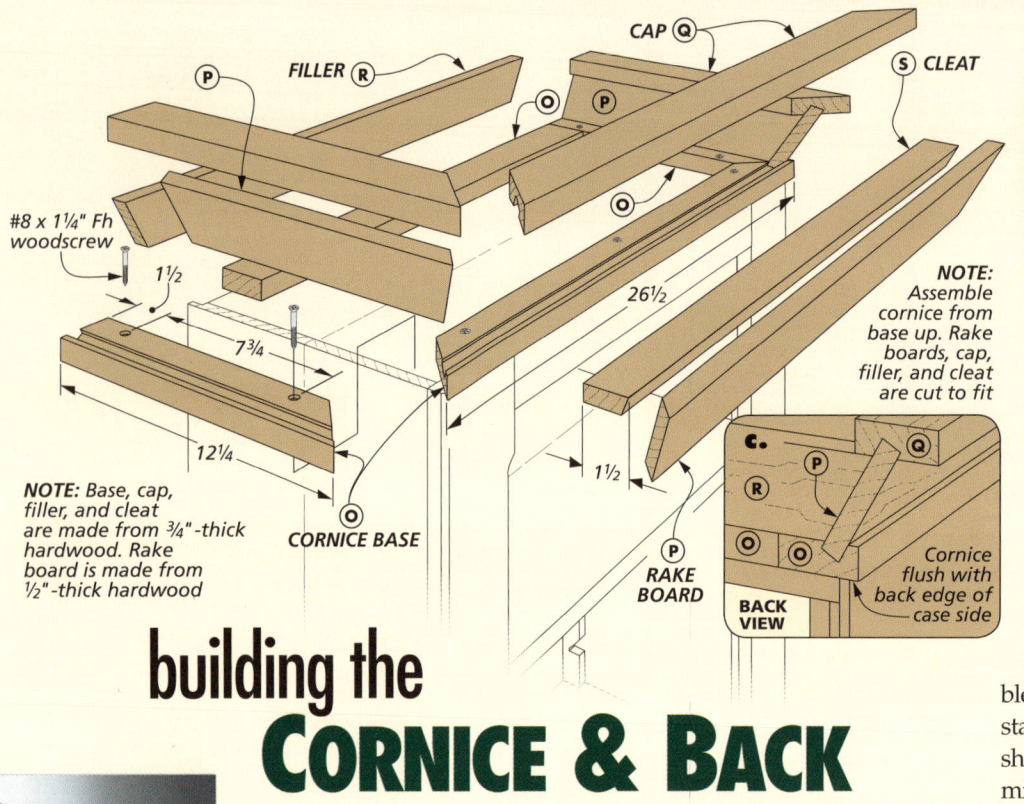

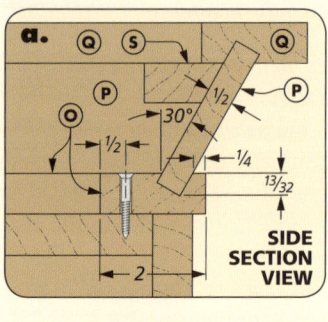

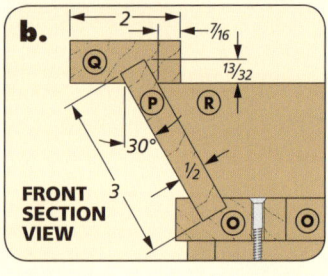

building the CORNICE & BACK

▲ The simple cornice features square edges and flat surfaces.

The cornice that tops the cupboard consists of a base and a cap frame that sandwich raking trim boards. To create a flat display surface on top, I installed a shelf across the upper frame. This shelf is made up of the same beadboards you'll fit to the cupboard back once the cornice is installed.

The construction of the cornice is a bit out of the ordinary. As you can see in details 'a' and 'b,' the rake trim fits into angled grooves in the frame pieces. This makes the whole assembly easier to build as well as very solid.

ANGLED GROOVES. You can start by cutting extra-long frame blanks to width — a front, two sides, and a back for the base, and a front and two sides for the cap. Now you'll need to install a ½"-wide dado blade in the table saw and tilt it to 30° to cut the angled grooves.

The box below shows how this goes. Note that the base pieces are cut with the outside edge against the rip fence while the cap pieces are cut with the inside edge against the fence. You'll need to adjust the rip fence setting between the two sets of cuts.

BASE FIRST. You're going to assemble the cornice from the bottom up starting with the base frame. As shown above, the front corners are mitered while the back rail is cut to fit between the side rails. Before gluing up the frame, I drilled the oversized countersunk screw holes to attach the cornice.

RAKE TRIM. The rake trim is next — a front piece and two sides. Due to the slant of the trim pieces, the corner joints are compound miters. The How-To box below shows an easy way to make these cuts on the table saw. I used an auxiliary fence on the miter gauge to support the pieces at 30°, then simply cut 45° miters.

I mitered one end of the front piece and one side piece from the left side of the blade, and then

How-To: Grooves & Compound Miters

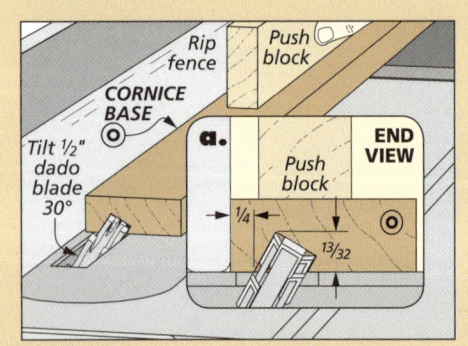

Base Grooves. Use a test piece to adjust the fence and blade height. Then make the cuts with outside edges against the fence.

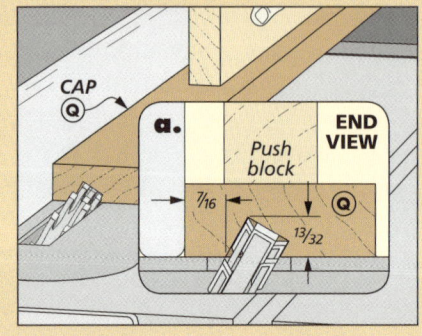

Cap Grooves. After readjusting the fence, cut the cap grooves with the inside edges against the fence.

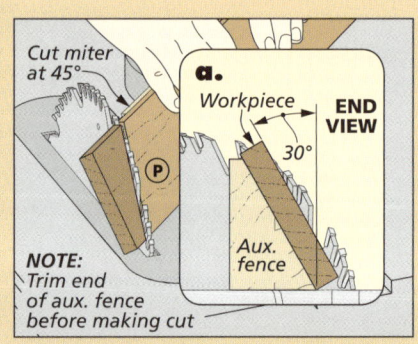

Compound Miters. A beveled fence attached to the miter gauge makes a simple job of mitering the rake trim.

switched to the right side to cut the mating miters. The back ends of the side pieces are cut square. Finally, I glued the pieces into the base using "hand" clamps to hold the joints while the glue set up.

THE CAP. Likewise, the cap pieces are cut and fit one at a time. I mitered the front piece to length first, then fit the two sides.

After gluing the cap pieces in place on the assembly, I installed the back filler and front cleat that support the shelf (details 'a' and 'c,' opposite). The ends of both pieces and the front edge of the cleat need to be beveled at 30°. Slide the cleat in from the back before installing the filler. And when all the pieces are in place, the cornice can be fastened to the cupboard with screws.

BACK & TOP SHELF

Your next task is to make and fit the beadboards that enclose the back and make up the cornice shelf. This authentic detail really adds a nice touch.

To allow for wood movement, the individual boards that form the back are joined together with floating ship-lap joints and fastened with nails (detail 'c'). The bead routed along one edge of each board disguises the joints as well as adds detail.

The How-To box at right shows how to make the beadboard at the router table and table saw. After routing a bead on each board, the ship-lap joints are created by cutting overlapping rabbets on opposite faces (detail 'c'). But take note that due to the presence of the bead on one edge, I cut the opposing rabbets to different depths.

With the ship-lap joints completed, you can cut the pieces to finished length for the back and the cornice. At this point, I went ahead and nailed down the shelf. It just takes is one nail at each end (except the end boards), as in details 'a' and 'c'). But since I intended to give the back an antiqued, milk paint finish, I held off on installing them.

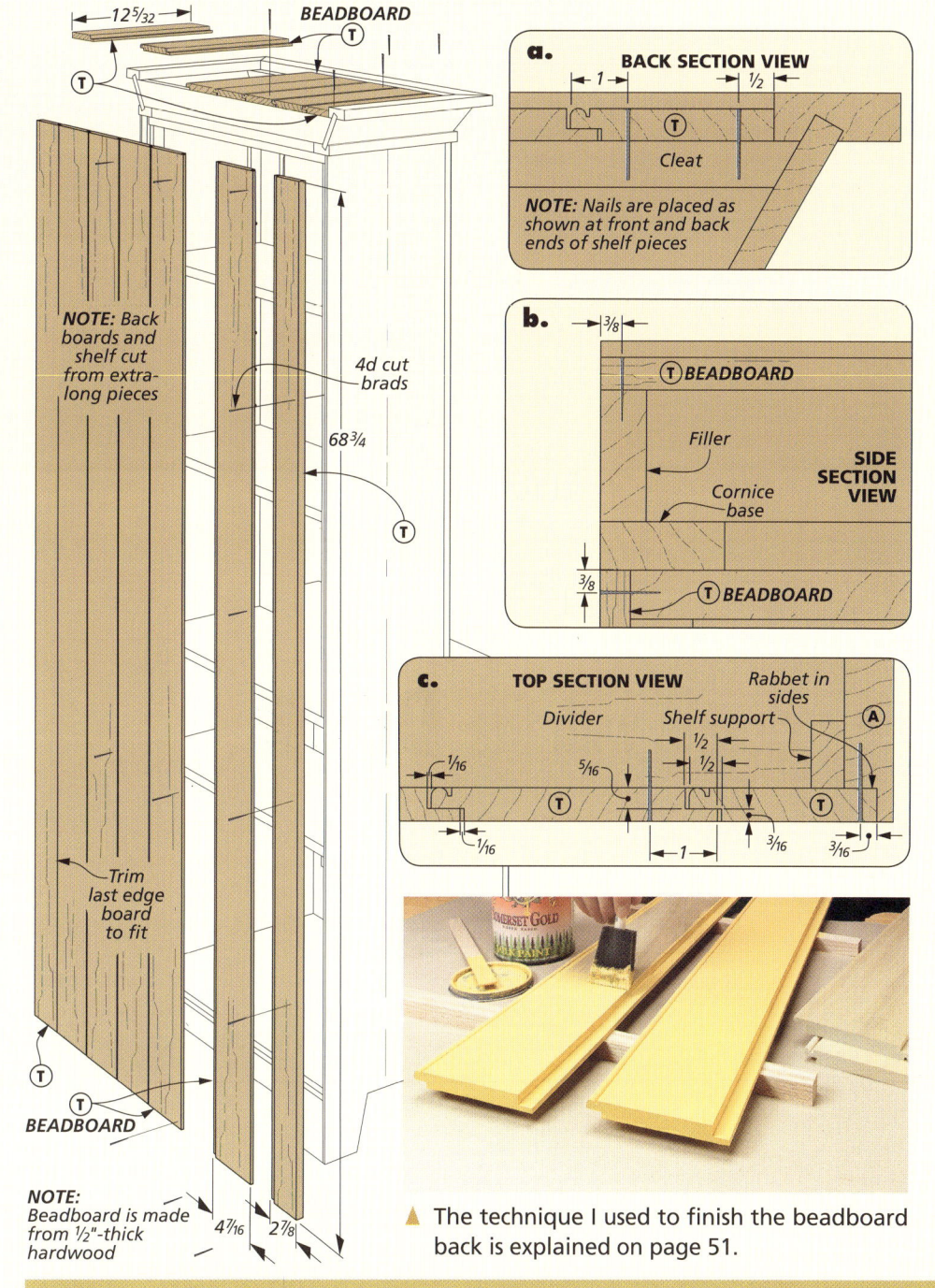

▲ The technique I used to finish the beadboard back is explained on page 51.

How-To: Beading

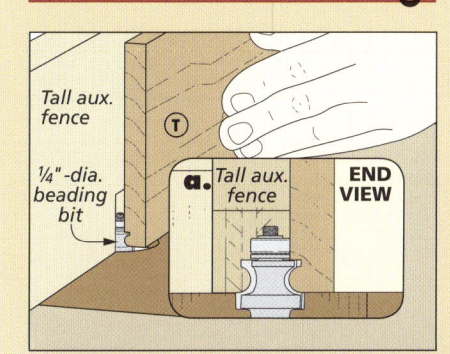

Edge Bead. Use a tall fence to help steady the workpiece on edge as you pass it across a beading bit.

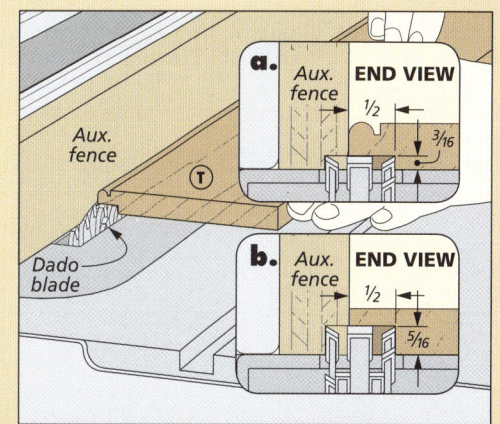

Two Rabbets. I cut the shallower rabbet behind the bead first. Then I raised the blade to cut the deeper rabbet on the opposite face.

closing with the DOOR

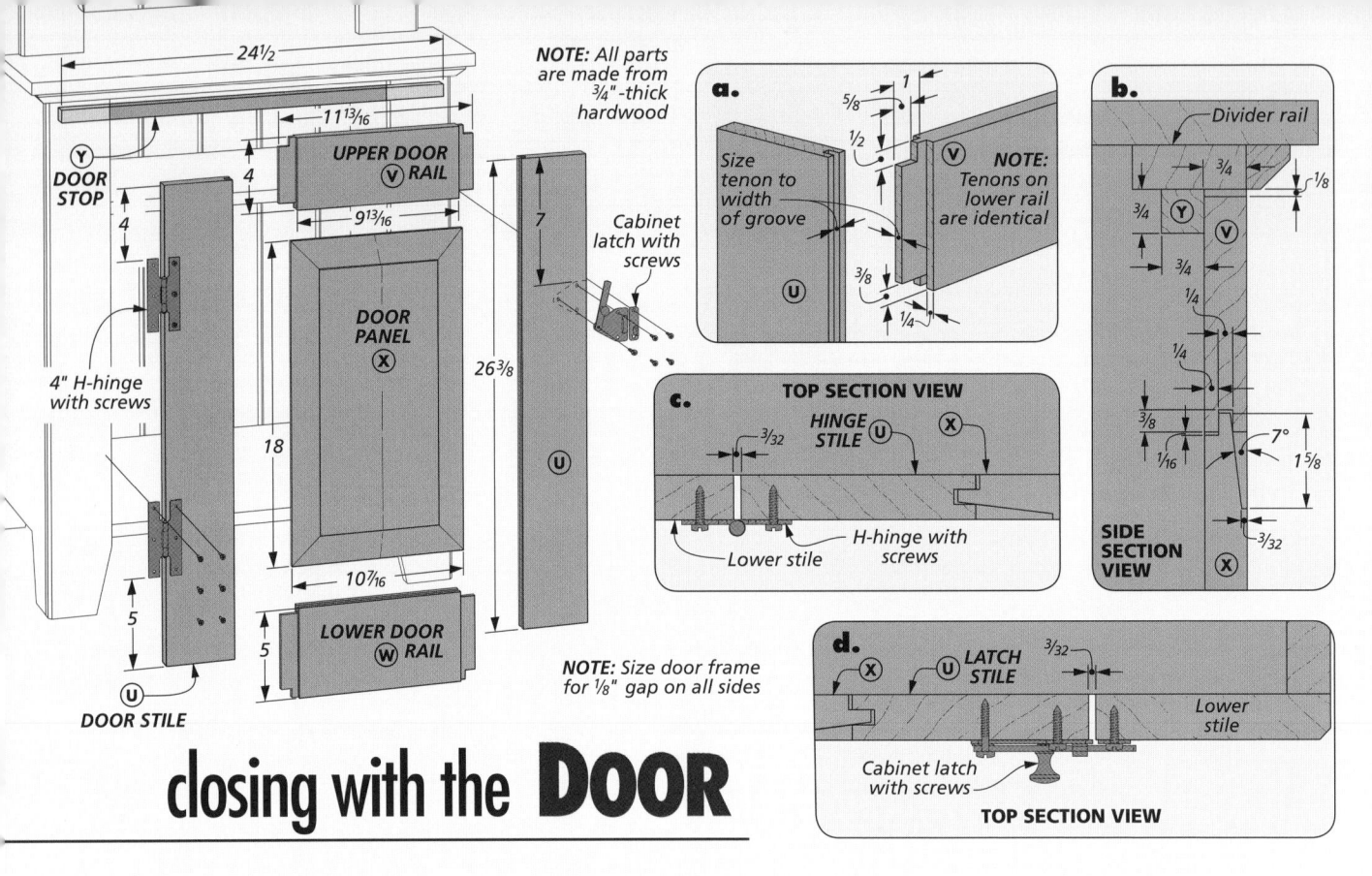

Your final task is to build and install the raised-panel door. Wide stiles and rails, haunched mortise and tenon joinery, and a traditional panel profile make it a perfect complement.

THE FRAME. I began work on the frame by cutting the wide stiles and rails to a final width and length. Note that the lower rail is wider than the upper rail.

Now, you'll want to take a look at the How-To box on the opposite page and detail 'a' for guidance with the joinery. The order is pretty straightforward. First, you'll cut centered grooves in all the pieces. Next, you can lay out and cut the mortises in the stiles — drilling out the waste at the drill press, then squaring them up with chisels at the bench.

A wide dado blade will make quick work of the haunched tenons. Just sneak up on a snug fit with the mortises. And cut tenon haunches a hair shy of bottoming out in the grooves.

THE RAISED PANEL. Your next step is to make the raised panel. Here, I used a very traditional profile — a wide, shallow bevel leading up to a short shoulder (main drawing and detail 'b'). And then once the profile is completed, the ¾"-thick panel is fit to the grooves by cutting rabbets around the perimeter. This design makes sizing the panel to the grooves easier.

The drawings in the How-To box below illustrates the table saw technique used to shape the panel. I started with shallow shoulder cuts, then tilted the blade and used a tall fence to complete

How-To: Shaping the Raised Panel

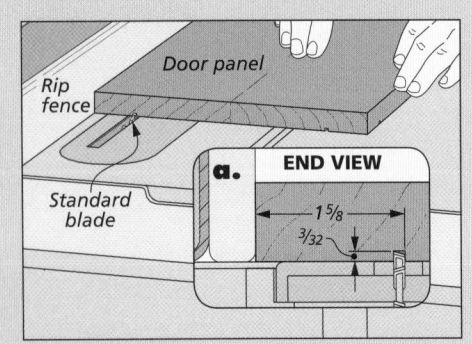

Shoulder Cuts. Start the profile with a very shallow (³⁄₃₂") shoulder cut around all four sides of the door panel.

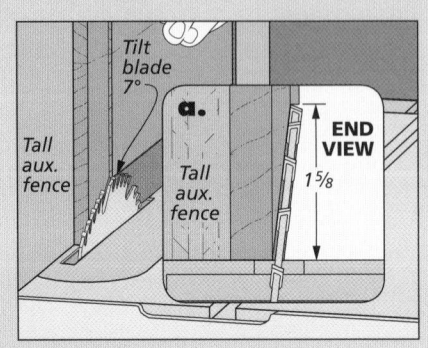

Bevel Cuts. Hold the panel firmly against the fence when cutting the profile to full depth in several passes.

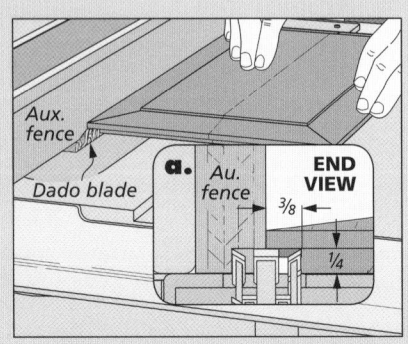

Rabbets. Start with the blade set low. Test the fit to the grooves as you raise the blade height between passes.

the profile. Set the blade height carefully and then cut the bevels to full depth with several passes.

RABBETS. Before cutting the rabbets, you'll want to clean up (sand or plane) the bevel cuts. I sized the width of the rabbets to create a 1/16" expansion gap all around (detail 'b,' opposite). Adjust the depth of the rabbets for a good fit to the frames.

When you're satisfied with the look and fit of the panel, go ahead and glue up the assembly. But don't glue the panel — let it float.

DETAILS. Before installing the door, I added a stop to the case (main drawing and detail 'b,' opposite). Finally, mount the reproduction hinges and latch.

Now you can take the rustic theme one step further and give the cupboard a slightly worn, glazed finish, as explained on page 51. It's almost like building a brand-new antique.

How-To: Door Joinery

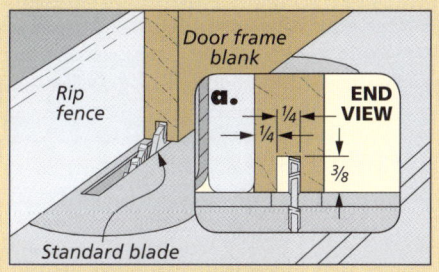

Centered Grooves. Center the grooves in the stiles and rails by flipping the pieces end for end between passes.

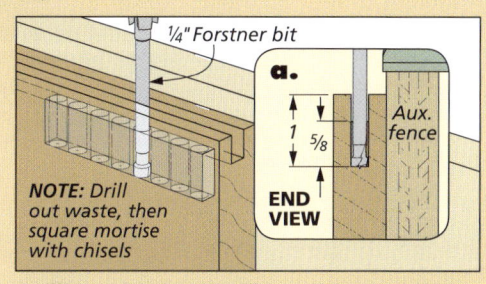

Drilling Mortises. Drill overlapping holes to remove most of the waste from the mortise. Then square it up with chisels.

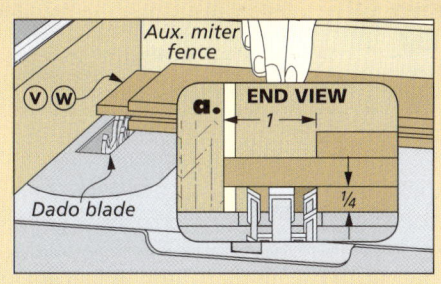

Tenon Cheeks. Raise the blade between sets of passes to size the tenons for a hand-pressure fit to mortises.

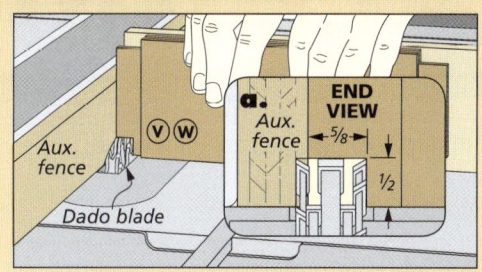

The Haunches. To cut the haunches, use a tall auxiliary miter gauge fence to support the rails on edge.

Materials, Supplies & Cutting Diagram

A	Sides (2)	3/4 x 17 1/4 - 73 1/4
B	Top (1)	3/4 x 10 3/4 - 25
C	Bottom (1)	3/4 x 16 3/4 - 25
D	Divider (1)	3/4 x 18 3/4 - 28 1/2
E	Divider Rail (1)	3/4 x 2 - 26
F	Lower Stiles (2)	3/4 x 4 - 30 1/2
G	Lower Case Trim (1)	3/4 x 3/4 - 48 rgh.
H	Back Base Rail (1)	3/4 x 4 1/2 - 25 1/2
I	Upper Stiles (2)	3/4 x 4 - 41 1/4
J	Upper Rail (1)	3/4 x 2 - 18
K	Shelf Supports (4)	1/2 x 1 - 40 1/2
L	Upper Shelf Cleats (4)	1/2 x 3/4 - 9 7/8
M	Lower Shelf Cleats (2)	1/2 x 3/4 - 10 3/8
N	Shelves (3)	3/4 x 10 5/8 - 24 3/8
O	Cornice Base (1)	3/4 x 2 - 80 rgh.
P	Rake Board (1)	1/2 x 3 - 58 rgh.
Q	Cap (1)	3/4 x 2 - 62 rgh.
R	Filler (1)	3/4 x 2 1/4 rgh. - 28 rgh.
S	Cleat (1)	3/4 x 1 1/2 - 28 rgh.
T	Beadboard (7)	1/2 x 4 7/16 - 82 rgh.
U	Door Stiles (2)	3/4 x 4 - 26 3/8
V	Upper Door Rail (1)	3/4 x 4 - 11 13/16
W	Lower Door Rail (1)	3/4 x 5 - 11 13/16
X	Door Panel (1)	3/4 x 10 7/16 - 18
Y	Door Stop (1)	3/4 x 3/4 - 24 1/2

- (1 pr.) 4" H-Hinges w/Screws
- (1) Cabinet Latch w/Screws
- (10) #8 x 1 1/4" Fh Woodscrews
- (4) #8 x 1 3/4" Fh Woodscrews
- (4) #8 x 1" Rh Woodscrews
- (1/4 lb.) 4d Headless Cut Brads
- (1/4 lb.) 5d Cut Finish Nails

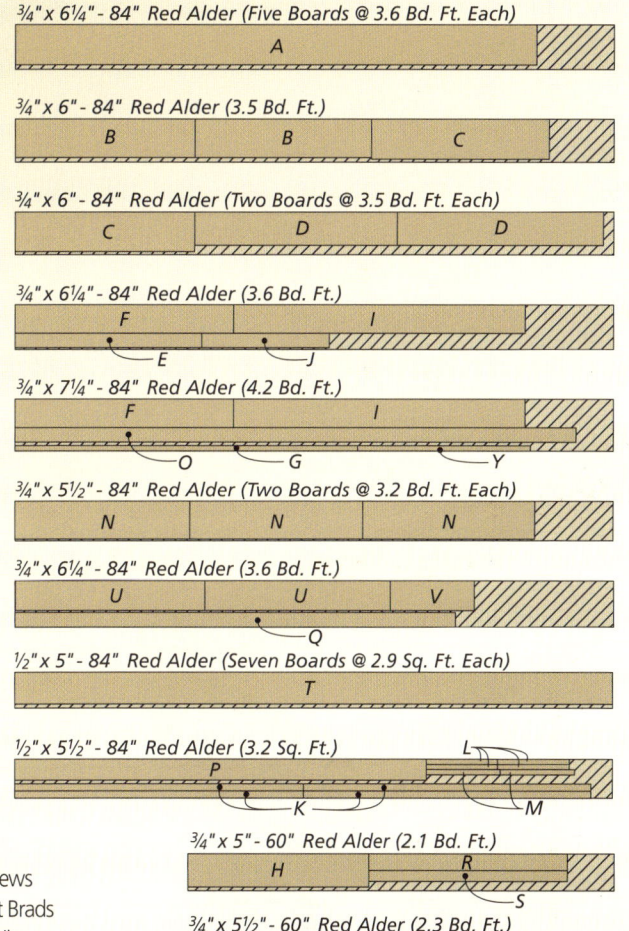

3/4" x 6 1/4" - 84" Red Alder (Five Boards @ 3.6 Bd. Ft. Each)
3/4" x 6" - 84" Red Alder (3.5 Bd. Ft.)
3/4" x 6" - 84" Red Alder (Two Boards @ 3.5 Bd. Ft. Each)
3/4" x 6 1/4" - 84" Red Alder (3.6 Bd. Ft.)
3/4" x 7 1/4" - 84" Red Alder (4.2 Bd. Ft.)
3/4" x 5 1/2" - 84" Red Alder (Two Boards @ 3.2 Bd. Ft. Each)
3/4" x 6 1/4" - 84" Red Alder (3.6 Bd. Ft.)
1/2" x 5" - 84" Red Alder (Seven Boards @ 2.9 Sq. Ft. Each)
1/2" x 5 1/2" - 84" Red Alder (3.2 Sq. Ft.)
3/4" x 5" - 60" Red Alder (2.1 Bd. Ft.)
3/4" x 5 1/2" - 60" Red Alder (2.3 Bd. Ft.)

woodworking essentials

mail-order Lumber

Get high-quality lumber for your projects with the click of a mouse.

▼ A 15-bd. ft. package of curly maple arrived in three days.

For some reason, many of us find it harder to shell out cash on quality wood than on tools. Common sense says that you can build great projects with a few basic tools, but you can only dress up run-of-the-mill wood in so many ways. Some projects beg for a little more character and uniqueness you can only get with highly figured wood or veneer.

WHERE TO BUY? The problem many of us face is locating sources for premium lumber and veneer. The big-box home centers are okay for a few basics like the occasional sheet of plywood, but their prices for lumber are off the chart and the quality is hit or miss. Your choice of species is pretty limited. Pine, oak, and poplar are standard fare. If you're lucky, you might find some maple or cherry, but that's about it.

Local lumberyards (where they still exist) have better quality, wider selection, and more knowledgeable staff to help you find what you need. Depending on where you live, you can rely on these local suppliers or a high-quality woodworking store. But in many places, you may not have ready access to these resources.

INTERNET LUMBERYARD

The good news is you can find just about anything you need online. There are a lot of suppliers looking for your business and they ship anywhere in the continental United States. And there are some benefits when you shop online.

UNLIMITED CHOICES. When you open up the market to online lumber vendors, you're not limited by the stock your local suppliers have on hand. Your choices in species and grain configurations become almost endless.

I look at it as having a team of buyers available to watch for unusual woods with beautiful grain patterns. Many vendors specialize in certain species, so you know they have a vested interest in offering you a wide selection.

SUPPORT THE LITTLE GUY. Remember those local lumberyards and mills? Many old, established mills have found that selling over the internet is a way to save the family business. They can offer high-quality wood to a much broader audience of potential buyers, no matter where they live.

WHERE TO START. If you use your favorite internet search engine and type in the phrase "online lumber," you'll end up with

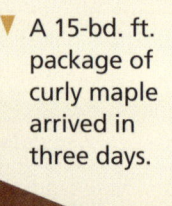

44 Woodsmith No. 195

dozens of potential vendors. But one resource I usually start with is *Woodfinder.com*. Their website serves as a portal for access to online lumber and veneer suppliers. You can narrow your search by locale, species, specialty woods, and many other parameters. It's worth checking out.

WHAT YOU SEE IS WHAT YOU GET. Most online vendors make sure you know exactly what you're getting. They'll have photos of each board or a representative sheet of veneer (see box below). And you'll know the exact measurements. The better vendors are also quick to answer any questions you may have.

DEALING WITH SHIPPING COSTS. The downside to ordering online is the cost of shipping. But there are ways to minimize its impact on your buying decision.

In some instances, the cost of the lumber is less than what you would pay locally. This can help balance the effect of the shipping cost on your pocketbook.

Another way to minimize shipping costs is to look for deals. Many vendors will have "bundle" deals with free shipping or give quantity discounts. It pays to subscribe to their email list or social networking page (like *Facebook*). This way, you're aware of any deals as they become available.

If you have woodworking friends looking to buy lumber or veneer, consolidate your order to maximize the quantity discount and save on shipping costs.

WHAT YOU GET. After placing your order and typing in your credit card information, what can you expect? In just a few days, you'll receive a package on your doorstep. The photos on the opposite page show a few packages I received. Most vendors package the wood with heavy cardboard and plastic to make sure it arrives dry and undamaged.

As you can tell in the photos above, you can get some pretty special and unusual pieces you may not be able to find locally. (I should note that I applied mineral spirits to highlight the grain.)

START SMALL. If you're new to buying wood online or don't have first-hand knowledge about a vendor, start with a small order. This way, you'll get a feel for the quality of service and product they can offer. If all goes well, you can go on to place larger orders. And like I said before, most vendors are happy to address any concerns or questions you have.

OTHER GOOD SOURCES. Besides online storefronts, there are a couple of other options for finding special wood. Online auction sites (like *eBay*) allow you to bid on a product. Often, you can get a great deal. As a matter of fact, some of the online vendors also use *eBay* to sell bundles of wood, veneer, or an especially figured, one-of-a-kind piece.

For a local option, check out sites like *craigslist.org*. You can often find wood in your own neighborhood or city.

SPECIALTY WOOD. For many projects, I'm perfectly content with the lumber I find locally. But if you want to try exotic and figured woods, buying online is the way to go. It's a great way to shop for that special piece that will really make your project stand out from the crowd. All it takes is a few clicks of a mouse. **W**

▲ Online vendors give you access to specialty wood and veneer you may not be able to find locally.

Buying Wood on the Internet

Browsing the internet for that special piece of wood, veneer, and even pre-made parts can be a little overwhelming at first. Fortunately, most of the online vendors make it easy for you to choose just the right material for your project.

When it comes to finding a highly figured piece of wood for a project, I start with *woodfinder.com*, as I mentioned above. Another good resource is *Ebay*. For a wide selection of veneer, one of my favorite resources is *Certainly Wood*. You can find them online at *certainlywood.com*.

For large projects like tables, it often makes sense to purchase premade parts like table legs. I like to use parts from *Classic Designs by Matthew Burak*. They're located online at *tablelegs.com*.

Woodsmith.com   Woodsmith   45

finishing room

working with
Milk Paint

This centuries-old favorite is just the ticket for lending an authentic look to distressed pieces and reproduction furniture.

▼ Powdered milk paint contains casein, just like the original version.

Choosing the right finish for a project is just as important as any of the joinery and molding details. And for furniture that's done in a rustic or antique style, I'll often use milk paint. It has a dull, flat sheen that looks great on traditional styles of furniture.

WHAT IS MILK PAINT? Milk paint is so named because milk was added to lime, chalk, and natural pigments to create the liquid paint. The protein casein in milk makes an excellent binder for the other ingredients. The result is a tough, long-lasting paint.

POWDERED PAINT. Fortunately, you no longer need to milk a cow or head to the dairy aisle of your grocery store to try milk paint. You can buy authentic, casein-based milk paint in a convenient powdered form, like that shown at left. All you have to do is mix the powder with water before using it (see photos directly above).

▲ With the powder measured into the jar, add an equal volume of water and stir.

▲ Even after vigorous stirring, it's still a good idea to strain the mixture to avoid lumps.

Powdered milk paint is available in twenty different traditional colors. (See page 51 for sources.) Best of all, milk paint is non-toxic, has very little odor, and dries so quickly you can apply a second coat in an hour. One thing to keep in mind, however, is that it's

▲ For an authentic, antique or distressed look, apply a thin coat of the first color.

▲ Next, sand some surfaces and the edges to bare wood and apply the second color.

▲ Finally, sand again after the second coat has dried to get the aged look you desire. Finish up with a glaze to add a dark layer.

best to mix only as much paint as you need. Because of the organic nature of milk paint, it will start to thicken and turn bad after a few days. (If you need milk paint with a longer shelf life, take a look at the box below.)

TECHNIQUES

What really makes milk paint stand out though is not how it's made, but how it's used. Milk paint lends itself to a number of different techniques that are great for creating custom effects or making a new project look old.

WASH COAT. For starters, you can a create a softer, faded look by using a "wash coat" of milk paint. Simply use more water when mixing up the paint to create a weaker color. The thinned-down paint acts more like a stain, allowing some of the character of the wood to show through the finish, such as you would find on a weathered piece.

BLENDING. You can also blend milk paint colors by combining the powders before adding the water. For example, adding white milk paint to any of the other colors will lighten the shade. This gives you a much wider range of tints.

LAYERING. One of the more interesting techniques that can be done with milk paint is to create a worn, distressed look with multiple layers and colors of paint. The photos at the top of the page give you an idea of how this is done.

The technique consists of layering two or more different colors of milk paint and sanding through some in a few areas. A glaze can also be used to give the wood an aged appearance. While the process is pretty straightfoward, it requires a little practice to achieve the right look. Essentially, you're trying to simulate the wear and tear that a piece of furniture might receive from being used and repainted over the years.

CRACKLE FINISH. One of my favorite milk paint effects is a crackle finish. As you can see in the photo at right, the top layer of paint is cracked, revealing a different color of paint beneath.

To create this effect, you apply a crackling agent between the first and second coats of paint. Within minutes of brushing on the second coat of paint, it begins to crackle. The effect is quite dramatic.

TOPCOAT. Although milk paint adheres very well, water or other liquids will leave stains on the dried paint. So it's a good idea to apply a clear finish over the paint, such as lacquer, polyurethane, or shellac. (Just avoid water-based finishes.)

Milk paint is a great finish for a wide range of projects. Once you give it a try, you'll be hooked. **W**

▼ A crackle finish is easy to apply and provides a unique look.

From the Can: Ready-to-Use Milk Paint

If you like the look of milk paint but don't enjoy mixing up a fresh batch for every project, you may want to consider *General Finishes'* line of milk paints. These paints come ready to use right out of the can. And unlike the powdered milk paints, they have a much longer shelf life.

In reality, these aren't true milk paints. (They aren't made from milk protein.) Instead, they're water-based latex paints that simulate the look and color of traditional milk paints. You can still use them to create a lot of the same effects shown above, which is why they were chosen for the beadboard on the step-back cupboard on page 34.

Like powdered milk paints, *General Finishes'* paints are available in a wide range of comparable colors. (See page 51 for sources.)

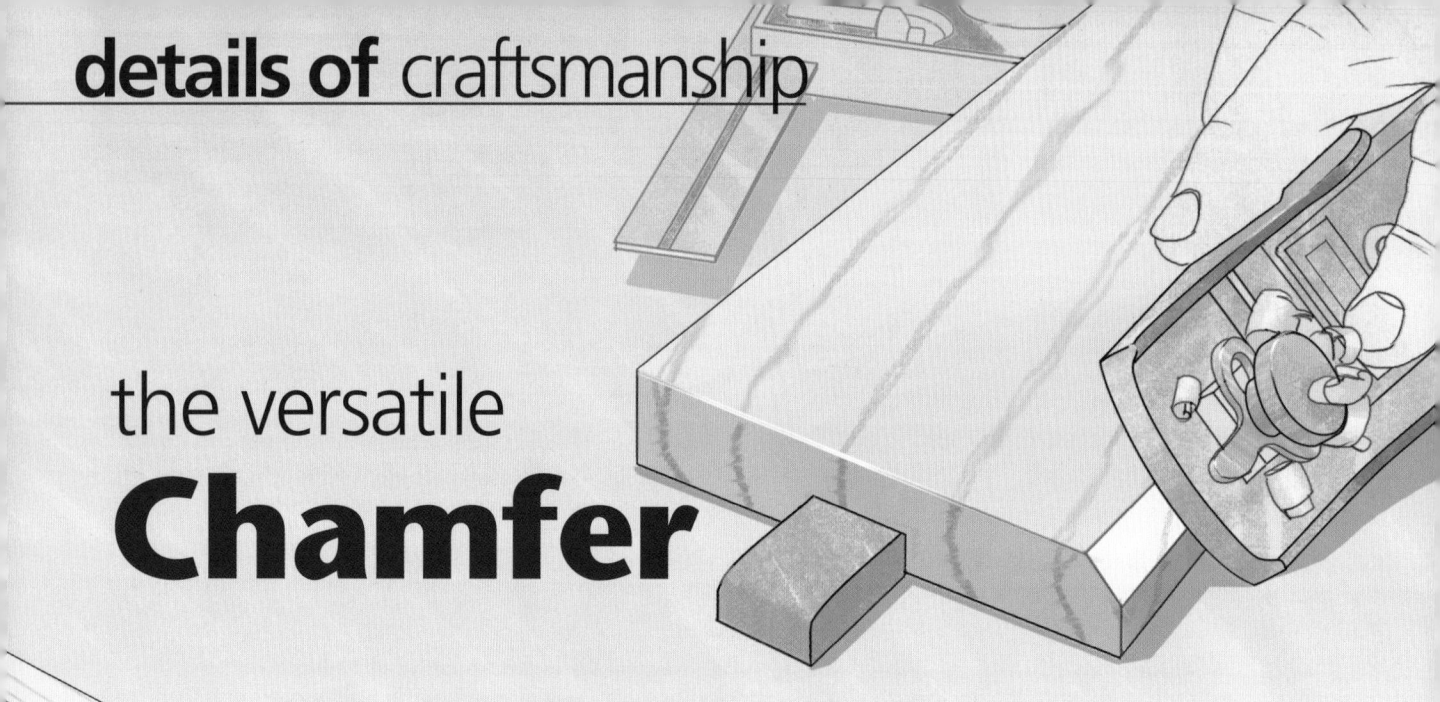

details of craftsmanship

the versatile Chamfer

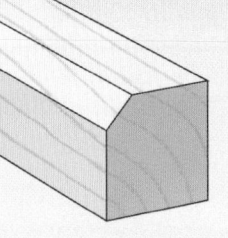

This simple profile looks great and both enhances the design and limits damage to your projects.

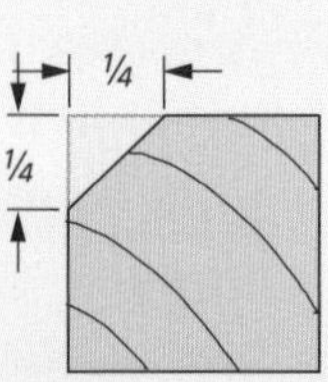

▲ Chamfers are typically dimensioned from the edge of the workpiece.

Molding profiles are often pretty style specific. For example, you wouldn't shape a fancy ogee profile on the edge of Shaker tabletop. However, there is one profile that works on virtually any period or style of furniture — the simple chamfer. No other profile offers as many design uses and possibilities. The trick is knowing how to incorporate chamfers into a design for the best practical function and aesthetic result.

WHAT'S A CHAMFER? Let's start with the basics. A chamfer is essentially a bevel cut along an edge or across a corner, as shown in the drawing in the left margin. Although a chamfer doesn't have to be cut at 45° to the adjacent surfaces, this is the most common angle. A flat profile cut at a shallower angle is often simply referred to as a bevel. But there's no rigid distinction between the two terms.

A chamfer is usually dimensioned along the relieved edges, not across the face. As shown in the drawing at left, a ¼" chamfer is formed by cutting back ¼" along each edge.

The simple profile of a chamfer is one reason why it's so versatile — it's very easy to shape. A chamfer can be made with a variety of hand tools (block plane or spokeshave), it can be routed, or cut on the table saw.

STOPPED OR FULL. Not all chamfers are the same. The drawings below show variations in the way a chamfer can be worked on an edge or edges. A full chamfer runs the entire length of an edge. It either ends free or butted up to a flat surface, as shown below. This type is often a good choice on outside edges.

However, full chamfers can also be shaped on the inside edges of a frame. As you see in the upper left example, the intersecting chamfers are joined with a mason's miter to form a sharp, square transition.

A chamfer can also stop short of one or both ends of the piece, in which case it's called a stopped chamfer. Stopped chamfers are often shaped on the inside edges of frames. And they're used on the outside corners of a case where a continuous chamfer might interfere with other intersecting moldings.

Another reason to use stopped chamfers is the design possibilities. The transition from the square edge to the chamfer can create a focal point for embellishment.

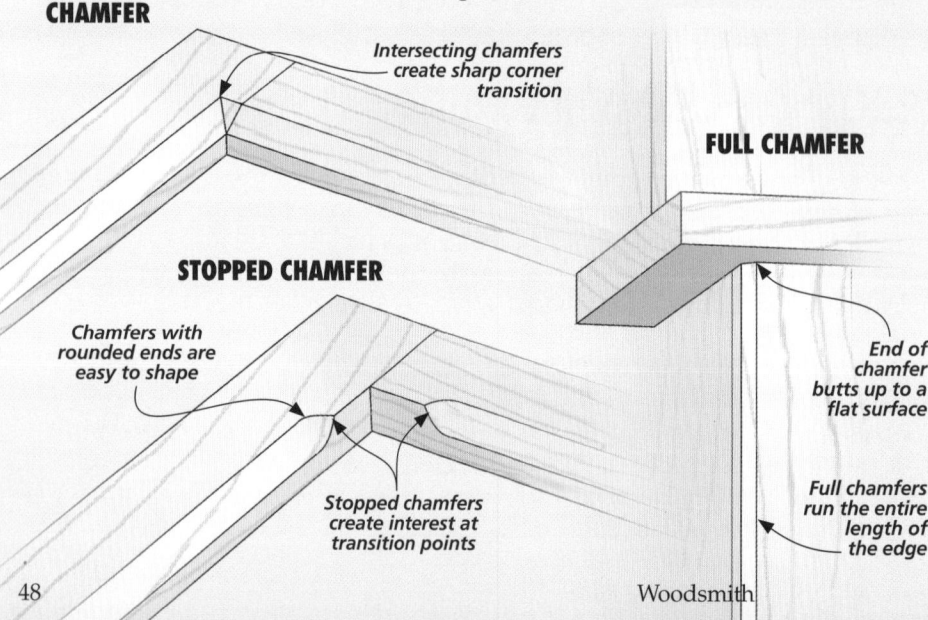

MASON'S MITER CHAMFER
Intersecting chamfers create sharp corner transition

STOPPED CHAMFER
Chamfers with rounded ends are easy to shape
Stopped chamfers create interest at transition points

FULL CHAMFER
End of chamfer butts up to a flat surface
Full chamfers run the entire length of the edge

The box at the bottom of the page shows several different ways to transition a chamfer.

WHY A CHAMFER? Chamfers can be added to a project to fill a number of roles. I'll give you some insight into just a few ways your projects may benefit from their use. The drawings at right help illustrate these points.

DAMAGE CONTROL. Sharp outside corners on a project are vulnerable to chips, dings, dents, or other abuse. Adding a small chamfer (as little as $\frac{1}{16}$") to ease the edge is often the answer. For example, the chamfer around the very bottom of the table leg shown at the far right helps minimizes damage when sliding the table across a floor.

Easing sharp edges with a small chamfer has another added benefit. The chamfer helps soften the edge to the touch, such as on a tabletop or drawer front.

FOR APPEARANCE SAKE. A chamfer may also be used like any other profile to add visual detail to an otherwise plain, square edge. Many of the projects you see in *Woodsmith* feature chamfers shaped for this reason. Chamfers that are $\frac{1}{4}$"-wide and up become focal points that play a role in the overall style of a project.

Keep in mind that the larger the chamfer, the more noticeable it will be. So it's important to scale the chamfer for the desired affect — subtle or bold.

CRISP & CLEAN. The crisp, unfussy appearance of a chamfer profile makes it a good fit with contemporary designs, as illustrated by the coffee table above. The sharp lines and flat surface add detail that complements a clean, uncluttered look.

ATTENTION-GRABBING. The picture frame at upper left demonstrates what I call the funnel effect. You may notice that several chamfers wrap around the inside edges of the frame and draw your eye inward. This focuses the attention to what's in the frame without being distracting.

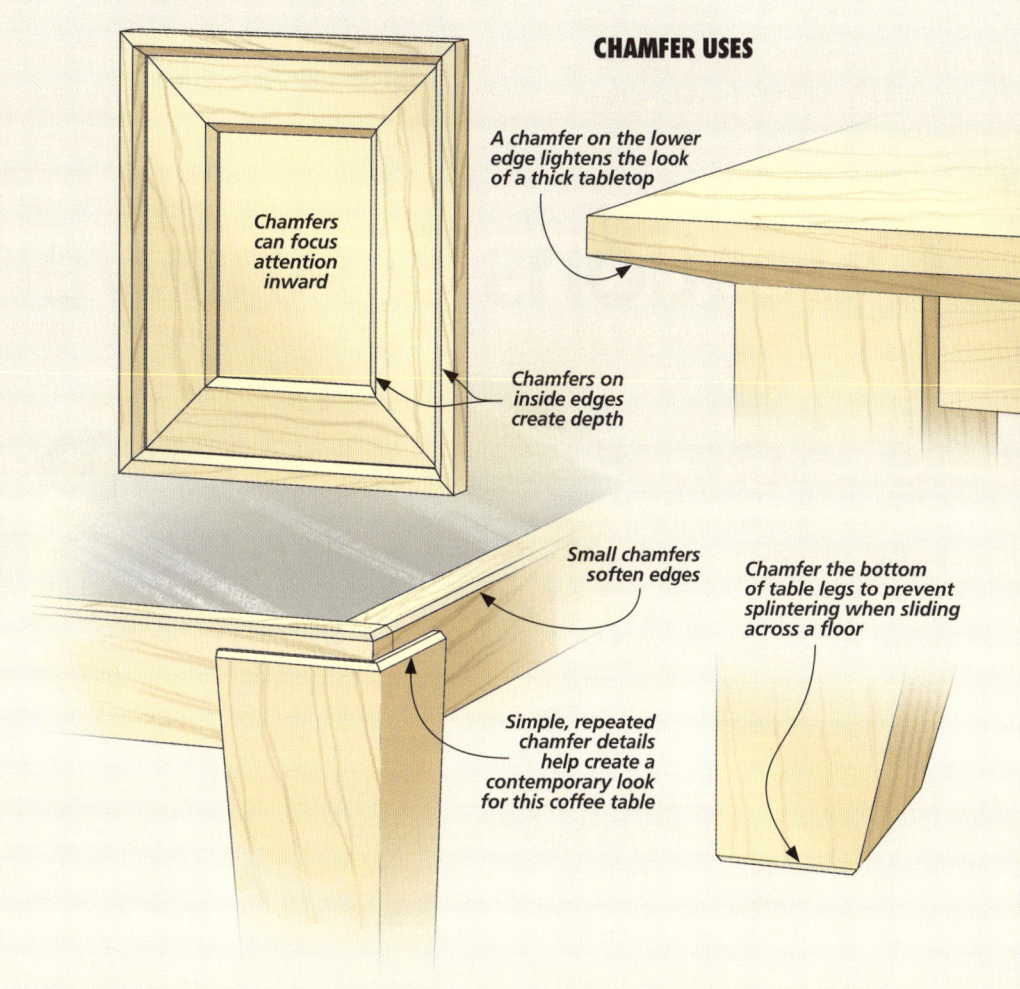

CHAMFER USES

Chamfers can focus attention inward

A chamfer on the lower edge lightens the look of a thick tabletop

Chamfers on inside edges create depth

Small chamfers soften edges

Chamfer the bottom of table legs to prevent splintering when sliding across a floor

Simple, repeated chamfer details help create a contemporary look for this coffee table

You'll find this same technique is used on the step-back cupboard on page 34. The stopped chamfers on the inside edges of the upper face frame stiles help direct your gaze to the contents of the cupboard's open shelves.

A LIGHTER LOOK. One final way to use a chamfer is to lighten the look of a bulky or thick part. A chamfer on the underside of a tabletop makes it appear thinner and works to draw the eye upward (upper right drawing). Likewise, a wide chamfer on the inside corner of a square table or chair leg reduces mass and the blocky shape is visually lightened and de-emphasized.

As you can see, the uses of the simple chamfer are wide ranging and impressive. This valuable design element deserves every woodworker's attention. **W**

A Closer Look: Chamfer Stops

Plain. The flat surface of this plain transition creates a crisp, eye-catching facet.

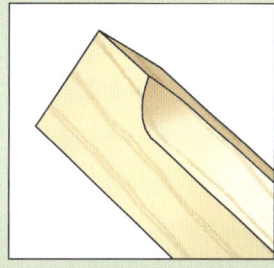

Rounded. The rounded chamfer stop is common and easy to shape.

Lamb's Tongue. This classic stop profile is seen on high-style furniture.

in the mailbox

Questions & Answers

Benchtop vs. Stationary Planers

Q *I'm thinking of upgrading my planer and was wondering if it's worth spending a little more to get a stationary planer instead of a benchtop model?*

John Piper
Salt Lake City, Utah

A Over the years, benchtop planers have gotten bigger and better with the addition of new features. At the same time, the cost of owning a stationary planer has come down due to the flood of inexpensive imported machines.

Today, only a few hundred dollars separate the top-of-the-line benchtop planers from the entry-level stationary planers. So it's worth taking a look at the pros and cons of each type. (See the drawings below for a quick comparison.)

WEIGHT. Benchtop planers are compact, self-contained units. They're often referred to as "portable" planers. While you probably won't want to carry one around, they're small enough to store under a worksurface and pull out when you need to use it. This makes a benchtop planer a great choice for infrequent use or a small shop.

By way of contrast, stationary planers are made of lots of cast iron and typically weigh several hundred pounds. This weight is great for dampening vibration, but can be a real hindrance if you don't have a dedicated spot in your shop for a planer.

MOTORS. All benchtop planers use universal motors (similar to the motor on your router). A universal motor spins at a high speed, but its RPM drops off significantly when placed under a load.

As a result, you won't be able to take heavy passes with a benchtop planer (particularly when planing wide boards). And you may have to take an occasional break during long planing sessions to avoid overheating the motor.

This isn't the case with the induction motors used on stationary planers. This type of motor is designed to run all day long. And it can hog off $\frac{1}{8}$" of material at a time without breaking a sweat, even on a full-width board. One possible downside, though, is just about all stationary planers require a 220-volt circuit.

NOISE. The noise factor is one of the most obvious differences between benchtop and stationary planers. The induction motors on stationary planers are noticeably quieter than the high-speed universal motors on the benchtops. You'll still need to use hearing protection with either type, but if your shop is in a basement or attached garage, a stationary planer won't drive everyone else out of the house.

MAINTENANCE. Most of the newer benchtop planers are equipped with self-indexing knives, making blade changes a snap. While some newer models of stationary planers also have this feature, many still lack it.

LONGEVITY. A stationary planer is a tool that you'll be able to hand down to your grandkids. Benchtop planers are essentially "disposable" tools. If the motor burns out, it's usually not cost-effective to have it repaired.

In the end, the decision between a benchtop or stationary planer really comes down to how you intend to use it. If you buy a lot of rough lumber and plane it down yourself, a stationary planer may be more suited to your purpose.

But if you're a typical home woodworker, building a few projects a year, a benchtop planer should meet all your needs just fine.

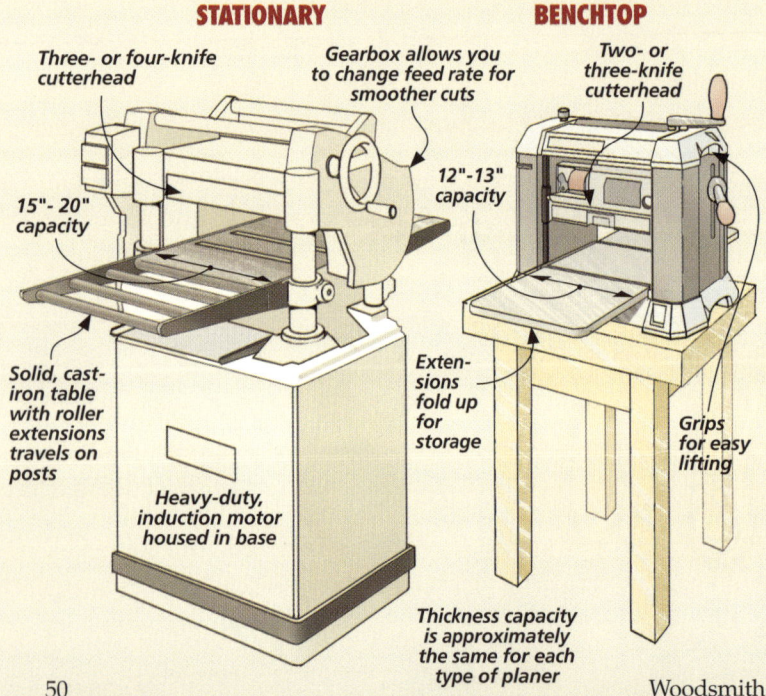

STATIONARY
- Three- or four-knife cutterhead
- Gearbox allows you to change feed rate for smoother cuts
- 15"- 20" capacity
- Solid, cast-iron table with roller extensions travels on posts
- Heavy-duty, induction motor housed in base

BENCHTOP
- Two- or three-knife cutterhead
- 12"-13" capacity
- Extensions fold up for storage
- Grips for easy lifting

Thickness capacity is approximately the same for each type of planer

hardware & supplies Sources

HIGH-TECH HINGES
The various hinges shown in the article on page 8 were all purchased from *Woodcraft* or *Rockler*. (Part numbers vary depending on the size and finish.) You can also find similar hinges from other sources.

BENCHTOP ROUTER TABLES
You can purchase benchtop router tables through many woodworking suppliers. The *Kreg* router table is sold through *Woodcraft* (148070) and *Kreg Tool* (PRS2000). We purchased the *Bench Dog* router table from *Rockler* (20253). Both of these router tables are also available from *Amazon*.

DRILL GUIDE
A drill guide is a great way to add accuracy to your hand drill. The *Wolfcraft* guide shown on page 12 is available from *Amazon* and *Rockler* (46441). The same guide is also sold by *Craftsman* (00967173000).

BOX JOINTS
The *Freud Box Joint Cutter Set* shown in the article on page 14 is available from several of the woodworking dealers listed in the margin at right.

WINE RACK
You won't need any hardware to build the wine rack on page 18. To give the cherry a warm look, we stained the project with a mix of three parts of *Zar Stain* (Cherry) and one part *WoodKote Jel'd Stain* (Cherry). This was followed by two coats of lacquer.

FOUR POSTER BED
Aside from some screws, the only hardware you'll need for the bed on page 24 is a set of bed rail brackets. We purchased these from *Rockler* (32077).

The stain used on the bed is *General Finishes' Gel Stain* (Java). Then I sprayed on two coats of lacquer.

STEP-BACK CUPBOARD
You'll need just a few pieces of hardware to build the step-back cupboard on page 34. The H-hinges (01X35.80) and cabinet latch (01X39.10) came from *Lee Valley*. The square finish nails (N-5) and headless cut brads (1½") were purchased from from *Horton Brasses*.

The case was finished with two coats of *General Finishes' Seal-a-Cell*. After lightly sanding through the finish on the corners and edges to simulate wear, a coat of *General Finishes' Gel Stain* (Java) was applied as a glaze.

The beadboard was painted with two colors of *General Finishes' Milk Paint* (Somerset Gold and Antique White). After lightly sanding through the top layer of paint in a few spots, I applied a coat of *General Finishes' Glaze* (Yellow Ochre).

MILK PAINT
The powdered milk paints discussed in the article on page 46 were purchased from *Woodcraft*. *Woodcraft* also carries *General Finishes'* line of pre-mixed milk paints sold in cans. **W**

Online Customer Service
Click on *Magazine Customer Service* at **www.woodsmith.com**
- Access your account status
- Change your mailing or email address
- Pay your bill
- Renew your subscription
- Tell us if you've missed an issue
- Find out if your payment has been received

MAIL ORDER SOURCES

Project supplies may be ordered from the following companies:

Woodsmith Store
800-444-7527
*Bench Dog Router Table,
Freud Box Joint Cutter Set,
Kreg Router Table*

Rockler
800-279-4441
rockler.com
*Bed Rail Brackets,
Bench Dog Router Table,
Freud Box Joint Cutter Set,
Hinges,
Wolfcraft Drill Guide*

Amazon.com
*Benchtop Router Tables,
Freud Box Joint Cutter Set,
Wolfcraft Drill Guide*

Craftsman
800-697-3277
craftsman.com
Craftsman Drill Guide

Horton Brasses
800-754-9127
horton-brasses.com
*Headless Cut Brads,
Square Finish Nails*

Kreg Tool
800-447-8638
kregtool.com
Kreg Router Table

Lee Valley
800-871-8158
leevalley.com
*Cabinet Latch,
H-Hinges*

Woodcraft
800-225-1153
woodcraft.com
*Freud Box Joint Cutter Set,
Hinges, Kreg Router Table,
Milk Paints*

Keep It All Organized!

Woodsmith Binders

As you build your *Woodsmith* library, here's a way to keep your issues organized. Each binder features durable vinyl covers and easy-to-read perforated number tags. Snap rings with a quick-open lever make it easy to insert and remove issues. And there's an extra pocket inside for storing notes. Each binder holds a full year (6 issues) of *Woodsmith*.

Visit **Woodsmith.com** to order or call **1-800-444-7527**.

Woodsmith Binder
○ **WB** (Holds 6 issues) $12.95

looking inside
Final Details

▶ *Four Poster Bed.* Tapered posts and clean lines give this bed a timeless look. Step-by-step plans for building it begin on page 24.

▲ *Step-Back Cupboard.* Open shelves make this cupboard ideal for storage or display. The compact footprint means you can use it in just about any room of the house. You'll find complete plans on page 34.

◀ *Wine Rack.* With a space-saving design and stylish good looks, this wine rack is at home whether sitting on a countertop or buffet. Detailed instructions for building the project start on page 18.

Tips & Tricks for Building Better Drawers — *Guaranteed!*

Tough Cuts Made *Easy* — Multipurpose Table Saw Jig

Woodsmith

Woodsmith.com

Vol. 33 / No. 196

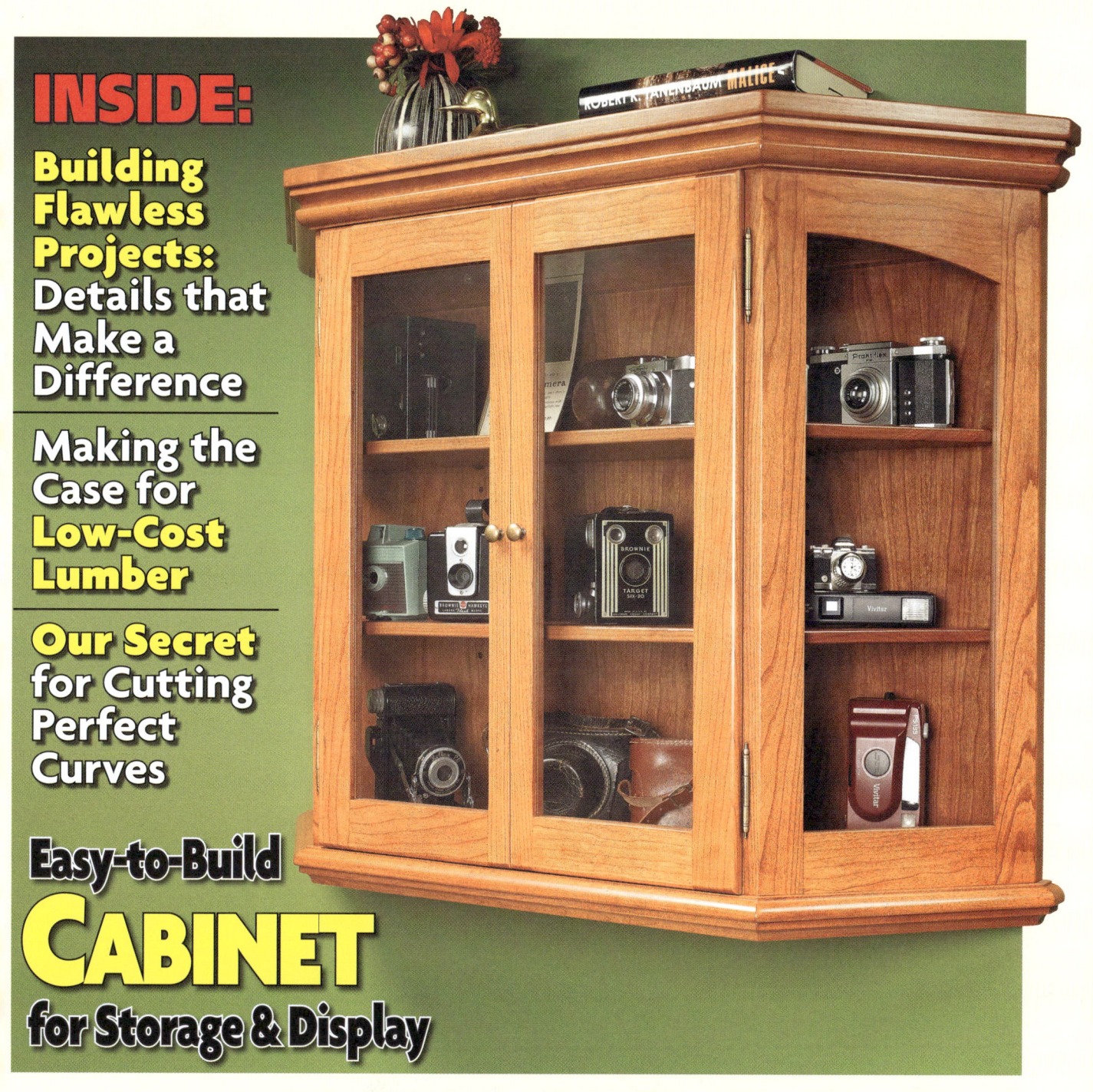

INSIDE:

Building Flawless Projects: Details that Make a Difference

Making the Case for Low-Cost Lumber

Our Secret for Cutting Perfect Curves

Easy-to-Build CABINET for Storage & Display

A Publication of August Home Publishing

looking inside

Table of Contents

from our readers
Tips & Techniques 4

all about
Cabinet Lighting 8
Find out what you need to know to select the right style of lighting for your next project.

tools of the trade
Hand Drills 10
Every shop needs a drill. Here's what to consider when choosing one for your shop.

jigs and fixtures
Tapering Jig 12
This versatile jig makes tough table saw cuts a lot quicker, easier, and safer.

woodworking technique
Veneering Large Panels 14
Learn the simple secrets to successfully veneering large surfaces.

tips from our shop
Shop Notebook 32

techniques from our shop
Building Better Drawers 42
Smooth-working drawers don't happen by accident. Make it a sure thing every time.

working with tools
Perfect Band Saw Cuts 44
We share some helpful tips for making dead-on, freehand cuts at the band saw.

finishing room
Finishing Poplar 46
We'll show you how the right finish can make this low-cost wood look like a million bucks.

details of craftsmanship
Setting Construction Goals 48
Paying attention to the right details is all it takes to build a great-looking project.

in the mailbox
Q & A 50

hardware and supplies
Sources 51

Curved-Handle Tray page 18

Veneered Credenza page 22

projects

weekend project
Curved-Handle Serving Tray 18
Round up some of those special scraps you've been saving and pencil in this eye-catching project for your next open weekend.

designer series project
Veneered Credenza 22
The "retro" styling of this handsome project is a nod to the not-too-distant past. It's a great opportunity to try something a little different.

heirloom project
Curio Cabinet 34
If you're a collector, this is a project you won't want to pass up — practical, attractive, and guaranteed to be an enjoyable shop experience.

Curio Cabinet page 34

Woodsmith.com

editor's note
Sawdust

My request for comments and suggestions on improving *Woodsmith* generated a lot of compliments, some great ideas, and few suggestions for improvement. I've read them all and I'm working to get back in touch with each of you. While I can't guarantee we'll be able to do everything that was suggested, we'll give it all serious consideration.

On to what really matters at this point — the issue that you hold in your hands. Inside, you'll find some great projects along with a couple of "back to basics" articles that I think are well worth perusing and are sure to improve your skills.

If you're looking for a great weekend project, check out the curved-handle serving tray on page 18. Matching the curved handle with the ends of the tray provides a nice woodworking challenge. And selecting a pair of contrasting and highly figured materials is the perfect way to create an eye-catching look.

When it comes to featuring a treasured collection, you can't go wrong with the curio cabinet shown on page 34. The glass doors and slanted sides of the cabinet provide a great view of any collection from any angle. And the simple moldings at the top and bottom of the cabinet give it a traditional look without a lot of time-consuming effort.

To round out the projects, there's an attractive, veneered credenza (page 22). It's designed in a style that's making a resurgence in some areas. Even if you don't build it, there's a lot of great information on large case construction and veneering that you can apply to any style of project you build down the road.

Finally, the article starting on page 48 about setting construction goals is a must-read. Regardless of what you're building, you'll find valuable nuggets of woodworking wisdom gained from years of experience.

Bryan

This symbol lets you know there's more information online at www.Woodsmith.com. There you'll see step-by-step videos, technique and project animation, bonus cutting diagrams, and a lot more.

Woodsmith 3

from our readers

Tips & Techniques

Handy Tool Stand

My collection of pliers was just thrown into one drawer with the idea that I'd build some suitable storage "some day." I finally grew tired of rummaging through my tool drawer every time I needed a pair of pliers.

The storage solution I came up with is shown in the photo and drawings. It's just an L-shaped stand with a slotted rack at the top to hold the tools. The rack is tapered so the pliers stay put. I made the base extra wide so it could stand on the workbench.

To build the stand, I cut the base and back to size first. Then I added a rabbet to the base and glued the two parts together.

Next, I built the rack assembly. Since the grooves in the front and back of the rack need to align, I cut them in an extra-wide blank first. After I ripped it in half, I cut the bevels on the rack front. To finish up, I cut hardboard dividers to size and glued up the assembly. A couple of screws through the back hold the rack on the stand. I added L-hooks so it could hang on pegboard. The base of the rack allows me to take it with me in my shop.

With this new caddy, my pliers are always right at hand.

Bob Zimmerman
Des Moines, Iowa

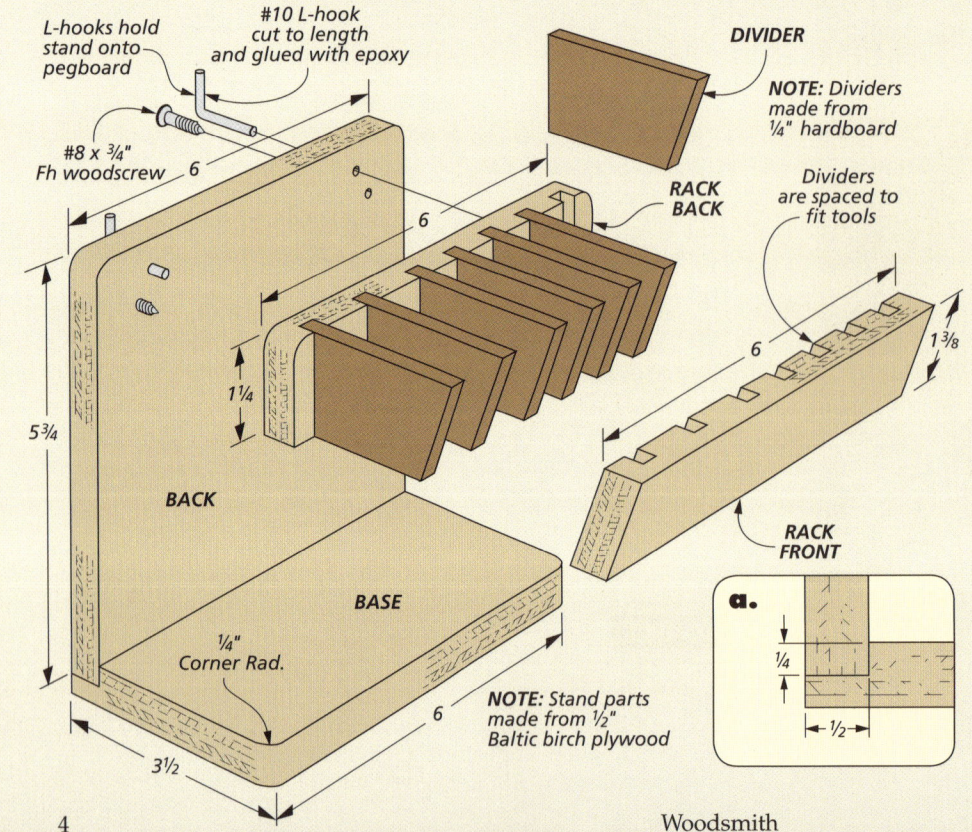

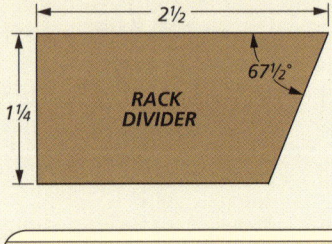

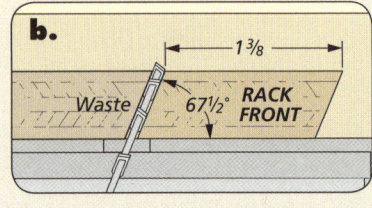

Change a Sanding Disk

Changing the disk on a disk sander is always a chore. You usually need to remove the table to have complete access to the plate in order to apply the new sanding disk. But I figured out a way to change the sanding disk without taking the table off.

First, I peel about half the backing off the disk and fold it down, as you can see in the top photo. Next, I slip the covered half behind the table and align the portion with the adhesive exposed with the plate. Finally, I turn the disk by hand 180° and remove the rest of the backing (lower photo).

The disk slips right into place without removing the table. I get the job done in a fraction of the time.

Chris Forgacs
Ravenna, Ohio

Dowel Extensions

I have a great router table that does everything I need it to do, until it's time to change the position of the fence. The bolts to loosen the fence are short and the knobs are close to the fence, making it almost impossible to turn them.

I remedied this problem with extensions made from 1"-dia. dowels about 4" long. First, I drilled a hole through the center of each dowel. Then I exchanged the bolts for longer ones. When I slipped the dowel over the bolt, it raised the knobs above the fence. Now it provides plenty of room for my fingers.

Bill Huber
Haslet, Texas

SUBMIT YOUR TIPS ONLINE

If you have an original shop tip, we would like to hear from you and consider publishing your tip in one or more of our publications. Go to:

Woodsmith.com
Click on the link,
"SUBMIT A TIP"

You'll be able to tell us all about your tip and upload your photos and drawings. You can also mail your tips to *"Woodsmith Tips"* at the editorial address shown at right. We will pay up to $200 if we publish your tip.

FREE TIPS BY EMAIL

Now you can have the best, time-saving secrets, solutions, and techniques sent directly to your email inbox. Just go to

Woodsmith.com
and click on
"Sign Up for Free E-Tips."
You'll receive one of our favorite tips each week.

Woodsmith
No. 196   August/September 2011

PUBLISHER Donald B. Peschke

EDITOR Bryan Nelson
MANAGING EDITOR Vincent Ancona
SENIOR EDITOR Ted Raife
ASSOCIATE EDITOR Dennis Perkins
ASSISTANT EDITOR Carol Beronich
CONTRIBUTING EDITORS Phil Huber,
Randall A. Maxey, James Bruton
EDITORIAL INTERN Abby Wolner

EXECUTIVE ART DIRECTOR Todd Lambirth
SENIOR ILLUSTRATORS David Kreyling, Harlan V. Clark, David Kallemyn
SENIOR GRAPHIC DESIGNER Bob Zimmerman
GRAPHIC DESIGNER Shelley Cronin
GRAPHIC DESIGN INTERN Becky Kralicek
CONTRIBUTING ILLUSTRATORS Dirk Ver Steeg, Peter J. Larson, Erich Lage

CREATIVE DIRECTOR Ted Kralicek
SENIOR PROJECT DESIGNERS Ken Munkel, Kent Welsh, Chris Fitch, Jim Downing, Mike Donovan
PROJECT DESIGNER/BUILDER John Doyle
SHOP CRAFTSMEN Steve Curtis, Steve Johnson
SENIOR PHOTOGRAPHERS Crayola England, Dennis Kennedy
ASSOCIATE STYLE DIRECTOR Rebecca Cunningham
SENIOR ELECTRONIC IMAGE SPECIALIST Allan Ruhnke
PRODUCTION ASSISTANT Minniette Johnson
VIDEO EDITOR/DIRECTOR Mark Hayes, Nate Gruca

Woodsmith® (ISSN 0164-4114) is published bimonthly by August Home Publishing Company, 2200 Grand Ave, Des Moines, IA 50312.
Woodsmith® is a registered trademark of August Home Publishing.
Copyright© 2011 August Home Publishing Company. All rights reserved.
Subscriptions: Single copy: $4.95.
Canadian Subscriptions: Canada Post Agreement No. 40038201. Send change of address information to PO Box 881, Station Main, Markham, ON L3P 8M6. Canada BN 84597 5473 RT
Periodicals Postage Paid at Des Moines, IA, and at additional offices.
Postmaster: Send change of address to Woodsmith, Box 37106, Boone, IA 50037-0106.

WoodsmithCustomerService.com

ONLINE SUBSCRIBER SERVICES
- **VIEW** your account information
- **RENEW** your subscription
- **CHECK** on a subscription payment
- **PAY** your bill
- **CHANGE** your mailing or e-mail address
- **VIEW/RENEW** your gift subscriptions
- **TELL US** if you've missed an issue

CUSTOMER SERVICE   Phone: 800-333-5075

SUBSCRIPTIONS
Customer Service
P.O. Box 842
Des Moines, IA 50304-9961
subscriptions@augusthome.com

EDITORIAL
Woodsmith Magazine
2200 Grand Avenue
Des Moines, IA 50312
woodsmith@woodsmith.com

AUGUST HOME PUBLISHING COMPANY   Printed in China

more tips from our readers

Drill Press Extension

I find it difficult to drill holes near the end of a long board. The board teeters on my small drill press table and I spend a lot of time trying to line up the bit before I even start the drill. So I built the auxiliary table you see in the photo.

It's just three pieces of lumber sandwiched together to make a long extension table that hooks over my existing drill press table. You can see how it works in the right drawing.

The key to this extension is the spacer between the support board on top and the hook board on the bottom. I planed a board for the spacer to the same thickness as my auxiliary table. This eliminates any play when I attach the extension table. It just slides into place and stays put. And when I don't need it, the low-profile design makes it easy to store out of the way.

Ian Ross
Smith Falls, Ontario

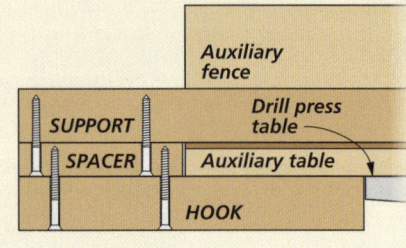

Temporary Pulls

Fitting drawers for a project is always a challenge. It takes a lot of trial and error (pulling drawers in and out of their openings many times) before I'm satisfied with how they fit in the case.

The problem is that I don't like to install the pulls until I'm sure the fit of the drawer is exactly right. That way I can align the pulls perfectly. But removing a drawer without a pull is difficult. So I use small pieces of duct tape as temporary drawer pulls. Now the drawers slide out easily.

Ken Munkel
Des Moines, Iowa

Disposable Glue Tray

When I glue up an assembly, I like to pour the glue in a tray so that I have easy access to brush it on joints. I've used all sorts of trays for this purpose, but found the cut off bottom of a windshield washer fluid container to be the best.

It's a great way to recycle a throw-away container. Plus, wood glue doesn't stick to this type of plastic. When I'm finished with the job, I can just pull the glue off after it dries, like you see in the photo. And it's ready to reuse again and again.

Charles Mak
Calgery, Alberta

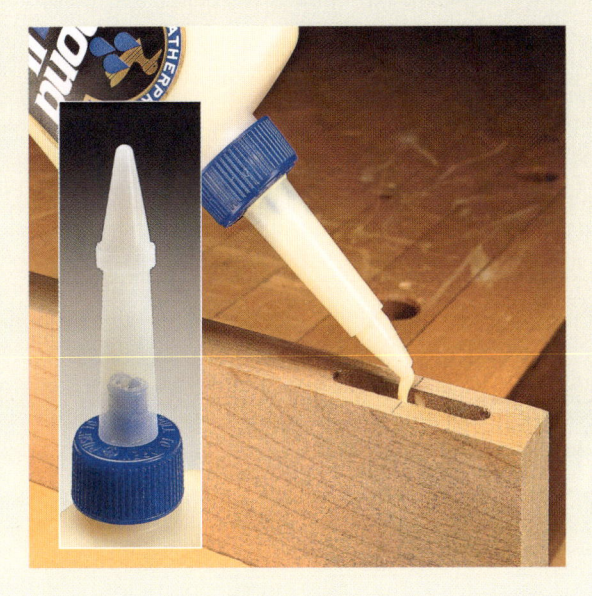

Glue Bottle Tip

No matter how careful I am, my glue bottle always seem to clog up after just a few uses. Rather than continually cleaning the nozzle and tip, I designed a better dispenser bottle.

First, I removed the stopper and nozzle from the glue bottle and made the opening slightly larger. Then I slid the nozzle from a tube of latex caulk over the stub. It's a perfect fit and the larger hole lets the unused glue run back to the bottle.

Dustin Hopper
Marshfield, Missouri

Quick Tips

PLASTIC DOWELS

When I'm painting or finishing a project in my shop, I use props to keep the project off the bench. But I seldom use wooden dowels. Instead, I use "dowels" cut from plastic coat hangers. The plastic cuts just like wood, but the finish won't stick to it. This makes clean-up a breeze.

Steve Fox
Gilberts, Illinois

REINFORCED SANDPAPER

When sanding with a finish sander, it's easy to wear through the sandpaper along the edges and corners where the paper gets the most friction. Often this happens before the sandpaper is used up, causing waste, lost time, and frustration. But I've found a quick, easy fix.

I apply duct tape to the back of the sandpaper. The duct tape reinforces the sandpaper against wear and tear so I get longer use out of it.

Jared Beck
Pocatello, Idaho

Inexpensive Remote

A remote control offers a handy way to turn on a shop vacuum when I need to collect dust from a routing or sanding job, since the vacuum is usually located in an out-of-the-way spot with the switch out of reach. But a remote control designed for workshop tools is relatively expensive. I found a cheaper alternative, though.

I use a remote control that's designed for outdoor lights. The two-piece remote, like the one shown in the photo, is available in the lighting department at most hardware stores or home centers. The amperage rating is high enough to run a shop vacuum without overloading the circuit. But the best part of using this remote is it costs about a third of the price of a shop remote.

Loren Apfel
Norfolk, Nebraska

Keep remote in shop apron

Plug shop vacuum into wall unit

SHORTEN PIN NAILS

I needed $1\frac{1}{2}$" pin nails to complete a project. But I only had 2" nails on hand.

Rather than make another run to the store, I simply snipped off the end of the 2" nails with a pair of tin snips. To sharpen the new ends, I held the strip of nails between scrap blocks of wood and reground them on my bench grinder. The shorter nails worked great in my pin nailer.

Serge Duclos
Delson, Quebec

WIN THIS BOSCH IMPACT DRIVER

That's right, send us your favorite shop tips. If your tip or technique is selected as the featured reader's tip, you'll win a *Bosch* impact driver just like the one shown here. To submit your tip or technique, just go online to w*oodsmith.com* and click on the link, "SUBMIT A TIP." You can submit your tip and upload your photos for consideration.

The Winner!

Congratulations to Ian Ross, winner of the *Bosch* impact driver. To find out how you could win this driver, check out the information on the left.

all about

choosing Cabinet Lighting

Installing the right lighting is the key to highlighting your treasures.

▼ Different types of bulbs emit light within a certain range of the color spectrum, either cool or warm.

12-volt fluorescent puck light

Xenon puck light

Battery-powered LED puck light

Fluorescent and LED strip lights create low-profile illumination

Incandescent canister lights create a spotlight effect

Adding interior lighting to a display cabinet is a great finishing touch. It draws attention to the project and the items on display. The only problem: There are a lot of choices. With so many options, it's easy to get overwhelmed.

Choosing the best lighting for a cabinet or shelf is easiest if you consider just two aspects: the source and the fixture. By the source I mean incandescent or fluorescent, among others. Knowing how these types of lights work helps narrow down the choice. Then you can decide on the type of fixture. Puck, strips, and canisters are a few of the choices.

LIGHT SOURCE

Only a few years ago there were just two choices for lighting: incandescent and fluorescent. But today there are almost as many light sources as there are fixtures.

INCANDESCENT. An incandescent light is the oldest, most common type of lighting available. Although the warm yellow glow is not quite as bright as other types of lighting, it's inexpensive. It's biggest drawback is that it produces a lot of heat. If you want to use it in an enclosed cabinet, it needs ventilation.

FLUORESCENT. Fluorescent light is at the opposite end of the color spectrum from incandescent. It casts a blue-violet glow. Because of how light is produced in the tube, it will take less wattage to produce the same amount of brightness as an incandescent bulb. That makes it more efficient to operate. The violet color of the light has a tendency to distort the color of objects, but you can find warm fluorescent light bulbs that are more natural looking and don't cast violet light.

Another design using the same technology is a compact fluorescent bulb. Most bulbs are made to fit in an incandescent light fixture, replacing incandescent bulbs to help reduce heat build up.

▲ Low profile LED strips can be linked together with special connectors (inset photo) and are easy to install in a cabinet.

Use the included dual-plug connector to link LED strips together

LIGHT EMITTING DIODES. If you want high-intensity light, then light-emitting diodes (LED) are the best choice. They're really tiny lights clustered together to make one bright light. These lights are lower in energy consumption and last longer than incandescent lighting. There are disadvantages to this light, though. They're expensive (about $20 per bulb) and their blue tint doesn't give the best color rendition.

HALOGEN LIGHTING. Another high-intensity option for lighting is halogen lights. Some of these lights are designed to fit incandescent fixtures, so you can get whiter light. They're more efficient to use and last longer than ordinary incandescent bulbs. They do burn hotter, so they need ventilation too.

XENON. Xenon lights may be the best choice of all. They burn cooler and still give off bright white light that mimic natural daylight. Often this is the best option when true color is important. The downside to xenon lights is that they're expensive (about $20 for a bulb).

FIXTURES

There are a wide variety of cabinet fixtures, but the size and shape of the fixture and where it needs to be located for optimal lighting may dictate which is best for a particular project.

CANISTER LIGHTS. An early popular shape of light was the canister light (lower left photo). Canister lights, which house incandescent, compact fluorescent, or halogen bulbs, shine light directly down. Some fixtures have the option to move side-to-side to a limited extent.

The downside to canister lights is that they have to be vented, so you can only use them in a cabinet that's designed to house the bulky canisters.

PUCK LIGHTING. A good alternative to canister lighting is puck lighting (lower right photo). Puck lights take up the least amount of space in a cabinet because they don't require venting. You can surface-mount them or recess them slightly. Still other puck lights are battery-powered and don't require special installation of any kind.

STRIP LIGHTING. To light multiple shelves with one light you can mount a strip light in the upper inside edge of a cabinet (photo above). This type of fixture comes with LED, fluorescent, or incandescent bulbs.

LINKABLE STRIP LIGHTS. One handy feature of strip lighting to look for is linkable strips. They have either short, pigtail connections or direct connectors, like the ones shown in the inset photo at the top of the page. You can connect multiple lights together to suit your needs for any project.

POWER SUPPLY. Regardless of what type of fixture you decide on, keep in mind that several of the fixtures here require voltage regulators or transformers to supply the correct amount of power. You'll need to consider this when planning for and installing lighting in a project.

Categorizing light sources and fixtures can help you narrow down the options. Then making the right choice will be easy. **W**

▲ Canister lights can create a dramatic effect, but require some clearance to install.

▲ Puck lights can be mounted on the surface of a cabinet or slightly recessed.

tools of the trade

choosing a
Hand Drill

Work faster and more efficiently using the right kind of drill for each job in the shop.

A hand-held drill is an essential tool for any woodworking shop. But when you consider the power supply, speed, size and capacity of different drills, finding the right drill for the task at hand might be a tough decision. One way to narrow down the choices is to focus on how the drill is powered: cordless, corded, or pneumatic. Each type of drill is best suited for specific tasks.

CORDLESS. Battery-powered drills are pretty much stantard fair in a woodworking shop. Since there's no cord to get in the way, you can take them anywhere. Newer models are available in a range of sizes and voltages. They're usually light and easy to handle, like the one shown in the top, right photo on the opposite page.

The newer, lithium ion batteries recharge quickly and hold a

▼ Each of these drill types are suited for different types of jobs.

For high torque, nothing beats a corded drill

Cordless drill/drivers offer go-anywhere versatility

Pneumatic drills are light-weight and powerful

Pneumatic drills work easily in tight spaces

10 · Woodsmith · No. 196

charge for months in storage. This means you don't have to charge the battery before each use, so you can just grab it and go.

Where a cordless drill excels is driving screws. Most drivers have a clutch on the chuck that regulates torque and allows you to drive screws gently without stripping out the holes or screw heads. The clutch actually disengages the chuck so it stops turning even though the motor is still running. Two speed range options also aid in driving screws (right inset photo). I use the slow speed to drive screws and the higher speed to drill small holes.

CORDED DRILLS. Cordless drill/drivers won't do every job, though. They don't have the power to drill large holes or drive long screws into hardwood. For that kind of work, it's best to use a corded drill.

The higher voltage of a corded drill provides more torque for heavy or extended use. For example, if I have a large hole to drill with a hole saw, a corded drill makes short work of it. (The drill shown in the main photo will handle a hole saw up to 1 3/8" diameter.)

I also like to use a corded drill for drilling holes for pocket hole joinery. With a corded drill the power never runs out or bogs down, so you can use it for drilling metal or other non-wood materials as well.

The weight of a corded drill can produce fatigue after prolonged use, though. And no clutch means driving screws takes more finesse.

PNEUMATIC DRILL. One type of power supply that's often overlooked is air. But if you have an air compressor, it's an option worth considering.

Air-powered tools combine the benefits of both the corded and cordless drill. First, they're light weight and easy to handle. Second their power is continuous, if your air compressor is large enough to provide the needed air. The air requirements for most drills are available from the manufacturer, so check the packaging to see if your compressor can handle the task.

While older air-powered drills only drive forward, newer models have reverse as well, like the one shown in the photo below. You can also vary the speed depending on how hard you pull the trigger. Because they use a common keyed chuck, pneumatic drills take the same bits and attachments as any other drill.

I like to use a pneumatic drill where I have limited clearance. They're great at getting into tight places, because the overall length is much shorter than most other drills. Since a pneumatic drill doesn't have a motor, they usually aren't as large as corded or even cordless drills. You can see what I mean in the lower, right photo on the opposite page.

While you can purchase an air-powered drill for around $35, a high-quality pneumatic drill will set you back about $200. But the tool has few working parts, so it will last virtually forever if kept oiled (left inset photo).

Depending on the type of work you do, you may want to have all three drills on hand in your shop. But if you're just getting started, match the drill to your current need, and you'll get better results with less frustration.

▲ The adjustable clutch feature on a cordless drill stops the drill before it strips a screw.

▲ Most cordless drills have two speeds: a low speed for driving screws with a light touch and a high speed for drilling (inset photo).

▲ Pneumatic drills are great for working in tight places. Keep them oiled for years of use.

jigs & fixtures

Rockler Taper Jig

Tapers and straight edges are a lot easier to cut with this handy tool.

Large, easy-to-grip handle for positive control

Adjustable fence helps position board for cutting tapers

Two, wide-body hold-downs clamp workpiece securely

Machined aluminum miter bar fits most saws

Sturdy, stable MDF covered with low-friction laminate

Wide abrasive strips prevent workpiece and fence from shifting

Handy measuring tape ensures accurate setups

I've made a few shop-built tapering jigs, but I have to admit I've never been completely satisfied with the performance of any of them. Either they were built for a specific task, then discarded or they were just a little too hard to set up and use safely. At the end of the day, I found this jig from *Rockler* to be well worth a look. It's not only well made, but super easy to set up and use.

SETUP. Made from flat, stable MDF and covered with low-friction laminate, the jig slides easily over the surface of any table saw. It also has an adjustable miter bar for an accurate fit in most miter slots. There are two positions for mounting the bar to fit most saw models. If the miter slot on your saw brings the base too close to the blade, you can simply trim the base of the jig to fit. I attached the miter bar to the jig and then used it as a guide to create a zero clearance edge on the base of the jig.

The jig also features a large handle for smooth, easy control throughout the cut. Keeping the workpiece on the jig

Woodsmith No. 196

is a snap with two wide hold-downs. They have non-marring rubber caps for a better grip (lower, center photo). Plus, the jig has three abrasive strips on the base to keep the workpiece from slipping during a cut (lower photo, opposite page).

MULTIPLE USES. The taper jig is designed to cut tapers on boards up to 6" wide. Or you can remove the miter bar and use it to cut a clean, straight edge on any width rough-sawn board (right photo).

TAPERING. The jig has markings for two ways to taper a board. Small holes on each end of the jig are used as indexing marks (left photo, below). Each mark represents one degree of taper. To use the indexing marks, set one end of the fence at the widest point in the taper. Then set the other end to the mark for angle of the taper to cut. With the setup complete, clamp the board against the fence and cut the taper.

DIMENSIONED TAPER. If a project has a dimensioned taper, you can use the measuring tape at each end of the jig to get the perfect setup for a leg or other tapered part. Again you set the lead end of the jig to cut the widest part of the taper. Then set the other end at the narrowest part of the taper. Begin the cut at the wide end of the workpiece for a cleaner cut.

▲ To cut a straight edge on wide boards, simply remove the miter bar from the base and guide the jig against the table saw rip fence. The result is a smooth, straight edge every time.

STOP. There's also a stop at the end of the jig to keep shorter workpieces from sliding backward (right photo, below). The stop can also hold a tapered leg firmly. For a four-sided taper, I save the cut offs and use them to prop the workpiece up for subsequent cuts. The cutoffs ensure a consistent taper on all four edges.

STRAIGHT EDGE. To cut a straight edge on rough lumber, I set the taper fence parallel to the saw blade and clamp the board on the base, as shown in the upper photo. For narrow boards, you can leave the miter bar in place and cut the irregular edge off the board. As I mentioned before, if the board you're cutting is too wide, you can remove the miter bar and use the jig with its edge against your rip fence.

SMALL PIECES. In addition to cutting tapers and trimming edges, this jig can also make cutting small workpieces safer, by holding them in place during a cut.

To sum things up, this jig is smooth, stable, and easy to use. Whether you're cutting tapers on a milled workpiece or cutting the edge off a piece of rough lumber, you'll have a jig that fills the bill. And for under $75, it will work for just about any budget. **W**

▲ Small holes at both ends of the jig make it easy to set the degree of taper.

▲ Large star-knobs make it easy to tighten the heavy-duty hold-downs.

▲ A handy, retractable stop catches the workpiece at the end of the jig. Slide the stop out of the way to cut longer boards.

woodworking technique

Veneering Large Panels

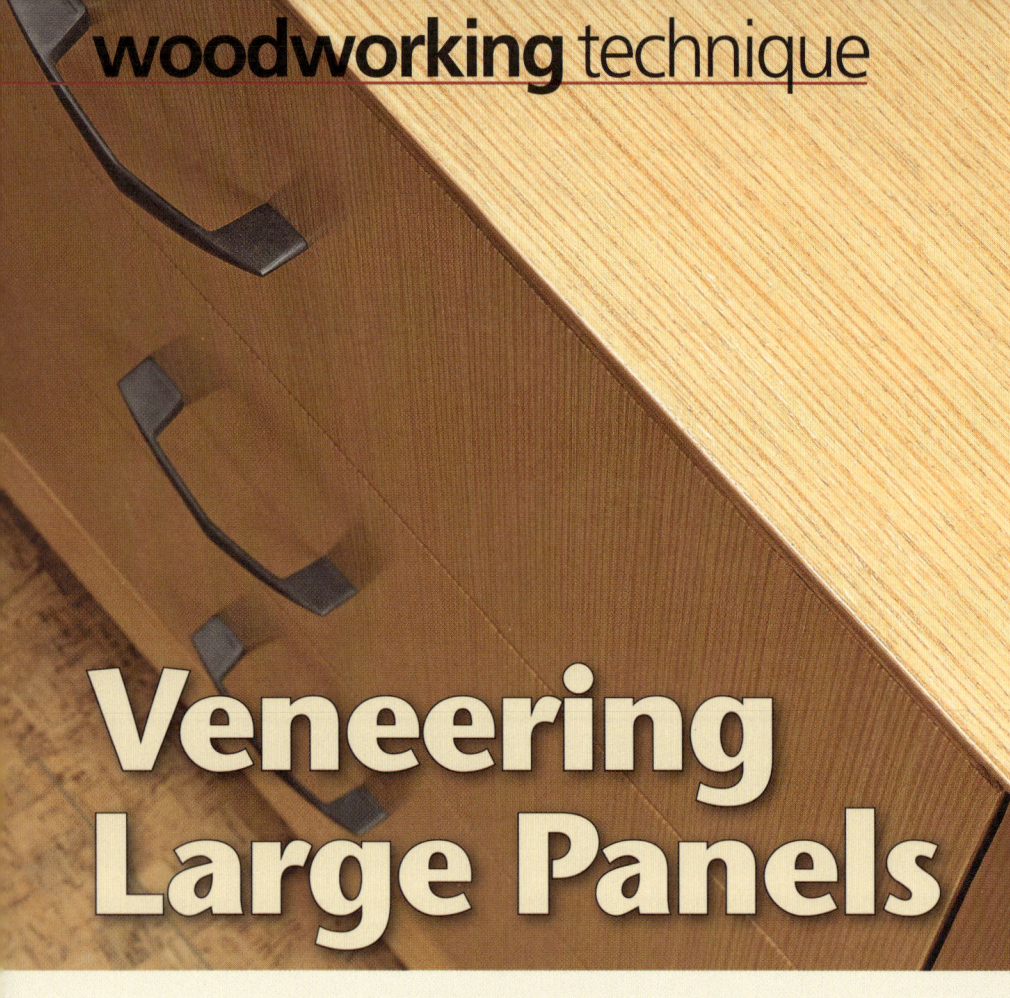

When applying veneer, careful preparation, a little bit of know-how, and a step-by-step approach guarantee a successful outcome.

▼ "Green" veneer looks virtually identical to the real thing.

Quartered Wenge

Zebrawood

Quartered Ebony

Quartered Douglas Fir

Veneer opens up a lot of design possibilities to woodworkers. The striking appearance of the credenza on page 22 is a great example. The linear grain pattern of the man-made veneer is a perfect complement to the clean lines and simple design details. This visual effect couldn't be achieved in any other way.

There are a handful of methods for applying veneer. The use of contact adhesive or a vacuum press can simplify the process. But contact adhesive is generally only suitable for paper-backed veneer. And due to the high cost, a large vacuum press system isn't a practical investment for occasional use.

CLAMP & CAUL. For applying the raw wood veneer to the large case and panels of the credenza, traditional caul and clamp veneering is a good option. The basic process is easy to understand. In a nutshell, you simply rely on a combination of platens (flat panels), cauls, and clamps to press the veneer onto the panel while the glue sets up.

The sheer size of the project may make this seem like a difficult task. But when you plan ahead and take it one step at a time, it should go smoothly.

"GREEN" VENEER. First, an introduction to the featured material is in order. If you didn't know better, you'd swear the faux vertical grain Douglas fir veneer used on the credenza was the real thing. This unique product is actually reconstituted from wood fibers and then dyed to match a particular species and figure pattern. Several of the available types are shown at left.

This material has several advantages over its natural counterpart. It comes in long, wide, full-yield sheets. The color and grain pattern are consistent within the sheet and from one sheet to the next. Additionally, the cost can be considerably less than natural veneer and it's a good "green" use of a limited resource.

THE TOOLS

Now, let's talk about the tools and supplies you'll need. A good starter set is small and generally inexpensive (top photo, opposite page). Here's a short description of the basic items.

CUTTING VENEER. You'll need something to cut the veneer with. I prefer to use a veneer saw. A veneer saw looks and cuts like a cross between a saw and a knife. The double-sided curved blade has individual teeth like a saw. However, the teeth are sharpened to a single bevel knife edge. A sharp utility knife also works but is more likely to tear or split the veneer, especially when making crossgrain cuts. A veneer saw only runs about $15 — a good investment. You'll also need a straightedge to guide the veneer saw. A three- or four-footer is adequate for most tasks.

VENEER TAPE. Another handy specialty item is veneer tape. It's used to join separate pieces of veneer as well as reinforce fragile veneer and repair cracks or splits.

Veneer tape is simply a very thin, although surprisingly strong, paper tape with hide glue applied to one side. To use veneer tape, you activate the glue by dampening it, then press the tape in place. (The tape is always applied to the outside face.) It can later be sanded or scraped off.

GLUE FOR VENEERING. A variety of glues can be used to lay veneer. However, my first choice is a product that's specifically formulated for this type of veneering. It's referred to as cold press veneer glue. *Titebond* is a commonly available brand.

It comes in liquid form so there's no mixing or heating involved. Its thick consistency minimizes bleed-through. And it dries to a very hard film that eliminates the chance of "creep" between the veneer and substrate.

When working on large panels, you'll need a quick, efficient way to spread the glue evenly over the surface. An inexpensive foam paint roller works great.

CLAMPING PRESSURE. Plenty of evenly distributed clamping pressure is essential to ensure complete adhesion of the veneer. F-style clamps, C-clamps, or handscrews will work well around the edges. However, when working with large panels, applying adequate pressure through the center is a challenge. Deep-throat clamps are one option. As you'll see on the following pages, a cheaper and equally effective solution is to use bowed cauls to transfer clamping pressure applied at the edge to the center of the panel.

GETTING STARTED

With the tools and supplies rounded up, you're ready to go. I'll start by explaining the process of laying veneer on the case. Then we'll talk about the slightly simpler task of completing the doors and drawer fronts.

SMOOTH & FLUSH. The preliminary steps are shown in the photos below. I started with some thorough surface preparation. Any irregularities will telegraph through the thin (1/40") veneer. So you'll need to fill any screw holes and small gaps in the joinery. Make certain the case joints, the beveled trim, and the filled screw holes are sanded perfectly smooth and flush to the surface.

THE VENEER. Your next task is to prepare the veneer. When you cut it to rough size, don't scrimp. I allowed an extra inch or more on all four sides. This makes initial positioning easier and it provides a little insurance if the veneer slips on the glue when clamping pressure is applied.

After cutting the veneer to size, it's a good idea to wrap the ends with veneer tape. This reinforces the veneer against splits.

▲ A small collection of tools and supplies is all that's required to successfully lay veneer.

Labels: Cold press veneer glue, Veneer tape, Straightedge, Foam roller, Plastic sheeting, Veneer saw, F-style clamps

▲ Apply filler to the screw holes and any other dings or gaps and then sand it smooth.

▲ Working on a sacrificial panel, clamp the straightedge down before cutting the veneer.

▲ To prevent splits from starting, wrap the ends of the cut pieces with veneer tape.

THE CLAMPING SYSTEM

A couple of the preliminary steps are out of the way. But some of the most important preparation is yet to be done. As I mentioned, the success of the job hinges on applying adequate pressure. So the next step is to get your clamping system organized. And then I strongly suggest a thorough dry run before getting out the glue.

CAULS & PLATENS. The veneer is applied to the two sides of the case first, and then the top. The same general setup is used for the different surfaces. I'll use the sides as my example.

To work on the sides, you'll want to stand the case on end, as shown in the drawing at right. It will be easier to position the veneer, cauls, and clamps.

The right drawing and detail show the clamping system I used to press the veneer onto the case. To make certain the veneer laid out flat and to help distribute the clamping pressure evenly, I used two pieces of ¾" MDF as my platen. A third piece of MDF is fit inside the case to balance the pressure. (It can be temporarily attached with double-sided tape.)

I sized the top platens larger than the case sides but slightly smaller than the piece of veneer. This allows you to observe any movement as the clamps are tightened. I also cut a piece of plastic sheeting to place between the veneer and the platens. This eliminates the chance of the veneer and platens sticking together.

As you can see above, I used three pairs of bowed cauls along the side to apply pressure across the platens. (Check out our web site for information on making bowed cauls.) Then I positioned individual clamps between the cauls for added pressure.

Woodsmith GO ONLINE EXTRAS
To learn how to how to shape bowed cauls, visit our website at Woodsmith.com.

LAYING THE VENEER

With the platens, clamps, and cauls ready, all the other necessary supplies at hand, and the dress rehearsal completed, you can begin laying the veneer. You'll find that once the glue goes on, things can get pretty hectic. And although you can get the job done single-handed, enlisting a helper can reduce the stress.

GLUE ON. The How-To box on the opposite page shows how to proceed. You start by spreading an even coat of glue on the case side. One option is to pour glue into a pan and dip the roller into it. But I think it's easier and faster to pour glue onto the surface and then use the roller to spread it.

A full, wet coat of glue is what you're after — not overly thick and pooling. Once you start applying glue, you have about 15 minutes to get everything in place and the clamps tightened, so you'll have to work quickly.

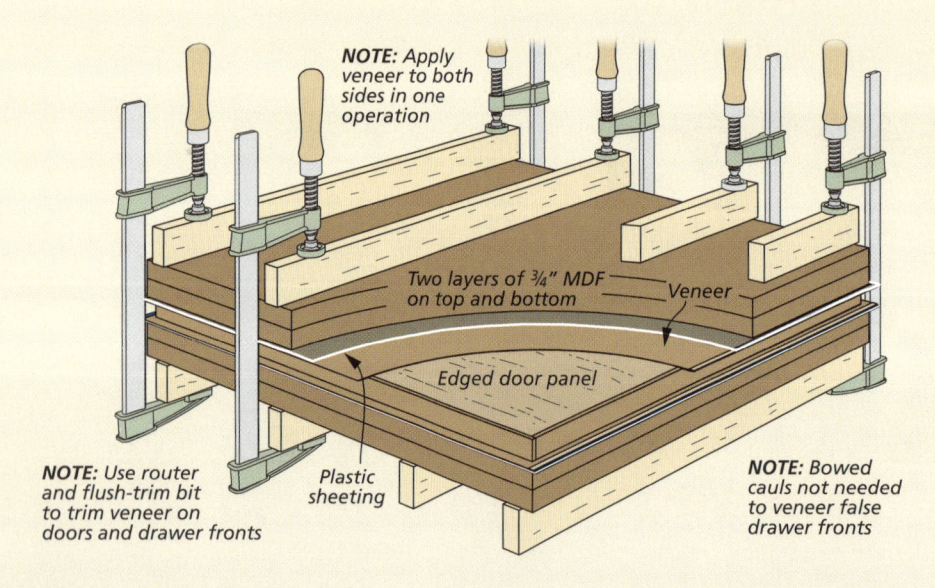

NEXT, VENEER. With the glue spread on the case side, you can carefully lay the veneer on the panel. The trick here is to position it right on the money with your first try. The glue grabs quickly and if you try to reposition the fragile veneer it will very likely split. This is where having a helper comes in handy.

PRESSURE. Now, quickly smooth the veneer with your hands, lay the sheet of plastic over it, and position the two platens. Take a final look to make sure everything is in order, then start adding the cauls and clamps. To prevent the veneer from shifting, apply pressure gradually by tightening each clamp a little bit at a time. Then you can relax.

CLAMPS OFF. Allow the glue to dry for a couple of hours before removing the clamps. You'll most likely be greeted by a smooth, flat surface. If you have spots of loose veneer or bubbles, check out the box below for an easy fix.

TRIM THE VENEER. Before applying the next piece, I carefully trimmed the veneer flush to the edges. The trick is to avoid lifting or chipping the veneer. Step Four shows how to do the job using a veneer saw. Sanding the edge lightly will complete the job.

Once both sides are veneered, the top piece can be laid. Obviously, you'll need larger platens and more cauls and clamps. I placed a caul about every 10". Step Five shows how to position the large sheet by "rolling" it out from one end to the other.

DOORS & DRAWER FRONTS. The technique used for the doors and drawer fronts is similar. The main difference is that both faces are veneered. And it's best to do this all in one step to avoid bowing the panels. The lower drawing on the opposite page shows how to build the "sandwich" one layer at a time. When veneering the narrower drawer fronts, you can dispense with the bowed cauls. Just use a few more clamps.

I think that when all is said and done, you'll find that the end result is well worth the effort.

How-To: Veneer the Credenza Case

STEP ONE
NOTE: Stand case on end
NOTE: Pour glue on surface and roll out evenly
Foam roller

Spread Glue. Pour glue onto the surface and use the roller to spread it evenly. A full, wet coat will ensure good adhesion.

STEP TWO
NOTE: Lay veneer and smooth out

Place Veneer. Position the veneer carefully on the wet glue and smooth it out. Once laid, don't try to reposition it.

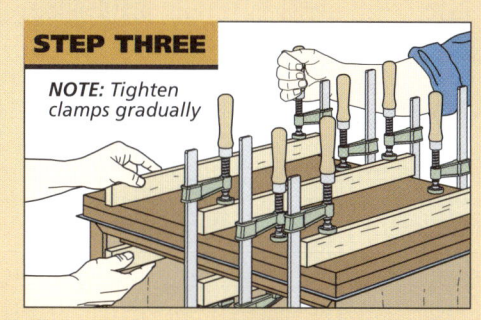

STEP THREE
NOTE: Tighten clamps gradually

Clamps On. Now quickly add the platens, cauls, and clamps. Tighten the clamps alternately, gradually increasing the pressure.

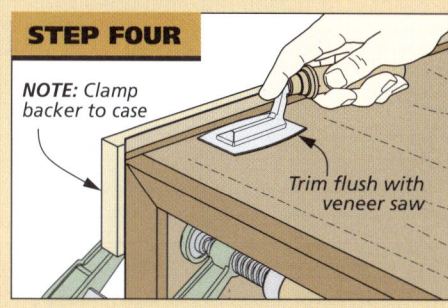

STEP FOUR
NOTE: Clamp backer to case
Trim flush with veneer saw

Trim the Veneer. A board clamped to the outside of the case backs up the veneer while you trim it flush with the veneer saw.

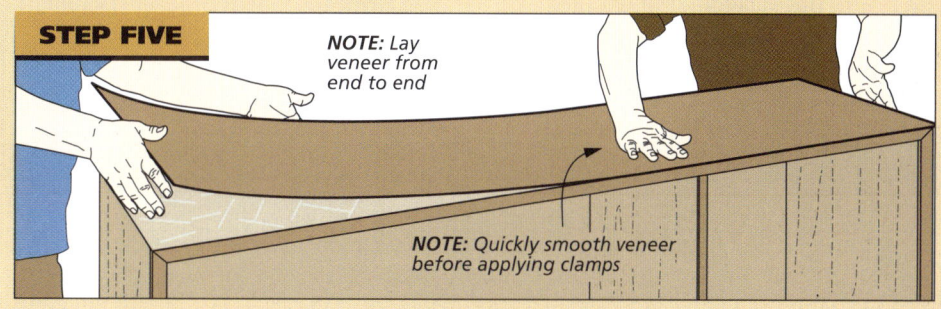

STEP FIVE
NOTE: Lay veneer from end to end
NOTE: Quickly smooth veneer before applying clamps

Two-Person Job. Positioning the long piece of veneer that covers the top of the case is definitely a job for two sets of hands. With one person holding each end, carefully position the veneer on one end and then "roll" it onto the surface. Then repeat the steps above.

Shop Tip: Iron Out Bubbles

If you find small patches or "bubbles" of veneer that didn't adhere well, don't worry, there's an easy fix. You can iron out the bubbles using heat to reactivate the dried glue.

Set a clothes iron to medium heat. Place a cotton cloth over the spot to be repaired and iron over the area. Check frequently to see when the veneer has flattened out and adhered.

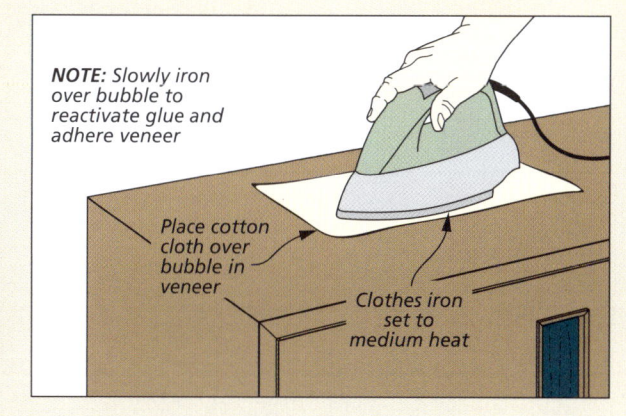

NOTE: Slowly iron over bubble to reactivate glue and adhere veneer
Place cotton cloth over bubble in veneer
Clothes iron set to medium heat

Weekend Project

curved-handle Serving Tray

Whether you use this tray to decorate your table or serve your guests, it will surely bring style and grace to your home.

Building a tray is a great way to practice new techniques in the shop. The joinery is often just as unique as the design. And this tray is no exception. It has splayed sides and arched ends that meet curved handles. This is a project that will look great on display in your home and will be a challenge to build too.

The splayed sides are easy to make and require just a couple cuts on the table saw. And the contrasting handles are cut on the band saw from a square blank, so there's no bending involved.

BUILDING THE TRAY

The design of the tray is based around the splay of the sides.

The other parts are sized to fit between them. For this reason I started with these.

Your first task is to cut the blanks for the sides. I cut them to length, but left them extra wide.

SPLAY THE SIDES. Cutting the joinery along the bottom edge of the sides is a multi-step process. The key is to create a square reference face for the bottom of the tray. This is done by making two bevel cuts. In addition, a groove in each side mates with a tongue cut along the edge of the bottom (detail 'a'). The How-to box at the bottom of the page steps you through the process.

To make the first bevel cut, I tilted the saw blade to 22½° and positioned the fence ⅛" from the blade. With the saw set up, you can hold the piece on edge and bevel the inside bottom edge of each side, as shown in the left drawing below.

GROOVE. As I mentioned, a groove in the face of the beveled edge holds a tongue on the bottom. To cut the groove, lay the workpiece flat on the table saw. You'll need to lower the blade to make the groove the proper depth, but leave the angle of the blade the same. The setup is shown in the second drawing from left, in the box below.

BEVEL. The second bevel cut squares up the edge to mate with the bottom. Your goal is to leave a ⁵⁄₁₆"-wide beveled face to match the bottom (third drawing below). Then you can trim the sides to width with a 90° cut along the top edge of each side.

NOTCHES. The final step for the sides of the tray is to cut a notch in each end for the handles you'll make later (detail 'b'). I did this with a dado blade in the table saw, standing the workpiece on end (right drawing, below).

After you've cut the notches, take a minute to cut an identical notch in a scrap piece of hardboard. You can use this later to gauge the thickness of the handles, as shown on page 20.

BOTTOM. The tray bottom is simply cut to size from straight-grain lumber. I used straight grain to reduce the chance of it cupping. Then you can rabbet each edge to create tongues (detail 'a').

GLUE UP. At this point, I took the time to glue the sides to the bottom. Clamping the splayed sides is a challenge, so I used tape to hold them in place.

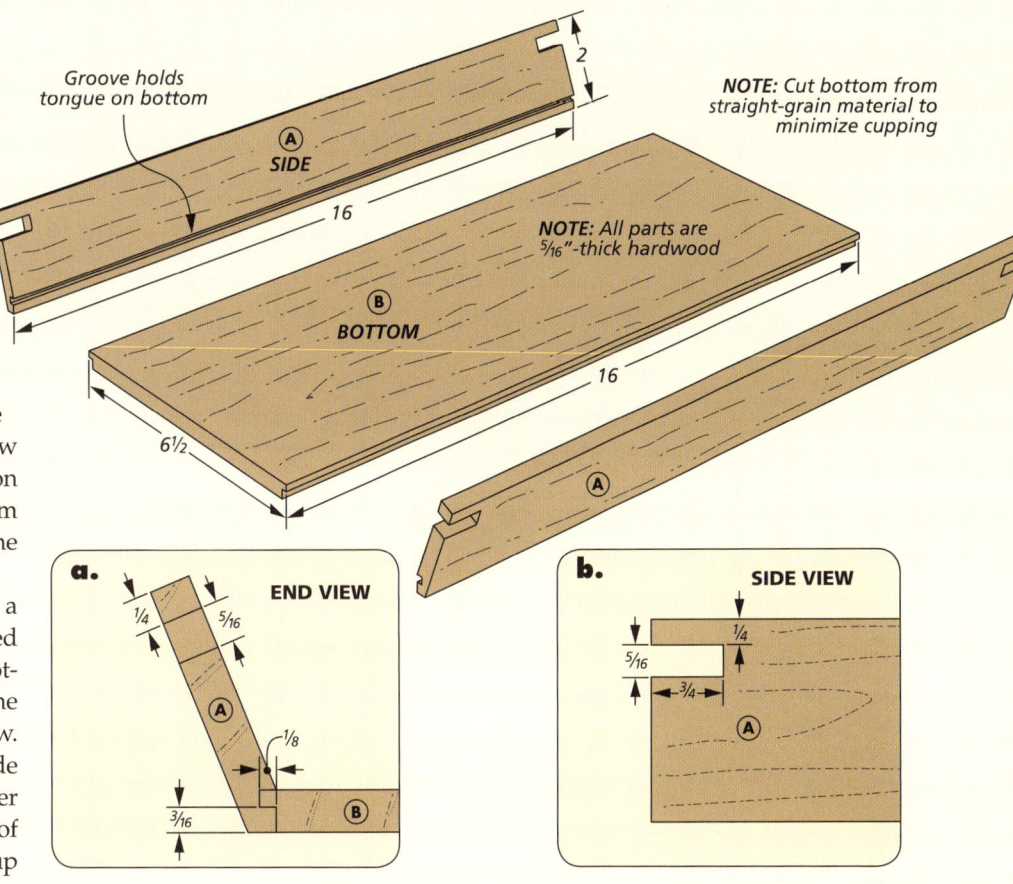

How-To: Make the Tray Sides

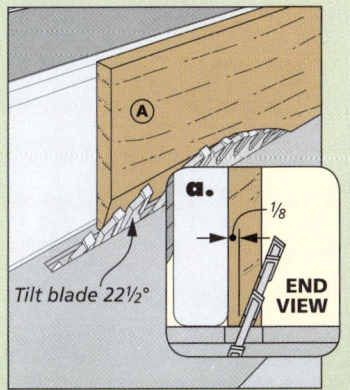

Bevel Edge. A beveled edge creates a surface to locate the cut for the groove.

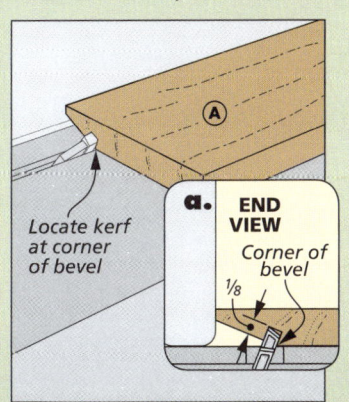

Groove. A groove cut along the face of the bevel will hold the tongue on the bottom.

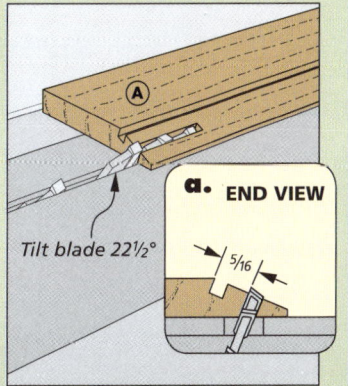

Second Bevel. A second bevel creates a flat so the tray sides are flush with the bottom.

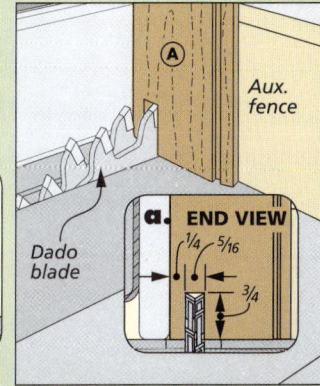

Handle Notch. Once the sides are cut to width, cut a notch to hold the curved handle.

Woodsmith.com　　　　Woodsmith　　　　19

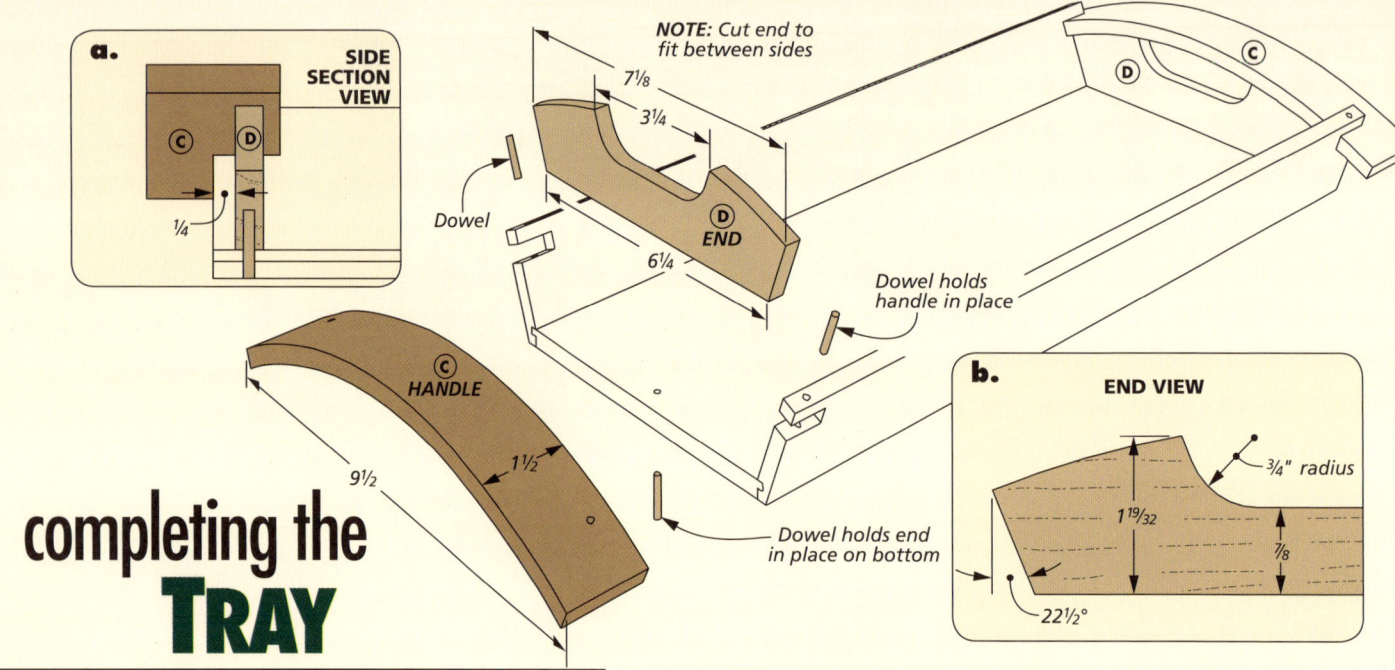

completing the TRAY

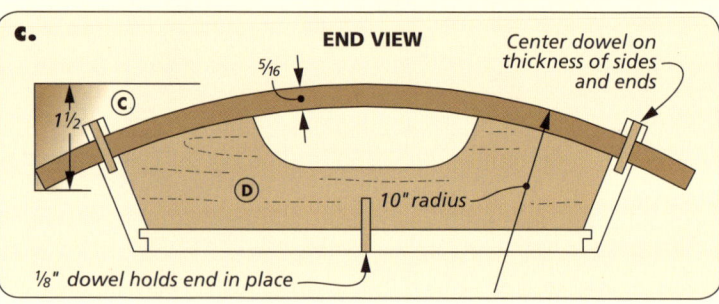

The tray is completed by adding the ends and handles. These integral parts fit together to close up the ends and give the tray its distinctive look. For this reason, the arc at the top of the end needs to match perfectly with the curve on the handle. To do this, I made the handle first and then used it as a template to shape the end.

HANDLE. Shaping the curved handle requires a couple of cuts on the band saw and some sanding. I started with an oversized blank. You can make a beam compass to mark the arcs on the side of the blank, as shown in the left drawing in the box below. Once the arcs are marked, bevel the blank on both ends to square the ends of the finished handle with the arc (center drawing below). Then cut the arcs on the band saw.

Cutting a smooth curve on the band saw can be difficult. But if you cut just outside the layout line, you'll find you have less material left to sand it smooth (right drawing). When the handles are cut to rough shape, you can clean up the inside curve with a sanding drum. Use a soft sanding pad to sand the top of the handle. As you sand, you can check the thickness of the handle with the hardboard gauge you cut earlier, as shown in the margin photo on the left.

▲ A hardboard gauge will help you check your progress when sanding.

How-To: Make the Handles

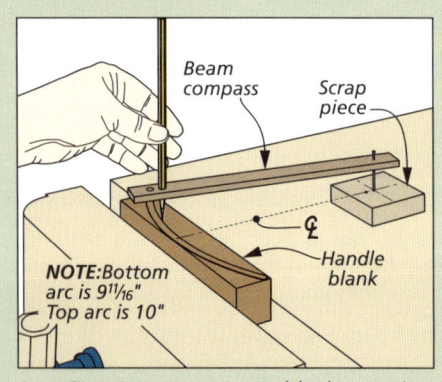

Lay Out Arc. Use a scrap block as a pivot point for the beam compass as you mark the arcs in the handle blank.

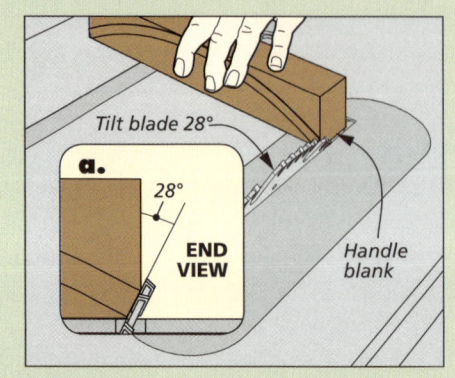

Trim Ends. Tilt the saw blade 28° to square the end of the handle. Then bevel the ends of the oversized block.

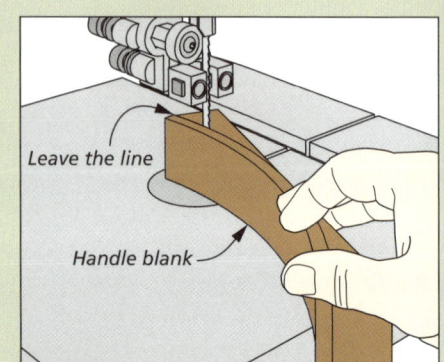

Band Saw Arc. A band saw will make short work of the arcs. After they're cut, sand the handle to remove saw marks.

How-To: Make the Ends

MAKE THE ENDS

The tray ends are also shaped with several cuts on the table saw and band saw. For this reason, I again started with a pair of extra-long, wide blanks.

BEVELS. The first step is to bevel the ends. They're cut at the same 22½° angle you used earlier for the sides. But this time you'll use a miter gauge. This is shown in Step One on the right. After you cut the bevels, check that the fit of each end is snug to the bottom and sides of the tray. You may need to sand the bevels a bit to get a good fit.

ARC. With the ends fit, you can slip the handles into the notches on the sides and mark the arc at the top of each end, as shown in Step Two on the right. When they're marked, cut the arcs on the band saw, leaving the line again (Step Three).

OPENING. To cut the finger opening on each end, I used the band saw, as shown in Step Four. The measurements are shown in detail 'b' on the opposite page. Then it's back to the sanding drum to clean up the cutouts, as shown in Step Five. Sand the ends too, until they fit snugly under the curve of the handle, as shown in the Shop Tip below.

FINAL ASSEMBLY. To attach the ends and handles to the tray, start by gluing the ends into place on the tray. Remember to recess them ¼" from each end of the bottom.

STEP ONE
Bevel Ends. With the miter gauge set at 22½°, bevel both ends of the blank to match the splay of the tray sides.

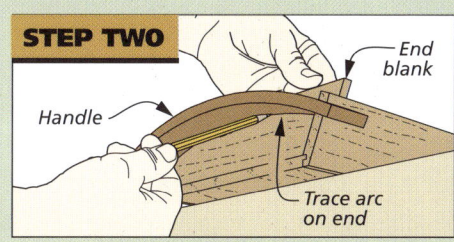

STEP TWO
Trace Handle. To fit the ends to the curved handle, insert the handle in the notches and use it as a guide to mark the curve.

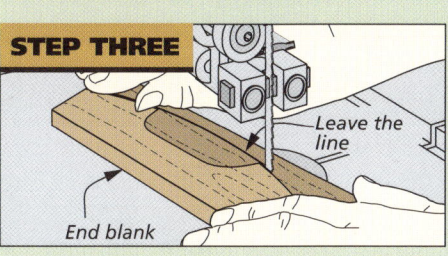

STEP THREE
Cut Arc. The arc at the top of the end is cut on the band saw. Cut on the waste side of the line to allow a custom fit.

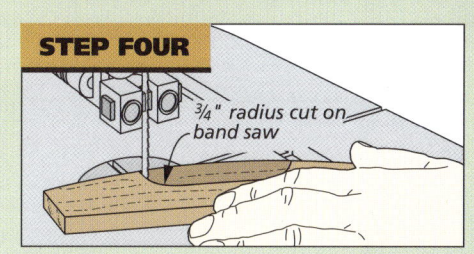

STEP FOUR
Cutout. The cutout for the handle openings is also cut on the band saw. Again, cut on the waste side of the line.

STEP FIVE
Drum Sand. After cutting away the waste, use a sanding drum to clean up the edges of the cutout and sand to the line.

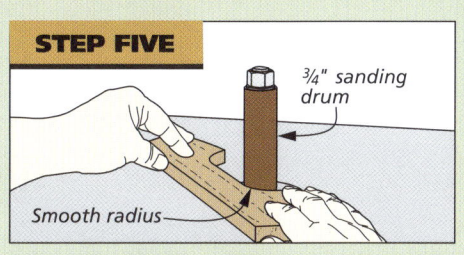

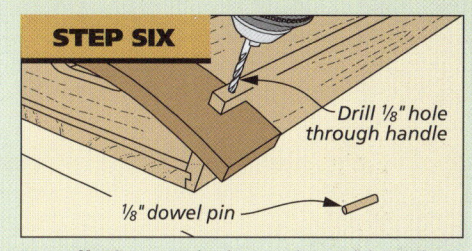

STEP SIX
Install Pins. With the ends and handle in place, drill a hole through the sides and into the handle, then insert a dowel pin.

Next, insert the handles in the notches and center them. You can drill holes from the top of the sides through the handles and insert dowels to hold them in place (Step Six). A final pair of dowels is inserted through the bottom to hold the ends. Finally, trim the dowels and sand them.

All that's left is to add a finish and fill your new tray with your favorite snack.

Shop Tip: Sanding to Fit

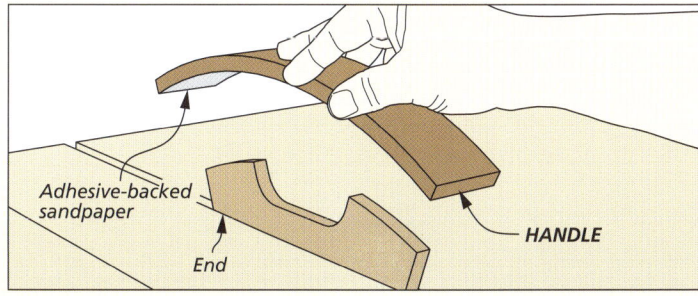

Fit End to Handle. In order to get a good fit between the end and the handle, use the handle as a sanding block to smooth the arc.

Materials & Cutting Diagram

A Sides (2)   5/16 x 2 - 16
B Bottom (1)   5/16 x 6½ - 16
C Handles (2)   5/16 x 1½ x 9½
D Ends (2)   5/16 x 1¾ - 7⅛
• Dowel (1)   ⅛"-dia. x 5" rgh.

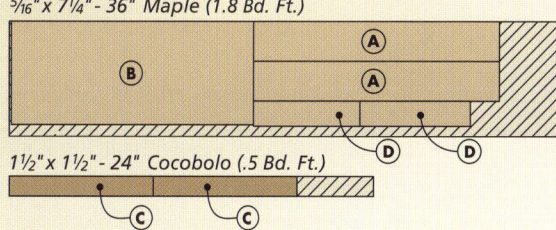

5/16" x 7¼" - 36" Maple (1.8 Bd. Ft.)

1½" x 1½" - 24" Cocobolo (.5 Bd. Ft.)

Designer Series Project

veneered Credenza

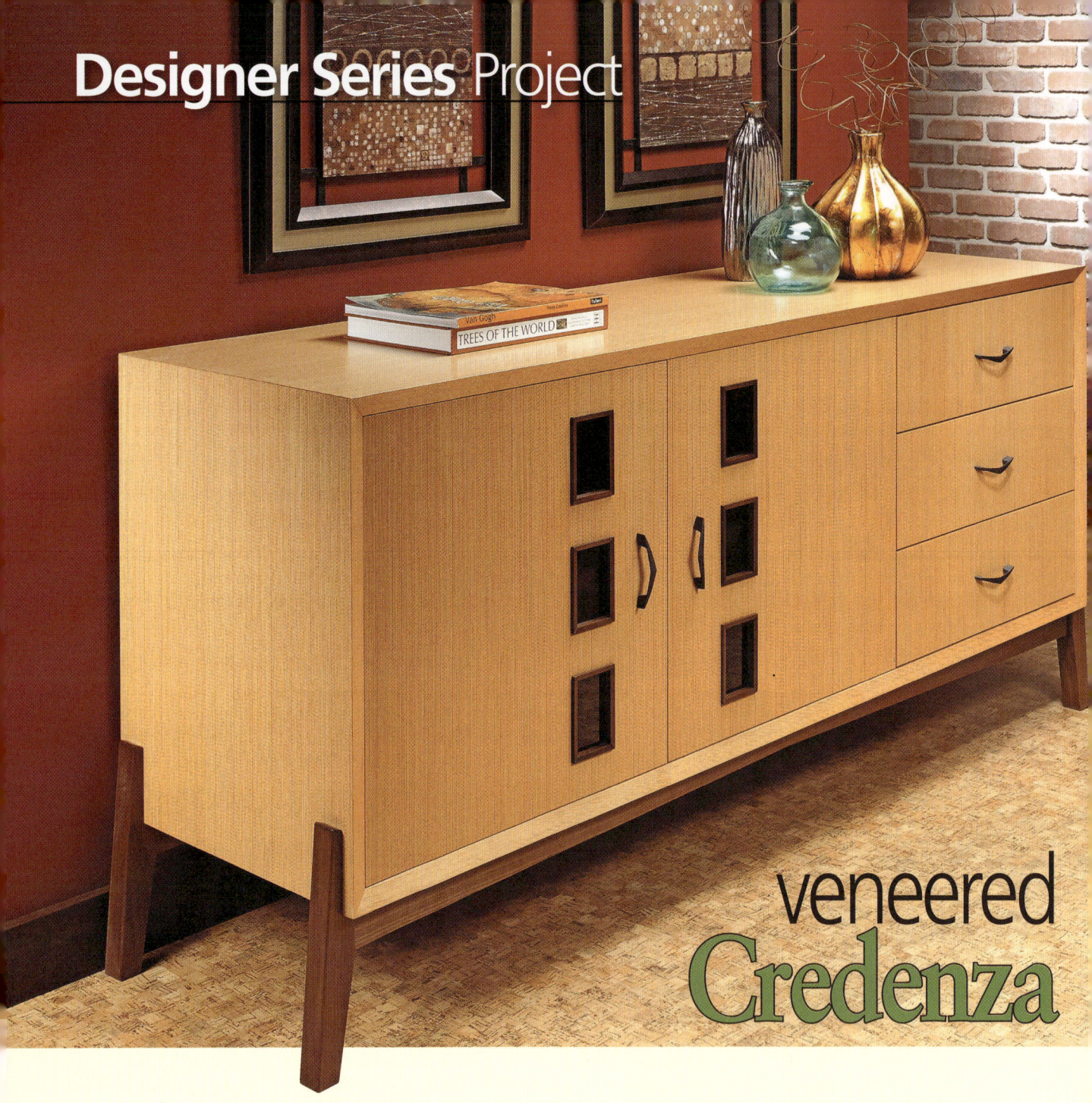

This project has a lot to offer — a sleek, eye-catching design, practical storage, and last but not least, a unique shop experience.

The clean, "retro" styling of this veneered credenza is a perfect example of the design concept "less is more." The idea is that you don't always need ornate detail to make a statement. Simply strip things down to the basics and allow a few, well-chosen design elements to carry the load. All it takes is a look at the photo above to realize how successful this minimalist philosophy can be.

I don't want to create the impression that this project is short on practical features and interesting woodworking. Nothing could be further from the truth. For starters, the storage possibilities are plain to see. The large drawers along with the enclosed shelf space offer versatile options. The credenza could find a home in the dining room, living room, office, or even the bedroom.

That decision can wait. First, you get to experience an enjoyable test of your shop skills. The basic casework is really pretty straightforward. But as I mentioned, it's the details that make the difference. The tapered legs, beveled case trim, the small, framed windows, and of course, the straight-grained fir veneer all present a great opportunity to take on some new challenges.

CONSTRUCTION DETAILS

OVERALL DIMENSIONS: 69¼"L x 20"D x 32"H

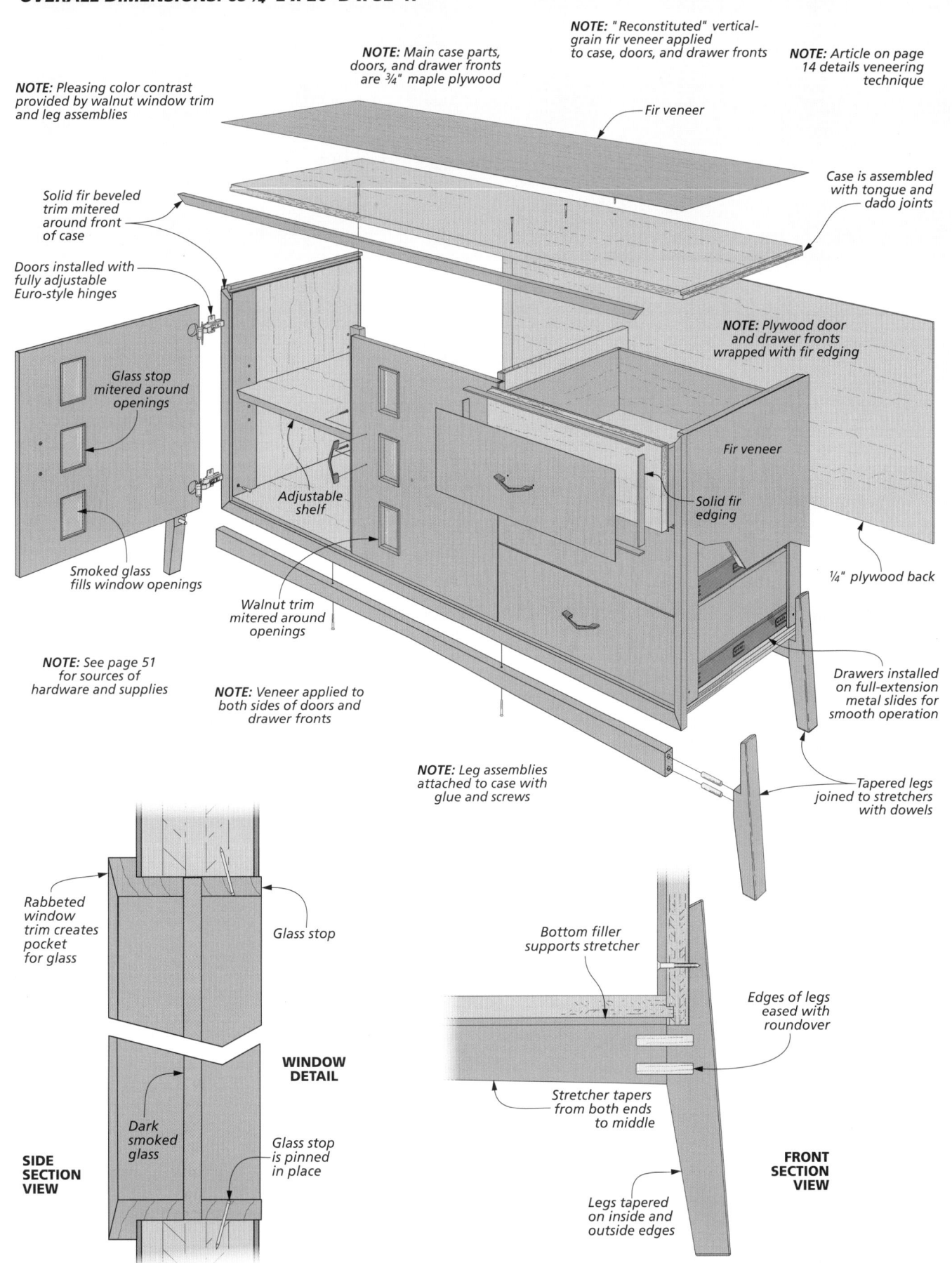

NOTE: Pleasing color contrast provided by walnut window trim and leg assemblies

NOTE: Main case parts, doors, and drawer fronts are ¾" maple plywood

NOTE: "Reconstituted" vertical-grain fir veneer applied to case, doors, and drawer fronts

NOTE: Article on page 14 details veneering technique

Fir veneer

Case is assembled with tongue and dado joints

Solid fir beveled trim mitered around front of case

Doors installed with fully adjustable Euro-style hinges

Glass stop mitered around openings

NOTE: Plywood door and drawer fronts wrapped with fir edging

Adjustable shelf

Fir veneer

Solid fir edging

Smoked glass fills window openings

¼" plywood back

Walnut trim mitered around openings

NOTE: See page 51 for sources of hardware and supplies

NOTE: Veneer applied to both sides of doors and drawer fronts

NOTE: Leg assemblies attached to case with glue and screws

Drawers installed on full-extension metal slides for smooth operation

Tapered legs joined to stretchers with dowels

Rabbeted window trim creates pocket for glass

Glass stop

Bottom filler supports stretcher

Edges of legs eased with roundover

WINDOW DETAIL

Dark smoked glass

Glass stop is pinned in place

Stretcher tapers from both ends to middle

SIDE SECTION VIEW

Legs tapered on inside and outside edges

FRONT SECTION VIEW

Woodsmith.com

Woodsmith

23

building the CASE

a. TOP SECTION VIEW — 3/8, 1/4" ply., Side, Bottom

b. FRONT VIEW — 1/4, 3/8, 3/8 Top, Side, 3/8, Bottom, 1/4, 1/4

Main drawing labels:
- NOTE: Cut rabbet in top, bottom, and sides for 1/4" plywood back panel (detail 'a')
- 65 1/4
- CASE TOP (B)
- 22
- (A) 3/4
- 19 1/4
- NOTE: Cut divider to final width and install only after beveled trim is added
- CASE SIDE (A)
- 24 1/4
- 23
- 19 1/4
- NOTE: Top and bottom dadoes in sides are not equal distance from ends (detail 'b')
- CASE BOTTOM (B)
- CASE DIVIDER (C)
- 22 1/2
- 18 3/8
- DIVIDER EDGING (D)
- NOTE: Cut divider edging to show vertical grain on face
- NOTE: Main case parts are cut from 3/4" plywood

c. FRONT VIEW — Case Top, 1/4, 3/4 ply., Case Bottom

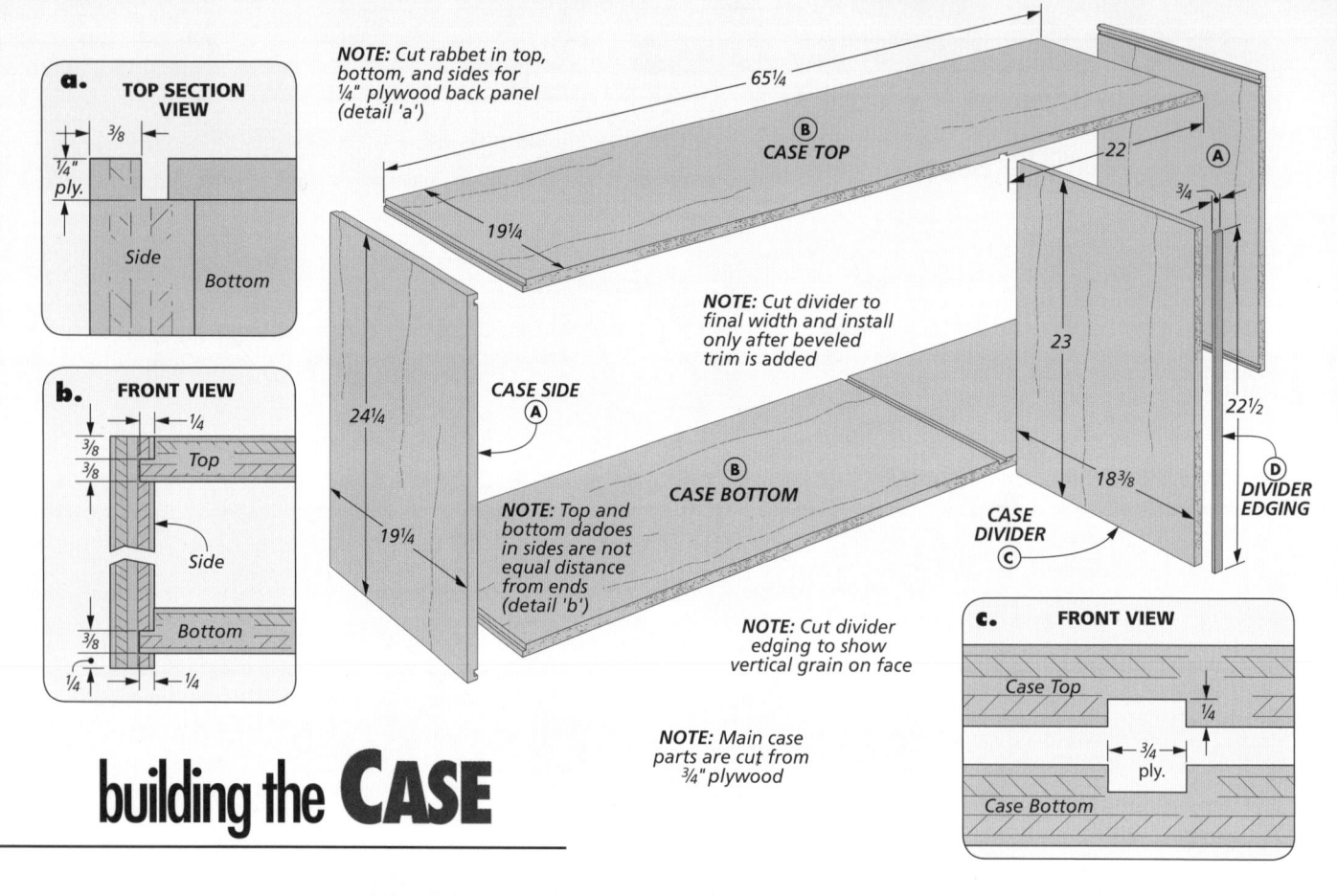

The project begins with assembly of the plywood case — two sides, a top, and a bottom. The front trim, divider, and a stop for the doors are then added, followed by the veneer. Installing the veneer after assembly covers the joinery.

SIMPLE JOINERY. Construction of the basic case is pretty straightforward. I used tongue and dado joints at the corners and full-width dadoes hold the divider. You can get started by cutting the sides, top, and bottom to final size from 3/4" plywood. The How-To box below illustrates the next several joinery steps.

REMINDERS. First up are the dadoes in the case sides. Note here that the top and bottom dadoes are not located an equal distance from the ends (detail 'b'). And when cutting the tongues on the top and bottom, remember that both pieces are oriented with the tongue down.

The dadoes for the divider should be sized to match the thickness of your plywood (detail 'c'). And be sure to cut them on the correct faces. Finally, rabbets to hold the plywood back complete this stage (detail 'a').

THE DIVIDER. Before cutting the plywood divider to size, I dry-assembled the case in order to take an accurate length measurement. I left it slightly wide so I could trim it for a custom fit a little later. Then I added a strip of 1/4"-thick vertical-grain fir to the front edge (main drawing).

How-To: Case Joinery

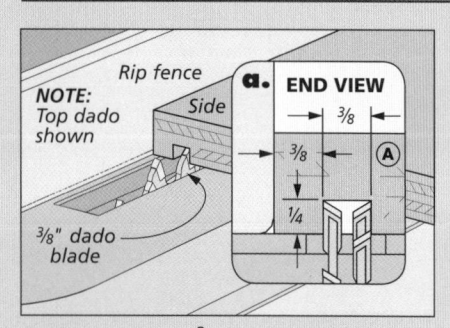

Dadoes. With a 3/8"-wide dado blade in the table saw, use the rip fence to locate the dadoes in the case sides. *(NOTE: Top dado shown; Rip fence; 3/8" dado blade; END VIEW: 3/8, 3/8, 1/4, (A))*

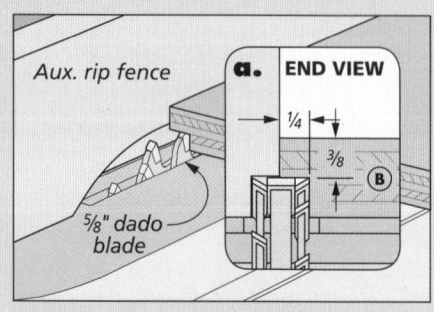

Tongues. Bury a wider dado blade in an auxiliary fence to cut the tongues. Sneak up on a snug fit to the dadoes. *(Aux. rip fence; 5/8" dado blade; END VIEW: 1/4, 3/8, (B))*

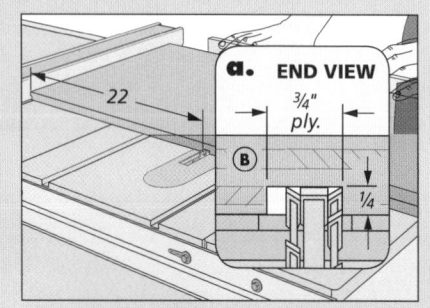

Divider Dadoes. I sized the dadoes to the thickness of the plywood by adjusting the fence between passes. *(22; END VIEW: 3/4" ply., 1/4, (B))*

24 — Woodsmith — No. 196

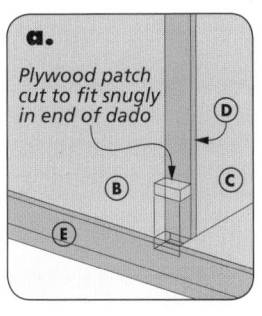

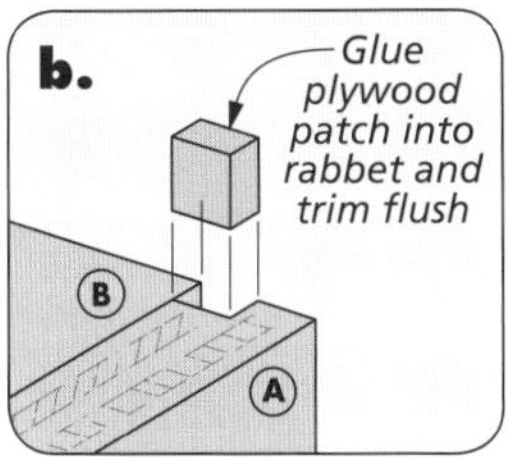

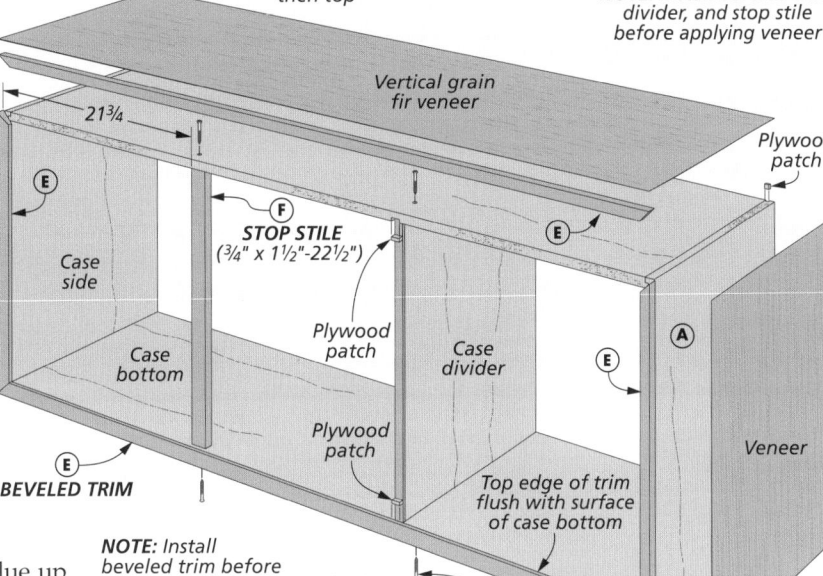

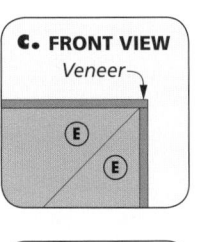

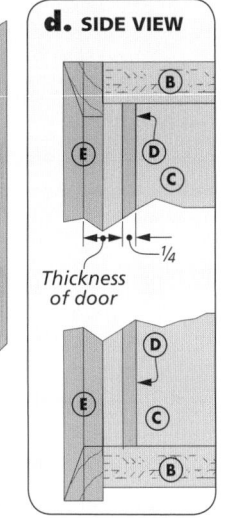

ASSEMBLY. Now you can glue up the top, bottom, and sides. The divider can be used as a spacer to help square up the assembly, but don't fasten it at this point.

BEVELED TRIM. Next, I made and installed the beveled trim that's mitered around the front of the case. A look at the box below will get you started. I'll just offer a little extra explanation.

I wanted the front edge of the trim to show a straight grain pattern so I cut the bevels on the face of ¾"-thick blanks. And since the same trim is applied to the front edge of the shelf, I made this extra piece at the same time.

When fitting the trim, note that the top and side pieces are flush with the outside of the case while the bottom piece is flush with the case bottom, as in detail 'd.'

The right drawing below shows a simple and effective way to clamp the beveled trim to the case. You'll find more on this in Shop Notebook on page 33.

DIVIDER & STOP STILE. With the trim in place, you can add the divider and stop stile. The trick is to position them a door's thickness from the edge of the beveled trim (detail 'd'). You'll need to measure the thickness of the plywood plus two thicknesses of veneer. (My total was $25/32$".) After trimming the divider to final width, you can install it with glue and countersunk screws.

The stop stile can be cut to fit and likewise fastened in place with screws. It's not centered across the opening so check the drawing above for the location.

PATCHES. Before applying the veneer, you have to do a little patching, as shown in details 'a' and 'b.' I cut plywood patches to fill the ends of the rabbets at the top of the case. Similar patches fit into the front ends of the dadoes that hold the divider.

TIME FOR VENEER. The man-made veneer added to the top and sides of the case (detail 'c') is a dead-ringer for vertical-grain Douglas fir. I applied it using veneer glue and plenty of clamping pressure. The in-depth article on page 14 will fill you in on all the details.

Beveled Trim

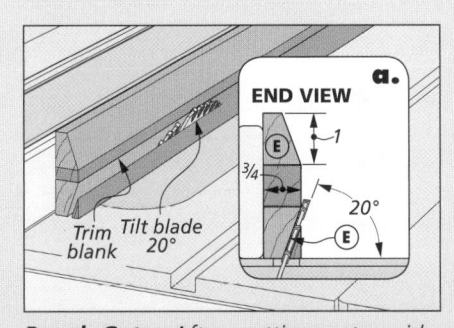

Bevel Cuts. After cutting extra-wide, extra-long blanks, hold them vertically against the rip fence to bevel each edge.

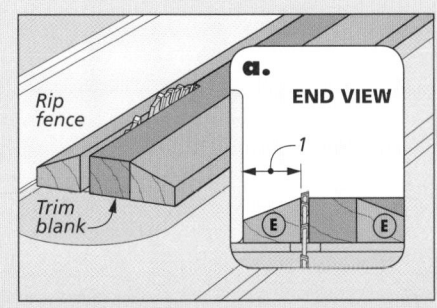

Rip to Width. Return the blade to 90° and adjust the fence to rip a 1"-wide trim piece from each edge of the blank.

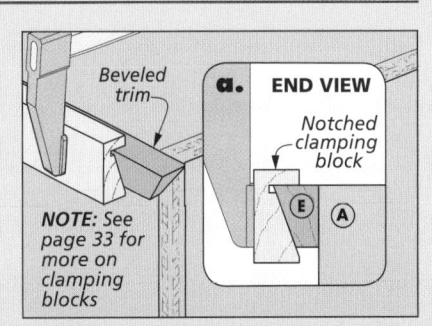

Clamping Helpers. When gluing the trim in place, notched blocks provide a flat, stable clamping surface.

Woodsmith.com   Woodsmith

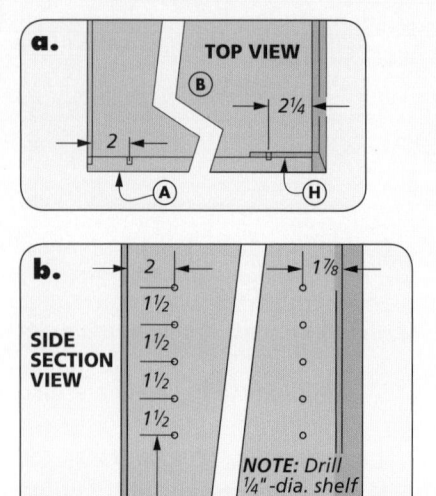

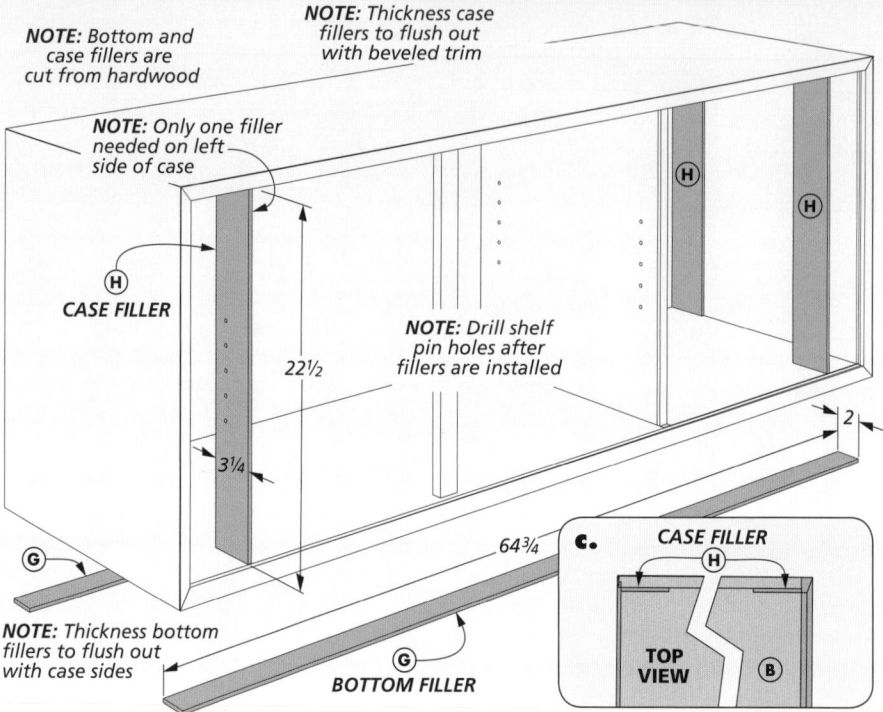

adding the LEGS

With veneer applied to the case, you can now start work on some of the important details. First, the case needs two different sets of hardwood fillers. Then after drilling a series of shelf pin holes in the left compartment, you can make and install the leg assemblies.

FILLERS. Fitting the fillers is easy — their purpose requires a little explanation. As you see in the main drawing above and detail 'b,' I glued two, long fillers to the underside of the case — one at the front and one at the back. They help support the leg assemblies. These pieces should fit flush with the case sides.

A second set of three identical fillers goes inside the case. A pair of fillers is added to the right side of the case for mounting the drawer slides (detail 'c').

The third piece is positioned in the front, left corner of the case. It's used to mount hinges for the door you'll install later (detail 'a'). Both front pieces should flush out with the beveled trim.

SHELF PIN HOLES. With the fillers in place, I completed work on the inside of the case by drilling shelf pin holes in the left side and the divider, as in the main drawing and detail 'b.' To do this, I made a simple template that registered on the bottom of the case.

LEG ASSEMBLIES. Now that the fillers are in place, you can start on the leg assemblies. The identical front and back assemblies each consist of a pair of tapered legs connected by a long stretcher. The legs are notched around the case to provide better support.

I began with the legs. The first step is to plane some walnut stock to 1½" thick. Then you can refer to the How-To box below for help shaping the legs. The pattern at right will provide all of the dimensions you need.

THE NOTCHES. Once the blanks are cut to overall size, the first step is

How-To: Make the Legs

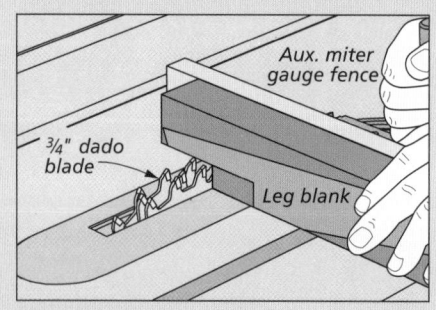

First, the Notch. With an auxiliary fence on the miter gauge to back up the blank, cut the notch in multiple passes.

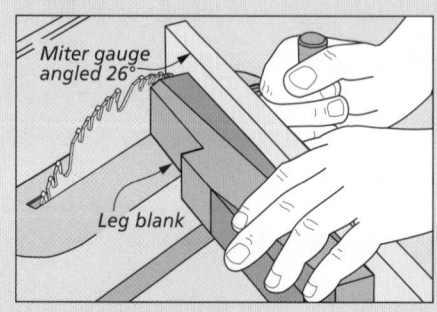

Top Bevel. Next, switch to a single blade and angle the miter gauge to cut the short bevel on the top of each leg.

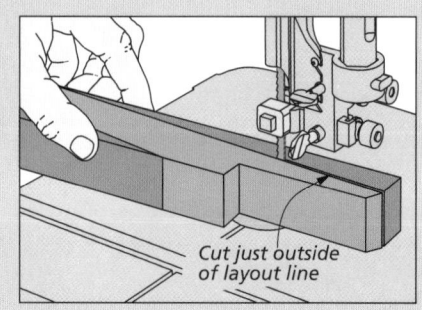

Two Tapers. When cutting the tapers, stick close to your layout line and you'll minimize the cleanup to follow.

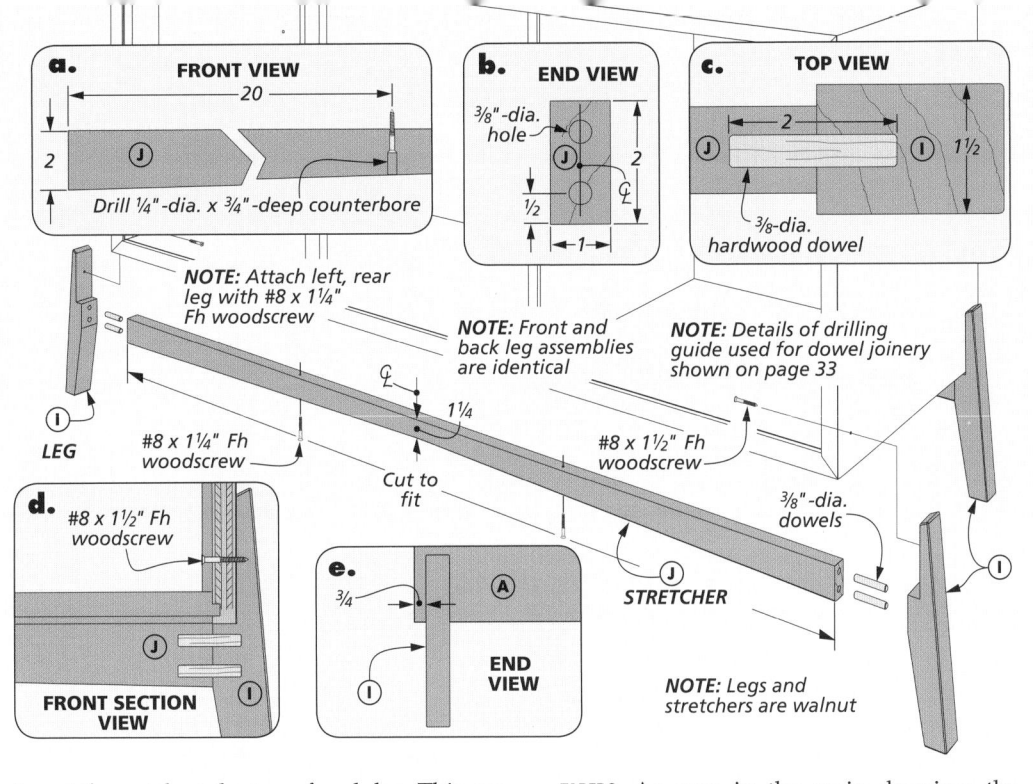

to cut the notch at the top of each leg. This can be accomplished quickly with a dado blade in the table saw. Just make sure the long face of each notch is smooth and flat.

BEVEL, TAPERS, & ROUNDOVERS. After cutting a slight bevel on the top of each leg, you can lay out and cut the tapers. All this takes is a quick trip to the band saw followed by some cleanup with a hand plane or sandpaper.

The final step is to round over the outside edges and the top and bottom of the legs. I routed the long edges. A little work with a sanding block took care of the top and bottom.

STRETCHERS. The stretchers that connect the pairs of legs are made from 1"-thick stock. However, before cutting the blanks to final size, you need to take an accurate length measurement. To get this dimension, I simply clamped each pair of legs in position at the bottom of the case and then measured between them.

TAPERS. As seen in the main drawing, the stretchers taper from each end to the centerpoint. I laid out the tapers and rough cut them on the band saw. A trip to the router table followed where I smoothed the cuts with a straightedge and flush trim bit. You can clean up the "peak" with a chisel or sanding block. Finally, drill a pair of counterbored screw holes in the lower edge of each stretcher (detail 'a').

ASSEMBLY. The legs and stretchers are joined with dowels (details 'b,' 'c,' and 'd'). The dowel holes can be drilled easily with a shop-made guide and a hand drill. You'll find information on making and using the guide on page 33.

INSTALLATION. Once the glueup is completed, installing the leg assemblies is pretty straightforward. First, I clamped them in position on the case and drilled pilot holes for the screws. After adding glue, reposition the assemblies, clamp them again, and insert the screws.

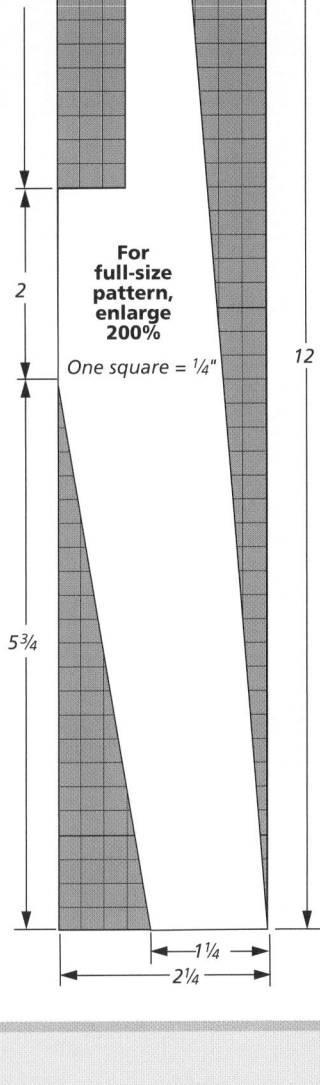

Shape the Stretchers

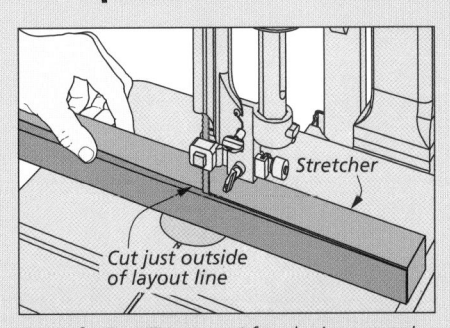

Rough Cut Tapers. After laying out the tapers on the stretchers, take them to the band saw to rough out the waste.

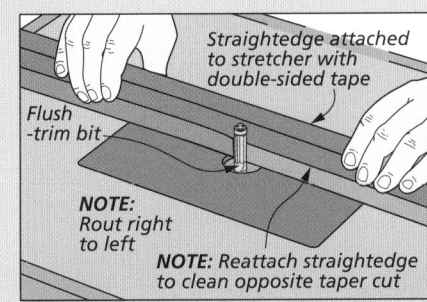

Smooth Tapers. I used a straightedge and a flush-trim bit in the router table to clean up the rough taper cuts.

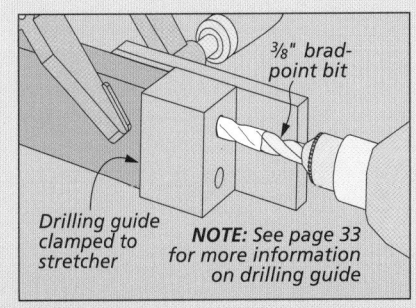

Drilling Guide. A simple drilling guide will ensure that the dowel holes match up and the pieces align properly.

Woodsmith.com   Woodsmith   27

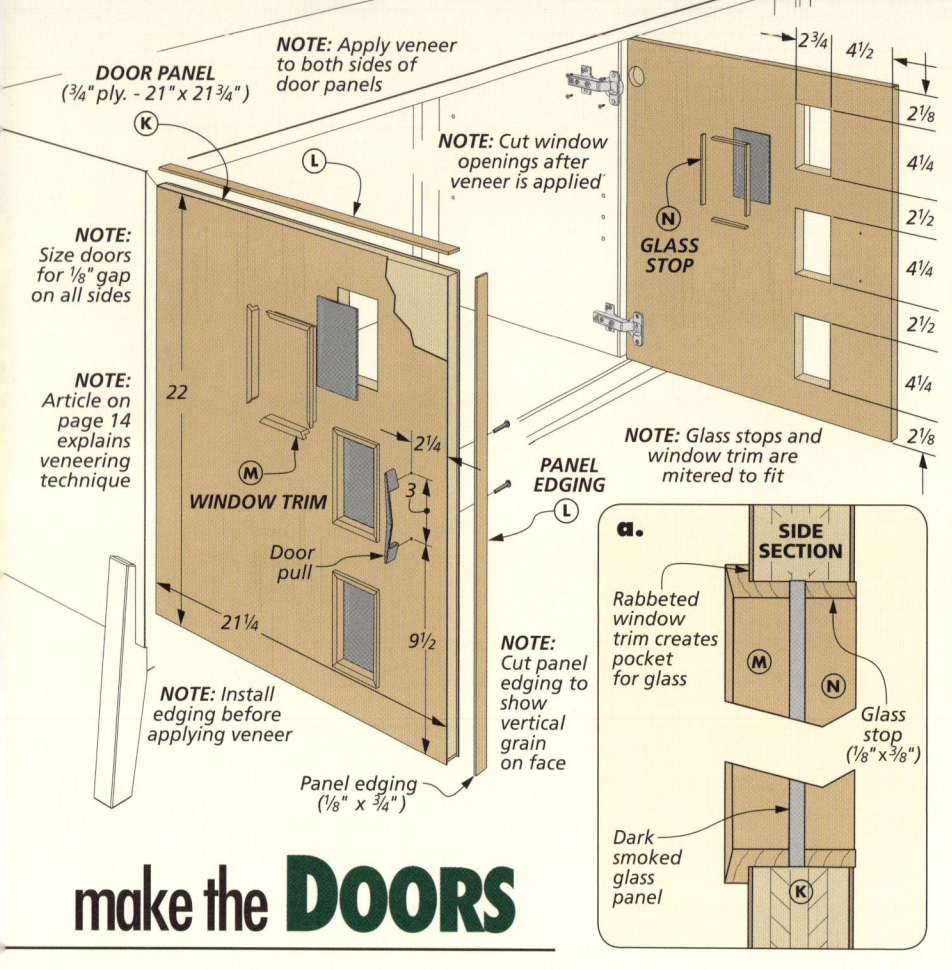

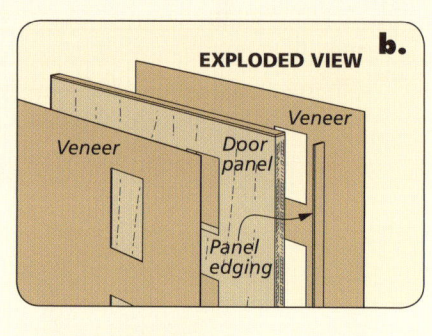

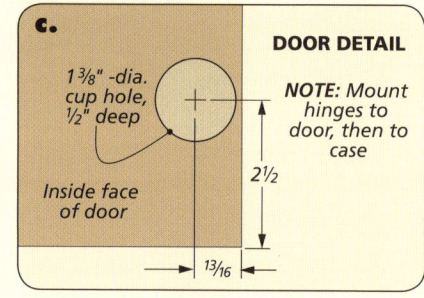

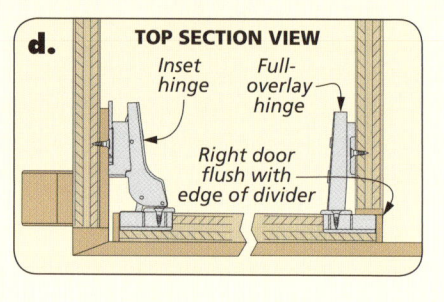

make the DOORS

That's it for the case construction. Your next task is to make and install the doors that enclose the left side of the case. Then all you need to do to finish up this section is make the plywood shelf.

THE DOORS. The doors start out as ¾"-plywood panels. The edges are hidden with thin strips of vertical-grain fir and then veneer is applied to both sides. Finally, you'll create the window openings and trim them out.

The first step is to cut the door panels to size. When doing this, take note of how the two doors fit the opening (detail 'd'). The edging will allow a little bit of fitting later on, but it's best to start with accurately sized panels.

EDGING. Now comes the thin edging. I didn't bother to miter it around the panels. I simply glued pieces to the top and bottom first, trimmed them flush, and then followed with the sides.

VENEER. With the fir edging installed, the door panels can be veneered. I applied veneer to both sides to make certain the stresses on the panel were balanced. However, compared to the large case, veneering the individual door panels will be a breeze. Again, you can refer to the article on page 14 for help.

WINDOW TEMPLATE. After trimming the veneer on the doors, your next task is to create the

▲ See page 32 for more details on the window template.

How-To: Window Openings

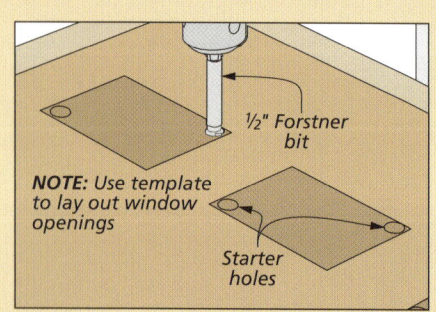

Starter Holes. After using the template to lay out the openings, drill ½"-dia. starter holes in opposite corners.

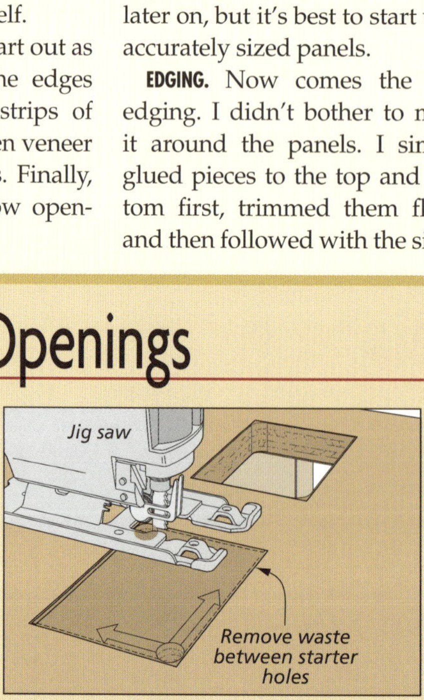

Rough Them Out. To avoid chipping, I used a fine-cutting jig saw blade and stayed well inside my layout lines.

Clean Up. With the template clamped over the opening, use a router and pattern bit to quickly clean it up.

window openings. To help with this, I put together a simple template. You can read about making and using it on page 32.

THE STEPS. The How-To on the opposite page shows several of the steps needed to form the openings. I'll fill in the blanks.

I began by using the template to lay out all the window openings. Then I drilled a pair of starter holes in each layout to accommodate a jig saw blade. When rough cutting the openings, I was careful to avoid chipping the veneer.

Now, it's more work for the template. As you can see, I used it along with a hand-held router and a pattern bit to clean up the rough openings. You'll get smooth, straight edges in short order. Finally, I again called on the template to guide my chisel while cleaning up the corners.

WINDOW TRIM. Next, you can form a pocket for the smoked glass by installing small, rabbeted trim pieces around each opening (detail 'a,' opposite page). The box below illustrates the three-step process used to make this contrasting, walnut trim. A small rectangular stop is installed on the inside to retain the glass. The end result really complements the overall design.

MITERS. With the trim and stop in hand, you fit it to the openings. I mitered the outside trim to fit and then glued it in place.

The glass stop can be fit with butt joints. You won't tack it in place until after the finish is applied and you're ready to install the smoked glass.

HINGES. The doors use easy-to-install, Euro-style hinges. However, each requires a different mounting style. The left door uses an inset hinge while the right needs an overlay hinge. But both are installed in the same way (details 'c' and 'd,' opposite page).

SHELF

The shelf will go quickly. It consists of a plywood panel with a piece of the same beveled trim used on the case glued to the front edge (detail 'a'). The only complication is that the shelf has to be notched to fit around the stop stile and the case filler.

The notches can be laid out directly by sliding the shelf into the case from the back and using a square to transfer their locations from the stile and case filler. You'll want to add a little extra for clearance. The Shop Tip above shows the setup I used to cut the center notch on the table saw.

Shop Tip: Notch

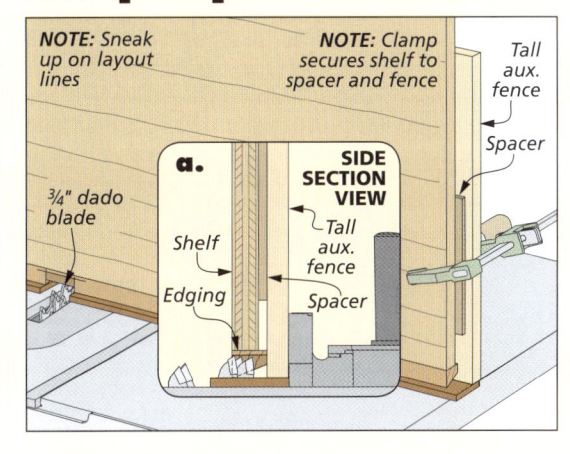

Window Trim

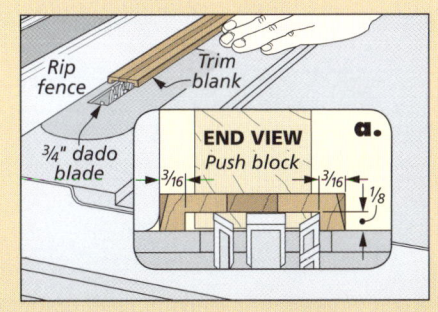

A Groove. Using a dado blade, cut a centered groove in the blank, leaving 3/16" of material along both edges.

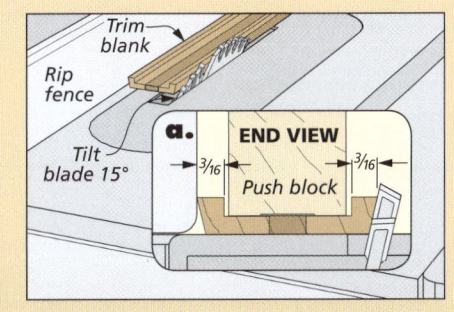

Bevel Cuts. Tilt the saw blade 15° and then position the rip fence to cut a bevel along each edge of the blank.

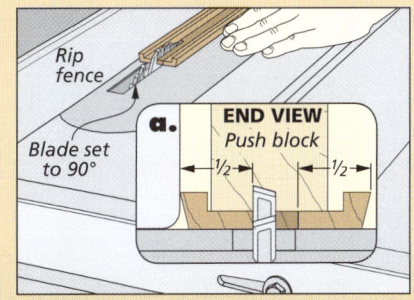

Two Pieces. Now, return the blade to 90°, reposition the rip fence, and rip the blank into two, 1/2"-wide pieces.

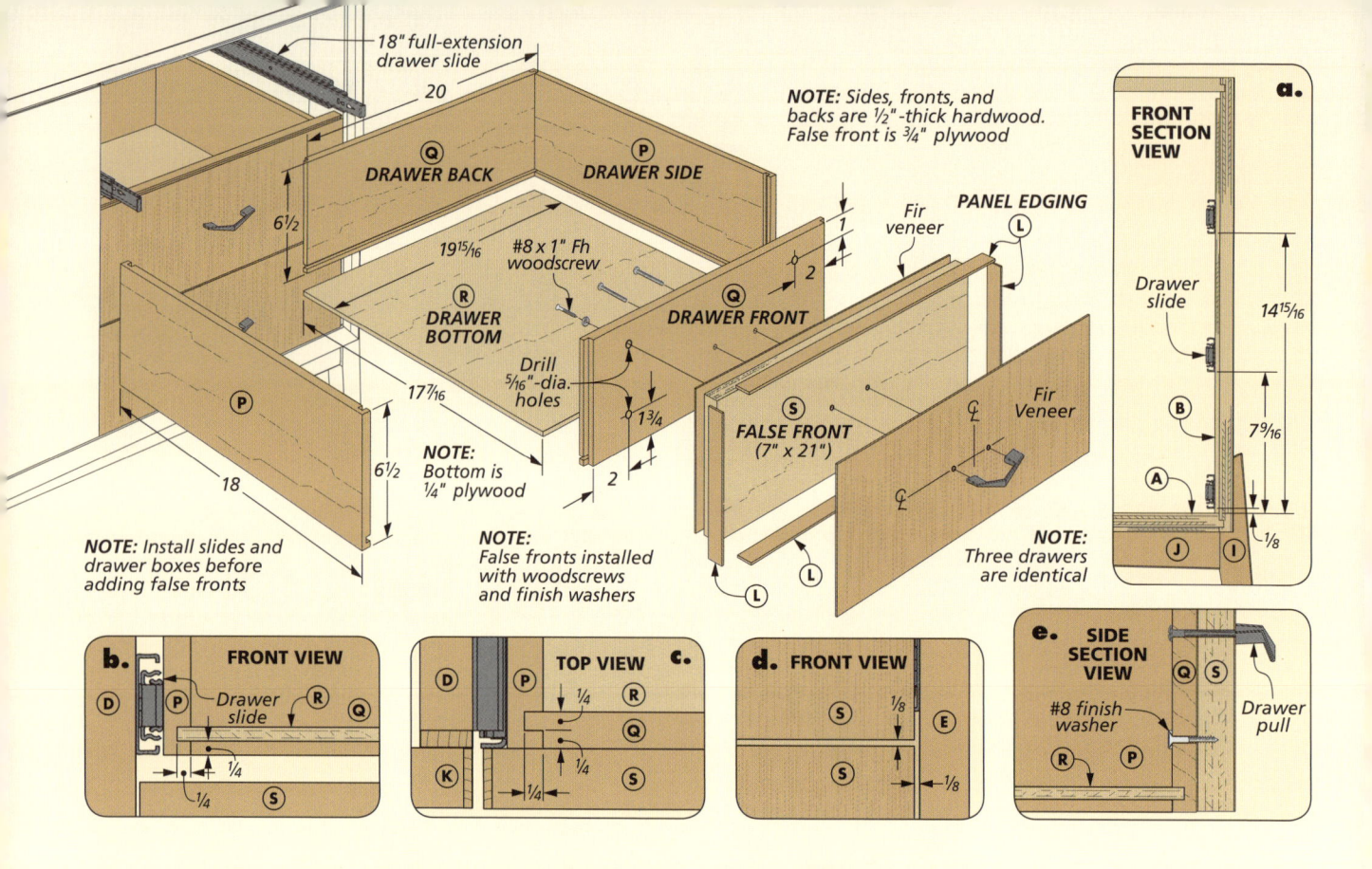

installing the DRAWERS & BACK

Building and installing the three identical drawers will wrap up the major construction. After this, all you'll have left to do is add the back panel to the case.

THE TASK AHEAD. As you can see above, the drawers are standard issue. I put together solid-wood drawer boxes with ¼" plywood bottoms using simple tongue and dado joinery. I made veneered false fronts and attached them with screws. Smooth, convenient operation is guaranteed by full-extension metal slides.

JOINERY. The How-To box below will guide you through the drawer joinery. In addition, you'll find some helpful drawer building tips on page 42.

When sizing the drawer boxes, be sure to allow 1" total side-to-side clearance to accommodate the slides. And before assembling the boxes, I drilled the oversized screw holes used later to fasten the fronts (detail 'e').

FALSE FRONTS. The false fronts start out exactly like the doors (main drawing above). I cut plywood panels to size, wrapped them with edging, and then applied veneer to both sides. The completed fronts are sized for a ⅛" gap on all sides (detail 'd').

INSTALLATION. Before attaching the false fronts, I installed the slides and drawer boxes in the case (detail 'a'). This makes it easier to position and adjust the fronts for even gaps all around.

With the slides in place and working smoothly, I used shims and double-sided tape to temporarily attach the false fronts. After drilling pilot holes in the fronts, remove the tape, and install the screws through finish washers.

BACK. You're in the home stretch. After adding the drawer pulls,

How-To: Drawer Joinery

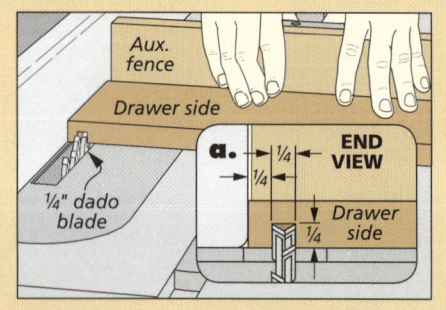

Side Dado. Cut the dadoes in the drawer sides first. A dado blade in the table saw will make short work of this task.

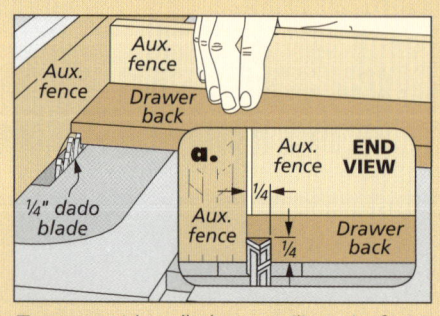

Tongues. I installed an auxiliary rip fence before cutting the tongues. Sneak up on a snug fit to the dadoes in the sides.

you can cut the ¼" plywood back to size and attach it with glue and brads, as shown at right.

THE END. Finish comes next. The "natural" look I settled on really highlights the contrast between the straight-grained fir and the walnut. You'll find finishing details on page 51. Finally, you can install the glass in the doors. Now it's time to scout out a good spot to display your "back-to-the-future" credenza.

CASE BACK (23¼" x 65½")

NOTE: See page 51 for finishing information

1" brads

NOTE: Case back is ¼" plywood

NOTE: Glue and nail case back in place

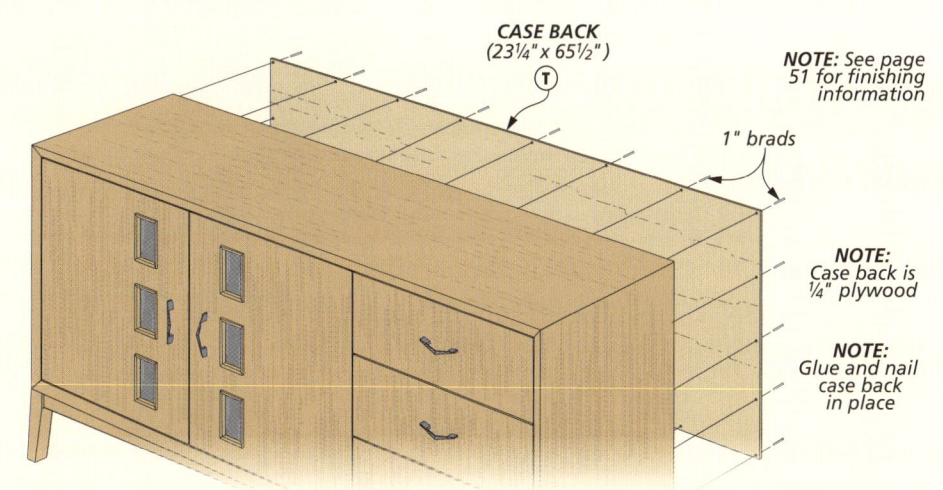

Materials, Supplies & Cutting Diagram

A	Case Sides (2)	¾ ply. - 19¼ x 24¼
B	Case Top/Bottom (2)	¾ ply. - 19¼ x 65¼
C	Case Divider (1)	¾ ply. - 18⅜ x 23
D	Divider Edging (1)	¼ x ¾ - 23
E	Beveled Trim (1)	¾ x 1 - 20' rgh.
F	Stop Stile (1)	¾ x 1½ - 22½
G	Bottom Fillers (2)	¼ x 2 - 64¾
H	Case Fillers (3)	¼ x 3¼ - 22½
I	Legs (4)	1½ x 2¼ - 12
J	Stretchers (2)	1 x 2 - 66 rgh.
K	Door Panels (2)	¾ ply. - 21 x 21¾
L	Panel Edging (1)	⅛ x ¾ - 32' rgh.
M	Window Trim (1)	¼ x ½ - 110 rgh.
N	Glass Stop (1)	⅛ x ⅜ - 110 rgh.
O	Shelf Panel (1)	¾ ply. - 17¹¹⁄₁₆ x 42⅛
P	Drawer Sides (6)	½ x 6½ - 18
Q	Drawer Fronts/Backs (6)	½ x 6½ - 20
R	Drawer Bottoms (3)	¼ ply. - 17⁷⁄₁₆ x 19¹⁵⁄₁₆
S	False Fronts (3)	¾ ply. - 7 x 21
T	Case Back (1)	¼ ply. - 23¼ x 65½

- (3) 26" x 99" Vertical-Grain Fir Veneer
- (5) Drawer/Door Pulls w/Screws
- (3 pr.) 18" Full-Extension Drawer Slides
- (1 pr.) Full-Overlay Euro-Style Hinges
- (1 pr.) Inset Euro-Style Hinges
- (4) ¼" Spoon-Style Shelf Supports
- (8) ⅜" x 2" Dowels
- (6) 2¹¹⁄₁₆" x 4³⁄₁₆" Dark Smoked Glass (⅛" thick)
- (1) #8 x 1¼" Fh Woodscrew
- (15) #8 x 1½" Fh Woodscrews
- (12) #8 x 1" Fh Woodscrews
- (12) #8 Finish Washers
- 1" Brads
- ½" Brads

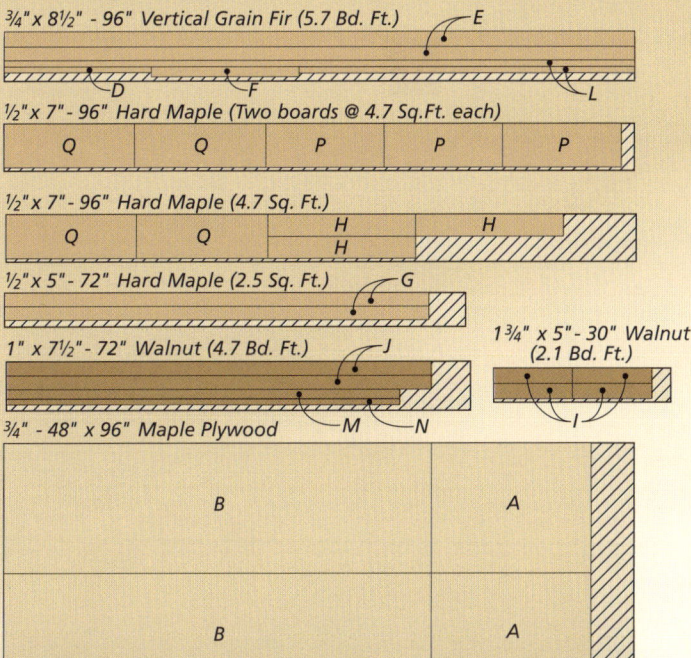

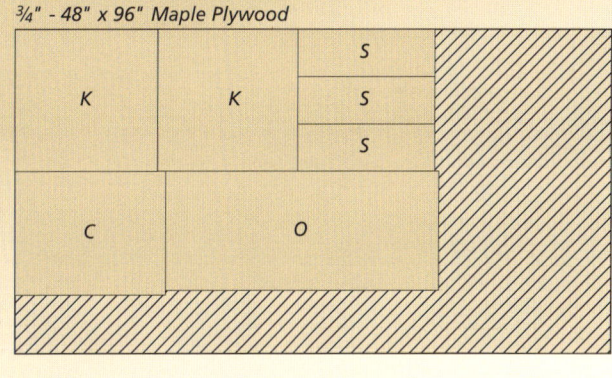

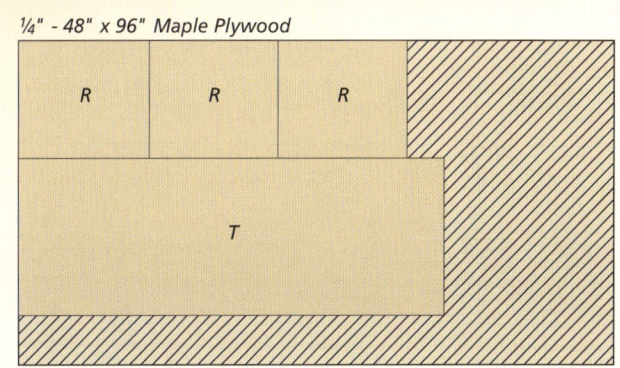

¾" x 8½" - 96" Vertical Grain Fir (5.7 Bd. Ft.)

½" x 7" - 96" Hard Maple (Two boards @ 4.7 Sq.Ft. each)

½" x 7" - 96" Hard Maple (4.7 Sq. Ft.)

½" x 5" - 72" Hard Maple (2.5 Sq. Ft.)

1" x 7½" - 72" Walnut (4.7 Bd. Ft.)

1¾" x 5" - 30" Walnut (2.1 Bd. Ft.)

¾" - 48" x 96" Maple Plywood

¾" - 48" x 96" Maple Plywood

¼" - 48" x 96" Maple Plywood

tips from our shop

SHOP NOTEBOOK

3-in-1 Template

The "windows" on the doors of the credenza on page 22 are one of the main focal points of the project. Because of this, you'll want to take the time to accurately lay them out and cut them. In order to make this process as foolproof as possible, I used a shop-made template, as shown in the photo.

TEMPLATE. As you can see in the drawing below, the template is made out of ½" plywood. In order to create the rectangular opening in the template, I glued it up out of four separate pieces, as shown below. Then I added a narrow cleat to the underside of the template to register it against the edge of the door.

USING THE TEMPLATE. The template can be used for three separate steps in making the windows. To start with, after laying out the top edge of each window opening, you can use the template to trace the openings on each door, as shown in Figure 1.

After drilling some starter holes and rough cutting the openings with a jig saw, I used the template and a pattern bit to trim the openings to final size. Simply clamp the template in place and trim the edges with the router (Figure 2).

As the final step to complete the windows, you can use the template as a guide for your chisel as you square up the corners of each opening, as shown in Figure 3.

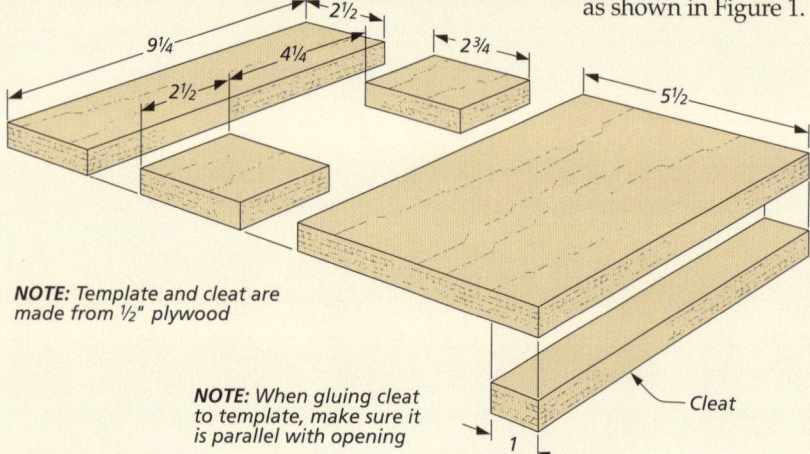

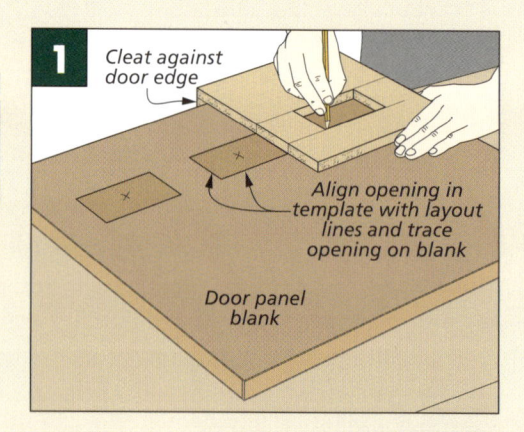

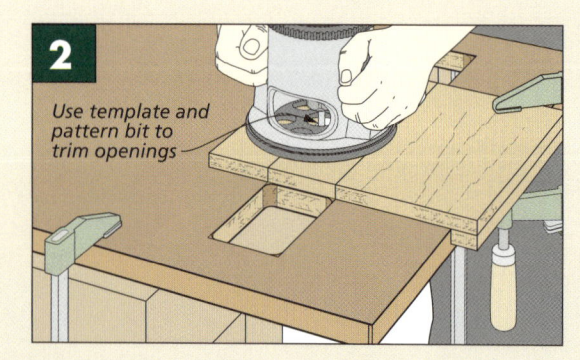

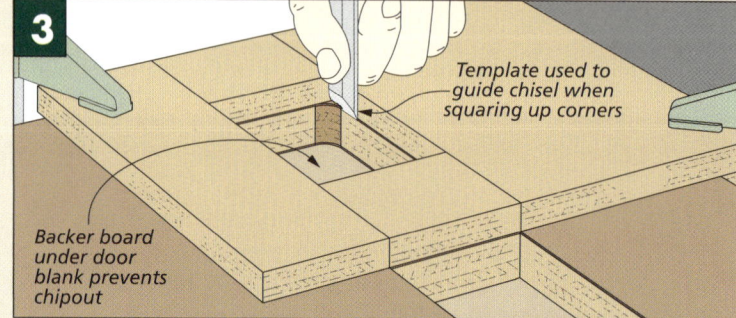

NOTE: Template and cleat are made from ½" plywood

NOTE: When gluing cleat to template, make sure it is parallel with opening

1. Cleat against door edge. Align opening in template with layout lines and trace opening on blank. Door panel blank

2. Use template and pattern bit to trim openings

3. Template used to guide chisel when squaring up corners. Backer board under door blank prevents chipout

Dowel Centers

The doors of the display cabinet on page 34 are held closed with small, rare-earth magnets and washers. The magnets are glued with epoxy into holes drilled into the door stops at the top and bottom of the case. And small, steel washers are installed in shallow counterbores on the inside face of each door.

The trick to installing the magnets and washers is keeping them aligned. An easy way to do this is to use dowel centers. The process is pretty simple. Before gluing the magnets into the cabinet, simply place a ¼"-dia. dowel center into the hole and close the door against it firmly to make an indentation (Figure 1).

After removing the door from the cabinet, you can use the mark left by the dowel center to line up your drill bit when drilling the counterbore for the steel washer (Figure 2).

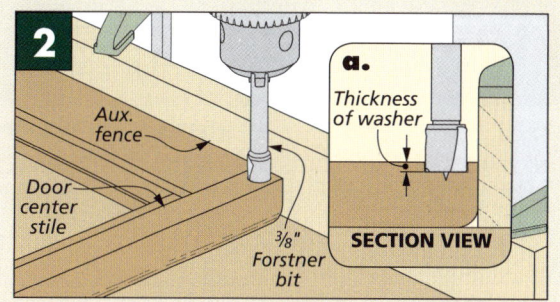

Notched Clamping Blocks

The front edges of the case of the credenza are covered with wide trim. But the beveled profile of the trim makes it difficult to clamp in place. To make the task easier, I created some custom clamping blocks that match the beveled profile of the trim.

To make the blocks, I started with some 1½"-wide strips of ¾"-thick stock. I created the beveled notch on the blocks by making two intersecting rip cuts on the table saw, as shown in Figures 1 and 2. Then you can cut the blocks to convenient lengths and place them over the trim as you clamp it in place (Figure 3).

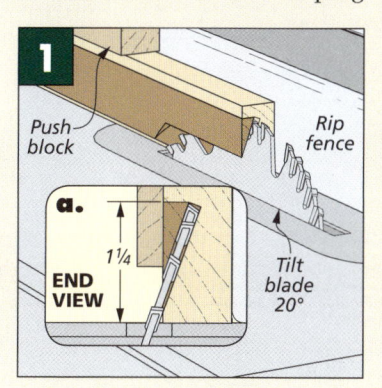

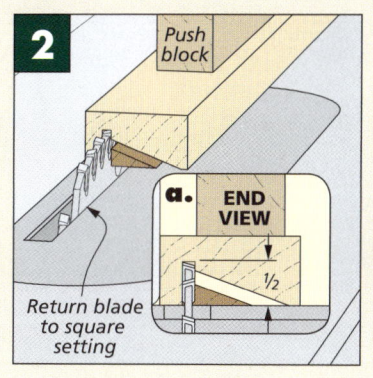

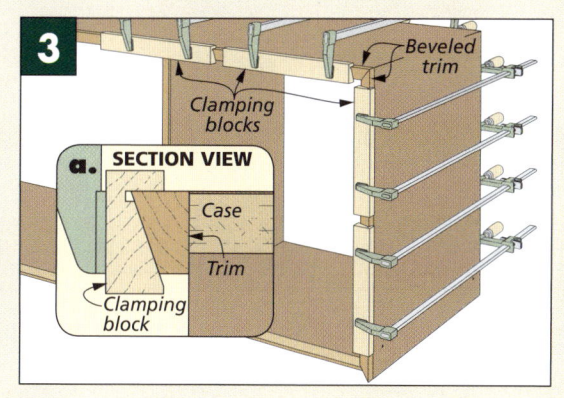

Drilling Guide

The legs and stretchers of the credenza are joined with dowels. But drilling the holes for the dowels presented a couple of challenges. First, you'll need to make sure the holes are properly aligned. And second, you need a way to guide the drill bit to prevent it from wandering, particularly when drilling into the end grain of the stretchers.

To accomplish both these goals, I made a simple drilling guide, like the one you see at right. The guide is just a block of wood with a pair of holes drilled through it. A fence attached to one side of the block allows you to clamp the guide to your workpiece. And a ¼"-thick spacer glued to one end of the fence allows you to use the same guide for drilling the holes in both the stretchers (Figure 1) and the legs (Figure 2).

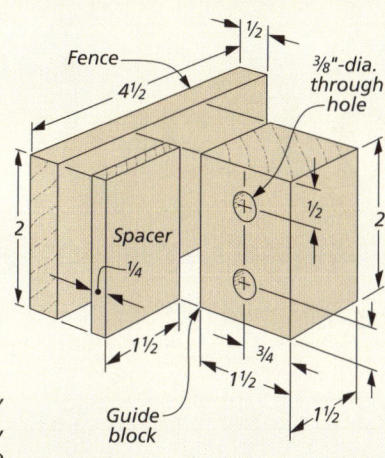

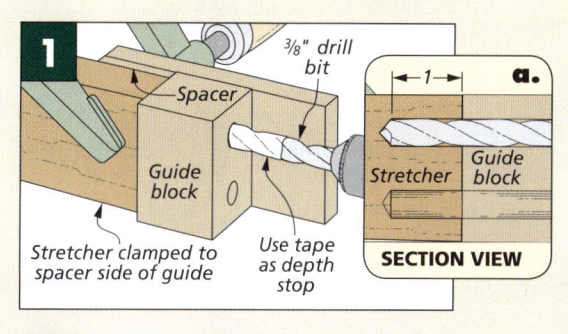

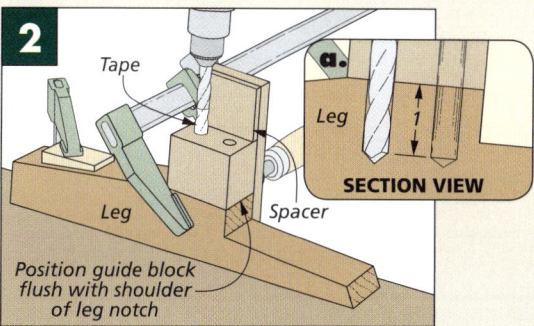

Heirloom Project

elegant Curio Cabinet

Keep the dust off of your collectibles and show them off in style with this attractive, wall-mounted cabinet.

An eye-catching curio cabinet, like the one shown above, offers a versatile way to spice up any room. Whether you use it to display a few special collectibles or simply some books and knick-knacks, it's sure to become the focus of the room.

But I have to admit, as much as I enjoy looking at the cabinet on the wall, I admire its construction even more. It combines several straightforward shop techniques to create a piece that's great looking but easy to build. From the built-up shop-made moldings on the top and bottom to the frame and panel doors, there's nothing here that's too difficult or requires any special tools.

I chose cherry for my cabinet, but it would look great in just about any hardwood. You can make one to match any decor.

CONSTRUCTION DETAILS

OVERALL DIMENSIONS: 37 11/16"W x 8 7/8"D x 27 5/8"H

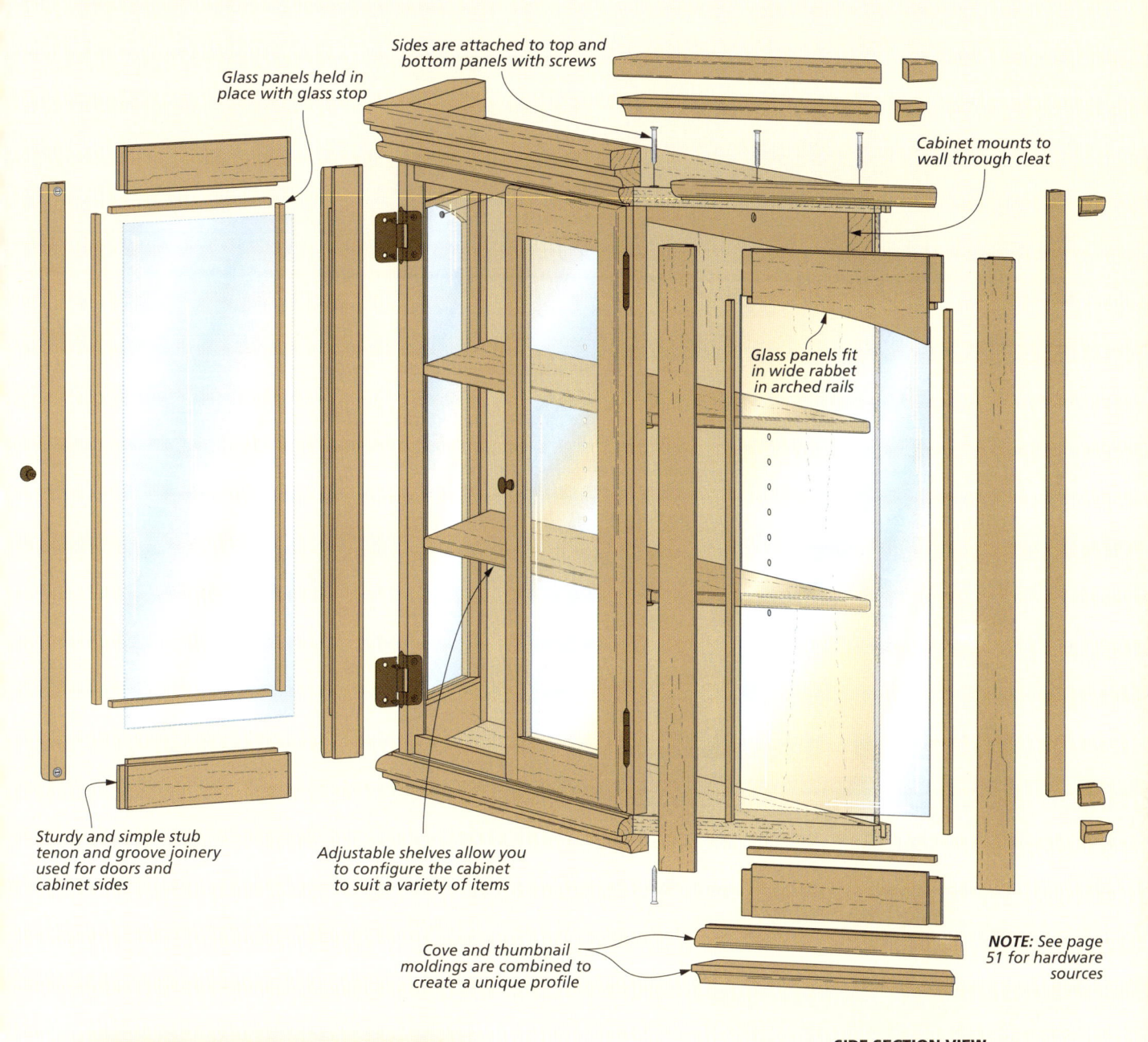

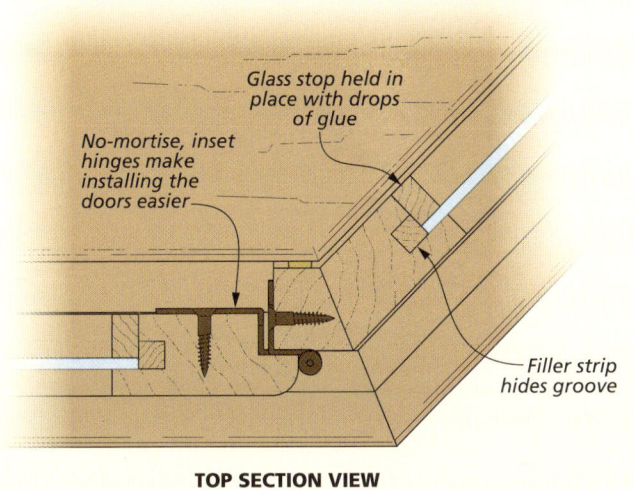

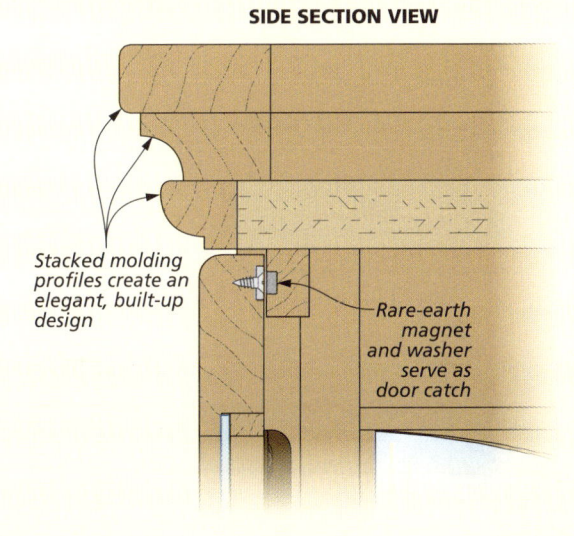

- Glass panels held in place with glass stop
- Sides are attached to top and bottom panels with screws
- Cabinet mounts to wall through cleat
- Glass panels fit in wide rabbet in arched rails
- Sturdy and simple stub tenon and groove joinery used for doors and cabinet sides
- Adjustable shelves allow you to configure the cabinet to suit a variety of items
- Cove and thumbnail moldings are combined to create a unique profile

NOTE: See page 51 for hardware sources

TOP SECTION VIEW

- No-mortise, inset hinges make installing the doors easier
- Glass stop held in place with drops of glue
- Filler strip hides groove

SIDE SECTION VIEW

- Stacked molding profiles create an elegant, built-up design
- Rare-earth magnet and washer serve as door catch

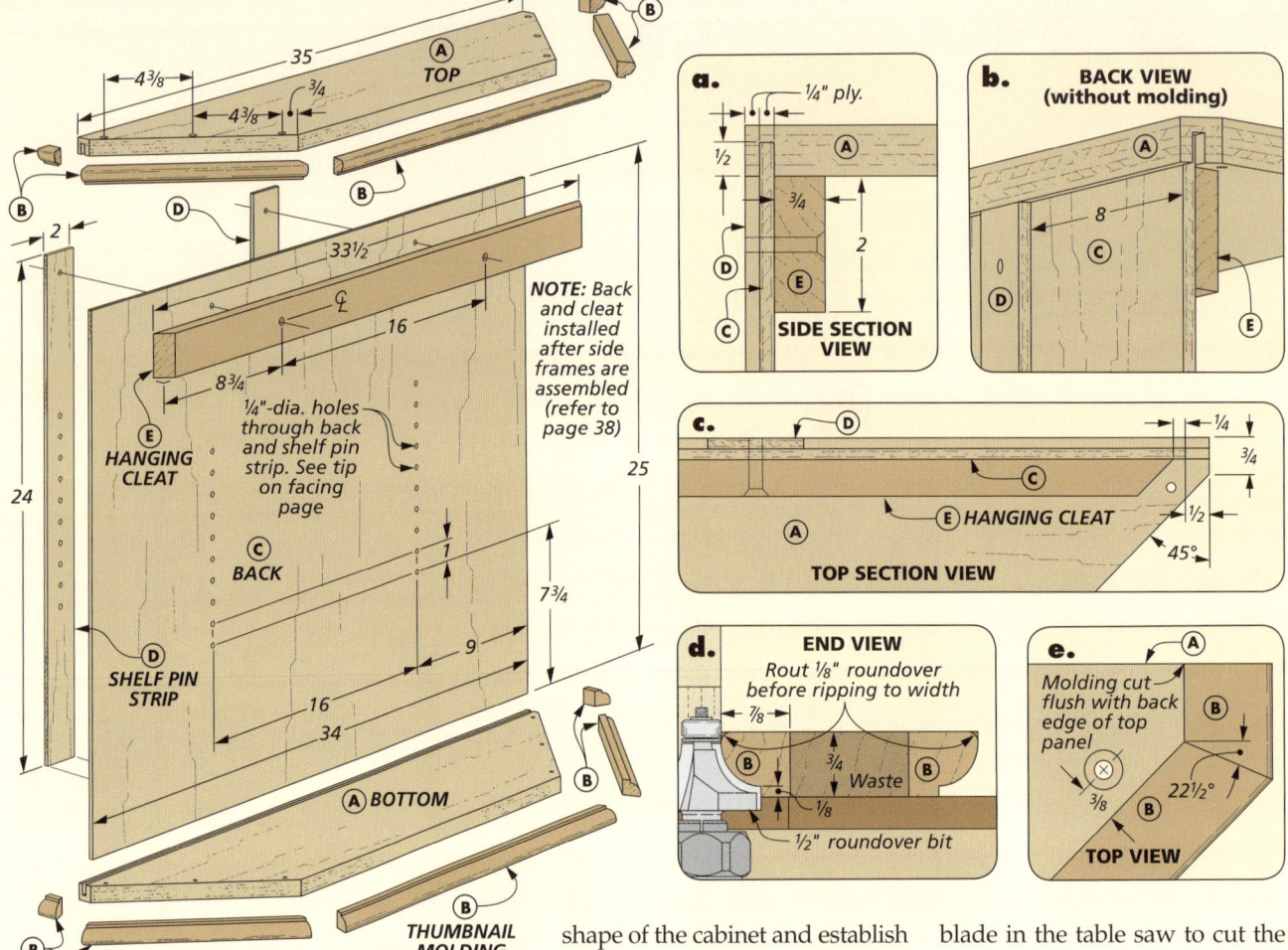

starting the CASE

The basic elements of the case provide the structural foundation for the cabinet. For this reason, I started with the plywood top and bottom panels. They define the shape of the cabinet and establish the angles for the rest of the pieces. After adding molding to cover the plywood edges, you'll make the back and hanging cleat and install them after you complete the side frames shown on page 38.

TOP & BOTTOM PANELS. You can begin by cutting the top and bottom panels to overall width and length. I used a combination blade in the table saw to cut the groove on the back edges of each piece to hold the back panel (left drawing, below). Using a single blade allows you to sneak up on a snug fit for the plywood back.

The next step is to bevel the ends of the panels. For this, I installed a long auxiliary fence on the miter gauge. As you can see in the box below, the extra

How-To: Cut the Top & Bottom Panel

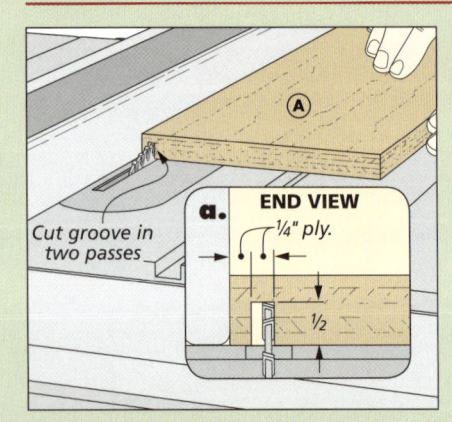

Groove First. While the panel is still square, cut the groove along the rear edge that houses the plywood back.

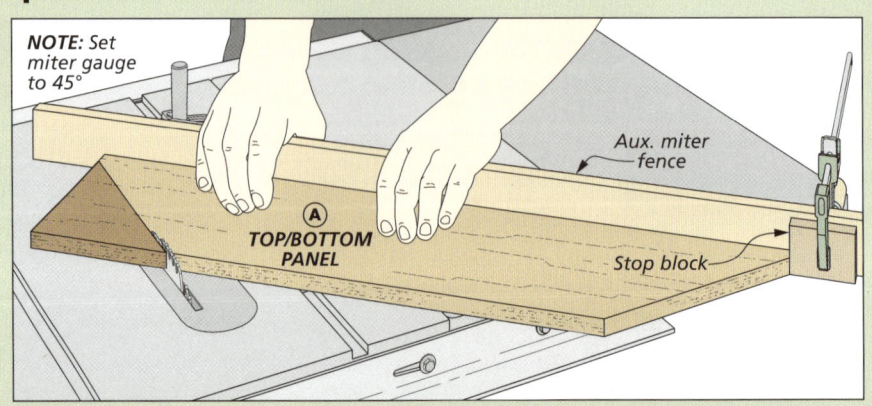

Bevel the Ends. To make sure that both panels are identical, clamp a stop block to an extra-long auxiliary fence. Make the first cut and adjust the stop block if needed. After cutting the bevel on one end, flip the workpiece to cut the opposite end.

Woodsmith No. 196

length not only makes it easier to manage the workpiece while you cut the bevels, but it also lets you use a stop block to make sure both panels end up the same shape. Note that the ends of the panels remain square (details 'c' and 'e,' opposite page).

You can complete work on the panels by drilling the countersunk screw holes shown in the main drawing and detail 'e' on the opposite page. You'll use these holes to attach the sides later.

THUMBNAIL MOLDING. To conceal the plywood edges, I used a simple, shop-made molding. Just rout the ½"-rad. profile on both edges of an extra-wide blank (detail 'd,' opposite page). After flipping the blank over to rout the ⅛" roundover, head back to the table saw to rip the molding strips free.

To cut the angles needed to install the molding on the plywood panels, I once again turned to the miter gauge and auxiliary fence. The drawing below shows the setup. It's a good idea to make a couple test cuts and double-check the results before cutting and fitting the final molding.

Once you have the angle set properly, you'll find it works best to cut and fit each piece individually. Do this in sequence, starting with the long, front pieces. I like to cut them just a hair long, then trim them to a perfect fit. After that, work your way around each end, carefully cutting the pieces for a gap-free fit.

An easy and effective way to install the molding is to use tape to clamp the pieces while the glue dries. Don't forget to put a little glue on the ends of each piece of molding while you're at it.

Shop Tip: Shelf Pin Holes

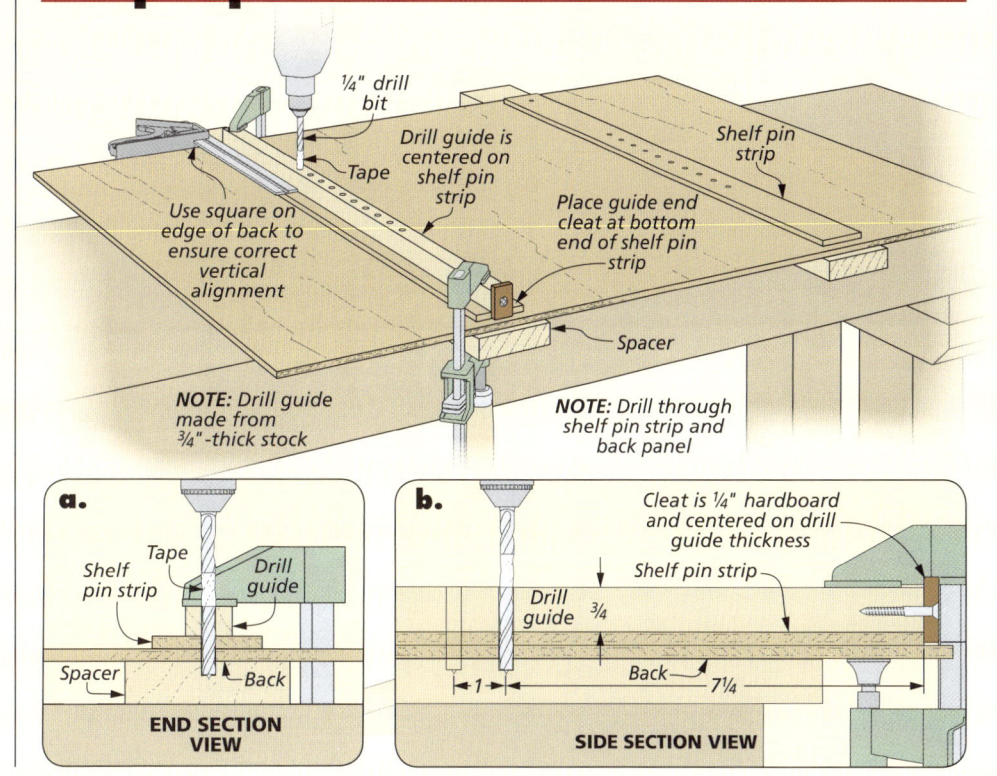

MAKE THE BACK. At this point, you're ready to make the plywood back. After cutting the back to final size, I cut the pair of shelf-pin strips to size as well. You can install the strips as shown in details 'a' and 'b,' opposite page.

After the glue dries, you're ready to drill the shelf-pin holes. The Shop Tip above shows how I used a shop-made guide to drill the holes. It's just a narrow piece of stock with the hole locations marked and drilled at the drill press. A cleat on one end registers the drilling guide from the bottom end of each strip to make sure the shelf-pin holes line up properly. (You'll use it again when you drill the matching holes in the side panels later.)

HANGING CLEAT. All that remains is to make the cleat you'll use to mount the cabinet on the wall. I used the miter gauge again to cut the cleat to length (detail 'c,' opposite page). After drilling the mounting holes, you can set the back and cleat aside while you work on the side frames.

Cutting the Molding

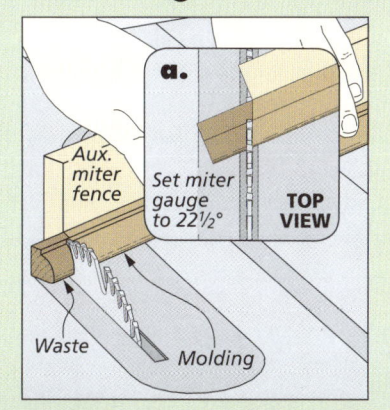

Molding. The auxiliary fence backs up the cut and prevents tearout as you miter the molding.

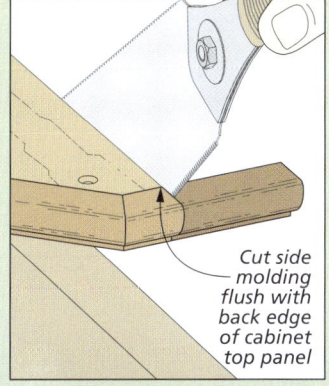

Flush Cut. A hand saw makes short work of trimming the molding flush with the back.

building the SIDE FRAMES

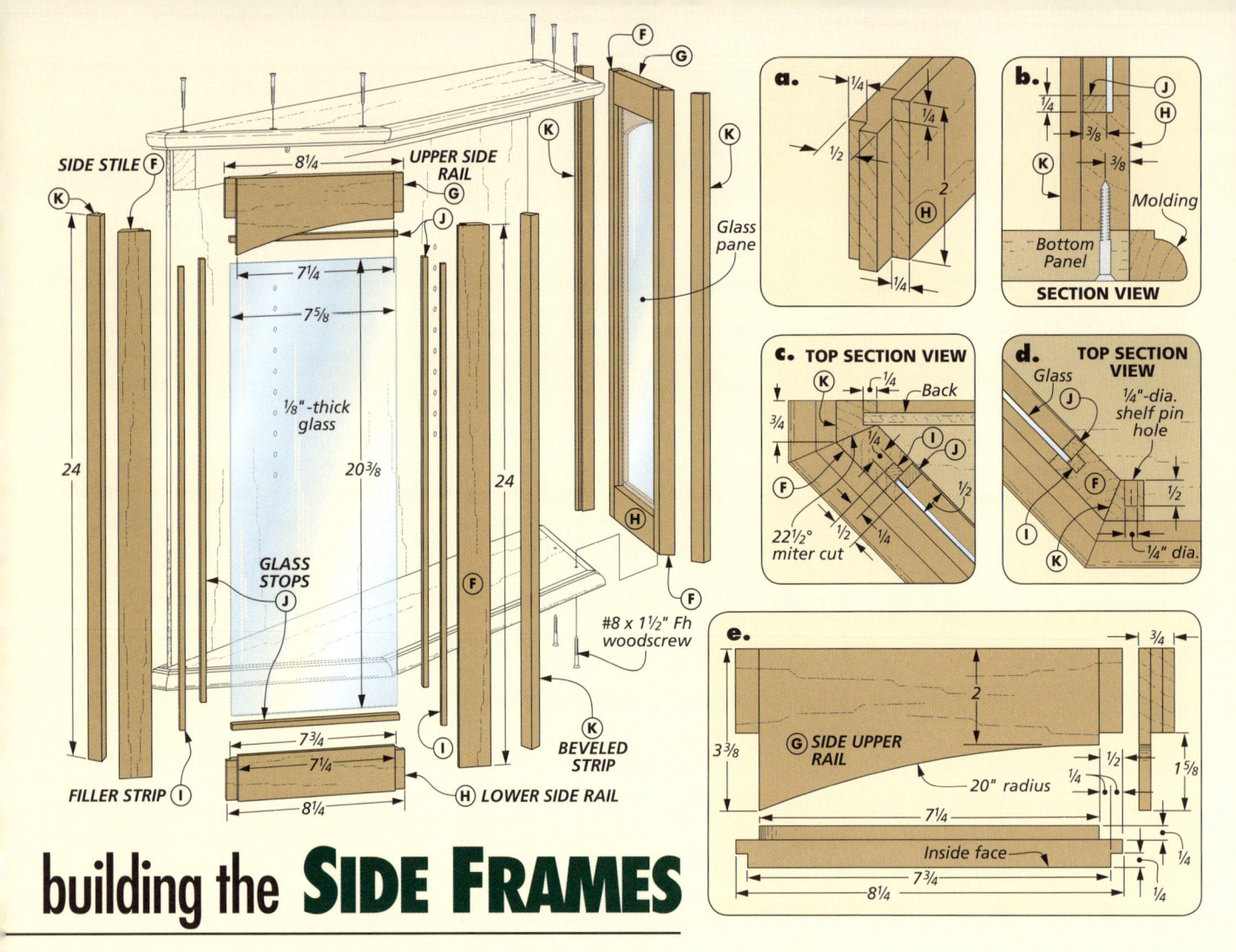

Adding a pair of side frames and four beveled strips makes the basic case rigid and provides a solid framework for mounting the doors. The frames feature arched upper rails and glass panels. To create a strong frame, I used a modified version of stub tenon and groove joinery. You'll find all the details in the drawings above. I'll explain how it all works, starting with the stiles.

CUTTING A GROOVE. Whenever I make this type of frame, I like to start by cutting the grooves. It's easier to match the thickness of the tenons to the groove than the other way around.

After cutting the stiles to final size, the How-To box below shows how to cut the centered grooves in each piece. Then just trim the inside edge to form a recess for the glass panel, as you can see in the right drawing below.

As I said earlier, there are a few aspects of the side frames that require special attention. The illustrations on the next page will help make everything clear.

RAIL TENONS. You can start by cutting the upper and lower side rails to final size. The upper rail starts out wider so you can cut the arched shape later.

Figure 1 shows how I cut the stub tenons on the ends of the rails. Because you trimmed off the back of the stile to form a recess for the glass, the tenon shoulders on the rails need to be offset to fit the stiles. Details 'a' and 'c' above show what this looks like.

How-To: Cutting Stile Grooves

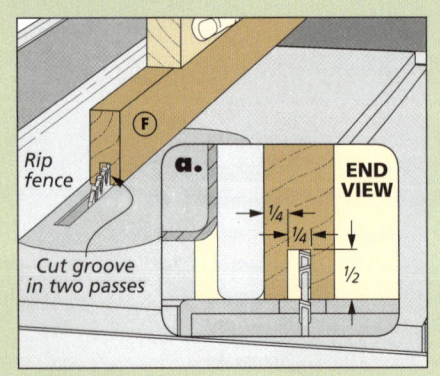

Centered Groove. Start with the workpiece slightly off center and make the first cut, then flip it end-for-end and repeat.

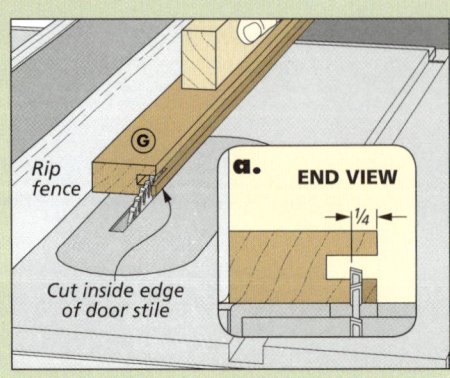

Trimming the Inside Edge. Cutting away the back, inside edge of the stiles results in a rabbet when the frame is assembled.

RABBETED RAILS. Next, you can cut the rabbets on the rails (Figures 2 and 3). You'll cut a wide rabbet on the upper rail. This allows you to fit the glass panel inside the frame without having to cut it to match the curve of the rail.

Now lay out the 20"-radius arc on the upper rails and cut it to shape at the band saw or with a jig saw. A little sanding to smooth the curves and you're done.

ASSEMBLY. The joinery helps keep the parts aligned and square during assembly. But it's still a good idea to check the overall assembly to make sure it's square as you add the clamps.

While the glue dried, I ripped some filler strips (details 'c' and 'd', opposite page). These fill in the grooves in the stiles between the rails. Once again, I made a couple test cuts to zero in on a snug fit. After cutting each to final length, I installed them with just a little glue in the grooves.

BEVELS & BEVEL STRIPS. The next step is to bevel the edges of the frames (Figure 5). Then you can get to work on the beveled strips that are attached to the edges of each frame. Both pairs of strips are cut from the edges of extra-wide blanks but they require some work before ripping them to final size (Figures 6 and 7).

The front strip serves as a hinge mounting strip for the doors. It also has holes drilled for shelf pins (Figure 6). The back strip has a groove to hold the plywood back of the cabinet, as shown in Figure 8. I used tape as a clamp to attach the beveled strips to the frames.

INSTALL THE GLASS. I found it easier to install the glass now, before assembling the case. Thin strips serve as glass stop. They're fastened with a few drops of glue to make them easy to remove if the glass ever needs replaced.

CASE ASSEMBLY. To assemble the case, I fastened the sides to the bottom, slid the back in place, and then attached the hanging cleat. Cap it off by fastening the top panel with screws.

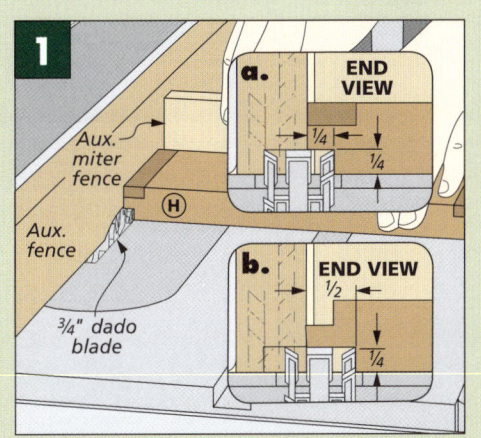

Stub Tenons. Cut the short cheeks of the tenon first (detail 'a'), then reposition the rip fence to cut the long cheek (detail 'b').

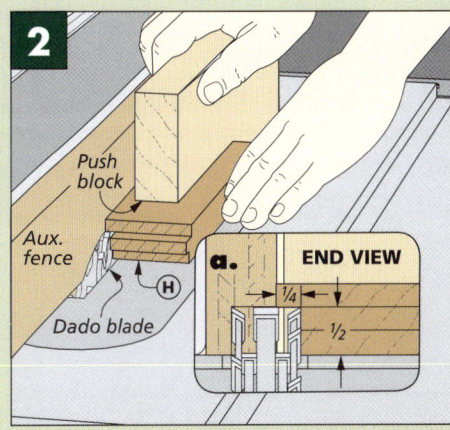

Lower Rail Rabbets. The rabbets in the lower rails are straightforward cuts using the dado blade and auxiliary fence.

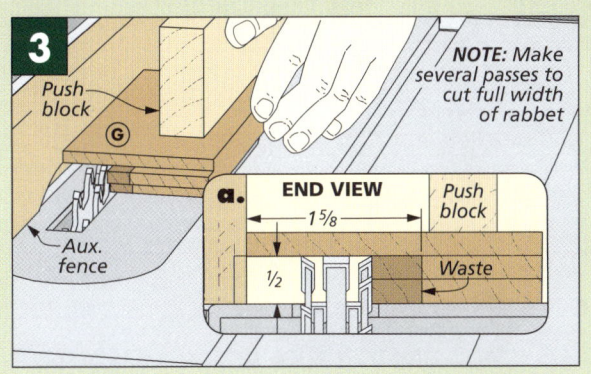

Upper Rails. Cut the wide rabbets on the upper rails using the same table saw setup. Use a push block and make a series of narrow cuts to remove the waste.

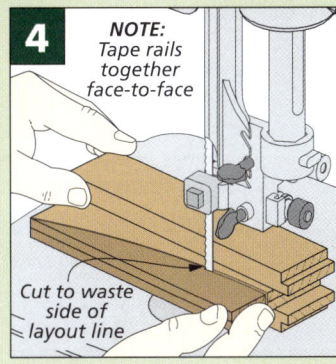

Upper Rail Arcs. Cut the arc in the rails at the band saw and sand the surfaces smooth.

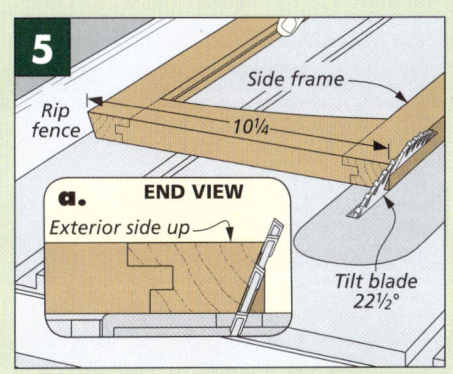

Edge Bevels. After assembling the frames and cleaning up glue squeezeout, rip the bevels on each edge by tilting the blade.

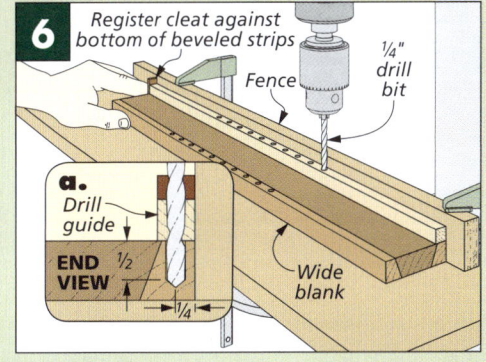

Shelf Pin Holes. The drilling guide is referenced against the bottom edge of the blank to make sure of a consistent alignment.

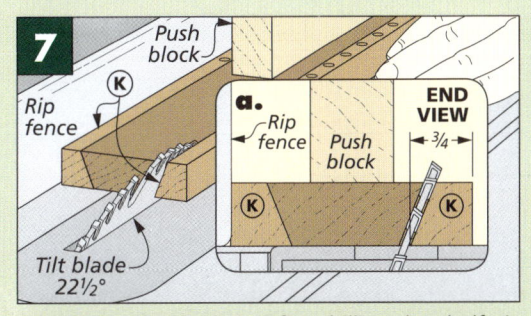

Front Beveled Strips. After drilling the shelf pin holes, rip the strips from the blank using the same blade angle to match the frames.

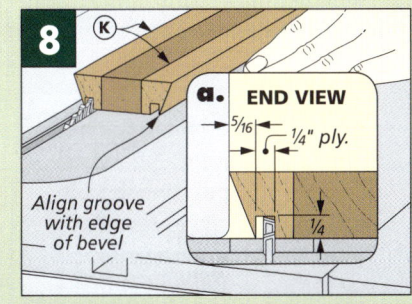

Rear Beveled Strips. You'll need to cut a groove to fit the plywood back before ripping the rear strips to width.

completing the CABINET

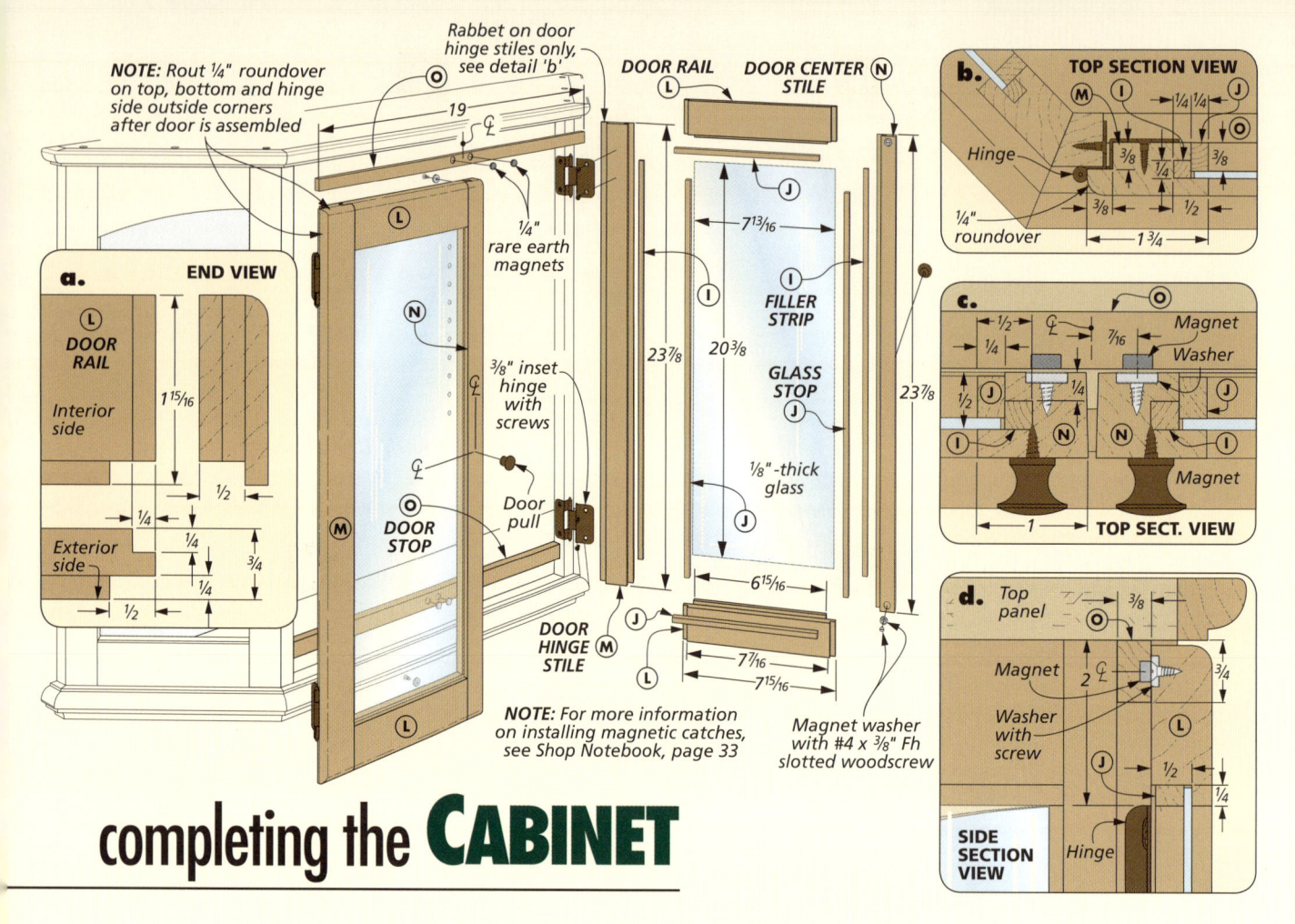

At this point, the cabinet is really beginning to take shape. All that remains now is to add the doors, some decorative molding on the top and bottom, and the two adjustable shelves.

DOORS. I used the same stub tenon and groove joinery technique to make the doors as was used for the sides. You can get started by cutting the rails and stiles to final size. (Note that the center door stiles are narrower than the outer, hinge stiles.)

GROOVES. Next, cut the centered grooves in the rails and stiles. Again, you'll need to cut away the inner edge of the rails to form a rabbet (detail 'a'). Likewise, on the stiles, the inner edge is cut back to accommodate the glass stop (details 'b' and 'c,' above).

TENONS. As before, I used the miter gauge to cut the offset stub tenons on the door rails. Test cuts on scrap pieces can help you sneak up on a perfect fit in the grooves in the door stiles.

ASSEMBLY & FINAL SHAPING. Now you can assemble the doors and install the filler strips in the grooves. Head over to the table saw and use a dado blade to cut a rabbet on the inside edge of the hinge stile. This allows the door to be inset $3/8$" into the frame. Then, round over the outside edge of the hinge stile as well as the top and bottom of the door frame at the router table. The drawings at left show the details of both operations. Finally, form a slight bevel on the inside edge of each door for clearance when opening and closing the doors (detail 'c').

FINISHING THE DOORS. With the door frames complete, you can install the glass. The process is the same as before. Then you can install the hinges and knobs, as shown in the drawings above. As you

How-To: Profile the Door Edges

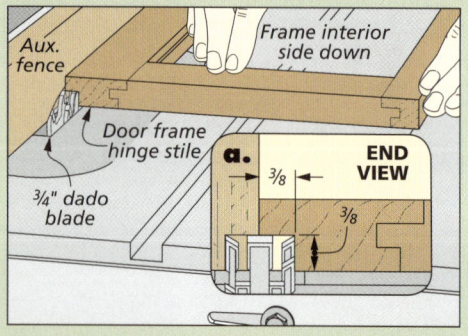

Door Hinge Stile. To create an inset fit for the doors, rabbet the inside edge of the hinge stile using a dado blade.

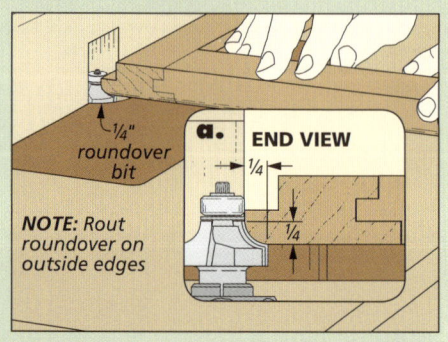

Roundover. Install a roundover bit in the router table and rout the profile on the top, bottom, and outside edges of the doors.

can see, the knobs are centered on the length and width of the center door stiles.

DOOR STOPS. I glued door stops to the top and bottom of the case with two rare-earth magnets embedded in each. The position of the magnets matches a pair of washers in the doors (detail 'c,' opposite page). For tips on installing the magnets and washers, turn to Shop Notebook, page 33.

COVE MOLDING. The cove molding installed on the top and bottom adds an attractive look to the cabinet. To make the cove molding, rout a ½" cove on the edge of a wide blank, as shown in detail 'a.' Then miter the pieces to length and glue them in place. Details 'b' and 'c' show the position of the molding.

TOP MOLDING. The top is completed with the addition of a top molding. For this, you just need to rout a ⅛"-rad. roundover on the two outside edges of a molding blank. Then you can install it as before, mitering the pieces to length and gluing them in place.

SHELVES. The two shelves are cut to size from ½"-thick stock. The ends are beveled at 45° and a ⅛" roundover is routed on all edges. The shelves rest on ¼" shelf pins that fit into the holes you drilled earlier in the back and sides.

After applying a finish to the cabinet, you're ready to hang it. For this, drive long screws through the hanging cleat and into a couple of wall studs.

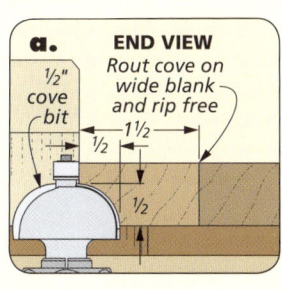

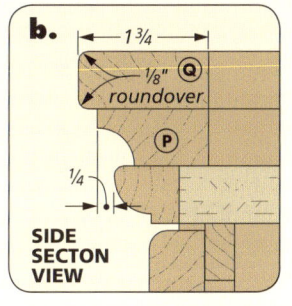

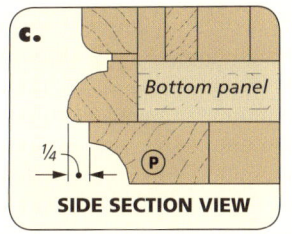

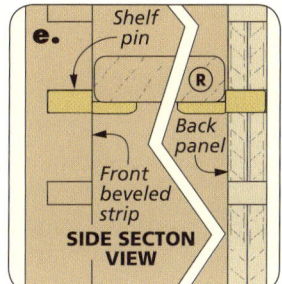

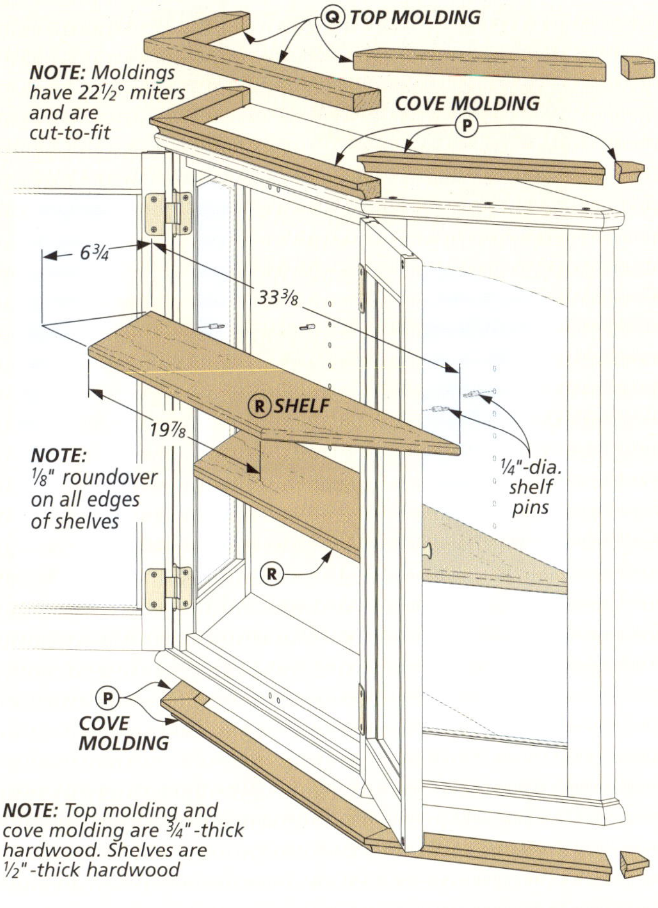

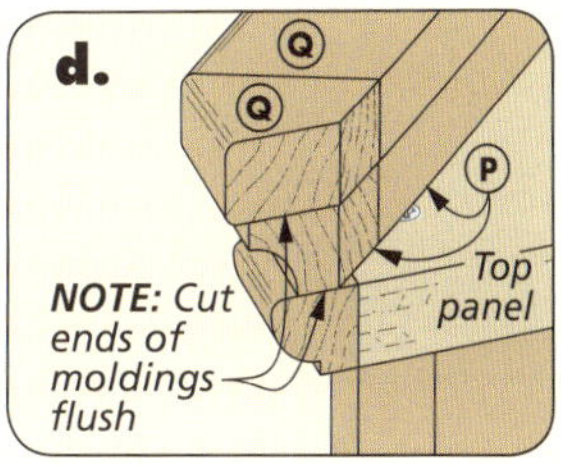

Materials, Supplies & Cutting Diagram

A	Top/Bottom Panels (2)	¾ ply. - 8 x 35
B	Thumbnail Molding (1)	¾ x ⅞ - 90 rgh.
C	Back (1)	¼ ply. - 34 x 25
D	Shelf Pin Strips (2)	¼ ply. - 2 x 24
E	Hanging Cleat (1)	¾ x 2 - 33½
F	Side Stiles (4)	¾ x 1½ - 24
G	Upper Side Rails (2)	¾ x 3⅜ - 8¼
H	Lower Side Rails (2)	¾ x 2 - 8¼
I	Filler Strip (1)	¼ x ¼ - 16' rgh.
J	Glass Stop (1)	¼ x 13/32 - 21' rgh.
K	Beveled Strips (4)	¾ x ¾ - 24
L	Door Rails (4)	¾ x 1 15/16 - 7 15/16
M	Door Hinge Stile (2)	¾ x 1¾ - 23⅞
N	Door Center Stile (2)	¾ x 1 - 23⅞
O	Door Stop (2)	⅜ x ¾ - 19
P	Cove Molding (1)	¾ x 1½ - 96 rgh.
Q	Top Molding (1)	¾ x 1¾ - 50 rgh.
R	Shelves (2)	½ x 6¾ - 33⅜

- (2 pr.) ⅜" Inset Hinges w/Screws
- (4) ¼" Rare-Earth Magnets & Washers
- (2) Door Pulls
- (8) ¼"-dia. Shelf Pins
- (12) #8 x 1½" Fh Woodscrews
- (8) #4 x ½" Fh Woodscrews
- (2) 7⅝" x 20⅜" Glass Panels (⅛" thick)
- (2) 7 13/16" x 20⅜" Glass Panels (⅛" thick)

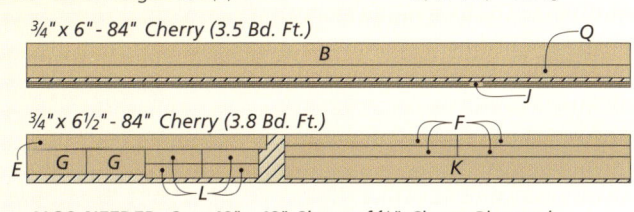

¾" x 6" - 84" Cherry (3.5 Bd. Ft.)

¾" x 6½" - 84" Cherry (3.8 Bd. Ft.)

¾" x 6½" - 84" Cherry (3.8 Bd. Ft.)

½" x 7" - 84" Cherry (4.1 Sq. Ft.)

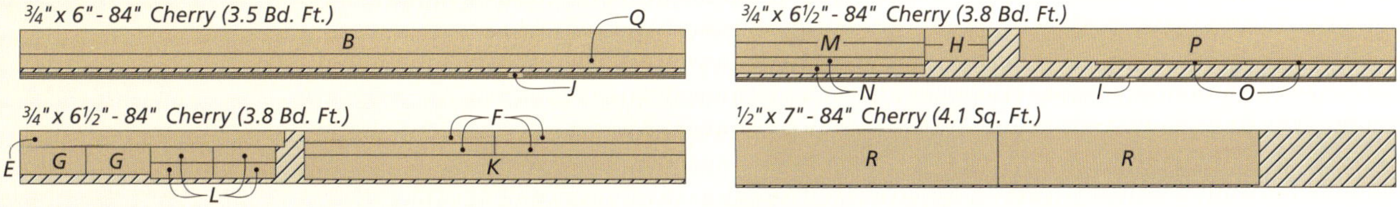

ALSO NEEDED: One 48" x 48" Sheet of ¼" Cherry Plywood
One 24" x 48" Sheet of ¾" Cherry Plywood

NOTE: Parts B, K, and P, cut from extra wide blanks.

techniques from our shop

successful Drawer Construction

When you get ready to build the drawers for a project, the first thing that comes to mind is the type of joinery you'll use. You have options as varied as classic, hand-cut dovetails to much simpler tongue and dado construction. But no matter what type of joinery you use to build the drawers, there are a lot of other factors that are just as important to achieving top-quality results.

I've put together a few guidelines that apply to all drawer construction — just common sense points I always keep in mind.

START WITH A PLAN. Whether you've designed your own project or you're working from a published plan, it's always a good idea to keep a list of parts at hand. For drawer building, that list should include how many sides, fronts, and backs you'll need and the final sizes of all pieces. Since the sides are often made from thinner stock than the front and back, make sure to list the pieces by thickness as well. This makes selecting stock easier.

SELECT YOUR STOCK. You can make the building process a lot easier by taking your time at the lumberyard. With your parts list or plan in hand, pick through the stacks to find enough straight, flat stock to fill the bill. One simple tip that I can offer is to always pick up 15-20% extra stock for tool setups and to save the day in case of a mistake.

Obviously, if you're planning to use plywood, this is less of a concern. However, if you do choose plywood, it's a good idea to stick to Baltic birch or similarly stable plywood free of voids.

MILL FLAT, SQUARE STOCK. You'll never get a good fit with out-of-square or twisted parts. Since a drawer needs to be not only square but also flat to slide properly, one bad piece can ruin the whole drawer. Don't fool yourself into thinking a piece will straighten out when it's clamped up. Taking the time to joint the workpieces flat on one face and then planing them to a uniform thickness is the first step in successful drawer construction (left drawing).

RIP TO WIDTH. Another good habit to get into is to rip all pieces of the same width with the same setup. In other words, set the rip fence of your table saw and use your parts list to rip enough stock to get all the pieces of that width

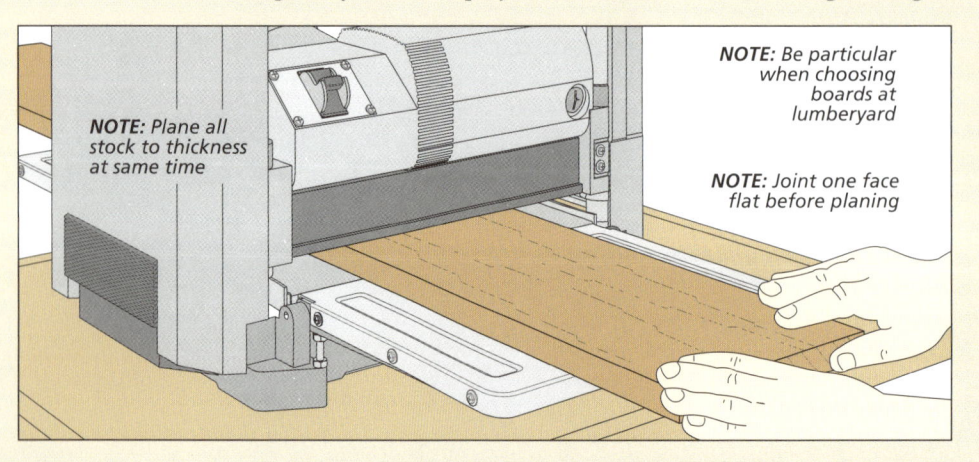

NOTE: Plane all stock to thickness at same time

NOTE: Be particular when choosing boards at lumberyard

NOTE: Joint one face flat before planing

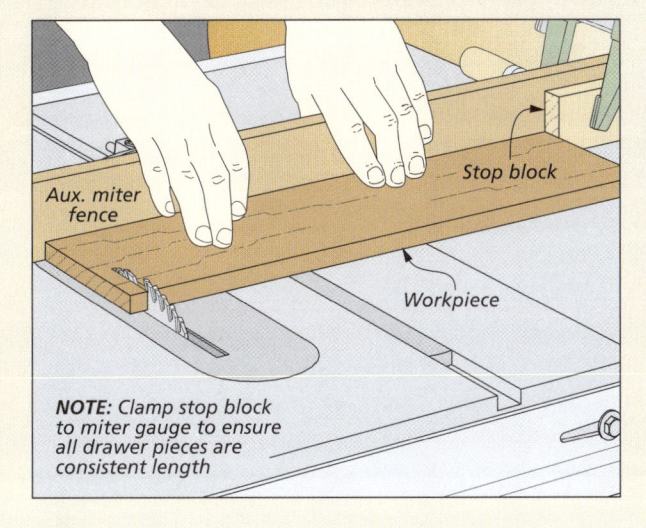

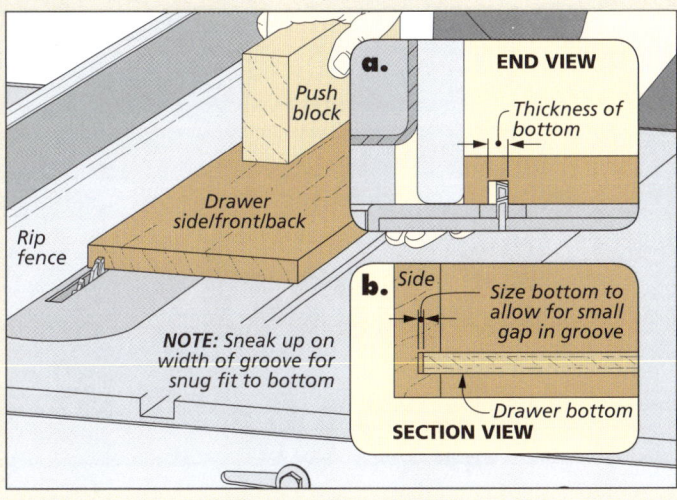

at one time. You'd be surprised how much variation you can get if you have to go back later to cut more stock to size.

ACCURATE LENGTH. No matter how careful you've been up to this point, if your sides aren't exactly the same length, you won't get a square drawer. The same is true for the fronts and backs. The best way to ensure this is to use a stop block when cutting the pieces to length (left drawing above). A scrap clamped to an auxiliary miter gauge fence is all you need.

MATCH & MARK STOCK. With the workpieces milled and sized, the next step is to lay out the pieces for each individual drawer. One important consideration is to get a nice look for the drawer fronts since they're often the highlight of the project. Whether the fronts are real or false, they should have a consistent grain pattern and good color match. This is less of a concern with the sides and the backs. But again, try to shoot for the best possible look.

Once you have the parts laid out and matched up, always label them clearly to avoid any chance of confusion when cutting the joinery. The Shop Tip below offers a quick, foolproof method of marking drawer parts.

DRAWER BOTTOMS. And when cutting the grooves for drawer bottoms in the parts, once again, make all the cuts using the same table saw setup. This makes it easier to size the grooves for a consistently snug fit to the bottom (right drawing above). However, it shouldn't be too tight. Then, to ensure a trouble-free assembly, size the drawer bottoms to allow for a small gap ($1/32$") at the bottom of the grooves.

ASSEMBLY. After clamping, set the drawer on a perfectly flat surface (the table saw or a flat piece of MDF on the benchtop) to make sure there's no twist in the glueup. It should sit flat without rocking. Finally, remember to check each drawer for square.

If you get in the habit of always following these simple tips when building drawers, you're sure to get top-notch results. And nothing highlights the quality of a project like attractive, smooth-working drawers.

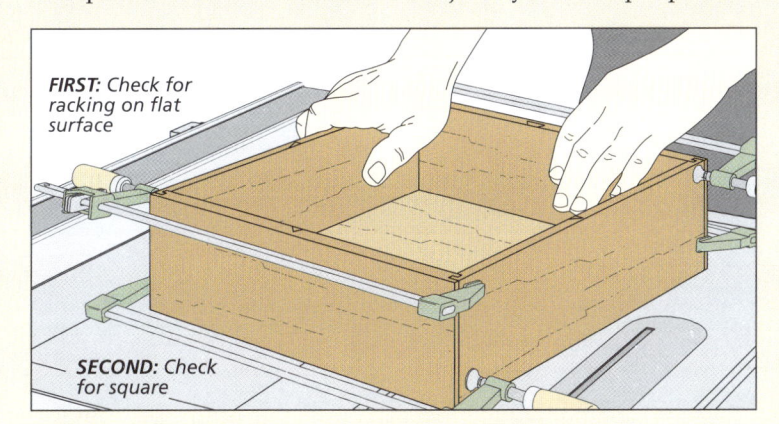

Shop Tip: Triangle Method

I've used this simple method for marking drawer parts for many years. It relies on triangles marked across the paired sides and front and back to tell you everything you need to know (photo at right).

The two sides are placed side-by-side and then a triangle is drawn across the top edge pointing forward. This tells you that the marked edge is the top, the open side of the marking on each piece is the inside, and the angled leg points to the front. The front and back are paired and similarly marked with the triangle also pointing forward.

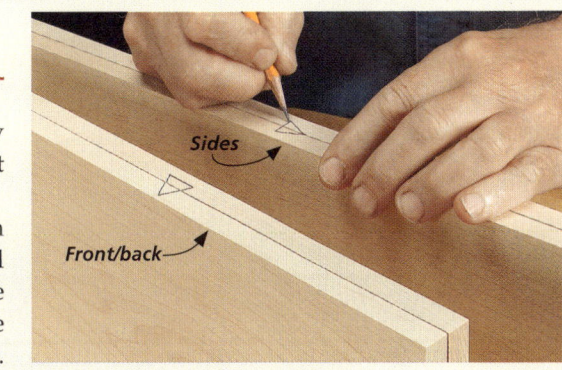

working with tools

perfect Band Saw Cuts

Attention to a few easy-to-master details guarantees accurate cuts.

During construction of a project, more often than not, I make at least one trip to the band saw. Usually this involves cutting a part to shape "free-hand." By this, I mean simply cutting to a layout line without the aid of a fence or other type of guide. This is essentially what the band saw is designed to do. The task can be as simple as making a straight taper cut or something more involved like shaping a complex profile.

The catch is that good results are not automatic. Inaccurate cuts with rough, burned edges can force you to perform a lot of tedious cleanup on the workpiece with a file, sandpaper, or sanding drum. But a poor result usually stems from a hasty setup and execution. All it takes is a little planning and the right approach to get clean, precise cuts.

SET UP THE SAW

The starting point is proper setup of the saw. And the first step is to choose the right blade for the job. There are two aspects to this — blade width and tooth count.

BLADE WIDTH. When cutting a profile, you need to match the width of the blade to the contour of the curve. In a nutshell, the narrower the blade, the tighter the radius it will cut. A blade that's too wide may not allow for the turns necessary to follow a layout line. On the other hand, very narrow blades tend to flex and can be difficult to keep on track.

Your best bet is to choose the widest blade that will still allow you to easily follow the layout line. The Shop Tip at left provides a handy turning radius reference.

TOOTH COUNT. Choosing a blade with the right tooth count involves a balance. More teeth creates a smooth surface but a slow cut. A slow feed may cause burning while the tendency to force the cut makes steering difficult. As is often the case, the middle ground is the best place to be. For general use, a 1/4"-wide blade with 6 teeth per inch works well.

GUIDES. Setting the height of the blade guides correctly is the second component of the setup. The guides should be as close to the surface of the workpiece as possible without blocking your view of the layout line (lower photo above). This helps minimize blade vibration and deflection.

▲ Position the saw's guides close to the workpiece for the best blade support.

Shop Tip: Blade Width

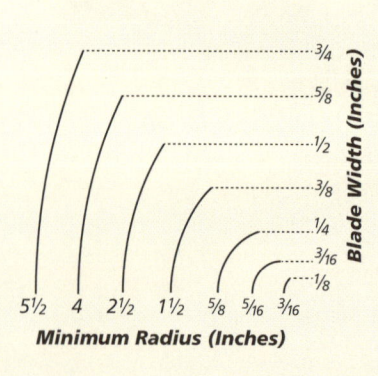

As shown at left, a blade's tightest turning radius depends on its width. When matching the blade width to the profile being cut, it's best not to push the limits.

Blade Width (Inches): 3/4, 5/8, 1/2, 3/8, 1/4, 3/16, 1/8
Minimum Radius (Inches): 5 1/2, 4, 2 1/2, 1 1/2, 5/8, 5/16, 3/16

THINK AHEAD

Once the setup is complete, don't be in a rush to start the cuts. Sometimes a little planning can actually help get the job done quicker and easier. Let me offer some food for thought.

First, when marking a profile on a workpiece, try to keep the layout lines 1/8" or more back from any edge (lower left drawing). The goal is to prevent the blade from breaking through the edge during the cut. A continuous cut in which the blade is always fully engaged will be much smoother.

THE FIRST CUT. When cutting a complex profile with multiple, intersecting curves, plan the order of the cuts in advance. If possible, you want to cut each separate section of the profile with a single cut. The drawing above illustrates this idea. The first cuts are simply relief cuts that allow the waste to be removed more easily.

You may also need to consider the best place to start a cut. Generally, it's easier to enter a cut at a steep angle (closer to 90°) rather than a shallow angle. At a very shallow angle the blade wants to skip along the edge. So when cutting a straight taper, enter from the end of the workpiece, as shown in the right drawing.

WATCH THE FRAME. Always remember that the saw has a frame that may obstruct completion of a cut. Running into the frame can be a problem when cutting profiles on longer workpieces. Think about which starting point will allow you to avoid the frame.

In some instances, you may need to flip the workpiece and mark the layout on the opposite face.

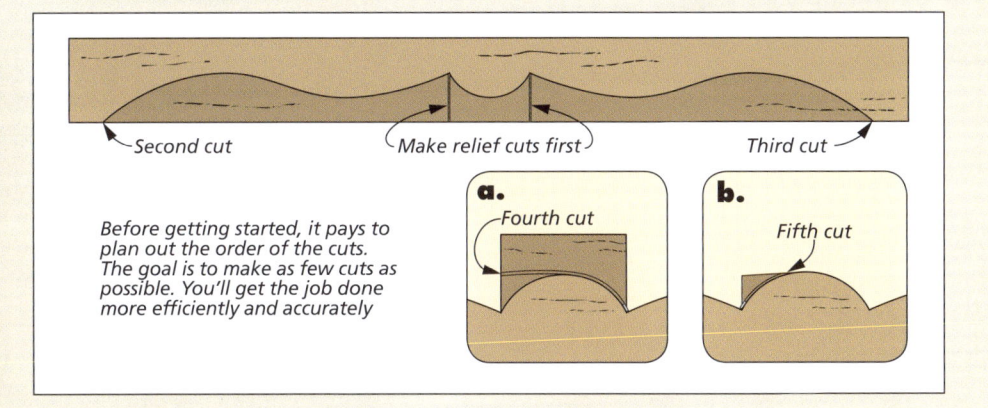

MAKING THE CUTS

Now that you're ready to start a cut, you have to ask, "how close to the layout line do I want to be?" If the saw is set up properly — the right blade and guide setting — you should be able to cut within about 1/32" of the line without fear of crossing over (right drawing below). This will leave you with a minimum of cleanup after the cut is completed.

SLOW & STEADY. A slow, steady feed rate makes it easier to follow a layout line. Avoid forcing the cut. You'll end up sacrificing control. However, to avoid burning and "hiccups" in the cut, always keep the workpiece moving.

I like to focus my eyes on the layout line just ahead of the point of the cut. This allows you to anticipate changes in direction and you'll be able to steer more easily and accurately.

TWO HANDS. I'm right-handed so I usually feed and control the workpiece with my dominant hand while using my left to guide it. You'll find that a light, sensitive touch with your guide hand produces the best result.

When making a straight cut, you can often use your guide hand as a rub fence. Place the thumb and index finger along the edge of the workpiece and use them to gently steer (drawing above). You'll find it's much easier to track a straight line.

ONE WAY. Sometimes it's necessary to back up at the end of a cut, but try to limit this. You'll usually score or burn the smooth surface. Back up just enough to exit the cut by removing a section of waste (far left drawing).

The only difficult thing here is remembering to slow down and take your time. This will end in a better result from less effort. **W**

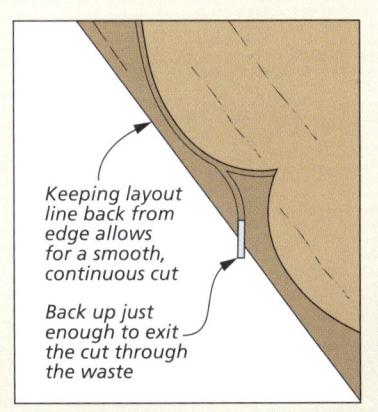

finishing room

tips for Finishing Poplar

Here's the secret to making this low-cost wood look like its expensive cousin.

▲ Fine-grained poplar is available in a variety of sizes at home centers and lumberyards.

When I build a big project, like an entertainment center or a bed, one of my first concerns is the cost of lumber. The board feet can really stack up on a project like that and if you use high-quality hardwood like cherry or walnut, the cost will add up too.

One way to save some money and still have a quality finished piece is to use a less-expensive wood like poplar. Poplar can be almost half the price of other premium hardwoods. It's stable and it machines well, making it easy to work with in the shop. Plus, the species has a fine, even grain with virtually no knots.

There's a downside to poplar, though. It can have heavy streaks and color variations that appear dark green to pale yellow, so most woodworkers have banished it to the unseen parts of projects, like drawer sides or web frames. But the wood can be painted or stained with great results. You can see examples of both in the main photo and the lower photo on the opposite page.

PAINT. The old saying "Paint covers a multitude of sins," was probably spoken first about poplar.

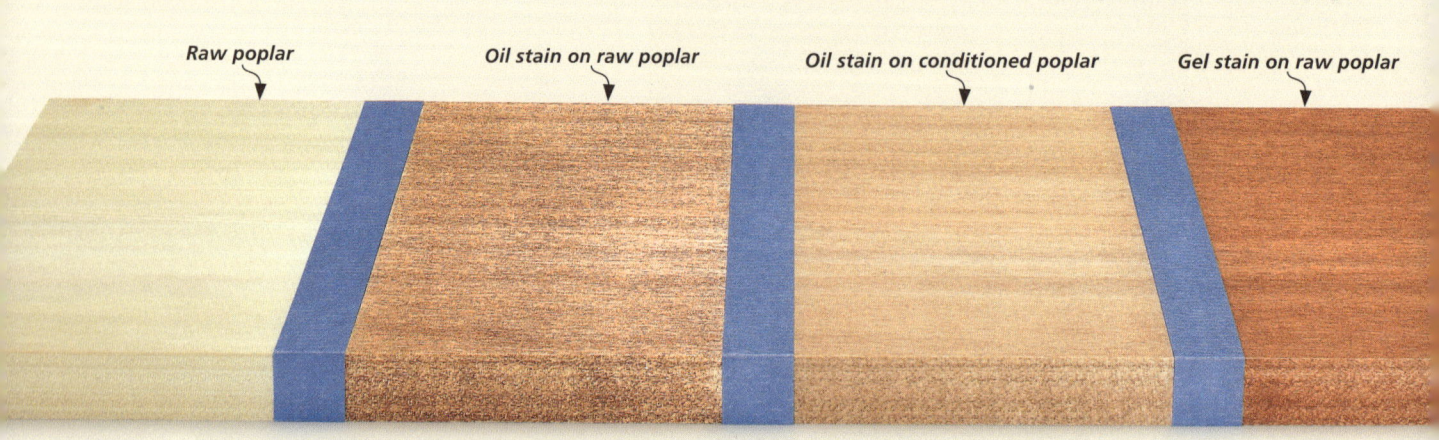

Raw poplar   Oil stain on raw poplar   Oil stain on conditioned poplar   Gel stain on raw poplar

46 Woodsmith No. 196

Light brown gel stain **Medium brown gel stain** **Red gel stain** **Dark brown gel stain**

This wood takes paint (oil-based or latex) extremely well. While paint looks good on poplar, you can make it look like more expensive, fine-grained woods. It just takes a particular type of stain.

OIL STAIN. Oil-based stains are very popular for most hardwoods because they help highlight the figure. But poplar can absorb stain inconsistently. This means you could end up with a project that looks blotchy, like the sample you see at the bottom of the opposite page.

CONDITIONER. If you prefer to work with oil stain, there is a solution to the blotchiness. You can apply a wood conditioner to the bare wood before you apply the stain. Most conditioners are a thinned varnish that seals the wood grain and gives you a more consistent surface on which to apply the stain. But there's a trade off in the process. As you can see in the photo on the opposite page, the conditioned wood is a lot lighter in color than the other finished surfaces. The process of sealing the wood also keeps the stain from penetrating. That's why I like to use gel stain.

GEL STAINS. Gel stains are exactly what the name implies: Mineral spirits and resin mixed with colorant to produce a thick gel.

If you've never used gel stain before, you'll be surprised when you open the can. It's about the consistency of mayonnaise (margin photo). Although it's oil based, a thickener in the stain gives it body. The resin keeps the color on the surface of the wood, but it's translucent. You'll see the wood grain, but not the original color of the wood.

Once you apply the gel, you'll immediately see the intensity of the color. It only takes one coat to get a rich, deep color on poplar. I like to use red gel stain for a project that looks like it's built from cherry without the expense of the finer wood. Dark brown stain works great to create the look of walnut. As with any stain, there is a wide selection of colors, so varied looks are easy to achieve.

To apply gel stain, I use a clean cloth with a healthy amount of stain on it (margin photo). As you apply the stain, you may notice streaks. These can be removed with a clean cloth while the stain is still wet. Apply the stain with a circular motion for maximum coverage. Then wipe with the grain to remove the excess stain and produce an even color. After the stain dries (about 8 hours) you can add your favorite topcoat.

You can apply a second coat of stain before the topcoat for a richer look. But I think you'll find that one coat of gel stain is all it takes to turn an ugly-duckling piece of hardwood into a striking, finished project.

▲ A gel stain looks almost like paint, but is transluscent. It dries to a rich, deep color that hides the greenish tint of poplar.

▲ The smooth texture and fine, clear grain make poplar a great choice for any project that will be painted. It accepts both oil-based and latex paint equally well.

details of craftsmanship

Setting Construction Goals

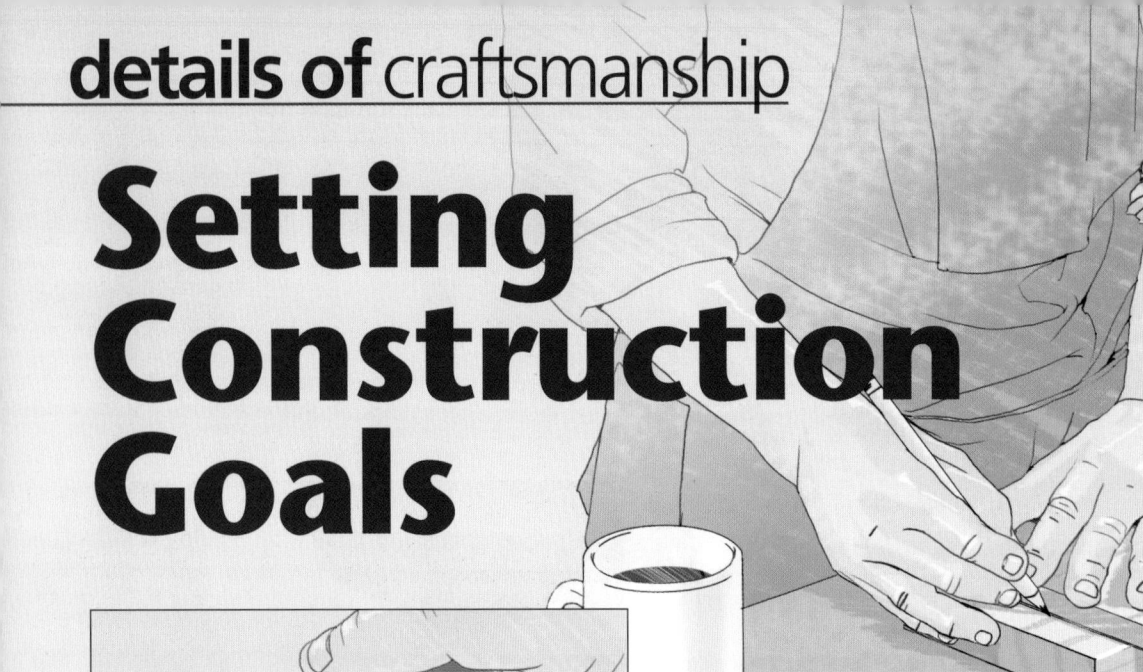

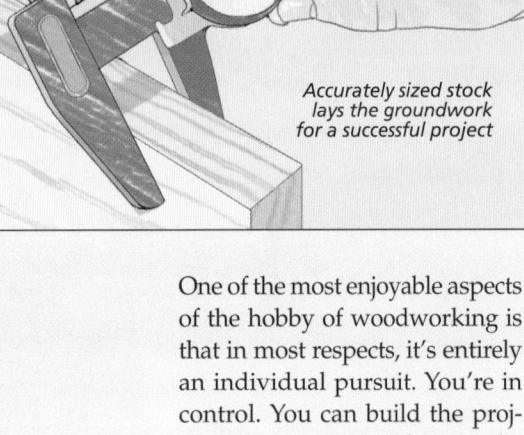

Accurately sized stock lays the groundwork for a successful project

It's the little things that make the difference. The key to building a top-notch project is attention to a few simple details.

One of the most enjoyable aspects of the hobby of woodworking is that in most respects, it's entirely an individual pursuit. You're in control. You can build the projects you want to build, using the tools and techniques you're comfortable with, and do the work at your own pace. And maybe most important of all, you get to set the goals and standards for the quality of the end result.

However, sometimes this last aspect can be a challenge.

When building a project, you have to decide — How good is good enough? To be honest, after many years of woodworking, I still sometimes struggle to find the right balance between my desire for a perfect outcome and the constraints of time and effort. It almost always comes down to a compromise. But the good news is that arriving at a happy medium isn't very difficult.

STRUCTURE, FUNCTION, & APPEARANCE. I approach every project with

Large surfaces draw extra attention. Make sure that they're true and flat

three general criteria in mind. First, a project should be structurally sound. Next, it needs to serve the function for which it was intended. Finally, I want every project I build to look good. You can't completely separate these three goals. Although each has its own criteria, they all come together in the final result.

A GOOD DESIGN. It all begins with a good design. As the saying goes, "You can't make a silk purse out of a sow's ear." You won't meet any of your goals unless the design is thoroughly hashed out beforehand and all the details are thought through. And having a good design even extends to careful wood selection.

However, once the design is set and meets the structural, functional, and appearance standards you've laid out, the quality of the end product depends on the work you do in the shop.

DON'T OBSESS. When doing the actual building — cutting, fitting, and assembling the parts — I like to think I'll achieve perfection at each step along the way. But in reality, I know that this is an impossible standard. So I don't obsess on this unrealistic goal. Instead, I focus on doing the best job that I can at each step along the way. Then I move on, putting thoughts of any minor imperfections aside. In other words, focus on the specific task at hand, but don't lose sight of the big picture. You'll find that if you adopt this practical attitude, chances are that the final product will turn out pretty darn good.

DON'T OVERLOOK. On the other hand, it's best not to let serious problems slide. Major shortcomings will only come back to bite you later on in the building process, and can compromise the end result. So when it's practical, correct these errors on the spot. If it's something that can't be fixed, keep in mind that you may need to adapt or compensate at a later point in the construction.

A WELL-BUILT PROJECT

The quality control aspects that I try to focus on when building can be condensed into a short and straightforward list. It all starts with accurately sized parts. Even small dimensioning errors have a way of compounding through the course of a project. So it's best to adopt the attitude that close is definitely *not* good enough.

GAP FREE & SQUARE. As well as being important structurally, the fit of the joints is one of the most noticeable aspects of a project. Gaps, heavy glue lines, or misaligned surfaces can stick out like a sore thumb. So shoot for joinery that's tight and flush. I always rely on a dry run and close inspection before the actual assembly to reveal any problems.

And nothing can be more confounding than having to "work around" an assembly that isn't square. It pays to check and double-check for square before and during the glueup. Then you can make the necessary adjustments rather than trying to compensate after the clamps come off.

A PLEASING EFFECT. Moldings are meant to draw attention and can help make or break the appearance of a project. For the best effect, make sure the joints fit tightly and the pieces are aligned properly (lower left drawing). Extra care taken here really makes a difference.

SMOOTH, FLAT & CONSISTENT. Surfacing (sanding, scraping, or planing) parts and assemblies is not my idea of a fun day in the shop. However, it's definitely not a place to cut corners.

I try to make sure that all large exposed surfaces are dead flat and smooth (lower drawing, opposite page). All the parts should be surfaced consistently (sanded to the same grit) and free of visible machine marks. A little extra sanding up front will pay off when the finish goes on.

But don't get carried away. Careful, controlled sanding is the key. Edges and profiles that are kept crisp and then softly eased look much nicer (right drawing).

If you check all assemblies for square and make corrections, you'll avoid problems later in the building process

DOORS & DRAWERS. When it comes to the fit of doors and drawers, I try to be very particular. Make sure the gaps are even and surfaces and edges align properly. All it takes is a little extra attention at the time of assembly to avoid racked doors and drawers.

Along the same lines, you want doors, drawers, table leaves, or other moving parts to operate smoothly and easily. Careful fitting and adjustment is the key.

The fact is, nothing here requires great skill. But when practiced together, the end result is fine craftsmanship. **W**

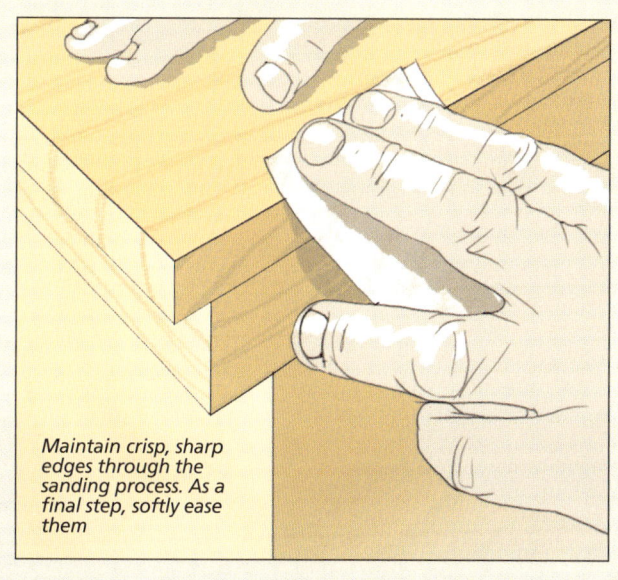

When fitting moldings, take the time to get it right. Shoot for gap-free and perfectly aligned joints

Maintain crisp, sharp edges through the sanding process. As a final step, softly ease them

in the mailbox

Questions & Answers

The Right Way to Rout

Q *I always have a hard time remembering which direction to rout when using a hand-held router. Is there a rule of thumb you follow, or does it even matter?*

Rafael Burgos-Mirabal
Cambridge, Massachusetts

A Determining which way to rout often causes some head scratching, especially when setting up for a routing procedure that's a little out of the ordinary.

As a rule, when using a hand-held router, you want to avoid routing in the same direction that the bit is spinning. If you don't, the router has a tendency to take off as soon as the bit contacts the workpiece. By routing in a direction against the rotation of the bit, you have more control.

This means that when routing a profile on the edge of a board, you want to rout from left to right as you face the workpiece. An easy way to remember this is that you should rout in the same direction that you read — from left to right.

DADOES & GROOVES. But there are some cases where it's a little more confusing. Routing a dado or groove with a fence to guide the router is one example.

At first glance, it wouldn't seem that the routing direction makes much difference since you're routing against a fence. But if you rout in the wrong direction, the rotation of the bit will pull the router off course and away from the fence.

So you still want to rout from left to right, but only if the fence is behind the router, like you see in the upper left drawing below.

If you're using two fences to rout both sides of a dado or groove, then you'll need to rout in a U-shape pattern, first along one fence and then in the opposite direction along the other (upper right).

FRAMES. Routing around the edges of a frame is another example. As you can see in the lower left drawing below, when routing the outside of the frame, you want to rout in a counter-clockwise direction. But when routing the inside of the frame, you'll want to rout in the opposite direction (clockwise).

RULE OF THUMB. No matter what it is you're routing, you can see a simple trick I use to jog my memory in the lower right drawing below.

Simply hold out your right hand, palm down, and extend your thumb and index finger. If you hold your thumb against the edge of the workpiece you wish to rout or the fence, your index finger will point you in the right direction. **W**

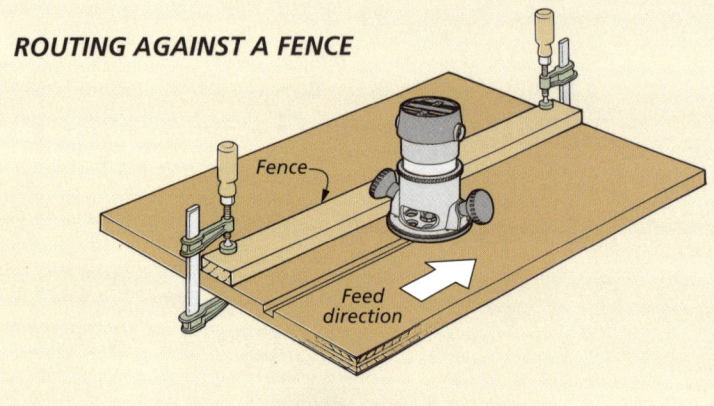

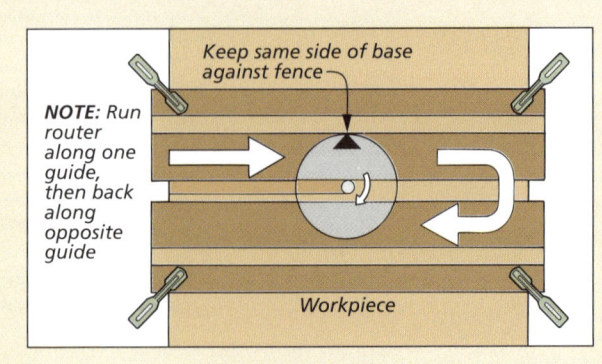

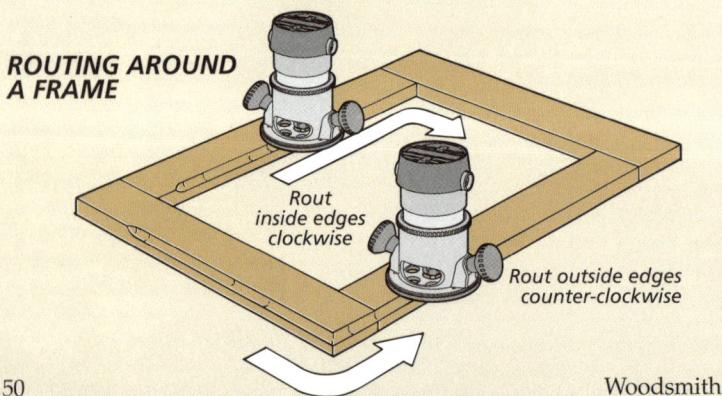

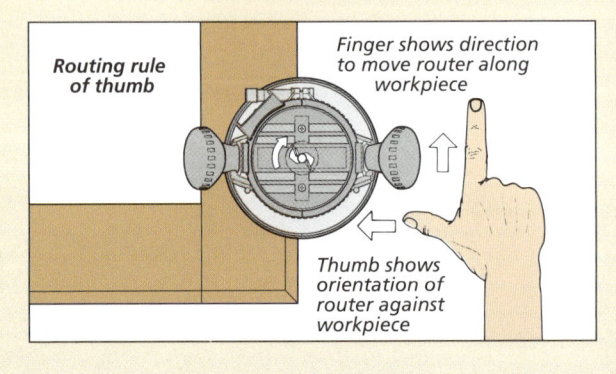

hardware & supplies Sources

CABINET LIGHTING
There are a multitude of cabinet lighting products available for woodworkers. Many of the lighting fixtures shown in the article on page 8 are available from *Rockler*, as well as other woodworking catalogs.

HAND DRILLS
Whether you're looking for a cordless, corded, or pneumatic drill, you'll find that you have plenty of choices available. Most home centers have a fairly good selection of drills. You can also find a large assortment of drills through online tool merchants such as *Amazon.com*.

TAPER JIG
The *Rockler Taper Jig* featured on page 12 works great for cutting tapers or ripping a straight edge on rough stock. The jig is available through *Rockler* (21597).

VENEERING
Veneering doesn't require a lot of equipment, but it does call for a few specialized tools and supplies, such as a veneer saw, veneer tape, and cold press glue. These items can be purchased through several of the woodworking sources listed in the margin at right.

SERVING TRAY
You won't need any hardware to build the serving tray on page 18. To finish the tray, we applied a coat of *General Finishes' Seal-a-Cell* and then sprayed on two coats of lacquer.

CREDENZA
To build the credenza on page 22, you'll need several hardware items. The drawer slides (02K36.18), inset hinges (00B15.24), and overlay hinges (00B15.20) were all purchased from *Lee Valley*. The spoon-style shelf supports (30437) came from *Rockler*. And the oil-rubbed door and drawer pulls (C8623) were ordered from *Rejuvenation*.

The smoked glass used for the windows in the doors was purchased at a local glass shop. Smoked glass is available in a couple different shades. We used a darker shade.

One of the most striking features of the credenza is the Douglas fir veneer. For this project, we used a man-made, "reconstituted" veneer product from *Certainly Wood*. It's available in large sheets, making it the perfect choice for this project.

For the finish, we applied a coat of *General Finishes' Seal-a-Cell* and then sprayed on two coats of lacquer.

CURIO CABINET
Most of the hardware used on the curio cabinet shown on page 34 came from *Lee Valley*. This includes the inset hinges (00H32.10), brass knobs (01A02.16) and rare-earth magnet sets (99K33.10). The shelf supports (30437) were purchased from *Rockler*.

The cabinet was stained with a mix of three parts *Zar* cherry stain and one part of *WoodKote Jel'd Stain* (cherry). After the stain was dry, the project was finished by spraying on a couple coats of lacquer.

Online Customer Service
Click on *Customer Service* at **woodsmith.com/magazine**
- Access your account status
- Change your mailing or email address
- Pay your bill
- Renew your subscription
- Tell us if you've missed an issue
- Find out if your payment has been received

MAIL ORDER SOURCES

Project supplies may be ordered from the following companies:

Woodsmith Store
800-444-7527
Corded & Cordless Drills, Veneering Supplies

Rockler
800-279-4441
rockler.com
Cabinet Lighting, Shelf Supports, Taper Jig

Amazon.com
Hand Drills

Certainly Wood
716-655-0206
certainlywood.com
Reconstituted Veneer

Constantine's
800-443-9667
constantines.com
Veneering Supplies

Lee Valley
800-871-8158
leevalley.com
Drawer Slides, Inset Hinges, Knobs, Overlay Hinges, Rare-Earth Magnet Sets

Rejuvenation
888-401-1900
rejuvenation.com
Pulls

VeneerSupplies.com
Veneering Supplies

Woodcraft
800-225-1153
woodcraft.com
Cabinet Lighting, Veneering Supplies

Keep it All Organized!

Woodsmith Binders

As you build your *Woodsmith* library, here's a way to keep your issues organized. Each binder features durable vinyl covers and easy-to-read perforated number tags. Snap rings with a quick-open lever make it easy to insert and remove issues. And there's an extra pocket inside for storing notes. Each binder holds a full year (6 issues) of *Woodsmith*.

Visit **Woodsmith.com** to order or call **1-800-444-7527**.

Woodsmith Binder
○ WB (Holds 6 issues)..........................$12.95

looking inside
Final Details

▲ *Curio Cabinet.* The glass doors and side panels of this cabinet allow you to show off your collection from just about any angle. Turn to page 34 to find everything you need to build the project.

▲ *Serving Tray.* The splayed, curly maple sides and curved, cocobolo handles combine to give this serving tray a distinctive look. Check out all the construction details beginning on page 18.

▼ *Credenza.* At home in just about any room of the house, this sleek cabinet offers plenty of storage. Detailed plans for building it begin on page 22.

ROUTER TABLE SECRETS You Need to Know | **Small Projects – BIG IMPACT** | **Q&A: LIFESAVERS!** Simple Tools Save the Day

Woodsmith

Woodsmith.com

Vol. 33 / No. 197

Tips & Tricks for
CUTTING SMALL PARTS

PLUS!

5 Great Ways to Add Storage to Your Shop

Secrets of a Master Craftsman: Creating Curved Parts

Discover a Foolproof Staining Method

A Publication of August Home Publishing

looking inside

Table of Contents

from our readers
Tips & Techniques 4

all about
Mahogany 8
The king of cabinet woods might be the best choice for your next project.

tools of the trade
Choosing an Air Compressor . . . 10
Every shop can benefit from air power. Learn how to find a compressor to fit your needs.

jigs and fixtures
5 Handy Tool Holders 12
If you're looking for an inexpensive way to add storage to your shop, we have the answer.

woodworking technique
Cutting Small Parts 14
Think the table saw is too big for the job? All it takes is the right approach.

tips from our shop
Shop Notebook 32

working with tools
Router Table Secrets 44
Two simple techniques that are guaranteed to make your router table more productive.

finishing room
Using Water-Based Dye 46
This easy-to-use stain produces vibrant color that lets the wood show through.

details of craftsmanship
Making Curved Parts 48
The trick is to match the method to the project. Here's what you need to know.

in the mailbox
Q & A 50

hardware and supplies
Sources 51

Gift Projects page 16

Folding Table page 24

2 Woodsmith No. 197

projects

weekend project
3 Small Gift Projects 16
I don't know what's more intriguing, the eye-catching look of these projects or the unique techniques used to make them. Why don't you take a look and decide for yourself.

designer series project
Folding Table 24
A compact table that doubles in size with next to no effort — who couldn't use that? But let's not overlook the classic Craftsman design and the stylish two-tone finish.

heirloom project
Jewelry Chest 34
This beautiful chest has everything you could want in a project and more. Loads of versatile storage, a truly unique design, and the chance to learn a new trick or two.

Jewelry Chest page 34

editor's note
Sawdust

While I like every project we feature in *Woodsmith*, there are some that draw my interest more than others. And that's usually the case with gift projects. Starting on page 16, you'll find three small projects that are attention grabbers. Because they're small projects, you can start building them and have them ready for the holidays — or any other time of the year for that matter.

All three projects are based on a technique of gluing up small workpieces of contrasting wood species. Depending on the step-by-step process you follow, you can create a bookmark, a lid for a small box, or a set of coasters. Working with small pieces is always a challenge, especially at the table saw. But we'll show you the techniques we use to cut them accurately and safely.

If you're looking for a project to take your woodworking skills to another level, check out the jewelry chest on page 34. Although it's a small project (and would make a great gift), it's loaded with woodworking. One obvious challenge is making the curved doors on the sides of the chest that give the project its unique look. To create them, we wrapped multiple layers of bending plywood around a custom form. Once the glue dried, the curve was locked in. After that, it was just a matter of adding some hardwood trim strips and figured veneer to the inside and outside of the door.

Speaking of challenges, while keeping up with our main task of producing and presenting interesting projects for the magazine, we've also been busy filming the fifth season of the *Woodsmith Shop*. It's hard to believe we've been at it for five years now, but we still have a lot of great projects, tips, and techniques we want to share with you. The new shows will start airing nationwide on local PBS stations this fall, so keep an eye out for it. If you'd like some sneak peeks of what's coming up, be sure to check out our website at *WoodsmithShop.com*.

Bryan

This symbol lets you know there's more information online at Woodsmith.com. There you'll see step-by-step videos, technique and project animation, bonus cutting diagrams, and a lot more.

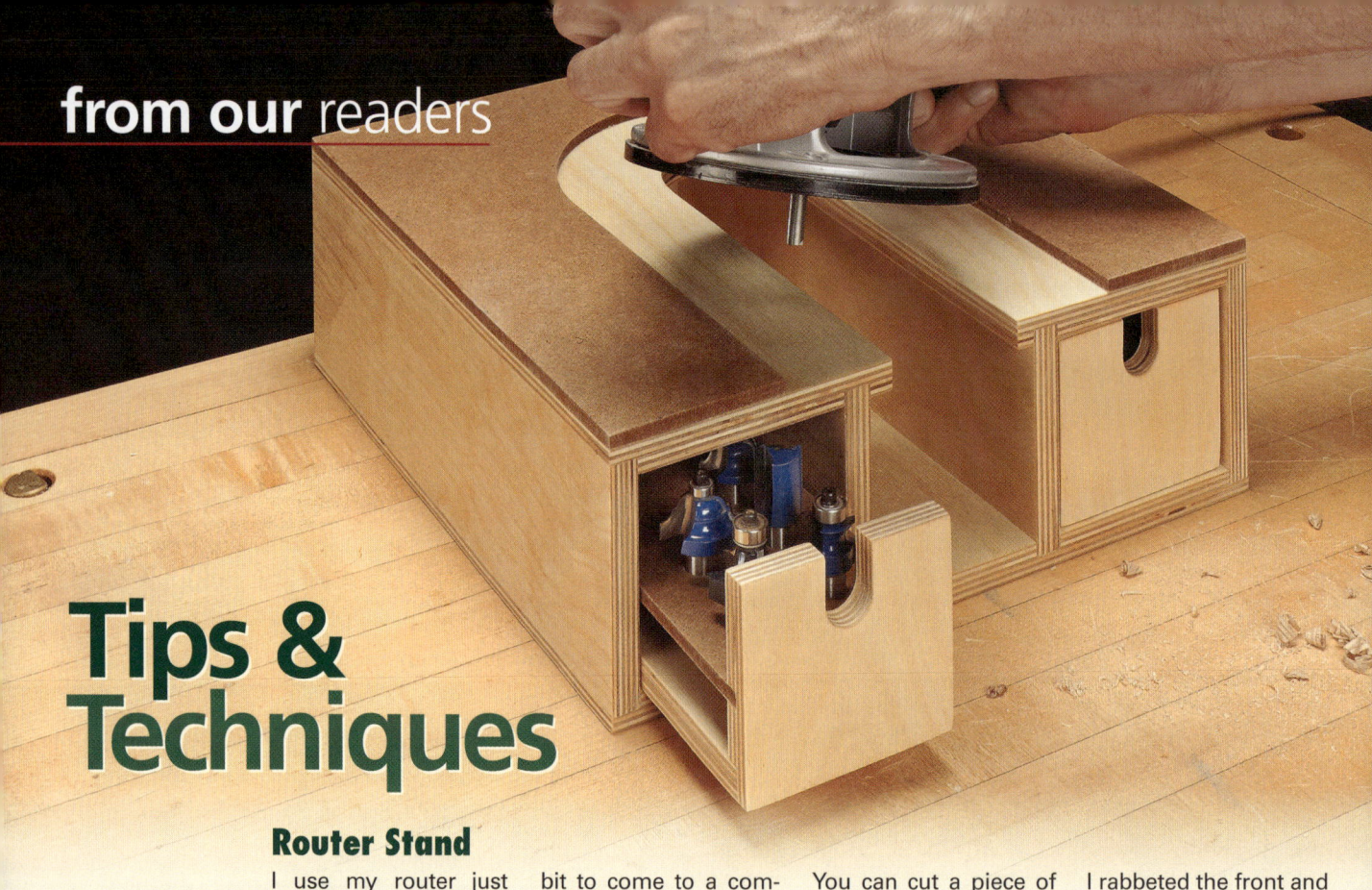

from our readers

Tips & Techniques

Router Stand

I use my router just about every time I'm in the shop. I wanted a stand for it that I could use on the workbench and would allow me to set the router down without waiting for the bit to come to a complete stop. So I built the router stand you see in the main photo.

As you can see, it has an opening in the top with a tray on one side for bits and a drawer on the other side for router accessories.

I kept the construction simple, so it was fast and easy to build.

You can cut a piece of plywood to size for the base and then rabbet the edges. Twin dadoes evenly spaced from the edges hold the dividers. The top is identical to the bottom except for a U-shaped opening.

After you cut the back, two sides, and dividers to size, you can glue up the stand. The tray and drawer are sized to fit the opening.

I rabbeted the front and back of the drawer to fit the bottom and sides, then glued the drawer together. The bit tray sits in a dado made on the front and back of the drawer. The final piece is a hardboard top that's cut to fit around your router base.

Now I have a place for a router at the bench.

Charles Mak
Calgary, Alberta

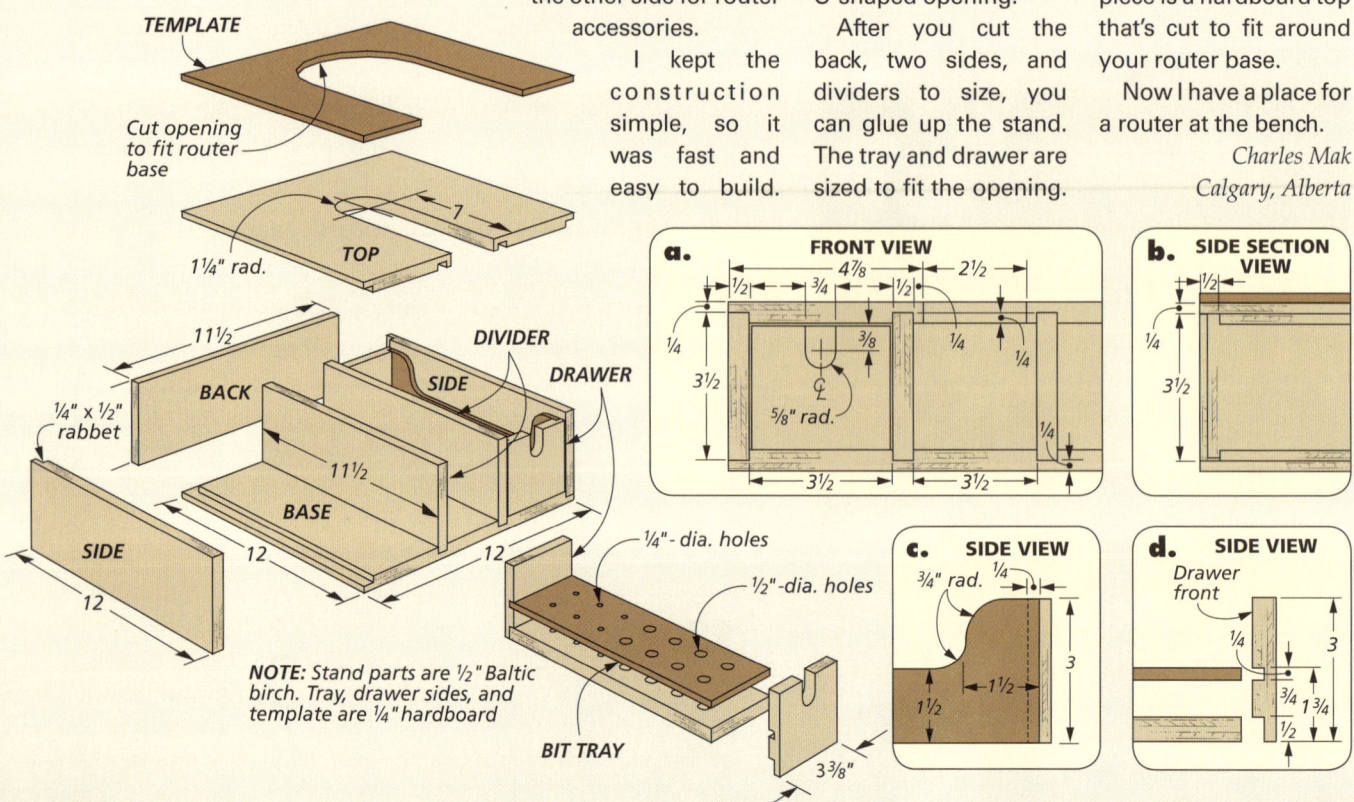

NOTE: Stand parts are ½" Baltic birch. Tray, drawer sides, and template are ¼" hardboard

Woodsmith No. 197

Woodsmith

No. 197 October/November 2011

PUBLISHER Donald B. Peschke

EDITOR Bryan Nelson
MANAGING EDITOR Vincent Ancona
SENIOR EDITOR Ted Raife
ASSOCIATE EDITOR Dennis Perkins
ASSISTANT EDITOR Carol Beronich
CONTRIBUTING EDITORS Phil Huber,
Randall A. Maxey, James Bruton
EDITORIAL INTERN Abby Wolner

EXECUTIVE ART DIRECTOR Todd Lambirth
SENIOR ILLUSTRATORS David Kreyling, Harlan V. Clark,
David Kallemyn
SENIOR GRAPHIC DESIGNER Bob Zimmerman
GRAPHIC DESIGNER Shelley Cronin
GRAPHIC DESIGN INTERN Becky Kralicek
CONTRIBUTING ILLUSTRATORS Dirk Ver Steeg,
Peter J. Larson, Erich Lage

CREATIVE DIRECTOR Ted Kralicek
SENIOR PROJECT DESIGNERS Ken Munkel,
Kent Welsh, Chris Fitch, Jim Downing, Mike Donovan
PROJECT DESIGNER/BUILDER John Doyle
SHOP CRAFTSMEN Steve Curtis, Steve Johnson
SENIOR PHOTOGRAPHERS Crayola England,
Dennis Kennedy
ASSOCIATE STYLE DIRECTOR Rebecca Cunningham
SENIOR ELECTRONIC IMAGE SPECIALIST Allan Ruhnke
PRODUCTION ASSISTANT Minniette Johnson
VIDEO EDITOR/DIRECTOR Mark Hayes

Woodsmith® (ISSN 0164-4114) is published bimonthly by August Home Publishing Company, 2200 Grand Ave, Des Moines, IA 50312.
Woodsmith® is a registered trademark of August Home Publishing.
Copyright© 2011 August Home Publishing Company. All rights reserved.
Subscriptions: Single copy: $4.95.
Canadian Subscriptions: Canada Post Agreement No. 40038201. Send change of address information to PO Box 881, Station Main, Markham, ON L3P 8M6. Canada BN 84597 5473 RT
Periodicals Postage Paid at Des Moines, IA, and at additional offices.
Postmaster: Send change of address to Woodsmith, PO Box 37274, Boone, IA 50037-0274.

WoodsmithCustomerService.com

ONLINE SUBSCRIBER SERVICES
- **VIEW** your account information
- **RENEW** your subscription
- **CHECK** on a subscription payment
- **PAY** your bill
- **CHANGE** your mailing or e-mail address
- **VIEW/RENEW** your gift subscriptions
- **TELL US** if you've missed an issue

CUSTOMER SERVICE Phone: 800-333-5075

SUBSCRIPTIONS
Customer Service
P.O. Box 842
Des Moines, IA 50304-9961
subscriptions@augusthome.com

EDITORIAL
Woodsmith Magazine
2200 Grand Avenue
Des Moines, IA 50312
woodsmith@woodsmith.com

AUGUST HOME PUBLISHING COMPANY

Printed in China

Drill Dock

I needed a handy place to store my hand-held drills and accessories. So I built a home for all my drills that gives me quick and easy access.

The result is the drill dock you see in the photo. To build the dock, I drilled holes in a simple shelf, large enough to hold the chuck on each drill.

Now all I have to do is slide a drill in one of the waiting docks. This way I always know where my drills are stored.

Donald Lile
Indianapolis, Indiana

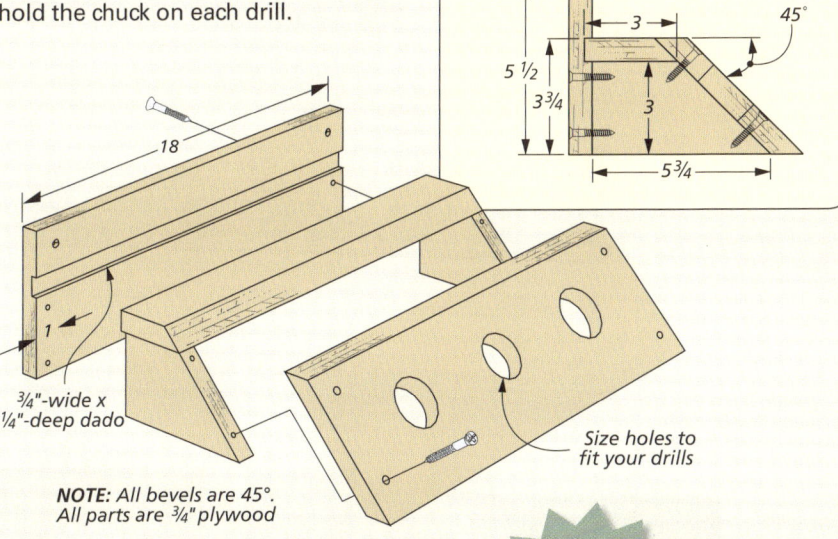

SUBMIT YOUR TIPS ONLINE

If you have an original shop tip, we would like to hear from you and consider publishing your tip in one or more of our publications. Go to:

Woodsmith.com
Click on the link,
"SUBMIT A TIP"

You'll be able to tell us all about your tip and upload your photos and drawings. You can also mail your tips to *"Woodsmith Tips"* at the editorial address shown at right. We will pay up to $200 if we publish your tip.

FREE TIPS BY EMAIL

Now you can have the best, time-saving secrets, solutions, and techniques sent directly to your email inbox. Just go to

Woodsmith.com
and click on
"Sign Up for Free E-Tips."
You'll receive one of our favorite tips each week.

more tips from our readers

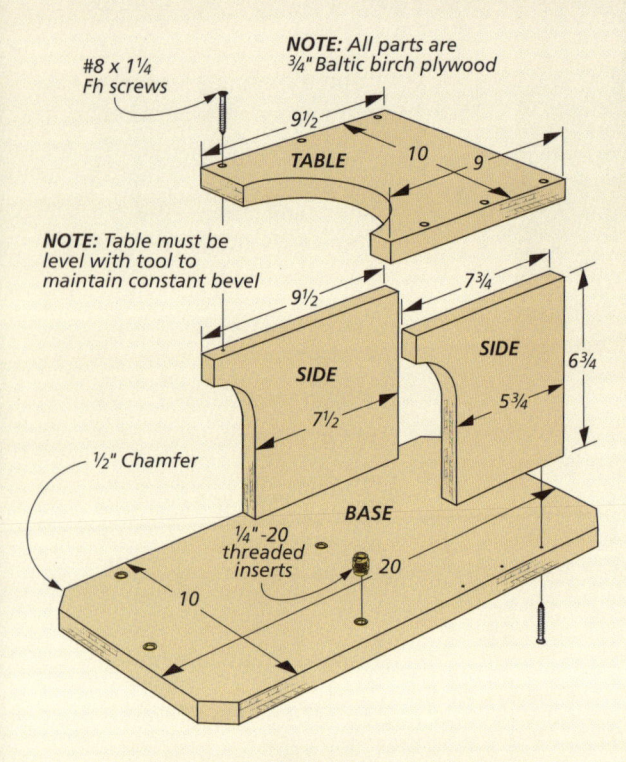

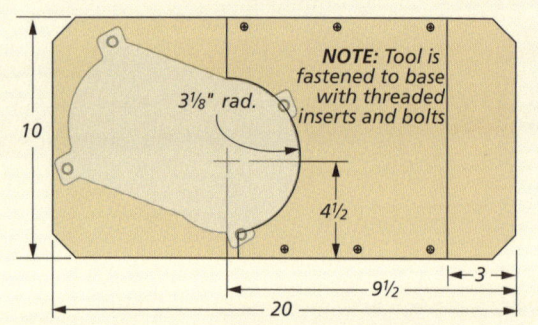

#8 x 1¼ Fh screws

NOTE: All parts are ¾" Baltic birch plywood

TABLE — 9½, 10, 9

NOTE: Table must be level with tool to maintain constant bevel

SIDE — 9½, 7½

SIDE — 7¾, 5¾, 6¾

½" Chamfer

BASE — ¼"-20 threaded inserts, 10, 20

TOP VIEW
3⅛" rad., 10, 4½, 9½, 3, 20

NOTE: Tool is fastened to base with threaded inserts and bolts

2" rad., 1, 3¾ — Right side / Left side

Work Sharp Upgrade

I have a *Work Sharp* to sharpen my chisels and plane irons. But some of my plane irons are wider than the tool rest on the machine.

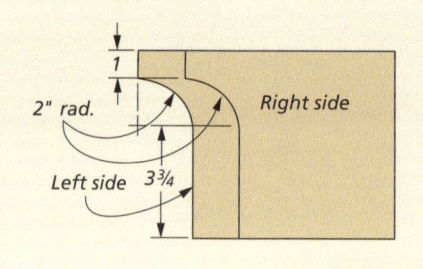

Rather than buy an attachment for wide blades, I built the stand you see in the photo above. With the aid of a honing guide, I can hold the blade at the right angle.

To build the stand I cut a base, two sides, and a table and screwed and glued them together. You can see how it's done in the drawings at left.

With this upgrade I can sharpen narrow and wide blades fast and with great accuracy.

Fred Mason
Waddell, Arizona

Cord Control

I grew tired of always fighting with the cord on my power tools. It just seemed to be in the way while sanding, drilling or using any other corded tool. So I hit on a simple solution to the problem, as you can see in the photo on the right.

You can take a long piece of wood and cut a slot on one end to hold the cord up and out of the way. Then round the edges of the square board on your router table so it will fit neatly in a dog hole on your bench. Now your cords are contained and never in the way.

Len Urban
Rancho Mirage, California

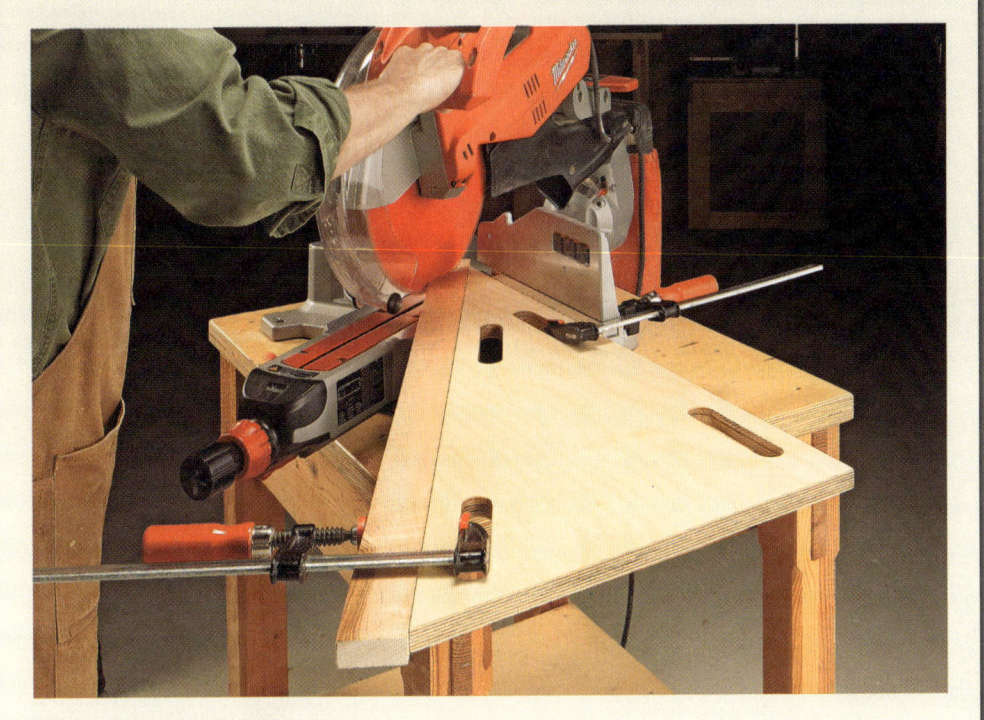

Acute Angle Miter Jig

I needed to cut an acute angle (less than 45°) on the end of a workpiece. So I built the simple miter saw jig you see in the photo.

This jig is flat and uses cutouts to hold the clamps. With the clamps at a low profile, you won't worry about bumping them during the cut.

To use the jig, just lay it next to the blade and clamp it at one end to the saw fence. The clamp spaces along the angled edge work well for clamping the workpiece to the jig.

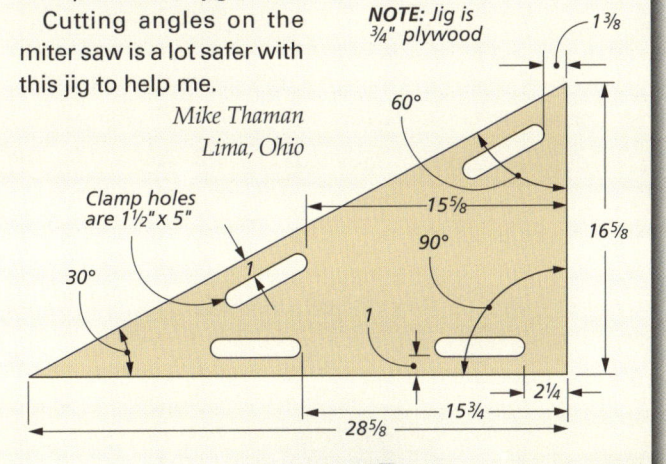

Cutting angles on the miter saw is a lot safer with this jig to help me.

Mike Thaman
Lima, Ohio

NOTE: Jig is ¾" plywood

Clamp holes are 1½" x 5"

30°, 60°, 90°

1 3/8, 15 5/8, 16 5/8, 28 5/8, 15 3/4, 2 1/4

Win This Bosch Impact Driver

That's right, send us your favorite shop tips. If your tip or technique is selected as the featured reader's tip, you'll win a *Bosch* impact driver just like the one shown here. To submit your tip or technique, just go online to Woodsmith.com and click on the link, "SUBMIT A TIP." You can submit your tip and upload your photos for consideration.

The Winner!

Congratulations to Charles Mak, winner of the *Bosch* impact driver. To find out how you could win this driver, check out the information on the left.

Quick Tips

SUBSTITUTE SANDING BLOCK

I like to use sanding sponges. But when I run out of them, I turn to polyethylene foam (not *Styrofoam*) blocks. They sometimes are used as padding in packaging or as space fillers in large or heavy shipments.

The foam cuts easily with a knife or band saw, and you can cut it into any shape. Adhesive-backed sandpaper will adhere well to the block too. This type of foam is also resistant to many solvents that you might use to clean wood projects.

Bill Styler
Priest River, Idaho

ATTENTION TO DETAIL

I make a lot of boxes and cabinets that use hinges. Whenever I put the final twist on the screws to hold the hinges, I make sure the slot in each screw is facing in the same direction. It's the little details that get a project noticed.

Elvin Perry
Valley Springs, California

TALC KEEPS RUST AT BAY

Paste wax is good at preventing rust from forming on metal tool surfaces. But it can also leave a residue on your workpiece. That's why I use talcum powder on my table saw, jointer, and planer to keep the rust at bay.

Just sprinkle the powder liberally on the surface and rub it in with a felt chalkboard eraser. The talc works its way into the pores of the metal to repel moisture and leaves a smooth surface.

Mathew Feehan
Ewa Beach, Hawaii

all about

demystifying Mahogany

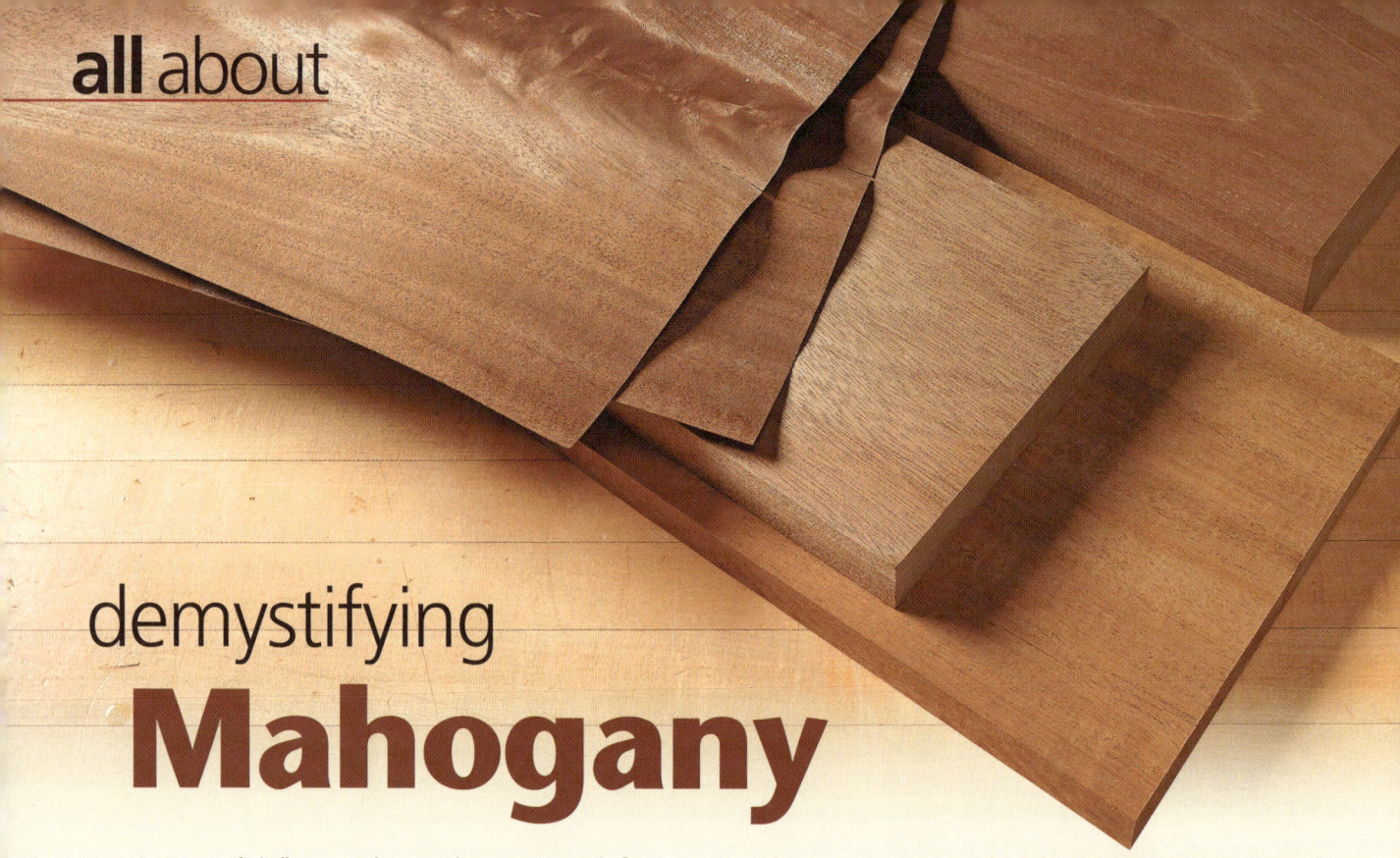

When choosing wood for a classic project, mahogany can't be beat. Here's what you need to know before heading to the lumberyard.

▼ Mahogany is the first choice for classic projects such as this Chippendale chest.

Mahogany has long been considered one of the premier cabinet woods of the world. And from my experience, I would definitely agree with that assessment. Mahogany combines all the characteristics that a woodworker desires in a project wood.

But this popularity and reputation for quality creates a measure of confusion and raises a few questions. Is all wood that's marketed as mahogany the same? And what makes mahogany such a desirable wood?

THE REAL ITEM. Let's start with a discussion of the first question. The simple answer is no, not all wood labeled as mahogany is the same. Due to its popularity, mahogany has a lot of imitators, look-alikes, and substitutes.

There are probably a dozen or more woods that are called mahogany of one sort or another. Some are related, while others are not. But only one species available today can honestly be called true mahogany — *Swietenia macrophylla*. (Two other closely related, true mahogany species are no longer commercially available.)

You'll find this species also referred to as genuine mahogany, Honduran mahogany, or South American mahogany. The trees grow throughout Central America and the northern part of South America. This mahogany is the reddish-brown cabinet wood that was quickly adopted by European and American cabinetmakers as early as the mid-17th century.

WHY MAHOGANY? Once you work with mahogany and get to know its characteristics, you'll be hard pressed to find any faults or shortcomings. No wood is perfect, but mahogany might come closer than any of the others.

APPEARANCE. Mahogany is first and foremost known for its attractive appearance. Although it can vary considerably, the initial color is usually a medium reddish brown. However, with exposure to light, the color gradually ages to a rich, dark reddish brown. If the color of the wood throughout a project is consistent and you can be patient, mahogany doesn't need a stain.

The figure of mahogany is extremely variable. And this feature also adds to the appeal. Some boards may exhibit a wild, swirling pattern while others appear more subdued. When mahogany is quartersawn, you get a striped or ribbon figure effect.

Although generally only available in veneer form, mahogany crotch figure is often used as an eye-catching accent (main photo on the opposite page).

STABILITY. All woods shrink and swell with changes in moisture content, but among different types of wood, the range can be considerable. This characteristic is called stability and mahogany has the distinction of being near the very top of the list. Mahogany exhibits little movement across the grain and little tendency to cup or warp. For woodworkers, this is a big plus.

WORKABILITY. In general, mahogany is a joy to work with. Mahogany has a pore structure similar to that of walnut. The pores are of moderate size and evenly distributed. This gives the wood an even texture and also contributes to the attractive appearance.

The density can vary, but falls in a range that makes it very easy to cut with both hand and power tools. You'll find that it holds fine details very well and is an excellent carving wood.

▲ The even texture and moderate hardness of mahogany make it perfect for carving.

Mahogany glues without any of the problems associated with some tropical species. Likewise, it accepts any finish. However, if a smooth surface is desired, you'll have to fill the pores.

AVAILABILITY & COST. In the distant past, 24"-wide tabletops made from a single mahogany board were not uncommon. But today, stock of this quality is hard to find. Mahogany is now monitored for sustainable harvests. This has the effect of limiting its availability and raising the cost. It's become one of the pricier woods in the rack, but is still below the cost of many other exotics.

RELATIVES & SUBSTITUTES. If you'd like to switch to a lower cost "mahogany-like" wood, you have a number of good choices. The photos at right and the chart below offer several options. Some of these look-alikes are botanically related to mahogany while others simply share a general resemblance to it. And although not the real thing, they're all quality woods in their own right.

African mahogany is a second cousin to genuine mahogany and based on appearance alone, the two can often be difficult to tell apart. As genuine mahogany becomes more difficult to obtain and more expensive, African mahogany is usually the substitute of choice for higher quality uses. It's not as stable, not quite as easy to work with, and won't age like true mahogany. But overall, it comes pretty close to the real thing. And you'll find the cost much easier on the wallet.

Wood marketed as Philippine mahogany (also called Lauan) is a different story. It's actually several species that are not related to mahogany. It simply looks similar. In the recent past, it was used extensively for trim, cabinets, and furniture. It has fairly good working properties, but the color and figure are less desirable.

Lyptus recently entered the market as a low-cost, all-around utility wood with a mahogany-like appearance. It's actually a hybrid of two Eucalyptus species. Very fast growing, it's considered a good "green" mahogany substitute. However, you'll find it rates considerably lower in both stability and workability.

True mahogany is a wood that's well worth seeking out for a special project. However, the best news is that there's a "mahogany" to suit almost any use. **W**

▲ The woods shown above all bear a resemblance to genuine mahogany and can be used as a substitute.

African mahogany
Philippine mahogany
Lyptus

Genuine Mahogany & Substitutes

	Appearance	Stability	Workability	Cost	Uses
Genuine Mahogany	Highly desirable	Very Stable	Very easy	High	Fine Furniture
African Mahogany	Excellent	Good	Easy	Moderate	Furniture
Philippine Mahogany	Good	Good	Easy	Moderate	General
Lyptus	Good	Fair	Average	Low	Utility

tools of the trade

choosing an
Air Compressor

Using air tools in your shop can make some tasks faster. Here's information that will help you make a decision about what to buy.

The first air compressor I owned was a small, pancake-style unit, similar to the one above. It worked great for powering a brad nailer. But some time later, I tried to use it with more demanding tools. That's when I discovered the compressor's limitations.

Whether you're buying your first compressor or thinking of upgrading, knowing what to look for will go a long way in helping you make a decision.

CRITERIA. There are three key aspects to consider when it comes to choosing an air compressor: air pressure, air flow (measured in cubic feet per minute, or CFM), and the amount of air that can be stored in the tank. Since air pressure, air flow, and storage all influence performance, it's important to know how they work together. Later, I'll talk about other features to look for when buying a compressor.

AIR PRESSURE. Air pressure is a simple concept. It's the number of pounds per square inch (PSI) of compressed air that the compressor can produce. Most tools run at 90 PSI (maximum). But it's a good idea to have a compressor that will produce a higher PSI than you need because the air pressure will drop as it's used. A good rule of thumb is to have at least 35% more than the required 90 PSI for the tool, or about 120 PSI. This way, you'll be assured of consistent pressure.

AIR FLOW. Air pressure isn't the only way to measure the output of a compressor. Another factor is the volume of air produced by the

▲ Most air compressors are fitted with a gauge to measure the air pressure.

Air Requirements for Popular Tools

Nailer	Spray Gun	Sander
1-4	2-4	6-13
CFM @ 90 PSI	CFM @ 90 PSI	CFM @ 90 PSI

10   Woodsmith   No. 197

compressor per minute (CFM). In order to operate tools at peak effciency, you need an adequate volume of air. Without it, you'll be disappointed in the tool's performance. In addition, operating high-demand tools with a compressor that has a low CFM rating may cause the compressor to run more frequently, resulting in faster wear and shorter pump life.

Most tools have a rating tag that states the CFM needed for optimum performance of the tool. The box at left gives you a range for a common woodworking tools. Compare these requirements to the air compressor so you make the right choice.

STORAGE. In addition to the PSI and CFM, another factor in determining the right compressor is the amount of air that can be stored in the compressor tank. Storage is measured by the size of the tank. So naturally, the larger the tank, the more compressed air it will store. And that means more compressed air is ready for the tool. If the tank is small, the compressor motor will have to work harder to keep up with the air demand. If it's larger, the motor won't run as often.

CONNECTION. As you can see, these three aspects of an air compressor are interrelated. You need to have enough CFM and a large enough tank to maintain the necessary air pressure to power tools without over-taxing the motor.

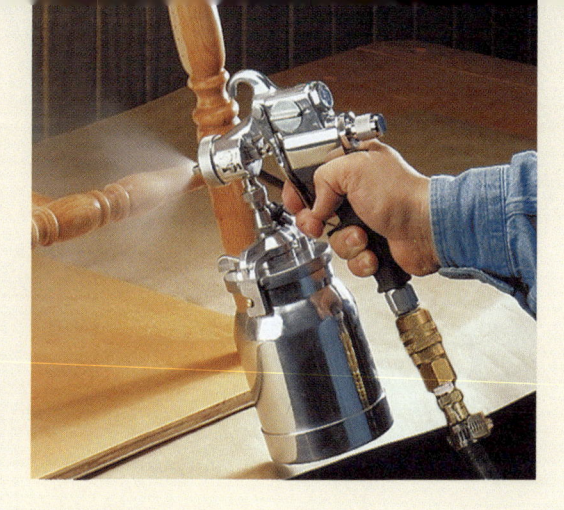

There are just a couple of other factors to consider before you decide on a compressor. Those are noise levels and electrical needs.

NOISE. Compressors tend to be noisy by nature. But some designs are louder than others. I've found that oil-less compressors make more noise than ones that use oil because the piston is usually small and runs faster than an oil-lubricated piston.

Another way to reduce the noise of a compressor is to buy one with a low RPM rating on the motor. A motor with a low RPM rating will make less noise and will cause less wear on the pump. And a belt-driven motor is also superior to direct drive. It's quieter and if the pump or the motor give out on the compressor, you don't have the expense of replacing both at the same time.

ELECTRIC SUPPLY. Most home-shop compressors can be plugged into a common, 110-volt outlet. But you'll need to make sure the circuit breaker is rated high enough to carry the load. For larger compressors, it's a good idea have to a dedicated 20-amp circuit.

CONSIDER YOUR TOOLS. Along with a basic understanding of air compressor performance, you should also consider the type of tools you'll want to use in your shop. Assuming you're going to use air in your shop for the occasional tacking job or to blow dust off your saw, a pancake compressor will do just fine (main photo).

If you have more tools to run in your home shop, then you'll need something a little larger, like the one in the top photo. A compressor this size will power a nailer, blow gun, drill, and an impact wrench without a problem. You'll find it fine for a spray finisher for short periods of time, and possibly a sander (if it's not used continuously). For longer periods of sanding or spraying, you'll need a larger compressor like the one shown in the left photo. This compressor delivers a higher CFM to power tools that demand a lot of air.

Armed with this information, the compressor aisle in the tool store won't seem nearly as intimidating as it did before. And you'll be able to make the right choice about an air compressor for your home shop.

▲ This 20-gallon compressor with a belt-drive motor provides enough air to spray for short periods of time.

◀ This air compressor has a higher CFM for heavy-duty woodworking tasks.

jigs & fixtures

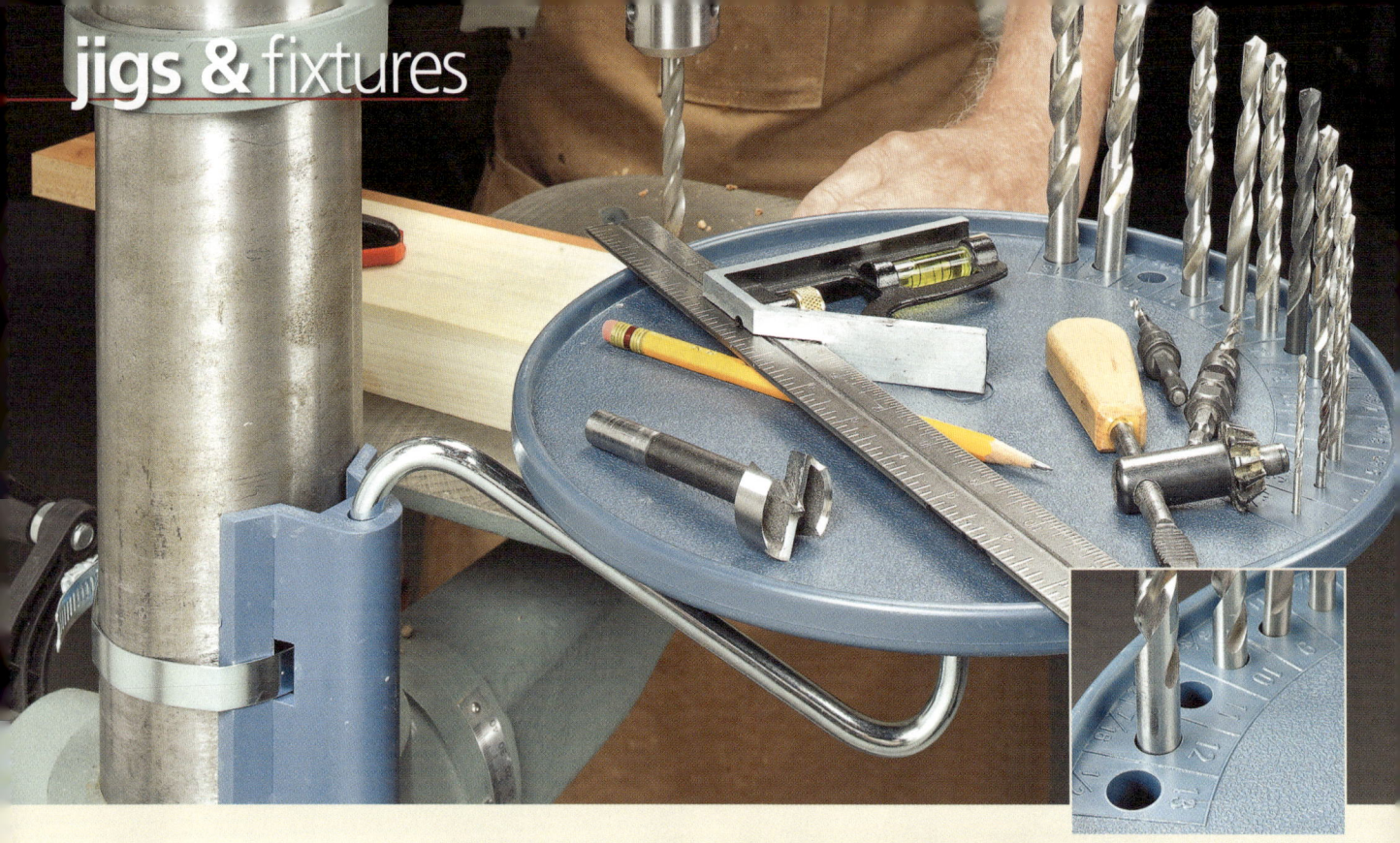

5 handy Tool Holders

Whether cutting, drilling, routing, or turning, having the things you need close at hand makes the job easier.

If your shop is anything like mine, there's a good chance that benchtop or countertop space is at a premium. It seems like there's an unwritten rule that states: "The tools and project parts you accumulate will expand to fill any available flat surfaces." And if you don't keep your shop clean, just finding a place to set down a tool can be a challenge. I recently tried out a few inexpensive items designed to help cut the clutter. They've proven to be really useful for some common storage needs.

Drill Press Tool Collector

The drill press is the first place I needed to find some help. More often than not, when I use the drill press there are going to be a few bit changes. On top of that, it's not unusual to have a countersink bit or a couple of sanding drums on hand for the same project.

Having the *Tool Collector* shown in the photo above has made life a lot easier. A large hose clamp holds the mounting bracket for the collector on the drill press column. This allows you to swing the storage tray into position when you need it. A series of holes in the tray keeps several of the most common bit sizes close at hand. And a lip on the edge of the round tray prevents things from rolling off. For under $15, you'd be hard pressed to find a more useful accessory.

Router Bit Storage Rack

Keeping router bits off the benchtop and out of drawers where they can roll around and easily be damaged is a priority. The bit rack shown below will hold both

▲ The sturdy metal storage rack can hold a sizeable collection of router bits. With holes for both ¼" and ½" shanks, the rack allows you to keep all your bits safe and secure.

½" shank bits (27) and ¼" shank bits (13). The mounting holes are spaced 16" on center, so you can even mount it to wall studs.

Lathe Tool Holder

Another place where I like to keep several tools and supplies near at hand is the lathe. The lathe tool holder shown at right has twelve slots for hanging your turning tools (six regular and six miniature). There's also plenty of tray space for sandpaper, calipers, or a can of your favorite finish. And it features a lip on the edge, so you don't need to worry about your supplies sliding off.

In order to bear the weight of tools and supplies, the tool holder is made of tough, high-impact plastic supported by a steel pivot arm. A sturdy mounting bracket fits into the slot on the bed of most standard-size or midi lathes.

◀ The lathe tool holder swivels to put the tools and accessories where you need them.

▲ The magnetic mounting tray is the perfect place to keep a few essentials within reach. Best of all, it's not designed for a specific tool, so you can attach one to any metal surface.

Magnetic Mounting Tray

For tools, accessories, small project parts, or hardware, this 4½" by 8¼" magnetic tray is perfect for wherever you're working. The sheet metal tray is rigid and built to last. And the magnets provide plenty of grip so the tray won't slide or move with tool vibration. The mounting tray also features a protective rubber bumper to help prevent it from scratching up your tools. As you can see in the left photo, I keep one on my band saw.

This collection of tool holders is guaranteed to make your time in the shop more productive. And to organize more tools, check out the tool apron in the box below. You can find where to buy each of these items in Sources on page 51. None of them will break the bank, but each will be a big help. **W**

Worth a Look: Storage Apron

No matter how hard I try to organize my shop, there are always a few items that just don't seem to fit anywhere. Oftentimes it's due to their odd size or shape. That's where the *Pack Rack Tool Apron* comes in handy.

Think of this as an apron for your shop (though few aprons can claim to have half as many pockets). Made of heavy denim and double-stitched for extra strength, the *Tool Apron* is sure to last a lifetime. On top of that, four steel grommets allow you to hang the apron on a wall, a roll-around shop cart, or clamp rack, as shown in the photo at right.

The pockets will hold chisels, screwdrivers, squares, or just about any other hand tool to keep them near the job. The innovative design of the pockets features a back row of narrow slots for chisels and screwdrivers, while the large pockets sit directly in front. It seems a little unconventional, but it really works out well. It might be the perfect solution for your storage needs.

▲ It's tough to beat the versatility of the *Pack Rack Tool Apron*. The double rows of pockets helps keep track of different size tools.

woodworking technique

tips & tricks for
Sizing Small Parts

The table saw is my tool of choice for cutting perfectly sized small parts. All it takes is the proper setup and the right technique.

The table saw works great for cutting accurate workpieces over a wide range of sizes. But when the parts get very small — such as those needed for the bookmark and coaster project on page 16 — a big table saw may seem like too much tool for the job. At this scale, maintaining safe control of the pieces while ensuring accuracy becomes a challenge.

But I've found that the trick to successfully ripping and crosscutting small parts to size is to adapt the table saw setup and your technique to the task. And I also take advantage of a few helpers.

RIP TO THICKNESS. When sizing larger parts, the order is pretty well set. You plane to thickness, rip to width, and then crosscut to length. But trying to plane really thin parts ($1/4$" or less) to thickness is often "iffy" at best. So when the width of the needed pieces allows it, I like to rip them to both thickness and width at the saw.

SAW SETUP. The first step is to adapt or scale down the saw to the job. To do this, I begin by installing a thin-kerf, general purpose (40-tooth) blade. Cutting a thinner kerf requires less effort and leads to cleaner, more accurate cuts. I've found that this type of blade will easily handle rip cuts in stock up to 2" thick.

Next comes a zero-clearance insert. This eliminates the worry of a thin piece or small cutoff slipping between the blade and the insert. A custom insert that includes an integral splitter is my choice, as in the lower left photo.

CHECK FOR SQUARE. A couple of quick checks and possible adjustments completes the setup. In order to end up with pieces of consistent thickness, the blade

Woodsmith GO ONLINE EXTRAS
For information on making a zero-clearance insert with a splitter, visit Woodsmith.com

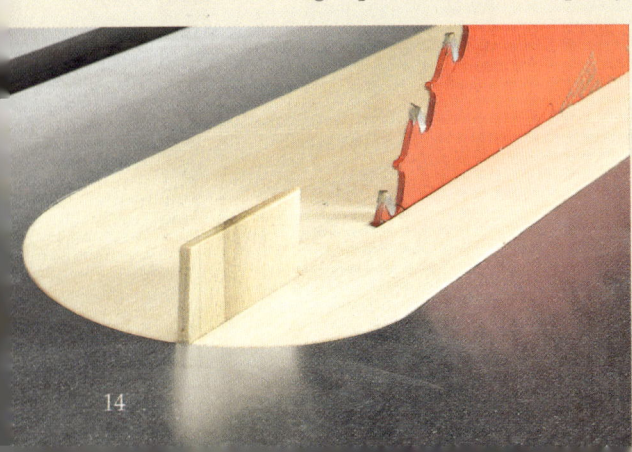

▼ Adding a zero-clearance insert along with a splitter ensures safer, cleaner cuts.

▲ A quick check ensures that both the blade and rip fence are square to the table.

▲ A set of calipers make checking pieces for accurate thickness quick and foolproof.

and the face of the rip fence both need to be perfectly square to the saw's table. I always like to double-check both (lower middle photo, opposite page).

PRECISE PARTS. When you're dealing with tolerances in small fractions of an inch, measuring parts may require more than a tape measure. Here's where a set of calipers can be a big help. You'll quickly know the exact thickness of the piece you just ripped.

REVERSE ORDER. Now you're ready to go. The process is pretty standard. You're going to start by cutting the multiple, thin pieces you need from thicker blanks (main photo on opposite page). Then you'll crosscut them to length. But there's a minor twist. I've found that it works best to reverse the usual order and rip the blanks to accurate width before ripping them to thickness. This way, you avoid having to re-rip the fragile, hard-to-control strips cut from the blank.

RIP TO THICKNESS. So once the blanks are ripped to the required width, the next step is rip thin pieces from them. The goal is to end up with strips that are accurate and consistent. The big challenge is to do the job safely. There are a number of approaches to the task, but for me, the simplest method works the best.

A close look at the main photo on the opposite page will give you the idea. For guaranteed consistency, I simply use the rip fence to gauge the thickness of the cutoffs. The strips are ripped between the fence and blade. The key to feeding and controlling the blank and the cutoff is a notched, MDF push block that can ride over the blade. It provides both the forward push and downward pressure necessary for good control.

You'll want to make a test cut or two to find an accurate fence setting. The calipers help me zero in. If you find that a strip is too thick, don't try to re-cut it. It will be too hard to control and chances are the results won't be accurate.

To guarantee accuracy, you'll need to maintain good pressure against the fence. I like to position my hand in front of the blade to act as a stationary featherboard. You may be more comfortable with the real thing, but you'll have to reposition it after every cut.

CROSSCUTTING. The last step is to crosscut individual pieces from the strips to final length. Again, the major issue is how to feed the thin pieces in a way that ensures a clean, accurate, and safe cut. My answer is shown in the drawing above and the left photo below — a scaled-down cutoff sled attached to the miter gauge. The sled carries the nestled workpiece through the blade with a minimal effort on your part. And both the blank and the cutoff are always under control.

When the pieces get very short — less than a couple of inches — I cut them to length on the right side of the blade. You can use the flip-stop shown below to guarantee accurate, repeatable results.

You'll discover that very thin, short pieces may crack as they're cut or be caught by the blade once they're loose. Making the cuts very slowly may help. If this doesn't work, try the solution shown in the Shop Tip below.

My last piece of advice is simple — just take it slowly. Starting out with crisply cut, accurate parts will save you time in the end. **W**

▲ A flip-stop clamped to the crosscut sled allows you to make precise and repeatable, short cutoffs. With the stop down, butt the workpiece against it, then raise it to make the cut.

Shop Tip: Tape It

Short, fragile cutoffs can be kept intact by reinforcing them. Apply a wide piece of masking tape and then turn up the leading edge as shown at right. The tape strengthens the piece during the cut and will also keep it in place afterward.

Weekend Project

parquetry Lidded Box & Bookmark

▲ You just might find that the eye-catching design of the bookmark shown above makes it difficult to concentrate on your reading.

Don't let the small size of this project fool you. It's sure to be a challenging and enjoyable test of your attention to detail.

This project will likely inspire a predictable reaction from admirers. Something along the lines of, "Wow, that's neat. How in the world did you do it? It must have been quite a challenge."

Well, I agree with the exclamation. The intricate, geometric pattern of the box lid and bookmark looks pretty cool. But as you might have guessed, there's a straightforward technique behind it. Granted, it takes patience — mostly time spent waiting for the glue to dry. But otherwise, the only trick is an easy-to-follow, step-by-step procedure.

SCALE IT UP. The secret to creating the detailed pattern is to increase the working scale to a more manageable size. To do this, the pieces are first assembled into a thick pattern blank. Then all you have to do is slice a box lid or bookmark from it. You're still working with small parts, but the larger size of the blank makes it easier to piece the pattern together.

What about the box? Once the lid is completed, making the box will be a breeze.

TRIM WHEN NECESSARY. Before starting a step-by-step description, let

Materials & Supplies

A Box Sides (2)   1/4 x 1 1/2 - 6 7/8
B Box Ends (2)   1/4 x 1 1/4 - 1 9/16
C Box Bottom (1)   1/4 x 2 1/16 - 6 7/8

- (1) 1/8" x 2" - 6 1/2" cherry
- (4) 1/8" x 2" - 6 1/2" maple
- (2) 1/32" x 2" - 6 1/2" walnut veneer
- (2) 1/16" x 2" - 6 1/2" walnut
- (3) 1/8" x 1 1/2" - 8" cherry
- (3) 1/8" x 1 1/2" - 8" maple
- (1) 1/16" x 1" - 10" walnut
- (1) 3/8" x 1" - 14" maple
- (1) 3/8" x 1" - 4" cherry
- (1) 1/8" x 1" - 20" walnut

Note: All pieces except veneer can be cut from 3/4"-thick stock

me offer a helpful heads-up. As I assembled the blank, I didn't try to fit pieces that were cut to finished size. With a few exceptions, everything was a little extra wide or extra long. Then I trimmed the partially assembled blank only when I needed a flush surface on which to fit more pieces. This approach gives you a fair amount of wiggle room and makes fitting the pieces easier.

THE PIECES. The first step is straightforward. You'll cut the strips of wood needed to make the parts for the blank. To create a pleasing contrast, I used cherry, walnut, and maple.

The most important dimension here is the thickness. So to guarantee consistency, I thicknessed all the pieces I needed right up front. The blank requires pieces that are 1/16", 1/8", and 3/8" thick. (I also included a layer of purchased 1/32"-thick walnut veneer.)

I didn't try to plane the thin pieces to thickness, but rather, I resawed all of them on the table saw from 3/4"-thick stock. You'll find an article on page 14 that describes how to do this safely and accurately. Don't worry if your pieces end up a hair thicker or thinner — consistency is what you're after. And I suggest you make a few extras so you'll be sure to have plenty.

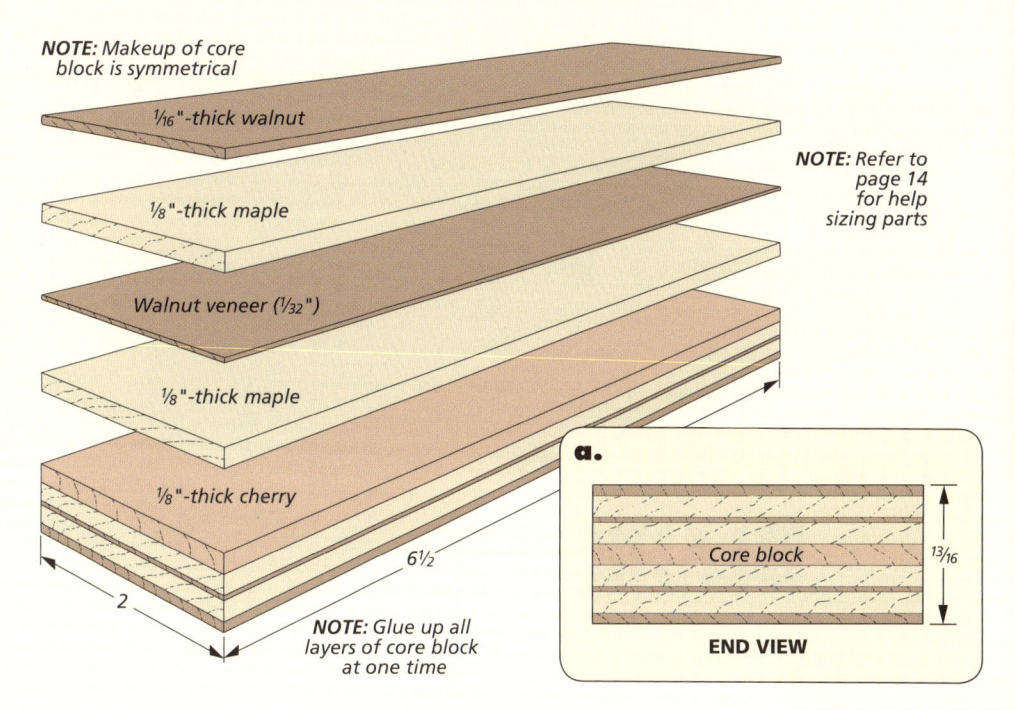

THE CORE BLOCK. With the stock prepared, you'll start on the blank by assembling a 2"-wide core block about 6½" long. The pieces added around the core block that complete the pattern will only be about 1" wide. The extra width of the block allows you to clamp it in a vise while adding the remaining pieces. It also provides a convenient "handle" when sanding the face or cutting off slices at the band saw.

The symmetrical makeup of the block is shown in the drawing above. It consists of layers of 1/8" cherry, 1/8" maple, and 1/32" and 1/16" walnut (main drawing).

I glued up the layers all at one time using a 1/2" MDF caul on each side to ensure a tight assembly (left drawing below). When you tighten the clamps, the edges of the pieces will want to slip out of alignment. You can realign them by simply standing the assembly on edge and pressing them down against the benchtop.

When the glue is dry and the clamps come off, you'll want to true up both long edges. You need smooth surfaces for layout purposes and as a reference when adding more pieces. I sanded one edge flat and then ripped the opposite edge as shown below.

▲ You'll find tips on sizing small parts in the article on page 14.

How-To: Glue & Trim Core Block

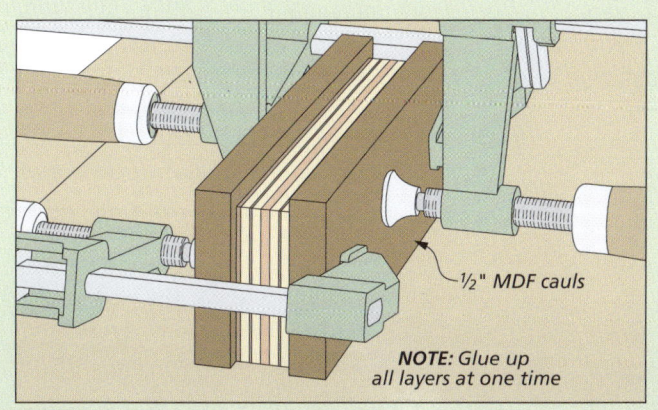

Cauls and Clamps. After applying glue to one face of each layer of the core block, stack them in the correct order, and clamp them tightly between a pair of 1/2" MDF cauls.

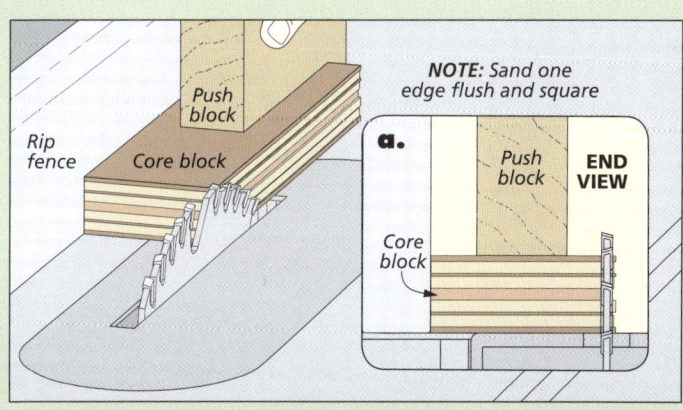

Flat and Square. Before adding more pieces, you need to true up the core block. After sanding one edge flat and square, I trimmed the opposite edge on the table saw.

completing the BLANK

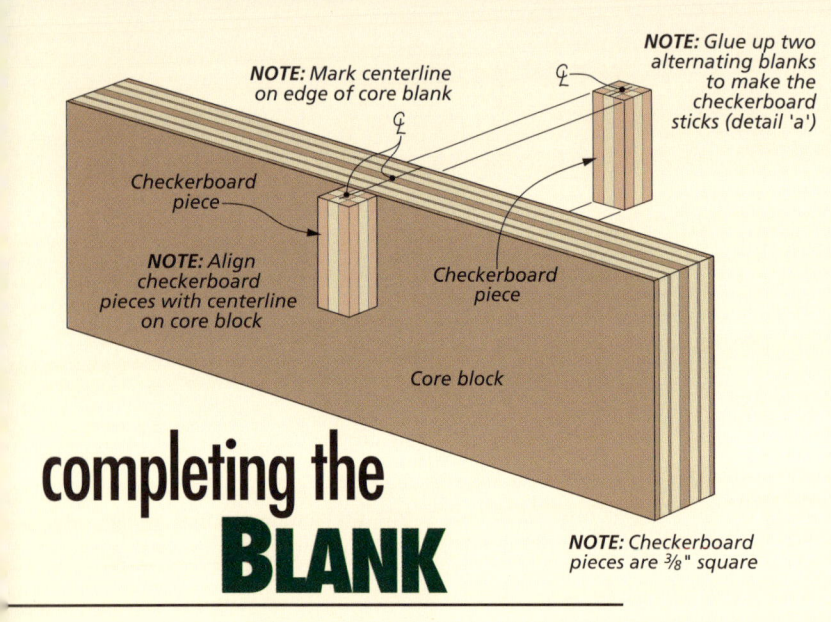

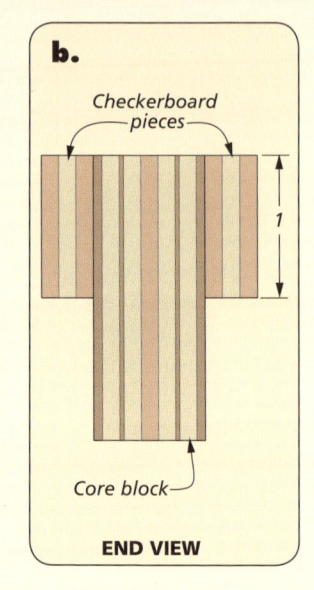

NOTE: Mark centerline on edge of core blank

NOTE: Glue up two alternating blanks to make the checkerboard sticks (detail 'a')

Checkerboard piece

NOTE: Align checkerboard pieces with centerline on core block

Checkerboard piece

Core block

NOTE: Checkerboard pieces are 3/8" square

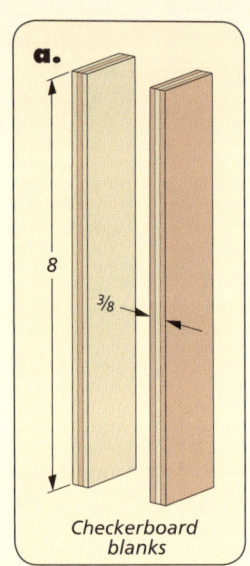

a. Checkerboard blanks (8, 3/8)

b. Checkerboard pieces, Core block, 1, END VIEW

From here on out, the pattern at the bottom of the opposite page will be your road map. First, note the interesting "checkerboard" designs. These are made as assemblies and then glued in place. Adding the two pieces centered along the sides comes next. But first you have to make them.

These pieces are simply short sections cut from a "stick" assembled in a checkerboard pattern. The sections are glued perpendicular to the edge of the core blank to expose the pattern on the end, as shown above.

ALTERNATING LAYERS. The box below provides an overview of making and adding these pieces. In a nutshell, you'll glue up two opposite blanks from alternating layers of maple and cherry, rip strips from the edges, and then assemble these strips into the pattern.

TWO BLANKS. The first step is to glue up each blank from three strips of maple and cherry. One of the blanks will alternate maple/cherry/maple and the other cherry/maple/cherry (detail 'a').

When the clamps come off, you'll want to square up one edge of each blank. To do this, I put together an edge sanding guide, as in the upper left drawing. It will come in handy later as well.

Your next task is to cut 1/8"-thick strips from each blank. You need two cherry/maple/cherry and one maple/cherry/maple strip to make a stick. Make sure the strips are right at 1/8" thick. If they're not, the stick won't be square.

ASSEMBLY. When you glue up the stick, the strips have to be kept aligned. Once the glue is dry, some minor cleanup is all you'll be able to do without throwing off the dimensions and the symmetry of the pattern.

One key to keeping the pieces in place is to use glue sparingly — just enough to ensure a good joint. This will limit the squeezeout and the slipping that occurs when the clamps are tightened down. The second piece of the puzzle is a rabbeted clamping "cradle" that keeps the pieces aligned, as in the upper right drawing.

TWO SECTIONS. With assembly of the checkerboard sticks completed, you can add two pieces

How-To: Checkerboard Sticks

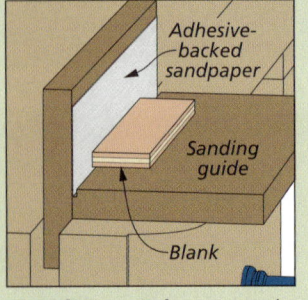

Sand One Edge. I used a sanding guide to square up one edge of each blank.
(Adhesive-backed sandpaper, Sanding guide, Blank)

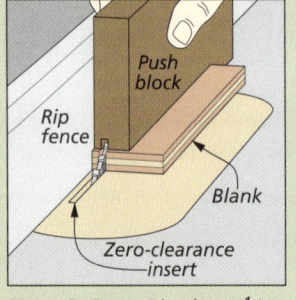

Two & One. Rip three 1/8"-thick strips from the blanks to make the stick.
(Push block, Rip fence, Blank, Zero-clearance insert)

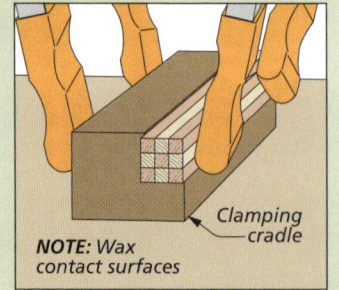

Three Layers. To create the pattern, glue up the sticks with alternating layers.
(Clamping cradle, NOTE: Wax contact surfaces)

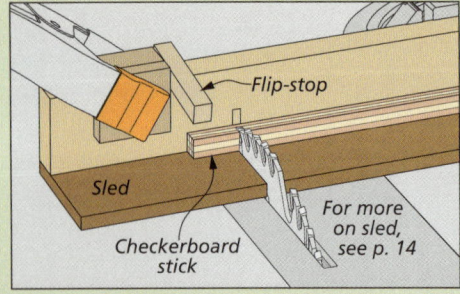

Cut to Length. The short sections can be cut to length safely and accurately on the table saw with a small parts sled.
(Flip-stop, Sled, Checkerboard stick, For more on sled, see p. 14)

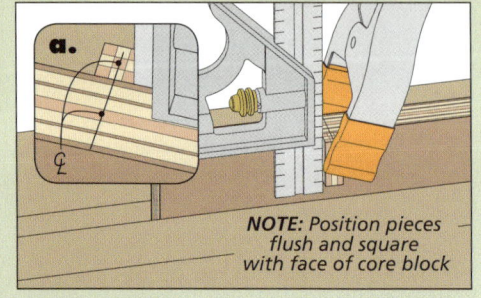

Precise Placement. I used a centerline marked on the block and a square to make sure the sections were positioned properly.
(NOTE: Position pieces flush and square with face of core block)

centered on the core block. I glued the 1"-long sections to the core block one at a time. A centered layout line marked on the edge will help you position them.

PIECE BY PIECE. Now the pace will start to pick up. The How-To box at right shows the order of assembly from here on.

As I mentioned previously, you'll only trim the partially assembled block when necessary. The first trim comes after some short pieces of walnut and four maple blocks are added to the blank, as shown in Figures 1 and 2. Measure and mark from your centerline and then square up both ends (Figure 3).

EXACT LENGTH. After a 1/16"-thick piece of walnut is applied to each end, the next step is to fit cherry blocks that align with the outer maple layers of the core block (Figure 5). These pieces have to be cut to accurate length.

THE BORDER. Once the remaining walnut strips and checkerboard blocks have been added, the blank is completed with a 1/8"-thick walnut border (Figure 8). You'll glue on the end border pieces first. I used the edge sander to "trim" the ends flush. Once the glue is dry on the end border pieces, you can repeat the process for the side pieces — sand, glue, and sand again.

FINAL SANDING. The final step is to sand the face of the blank. As illustrated in Figure 9, a piece of adhesive-backed sandpaper attached to the table saw or benchtop will get the job done.

How-To: Assembling the Blank

1. Walnut. Glue a short piece of 1/16"-thick walnut to both sides of the checkerboards. 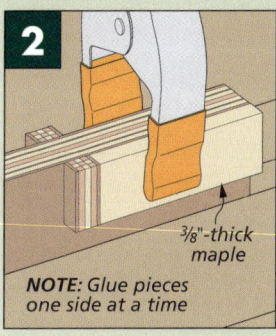
NOTE: All pieces can be glued at one time

2. Now, Maple. I filled the remaining space on both sides with maple blocks. 
NOTE: Glue pieces one side at a time

3. First Trim. With the maple blocks added, take the blank to the saw and trim both ends. 
NOTE: Trim blank to 5 3/4" in length

4. Walnut Caps. The next step is to cap the ends with pieces of 1/16"-thick walnut.

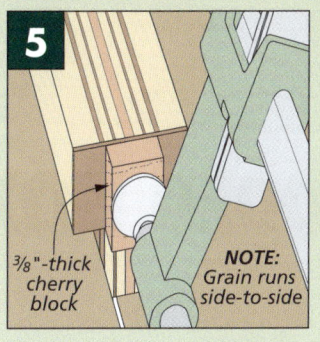

5. Cut to Fit. Cherry blocks are sized to align with the core block's outer maple layers. 
NOTE: Grain runs side-to-side

6. More Walnut. Now you add a walnut strip to each side of the cherry blocks. 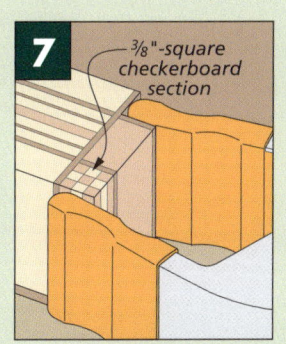
NOTE: Glue both pieces at one time

7. The Corners. The empty corners are filled with checkerboard sections.

8. A Border. Sand the edges of the blank flush before adding the border pieces. 
NOTE: Add end border, then side border

9. A Smooth Face. When sanding the blank, try to keep the face square to the sides.

FULL-SIZE PATTERN

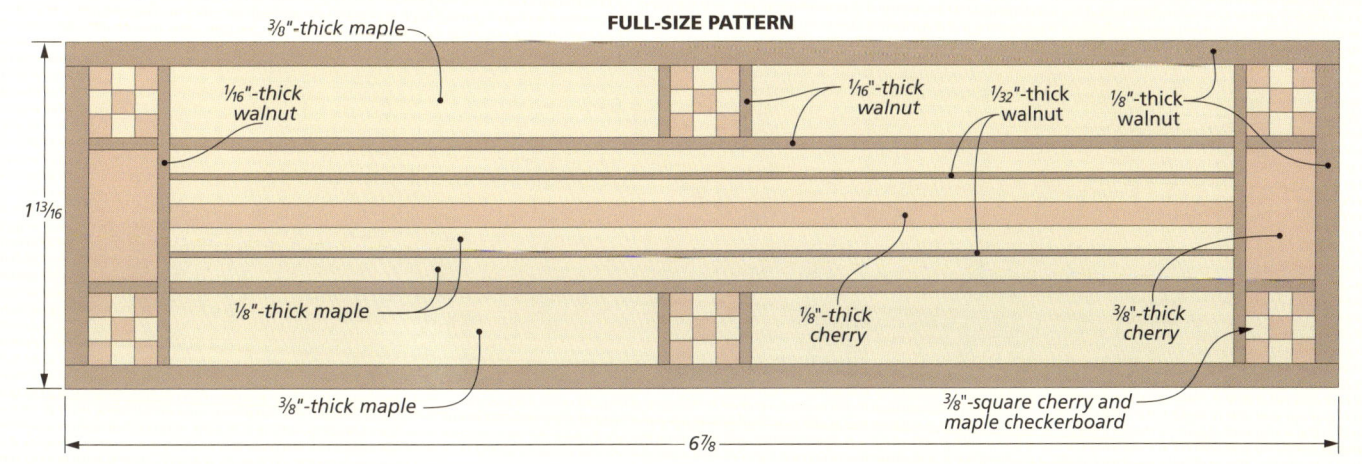

3/8"-thick maple
1/16"-thick walnut
1/16"-thick walnut
1/32"-thick walnut
1/8"-thick walnut
1/8"-thick maple
1/8"-thick cherry
3/8"-thick cherry
3/8"-thick maple
3/8"-square cherry and maple checkerboard

1 13/16"
6 7/8"

building a LIDDED BOX

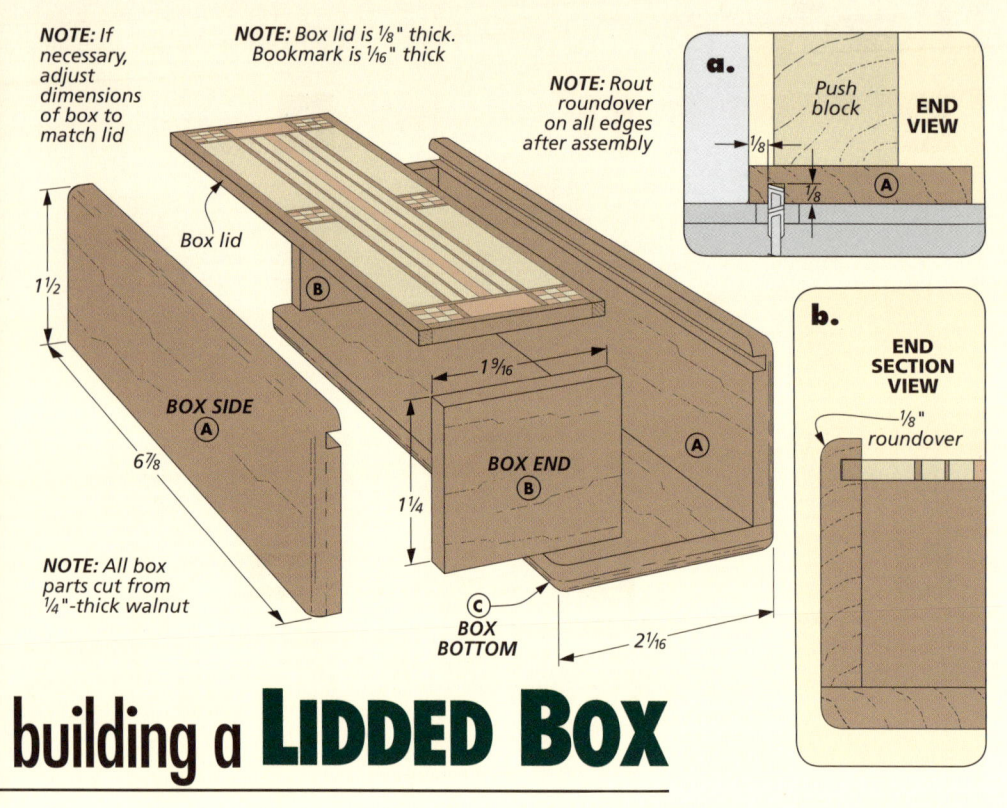

NOTE: If necessary, adjust dimensions of box to match lid

NOTE: Box lid is 1/8" thick. Bookmark is 1/16" thick

NOTE: Rout roundover on all edges after assembly

Box lid
BOX SIDE (A)
1 1/2
6 7/8
NOTE: All box parts cut from 1/4"-thick walnut

1 9/16
BOX END (B)
1 1/4
(A)
(C) BOX BOTTOM
2 1/16

a. Push block — END VIEW — 1/8", 1/8", (A)

b. END SECTION VIEW — 1/8" roundover

With its face sanded, the blank looks impressive. However, to make something useful, you'll need to cut off a thin layer or layers — 1/16" thick for a bookmark, 1/8" thick for a box lid.

SLICE & SAND. The How-To box below shows the simple two-step procedure I used to create the box lid and bookmark. First, you'll carefully cut off a thin section at the band saw and then you'll sand the cut face smooth.

THE BAND SAW. The thin blade of the band saw will allow you to maximize the number of sections you'll get from the blank. However, to get a slice with a consistent thickness, it works best to use a fairly wide blade — 3/8" or 1/2". You'll get a smoother cut with less chance of the blade wandering or deflecting. And before making the cut, be sure that the blade and fence are parallel and square to the table.

I cut the sections slightly thick to allow for sanding. A test cut with a scrap can help you set the fence. Keep in mind that a smooth, accurate, and consistent cut requires less sanding.

SANDING. If you're wondering how to sand the cut face of the thin sections, I'll share my simple trick. I stuck a piece of double-sided tape to a block of wood and "dirtied up" the outside face to make it less tacky. Stick the cut section to the block and sand it on a flat surface. Go easy and check your progress often to ensure a consistent thickness.

THE BOX. I can assure you that once the lid is completed, making the box to go along with it goes a lot quicker. The details are shown in the drawings at left.

Since the lid is already made, you'll size the box to fit it. The box consists of two sides, two ends, and a bottom all glued together with butt joints.

I cut full-length grooves in the sides sized to hold the sliding lid (details 'a' and 'b'). Both ends are sized to fit flush to the bottom of the grooves. This allows the lid to slide in both directions.

Once the box was assembled, I routed a 1/8" roundover on all the outside edges. And after several coats of spray lacquer, your box is ready for the compliments. **W**

How-To: Make the Lid & Box

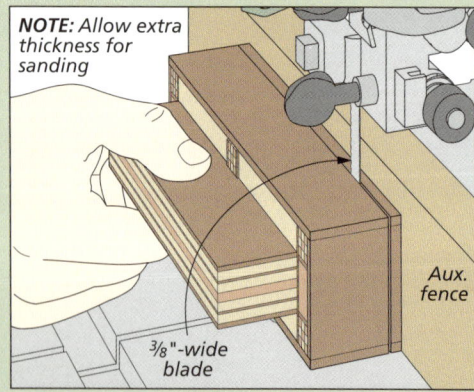

Slice the Blank. After smoothing the face of the blank, I used a wide band saw blade to cut thin sections for the box lid and bookmark.

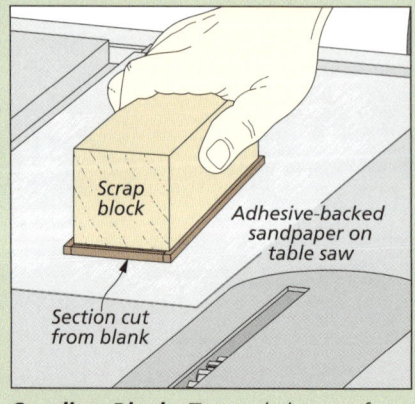

NOTE: Allow extra thickness for sanding — Aux. fence — 3/8"-wide blade

Sanding Block. To sand the cut face, attach the section to a block using slightly tacky double-sided tape.

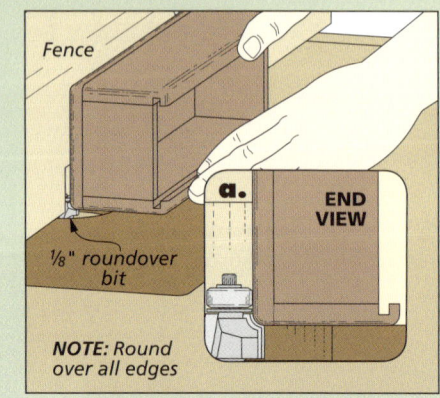

Scrap block — Adhesive-backed sandpaper on table saw — Section cut from blank

Ease the Edges. Once the box is assembled, you can round over all the outside edges at the router table.

Fence — **a.** END VIEW — 1/8" roundover bit — *NOTE: Round over all edges*

20 Woodsmith No. 197

Coaster Set

The technique here is easy to master — the end result is sure to draw attention.

Judging from the look of the end result, you might think the technique used to make these unique coasters is complicated and difficult to execute. The way the gently curving contrasting bands crisscross the coaster — how could it all fit together so well?

Well, the reality is just the opposite. Once you learn the secret and give it a try, you won't believe how easy it is. And if you're like me, you'll be hooked.

THE BASICS. Here's a quick lesson. You start with a square blank. Next you lay out a gentle curve across the blank. The band saw is your next stop. Here, you cut the blank into two pieces along the curved layout line. This is really the only challenge. You want the cut to be as smooth as possible.

Now you simply glue the blank back together with a thin, flexible band of wood sandwiched between the two pieces. Lay out another curve and repeat the process over and over until the pattern is complete. Finally, you trim the blank to final size, add the border, and slice off coaster sections at the band saw.

One big plus is that you don't need to worry about matching the pattern precisely. Almost any design is guaranteed to look great. And once you learn the basic technique, you can easily create you own patterns and projects.

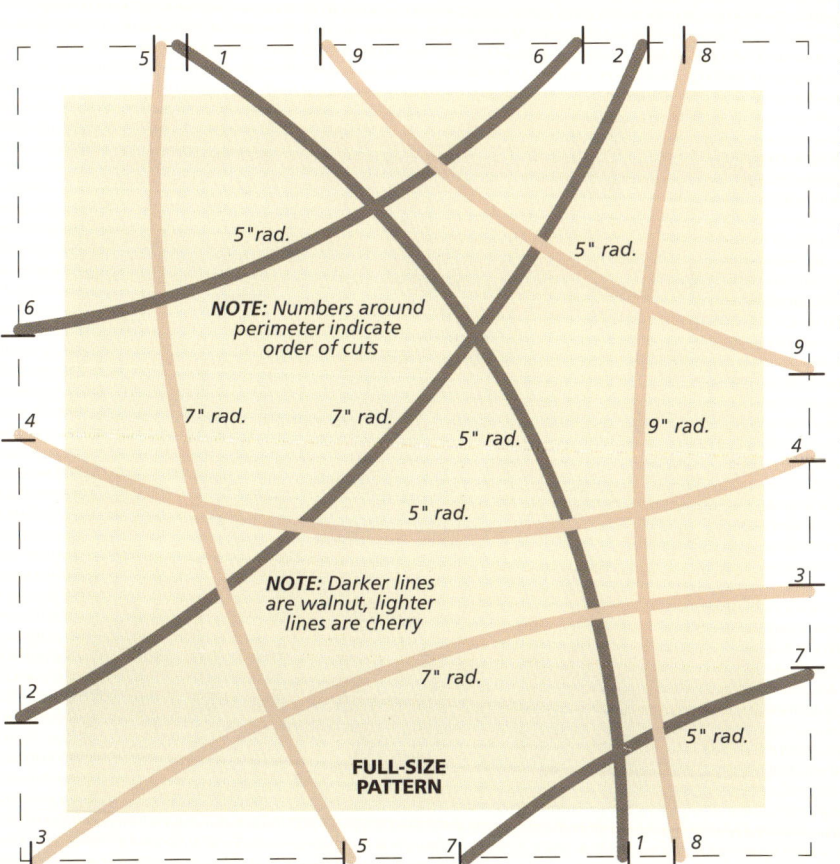

FULL-SIZE PATTERN

NOTE: Numbers around perimeter indicate order of cuts

NOTE: Darker lines are walnut, lighter lines are cherry

5" rad.
5" rad.
7" rad.
7" rad.
5" rad.
9" rad.
5" rad.
7" rad.
5" rad.

Materials & Supplies

A	Maple Coaster Blank (1)	1½ x 4¼ - 4¼
B	Walnut Band (1)	1/16 x 1½ - 24 rgh.
C	Cherry Band (1)	1/16 x 1½ - 28 rgh.
D	Walnut Coaster Border (1)	3/8 x 1½ - 20 rgh.
E	Maple Tray Bottom (1)	¼ x 4 9/16 x 4 9/16
F	Maple Tray Sides (4)	¼ x 1¼ - 5 1/16

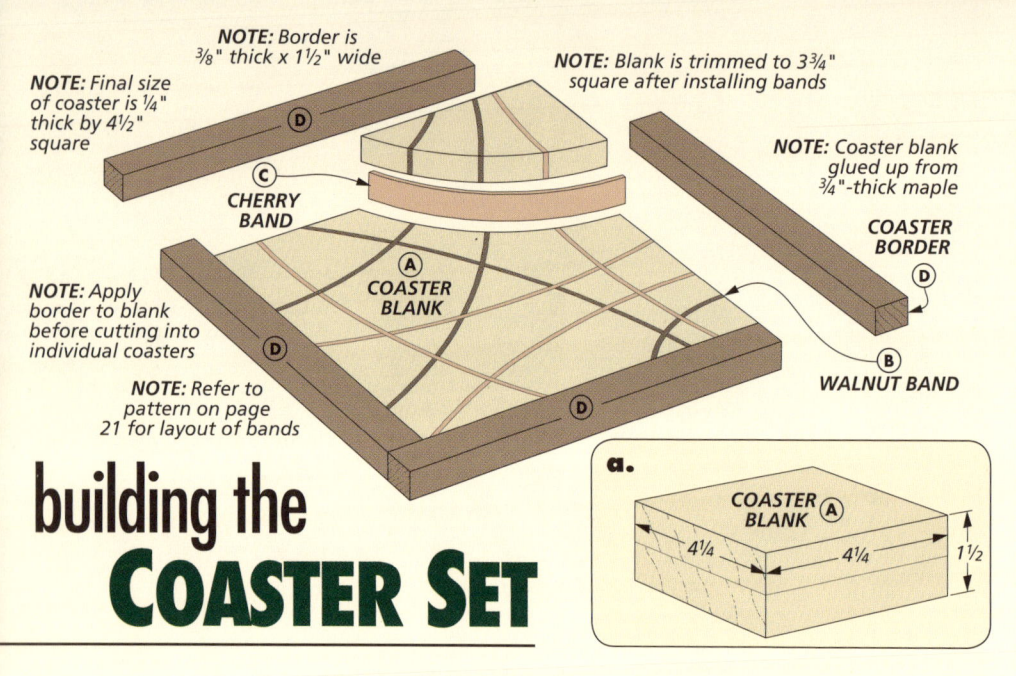

building the COASTER SET

NOTE: Final size of coaster is ¼" thick by 4½" square

NOTE: Border is ⅜" thick x 1½" wide

NOTE: Blank is trimmed to 3¾" square after installing bands

NOTE: Coaster blank glued up from ¾"-thick maple

- Ⓒ CHERRY BAND
- Ⓐ COASTER BLANK
- Ⓓ COASTER BORDER
- Ⓑ WALNUT BAND

NOTE: Apply border to blank before cutting into individual coasters

NOTE: Refer to pattern on page 21 for layout of bands

a. COASTER BLANK — 4¼ x 4¼ x 1½

I've given you the condensed version. Now I'll go through the process again, filling in all the details. A look at the drawings below will help you follow along.

PARTS. To get started, you'll need a 1½"-thick by 4¼"-square maple blank. (Later, the blank will be trimmed to 3¾" square.) I made the blank by gluing up two pieces of ¾"-thick stock (detail 'a').

Next, I cut some thin walnut and cherry bands on the table saw. I thicknessed the bands to fit the kerf made by the ¼"-6 TPI band saw blade I planned to use (about ¹⁄₁₆"). Their width should match the thickness of the blank.

TEMPLATE. The curves that made up my pattern had three different radii — 5", 7", and 9". So to help lay out the curves, I made a hardboard template with each radius on a different edge.

MARK FIRST CURVE. It works best to lay out each curve only as needed. This way, there's no chance of getting confused. So with everything ready to go, you can mark for the first cut (Line 1 on the pattern).

An easy way to do this is to copy the full-size pattern on page 21 and lay it over the blank. (You can also lay the blank over the pattern on the page.) Then mark the end points and draw the proper radius curve between them.

CUT FIRST CURVE. A quick trip to the band saw follows. The key is to make a smooth, continuous cut. I tried to cut right along the inside curve of my layout line. If you get off the line a bit, don't worry, just keep cutting. A smooth curve is all you're after.

How-To: Make the Coaster Blank

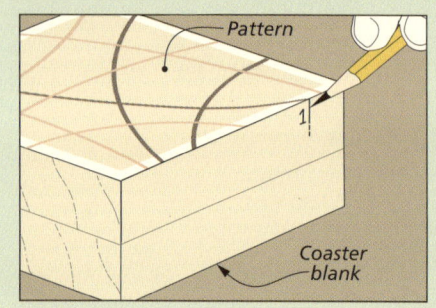

Mark the First Curve. You can lay the pattern over the blank to mark the two end points of the curve.

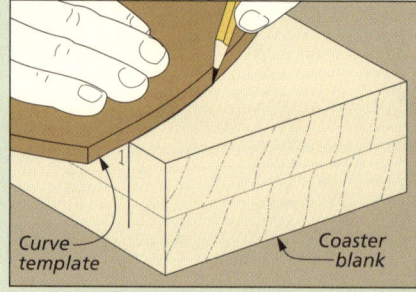

Lay Out the Curve. I used a hardboard template with the three different radii to lay out the curves on the blank.

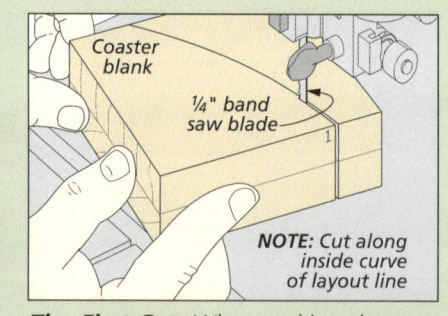

The First Cut. When making the cuts, I tried to stick to the inside edge of the layout line. A smooth cut is the goal.

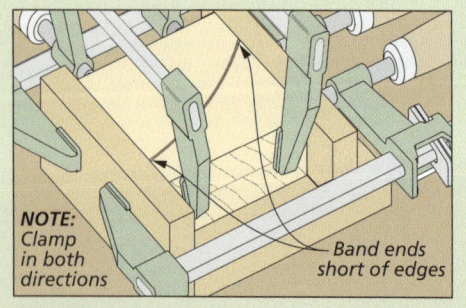

Clamping Fixture. Once glue is applied to both halves, place the parts in the fixture and apply clamps in both directions.

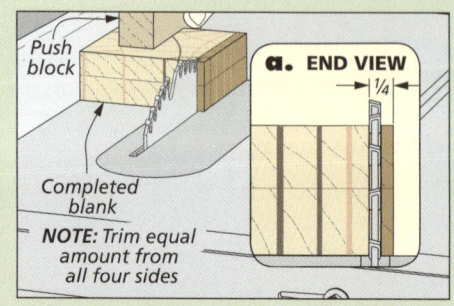

NOTE: Clamp in both directions — Band ends short of edges

Final Size. Use the rip fence to trim ¼" off two adjacent sides. Then reset the fence to trim the blank to its final 3¾"-square size.

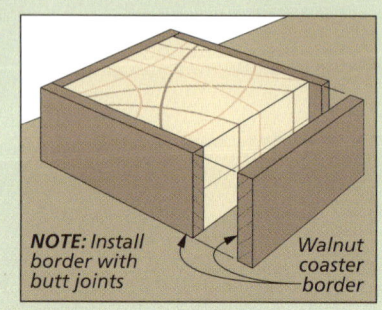

a. END VIEW — ¼ — NOTE: Trim equal amount from all four sides

Border. Work around the blank applying the border pieces slightly long. Then sand the ends flush.

NOTE: Install border with butt joints — Walnut coaster border

FIRST BAND. Cutting a band to fill the kerf is next up. It should end slightly short of both edges of the blank. This makes gluing the blank back together easier. Just bend a piece around the curve, mark it, and cut it to length.

CLAMPING. It's time for glue and clamps. When gluing the blank back together, the goal is to try to maintain alignment of the edges and the original square shape. The catch is that the sections want to slip when clamping pressure is applied. To overcome this problem, I made the clamping fixture shown on the opposite page. You'll find more information on this on page 33.

OVER & OVER. When the glue is dry, you can remove the clamps and get ready to cut the second curve. You'll want to keep both faces of the blank clean of glue squeezeout and reasonably flat. This makes laying out the curves and cutting them much easier.

Now, you can settle into a routine. Keep repeating the process until the pattern is complete. Many of the later bands will cut across ones already installed. This is part of the appeal of the pattern. Here, the key to maintaining the smooth shape of all the curves is to keep the sections aligned during the glueup. But don't worry if they're off a hair. In the overall design, this won't be noticeable.

TRIM TO SIZE. After the last band has been installed, the blank can be trimmed to final size at the table saw. Just remember to trim all of the sides equally.

THE BORDER. Before slicing the coasters from the blank, I added the walnut border. I made this easy by installing the pieces "pinwheel" fashion, as shown in the main drawing on the opposite page. Each piece can be cut long and then sanded flush after all the pieces are glued on.

FOUR COASTERS. At this point, you're ready to turn the blank into four coasters at the band saw. I sanded both faces nice and flat and then set the band saw fence to take a slice just over ¼" thick. The Shop Tip at right shows the simple push block I used to keep my fingers well away from the band saw blade.

After the first cut, resand the face of the blank and take another slice. Follow with two slices from the opposite face. And once all four coasters are cut, you can sand the faces using the "tacky" block method described on page 20.

THE TRAY. Building a tray to hold your set of coasters won't take long. All of the details are shown in the How-To box below.

The tray consists of four sides mitered around a bottom panel. Once the tray was glued up, I added finger slots to two opposite sides. The rounded slots can be formed quickly by drilling an off-center hole through the sides with a Forstner bit, as illustrated.

Finally, in anticipation of a lot of use, I gave both the coasters and the tray a couple of coats of polyurethane varnish.

Shop Tip: Push Block

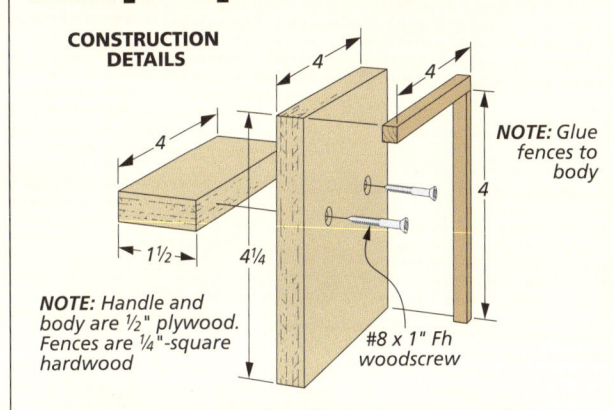

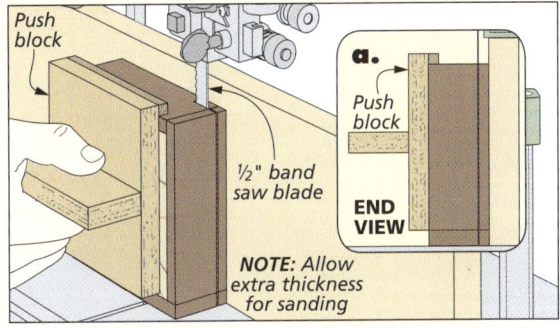

CONSTRUCTION DETAILS

NOTE: Glue fences to body

NOTE: Handle and body are ½" plywood. Fences are ¼"-square hardwood

#8 x 1" Fh woodscrew

½" band saw blade

NOTE: Allow extra thickness for sanding

Safe, Firm Control. I installed a tall auxiliary fence on the band saw and used a custom push block to feed the blank safely through the blade.

How-To: Build a Coaster Tray

NOTE: Finger slots formed after assembly

Soften edges with sandpaper after assembly

FRONT SECTION VIEW — Bottom edge of side flush with tray bottom

TRAY BOTTOM — 4⁹⁄₁₆

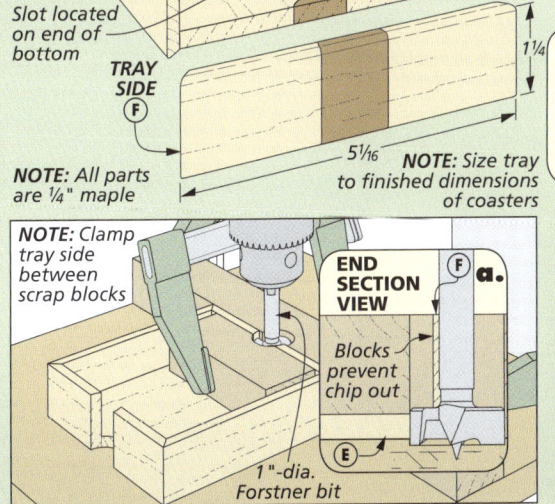

Slot located on end of bottom

TRAY SIDE — 5¹⁄₁₆ — 1¼

NOTE: All parts are ¼" maple

NOTE: Size tray to finished dimensions of coasters

TOP VIEW — ½"-rad.

NOTE: Clamp tray side between scrap blocks

END SECTION VIEW — Blocks prevent chip out — 1"-dia. Forstner bit

Drilling Finger Slots. The finger slots can be formed by drilling off-center holes through the tray sides. You'll need to clamp backup blocks in place.

▲ The wide finger slots make it easy to remove the coasters from the tray.

Designer Series Project

all-new Folding Table

This innovative Craftsman-style design makes better use of space in a dining area.

A folding table is a versatile way to make the most of limited space in a kitchen or dining room. It can double as a work table in the kitchen or a handy place to grab a snack. When it's time for dinner or company, this counter-height table folds out to create extra room for family and friends.

From a woodworking standpoint, the table presents some interesting challenges. There are several mortise and tenon joints that connect the legs and rails.

And the decorative panels in the end frames complement the Craftsman-style design. I took the difficulty out of creating the openings in the panels by making them three-piece glueups.

The most unique aspect of this table is its ability to double in size when it's folded out. This is accomplished by a pair of hinged end frames that swing out to support the hinged top. When the table is folded, the end frames store flat against the table base.

CONSTRUCTION DETAILS

OVERALL DIMENSIONS: 48"L x 21"W x 36"H (Folded)
48"L x 42"W x 35"H (Expanded)

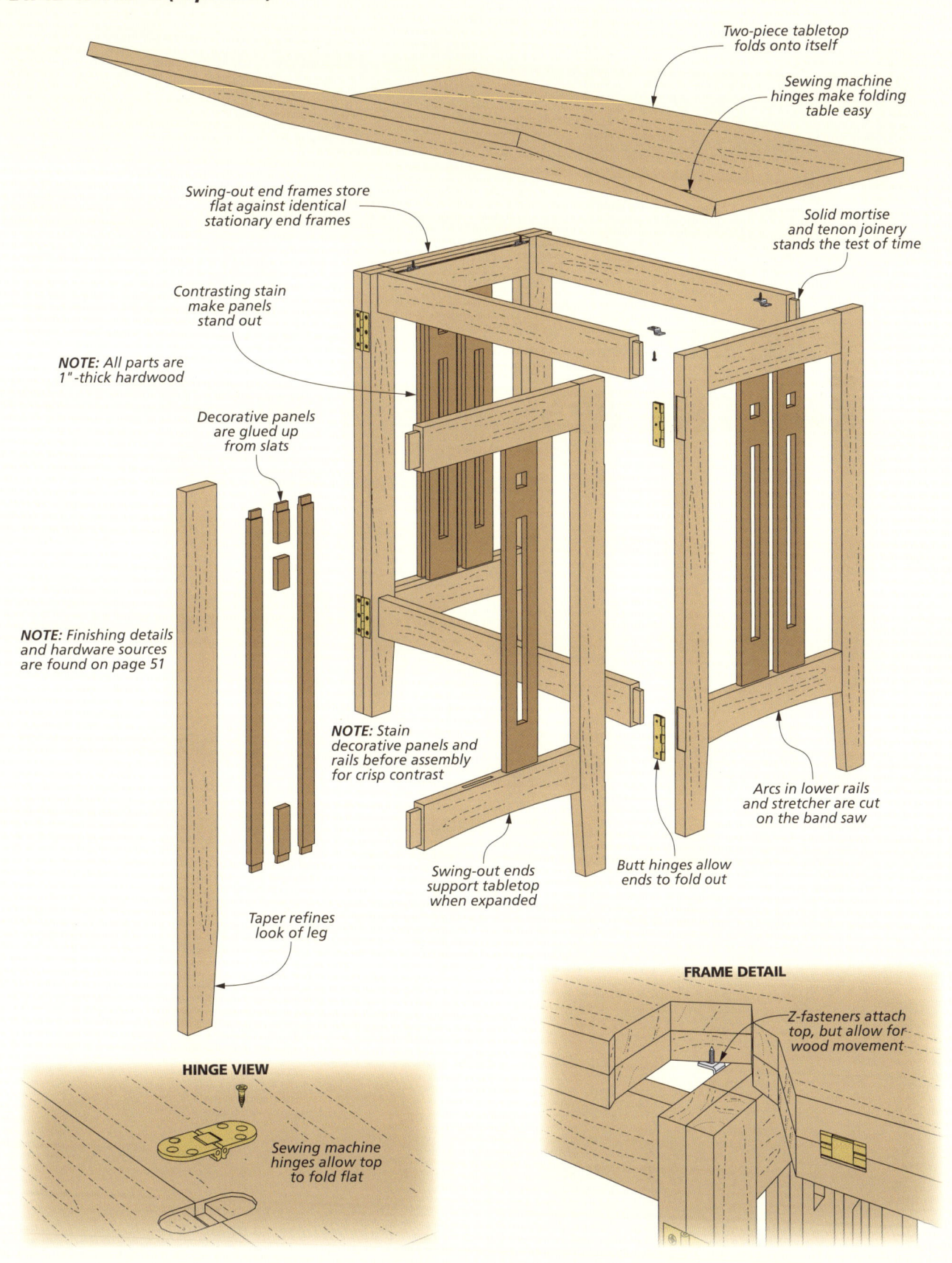

Two-piece tabletop folds onto itself

Sewing machine hinges make folding table easy

Swing-out end frames store flat against identical stationary end frames

Solid mortise and tenon joinery stands the test of time

Contrasting stain make panels stand out

NOTE: All parts are 1"-thick hardwood

Decorative panels are glued up from slats

NOTE: Finishing details and hardware sources are found on page 51

NOTE: Stain decorative panels and rails before assembly for crisp contrast

Swing-out ends support tabletop when expanded

Butt hinges allow ends to fold out

Arcs in lower rails and stretcher are cut on the band saw

Taper refines look of leg

HINGE VIEW
Sewing machine hinges allow top to fold flat

FRAME DETAIL
Z-fasteners attach top, but allow for wood movement

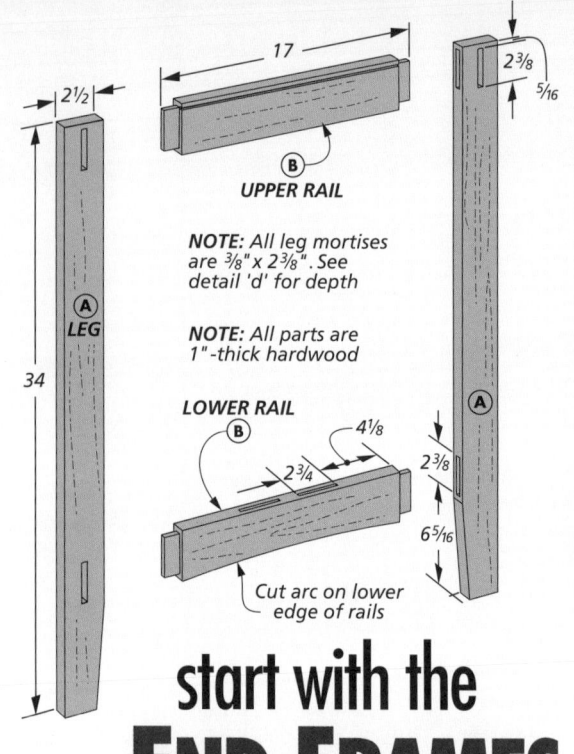

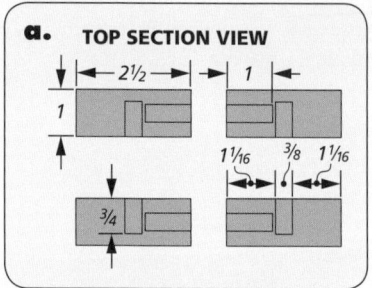

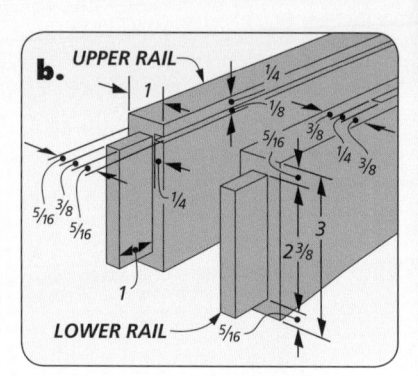

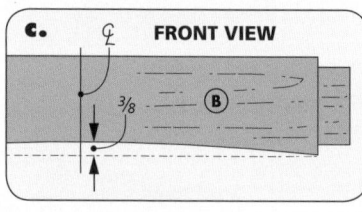

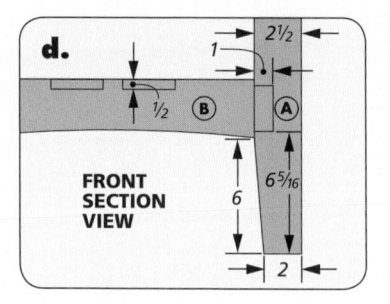

start with the END FRAMES

The base of the table starts with four end frames. The two inner frames are connected by stretchers to form the fixed base. The outer frames are hinged to support the top when it's folded out.

I started the table by building the frames first. Each frame consists of two legs, an upper and lower rail and a pair of decorative panels.

LEGS & RAILS. After the lumber is planed to thickness, cut the legs and rails to length and width. There are a number of mortises in each leg and rail. To keep all these mortises straight and orient the uncut boards properly, I marked each workpiece with a part letter before I started laying out the mortises. It also helps to mark the top, bottom, inside and outside of each leg. The mortises on the edges of the legs receive the rails and those on the face of the leg receive the stretchers. Note that there is only one lower stretcher, so only two legs will have a face mortise on the lower end. The remaining mortises are cut in the rails to hold the panels.

LAYOUT. With each part marked, I laid out all the mortises, as shown in details 'a' and 'd.' It's a good idea to lay out matching mortises at the same time, as shown in the left drawing in the box below. Then you can spread the parts out as they will be assembled and check to make sure opposite mortises face each other.

MORTISES. When you have the workpieces marked, you can take them over to the drill press and drill out the mortises (center drawing, below). Then use a chisel to square up each mortise for a snug, seamless fit.

TENONS. After the mortises are complete, you can cut tenons on the upper and lower rails to fit the mortises. The measurements are shown in detail 'b.'

FASTENER GROOVE. Two of the upper rails have a groove cut near the top of the inside face for the tabletop fasteners. Cut the groove now before assembly.

How-To: Make Mortises & Lay Out Arc

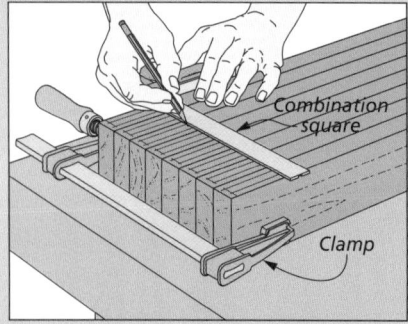

Gang Layout. A fast and easy way to mark all the mortises at once is to clamp the legs together.

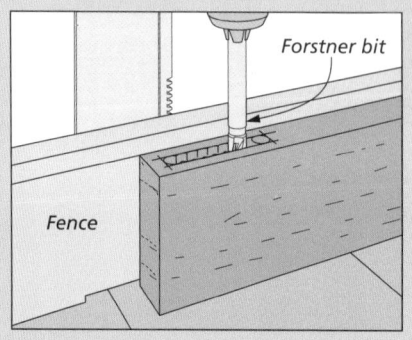

Drill Mortises. Use a Forstner bit to drill out the waste in each mortise. Then clean up the walls with a chisel.

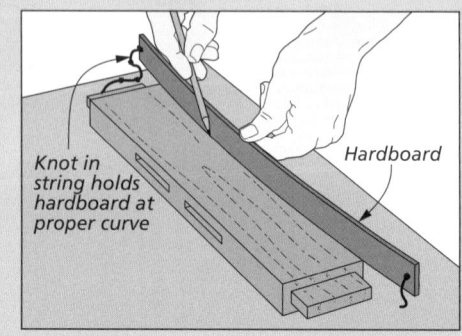

Lay Out Arc. A narrow strip of hardboard can be flexed into a curve and used as a template to draw the arc on the rails.

TAPERS. The final step for the legs is the tapers. Take care when marking the legs for the tapers. They should be on the same face as the mortise (main drawing). To cut the taper, I used a simple shop-made jig like the one shown in Shop Notebook on page 32.

ARCS. You'll need to cut the arc on the lower rails before assembling the end frames. To mark the arcs, you can use a long, flexible hardboard strip, as shown in the right drawing on the opposite page. Be sure to make the cuts on the lower edge of the rails.

DECORATIVE PANELS

Each end has a pair of decorative panels glued up from pieces of ½"-wide lumber. Two full-length slats are separated by three shorter pieces to create two openings at the top and center of each panel.

MILLING. I cut the slat pieces for the panels from the edge of a 1"-thick board. You can cut them slightly thick and plane the panels to finished thickness after they're assembled.

PANEL ASSEMBLY. As with the mortises, you'll find it easy to gang the slats together to mark them, as shown in the left drawing below. To assemble the panels, I glued the short, center slats to one long slat. Then after letting the glue set up, I glued another long slat to the opposite side (second and third drawing, below).

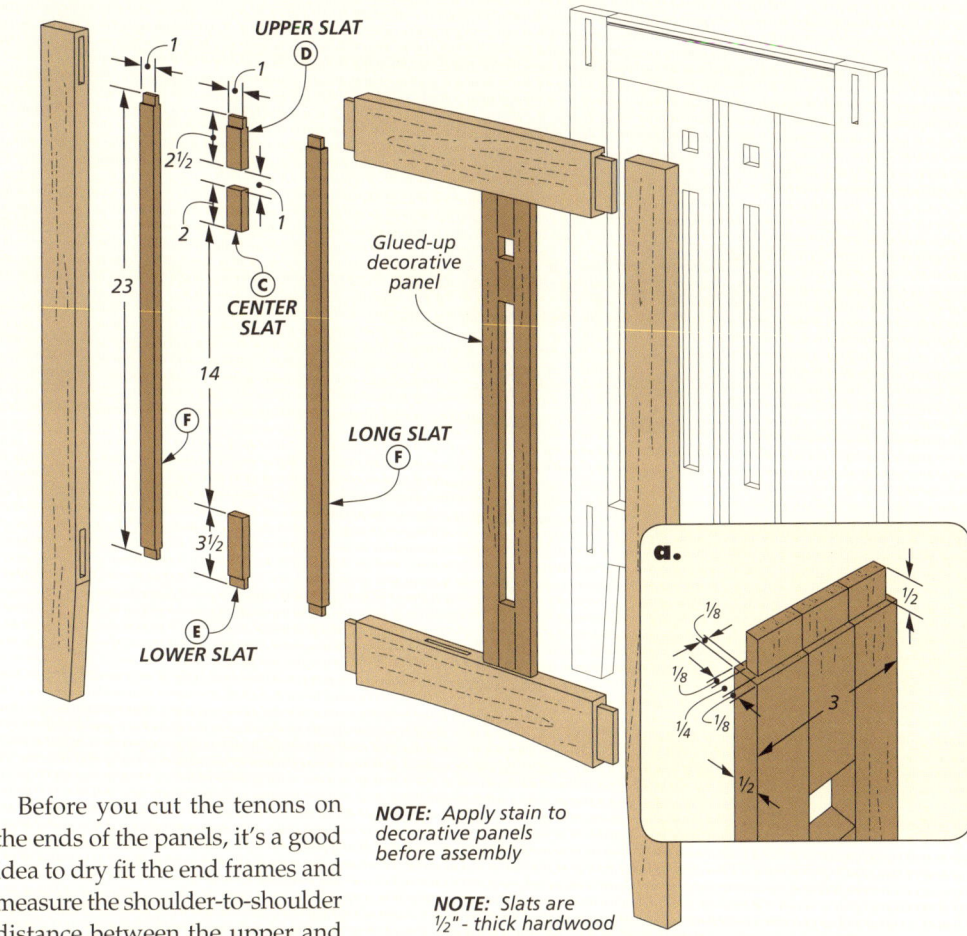

Before you cut the tenons on the ends of the panels, it's a good idea to dry fit the end frames and measure the shoulder-to-shoulder distance between the upper and lower rails. With this measurement in hand, you can cut the tenons to length.

PRE-STAIN. After the assembly is complete, go ahead and apply the contrasting stain to the panel. I used ebonizing dye to color the panels black. You'll find details about the dye I used in Sources on page 51. Mask off the tenons on the panels before you apply the dye so they won't swell. I also stained the rails before assembly. This way you won't have to worry about getting stain on the black panels.

END FRAME ASSEMBLY. I didn't use any glue to hold the decorative panels between the rails, since they're trapped. Once the panels are in place, glue the mating legs on either end of the rails and make sure the frame is flat.

Slat Assembly & Joinery

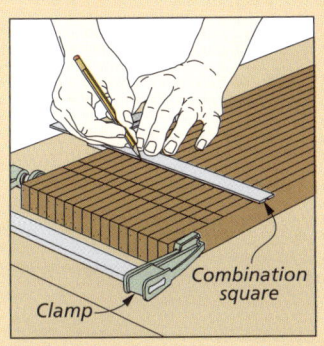

Gang Layout. To lay out locations for the short center slats, clamp the long slats together.

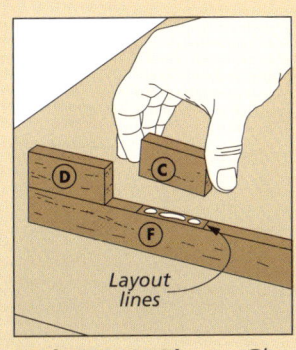

Tack Center Pieces. Glue the center slats between the layout lines.

Final Glueup. Glue and clamp the second long slat to finish the panel.

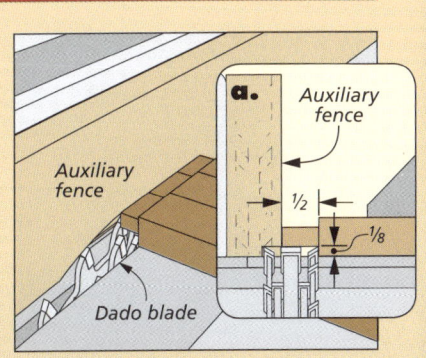

Slat Tenons. Bury a dado blade in an auxiliary fence to cut the tenons on the decorative panels.

making the STRETCHERS

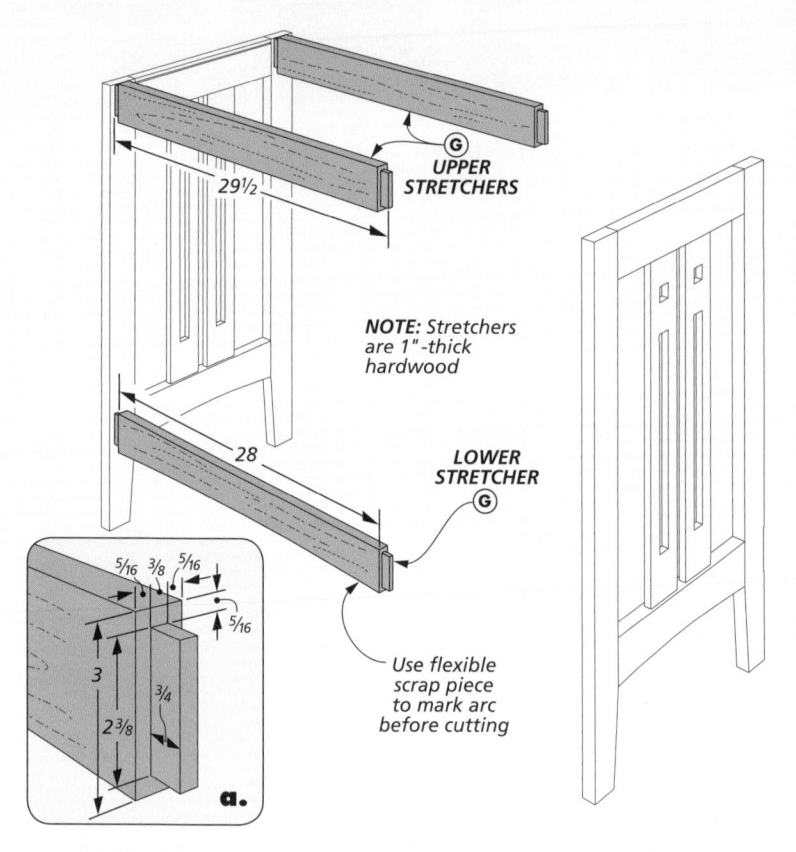

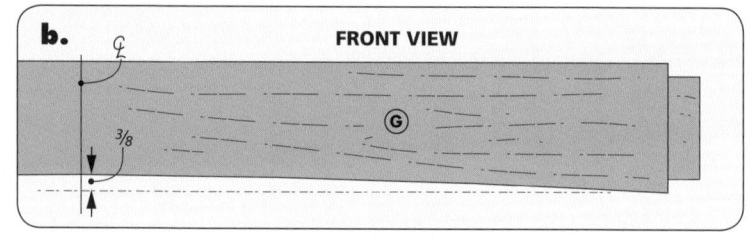

In this stage of the construction, you'll join two end frames to create a fixed base for the table. Then you'll attach the remaining frames with hinges so they fold out to support the extended table.

Three stretchers join the two fixed frames of the table. The single lower stretcher has an arc similar to the frame rails, but the two upper stretchers are square.

I located the lower stretcher on the hinge side of the fixed base. This way when the table is folded out, the lower stretcher will stay in the center of the table, leaving leg room on both sides of the table. When the table is folded up, it can sit with the stretcher against the wall. This will leave leg room on the side that faces into the room.

STRETCHERS. To make the stretchers, first cut them to size. Then go ahead and cut the tenons to fit the mortises, as shown in the How-To box below. To cut the arc in the lower stretcher I again used a flexible hardboard scrap to lay out the arc. Then I cut it on the band saw. A sanding drum in the drill press makes quick work of sanding the arc smooth.

BASE ASSEMBLY. When the stretchers are ready, you can assemble the base. Your first task is to glue the stretcher tenons in the mating mortises. Since there are only three stretchers, keeping the assembly square during

How-To: Cut Tenons & Arcs

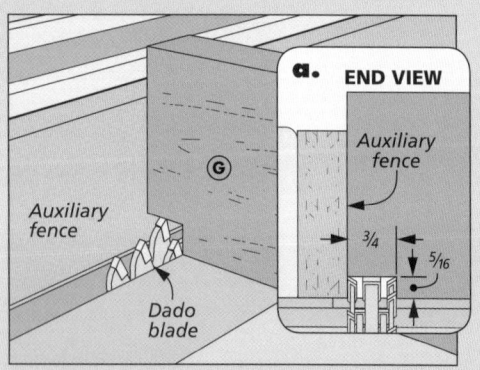

Cut the Shoulders. You can cut the shoulders on the table saw with a dado blade. Use an auxiliary rip fence as a stop.

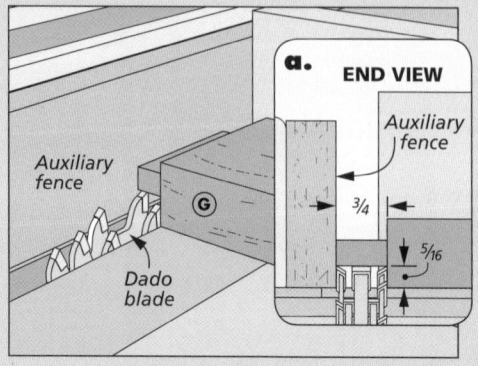

Cut Cheeks. Both the shoulders and cheeks are cut to the same depth. You won't have to adjust the blade height or fence settings.

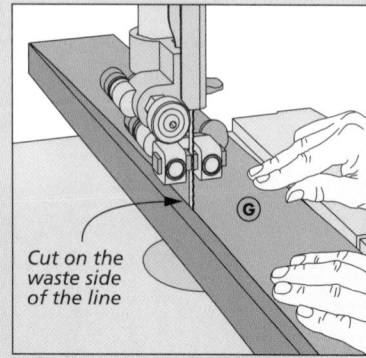

Cut the Arc. Use the band saw to cut the arc in the stretcher. Then clean it up with a sanding drum.

the glueup presents a challenge. To remedy this, you can cut a scrap board to the same length as the shoulder-to-shoulder measurement of the stretchers. This allows you to add an extra clamp at the lower edge of the unhinged side of the base and keep the assembly square.

HINGED PANELS. To complete the base assembly, attach the matching end frames with hinges. Here I used mortised butt hinges. Butt hinges open flat and fold up on themselves. This allows the hinged part of the base to lay flat against the stationary base when the table is folded up. The hinges are recessed slightly to allow for the thick hinge pin.

INSTALL HINGES. To rout the hinge mortises, you can build a simple template like the one shown in the lower left drawing. As you can see in the box below, a dado clean-out bit works best. (Rout deep to accommodate pins.)

I routed the mortise on the fixed frame first and then clamped the other frame to it, aligning them to mark the placement of the other leaf. Make sure that the top edges of the frames are flush so the table will be supported at all points. When you've finished routing, clean up the corners of the mortises with a chisel, and attach the hinges with screws.

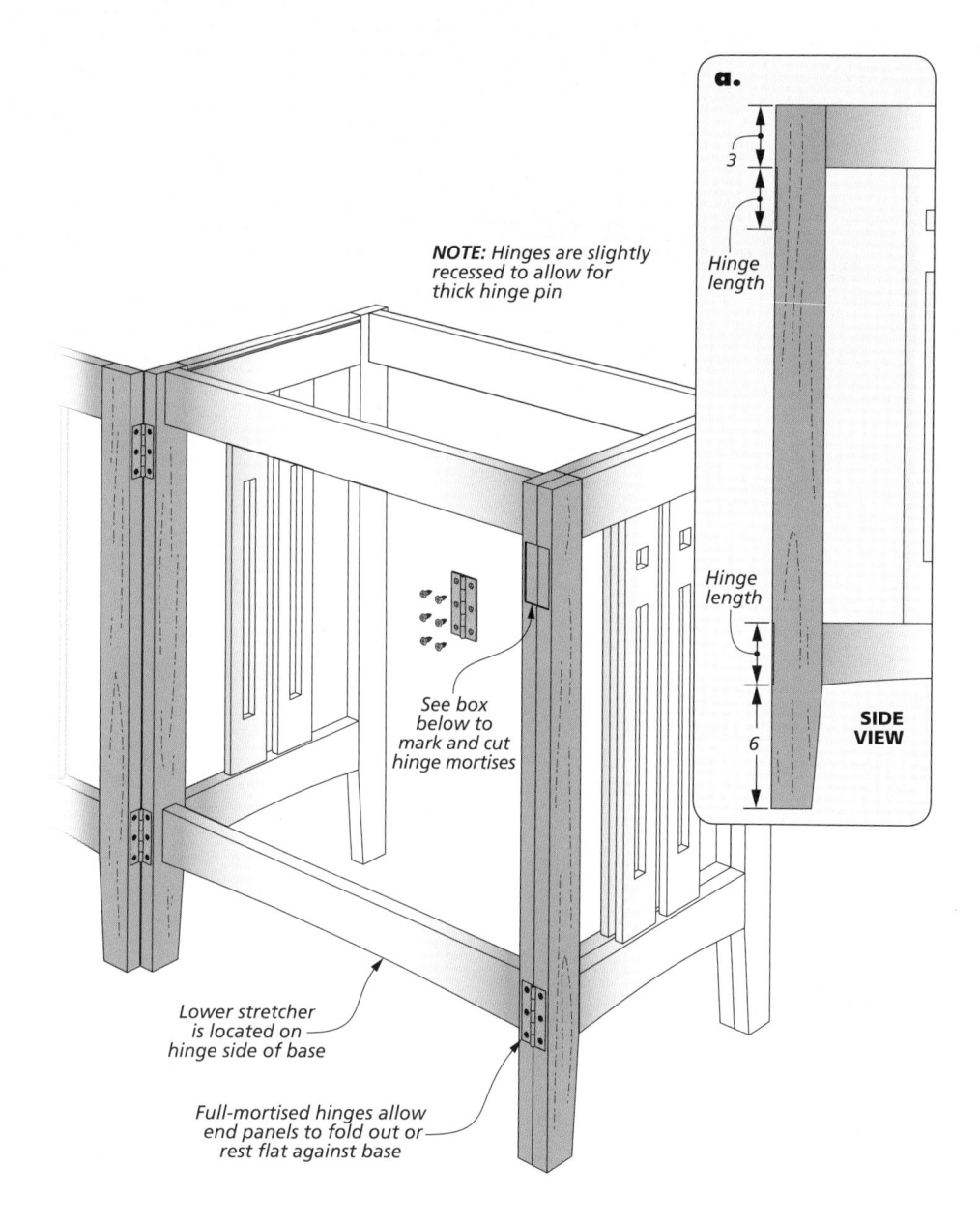

NOTE: Hinges are slightly recessed to allow for thick hinge pin

See box below to mark and cut hinge mortises

Lower stretcher is located on hinge side of base

Full-mortised hinges allow end panels to fold out or rest flat against base

a.
3
Hinge length
Hinge length
6
SIDE VIEW

Hinge the End Frames

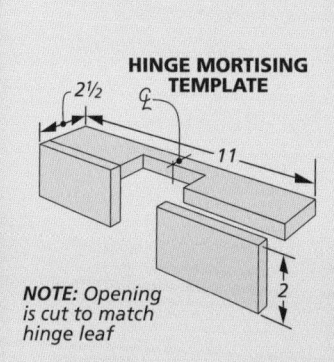

HINGE MORTISING TEMPLATE
2½
11
2

NOTE: Opening is cut to match hinge leaf

Router baseplate
Dado clean-out bit
Template

Mark mating frame for hinges while clamped together

Use screwdriver to install brass screws

Template. Glue up pieces of MDF and cut an opening for the hinge template.

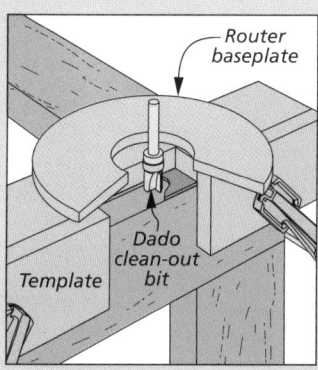

Rout for Hinges. Use a dado clean-out bit and the template to rout the hinge mortises.

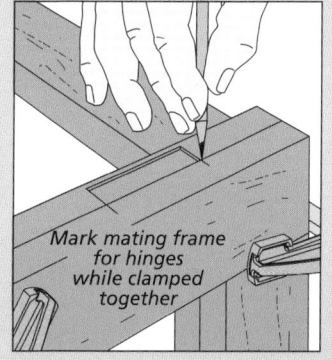

Transfer Layout. Align the ends and mark the location of the mating hinge leaf.

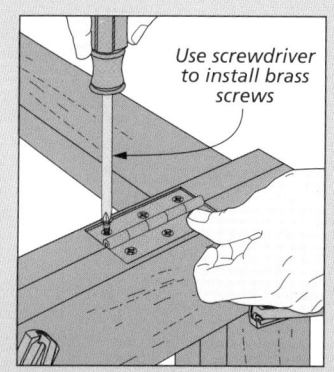

Install Hinge. Clamp the two end frames together and install the hinges.

Woodsmith.com   Woodsmith

next up, the TABLETOP

The top consists of two glued-up panels connected with sewing machine hinges. The hinges are mortised flush and allow the top to fold over on itself or lay flat when open. You can see details about these hinges on the opposite page.

TABLETOP. To build the top sections, glue up two panels. After flattening, cut them to final length and width.

HINGES. To install the hinges, first clamp the top sections together. Next, rout the stepped mortises using the jig shown in the How-To box on the opposite page. Finally, install the hinges.

FINISH. You can use a soft sanding block to ease the edges of the tabletop before you apply the finish. Since both sides of the tabletop will be visible, I applied the stain and topcoats to both sides. You can go ahead apply the remaining stain and top coats to the base too.

ATTACH THE TOP. To attach the top to the base of the table, I folded the top and placed the base upside down on top of it. Center the base on the top and make sure that the hinge side of the top and the hinge side of the base are on the same side. A pair of Z-fasteners attach the tabletop to the base at each end. They fit in the grooves on each end of the fixed frame. This type of fastener allows for wood movement in the top assembly.

Once the top is in place, you're ready to set the table and enjoy lunch. **W**

Materials, Supplies & Cutting Diagram

A	Legs (8)	1 x 2½ - 34
B	Rails (8)	1 x 3 - 17
C	Center Slats (8)	1 x ½ - 2
D	Upper Slats (8)	1 x ½ - 2½
E	Lower Slats (8)	1 x ½ - 3½
F	Long Slats (16)	1 x ½ - 23
G	Stretchers (3)	1 x 3 - 29½
H	Tops (2)	1 x 21 - 48

- (3) Sewing Machine Hinges w/screws
- (4) 1⅝" x 3" Brass Butt Hinges w/screws
- (4) Z-fasteners

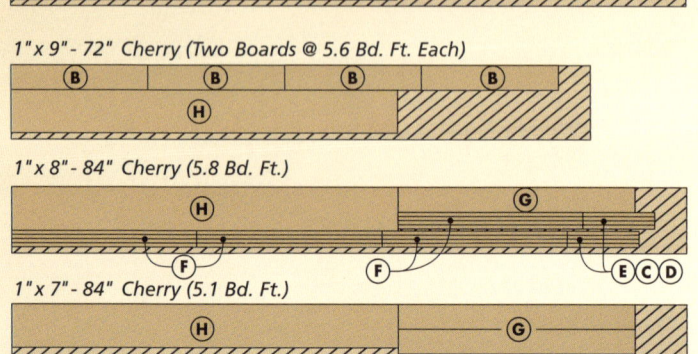

Hinges

Sewing machine hinges get their name from their original purpose: for sewing machine cabinet tops that fold out to create a worksurface. They work great because they create a tight seam when extended and sit flush with the tabletop.

The design of the hinge I used for this table has a knuckle that is recessed when the hinge is opened or closed. This way the knuckle doesn't get in the way.

You can see the step-by-step installation in the drawings below. You'll just need a router and a sharp chisel.

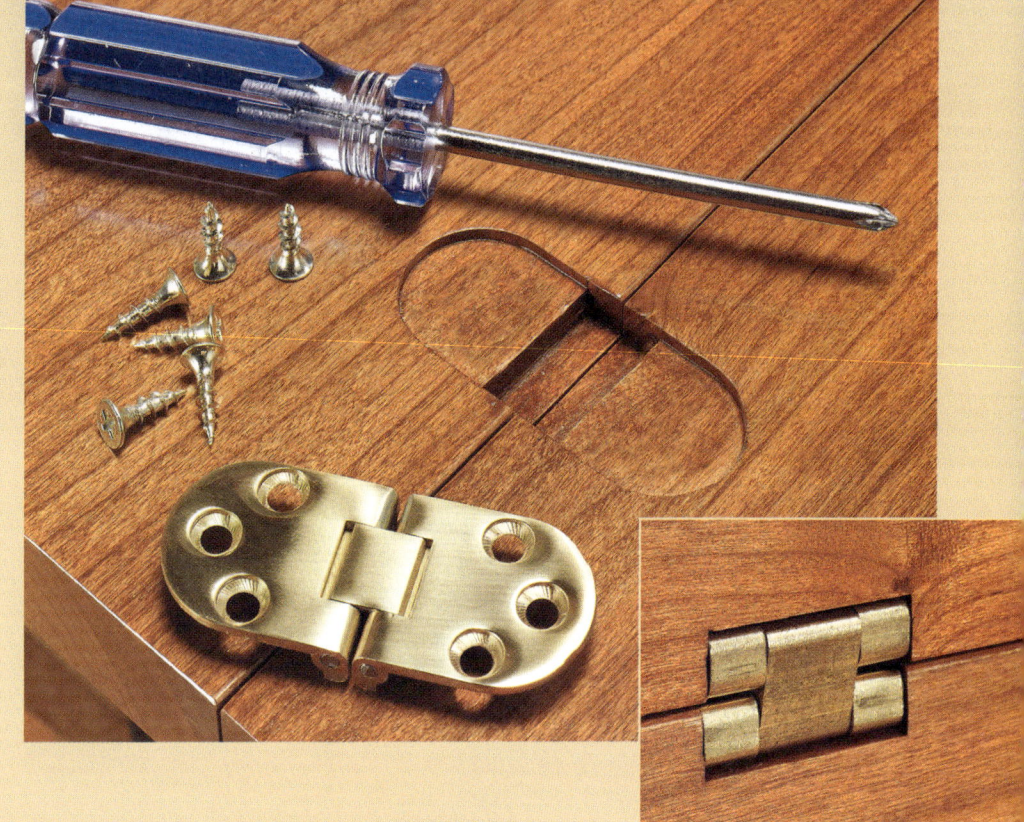

How-To: Install Sewing Machine Hinge

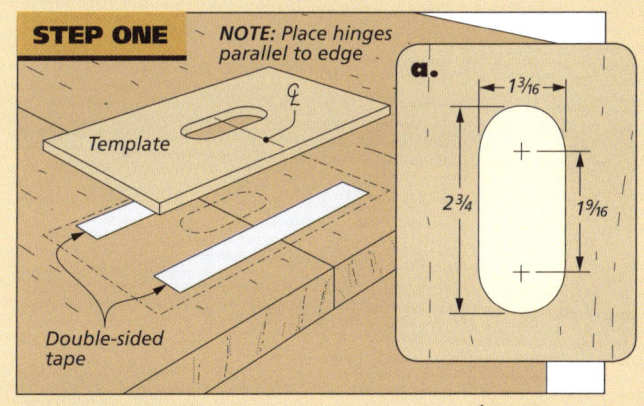

STEP ONE
NOTE: Place hinges parallel to edge

Template, Double-sided tape

Detail a: 1 3/16, 2 3/4, 1 9/16

Template Routing. Make a template from 1/4" plywood with the dimensions as shown in detail 'a.' Use double-sided tape to secure the template to both table halves.

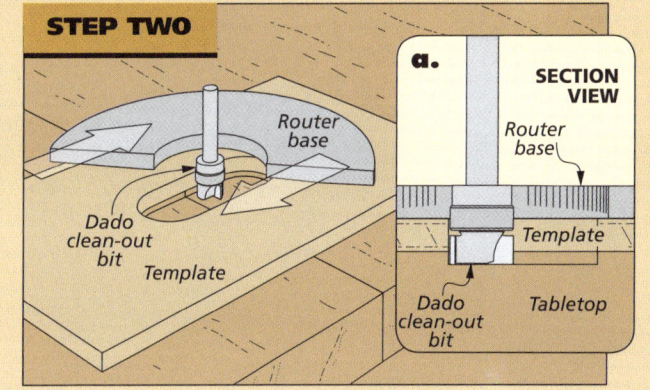

STEP TWO
Router base, Dado clean-out bit, Template

Detail a. SECTION VIEW: Router base, Dado clean-out bit, Template, Tabletop

Rout First Pass. Set the depth of the dado clean-out bit to equal the thickness of the hinge leaf. Since the hinges are rounded, there's no need to square up the ends.

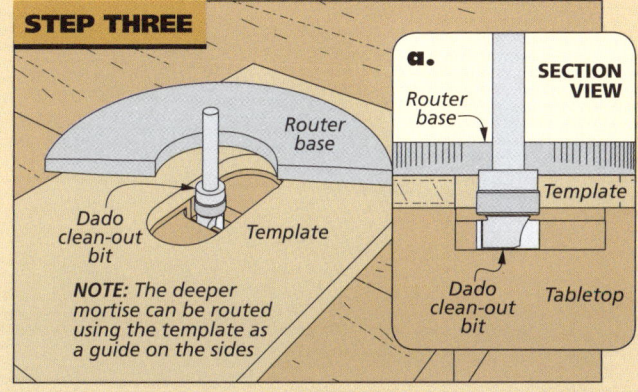

STEP THREE
Dado clean-out bit, Router base, Template

NOTE: The deeper mortise can be routed using the template as a guide on the sides

Detail a. SECTION VIEW: Router base, Template, Dado clean-out bit, Tabletop

Rout for Knuckle. The deeper section of the stepped mortise is determined using a folded hinge. Set the bit depth to rout a recess for the knuckle of the hinge.

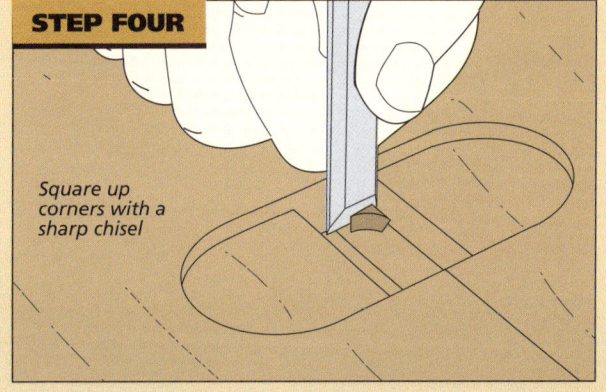

STEP FOUR
Square up corners with a sharp chisel

Chisel Cleanup. When you're finished routing the opening for the hinge pins, you can use a chisel to square up the corners and edges of the knuckle recess.

tips from our shop

SHOP NOTEBOOK

Bending Form

Creating the curved doors for the jewelry chest on page 34 isn't nearly as difficult as it might seem. The secret is to use a special, bendable type of plywood, along with a shop-made form like the one shown at right.

The bending form is made out of MDF. Several cauls allow you to clamp the layers of plywood together and hold them in place while the glues dries.

As you can see below, the form is made up of two sides and a pair of braces — a wide brace on the top and a narrow one at the front. The front corner of each side is rounded to match the inside radius of the doors of the jewelry chest. A row of holes is drilled in each side for clamps.

After screwing the sides to the braces, a cleat is added to the front of the form. This cleat prevents the plywood layers from slipping as you apply the clamps. It also acts as a registration stop for the front edge of the door, so it's important to attach the cleat square to the sides of the form.

CAULS. The last parts to make are the cauls. The top caul is simply a piece of ¾" MDF. The front caul is cut from a strip of hardwood. And finally, to make certain the layers of plywood conform to the rounded corners of the form, I made a couple of curved cauls to match the outside radius of the doors. To do this, I simply drew a 2" radius on the end of a couple of blanks and then cut the curves on a band saw. After a little sanding, the cauls matched the radius of the curved door perfectly.

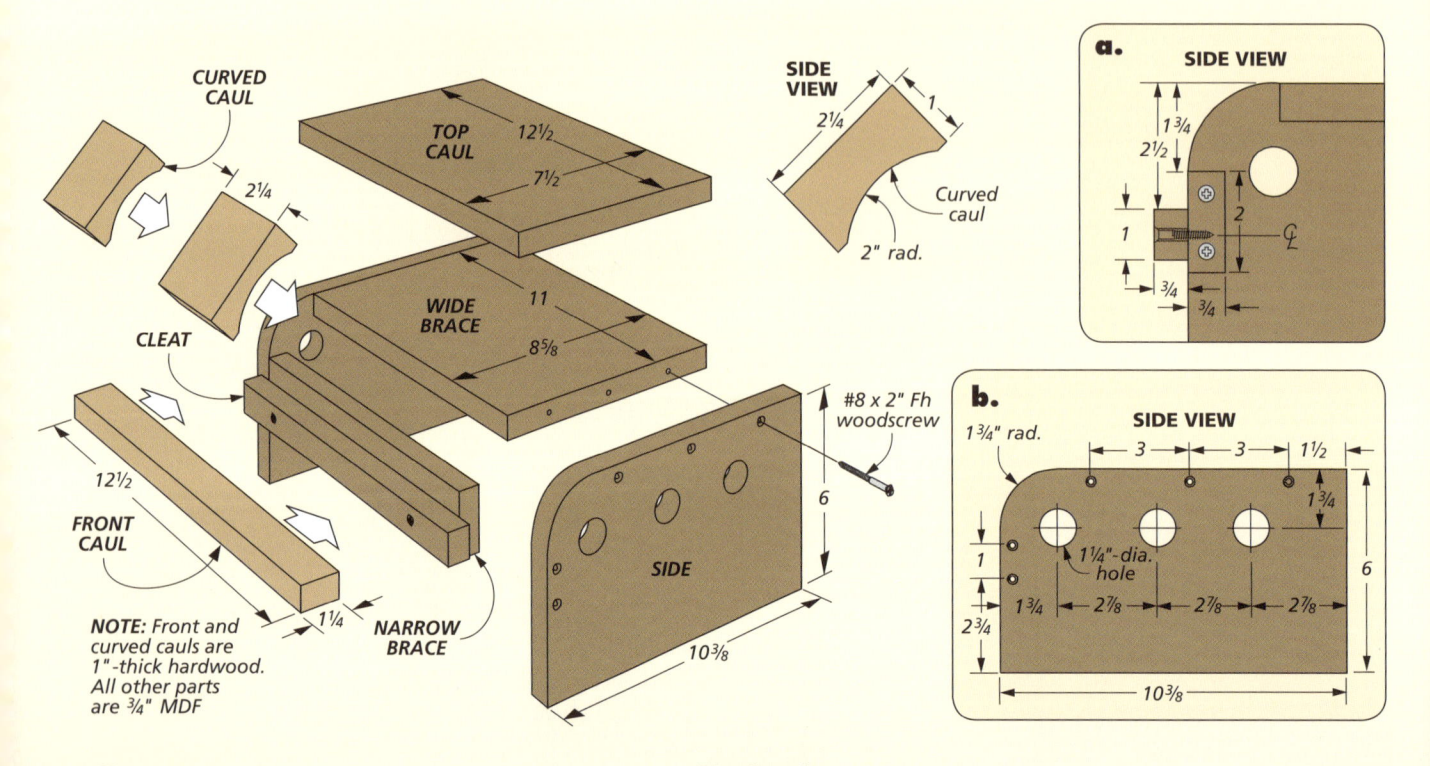

Woodsmith

Taper Jig

Cutting the short tapers on the legs of the folding table on page 24 is a simple job on the table saw. All you need is a jig to hold the leg at the proper angle.

The jig I used is shown at right. It consists of nothing more than an MDF base with a few cleats to position the leg blank.

To make the jig, I started by laying out the taper on one of my leg blanks. Then I placed the blank on the base of the jig, lining up the taper with the edge of the base. While holding the blank in this position, you can glue the cleats to the base of the jig — one at the end of the blank and two along the side. Then remove the leg blank while the glue dries.

To cut a taper, simply attach the leg blank to the base of the jig with double-sided tape.

Clamping Jig

Gluing up the blank for the coasters on page 21 is a bit of a challenge. To prevent the pieces from slipping, I made this simple clamping jig. It's just two pieces of hardwood screwed together — a base and a fence. A separate clamping caul traps the pieces against the fence. And the open ends allow you to clamp the pieces from both directions.

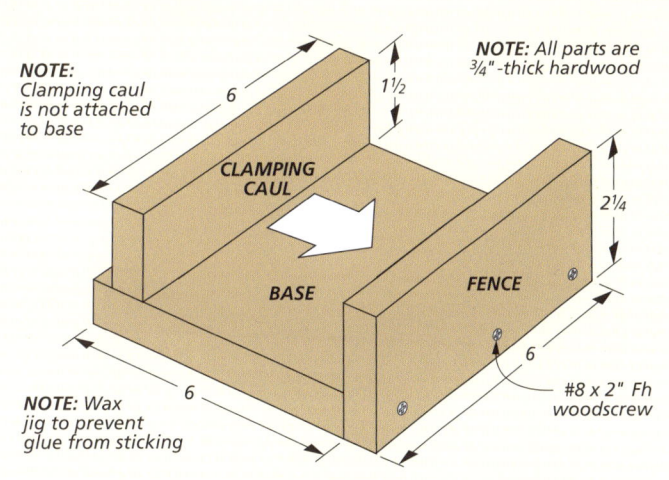

Feet Profile

To create the 1"-rad. cove profile on the feet of the jewelry chest, I used a Forstner bit in the drill press. As you can see below, I sandwiched the blanks between a couple of scrap pieces of ¾" MDF.

A spacer block placed between the blanks provides a centerpoint for the drill bit. With the "sandwich" clamped to the drill press, it's a simple matter to drill out the waste for the coves.

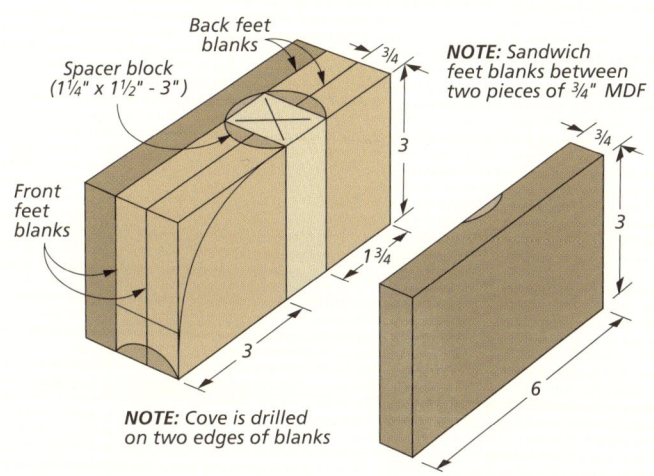

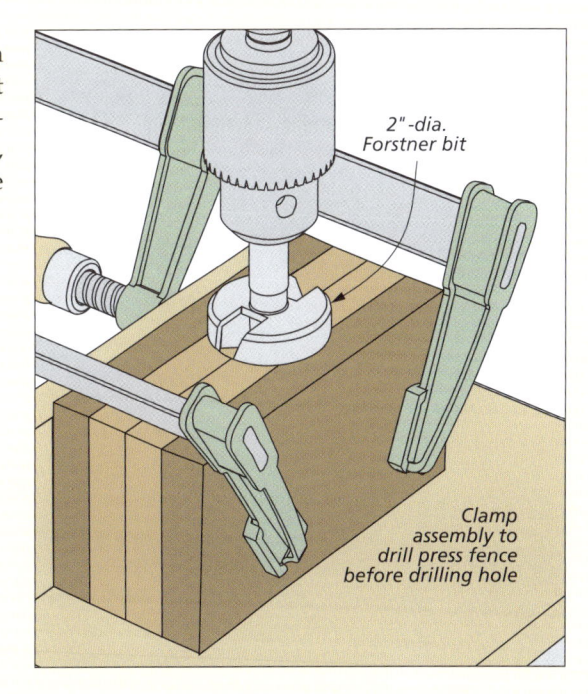

Heirloom Project

curved-door Jewelry Chest

This project will test your woodworking skills and give you an opportunity to learn a few new techniques.

There aren't many gifts that will put a smile on the face of the recipient like a hand-made jewelry chest. And since it's such a personal gift that will last a lifetime, it will always remind the owner of the craftsmanship and thought that went into building it.

The design shown above is sure to get plenty of "oohs" and "aahs," as well. The use of contrasting woods is a sure way to catch the eye. (I used maple and wenge.)

For the bulk of the jewelry chest you'll use pretty straightforward woodworking techniques. For instance, the case is assembled using tongue and dado joinery. Then, the top and bottom are attached with dowels.

But it's the curved doors that really grab your attention. And they'll give you an opportunity to try out a wood-bending technique. I used a special bending plywood to form the doors and then covered them with veneer. If you've never attempted bending wood before, this project is a great chance to give it a try.

CONSTRUCTION DETAILS

OVERALL DIMENSIONS: 13$\frac{13}{16}$"H x 14"W x 8$\frac{3}{4}$"D

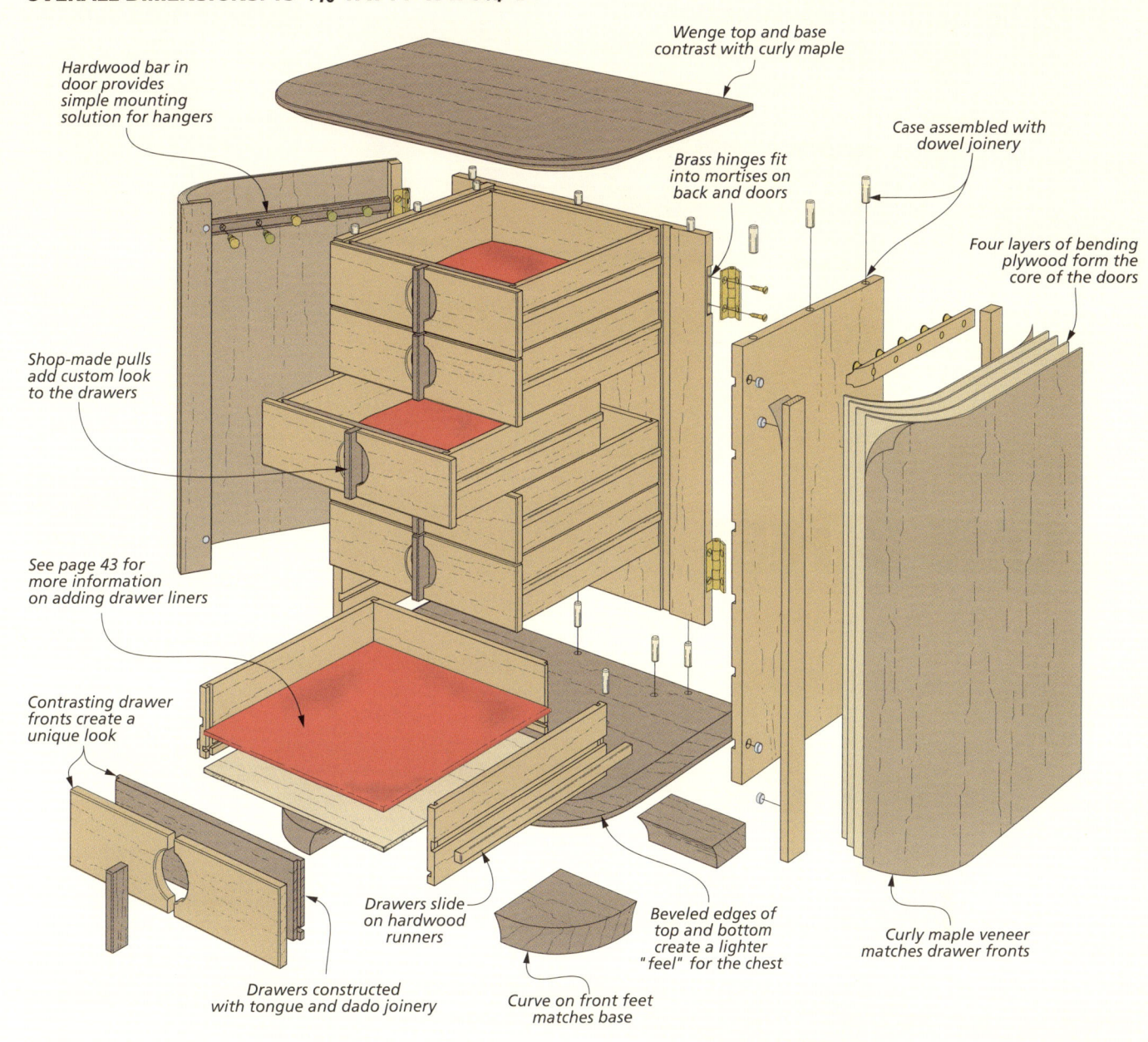

- Hardwood bar in door provides simple mounting solution for hangers
- Wenge top and base contrast with curly maple
- Brass hinges fit into mortises on back and doors
- Case assembled with dowel joinery
- Four layers of bending plywood form the core of the doors
- Shop-made pulls add custom look to the drawers
- See page 43 for more information on adding drawer liners
- Contrasting drawer fronts create a unique look
- Drawers constructed with tongue and dado joinery
- Drawers slide on hardwood runners
- Curve on front feet matches base
- Beveled edges of top and bottom create a lighter "feel" for the chest
- Curly maple veneer matches drawer fronts

▲ The jewelry chest features specially designed storage for necklaces, jewelry, and other valuables.

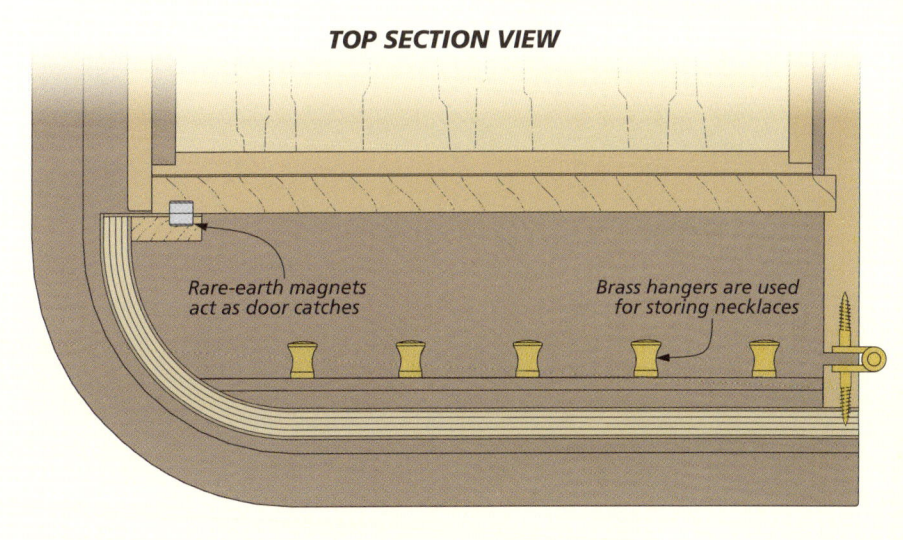

TOP SECTION VIEW

- Rare-earth magnets act as door catches
- Brass hangers are used for storing necklaces

Woodsmith.com · Woodsmith · 35

start with the CASE & FEET

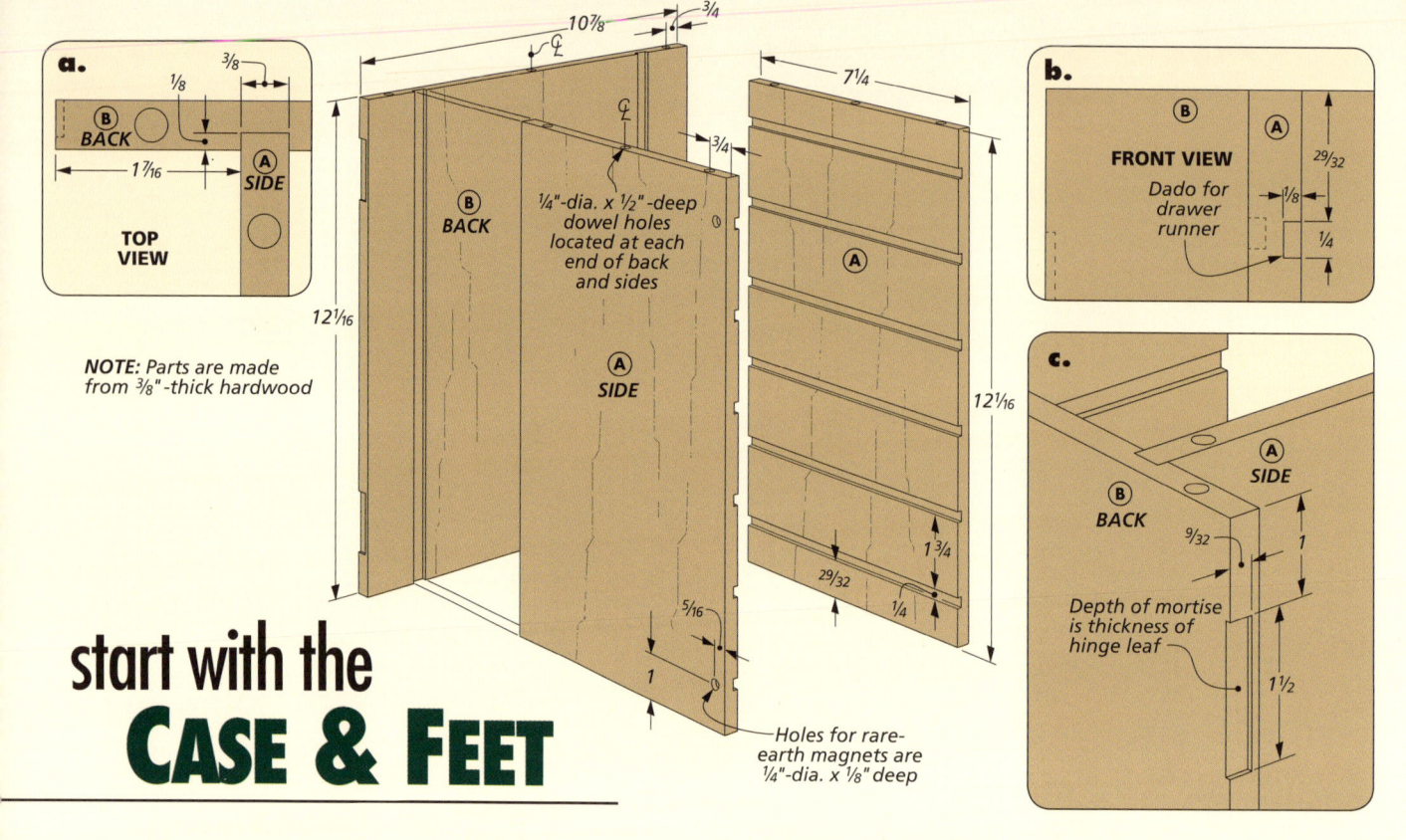

The basic case of the jewelry chest is formed by the back and sides. The back has a pair of grooves to hold the sides, and the sides are dadoed to receive the drawers. After they're assembled, the top and bottom are installed with dowels and glue. I started by making the sides.

SIDES. You'll need to begin by planing your stock to 3/8" thick. Then, cut the sides to final size. With a dado blade in the table saw, cut the matching dadoes for the drawers in both sides.

MAGNETIC CATCHES. Next, drill the holes for magnetic door catches as shown in the main drawing above. But don't install the magnets until the final assembly.

BACK. Now you can cut the back to final size and cut the two grooves on the inside face. I also routed the shallow hinge mortises in the back (detail 'c'). To do this, I sandwiched the workpiece between two pieces of thick scrap to make sure the router had plenty of surface to ride on (center drawing, below). Then, square up the cuts with a chisel.

DOWEL HOLES. I also drilled holes in the ends of the sides and back at the locations shown in the main drawing. These holes house the dowels used to attach the top and bottom. I used a doweling jig to make sure the bit didn't blow out the sides (right drawing, below).

How-To: Dadoes, Hinge Mortises & Dowel Holes

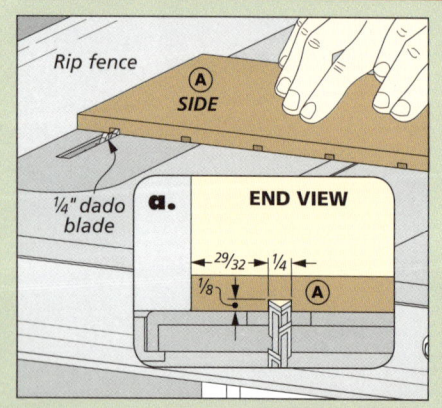

Dadoes. With a 1/4" dado blade in the table saw, cut the dadoes for the drawer runners in both sides.

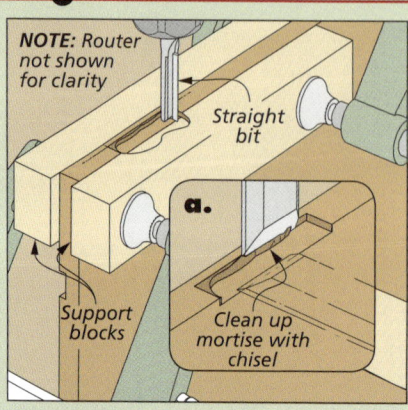

Rout the Hinge Mortise. Clamp the back between two blocks to support the router and then rout the mortise.

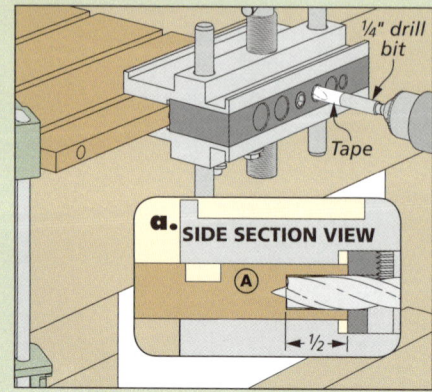

Dowel Holes. After marking the hole locations, use a doweling jig to drill straight holes in the back and sides.

SUB-ASSEMBLY. Now add glue in the grooves on the back and insert the sides, making sure the magnet holes are at the front. Take a moment to check that the sides are perfectly square to the back.

TOP & BOTTOM. With the sides and back assembled, you can move on to making the top and bottom. I used wenge, known for its rich, dark color and spectacular grain. I started by planing it to ½" thick.

After cutting the top and bottom to final size, the next step is to round the front corners of both pieces. For this, I marked the layout using a compass and then cut the corners at the band saw. The drawing below shows the process.

CHAMFER THE EDGES. At the router table, install a 60° chamfer bit and rout the edges of both pieces (center drawing, below). I routed the chamfer in light passes to avoid splintering the wenge. It's a good idea to finish with a very shallow cleanup pass.

I used ¾"-thick wenge for the front and back feet. The edges have a cove profile. The front feet are also rounded (lower right drawing). You can find details for making the coves in Shop Notebook on page 32. After sanding, glue the feet in place on the bottom.

ASSEMBLY. Before assembly, you'll need to mark the dowel hole locations on the top and bottom. An easy way to do this is to place ¼"-dia. dowel centers in the holes in the sides and back. Then, set them in place on the bottom. After checking to make sure the position is even and square, tap the sides and back. Now all you need to do is drill holes at the site of the marks. Repeat this process to mark the top. Finally, attach the back and side sub-assembly with glue and dowels.

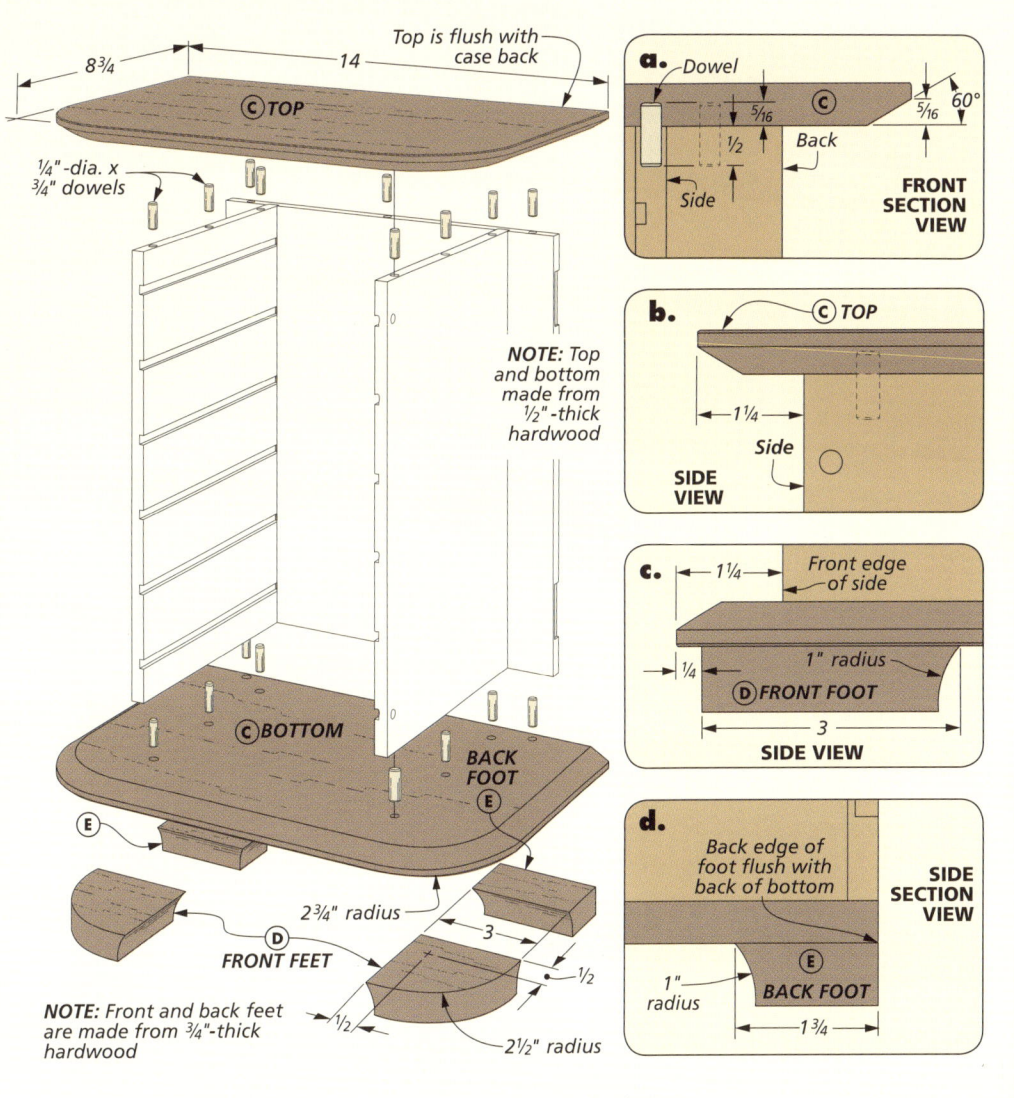

Shaping the Top, Bottom & Feet

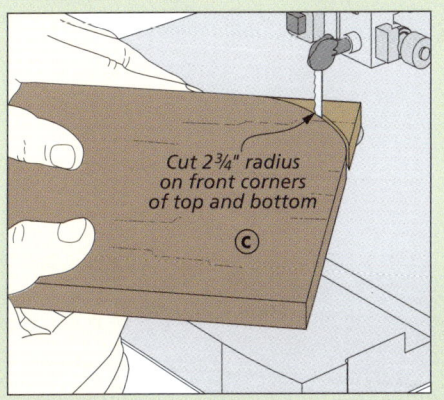

Rounding the Corners. First, lay out the radius on the corners with a compass, then cut to the line at the band saw.

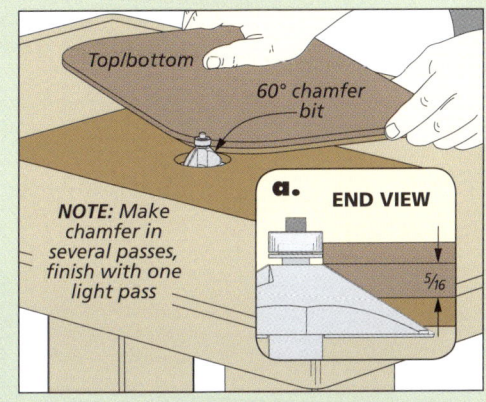

Chamfer the Edges. Use the 60° chamfer bit to add the decorative profile on the edges. Making light passes will help prevent tearout.

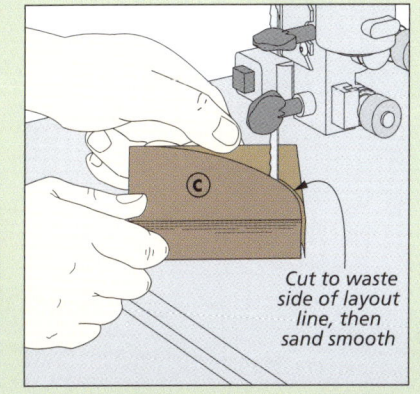

Cutting the Feet. After cutting the cove profiles on the feet blanks, round the corners at the band saw.

constructing the DRAWERS

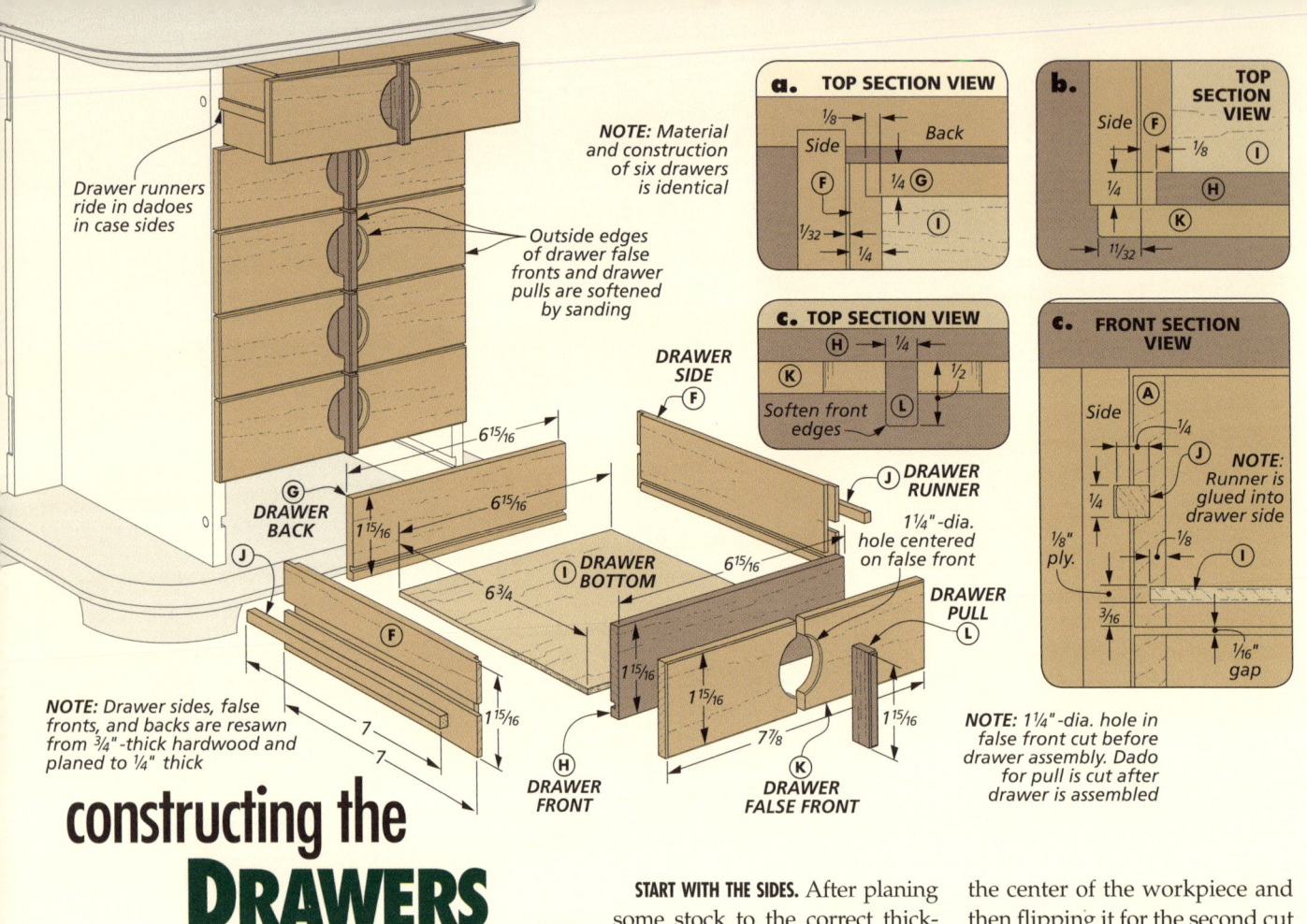

With the case complete, you can turn your attention to the drawers. The six drawers are identical, so that makes things pretty straightforward. I used rabbet joints since the drawers won't be holding much weight. As you can see in the drawings above, the drawers slide on simple hardwood runners.

START WITH THE SIDES. After planing some stock to the correct thickness, cut the sides to final size. You can then cut the rabbets on the ends at the table saw. For this, I relied on a miter gauge with an auxiliary fence to prevent tearout. The left drawing below shows how I made the cuts.

On the outside faces, cut a centered groove for the drawer runners by making the first cut near the center of the workpiece and then flipping it for the second cut (center drawing, below).

DRAWER FRONTS, BACKS, & BOTTOMS. Even though the drawer fronts are wenge and the backs are maple, they're identical in dimension and installation. When you've finished cutting them all, set the rip fence and cut the groove for the drawer bottoms as shown in the right drawing below.

How-To: Cut the Drawer Sides

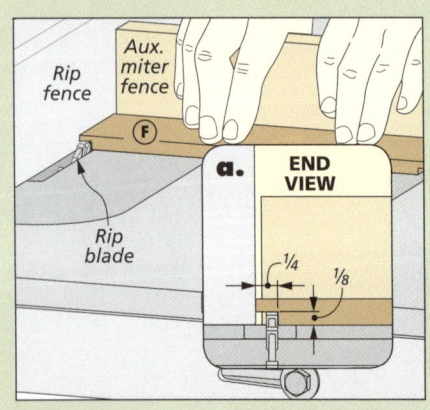

Rabbets. With an auxiliary fence on the miter gauge, you can use the rip fence as a stop to cut the rabbets on the ends.

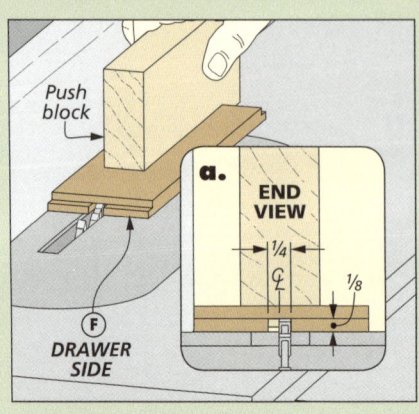

Groove. Cut the centered groove in the drawer sides with a rip blade by flipping the piece end-for-end between cuts.

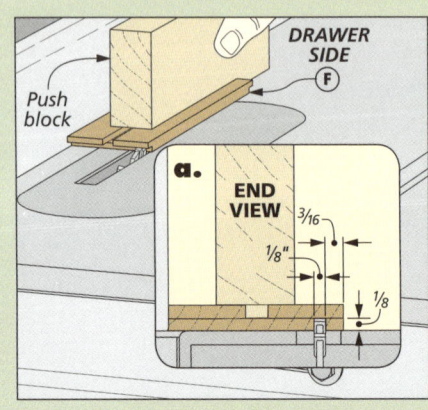

Groove for the Drawer Bottom. Set the rip fence and cut the shallow groove in the fronts, backs, and sides.

I used 1/8" birch plywood for the drawer bottoms. All you need to do is cut each one to final size and you're ready to test fit the drawer assemblies.

ASSEMBLY. At this point, you can assemble the drawers using glue in the rabbets and in the grooves for the drawer bottoms. Make sure to check each drawer box for square as you clamp them up and allow them to dry.

DRAWER RUNNERS. The next step is to add the runners to the drawers. First you'll need to rip the narrow strips at the table saw. Then cut them to final length and glue them into the grooves on the drawer sides. Test fit each one in the case and lightly sand the runners if necessary for a good fit.

FALSE FRONTS. One of my favorite design features about this project is the curly maple false front over the dark wenge. The main drawing on the opposite page shows how it works. When you drill the hole and cut the dado for the drawer pulls, it exposes a nice contrast. The drawings at right explain the steps needed to add the false fronts and drawer pulls.

With the drawers installed in the case, I positioned the false fronts on the drawer boxes. Starting at the bottom drawer, use tape to hold the false front in position.

Next, add glue and spring clamps to complete the assembly. Try to avoid squeezeout near the hole in the false front.

After the glue dries, head over to the table saw and cut the centered dado in the fronts. This is best done with a tall auxiliary fence on the miter gauge and a stop block to make consistent cuts. I used a cut-and-flip method to make sure the dado was centered.

ADD THE PULLS. Finally, I ripped 1/4"-thick wenge into 1/2"-wide strips to use as drawer pulls. I also did a little bit of gentle sanding to break the sharp front edge of the stock. Then, simply cut the pulls to length and install them in the dadoes on the fronts with glue and clamp them in place.

How-To: Add False Fronts & Pulls

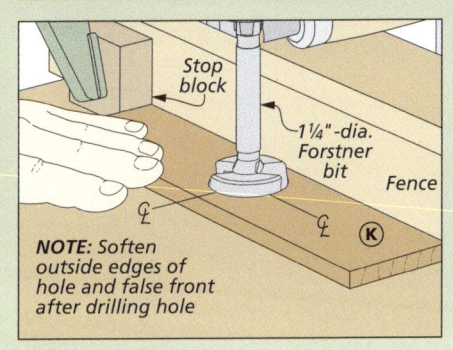

Drilling. After marking the centerpoint of the false front, align it with the bit and set the fence and stop block.

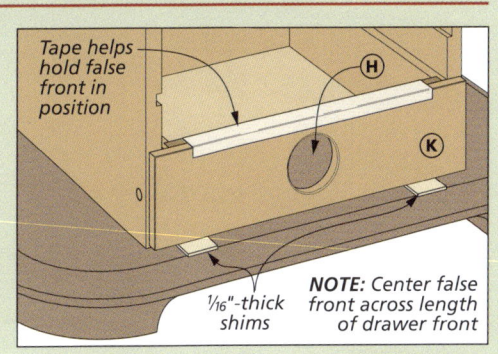

NOTE: Soften outside edges of hole and false front after drilling hole

False Fronts Spacing. With the drawer in place in the case, use a strip of tape to position the false front vertically and horizontally.

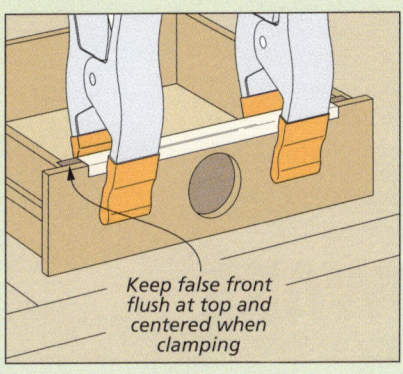

NOTE: Center false front across length of drawer front

Clamping. Spring clamps provide plenty of clamping pressure for the glueup and the tape prevents slipping.

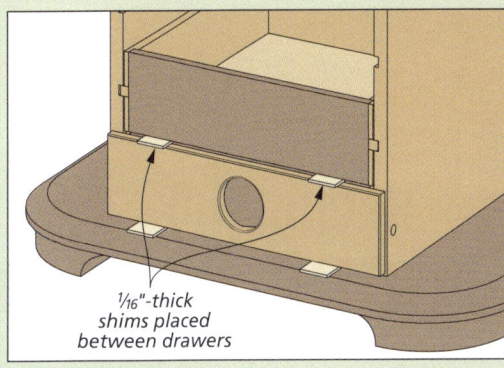

Add the Rest. Continue adding false fronts to the drawers by positioning each drawer in its spot and repeating the glue-up process.

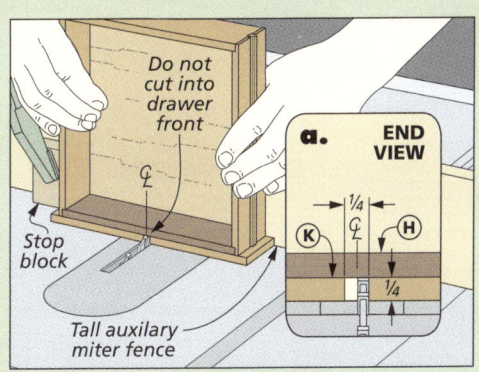

Centered Dado. Once again, I used a "cut-and-flip" technique to cut a centered dado in the false fronts for the drawer pulls.

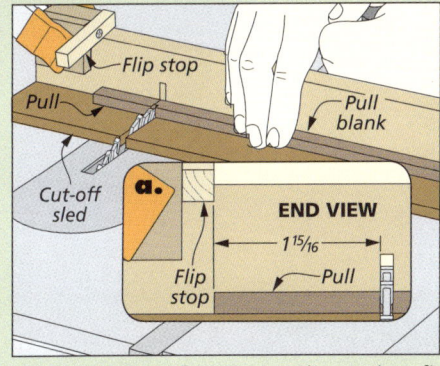

Drawer Pulls. After planing the stock to fit the dadoes, simply cut them to length. (See page 14 for tips on cutting small parts.)

◄ The hole and wenge strips combine to create a unique drawer pull.

adding the
DOORS & HARDWARE

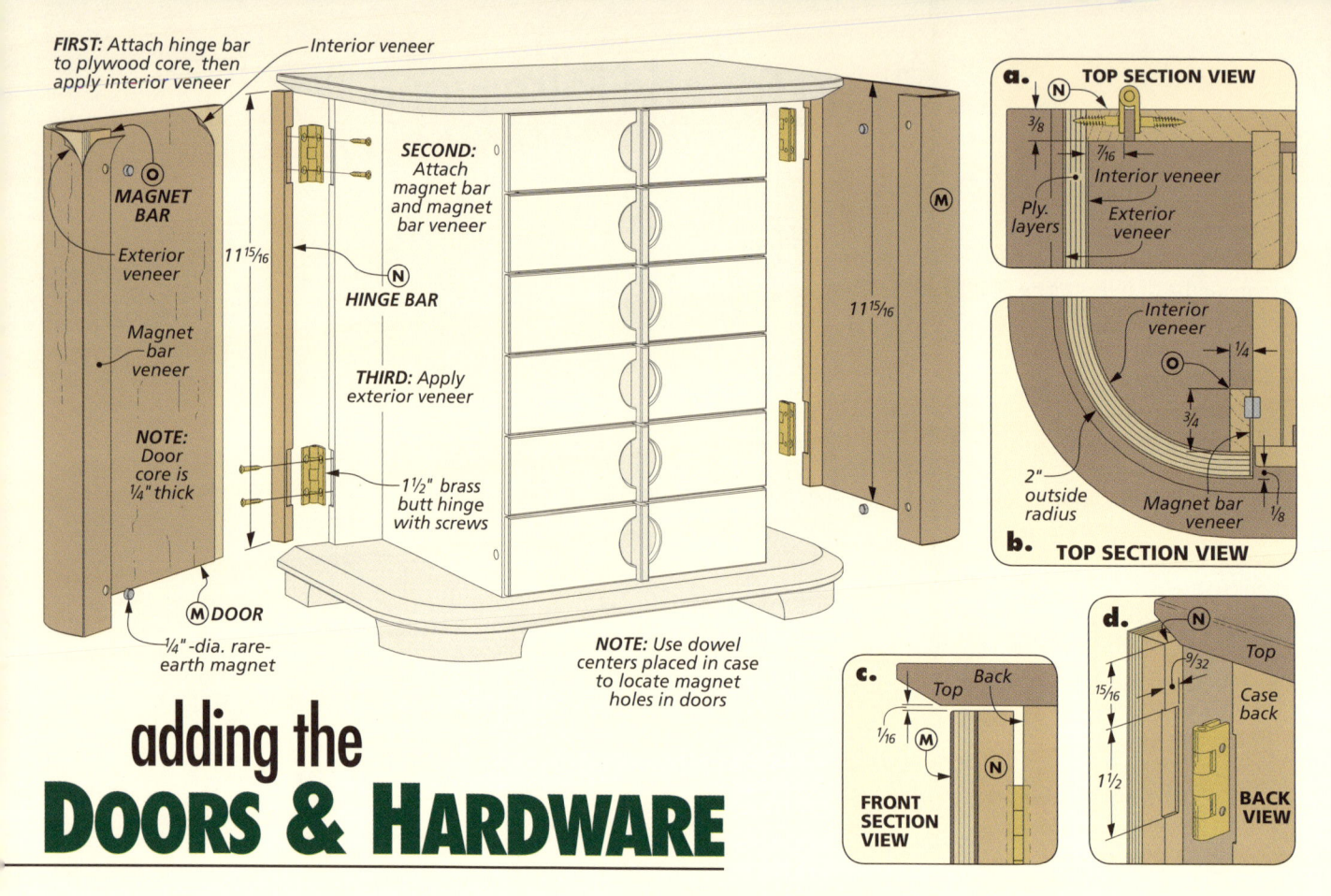

One of the highlights of this jewelry chest is the distinctive curve of the doors. The secret to making them is to use $1/16$"-thick bending plywood. This plywood is manufactured with the grain running the same direction in all the plies so it bends easily. After laminating a plywood core, you'll cover it with a veneer, like the curly maple I used. Opening the doors reveals several brass necklace hangers.

BENDING FORM. I started by making a plywood bending form. You can find the details you'll need to build it in Shop Notebook on page 32. The form features a round edge for the curves and an array of holes in the sides, allowing plenty of access for clamps.

PREPARING THE PLYWOOD. After building the form, cut the four pieces of bending plywood slightly oversize. I started with the pieces roughly 11" x $12\frac{1}{2}$". This will allow you to trim the edges and clean up the squeezeout after the glue sets up. You'll also want to make sure the sheets are aligned to bend in the same direction. (You can easily feel the right direction to bend the plywood.)

Before adding the glue to the laminations, I did a dry run to get a feel for the bending process. The drawings on the opposite page walk you through the steps.

You can start by clamping the front edge of the stacked pieces in the form with a caul on the outside. Then I made sure the rest of my clamps and cauls were within easy reach, ready to go.

BENDING & GLUING. After the dry run, apply an even coat of glue over one side of each sheet. Stack the plies in the form and add the clamps and cauls. I used cold-press veneer glue to help avoid springback in the lamination.

After the glue has dried, inspect the doors for a gap-free lamination and twist. Then, you can clean up the edges with a plane and square them at the table saw.

How To: Attach Door Hardware

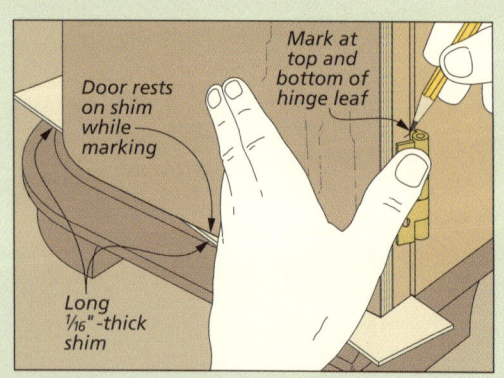

Marking Hinge Location. Use a thin shim to support the door while you position it against the case and mark the mortise location.

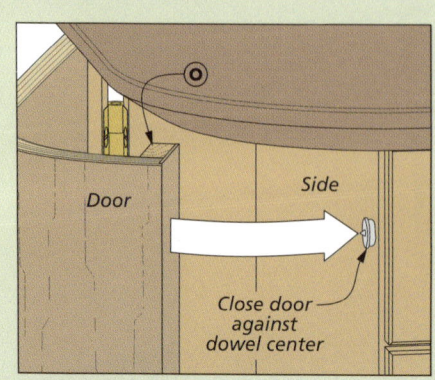

Locating the Magnets. Slip a $1/4$" dowel center in the hole in the case to mark the mating hole for the magnet.

I cleaned up the top edge with a block plane, then set the rip fence to trim the bottom edge on the table saw. Then, I used the miter gauge and an auxiliary fence to square up the front and rear edges of the doors. The important thing here is to trim the front edge of the door clean and square. You'll use this edge to align the door with the drawer fronts and then trim the back edge to final length.

HINGE BAR. A hardwood hinge bar is attached to the rear edge of the door. As you can see in details 'a' and 'd' on the opposite page, this bar is mortised for the hinge.

After gluing the bar in place, use shims to position the doors. Then mark the hinge location to match the mortise on the case (see the box on opposite page).

Once you've cut the mortises, test fit the hinges to make sure the doors align properly. Remove the doors for now and set the hinges aside until final assembly.

VENEERING. At this point, you're almost ready to veneer the inside face of the doors. But first, I added a seal coat of finish to the raw plywood. This guarantees a better bond with the self-adhesive veneer. Lightly sand the finished doors. Then, add the veneer and use a roller to remove any air bubbles. The bottom two drawings at right show the order you need to follow as you add the veneer and the magnet bar.

MAGNET BAR. After trimming the inside piece of veneer, I attached a magnet bar on the front edge of the doors. This houses the rare-earth magnets that match up with the ones in the case. The box at the bottom of the opposite page shows how to locate the holes.

COMPLETING THE VENEER. With the bar glued in place, you can install the rest of the veneer. Begin by attaching a narrow strip of veneer to the magnet bar. Then you can add veneer to the outside face of the doors. As before, use a roller to press the veneer in place and get a good glue bond. Finally, trim the veneer around all the edges.

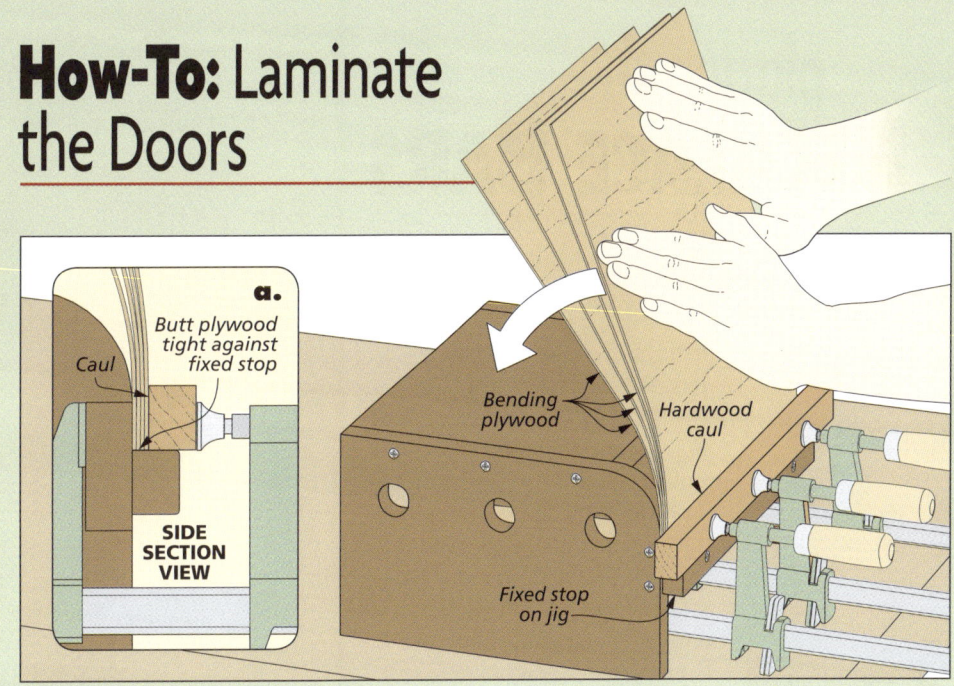

How-To: Laminate the Doors

Bending the Plywood. It's a good idea to do a dry run of the bending process. Start by clamping the sheets at the front edge. Then, use hand pressure to bend the sheets over the curved form. Finally, lay out all the clamps and you're ready to add glue.

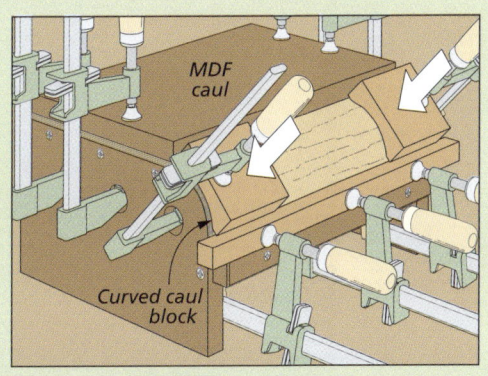

Clamping the Bent Sheets. Use curved cauls to clamp the sheets around the bends and a flat caul to apply even pressure to the top.

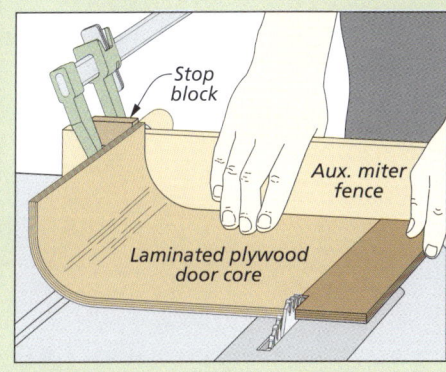

Cutting Door to Final Size. Use a stop block and an auxiliary fence on the miter gauge to hold the door and cut it to size.

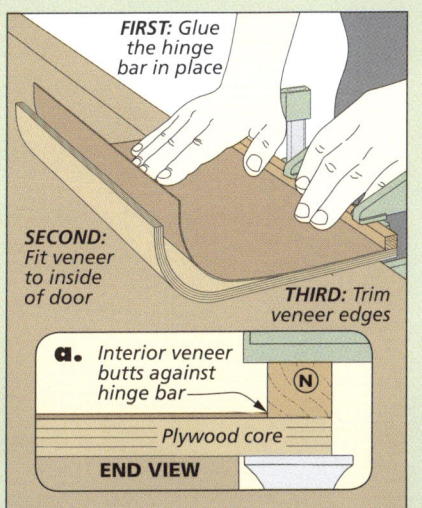

Veneering. After gluing the hinge bar in place, butt the veneer up to the edge and press it into place.

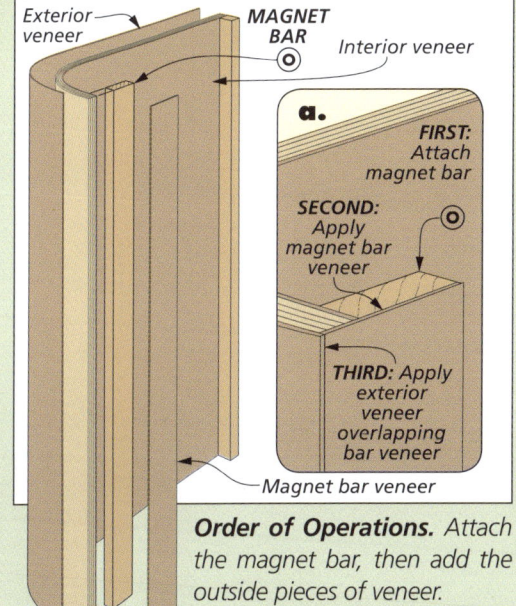

Order of Operations. Attach the magnet bar, then add the outside pieces of veneer.

placing the
NECKLACE BARS

There are only a few more steps needed to complete the jewelry chest. First, you'll need to attach the necklace bars and hangers to the doors. Then, it's just a matter of adding the drawer lining and dividers, installing the doors, and putting a nice finish on the piece.

NECKLACE BARS. The wenge necklace bars hold the attractive brass hangers. The way to make them is shown in the box at right. It starts with an extra-wide blank. This makes it easier and safer to rout the coves on the edges.

Next, you simply rip the bars free and drill the holes for the hangers. I used the band saw to cut a rounded profile to match the inside curve of the doors. A little sanding will help you fine-tune the fit. Finally, just glue them in place on both doors.

FINISH. I finished the piece with wiping varnish to bring out the curl of the maple and the richness of the wenge. After that, I made some drawer dividers and lined the drawers. For those steps, see the tips on the opposite page.

▲ With the necklace bar and brass hangers installed, the doors become extra storage space.

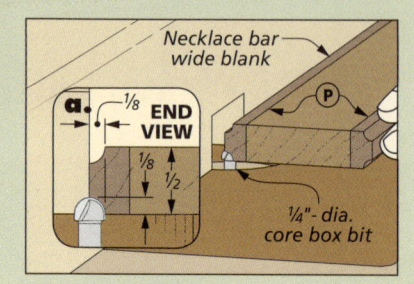

Routing Profiles. Starting with an extra-wide blank makes routing the necklace bars easier and safer.

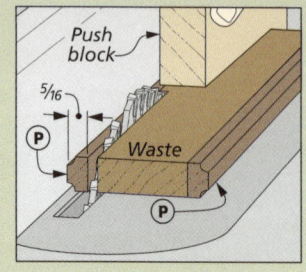

Rip to Width. Ripping the necklace bars to final width is a breeze at the table saw.

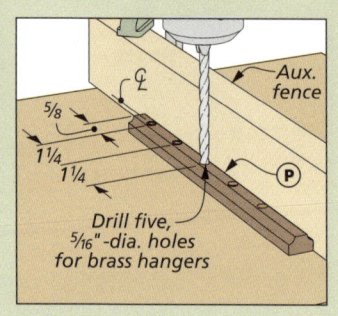

Drilling. With the hole locations laid out on the blank, use a fence to keep them in line.

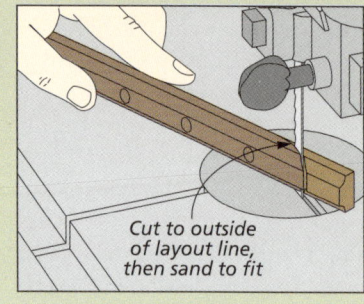

Cutting Curve. After marking the curve on the blank, head to the band saw and cut close to the line.

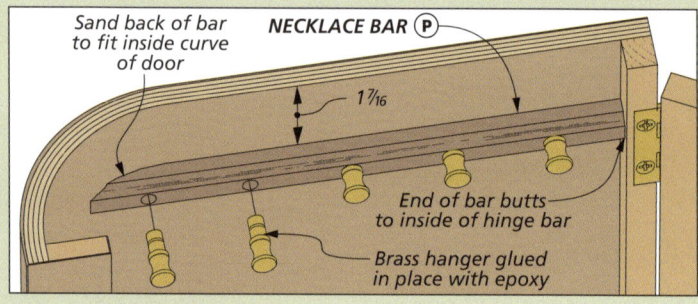

Fitting the Necklace Bar. With the holes drilled and the bar cut to shape, the final adjustments are made by sanding the curve for a gap-free fit before gluing the bar in place.

Materials, Supplies & Cutting Diagram

A Sides (2)	3/8 x 7 1/4 - 12 1/16	
B Back (1)	3/8 x 10 7/8 - 12 1/16	
C Top/Bottom (2)	1/2 x 8 3/4 - 14	
D Front Feet (2)	3/4 x 3 - 3	
E Back Feet (2)	3/4 x 3 - 1 3/4	
F Drawer Sides (12)	1/4 x 1 15/16 - 7	
G Drawer Backs (6)	1/4 x 1 15/16 - 6 15/16	
H Drawer Fronts (6)	1/4 x 1 15/16 - 6 15/16	
I Drawer Bottoms (6)	1/8 ply. - 6 3/4 x 6 15/16	
J Drawer Runners (12)	1/4 x 1/4 - 7	
K Drawer False Fronts (6)	1/4 x 1 15/16 - 7 7/8	
L Drawer Pulls (6)	1/2 x 1/4 - 1 15/16	
M Doors (2)	1/4 ply. - 10 rgh. x 11 15/16	
N Hinge Bars (2)	3/8 x 7/16 - 11 15/16	
O Magnet Bars (2)	1/4 x 3/4 - 11 15/16	
P Necklace Bars (2)	1/2 x 5/16 - 7	

- (18) 1/4"-dia. x 3/4" Fluted Dowels
- (2 Pair) 1 1/2" Brass Hinges
- (8) 1/4"-dia. Rare-Earth Magnets
- (10) 5/16" x 3/8" Brass Knobs

3/4" x 8" - 96" Maple (5.3 Bd. Ft.)

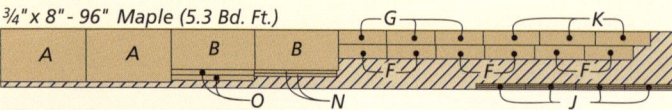

3/4" x 10" - 48" Wenge (3.3 Bd. Ft.)

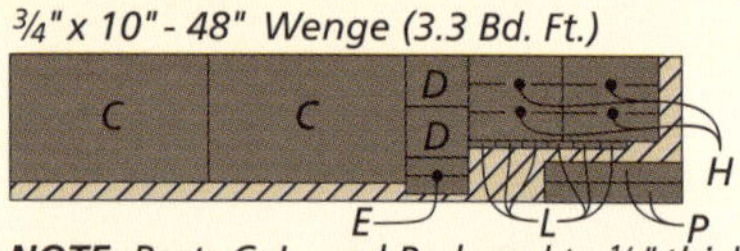

ALSO NEEDED: Four pieces 10 1/2" x 12 1/2" self-adhesive veneer

NOTE: Part P is cut from an extra-wide blank

25" x 25" - 1.5mm Bending Plywood (2 sheets needed)

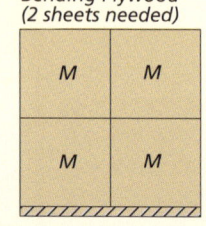

24" x 24" - 1/8" Birch Plywood

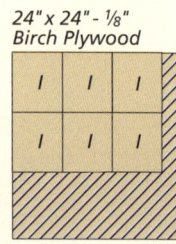

NOTE: Parts C, L, and P planed to 1/2" thick. Part H planed to 1/4" thick. Parts F, G, and K are resawn and planed to 1/4" thick. This yields two of each part shown in the cutting diagram

Enhance Your Jewelry Chest: Liners & Dividers

Drawer Liners

If you want to go one step further and add a few luxuries to your completed jewelry chest, then fabric-covered padding is the place to start. Our online extra includes all you need to know about fabric and padding choices, glue and posterboard options, the tools you need to work with fabric, and a step-by-step guide to help you through lining each drawer.

I used velveteen to line the bottoms of the drawers, as shown in the right photo. But there are a host of other choices for both fabric and padding.

Drawer Dividers

In order to customize the drawers and prevent the contents from sliding around, I made a few different types of drawer dividers. And though the size and number of partitions varied, you can use the same technique to build them all.

You can start by resawing and planing some stock to $\frac{1}{8}$" thick. This thickness is perfect for the small drawers. Then, I used a very simple, half-lap joint to make the different sized dividers. It's easy to cut this joint at the table saw. I also varied the height of the dividers for different contents.

Ring Cushions

Making a special area in the jewelry chest to hold rings is a nice touch. It's also an easy process. I found most people prefer to have rings in a removeable tray, so that's the place to start. The online plans have the details.

Once you've built the tray, all you need to do is glue rolls of padding onto posterboard and then wrap the rolls with fabric. And there's no need to worry about sewing. All the materials were glued in place using specially formulated glue designed to instantly bond fabric.

Woodsmith GO ONLINE EXTRAS

For detailed plans of the optional drawer liners, dividers, and ring cushion, visit our website at Woodsmith.com

working with tools

make it round on the
Router Table

Who says you can't teach an old router table new tricks? Here are a couple of handy techniques that will expand its repertoire.

The router table is without a doubt, a versatile tool. Rabbets, dadoes, grooves, tenons, box joints, moldings and profiled edges — you name it, the router table can usually handle it. However, you might think that turning to the router table to shape round workpieces sounds like a stretch.

Pardon the pun, but the truth is that there are a couple of very straightforward router table techniques that allow you to create perfectly shaped circular panels or dowels. I'll share the basics of each one with you.

TURNING CIRCLES

You may be familiar with the technique for using a router fixed in a trammel to "spin" a perfectly circular workpiece. It's a great way to shape round tabletops or other large, circular pieces. Making round workpieces on the router table works similarly, only here the router and bit are stationary while the workpiece rotates.

A SIMPLE JIG. The key is a barebones jig made up of an auxiliary tabletop, a swing arm, and a stop (lower left drawing). Construction of the jig is very easy. All of the pieces can be made from ¼" hardboard.

To accommodate the swing arm, I sized the top to overhang the sides and front of the table. Then I laid out and drilled a 1"-dia. hole for the router bit. After drilling a series of pivot pin holes in the swing arm, it's attached

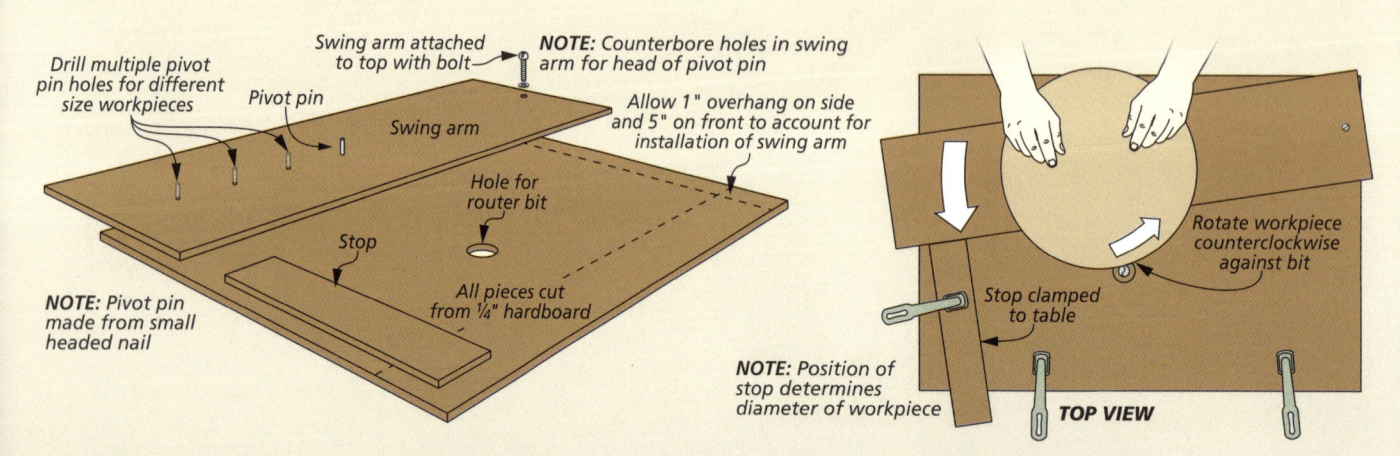

Drill multiple pivot pin holes for different size workpieces

Pivot pin

Swing arm attached to top with bolt

NOTE: Counterbore holes in swing arm for head of pivot pin

Swing arm

Allow 1" overhang on side and 5" on front to account for installation of swing arm

Hole for router bit

Stop

All pieces cut from ¼" hardboard

NOTE: Pivot pin made from small headed nail

Rotate workpiece counterclockwise against bit

Stop clamped to table

NOTE: Position of stop determines diameter of workpiece

TOP VIEW

44   Woodsmith   No. 197

near the front left corner of the top with a bolt, washers, and nut. The stop is just a narrow cutoff.

SET UP. A look at the drawings on the opposite page and a brief explanation are all it takes to understand how the jig works. To set up, a straight bit is installed in the router table (I like to use a spiral flute up-cut bit) and the auxiliary top is positioned over it and clamped down. Then, after drilling a small centered hole in the rough-shaped workpiece, it's placed over the pivot pin (a nail) in the swing arm. Finally, you'll clamp the stop in place to limit the travel of the swing arm and produce the desired diameter.

THE SPIN. With everything ready to go, you simply turn on the router and pivot the arm and workpiece toward the bit. When the arm contacts the stop and the bit is engaged, you slowly and steadily rotate the workpiece counterclockwise. After a full turn or more, retract the arm with the trimmed workpiece.

A FEW TIPS. It often works best to sneak up on the final diameter by trimming the workpiece incrementally, especially when routing solid wood. You'll get a smoother end result. You simply move the stop back a little bit between passes.

Be sure to maintain a good grip with both hands as you rotate the workpiece. And you'll need to apply constant forward pressure to keep the arm in contact with the stop. I'll usually make a couple of revolutions to be certain I've cut to full depth all around the perimeter of the circle.

MAKING DOWELS

Making dowels of many standard diameters (down to $\frac{3}{8}$") in any kind of wood is as simple as routing a roundover — or rather, four roundovers. In a nutshell, a square blank is "turned" round by knocking off all four edges (corners) with roundover cuts.

GET READY. I'll illustrate with an example. You start by milling an extra-long, square blank matching the diameter of the dowel you want to make — let's say $\frac{3}{4}$". Then you install a roundover bit in the router table that corresponds to the dowel's radius. This would be a $\frac{3}{8}$" bit.

Next, I add a long auxiliary fence to the router table. This simply provides the support you need to make longer dowels, as you'll see (drawing below).

The fence is aligned flush with the bearing of the bit. The height of the bit is adjusted to align with the fence's base (detail 'b').

MAKE A DOWEL. When you make the four roundover cuts, you need to maintain square reference edges to keep the blank from rolling. You can do this by not routing a short section at both ends of the blank. I like to mark a reference line about 2" to either side of the bit to show me where to start and stop the roundover cuts.

That's the hard part. The rest is easy. With the router turned on, align the left end of the blank with the start line, pivot it into the bit and feed it slowly until the right end reaches the stop line (detail 'a'). Then give the blank a quarter turn and repeat the process.

When routing larger diameter dowels, you'll get a better result by working down to round. Set the fence for a partial cut and then move it after a series of passes.

Once all four edges have been rounded, the ends of the blank can be cut off. The dowel will be perfectly round or pretty close to it. A minor sanding will be all you need to smooth the surface. **W**

▲ It's easy to make dowels in a variety of sizes from any type of wood.

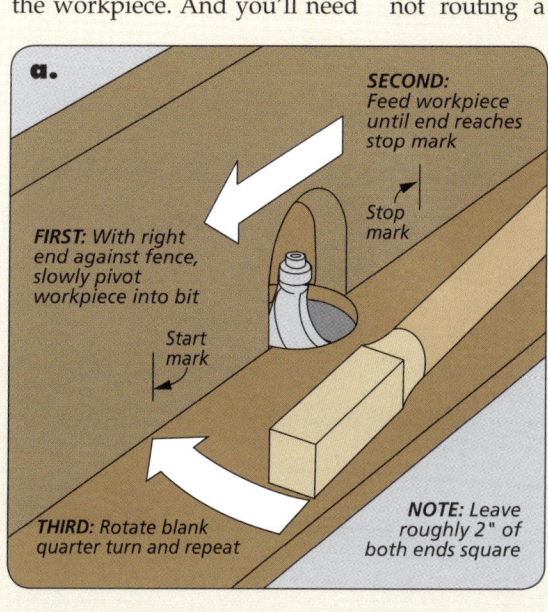

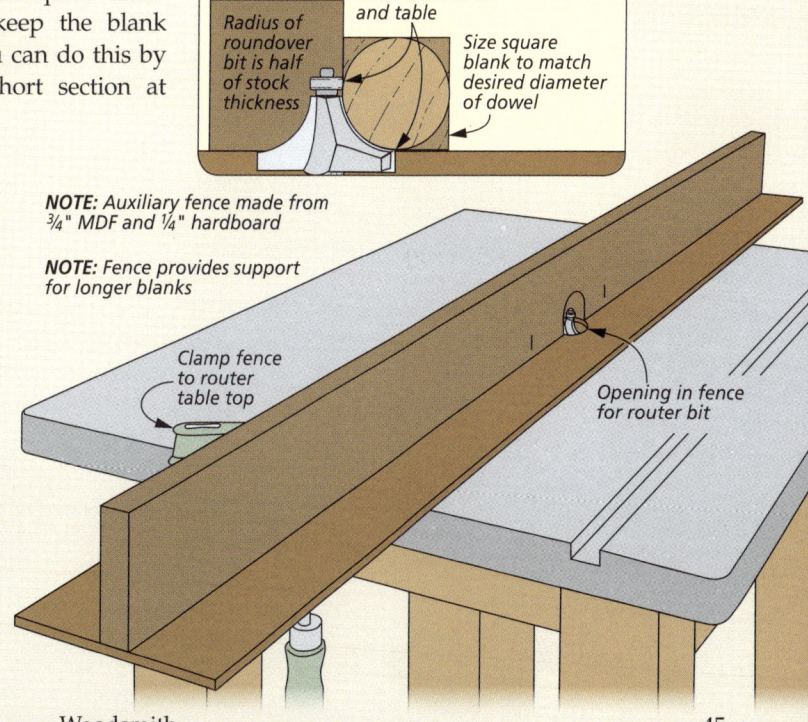

finishing room

great color with
Water-Based Dyes

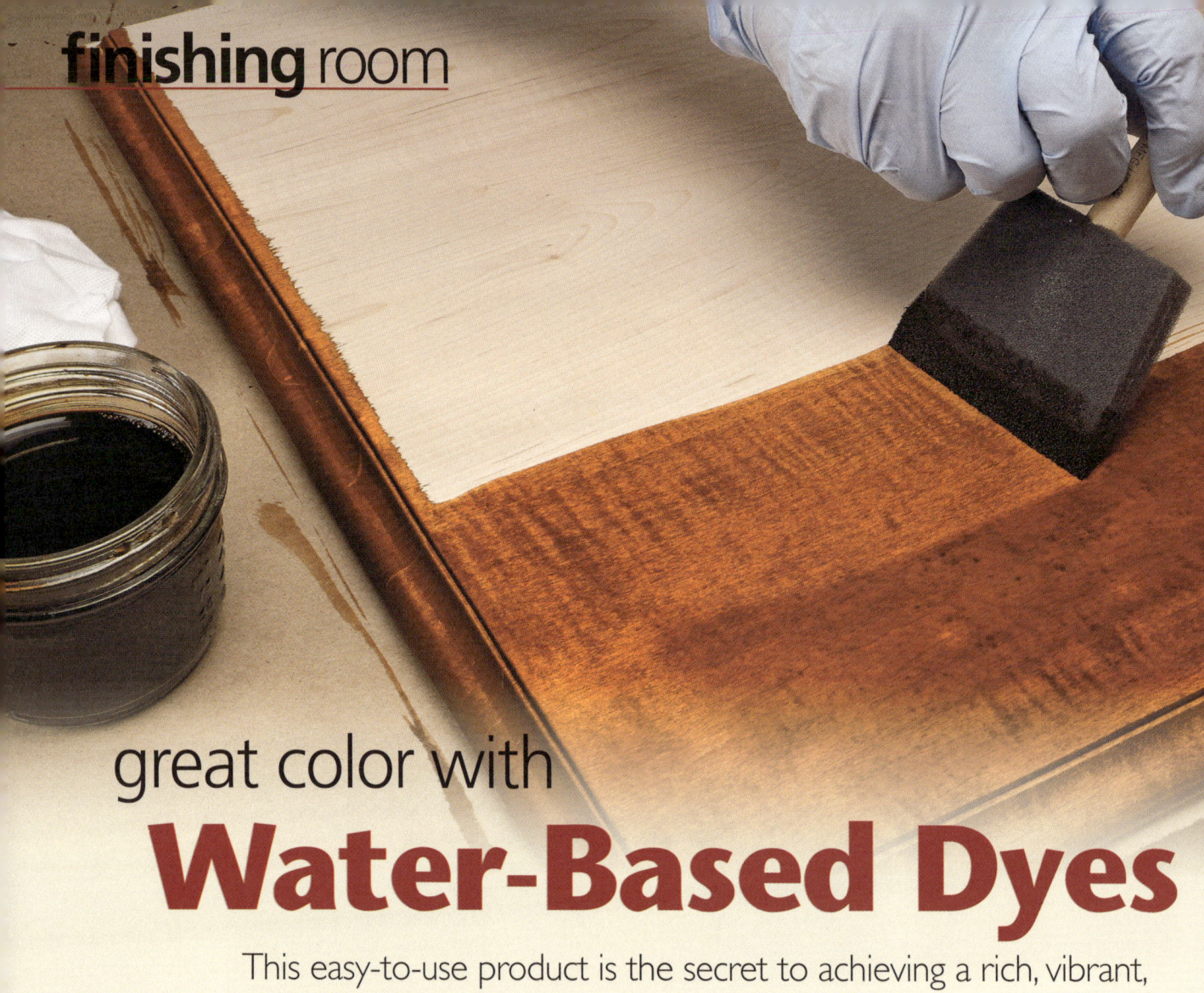

This easy-to-use product is the secret to achieving a rich, vibrant, and natural-looking color on your next project.

▼ Water-based dyes can be mixed from powders or liquid concentrates (see Sources on page 51).

Staining is often a finishing step that can make or break the appearance of a project. And unfortunately there's no magic bullet that will guarantee a good outcome. But the more options you have to choose from, the better the chance of getting top-notch results. This is why I keep water-based dyes on hand.

WHY? A water-based dye can give you a look that's very different from a typical oil stain. Oil stains contain large pigment particles that are simply suspended in a solvent. When the stain is applied, the pigments essentially sit on the surface of the wood to give it color. However, this can sometimes make it difficult to produce a deep, natural color without obscuring the figure of the wood.

Water-based dyes work differently. The dye particles are very small and actually go into solution — like sugar in water. This allows the water to carry the dye particles deep into the wood fibers. The resulting look is more transparent and natural. You end up with a very rich, penetrating color that still lets the figure of the wood show through.

As you can see in the photo above, a dye can really "pop" the beautiful figure of woods such as curly or birdseye maple. And the penetrating nature of a dye makes it a good choice when a deep, dark color is required. A good example is the ebonized effect used on the decorative panels of the folding table on page 24.

MIX IT UP. You'll find dyes that are formulated for use with different solvents — water, alcohol, and oil-soluble types. However, because of their slower drying time, water-based dyes are by far the easiest to use, especially on large surfaces and projects.

A water-based dye can be mixed from a powder or a liquid concentrate (photo at left). The dyes come in a wide range of colors — both wood tones and "pure" colors. Two or more can be combined to create virtually any shade in the rainbow.

When you mix a powdered dye, always use precise measurements and keep track of the formula. This way, you can easily match the same color again, if necessary. For me, it's easiest to simply measure by volume, but you can also weigh out the powder.

Although the instructions on the dye packet provide a recommended concentration, this is just a loose guideline. The base dye color can be lightened or darkened by changing the proportions of dye and water (photo below). Coming up with the desired color can involve experimentation. You'll find that a small amount of dye goes a long way.

The dye powder will dissolve better in hot water. If any powder doesn't dissolve, you'll want to strain it out before applying the dye to the wood.

APPLICATION. Applying a water-based dye requires a slightly different technique than that used for an oil stain, but it's just as easy. The How-To box below illustrates the basic routine.

The first thing you need to know is that, as you might guess, a water-based dye can raise the grain and leave a fuzzy surface. The solution to this drawback is to beat the dye to the punch by pre-raising the grain. Lightly dampen the surface, let it dry, and then sand away the raised fibers with 220-grit sandpaper.

A water-based dye can be brushed, wiped, or sprayed on. I like to use a foam brush (main photo). You can apply the dye quickly and it's easier to get into all the nooks and crannies.

When applying a water-based dye, the goal is to avoid streaks and lap marks that result from not maintaining a wet edge. The relatively slow drying rate helps you accomplish this. The trick is to flood the surface and keep it wet until the area you're working on is completely coated. Then you wipe off the excess dye with a clean cloth. You'll get consistent penetration and even color.

The color can be further darkened by applying a second coat once the first coat has dried thoroughly (30 minutes). Or, you can modify the color by applying a different shade over the first.

A TOPCOAT. Dyes don't have an oil binder like pigment stains. So when the water evaporates, the color will appear drab. But once the topcoat is applied, the rich, vibrant look will return.

Water-based dyes are compatible with most topcoats. The exception is a water-based finish. Applying a water-based topcoat can redissolve the dye and leave a streaky mess. If you want to use a water-based finish, you'll need to seal in the dye with a coat of shellac or wiping varnish.

So the next time you're debating the best color for a project, consider using a dye. I think you'll be glad you did.

▲ Applying a topcoat brings back the vibrant color you observed while the dye was still wet.

▲ The photo shows how the color of the dye is dependent on the concentration of the mixture. The left sample is ¼ teaspoon to 8 ounces of water while the right sample uses a full teaspoon.

How-To: Apply a Water-Based Dye

▲ Before applying the dye, it's a good idea to pre-raise the grain by dampening the surface.

▲ A thorough sanding with 220-grit sandpaper will then prevent the dye from raising the grain again.

▲ Once an area is completely coated and still wet, wipe the excess dye from the surface.

details of craftsmanship

techniques for Bending Wood

Adding curves to your designs is just a matter of using the right method for the project.

Making curved parts using the bent lamination technique begins by cutting thin strips

The jewelry chest project that begins on page 34 features a pair of attractive curved-front doors. It's a good example of the dramatic effect adding curves to a project can have. For that project, I laminated bending plywood around a form. But there are other options for adding bends and curves to your work. Here's a quick look at a few of the different techniques you can put to use in your shop.

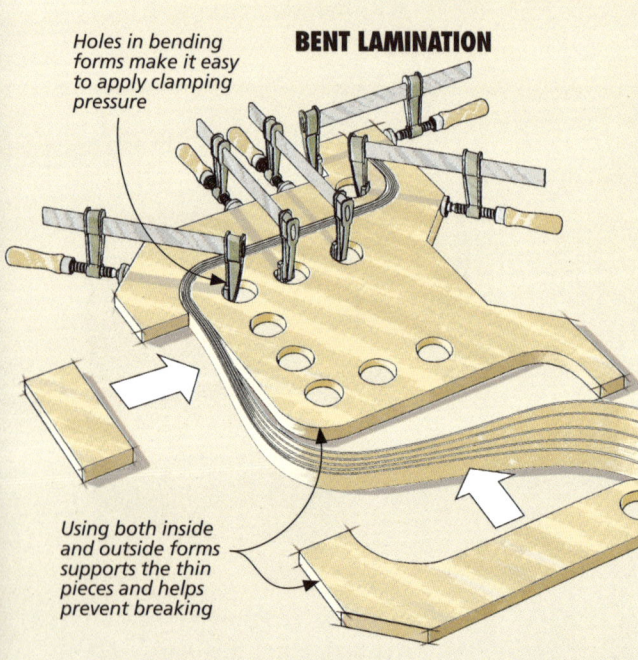

BENT LAMINATION

Holes in bending forms make it easy to apply clamping pressure

Using both inside and outside forms supports the thin pieces and helps prevent breaking

BENT LAMINATION

Bending plywood is a great choice for wide project parts, like the doors on the jewelry chest. But a similar technique can be used to bend thin laminations of hardwood in a bending form. By resawing hardwood stock into very thin slices, usually $\frac{1}{16}$" to $\frac{1}{8}$" thick, you can stack the individual pieces and glue them together to retain the desired shape.

The bent lamination technique can be used for all sorts of applications. It's perfect for making small parts like simple, curved door handles. But it can also be adapted for more complex shapes.

BENEFITS. One big advantage of a laminated part over one simply cut to shape is the strength of the laminated piece. With a part made using this technique, you're always assured of strong, long-grain wood throughout the length of the part.

Another reason to choose bent lamination over other options is the variety of shapes you can create. For instance, if you need a very tight-radius curve all you need to do is reduce the thickness of the plies to accommodate just about any bend. Making a 1"-radius bend is difficult with any other technique. But it's a breeze with thin laminations.

Finally, when it comes to making multiple parts, there's no other method that comes close. Once you've built a form, you can turn out identical parts in whatever quantity you need.

HOW IT'S DONE. It all starts with cutting the thin strips. I prefer to cut the plies for bent laminations on the band saw, like in the drawing above. But you can also cut the pieces at the table saw. The goal is to keep them a uniform thickness. A simple mark on the end or edge of the workpiece helps you reassemble the strips in sequence to preserve the grain pattern.

Now, all you need is a bending form. I like to use MDF to make the forms because it's easy to work with and has no grain direction. This is a big plus when shaping curved forms.

Using inside and outside forms, like those shown in the drawing at left, almost guarantees a gap-free lamination. They apply equalized clamping pressure to the whole length of the lamination. It's also a good idea to wax the forms to prevent the glue from sticking.

KERF BENDING

A popular technique for making curves in plywood is kerf bending. As the name implies, a series of saw kerfs are cut on the inside face of the section to be bent. The kerfs are cut nearly through the final core ply, stopping just short of the veneer (detail 'a'). This creates a relief space which allows the veneer to bend.

This technique borrows a page from the finish carpenter's book. It's often used in custom-made built-ins or stairways. But it also has a place in furniture building. You'll often find kerf-bent pieces in large furniture like wardrobes and credenzas. It's also a popular technique for making table aprons.

CONSIDERATIONS. Kerf bending is probably the easiest way to add curves to a project. It doesn't require any special equipment or complicated jigs. All you need is a table saw and some cabinet-grade plywood.

On the down side, the inside of the kerf-bent piece will show the unattractive kerfs. Of course, you can cover that face with veneer or a number of other options, but it does add to the work.

SPACING. How far apart you cut the kerfs depends on the radius of the curve you want to create. The drawings at right give you an idea of how the radius of the bend affects the spacing of the kerfs.

FIXING THE BEND. Unlike bent laminations, kerf-bent pieces won't retain their shape. To fix the curved piece in position I usually attach it to a curved framework or other pieces in the case.

Kerf bending and bent laminations both have a variety of uses in furniture making. But if your project requires bending solid wood, the box below describes how to do it with steam. **W**

A tight radius bend requires the kerfs be placed close together

Larger radius curves have more distance between saw kerfs

Cutting the kerfs is a simple matter at the table saw

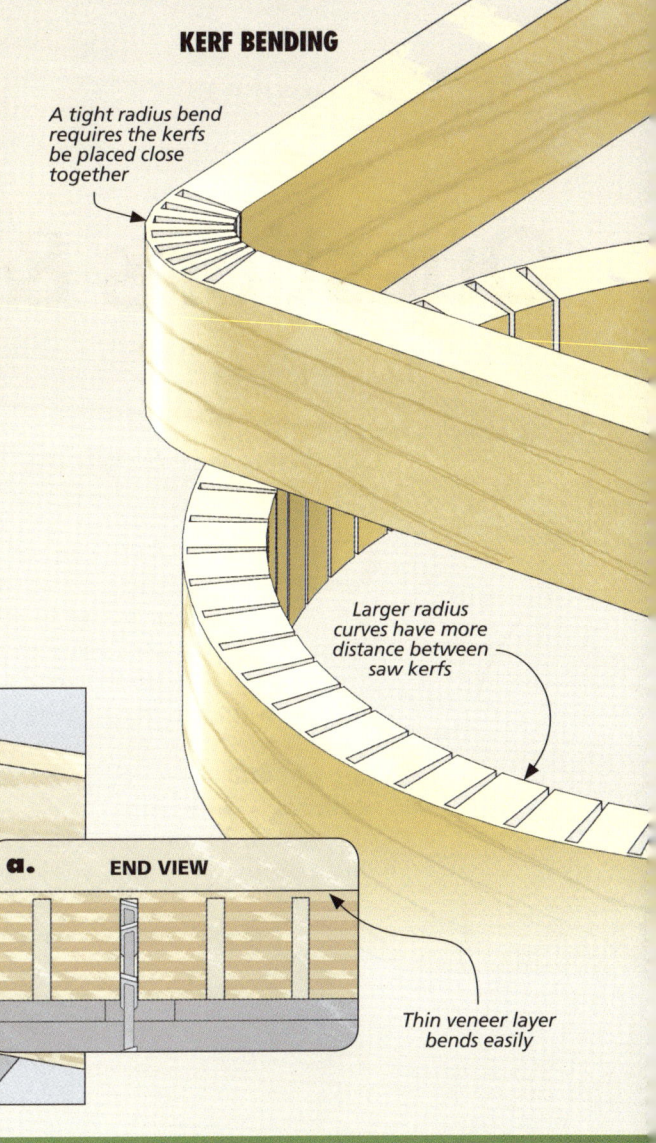

a. END VIEW

Thin veneer layer bends easily

Worth a Look: Steam Bending

Steam bending has a long tradition in woodworking. The concept is to heat up and add moisture to the wood until the cells become elastic enough to bend in a form.

The most popular method is to enclose the workpiece in a steam chamber. As the drawing at right shows, a fairly simple setup can be made from common kitchen items like a tea kettle and a hotplate. But there are also dedicated steamers available if you intend to do a lot of bending.

This technique is used to bend along the long grain of the wood. The choice of wood is also important. Some woods like oak and ash bend very well. Others, like maple, are a little more stubborn.

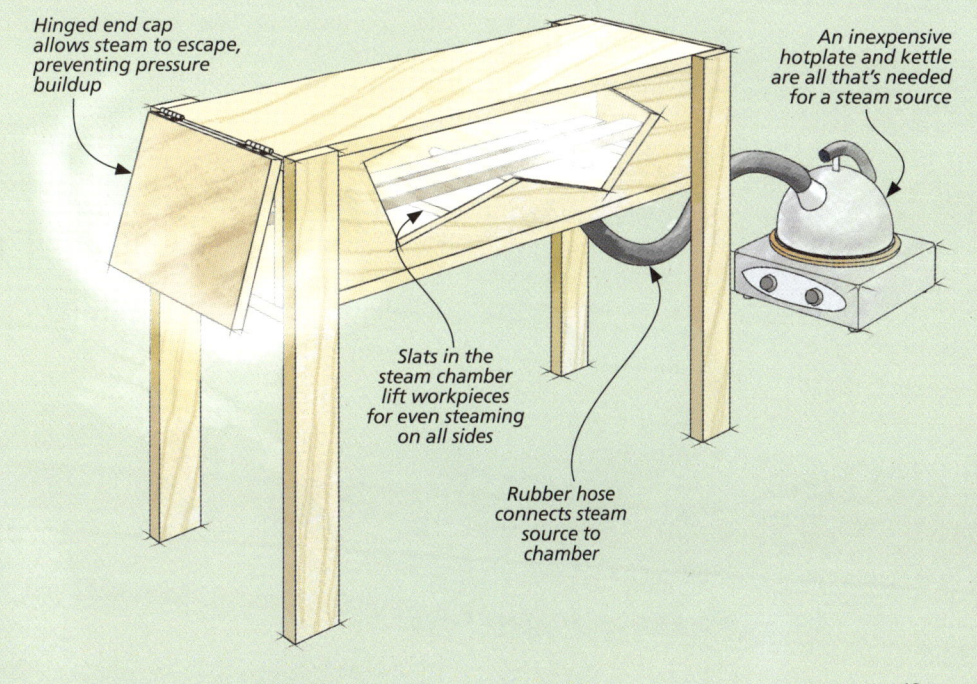

Hinged end cap allows steam to escape, preventing pressure buildup

An inexpensive hotplate and kettle are all that's needed for a steam source

Slats in the steam chamber lift workpieces for even steaming on all sides

Rubber hose connects steam source to chamber

in the mailbox

Questions & Answers

Removing Broken Screws

Q I broke off the head of a screw while installing a hinge. I need to put a new screw in the same location, but I don't know how to get the old one out without damaging the wood. Is there any reliable way to do this?

Larry Pedersen
Rolfe, Iowa

A I think it's safe to say we've all been there. Broken screws and stripped heads are common occurrences. Fortunately, there are a couple of inexpensive tools that offer solutions. One grabs the screw body and backs it out. The other drills a plug (containing the screw) out of the wood.

SCREW EXTRACTORS. For #10 or larger screws, I like to use an extractor bit to remove the shaft of the screw. As you can see in the photos below, these bits have a tapered, counterclockwise thread. This thread allows the bit to bite into the screw and back it out.

The key to making it all work is to use the drilling end of the bit to drill a small pilot hole in the remnant of the screw. You'll need to reverse the drill to do this. Then, reverse the bit and place the tip of the extractor in the pilot hole. Keep firm downward pressure on the drill and keep the drill speed very low as you extract the screw.

If the extractor doesn't bite, remove the bit from the drill. Then use a hammer to give it a light tap in the hole.

CUTTING A PLUG. In the case of smaller diameter screws, it can be difficult to get a bite on the shaft. In that event, a plug-cutting extractor is the answer. The sawtooth bit shown in the photos above fits into your drill and removes the wood surrounding the screw. Then you can simply pop out the plug and glue in a small dowel of the same diameter (the bits are sold in standard sizes). The drawing above shows the process.

The coarse teeth can make it hard to get the cut started without the tip of the bit "wandering". An easy fix is to make a guide by drilling a hole matching the diameter of the extractor in a piece of scrap. Then all you need to do is hold the guide in place in line with the screw and drill the plug.

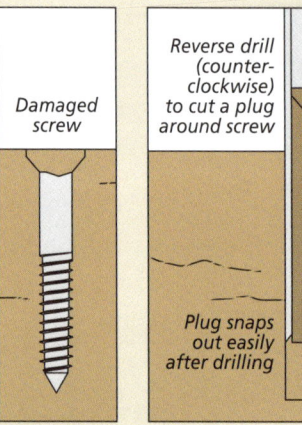

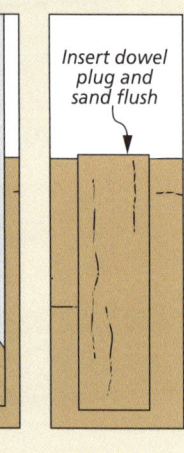

▼ These screw extractors can save the day when you strip or break a screw.

Reverse screw threads extract screw

Drill broken or stripped screw with this end

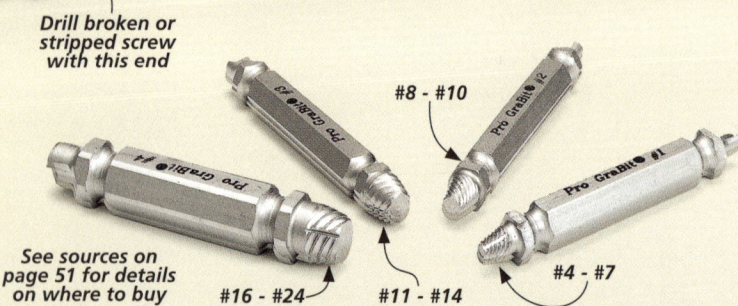

Sawtooth design drills a plug

Damaged screw

Reverse drill (counter-clockwise) to cut a plug around screw

Insert dowel plug and sand flush

Plug snaps out easily after drilling

See sources on page 51 for details on where to buy

#16 - #24   #11 - #14   #8 - #10   #4 - #7

Do you have any questions for us?

If you have a question related to woodworking techniques, tools, finishing, hardware, or accessories, we'd like to hear from you.

Just write down your question and mail it to us: Woodsmith Q&A, 2200 Grand Avenue, Des Moines, Iowa 50312. Or you can email us the question at: woodsmith@woodsmith.com.

Please include your full name, address, and daytime telephone number in case we have questions.

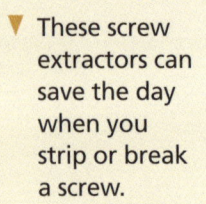

hardware & supplies
Sources

TOOL HOLDERS
Any of the tool holders on page 12 will instantly add storage space to your shop. All of the items shown in this article are available from *Rockler*. This includes the drill press tool collector (93386), the router bit storage rack (32602), the lathe tool holder (31107), and the *Pack Rack Tool Apron* (41486).

BOOKMARKS / COASTERS
You won't need any hardware to build the bookmark, pencil box, or coaster set on page 16. And you'll probably be able to find most of the wood you need for these projects in your scrap bin.

To finish the bookmark and the box, I wiped on a coat of *General Finishes' Seal-a-Cell* and then sprayed on a couple coats of lacquer. But for the coasters, I wanted a more water-resistant finish. So I applied three coats of polyurethane.

FOLDING TABLE
The folding table on page 24 requires just a few hardware items. You'll need some tabletop fasteners (34215), two pairs of brass hinges for the legs (32978), and a pair of sewing cabinet hinges for the top (26765). I was able to purchase all of these items from *Rockler*.

The two-tone finish was achieved by first staining the slats with an ebony dye and then staining the rest of the table with a mix of three parts *Zar* stain (cherry) and one part *WoodKote Jel'd Stain* (cherry). Then the table was finished with two coats of lacquer.

JEWELRY CHEST
Choosing the right hardware is important for any project, but particularly so for a fine project like the jewelry chest on page 34. The brass hinges (32908) came from *Rockler*. The brass knobs (01A01.10) used for the necklace hangers and the rare-earth magnets (99K31.01) were purchased from *Lee Valley*.

The bending plywood used to make the doors is also available from *Lee Valley* (03A10.04). And we purchased the adhesive-backed, curly maple veneer from *VeneerSupplies.com*.

To finish the jewelry chest, we simply wiped on a coat of *General Finishes' Seal-a-Cell* and followed up with two coats of sprayed lacquer.

WATER-BASED DYES
For clear, vivid colors, it's hard to beat water-based dyes. You can find dyes in a wide variety of wood tones as well as bright colors, in both powder and liquid form. They are sold through a number of the woodworking retailers shown in the margin at right.

SCREW EXTRACTORS
Few things in woodworking are more frustrating than breaking off the head of a screw in a nearly completed project. Fortunately, the screw extractors shown on page 50 can often save the day. The *GraBit* screw extractor set (35498) will handle several sizes of screws. It's sold by *Rockler*. The plug-cutting extractors are also sold by *Rockler*, in three individual sizes.

Online Customer Service
Click on *Magazine Customer Service* at **www.woodsmith.com**
- Access your account status
- Change your mailing or email address
- Pay your bill
- Renew your subscription
- Tell us if you've missed an issue
- Find out if your payment has been received

MAIL ORDER SOURCES
Project supplies may be ordered from the following companies:

Woodsmith Store
800-444-7527
Water-Based Dyes

Rockler
800-279-4441
rockler.com
Folding Table Hardware, Screw Extractors, Tool Holders, Water-Based Dyes

Lee Valley
800-871-8158
leevalley.com
Bending Plywood, Brass Knobs, Rare-Earth Magnets, Water-Based Dyes

Van Dyke's Restorers
800-558-1234
vandykes.com
Brass Jewelry Chest Hinges

VeneerSupplies.com
Adhesive-Backed Veneer

W.D. Lockwood
866-293-8913
wdlockwood.com
Water-Based Dyes

Woodcraft
800-225-1153
woodcraft.com
Rare-Earth Magnets, Water-Based Dyes

Woodworker's Supply
800-645-9292
woodworker.com
Water-Based Dyes

Keep it All Organized !

Woodsmith Binders

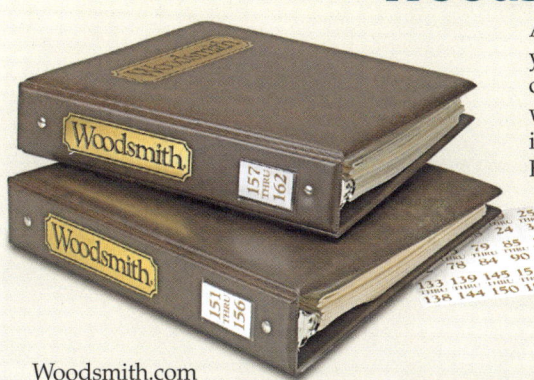

As you build your *Woodsmith* library, here's a way to keep your issues organized. Each binder features durable vinyl covers and easy-to-read perforated number tags. Snap rings with a quick-open lever make it easy to insert and remove issues. And there's an extra pocket inside for storing notes. Each binder holds a full year (6 issues) of *Woodsmith*.

Visit **Woodsmith.com** to order
or call **1-800-444-7527**.

Woodsmith Binder
○ **WB** (*Holds 6 issues*).................$12.95

looking inside
Final Details

▲ *Gift Projects.* The idea is simple — glue up small pieces of contrasting woods, then cut "slices" from the blank to create any of these three eye-catching projects. We'll take you through the process in the article starting on page 16.

▲ *Jewelry Chest.* Curved doors, curly maple, and wenge accents combine to create a stylish home for jewelry or any collection of small items. Turn to page 34 to find everything you need to build the project.

Folding Table. ▶ The small footprint of this table makes it suitable for just about any room in the house. But by folding out the legs and top, it quickly doubles in size. Complete plans begin on page 24.

5 Tools to **MAKE YOU** a **BETTER** Woodworker

Face Frames: The Secret to **SUPER-STRONG** Cabinet Construction

Woodsmith

Woodsmith.com

Vol. 33 / No. 198

Cherry
ARMOIRE

> **Rock-Solid Frame & Panel Construction**

> **Versatile Storage Options**

> **Simple Moldings Add Elegant Details**

Also:
Build It Right: From Paper Plan to Perfect Project

Clean Cuts Every Time — 3 Must-Have Table Saw Blades

A Publication of August Home Publishing

looking inside

Table of Contents

from our readers
Tips & Techniques 4

all about
Clean Cuts Every Time 8
You only need three blades to get smooth, tearout-free cuts from your table saw.

tools of the trade
5 Top Hand Tools 10
Every power tool woodworker should have these five hand tools to get top-notch results.

jigs and fixtures
The Versatile Fast Joint Jig 12
With a simple jig and a set of templates, you can make a wide range of decorative joints.

working with tools
Shop Tips for Tight Dovetails ... 14
Perfect-fitting half-blind dovetails are a snap when you follow these handy tips and tricks.

tips from our shop
Shop Notebook 28

techniques from our shop
From Plans to Perfect Projects ... 42
Here's what you need to know to get the best results from any set of project plans.

finishing room
Fast, Foolproof Finishing 46
Laying down a smooth, even finish starts with the right tool. Here's what we use.

details of craftsmanship
The Secret of Face Frames 48
Face frames are the key to rock-solid cabinet construction that looks great.

hardware and supplies
Sources 51

Entry Bench page 16

Craftsman Lamp page 22

projects

weekend project
Classic Entry Bench..........16
The casual look of this small bench comes from its graceful curves and sculpted seat. To ensure it lasts for years to come, it's built with traditional mortise and tenon joinery.

designer series project
Craftsman-Style Lamp 22
Stained glass panels set in solid-wood frames give this lamp an unbeatable look. The best part is that creating the stained glass panels is surprisingly simple to do.

heirloom project
Cherry Armoire 30
This stylish armoire has a lot going for it. First, with the two-tone finish and simple details, it looks great. Second, there's loads of storage. And finally, the construction is quick and easy.

Cherry Armoire page 30

editor's note
Sawdust

While I'm always happy about the projects and department articles we feature in each issue of *Woodsmith*, there's one new project development I'm really excited about. And that's the release of a DVD collection of the first four seasons of the *Woodsmith Shop* television show.

Each season consists of 13 episodes (30-minute shows) that are on a pair of DVDs. If you've watched the shows, you know we mention the free plans, articles, and extra videos that are available online. But we've included all that information on a separate CD (that's included with the DVD set). So, everything that was shown on the original TV show and online, is now in the boxed set.

Now, you can watch any episode at your convenience. If you didn't catch something the first time, it's a simple matter to view any segment of a show as often as you'd like. You can find out how to order the complete DVD set (or individual seasons) by turning to Sources on page 51.

Finally, we're closing in on the publication of our 200th issue, which you'll receive in a few months. We're working on making the issue extra special. But rest assured, it will still feature the same great projects, techniques, and tips that you've come to expect. Many of you have been with us from the beginning, while for some it's only been a few years. For that, the entire staff and I would like to thank you for your support and encouragement. We couldn't have done it without you.

Bryan

STATEMENT OF OWNERSHIP, MANAGEMENT, AND CIRCULATION
(Required by 39 U.S.C. 3685)

1. Publication Title: Woodsmith. 2. Publication No.: 0164-4114 3. Filing Date: October 3, 2011. 4. Issue Frequency: Bimonthly. 5. No. of issues published annually: 6 (six). 6. Annual subscription price: $24.95. 7. Complete mailing address of known office of publication: 2200 Grand Avenue, Des Moines, (Polk County), Iowa 50312-5306. 8. Complete mailing address of the headquarters or general business offices of the publisher: 2200 Grand Avenue, Des Moines, (Polk County), Iowa 50312-5306. 9. Full names and complete mailing addresses of publisher, editor, and managing editor: Publisher: Donald B. Peschke, 2200 Grand Avenue, Des Moines, Iowa 50312; Editor: Bryan Nelson, 2200 Grand Avenue, Des Moines, Iowa 50312; Managing Editor: Vincent Ancona, 2200 Grand Avenue, Des Moines, Iowa 50312. 10. Owner: August Home Publishing Company, 2200 Grand Avenue, Des Moines, Iowa 50312; Donald B. Peschke, 2200 Grand Avenue, Des Moines, Iowa 50312. 11. Known bondholders, mortgagees, and other security holders owning 1 percent or more of total amount of bonds, mortgages or other securities: None. 12. (Does not apply.) 13. Publication Title: Woodsmith. 14. Issue Date for Circulation Data Below: August/September 2011 15. Extent and nature of circulation:

	Average no. copies each issue during preceding 12 months	Average no. copies of single issue published nearest to filing date
A. Total number of copies (net press run)	234,030	230,709
B. Paid circulation (by mail and outside the mail):		
1. Paid/requested outside-county mail subscriptions stated on PS Form 3541	191,040	191,102
2. Mailed in-county paid subscriptions stated on PS Form 3541	0	0
3. Paid distrib. outside the mails (sales through dealers/carriers, street vendors, counter sales, and other paid distrib. outside USPS)	13,550	11,941
4. Paid distribution by other classes of mail through the USPS	0	0
C. Total paid distribution	204,590	203,043
D. Free or nominal rate distribution (by mail and outside the mail)		
1. Free or nominal rate outside-county copies included on PS form 3541	169	182
2. Free or nominal rate in-county copies included on PS Form 3541	0	0
3. Free or nominal rate copies mailed at other classes through the USPS	0	0
4. Free or nominal rate distribution outside the mail (carriers or other means)	0	0
E. Total free or nominal rate distribution	169	182
F. Total distribution	204,759	203,225
G. Copies not distributed	29,271	27,484
H. Total	234,030	230,709
I. Percentage Paid and/or requested circulation	99.92%	99.91%

16. Publication of Statement of Ownership. Will be printed in the Jan. 2012 (#198) issue of this publication.
17. I certify that all information furnished on this form is true and complete. (signed) Bryan Nelson, Editor

On occasion, we allow companies whose products and services may be of interest to you to send advertising mail to our subscribers. We are careful to choose ethical companies that have information of genuine interest to our subscribers. Most of our subscribers appreciate these materials. However, if you prefer to have your name deleted from the mailing list made available to other companies, please write to us at Woodsmith, 2200 Grand Avenue, Des Moines, IA 50312

from our readers

Tips & Techniques

Adjustable Sanding Jig

There are times when I need to sand a miter cut on a workpiece to get a tighter fit. The trouble is, it can be difficult to hold the workpiece at the correct angle to the sander. So I built the sanding jig in the photo. This fence gives me better support for my workpiece than a miter gauge could, which makes the miter more precise.

The base of the jig is a piece of plywood with a radius cut on one corner (drawing below). On the underside of the base, I attached a miter bar to register the sander to the table.

In one corner of the base, I attached an adjustable pivoting fence. One end of the fence is bolted to the base with a carriage bolt. The other end is held in place by a three-piece clamp tightened with a knob and carriage bolt.

You can use a protractor or a bevel gauge to adjust the fence to the angle that you need to sand. Then slide the workpiece against the fence for an accurate sanded miter.

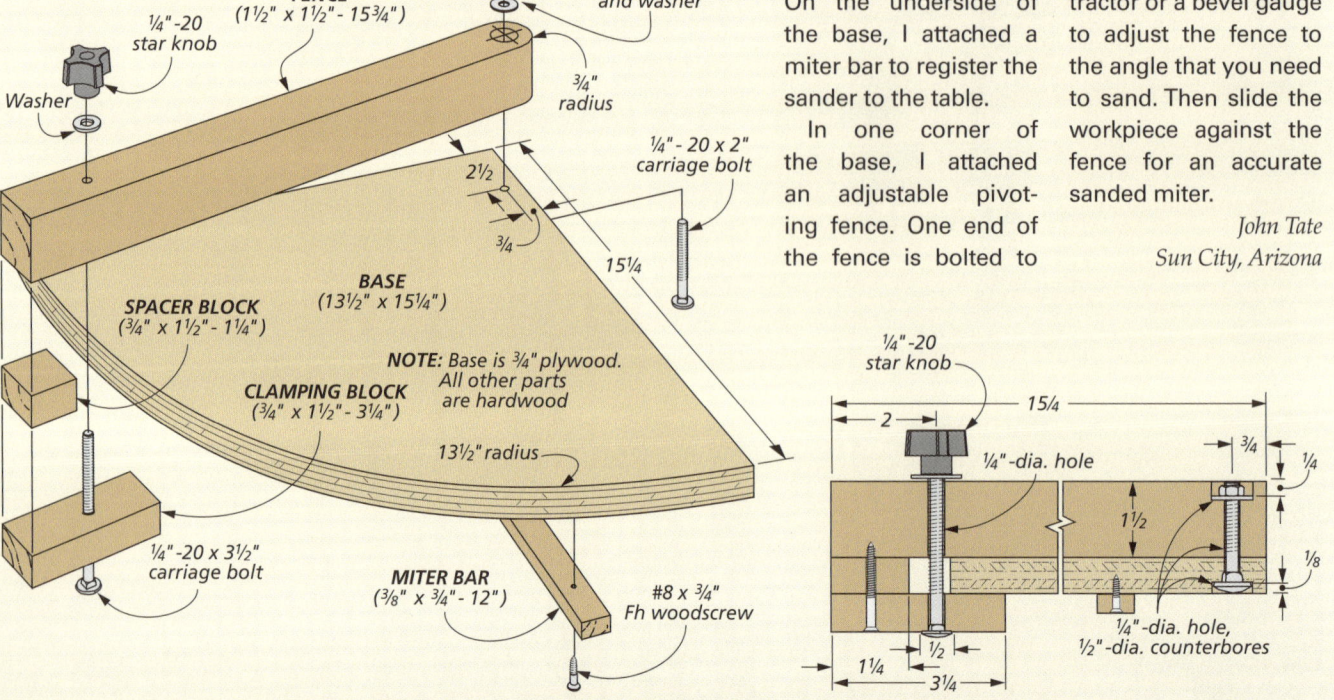

John Tate
Sun City, Arizona

4   Woodsmith   No. 198

Finish Shelves Fast

I had to apply finish to a number of bookcase shelves, and I didn't want to wait for one side to dry before I finished the other side. The drying rack you see in the drawing is my solution.

It's just a couple of 2x4s set on edge across two sawhorses. To hold the shelves, I drove finish nails in the ends of each shelf so they could rest on the 2x4s. The nails also serve as handles to flip the shelves when one side is complete. This keeps my fingerprints out of the finish and allows both sides to dry at once.

Tony Gallo
Brampton, Ontario

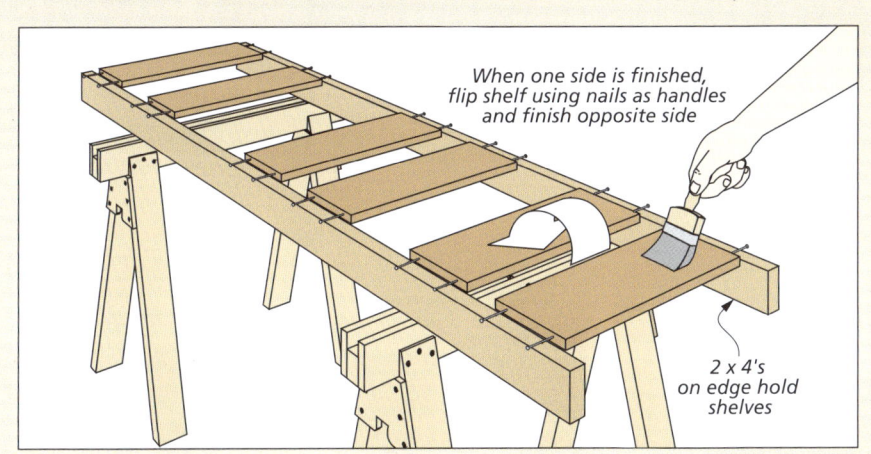

When one side is finished, flip shelf using nails as handles and finish opposite side

2 x 4's on edge hold shelves

Scraper Caddy

I have a number of card scrapers in different thicknesses and shapes. I needed a place to keep them organized and sharp. A simple caddy that goes to my bench was just the ticket.

As you can see in the photo, it's just a block of wood with several kerfs cut across it. I found the kerf from a hand saw made perfectly sized slots.

With this caddy, I now have all my scrapers in one location and the edges are safe from dings and dents. Plus, it stores easily on a shelf.

Donald Henderson
Orleans, Ontario

SUBMIT YOUR TIPS ONLINE

If you have an original shop tip, we would like to hear from you and consider publishing your tip in one or more of our publications. Go to:

Woodsmith.com
Click on the link,
"SUBMIT A TIP"

You'll be able to tell us all about your tip and upload your photos and drawings. You can also mail your tips to "Woodsmith Tips" at the editorial address shown at right. We will pay up to $200 if we publish your tip.

FREE TIPS BY EMAIL

Now you can have the best, time-saving secrets, solutions, and techniques sent directly to your email inbox. Just go to **Woodsmith.com** and click on "Woodsmith Tips" You'll receive one of our favorite tips each week.

Woodsmith
No. 198   December/January 2012

PUBLISHER Donald B. Peschke

EDITOR Bryan Nelson
MANAGING EDITOR Vincent Ancona
SENIOR EDITOR Ted Raife
ASSOCIATE EDITOR Dennis Perkins
ASSISTANT EDITOR Carol Beronich
CONTRIBUTING EDITORS Phil Huber,
Randall A. Maxey, Wyatt Myers, James Bruton
EDITORIAL INTERN Abby Wolner

EXECUTIVE ART DIRECTOR Todd Lambirth
SENIOR ILLUSTRATORS David Kreyling, Harlan V. Clark,
Erich Lage, David Kallemyn
SENIOR GRAPHIC DESIGNER Bob Zimmerman
GRAPHIC DESIGNER Shelley Cronin
GRAPHIC DESIGN INTERN Becky Kralicek
CONTRIBUTING ILLUSTRATORS Dirk Ver Steeg,
Peter J. Larson

CREATIVE DIRECTOR Ted Kralicek
SENIOR PROJECT DESIGNERS Ken Munkel,
Kent Welsh, Chris Fitch, Jim Downing
PROJECT DESIGNER/BUILDER John Doyle
SHOP CRAFTSMEN Steve Curtis, Steve Johnson
SENIOR PHOTOGRAPHERS Crayola England,
Dennis Kennedy
ASSOCIATE STYLE DIRECTOR Rebecca Cunningham
SENIOR ELECTRONIC IMAGE SPECIALIST Allan Ruhnke
PRODUCTION ASSISTANT Minniette Johnson
VIDEO EDITOR/DIRECTOR Mark Hayes

Woodsmith® (ISSN 0164-4114) is published bimonthly by August Home Publishing Company, 2200 Grand Ave, Des Moines, IA 50312.
Woodsmith® is a registered trademark of August Home Publishing.
Copyright© 2011 August Home Publishing Company. All rights reserved.
Subscriptions: Single copy: $4.95.
Canadian Subscriptions: Canada Post Agreement No. 40038201. Send change of address information to PO Box 881, Station Main, Markham, ON L3P 8M6.
Canada BN 84597 5473 RT
Periodicals Postage Paid at Des Moines, IA, and at additional offices.
Postmaster: Send change of address to Woodsmith, PO Box 37274, Boone, IA 50037-0274.

WoodsmithCustomerService.com

ONLINE SUBSCRIBER SERVICES
- **VIEW** your account information
- **RENEW** your subscription
- **CHECK** on a subscription payment
- **PAY** your bill
- **CHANGE** your mailing or e-mail address
- **VIEW/RENEW** your gift subscriptions
- **TELL US** if you've missed an issue

CUSTOMER SERVICE   Phone: 800-333-5075

SUBSCRIPTIONS
Customer Service
P.O. Box 842
Des Moines, IA 50304-9961
subscriptions@augusthome.com

EDITORIAL
Woodsmith Magazine
2200 Grand Avenue
Des Moines, IA 50312
woodsmith@woodsmith.com

AUGUST HOME PUBLISHING COMPANY   Printed in China

more tips from our readers

Board Jack

I sometimes have long or wide boards that I need to clamp at my workbench. The face vise will hold one end, but the opposite end needs support. So I built this board jack to support the end opposite the vise.

To build the jack, I routed a narrow slot in the center of a board and then drilled a hole at one end to attach a dowel. The dowel slips into a hole in the front edge of your workbench. An adjustable support is fixed to the slotted board to hold one end of the workpiece.

I drilled a hole in the face of the shelf and inserted a carriage bolt through the hole and into the slot. Then added a knob that I threaded over the carriage bolt. When I tighten the knob, it keeps the shelf at the proper height to support the board, while the other end is in the vise.

Oneil Long
Mound City, Missouri

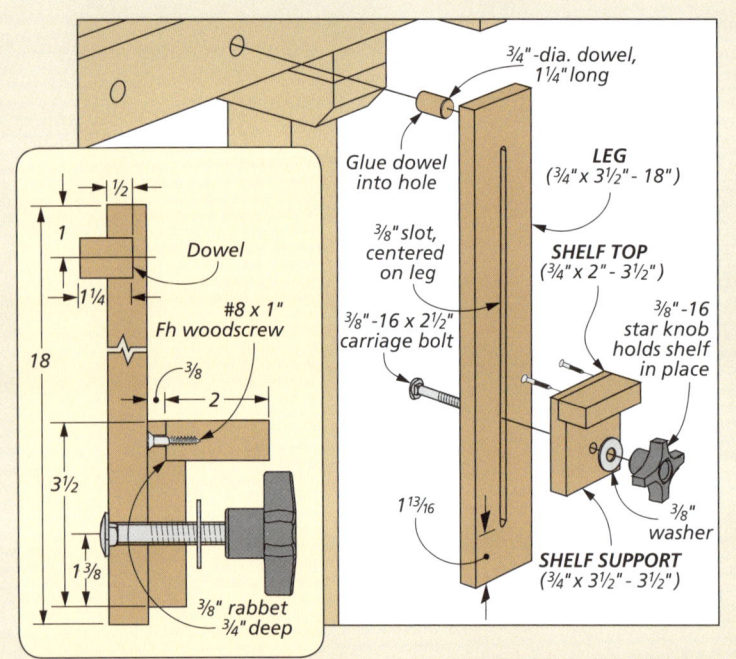

Nail File Sander

I often find that the smallest glueup flaws in a project are the hardest to clean up. But a metal fingernail file is just the right size for getting into those hard-to-reach areas where glue squeezes out.

I picked up the file shown in the photo at the drugstore. To make it easier to work with, I ground the tip of the file to a 45° angle. Then I put a sharp bevel on the tip to create a mini-chisel. The edge on the file gets into the smallest nooks of my project to clean up any trouble spots.

Peter Sherrill
Forestville, Wisconsin

Outfeed Roller Storage

I use an outfeed roller a lot in my woodworking shop. But I don't need one set up all the time. Even though it folds flat, I keep it out of the way by storing it overhead. The ceiling joists are a perfect place to hang it.

To do this, I hung three bicycle hooks from the joists in my garage shop. When I need to store the stand, I just hook the legs onto two of the hooks (left drawing). Then I swing up the other end and slip it into a third hook (lower drawing) to secure the stand to the ceiling.

Now I don't need to use valuable floor space to store my roller stand. But it's at the ready when I need it.

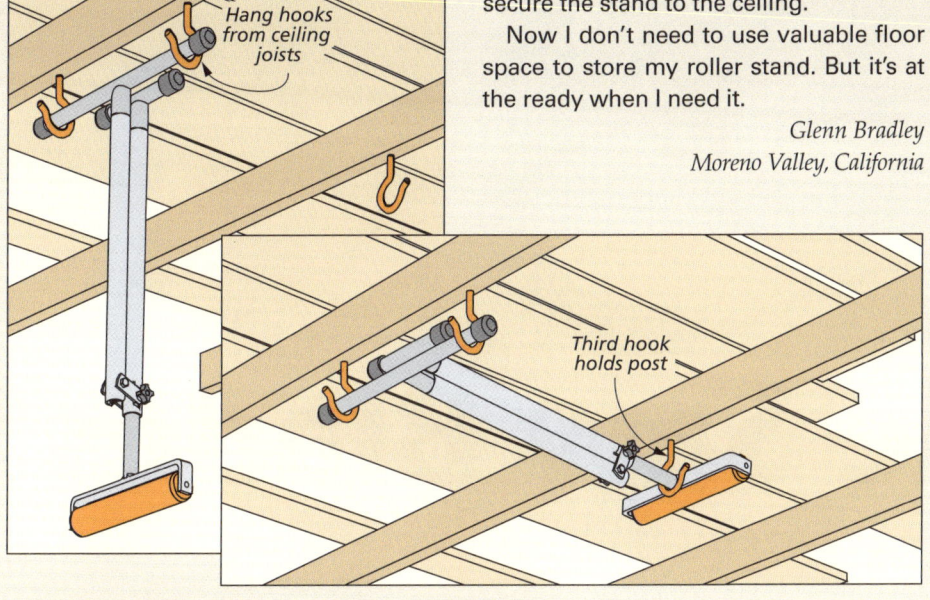

Glenn Bradley
Moreno Valley, California

Mini Scraper

Utility knife blades make great mini scrapers. But the small blades are hard to hold onto. A wood handle keeps it stable.

I just cut a slot in the end of a thin scrap piece, about the same thickness as the blade. Then I inserted the blade in the slot, using a piece of masking tape to grip it securely.

Ron Duchek
St. Louis, Missouri

WIN THIS BOSCH IMPACT DRIVER

Simply send us your favorite shop tips. If your tip or technique is selected as the featured reader's tip, you'll win a *Bosch* impact driver just like the one shown here. To submit your tip or technique, just go online to W*oodsmith.com* and click on the link, "SUBMIT A TIP." You can submit your tip and upload your photos for consideration.

The Winner!

Congratulations to, Oneil Long, winner of this Bosch impact driver. To find out how you could win this driver, check out the information on the left.

Quick Tips

ROUTER STABILIZER

I like to keep a guide bushing installed in one of my routers. But the bushing prevents the router from sitting flat for storage.

My solution is to stand the router upright on top of a small V-belt. The belt is just high enough to provide clearance for the bushing and allows the router baseplate to rest on the belt.

Serge Duclos
Delson, Quebec

EMERGENCY BUFFER

I needed to buff out a large tabletop that I had applied wax to, but I didn't have a pad or a buffer.

To accomplish the task, I decided to use a piece of a soft terry cloth towel cut to fit my orbital sander. It worked great and the towel stuck well to the hook and loop pad on the sander. When I was done, I just tossed the piece of towel.

Ross Henton
Frisco, Texas

FITTING DRAWERS

When I'm fitting drawers in a cabinet, I find that getting a drawer out that's slid in flush presents a problem. Since the drawer doesn't have a knob or handle on it yet, I need a simple way to remove it from the cabinet. But I don't want to mar the drawer by prying it out with a tool.

Instead, I turn to my shop vacuum. The suction from the vacuum holds tight to the front of the drawer and doesn't leave any marks on the unfinished wood.

Melissa DeLay
Shoreview, Minnesota

all about
selecting
Table Saw Blades

Matching the right blade to the type of cut you're making is the key to getting professional-quality results from your table saw.

Tooth Configurations

- Flat Top
- Alternate Top Bevel (ATB) 
- Combination (ATB-R) 
- High-ATB 
- Triple Chip Grind (TCG) 

If you were to peek into most woodshops, chances are you'd find a table saw near the center of each one. With it, you can rip stock to width, crosscut workpieces to length, and create many different kinds of joinery.

It will only do these things well if you install the right blade for each task. If you don't, you might get rough cuts, tearout, or burnt edges. Worse yet, you could risk kickback during a cut.

WHAT'S THE DIFFERENCE? In order to learn how blades are designed for different tasks, you need to understand the common parts of the blade. You can start by taking a look at the drawing at right. As you can see, the blade begins with a steel plate, and ends in teeth tipped with carbide.

Another feature of blade design is the laser cutouts in the plate. As technology improved, laser-cut expansion and anti-vibration slots were added to improve performance. These slots reduce vibration and help keep the blade cool, reducing blade warp due to heat build-up.

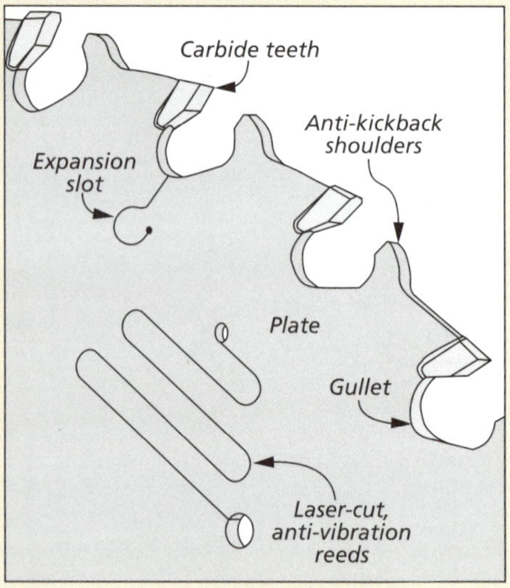

But it's mainly the teeth and gullets that differentiate the three major types of blades — rip, crosscut, and combination. I'll take a look at each of these blades individually.

The type, number, and configuration of the teeth vary according to the task. The drawings in the margin show the shapes of the teeth and the different combinations.

RIP BLADES. Rip cuts are made along the length of a workpiece, in

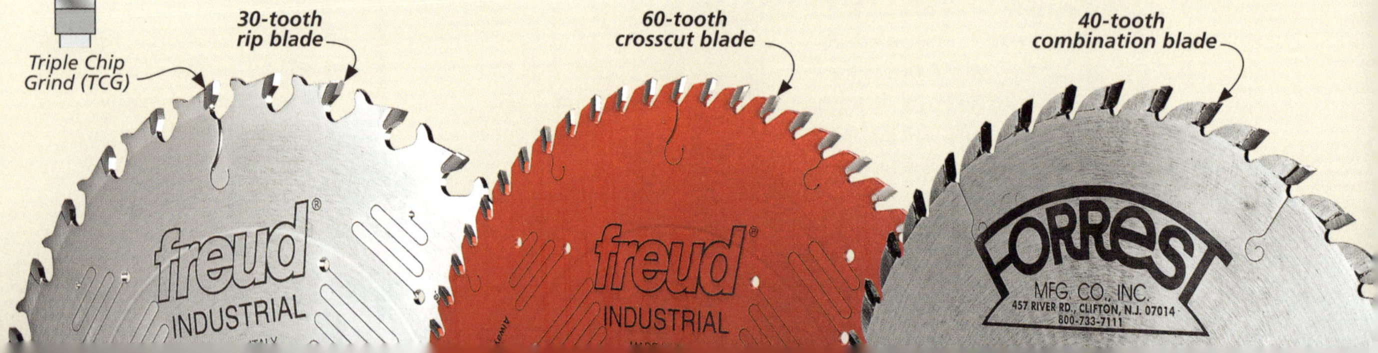

Diagram labels: Carbide teeth, Anti-kickback shoulders, Expansion slot, Plate, Gullet, Laser-cut, anti-vibration reeds

30-tooth rip blade

60-tooth crosscut blade

40-tooth combination blade

line with the direction of the grain. As the name implies, this cut separates the grain by ripping between the layers. For this type of cut, you don't need a lot of teeth. In fact, too many only cause the wood to burn. A blade with 24-30 teeth and a flat-top configuration is perfect. The combination of fewer teeth and flat-top design help prevents the saw from bogging down in thick stock.

In addition to the flat-top teeth, rip blades also have deep gullets. It's the gullets that allow the large amount of chips and dust to be carried out of the cut. If the chips can't escape, the blade will heat up and burn the edge of the workpiece.

CROSSCUT BLADES. At the other end of the spectrum is the crosscut blade. Since a crosscut is perpendicular to the grain direction, you want more teeth to slice through the fibers rather than ripping them. The right tooth for this kind of cut has to be sharp enough to score the fibers and slice them cleanly. The alternate top bevel (ATB) teeth fill the bill perfectly. The result is a clean cut in solid wood.

You'll find that a 60-tooth count is the norm for table saw crosscut blades. As you can see in the drawings at right, the gullets of crosscut blades are shallower than the rip blades. These shallower gullets are all you need to carry away the smaller chips from a crosscut.

COMBINATION BLADE. A combination blade is a compromise between a rip and crosscut blade. It will do either task reasonably well, depending on the thickness of the stock. It also works well for plywood and other sheet goods.

You'll normally find 40-50 teeth on a combination blade. Many combination blades add a flat-top or raker tooth to the ATB design for smoother rip cuts. This ATB-R has become common on combination blades from many manufacturers.

THIN-KERF BLADES. Another feature to consider when shopping for blades is the thickness of the blade.

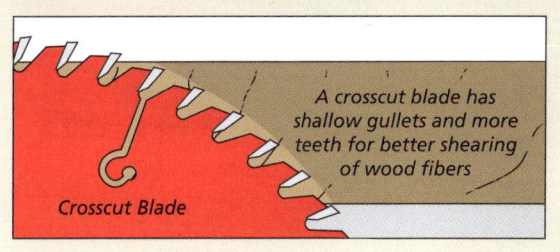

Crosscut, rip, and combination blades are available in both standard and thin-kerf designs. Thin-kerf blades are a great choice for most saws. The plate and teeth are 25% thinner than conventional blades (usually around $3/32$" instead of $1/8$"). This reduces the workload for the saw and makes it easier to cut thick stock with a lower-powered saw. I keep a thin-kerf combination blade on my saw most of the time.

Finally, my best advice is to buy a top-quality product (refer to Sources on page 51). It will pay you back every time you use your saw. No matter what the task, the right blade can improve the quality of your work. **W**

The deep gullets of a rip blade remove large amounts of material when cutting with the grain

Rip Blade

A crosscut blade has shallow gullets and more teeth for better shearing of wood fibers

Crosscut Blade

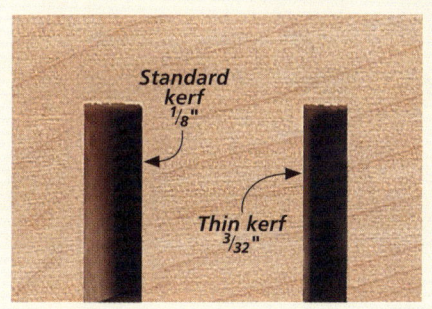

▲ A thin kerf might not seem like much of a difference, but it reduces the workload on your saw by 25%.

Standard kerf $1/8$"
Thin kerf $3/32$"

Top-Notch Blade: Freud's Premier Fusion

I've been a fan of *Freud* blades for many years. For me, it's tough to beat the quality of their products for the price. Recently, I tried out their *Premier Fusion* combination blade. This blade is priced about 50% higher than their conventional blades, so I was anxious to see if the performance justified the cost.

WHAT IS IT? At first glance, the *Premier Fusion* looks like most *Freud* blades, right down to the familiar red, non-stick coating.

The teeth are made from *Freud's* unique micro-grain carbide called TiCo — a combination of titanium and cobalt. But what's different here is the profile of the teeth. The Hi-ATB configuration also relies on a special double side grind in the sharpening process (see inset photo at right). This creates two cutting surfaces for a smooth face on all sorts of cuts.

As you can see in the photos at right, the *Fusion* crosscut the face veneer of some cabinet-grade plywood without leaving a splinter. Not many blades can boast a cut that clean. Best of all, it did that and virtually every other type of cut day after day. If you really don't like changing blades, this is the one for you.

▼ Cutting cabinet-grade plywood with no tearout is the sign of a good blade.

Double side grind

No tearout

tools of the trade

build better with
Top 5 Hand Tools

To take the quality of your work to the next level, turn back the clock and learn about some "old-school" tools.

In the debate over hand tools versus power tools, my position is a simple one: Use the tool that makes the most sense for a particular task. For most woodworkers doing furniture projects, that means power tools. But even if you're a power-tool woodworker, there are still a few hand tools you shouldn't be without. And I don't mean just the measuring and marking tools that we all need.

As a rule, your power tools get you most of the way toward high-quality results. But a few hand tools will make them even better.

Hand tools can impart a bit of "finesse" to your woodworking projects by allowing you to work in small increments (often thousandths of an inch). And the more you use them, the more you'll appreciate the tools and the results.

You can find most of these tools in the online woodworking suppliers. Sources on page 51 has the information on the websites.

1 Card Scrapers

It's hard to imagine a tool that provides more bang for the buck than a card scraper. This simple, flat piece of steel can smooth a workpiece quickly and leave a beautiful surface that you won't need to touch with sandpaper. The secret is the cutting edge.

The scraper relies on a hook-shaped burr on the edge rather than a conventional, beveled blade. When properly sharpened, the hook produces wispy shavings.

Another nice thing about scrapers is that they're available in different profiles. One common type, the gooseneck, has a round shape that can be used to smooth convex surfaces. And by simply adjusting the angle, you can scrape more than a single radius curve.

I'm not saying you should throw away your sander. But the more proficient you become with a card scraper, the more you'll find yourself turning to it.

2 Shoulder Plane

When it comes to shaving a hair off of a tenon or cleaning up the bottom of a dado or groove, a shoulder plane is the tool for the job. There are a couple of unique features that make a shoulder plane a must-have tool.

First, the blade is just slightly wider than the body (usually only about $\frac{1}{64}$"). And the blade is bedded at a low angle. This allows it to cut a crisp corner on the cheeks and shoulders of a tenon (hence the name).

Shoulder planes are sold in several sizes. I like a medium size, $\frac{3}{4}$"-wide version. If you cut tenons at the table saw, you'll appreciate how well this plane cleans them up, as shown in the photo.

3 Set of Chisels

I don't think there can be much debate regarding the necessity of chisels — even in a power-tool shop. No matter what kind of work you do, a good set of chisels is one of the best tool investments you can make. They're essential for fine-tuning joinery, squaring up corners, and dozens of other common tasks.

The good news is, you don't have to spend a fortune to find a set of high-quality chisels. Several brands sold today combine value with long-lasting performance. There are a number of six-piece chisel sets for $60-80.

Look for a blade hardness of Rc58-62. This is hard enough to hold an edge well, but still soft enough to sharpen easily.

4 Ryoba Saw

No matter how confident and proficient you are at the table saw, there are plenty of cuts that are simpler and safer to make using a hand saw. And there's a perfect combination of value and quality in a Japanese-style *ryoba* saw. This double-edged saw has both crosscut and rip teeth.

The steel teeth are impulse hardened, so you'll never need to sharpen them. Instead, you can simply replace the blade.

Of course, if you prefer the Western alternative, then a couple of good back saws (one with rip teeth and the other crosscut) will serve the same purpose.

5 Block Plane

As a power-tool woodworker, I admit I was always a little bit intimidated about using a hand plane. There are so many different sizes and styles that I found it easier to simply ignore them all.

After a few years, however, I broke down and bought a block plane and I never looked back. There's just about no limit to what you can do with a high-quality, well-tuned block plane. From shaving down a proud dovetail or box joint (using a low-angle model) to chamfering an edge, once you learn to properly set up and use a block plane, you'll wonder how you ever got by without one.

Fortunately, it's not hard to find a good one, either. I'd advise buying a block plane that makes it easy to adjust the depth of cut. The planes from *Lie-Nielsen* and *Veritas* for instance, incorporate easy-to-use depth controls and are ready to use out of the box. W

jigs & fixtures

Key joint

▲ The key template is included with the basic jig.

decorative joinery with the
Fast Joint Jig

▼ Everything you need to make attractive, strong joints is included with the jig.

The easy-to-use jig allow you to make amazing joinery that adds a distinctive look to any drawer or box.

Clamps
Fence
Jig base with hold down clamps
Setup blocks
End
Templates
Spring lock washer
Dovetail bit
Spiral bit
Router bushings
Centering cone

Dovetail joinery is a reliable and traditional way to join drawer parts. That's why there are a lot of dovetail jigs out there. But most only cut dovetails and box joints. Besides dovetails, the *Fast Joint Precision Joinery System* can be used to cut other decorative joints.

This jig takes routed joinery a step further by offering several distinctive designs, as you can see in the margin photo on the opposite page. And this is just a small sample. You'll find templates for other designs available with the jig, including conventional half-blind and through dovetails (see page 51 for sources).

THE BASICS. The jig consists of a base and two end fences that hold a pair of templates. The templates are referred to as "male" and "female" (more familiar terms are tails and pins). One side of the box or a drawer side is clamped flat to the jig and routed on a router table with the included bit, following the male template. The mating side of the box or drawer front is clamped upright against a fence and routed using the female template. All you need to do is guide the template against a bushing mounted in the insert plate.

ALL INCLUSIVE. Everything you need to make decorative joints is included with the joinery system (left photo). The jig needs some assembly, but all the parts are cut to exact specifications. During assembly you'll want to take extra care to square the side fences to the base. This helps you rout precise joints.

ROUTER SETUP. Before using the jig, be sure to take some time to tune up your router table. You'll want to make sure the insert plate is flush with the router tabletop. And you'll need a router plate that accepts standard *Porter-Cable*-style bushings. Once the jig is assembled and your router table is ready, you can start making joints.

STEP-BY-STEP. Working with the jig is pretty easy if you follow a few basic guidelines. The jig includes a detailed instruction book that steps you through the process, so I'll just give you the highlights and a few pointers.

Your first step is to make sure your workpieces are the correct thickness. If you're making drawers, it's okay to have thinner drawer sides, but the drawer fronts for some of the larger joints need to be at least ¾" thick. For instance, the crown joint shown in the margin photo is approximately ⅝" tall. You can see how the joint wouldn't fit on the edge of a ½" workpiece.

ROUTER BIT. There's just one more thing to mention before you turn on your router. The router bit included with the jig is a specially made, high-speed steel bit. You won't be able to pick one up at the local hardware store, so you might want to have an extra bit on hand just in case you need it.

PRACTICE JOINTS. You'll want to make some test cuts to get a feel for the jig. My first joints were a little loose and had some tearout. But after I made a few more test cuts, I found the jig to be extremely accurate. That's when it all came together for great-looking joints.

AVOIDING TEAROUT. Because there are so many intricate details with some of these joints, it's not unusual to experience tearout on the edges of the workpieces. For example, on the lock and arrowhead joints (right photos), I noticed that as I moved the bit out of the indented part of the male portion of the joint, the protruding edge would chip. Rout slowly around the details to avoid this tearout.

Tearout at the edges of a workpiece may also be a problem when you're routing the male side. You can backrout (move the workpiece in the same direction as the spinning bit) on the end of the workpiece to cut down on tearout. Again, if you take a small bite on the workpiece, you won't have any trouble backrouting.

CLEAN ROUTING. Besides tearout, there are just a couple other issues to be aware of. Like any dovetail jig, the *Fast Joint Jig* creates a lot of chips. And the template has a tendency to collect these woodchips and dust in the recesses where the bushing rides. So be sure to clean out the templates (I used an air compressor) before you make the final pass on the router table.

BLIND ROUTING. I didn't find much about the jig design that caused me concern. But one thing to point out is that sometimes you're routing blind. So you can't really see the results of your work until you lift the jig off the table. If you're working with a large workpiece, this could be a challenge.

ROUT SLOWLY. I also had one mishap with the bit. It broke after making just a few test joints. I'm pretty sure this was due to trying to take off too much material in one pass. After I started taking smaller bites with the router, I didn't break any more bits.

Overall I like the jig. It makes tight-fitting decorative and traditional joints with ease. And for about the cost of a conventional dovetail jig you can make joinery in a variety of patterns on workpieces of different thicknesses. That makes this a worthwhile tool for your shop. **W**

▲ Routing the "female" side of the joint, which is usually placed in the drawer front, is done with the workpiece clamped vertically in the jig against the fence.

▼ Additional templates are available to create these and other joints for about $20 each.

Lock joint

Arrowhead

Crown

Bird's Eye

Dovetails, Too!

The *Fast Joint Precision Joinery System* creates dovetails using a set of templates just like the other joints. A dovetail bit is included with the jig.

You'll rout each side separately, like the other joints. And the templates help you get a precise fit for dovetail joints just as easily as any dovetail jig.

▲ Half-blind and through dovetails are a snap with the *Fast Joint* jig.

working with tools

12 tips & tricks for perfect
Dovetailed Drawers

Here's an easy-to-follow checklist that will guarantee your foolproof dovetail jig won't make a fool out of you.

A dovetail jig and a router make building drawers with half-blind dovetail joints a sure thing — assuming everything works the way it's supposed to. However, in the real world a dovetail jig can prove to be a bit finicky. And this sometimes makes routing dovetails an exercise in frustration.

But like every woodworking operation, ensuring success is simply a matter of knowing what can go wrong and how to avoid or fix the problem. Every dovetail jig is a little bit different, but there are some universal tips, tricks, and guidelines that guarantee you'll get the perfect-fitting dovetail joints you're after.

SIZING & SPACING. When planning your project, it's important to think ahead and size the height of the drawer openings and drawers to match the template spacing of your jig. The two most common spacings are on ⅞" and 1" centers. The goal is to end up with a half pin (or close to it) at the top and the bottom (margin photo). For example, if your jig uses a 1" spacing, the height of the drawers should be in even increments of 1".

ACCURATE PARTS. You won't get nice-fitting joints or drawers if you start with inaccurate or inconsistent parts. So always make sure your workpieces are flat, square, and uniformly sized.

EASY ACCESS. I like to position the jig at a comfortable working height and make sure it's clamped down tightly (photo below). You'll also find it's advantageous to work at a height that gives you a clear view of the cut. Finally, eliminate any clutter in the work area that might snag the router's power cord.

A CENTERED BUSHING. The jig's template and the bushing in the router base work together to guide the router and bit. If the bit isn't perfectly centered in the bushing, the cuts may not be consistent. So it's a good idea to center the bit before getting started.

▼ Plan the height of the drawers to accommodate a half pin at the top and bottom.

◀ Position the dovetail jig at a height that gives you easy control of the router and also allows you to view the scene of the action.

Woodsmith

Actually, since the bit is fixed in the collet, what you're doing is centering the bushing around the bit. This can be done easily with an inexpensive centering cone as shown in the photo at right.

SECURELY CLAMPED. You never want the workpieces to shift while you're routing the joint. So it pays to make sure they're held firmly beneath the clamping bars. If your jig doesn't have grip tape on the clamping bars, consider adding some adhesive-backed sandpaper to create a non-skid surface. And when clamping narrow parts, I place a spacer under the clamping bars to keep them from racking (main photo, opposite page).

BIT HEIGHT. The fit between the pins and tails is determined by the bit height in the router. This is your main adjustment when setting up to cut the dovetails. So the first thing I do is adjust the bit height with test cuts using stock identical in thickness to that of the drawer parts.

If the fit of the joint is too tight, you'll need to lower the bit. The bit will then cut narrower tails and wider sockets. Too loose, and you should raise the bit to produce the opposite effect. I rely on a simple verse to help me remember which way to go, "Lower to loosen — heighten to tighten."

A GOOD FIT. It's always hard to know when the fit is just right. I shoot for a joint that can be assembled with only moderate pressure. You should be able to fit the tails halfway into the sockets by hand. Then a few light taps with a mallet should fully seat the tails (lower right photo).

SCORING PASS. It's not uncommon to experience minor tearout along the inside edge of the tail piece. This can be avoided by starting with a light scoring pass across the front of the workpiece traveling from right to left (main photo, opposite page). Backrouting this shallow shoulder will eliminate the chance of tearout when making the full-depth cuts.

BACK & FORTH. When following the fingers on the subsequent pass, I work on keeping the router flat on the template. Since only half of the router's base is supported by the template, the trick is to concentrate on keeping its weight balanced. And then once the first left-to-right pass is completed, I like to make a second right-to-left "insurance" pass to be certain that all the sockets and tails are cut to full depth.

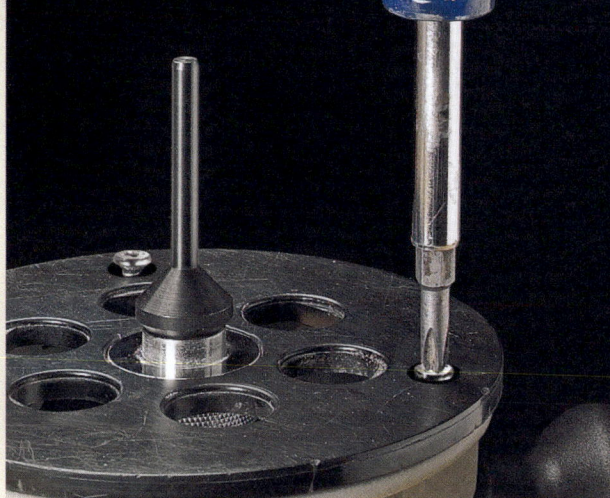

FLUSH EDGES. Even when the pins and tails fit well, the edges of the pieces may not align (upper left photo below). The cause? One piece was not snug against the stop. The simple cure is to check the position of both workpieces before turning on the router. They should be tight against the stop as well as snug to one another and the template.

IN OR OUT. You can encounter a similar problem where the sides aren't flush (proud or recessed) with the front and back. The fix here is to adjust the depth of the sockets by moving the template or stop bar forward or back.

NO CLAMPS. Since dovetails form a locking joint, relying on clamps at assembly is optional. My choice is to leave the clamps in the rack. It's less stressful and it's easier to square up the drawer. Just apply glue sparingly to the sides of the tails and sockets, tap the joint flush, and finally, check for square on a flat surface.

▲ Installing the bushing and baseplate with a centering cone will ensure the bit is perfectly centered.

▲ Misaligned edges or surfaces can be avoided with careful setup and adjustment.

▲ You want to shoot for an easy-to-assemble fit between the pins and the tails. It shouldn't take more than a few light taps with a mallet to seat the tails flush with the pins.

Weekend Project

classic Entry Bench

Mortise and tenon joinery, a sculpted seat, and curved legs combine to make this bench an elegant addition to your home.

A bench is a great addition to an entryway or hall in your home. It also creates a comfortable place to cozy up by the fireplace or as a dressing seat at the foot of the bed. It's really a versatile piece of furniture in any home.

This bench will grace any area with style, too. The sculpted seat and wedged, through tenons add to the attractiveness of the bench. In addition, the splayed legs and curved rails and stretchers create eye-catching lines on the base.

Even with the angles and contoured seat, the bench isn't complicated to build. The legs are easy to cut on the table saw with a simple shop-made jig. And another easy-to-build jig guides a router to form the contoured seat. Plus, it's all done with power tools. This eliminates a lot of involved handwork, so you can have this bench completed in short order.

The only difficult part about building the bench is deciding where it will be located, because you'll want to show off this impressive bench.

making leg TENONS

You'll start on the bench by making the four tapered legs. The legs are mortised to accept the rails and stretchers, and a tenon is cut on the top of each leg to fit through mortises in the seat.

TENON FIRST. I cut each leg from a wide, rectangular blank. Your first step is to cut the tenons on the end of the leg blanks, as shown in detail 'a.' Because of the curved shape of the leg, the tenon at the top is offset. After the leg is cut to shape, the tenon will be centered.

To create a clean shoulder at the top, I first scored all four shoulders of the leg with a standard blade, as shown in the How-To box below. (You'll need to adjust the blade height for each side.) The shoulder on the curved side of the leg is too deep to cut with a dado blade, so you'll need to make a series of cuts on the table saw and clean up the cheek with sandpaper. Then you can finish up the tenon with a dado blade, as shown in the center drawing in the box below.

RELIEF KERF. There are just a couple more steps to complete the tenons. Later, when you attach the seat to the base, you'll use wedges to lock the tenons in the mortises. So you'll need to cut the kerfs now for the wedges. First I drilled a relief hole for the end of each kerf to prevent the leg from splitting when the wedge is added. The holes also act as glue catches at the bottom of the wedge. You can locate the relief holes in the tenons, as shown in the right drawing below.

Then lay out the lines for the relief kerfs. Finally, cut them on the band saw (drawing below).

With the tenons complete, your next step is to finish up shaping the legs and drilling out the mortises.

How-To: Cut the Tenons

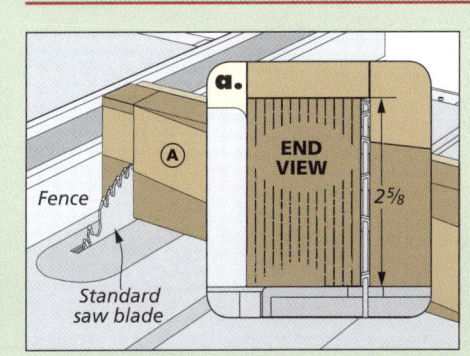

Tenon Cuts. *The tapered side of the leg requires deep cuts, so use a standard blade to make multiple cuts, removing the waste.*

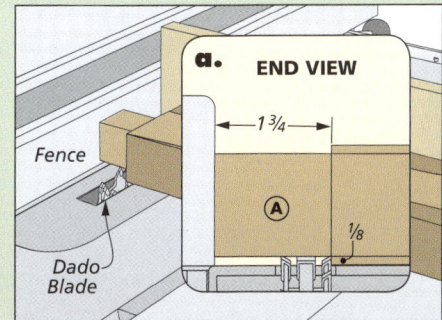

Finish the Tenon. *The remaining three sides of the tenon can be cleaned up with a dado blade. Use the rip fence as a stop.*

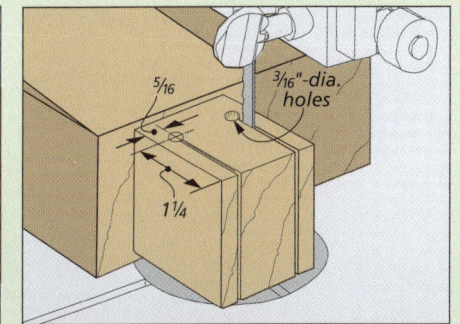

Relief Kerfs. *Use a band saw to make two kerfs in the end of the tenon. During assembly you'll insert wedges in the kerfs.*

completing the BASE

To complete the legs, you'll need to taper the inside edge and cut a curve on the opposite edge. In addition to shaping the legs, you'll also drill out the mortises for the rails and stretchers.

TAPER. The first step is to cut the taper on the edge of the leg (left box below). The jig I used to make this cut is shown in the left margin. Save the leg cutoffs to use as a caul during the glueup later.

MORTISES. Next up is the stretcher mortise on each tapered edge of the leg. You'll want to lay out the mortises on each leg so that you end up with two sets of mirrored legs. I formed the mortises before I cut the curve on the opposite edge. This way, you still have a flat edge to register against the drill press table, as shown in the center drawing below.

When the stretcher mortises are complete, it's time to cut the mortise on the face of the leg for the rails. This time you'll lay the tapered edge of the leg against the drill press fence. This will automatically keep the mortise parallel with the tapered edge, as shown in detail 'a.'

CURVE. Laying out and cutting the curve is the final step for the legs. You can use a narrow strip of hardboard and string to strike a layout line (right drawing below). Then make the cut on the waste side of the line at the band saw and clean up the edge with a sanding drum.

Once the legs are shaped, round over all the edges on the router table. I like to do this on the bottom edges of the legs, too. This way if the bench is moved, the legs won't chip.

RAILS & STRETCHERS

Each pair of legs is attached to a rail to make an end section. Although the rails sit at a slight angle, they're cut square. Likewise, the tenons are cut square.

RAIL. Since the tenons on the rails are pretty straightforward, I went ahead and installed a dado blade to cut them. Use the rip fence on your table saw as a stop to size the tenon.

How-To: Shape the Leg

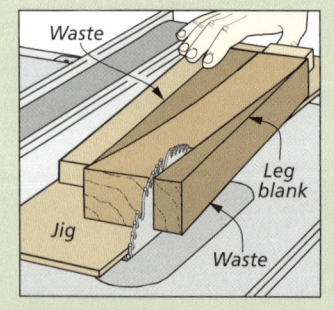

Taper Cut. Use a taper jig (above) to cut a taper on the inside edge of each leg.

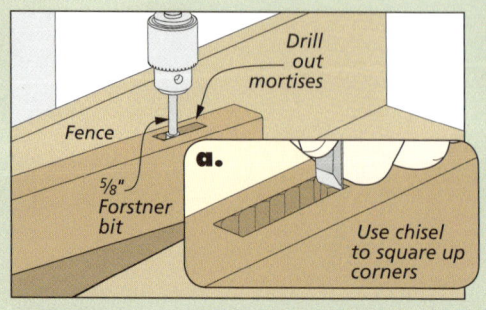

Drill Mortises. Drill out the mortises for the stretchers in the tapered edge of the leg. Then clean up the sides with a chisel.

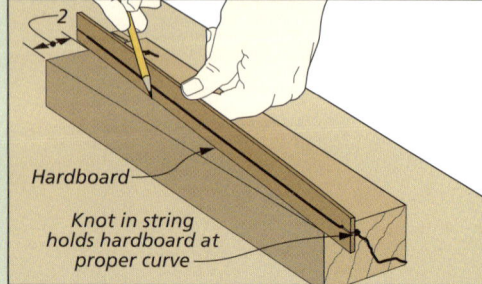

Cut Curve. Use a narrow strip of hardboard and a string to lay out the curve on the outside edge of the leg. Cut it on the band saw.

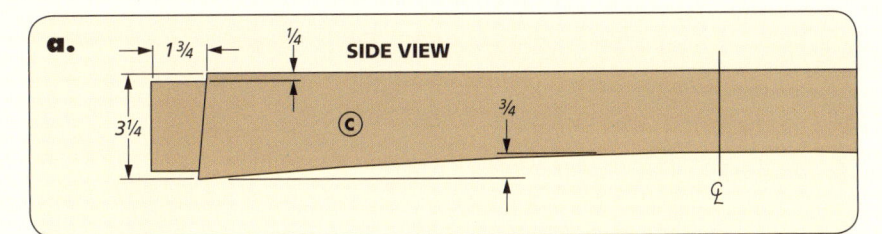

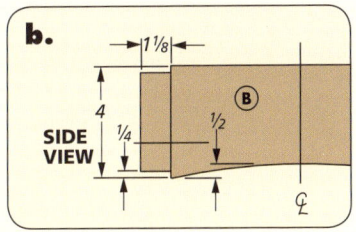

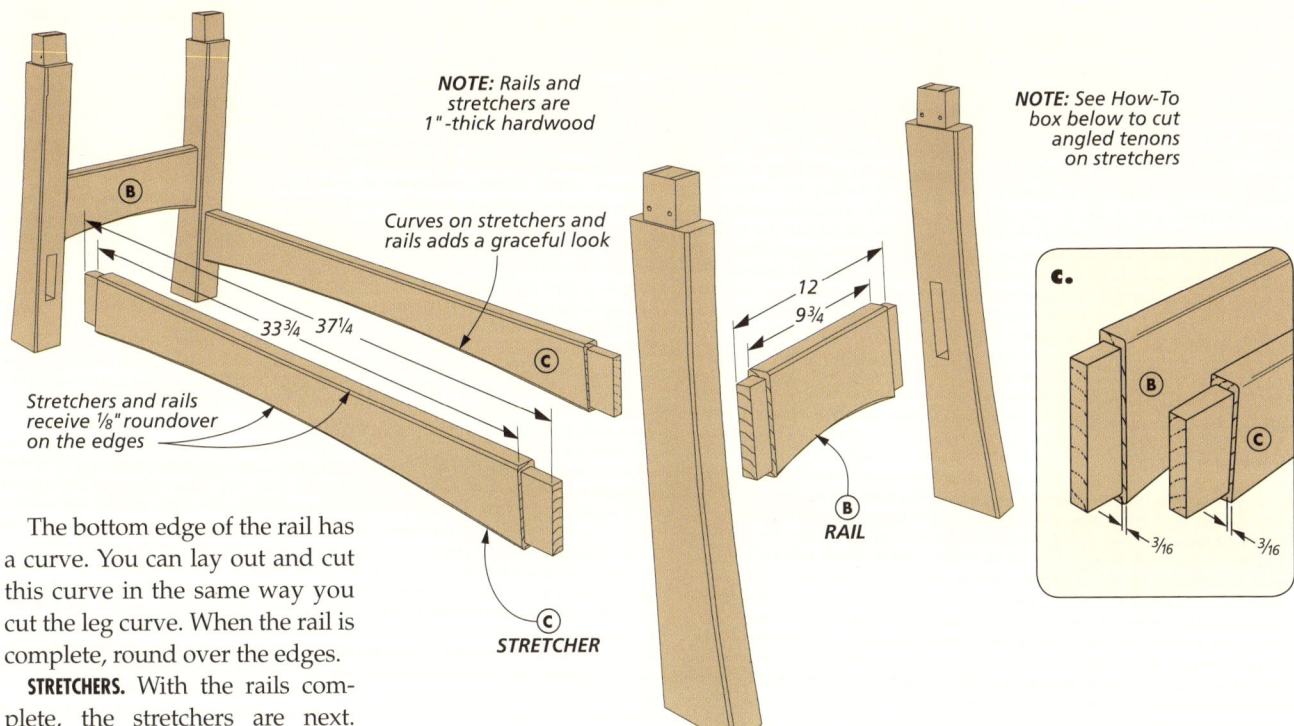

The bottom edge of the rail has a curve. You can lay out and cut this curve in the same way you cut the leg curve. When the rail is complete, round over the edges.

STRETCHERS. With the rails complete, the stretchers are next. You'll need to cut the tenon shoulders on the stretchers at 5° to match the splay of the legs, as shown in the box below. I started by cutting the stretcher to overall length and width. To cut the cheeks of the tenon, follow the step in the left drawing below. Then flip the workpiece and angle the miter gauge in the opposite direction to cut the other cheek.

As you can see in the center drawing, there are two setups for the edge shoulders. You'll need to reposition the rip fence for each cut. The key here is to leave a little bit of waste when making these cuts and then trim the shoulders back with a chisel.

To finish up the stretcher, cut the curve on the lower edge. Then round over all the edges.

ASSEMBLY. With the workpieces completed, it's time to get busy assembling the base. To create two end sections, I glued each rail to a pair of legs. Then I connected the end sections with the stretchers, using the waste from the curved cuts earlier as cauls to hold the clamps during the glueup. When the glue is dry, you can start on the seat.

Angled Tenon

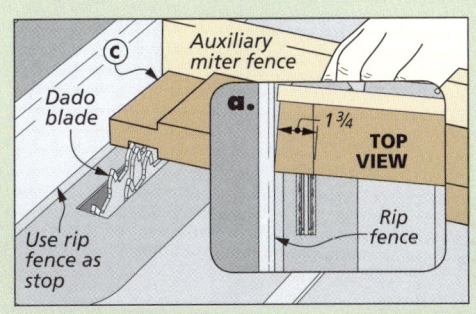

Stretcher Tenon. Set the miter gauge at 5° to cut the first cheek. Without moving the rip fence, reverse it to cut the other cheek.

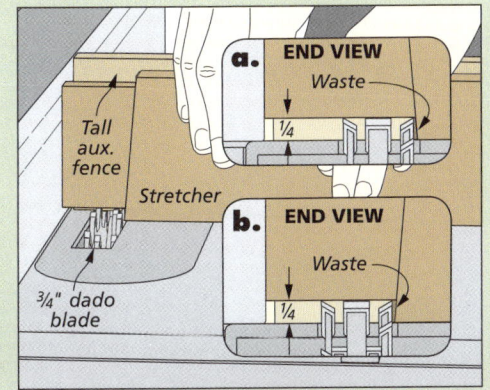

Edge Shoulder. Set the saw blade at 90° for the edge shoulder cut. Make the cuts just a little shy of the cheek cut.

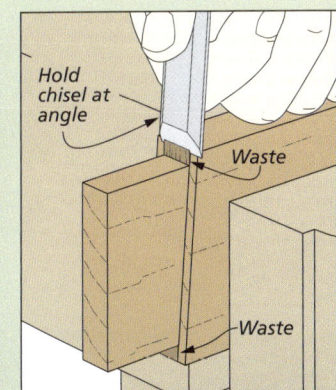

Clean Up. Use a sharp chisel to clean up the edge shoulder to meet the cheek shoulder.

make a SCULPTED SEAT

NOTE: Refer to page 29 for information on cutting wedges

WEDGES

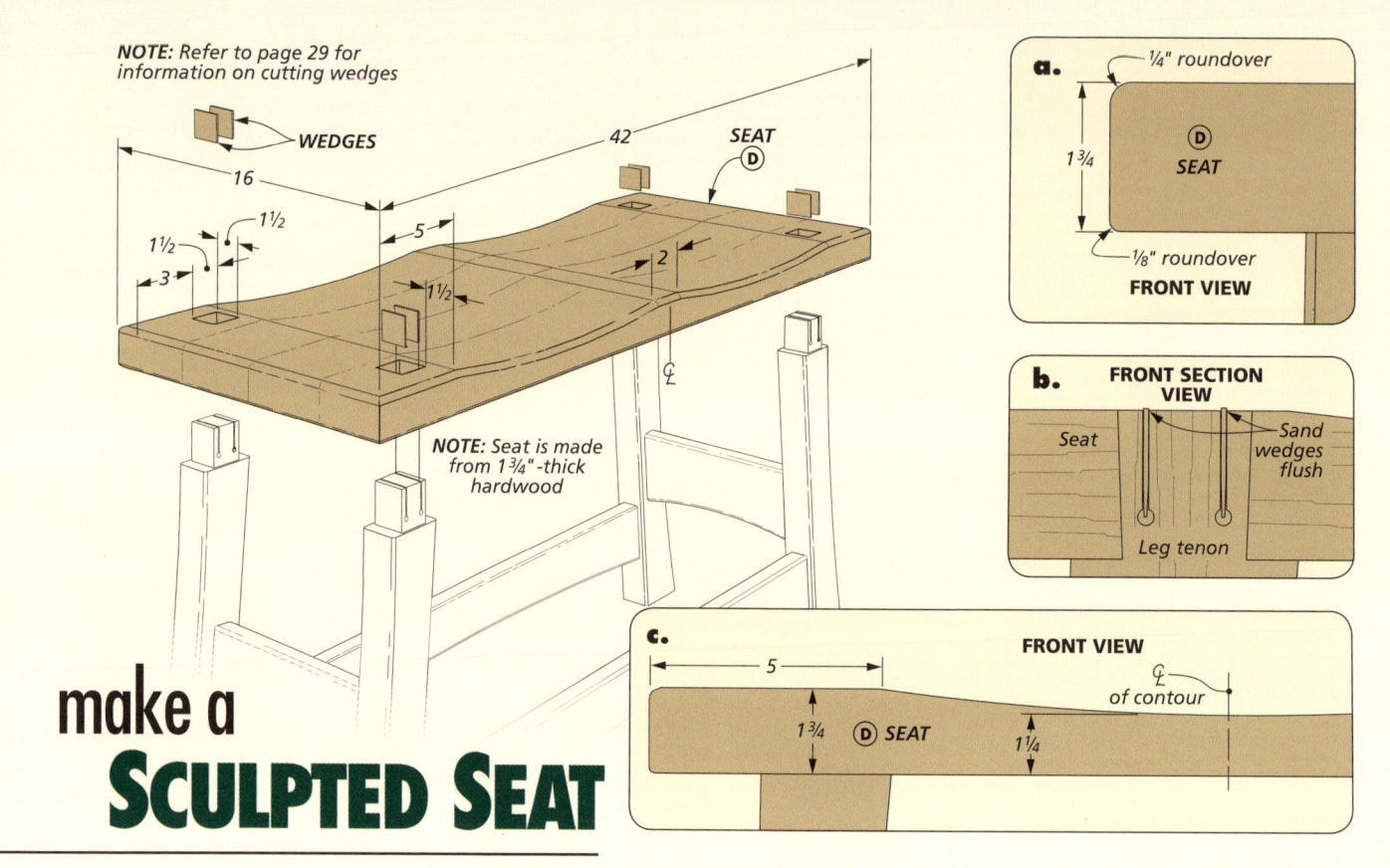

16 — 42 — SEAT (D)

1½ — 1½ — 3 — 5 — 1½ — 2

NOTE: Seat is made from 1¾"-thick hardwood

a. ¼" roundover — 1¾ — SEAT (D) — ⅛" roundover — **FRONT VIEW**

b. FRONT SECTION VIEW — Seat — Sand wedges flush — Leg tenon

c. FRONT VIEW — 5 — 1¾ — SEAT (D) — 1¼ — ℄ of contour

The seat for the bench starts with a glued-up panel. Then it's shaped with a simple shop-made router jig. Finally, mortises are cut in the seat to hold the leg tenons.

CONTOURS. When the seat is cut to size, you can start to work on the seat contours. Use the shop-made jig shown on page 28 with a router to sculpt the seat. The step-by-step process of routing each end of the seat is shown in the How-To box below.

To get started, mark layout lines for the contoured area on the seat (detail 'c'). Then set up the jig to begin routing, as shown in the center drawing below.

I used spacer blocks on the edges of the seat, so I could rout all the way to the edge of the seat and avoid routing into the guide rails. You'll rout one end of the seat at a time, removing small amounts of material with each pass (right drawing).

The router will have a tendency to pull into the waste as you rout in one direction and away from the waste when you push the router in the opposite direction. If you find the router hard to handle, you can minimize this effect by taking lighter passes. Rout to within about an inch of the layout lines. When the bulk of the waste has been removed, make a few light passes to sneak up on the layout lines. Repeat the process on the opposite end of the seat. Finally, sand the entire seat, blending in the edges with the seat contour and smoothing the surface with a soft sanding block.

POSITION MORTISES. As I mentioned, the seat is attached to the base with wedged tenons in through mortises. To locate the mortises,

How-To: Shape the Seat

Shop-Made Router Jig. You'll find details on the jig I used to shape the seat on page 28.

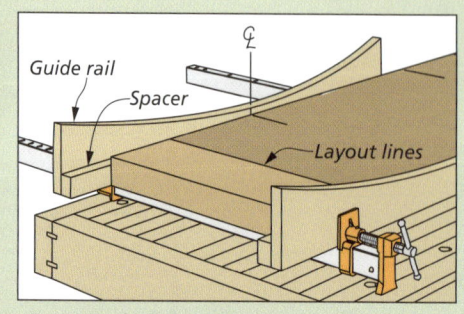

Set Up the Jig. Align the center of one side of the seat with the guide rails, add the spacers, and clamp them to the seat.

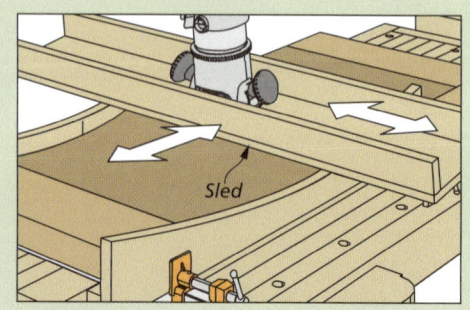

Using the Jig. With the bit set to take a light cut, let the router come up to full speed and then ease into the cut.

place the seat upside down on the workbench and center the base on the seat. Because the seat is large and heavy, I came up with a technique to use a hand-held router to cut the mortises (right drawings).

I attached strips of hardboard around each tenon with double-sided tape, as shown in Figure 1. These strips act as a template when cleaning the side of the mortise with a flush-trim bit and a pattern bit.

With the template strips in place, you can drill out the center of the mortise with a handheld drill (Figure 2). You'll need to place a scrap piece under the workpiece to act as a backer. Once the hole is drilled, use a pattern bit to remove the waste up to the template on the underside (Figure 3). To continue, flip the seat over and use a flush-trim bit to remove the waste on the top side (Figure 4). The round corners left by the router can be cleaned up with a sharp chisel.

BEVEL. The final step in creating each mortise is to sand a slight bevel on two sides of the mortise to allow the tenon to splay out as the wedges are driven in. You want to bevel the two sides that are parallel to the wedge kerfs you cut earlier in the top of the leg tenons. You don't have to remove much material. I just sanded the sides with some 60-grit sandpaper and a narrow sanding block (Figure 5).

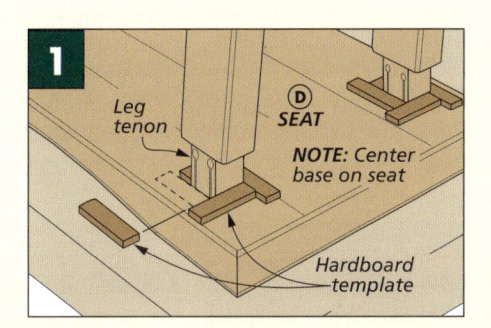

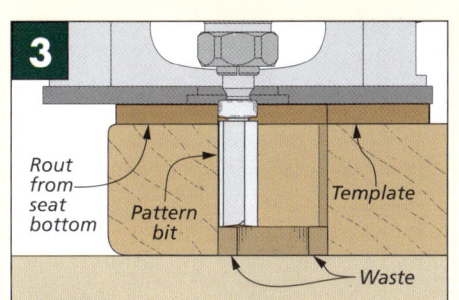

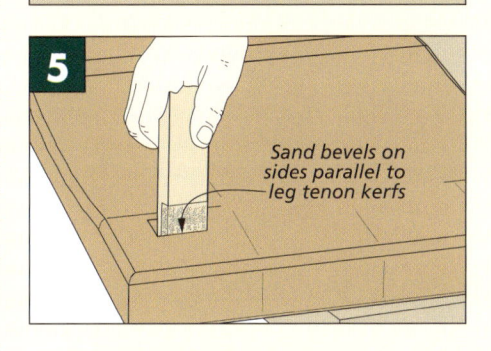

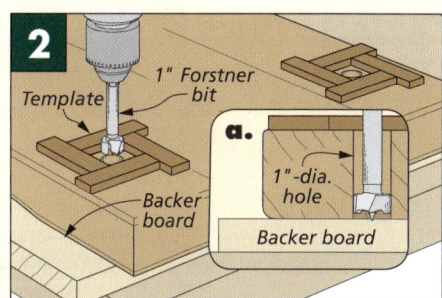

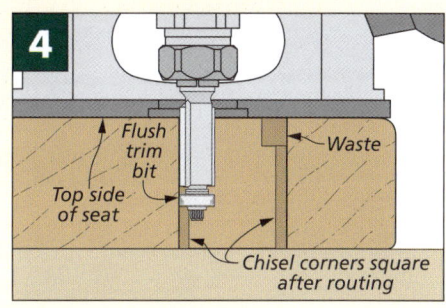

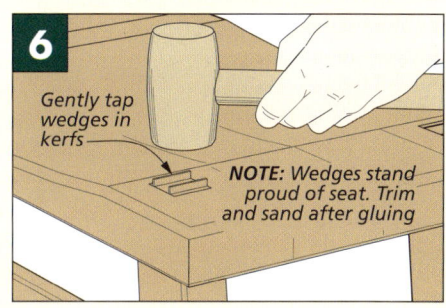

WEDGES & ROUNDOVERS. Before you attach the legs to the seat, there are two things you need to do. First, you'll need to cut wedges for the tenons (refer to page 29). Then you'll want to rout the roundovers on the top and bottom of the seat. This is much easier to complete before you assemble the bench.

ADD THE SEAT. When you've completed the roundovers, glue the seat to the base through the mortises, spread some glue in the kerfs, and drive the wedges in place (Figure 6). When the glue is dry, you can trim the wedges and sand everything flush with the seat.

Once you've applied the finish (refer to Sources on page 51), you can find a prominent spot in your home to show off your new classic-style bench. **W**

Materials & Cutting Diagram

A	Legs (4)	$1^3/_4$ x $4^3/_4$ - 19	**C**	Stretchers (2)	1 x $3^1/_4$ - $37^5/_{16}$
B	Rails (2)	1 x 4 - 12	**D**	Seat (1)	$1^3/_4$ x 16 - 42

$1^3/_4$" x 5" - 72" Oak (Four boards @ 5 Bd. Ft. each)

1" x 5" - 60" Oak (Two boards @ 2.6 Bd. Ft. each)

Designer Series Project

stained glass
Craftsman Lamp

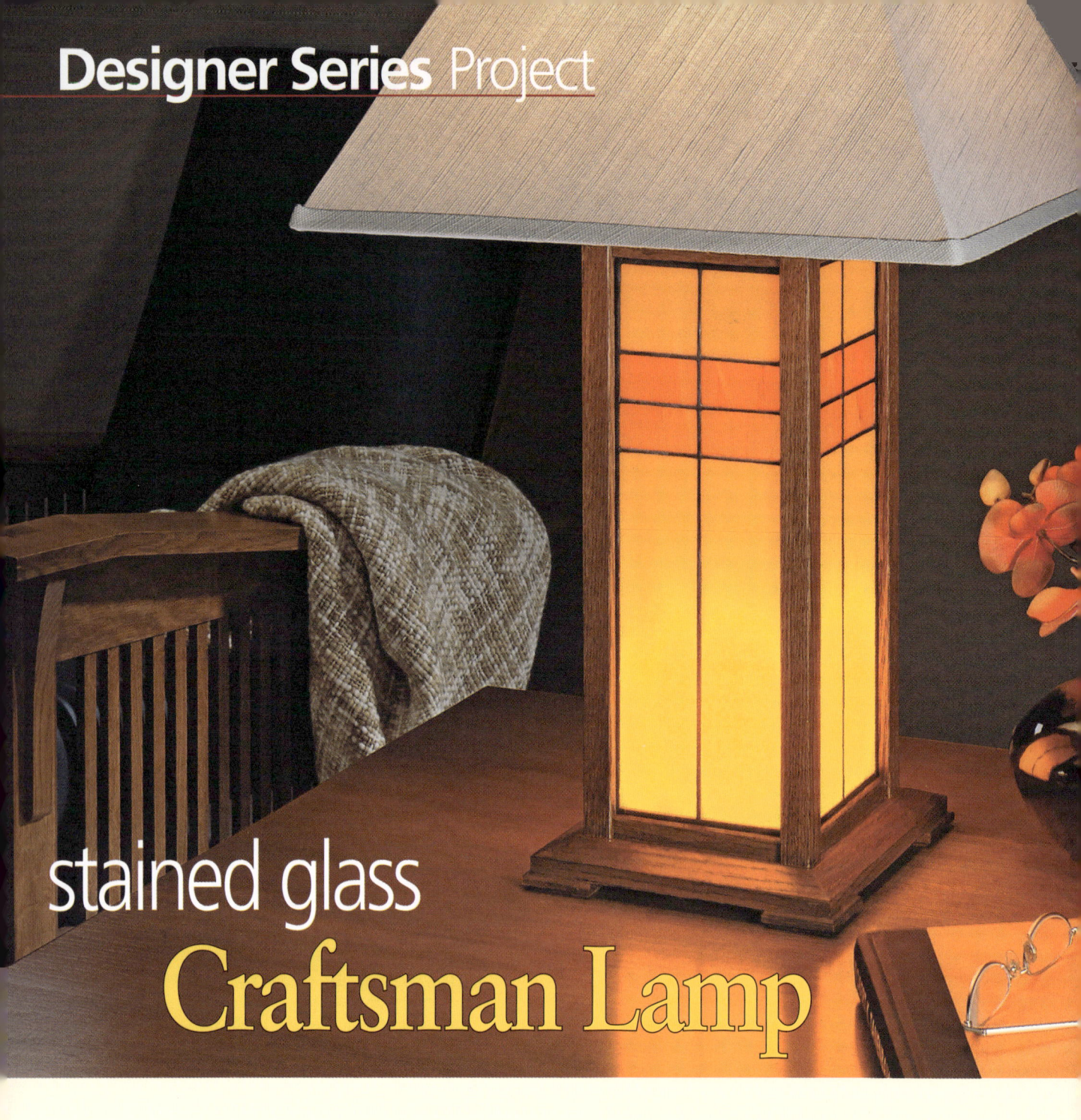

Words like "timeless" and "classic" get thrown around a lot when describing furniture. In this case, they're both appropriate.

A good lamp can do a lot more than light up a dark room. It can help define the style and function of any space in your home.

The stained glass lamp shown above does exactly that. The signature lines of the Craftsman style are evident throughout. Each panel of the stained glass base is framed with oak. The feet and base are typical of Craftsman-style furniture, as well.

Whether you're a beginner or an old hand at woodworking, this is a great project. It's not too difficult, but your attention to detail will be well-rewarded. And it's also a perfect introduction to working with stained glass. All the cuts are straight lines, and I've used a very simple soldering technique to assemble the panels. Even the wiring is very straightforward. I'll take you through the whole process, step by step.

In the end, you'll have learned a few new techniques. But better still, you'll have a beautiful addition to your home. A timeless classic if there ever was one.

CONSTRUCTION DETAILS

OVERALL DIMENSIONS: 8¼"W x 8¼"D x 16½"H (without shade); 27"H (with shade)

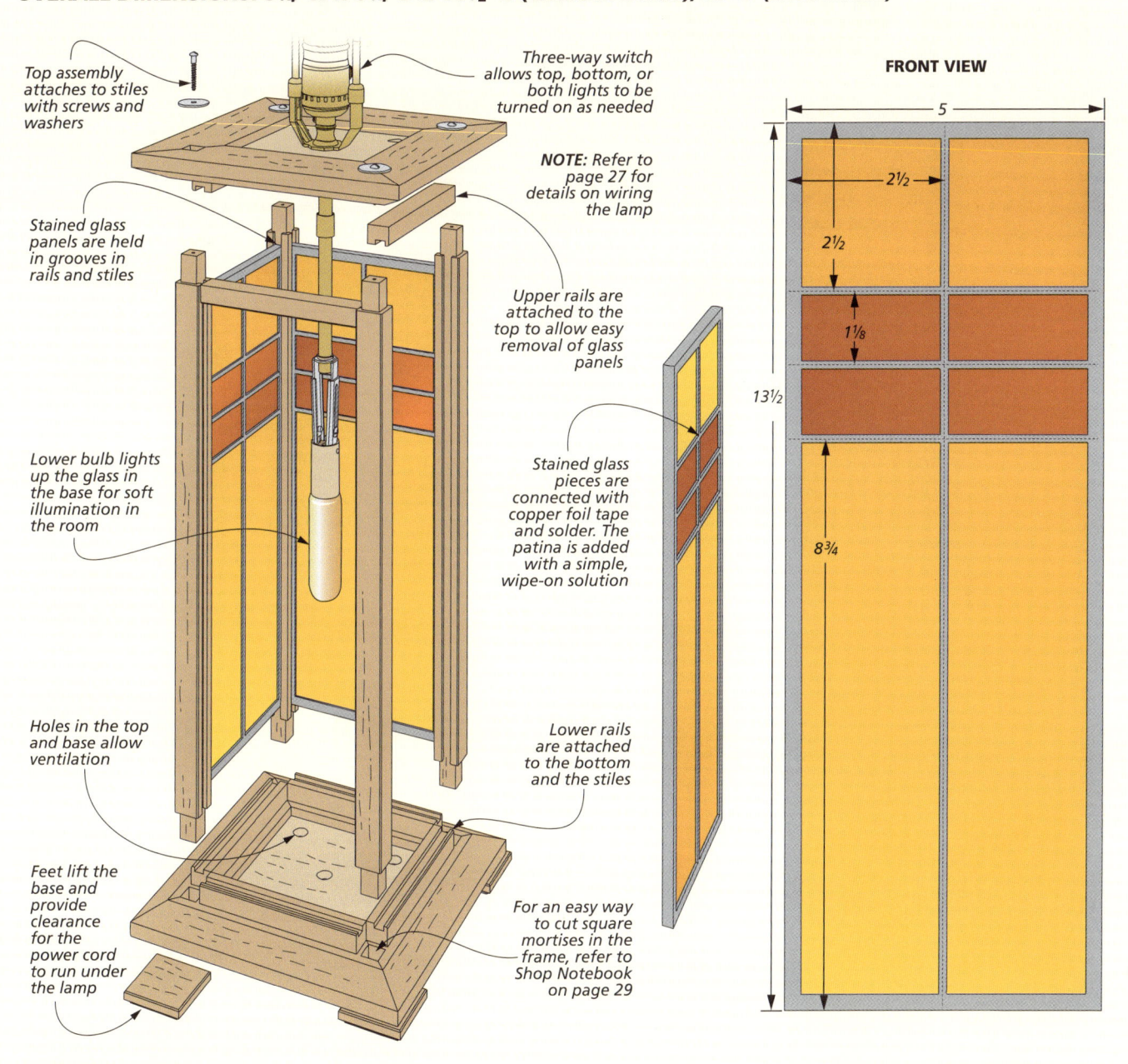

- Top assembly attaches to stiles with screws and washers
- Three-way switch allows top, bottom, or both lights to be turned on as needed
- Stained glass panels are held in grooves in rails and stiles
- **NOTE:** Refer to page 27 for details on wiring the lamp
- Upper rails are attached to the top to allow easy removal of glass panels
- Lower bulb lights up the glass in the base for soft illumination in the room
- Stained glass pieces are connected with copper foil tape and solder. The patina is added with a simple, wipe-on solution
- Holes in the top and base allow ventilation
- Lower rails are attached to the bottom and the stiles
- Feet lift the base and provide clearance for the power cord to run under the lamp
- For an easy way to cut square mortises in the frame, refer to Shop Notebook on page 29

FRONT VIEW
- 5
- 2½
- 2½
- 1⅛
- 13½
- 8¾

Materials, Supplies & Cutting Diagram

A	Top/Bottom Frame Pieces (8)	¾ x 1⅞ - 8
B	Frame Panels (2)	¼ ply. - 4¾ x 4¾
C	Feet (4)	⅜ x 1¾ - 1¾
D	Top Glass Panels (8)	¼ glass - 2½ x 2½
E	Center Glass Panels (16)	¼ glass - 2½ x 1⅛
F	Bottom Glass Panels (8)	¼ glass - 2½ x 8¾
G	Stiles (4)	¾ x ¾ - 15¾
H	Rails (8)	½ x ⅝ - 4¾

- (1 roll) ¼" Copper Foil Tape
- (1 roll) 60/40 Solder
- (1 Bottle) Flux
- (1 Bottle) Patina
- (1) Three-Wire Socket
- (1) Candelabra Base Socket
- (1) 35W Tubular Bulb
- (1) Brass Neck
- (1) 3" Brass Nipple
- (1) 4" Brass Nipple
- (1) Brass Coupling
- (1) Brass Hexagon Lock Nut
- (1) 18-gauge Lamp Cord (8'-long)
- (1) Harp
- (1) Shade
- (4) #6 x 1" Rh Woodscrews
- (4) 5/32" x ⅞" Fender Washers
- (1) 22-gauge Lamp Cord (12"-long)

¾" x 5" - 72" Red Oak (2.5 Bd. Ft.)

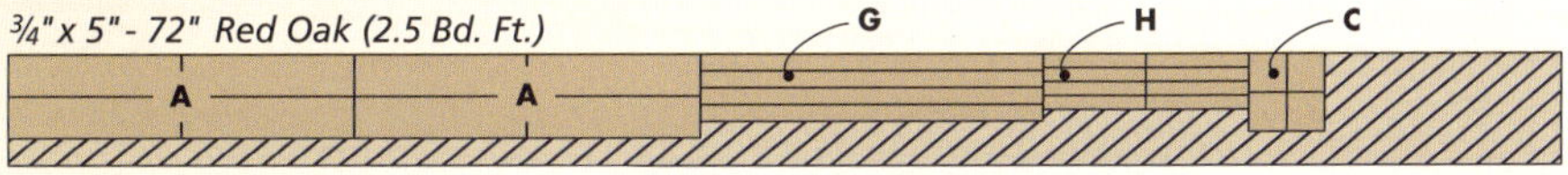

¼" x 6" - 12" Red Oak Plywood

making the
TOP & BOTTOM

The stained glass base of the lamp is sure to get a lot of attention. It starts with two identical frames, one on the bottom, the other serving as the top. These frames anchor the side panels that hold the stained glass. They also hold ¼" plywood panels that the electrical components are mounted to.

FRAMES. I made the top and bottom frame and panel assemblies using the techniques shown in the box below. The mitered frame pieces are beveled on the outer edge. A plywood panel fits into a groove on the inside edge. As you can see in the main drawing, I also drilled five holes in each plywood panel to allow airflow through the base to minimize the heat build up.

One unusual feature is the mortise that holds the stiles. I formed the mortise by cutting a notch in the end of each frame piece. You can find the details in Shop Notebook on page 29.

ASSEMBLY. Assemble the frames using glue and clamps. Be sure to align the notches carefully to form a square mortise. After the glue dries, you can turn your attention to the four small feet that fit on the bottom frame.

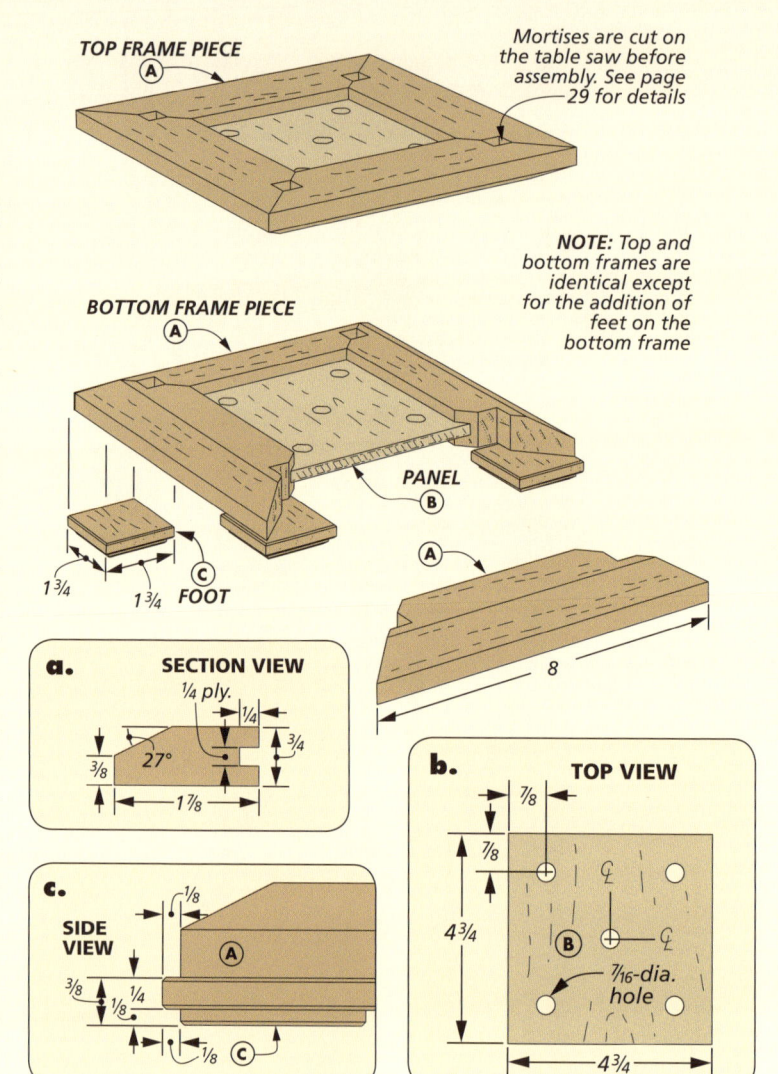

FEET. Four feet raise the frame and make room for the power cord. The far right drawing below shows how to cut the rabbets on all four sides of each foot. Then lightly sand a chamfer on the edges and glue the feet in place.

NOTE: Top and bottom frames are identical except for the addition of feet on the bottom frame

Mortises are cut on the table saw before assembly. See page 29 for details

STAINED GLASS

The stained glass panels are the highlight of the lamp. If you've never worked with glass, this is an easy place to start. The process is straightforward: Cut the glass pieces to size, wrap copper foil

---

How-To: Make the Frames & Feet

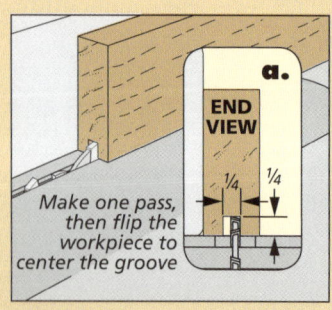

Notch. Start shaping the frame pieces by cutting a centered groove for the plywood panels.

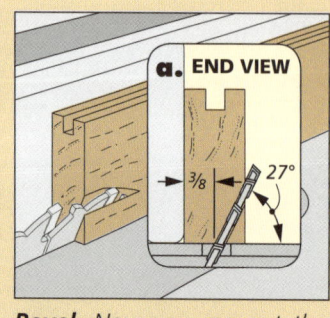

Bevel. Now you can cut the decorative bevel on the outside edge of the pieces.

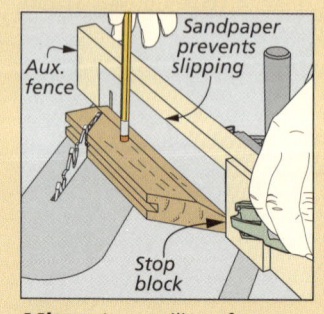

Miter. An auxiliary fence on the miter gauge makes cutting accurate miters a snap.

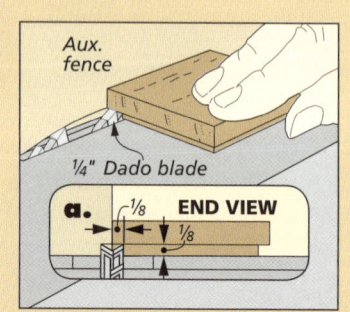

Feet. With most of the blade buried in an auxiliary fence, cut the shallow rabbets on the feet.

24 Woodsmith No. 198

tape on the edges, flux the tape, and solder them together. Sources on page 51 has information on finding the materials you'll need.

GETTING STARTED. The step-by-step instructions at right walk you through the process of making the panels. I made a simple jig with stops on the top and left edges to help keep the panel square while you cut and assemble the pieces (Step 1). Also, take a minute to identify the inside and outside faces of the glass. (The shiner face is the inside.)

WORKING WITH GLASS. Using a glass cutter to score the glass can take a little practice. I made a few practice cuts to get started, then cut the first panels to size. Keep a straightedge on the workpiece to steady the cut. Then use a quick snapping motion to break the glass along the scored line.

Steps 2 and 3 show how to wrap the tape around the edges and burnish it in place. Remember that it's really the tape that will hold everything together, so burnishing is a critical step.

ASSEMBLING THE PANELS. Flux allows the solder to flow easily into joints for a good bond. After brushing flux onto the taped edges, lay out the fully wrapped pieces on your worksurface (Step 5).

Now you can flow the solder into the joints by using the tip of the iron to heat the solder. I found this worked well and allowed me to make a consistent bead on the joints. The key is to keep moving.

I soldered the inside face first to help develop a good technique. Since this face isn't visible, you can refine your touch here and ensure a better finished product.

After soldering the outside joints, you can add another strip of tape to the outside edges (Step 7). Applying solder to this piece gives the panel a finished look.

Finally, you're ready for a little cleaning up. Lacquer thinner works well to remove finger oils and flux residue. Then just brush on the patina as shown in Step 8 to darken the solder.

GO ONLINE EXTRAS — To find a plan for the cutting and assembly jig, go to our website at Woodsmith.com

STEP ONE. With the proper tool, cutting glass is as easy as scoring and snapping. This jig and a spacer block make cutting a breeze.

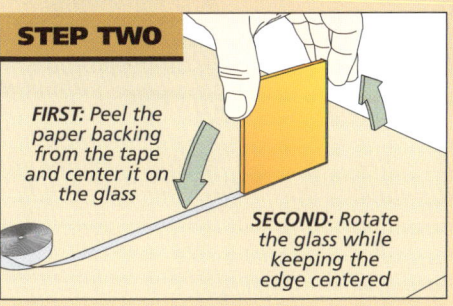

STEP TWO — Tape. Wrap the edges of each piece with the copper foil tape. By using a rolling motion, it's easy to keep the tape centered. 
FIRST: Peel the paper backing from the tape and center it on the glass.
SECOND: Rotate the glass while keeping the edge centered.

STEP THREE — Burnish. The end of the glass cutter is ideal for burnishing the tape onto the glass. This step fixes the tape to the edge for a solid joint.

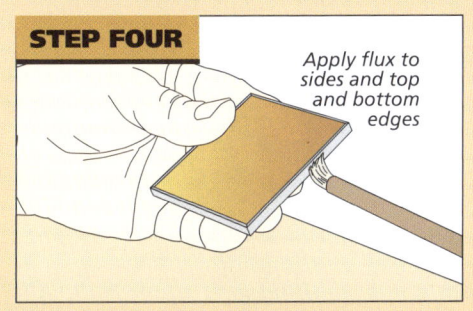

STEP FOUR — Flux. Apply the flux with a brush. Be sure to cover all of the copper foil tape to allow the solder to flow into the joint. Apply flux to sides and top and bottom edges.

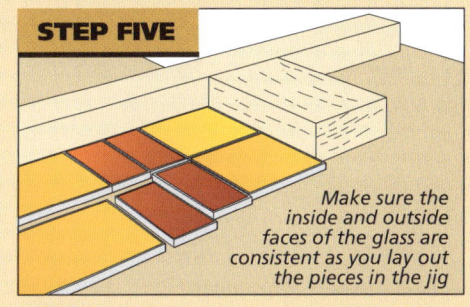

STEP FIVE — Assembly. The cutting jig now serves as an assembly platform to hold the pieces in perfect alignment for soldering the joints. Make sure the inside and outside faces of the glass are consistent as you lay out the pieces in the jig.

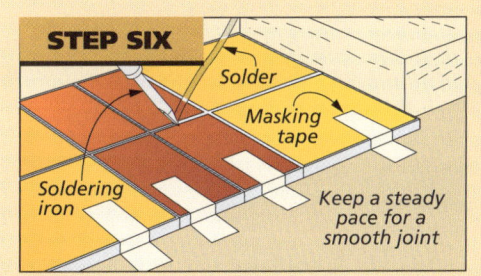

STEP SIX — Solder. You can rest your hands on the jig to hold them steady as you heat the solder and flow it into the joints. Try for an even bead. Soldering iron, Solder, Masking tape. Keep a steady pace for a smooth joint.

STEP SEVEN — Tape the Edges. Now you can add the tape on each edge and solder this piece, before you add the patina (for a uniform look). Add a strip of copper tape to the outside edge of the face of the panel.

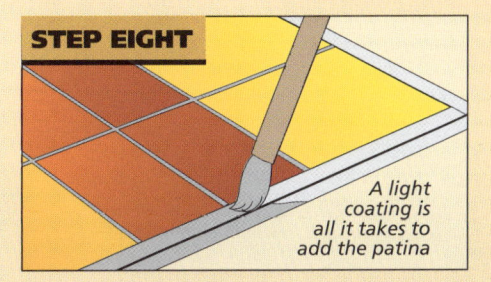

STEP EIGHT — Patina. After the soldering is complete, brush on a coat of patina fluid. The effect is instant, so you can easily see any spots you miss. A light coating is all it takes to add the patina.

▼ The finished glass panel looks authentic to the Craftsman style.

completing the LAMP

With the frames complete, you can turn your attention to the rails and stiles that house the stained glass panels. The top and bottom frames are connected to the four long stiles with a mortise and tenon joint. The joint is glued in the bottom frame, but secured with screws at the top.

The upper rails are glued to the top only. This allows the top frame to be removed to replace bulbs and access the stained glass panels in case they're damaged.

RAILS & STILES. The main drawing at right shows the dimensions of the rails and stiles. Details 'b' and 'c' show the profiles of each piece. The rails start out as ¾"-wide blanks that are ripped to final width after cutting the groove. You can see how I made them in the box below.

The thing to keep in mind is that the glass panels should slide easily into the grooves. Also, you may need to make the grooves deeper if your panels finish a bit wider than the plan shows.

When you've completed those tasks, you can finish up by drilling centered ³⁄₃₂"-dia. holes in the ends of the tenons. These are the pilot holes for screws that attach the stiles to the upper frame (far right drawing at the bottom of the opposite page).

CHAMFER. The outside edges of the stiles and the one outside edge of the rails are chamfered as shown in details 'b' and 'c.' I used a sanding block for this.

How-To: Make the Rails & Stiles

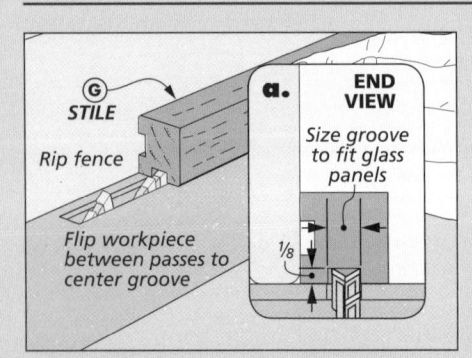

Make the Stiles. With a dado blade installed, cut the shallow grooves on two adjacent faces to hold the glass.

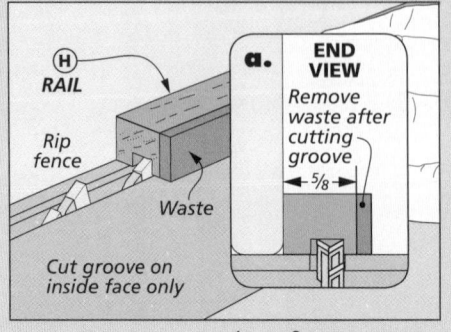

Rails. Starting with a ½" x ¾" blank, first cut a centered groove, then install a rip blade and rip the blank to final width.

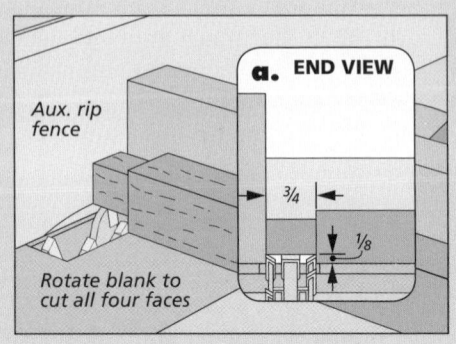

Tenons. Install an auxiliary rip fence and use a ¾" dado blade to cut the tenons on the ends of the stiles.

26   Woodsmith   No. 198

It's a good idea to dry fit the entire assembly, including the glass panels. The tenons should fit snugly into the mortises on the top and bottom frames.

ASSEMBLY. At this point, glue the rails and stiles to the bottom frame (left drawing, below). Next, fit the top in place on the stiles and glue the upper rails to the top frame.

STAIN & FINISH. After the glue dries, you can stain the lamp. Sources on page 51 has the details on the finish I used. Once the stain dried, I added the clear finish.

WIRING. Wiring the lamp isn't too difficult, but if you're uncomfortable, it's probably best to hire an electrician to wire it for you or take it to a lamp store for help.

The unique thing about this lamp is the three-wire switch on the upper socket. This switch controls both the upper and lower lights. The socket has two "hot" leads and a single neutral post. One hot is for the lamp, and the other connects to a separate fixture, in this case the candelabra socket in the base. The drawings at right show the assembly of the lamp parts, as well as the wiring plan.

With this type of switch, it's best to "pigtail" the lower socket to the upper one. I used 22-gauge lamp cord to make the connection from the socket to bottom fixture. This way, you simply connect the cord to the upper socket and avoid the need to splice wires.

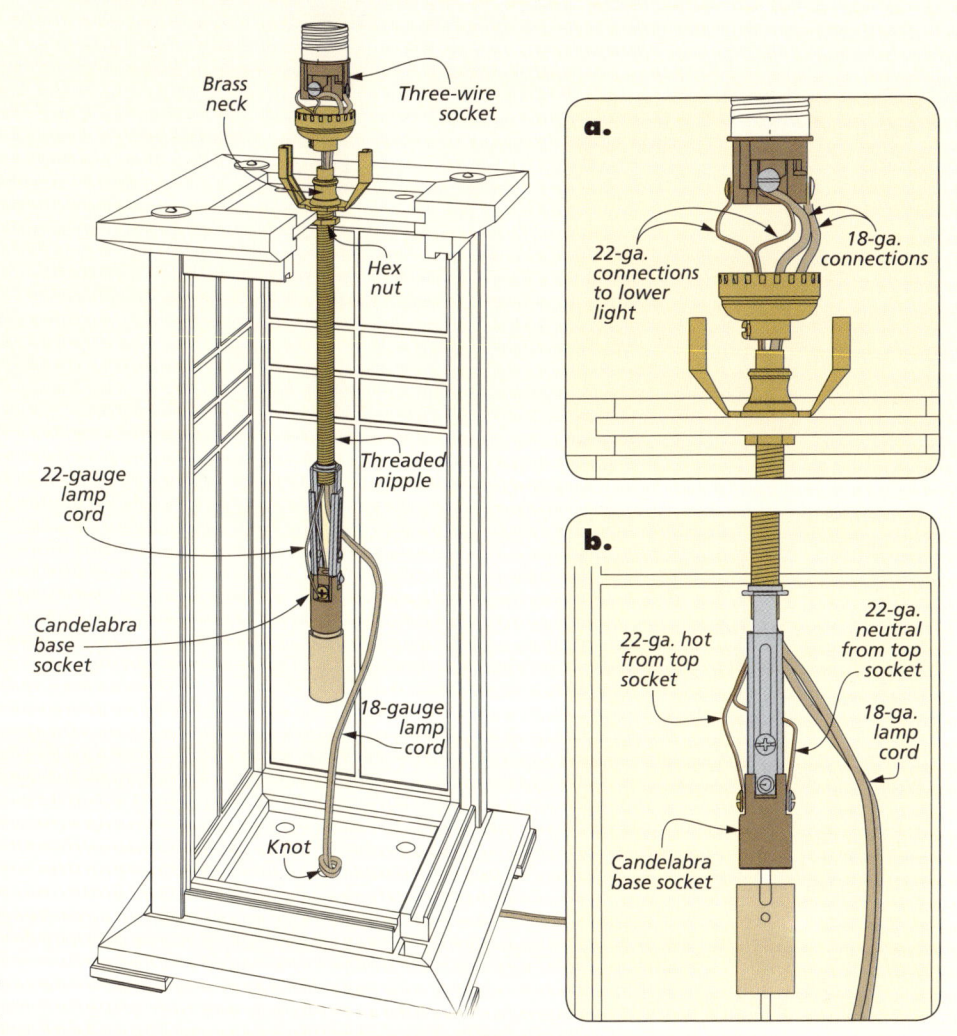

You can start by tying a knot in the 18-gauge cord near the base to prevent it from pulling off the connections. After that, thread the 18-gauge cord and a short length of 22-gauge cord up through the nipple to the three-wire socket. Then, connect the hot and neutral wires to the socket. Now you can attach the 22-gauge wire to the hot post that controls the socket and neutral posts on the socket, as well.

After connecting to the lower socket, test to make sure that all the switch positions work. Then, all that remains is to install the glass panels, secure the top, and attach the lamp shade.

Assemble the Lamp

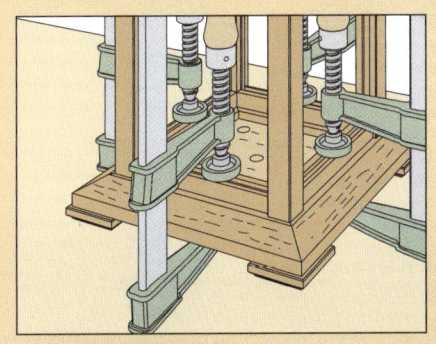

Assemble the Base. Glue the stiles into the mortises and the rails to the face. A snug fitting tenon doesn't require a clamp.

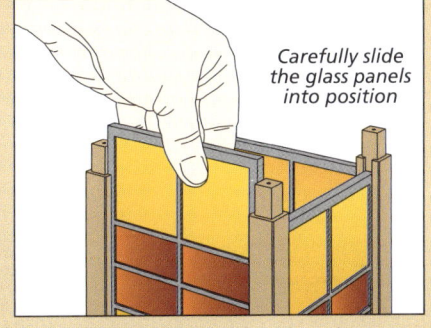

Add the Glass Panels. The glass panels should slide into the grooves in the stiles without binding.

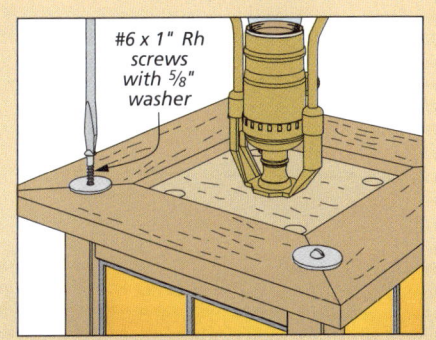

Install the Light. After fitting the upper socket into the frame, attach the frame using screws and washers.

tips from our shop

SHOP NOTEBOOK

Bench Seat Jig

Creating the sculpted seat for the bench on page 16 is a lot easier than it looks. The secret is to use a jig to support your router while you "scoop" out the seat, as shown in the photo at right.

The router is attached to a long sled that rides on a pair of curved rails. The rails guide the router in a gentle arc. By making a series of overlapping, curved passes across the width of the seat blank, you create a hollow.

THE JIG. As you can see in the drawing below, the jig is really pretty simple. The sled is just a piece of ½" plywood with a pair of hardwood cleats added as stiffeners. And the guide rails are cut from hardwood. A spacer is glued to one face, flush with the bottom edge. This provides clearance for the router bit.

To use the jig, start by laying out the ends and centerline of the two hollows on the seat blank. Then clamp the guide rails of the jig against the edges of the blank. An index mark at the center of the guide rails helps with positioning the rails on the seat blank.

When it comes to the actual routing, you'll want to take light passes, removing no more than ¹⁄₁₆" of material at a time.

▼ A bowl and tray bit is used to shape the bench seat.

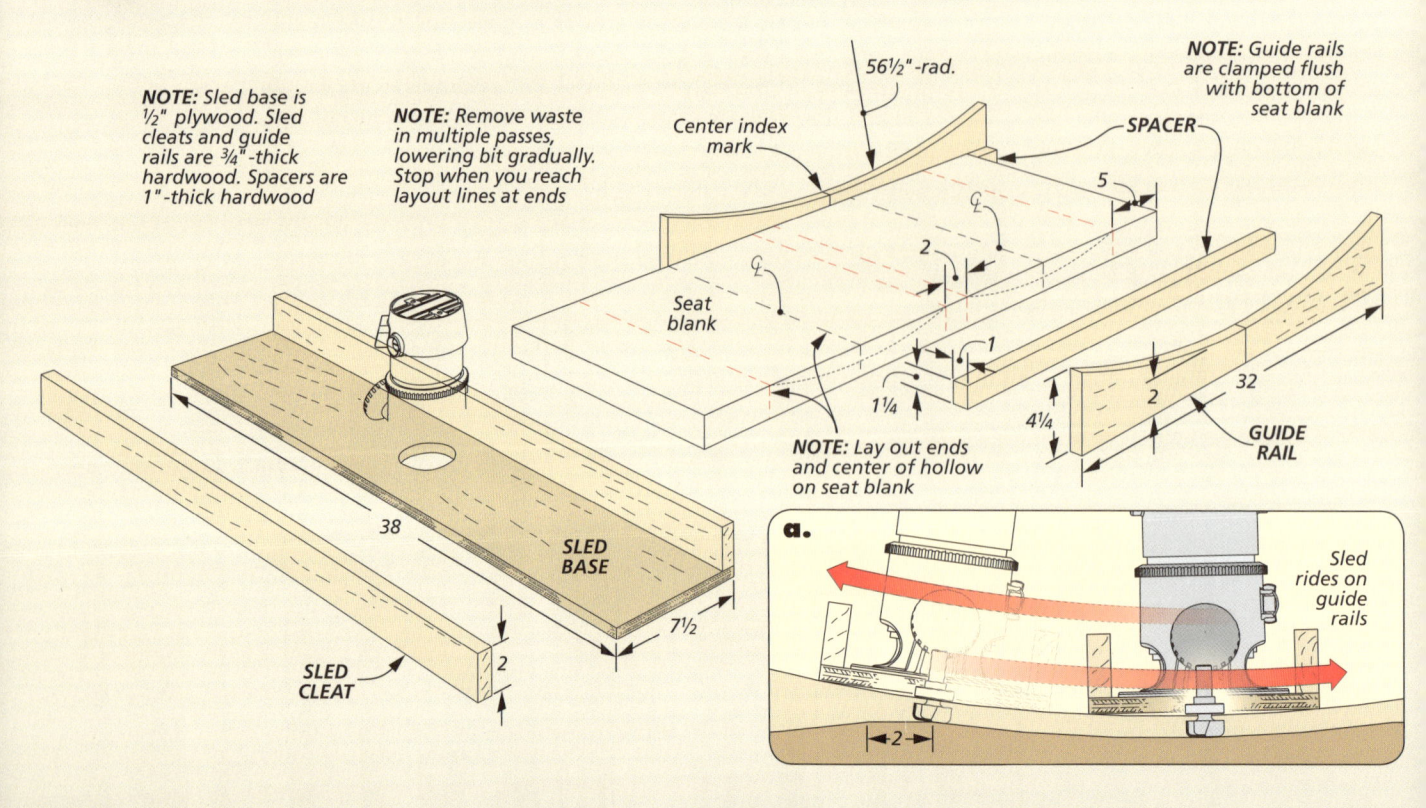

NOTE: Sled base is ½" plywood. Sled cleats and guide rails are ¾"-thick hardwood. Spacers are 1"-thick hardwood

NOTE: Remove waste in multiple passes, lowering bit gradually. Stop when you reach layout lines at ends

NOTE: Guide rails are clamped flush with bottom of seat blank

NOTE: Lay out ends and center of hollow on seat blank

Wedged Tenons

The seat of the bench on page 16 is joined to the base with wedged mortise and tenon joints. The wedges prevent the tenons from working loose. Because they're so thin, I cut them at the band saw.

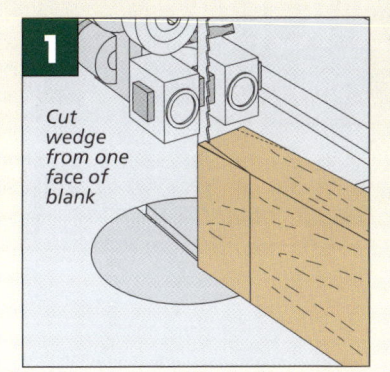

I started by ripping a blank to match the width of the tenon. At the band saw, I cut a thin wedge off one face of the blank (Figure 1). Next, I cut a second wedge off the opposite face (Figure 2).

Before cutting the next pair of wedges, I simply crosscut the end of the blank, using a miter gauge, as shown in Figure 3.

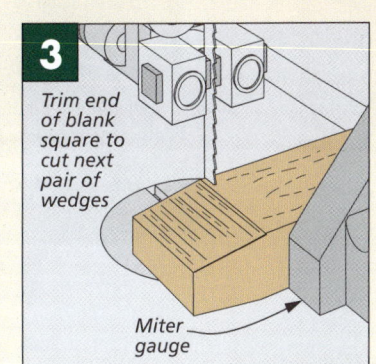

▲ Thin wedges driven into the end of the tenon locks it in place.

1 Cut wedge from one face of blank

2 Cut wedge from second face of blank

3 Trim end of blank square to cut next pair of wedges

Square Mortises

Unless you own a mortising machine, creating a square mortise usually means drilling a hole and squaring up the sides with a chisel. Getting a tight fit is always a challenge, especially when you're dealing with through mortises, like the ones on the lamp on page 22.

Fortunately, in this case, there's an easier way. Because the mortises are centered on the joint lines of the mitered frames, you can actually cut the mortises on the table saw. The trick is to cut a notch on the end of each mitered piece to create half of the mortise, as shown in the upper left drawing. I used a stop block on my miter gauge fence in order to position all the notches identically.

When the frames are glued up, the notches will come together to form perfect, square mortises.

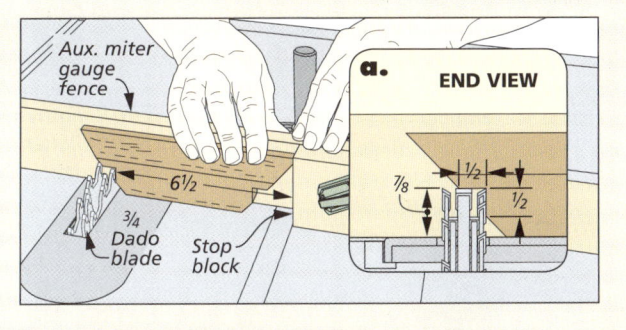

Mortise is formed by notches in miter joint

Shelf Pin Template

In order to drill the shelf pin holes in the case of the armoire on page 30, I made the simple drilling template shown at right. It's nothing more than a piece of hardboard with a row of ¼" holes drilled in it at the drill press. Cleats are added to both faces of the template to help position it against the case of the armoire.

To drill the holes at the front of the armoire, simply place the template so the cleat registers against the front edge of the case (Figure 1). Then to drill the back holes, place the template so the cleat registers against the shoulder of the rabbet cut in the back of the case (Figure 2).

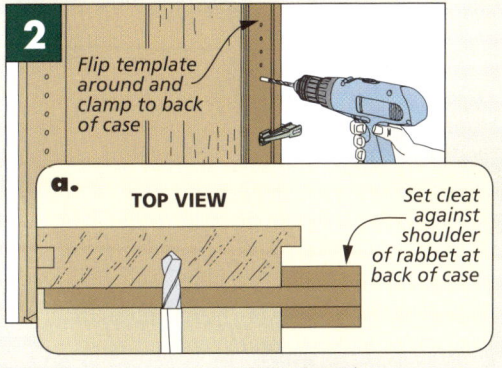

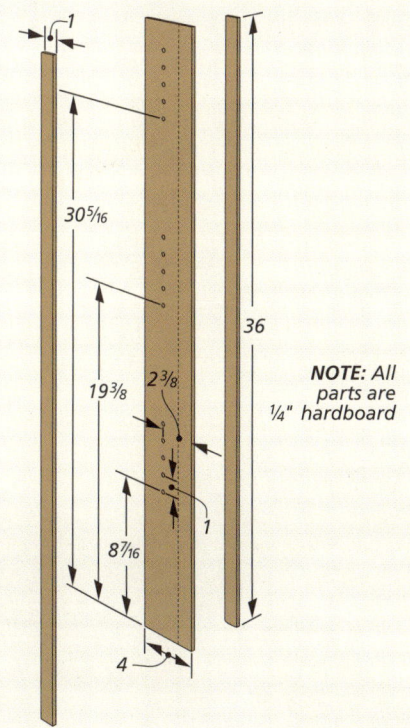

1 Clamp template to front edge of case

2 Flip template around and clamp to back of case

a. TOP VIEW — Set cleat against shoulder of rabbet at back of case

NOTE: All parts are ¼" hardboard

Heirloom Project

cherry Armoire

Offering three types of storage in a single, compact package, this stylish project serves all your needs.

Having an abundance of storage options in the bedroom is an ideal situation. Of course, first off you need hanging "closet" storage. Then add to this some easy-access shelving. And don't forget a set of drawers to contain all the odd and ends. Now, how about incorporating all of these needs into one project? What you'd have is the attractive armoire shown at left — a versatile, all-in-one bedroom storage unit.

I won't try to fool you by downplaying the size of this project. But considering all the storage it supplies, the footprint is relatively compact — only about 2' by 3'. And honestly, the construction is a breeze. You'll find that the woodworking is straightforward and definitely pleasurable. I used an efficient mix of solid wood and plywood — no large panel glueups are required. Likewise, the joinery strikes a nice balance between strength and practicality.

As you can clearly see, this armoire is more than just a big box. Although simple, the details really hit the nail on the head. From the flared feet of the base to the simple crown, it all works together perfectly. So what are you waiting for?

CONSTRUCTION DETAILS

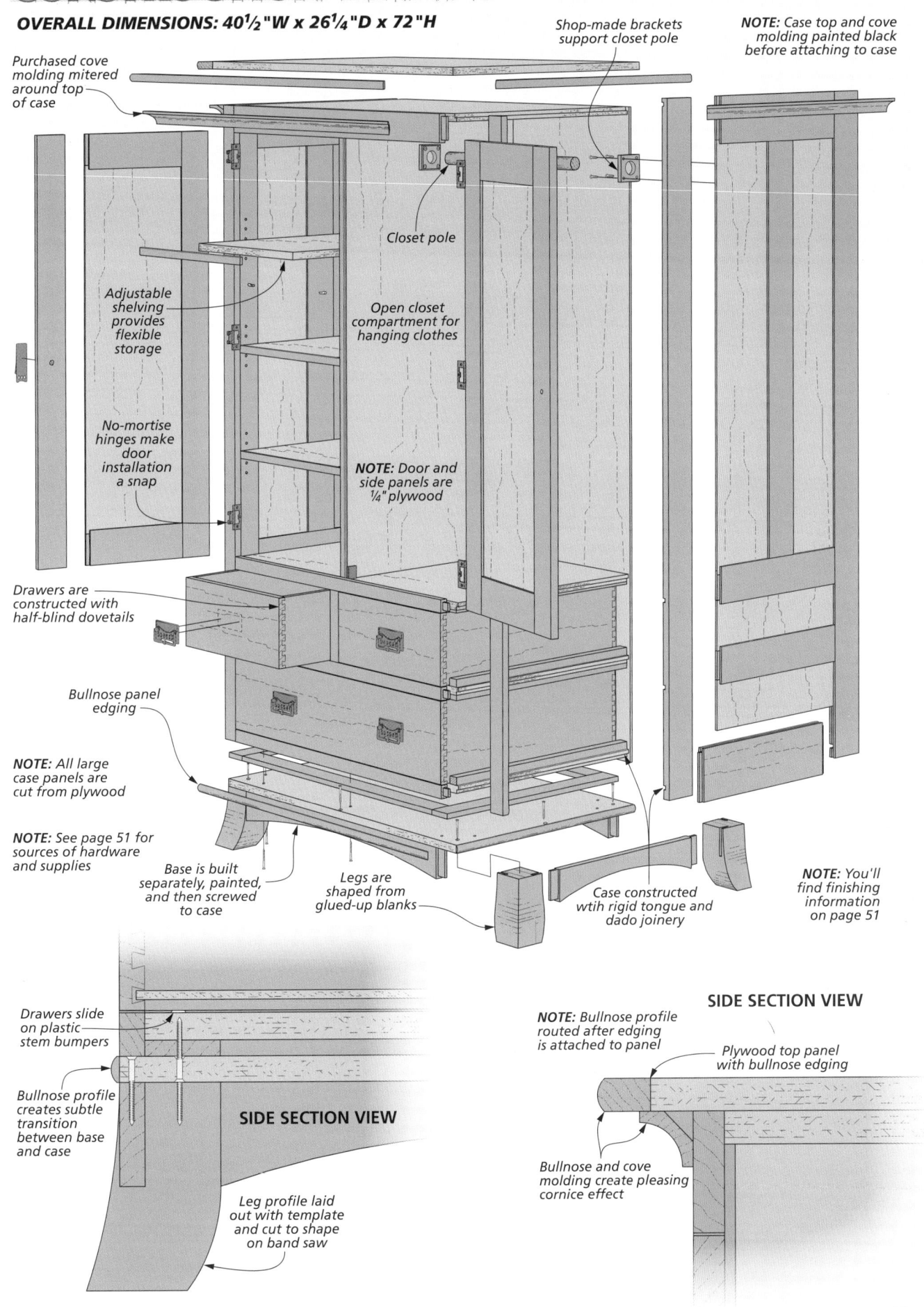

OVERALL DIMENSIONS: 40½"W x 26¼"D x 72"H

Purchased cove molding mitered around top of case

Shop-made brackets support closet pole

NOTE: Case top and cove molding painted black before attaching to case

Closet pole

Adjustable shelving provides flexible storage

Open closet compartment for hanging clothes

No-mortise hinges make door installation a snap

NOTE: Door and side panels are ¼" plywood

Drawers are constructed with half-blind dovetails

Bullnose panel edging

NOTE: All large case panels are cut from plywood

NOTE: See page 51 for sources of hardware and supplies

Base is built separately, painted, and then screwed to case

Legs are shaped from glued-up blanks

Case constructed with rigid tongue and dado joinery

NOTE: You'll find finishing information on page 51

Drawers slide on plastic stem bumpers

Bullnose profile creates subtle transition between base and case

SIDE SECTION VIEW

Leg profile laid out with template and cut to shape on band saw

NOTE: Bullnose profile routed after edging is attached to panel

SIDE SECTION VIEW

Plywood top panel with bullnose edging

Bullnose and cove molding create pleasing cornice effect

Woodsmith.com   Woodsmith   31

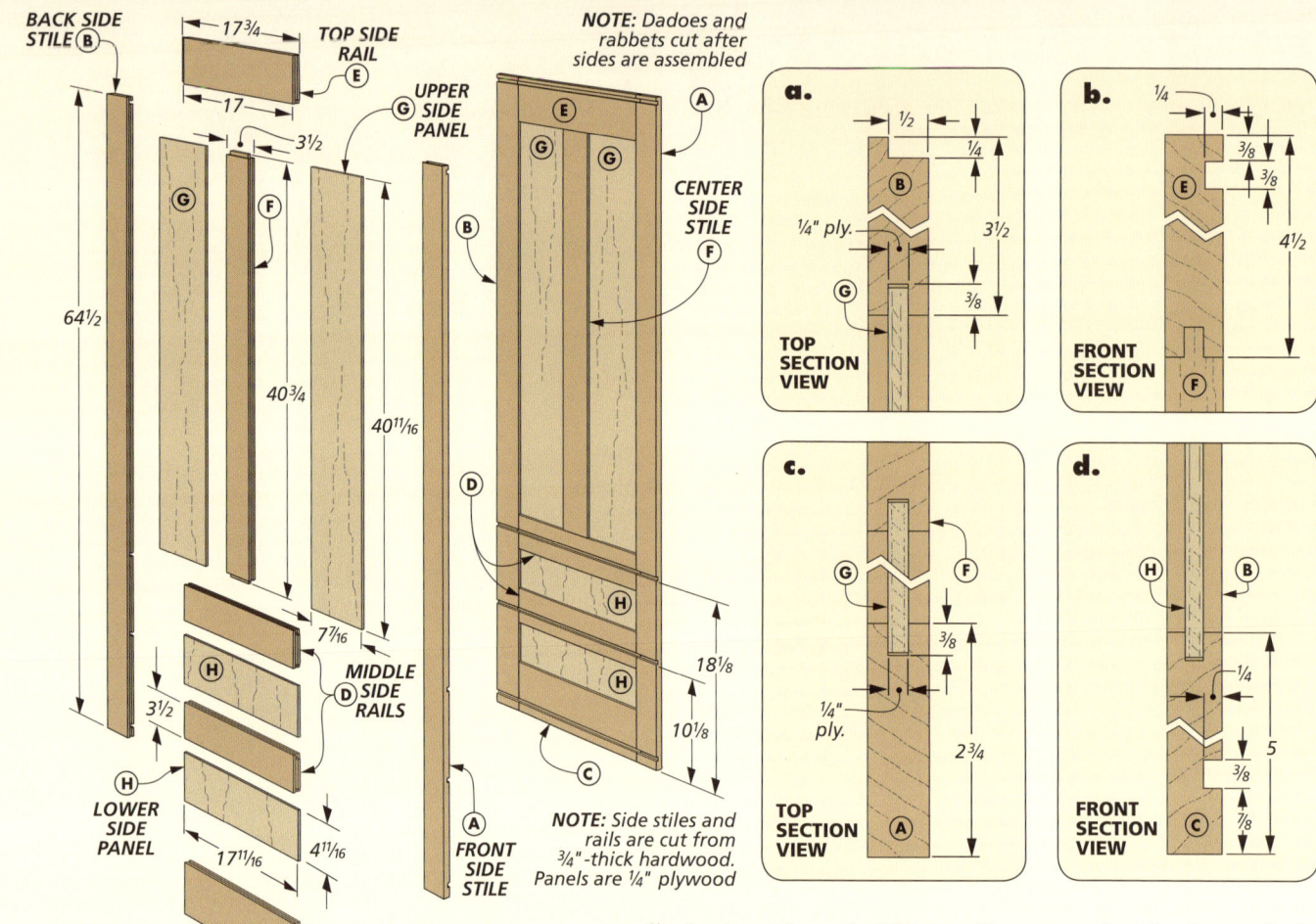

assembling the SIDES

One of the features that contributes to the stylish look of the armoire is the makeup of the frame and panel sides — two large vertical panels over two smaller horizontal panels. This is where the project gets underway. You'll assemble the two sides with stub tenon and groove joinery. Then the next step is to connect them into a rigid case with a set of plywood dividers.

THE PARTS. Before you get busy cutting the frame rails and stiles to size, let me point out a couple of important details.

First, note that the front stile is ¾" narrower than the back stile. This difference in width simply accommodates the thickness of the face frame you'll add later. This also means the two sides need to be built as mirror images. Likewise, when you look at the drawing above, you'll see that the frame rails are cut to three different widths.

CENTERED GROOVES. As I mentioned, the sides are constructed with stub tenon and groove joinery. So the next step is to cut centered grooves in all the pieces.

The goal is to size the grooves for a snug fit over the ¼" plywood you're going to use for the panels. The left drawing in the How-To box shows a good way to get this done at the table saw. With a standard blade in the saw, start with a cut near the center of the edge. Then, flip the piece end-for-end and make a second cut. Adjust the rip fence and repeat the process until you're satisfied with the fit. Don't forget that the center stile and two middle rails will need a groove on both long edges.

How-To: Stub Tenon & Groove

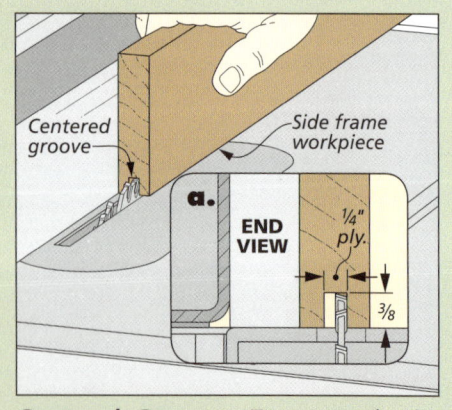

Centered Grooves. To accurately size and center the grooves, flip the pieces end-for-end between passes.

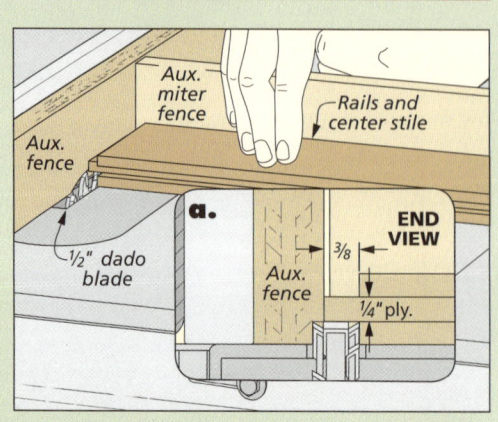

Stub Tenons. After adjusting the rip fence, sneak up on the thickness of the tenons by raising the blade between sets of passes.

STUB TENONS. Now you can swap out the standard blade for a dado blade to cut stub tenons on both ends of the rails and center stile. In the right drawing in the box on the opposite page, you'll notice that I buried the blade in an auxiliary fence. This allows you to cut the full length of the tenon in a single pass. However, you'll still want to sneak up on the thickness of the tenons. A gap-free fit to the grooves will produce the strongest glue joint.

PANELS. Once the panels are cut to size, the side frames can be glued up. To ensure that the assembly went smoothly, I sized the panels for an overall $1/16$" clearance in both dimensions.

PIECEMEAL GLUEUP. When it comes to involved glueups, I've always favored a relaxed, multi-step approach. Here, both the size and complexity of the assemblies make this especially appealing. The drawings in the box at right break it down for you.

Since wood movement won't be a problem, you can glue the plywood panels into the grooves for a stronger assembly. And remember to check for square at each step along the way.

DADOES. The four horizontal dividers connect the sides with tongue and dado joints — a good choice for maximum racking resistance. So when the clamps come off and the assemblies are cleaned up, cutting the dadoes in the sides is your next task.

The box at right shows how I did this with a $3/8$" dado blade in the table saw. The large side assemblies are a little bit unwieldy, but with some outboard support positioned to the left of the saw, it shouldn't be a problem. Make sure you cut the dadoes in pairs so they align accurately.

BACK RABBET. After cutting all four pairs of dadoes, I completed this stage of the work by cutting rabbets to hold the $1/4$" plywood back panel. You can use the same dado blade but you'll need to bury it in an auxiliary rip fence.

Shop Tip: A Step-By-Step Glueup

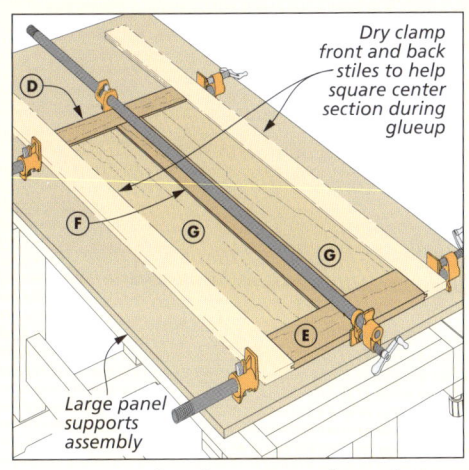

Step One. Glue the center stile and upper panels between the top and upper middle rail. The outer stiles keep things square.

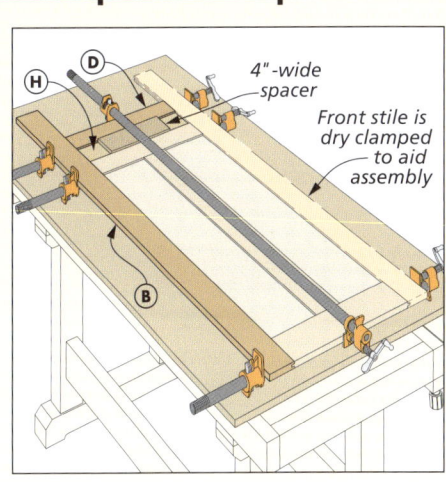

More Parts. Next, add one outer stile, the upper horizontal panel, and the lower middle rail. A spacer helps position the rail.

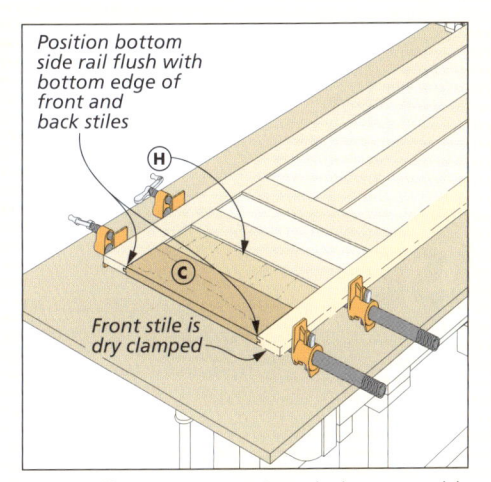

A Small Step. I continued the assembly with an easy addition — the bottom rail and the lower horizontal panel.

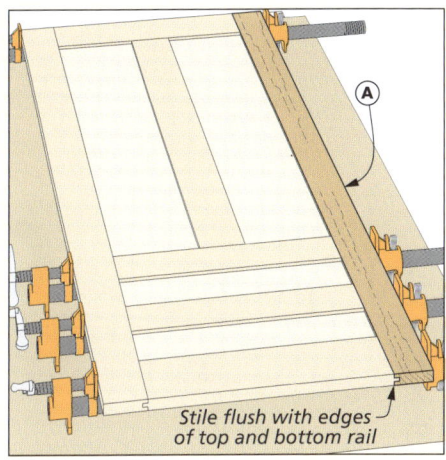

Wrap It Up. After doing its part to help keep everything aligned and square, the front stile can now be glued in place.

How-To: Dadoes & Rabbet

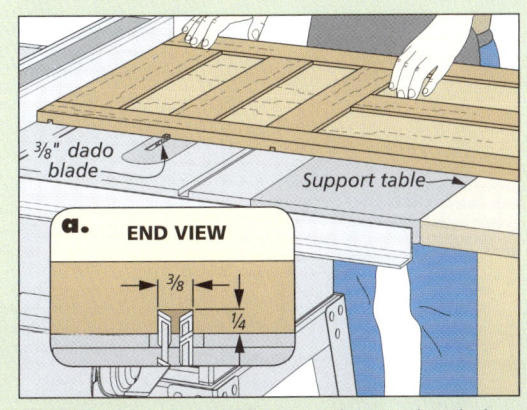

Dadoes. Use the rip fence to locate the dadoes in the side assemblies. Cut the corresponding dadoes in both sides before readjusting the fence.

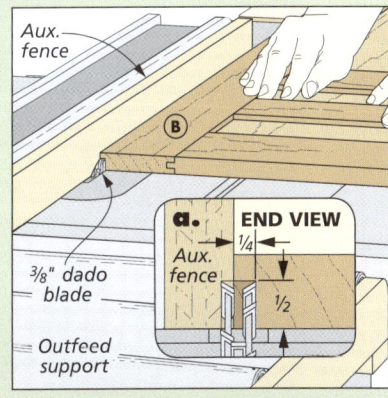

Back Rabbet. You'll have to bury the blade in an auxiliary rip fence to cut the rabbets for the plywood back.

Woodsmith.com

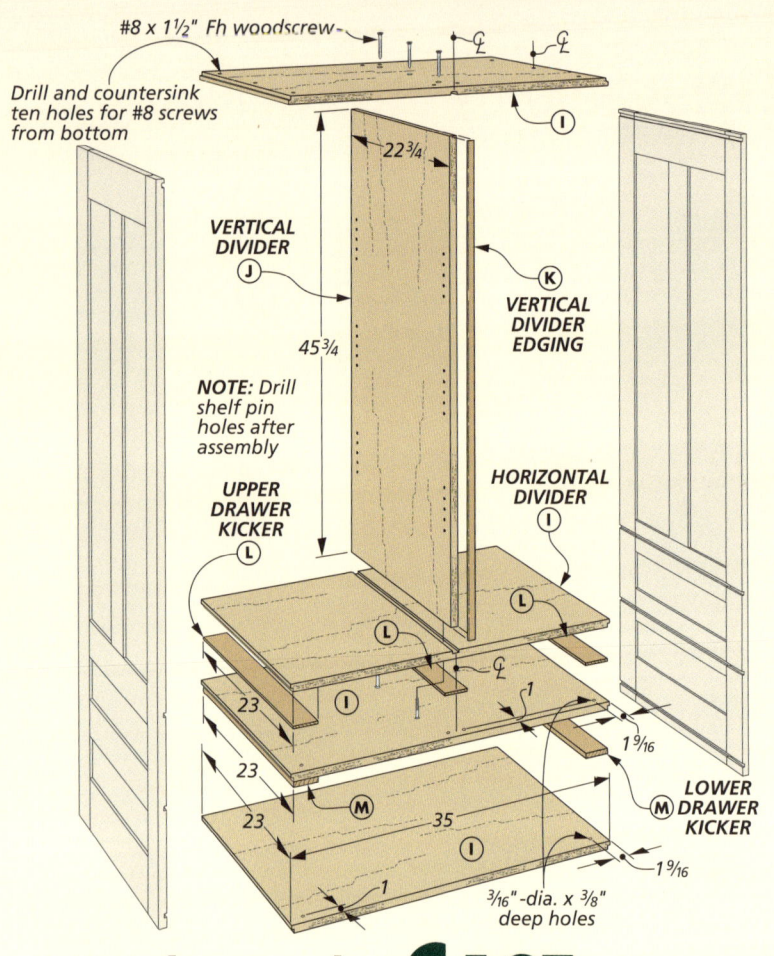

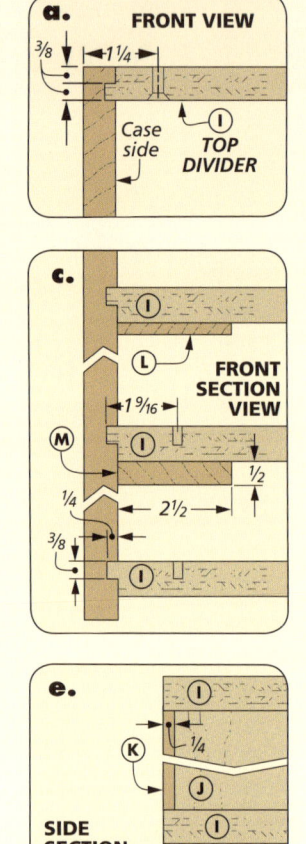

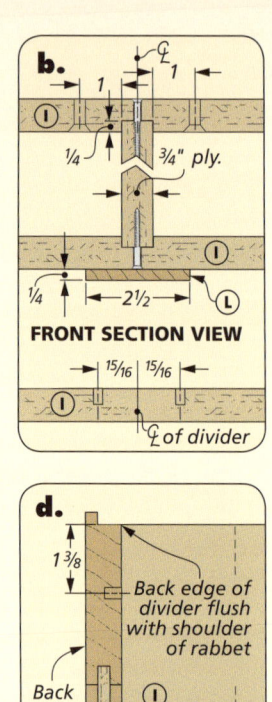

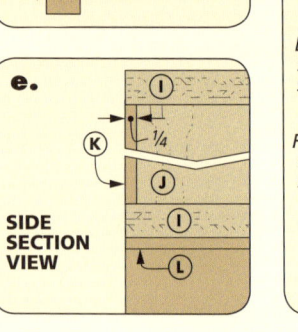

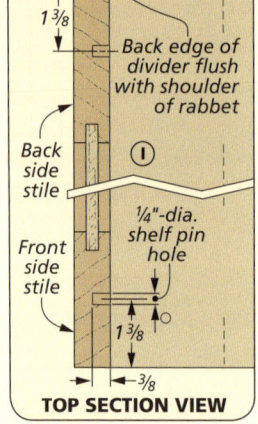

completing the CASE

With the sides completed, the pace of progress is going to pick up. After fitting the horizontal and vertical dividers, you can assemble the case and then add a face frame and the back.

THE DIVIDERS. The four identically sized horizontal dividers should be cut to fit from the front edge of the sides to the shoulder of the rabbet for the back (detail 'd'). Then you can switch to a dado blade to cut a tongue on each end, as shown in the box below and details 'a' and 'c.'

The vertical divider is captured in a pair of centered dadoes in the top and upper middle horizontal divider (How-To box and detail 'b'). Just take care to cut these dadoes on the correct faces.

The front edge of the vertical divider won't be covered by the face frame. So after cutting this

How-To: Divider Joinery

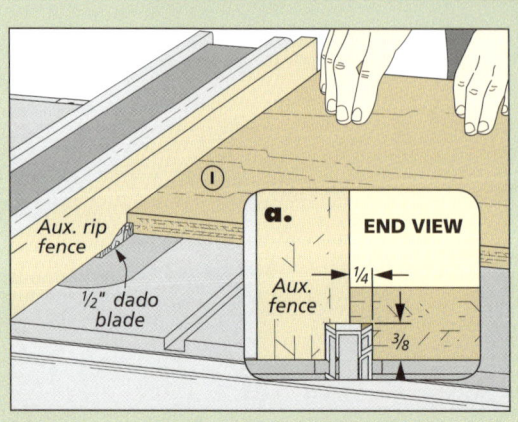

Tongues. I buried a dado blade in an auxiliary rip fence to cut tongues on the horizontal dividers. Gradually tweak the blade height for a snug fit.

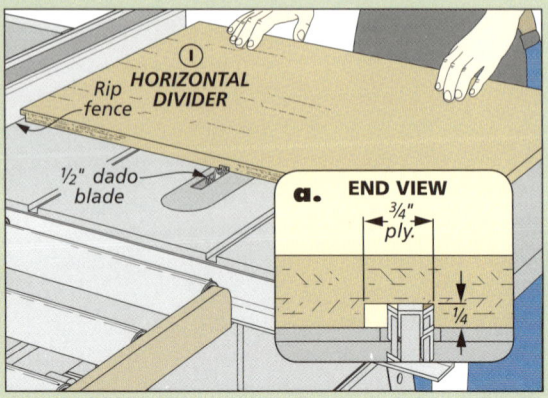

Centered Dadoes. To accurately center and size the dadoes for the vertical divider, make two passes flipping the panels end-for-end in between.

34   Woodsmith   No. 198

part to size, you'll need to add a piece of ¼"-thick edging, as shown in detail 'e,' opposite.

LOTS OF HOLES. Now before you begin putting the pieces together, you have several "boring" tasks to take on. First, the bottom and lower middle divider need holes for stem bumpers that act as drawer glides (details 'b' and 'c,' opposite). The top and upper middle divider each get a set of countersunk screw holes used to fasten the vertical divider (detail 'b,' opposite). Finally, the top divider has a set of countersunk holes used to attach the top.

A RELAXED ASSEMBLY. Like the side frames, it works best to tackle the assembly in stages. I started by fastening the vertical divider between the top and upper middle divider with glue and screws. Then, I glued this assembly to one side. I followed up with the remaining dividers, and finally added the second side.

INTERIOR DETAILS. When the clamps come off, you can finish up a few interior details. First, the upper left compartment needs holes for shelf pins. As shown on page 29, these can be drilled accurately with the aid of a template. The margin drawing on the opposite page shows where they go.

And while access was still wide open, I added a set of kickers to the drawer openings (main drawing and detail 'c,' opposite page).

A FACE FRAME. The case is now ready for a face frame. As you can see above, I constructed the large face frame with mortise and tenon joints to take advantage of the rigidity this joinery provides. Aside from the size, building the face frame is really pretty straightforward.

After cutting all the pieces to size, I laid out the mortises in the stiles and two of the rails. If you position the corresponding pieces side-by-side, you can get this done quickly and accurately. Let me note that while the two lower rails flush out with the top of the dividers, the upper middle rail is positioned to form a ¼" tall containment lip at the front of the upper compartment (detail 'c').

From here on out, the How-To box at left is your guide. I drilled out the mortises at the drill press and then squared them up at the bench. A dado blade in the table saw will take care of the tenons. And once assembled, the face frame is simply glued to the front of the case. Plenty of clamps and cauls is the key here.

THE BACK. The case can be wrapped up by adding the plywood back. To allow it to be removed for access, I installed it with screws only (detail 'd').

Face Frame Joinery

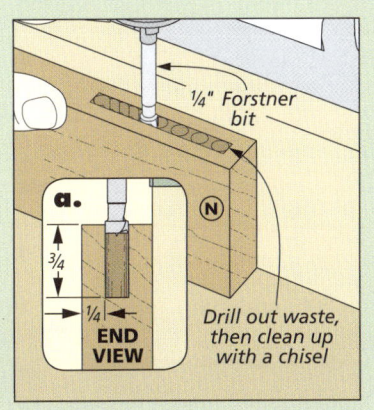

Mortises. Start by drilling a series of unconnected holes, then remove the waste between them.

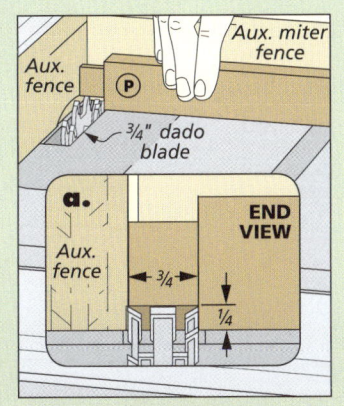

Tenons. After cutting the tenons to thickness, you'll need to trim the edge shoulders.

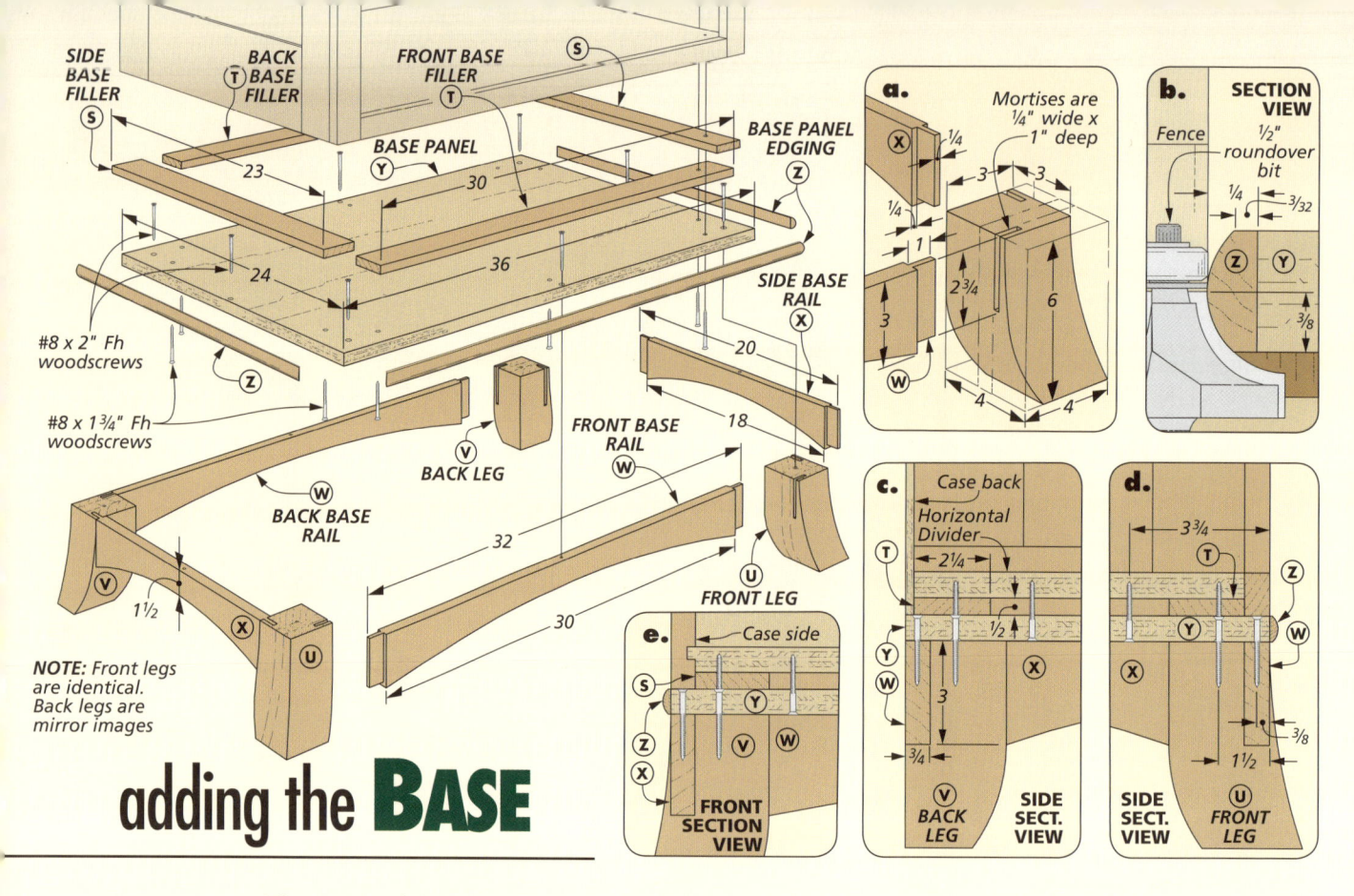

adding the BASE

The curves of the base are a nice complement to the straight lines of the case. Making and installing this assembly was next on my list.

FILLERS. Before tackling construction of the base, I thought I'd better prepare the case for it. All this takes is the addition of a set of fillers to the underside of the case, as in the main drawing.

LEGS FIRST. The base starts by assembling a frame made up of four legs and four rails.

A plywood base panel with molded edging is then added to the top of the frame.

I started on the base by shaping the four flared legs. As you see in details 'c' and 'd,' the front and back legs are slightly different. While both outside faces of the front legs flare outward, the rear face of the back legs is flat. However, as you'll see, the procedure for making both sets follows essentially the same course.

All the legs start as 4"-square by 6"-long blanks. So I glued up one long blank by sandwiching a layer of ¾"-thick stock between two layers of 1¾"-thick stock. Then I planed it to final thickness before cutting the leg blanks from it.

STEP-BY-STEP. At this point, you can refer to the box on the following page for step-by-step guidance. I'll fill in any blanks.

The front legs are identical while the back legs end up as

You'll find a full-size pattern for the legs on our website at Woodsmith.com

How-To: Make the Base Rails

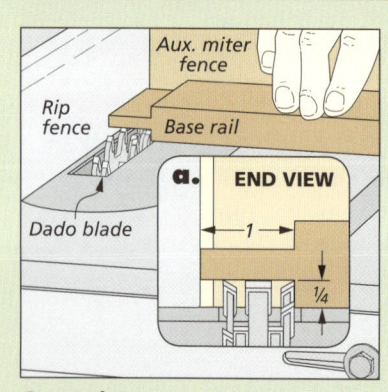

Several Passes. I cut the 1"-long tenons on the rails with a couple passes across a wide dado blade.

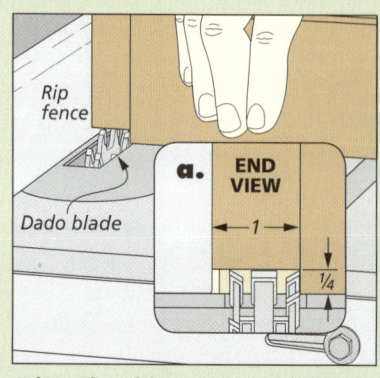

Edge Shoulders. Next, you'll need to cut a short shoulder on only the lower edge of each tenon.

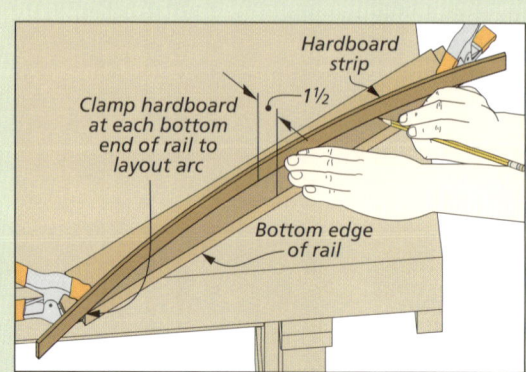

Rail Profiles. Mark the height of the profile at the rail's centerpoint. Then bend a flexible strip of hardboard to your mark and trace along it.

36   Woodsmith   No. 198

a mirror-image pair. And even though they have different final dimensions and shapes, it's easier to begin the job from the same point. Then, along the way you can simply skip one of the profile cuts on the back legs and replace it with a straight trim cut. However, I did take a minute to clearly mark which blank would go where.

MORTISES. The legs are connected to the base rails with open end mortise and tenon joints. You'll want to lay out and cut the mortises while the blanks are square.

THE SHAPING. There are really only a couple tricks to shaping the legs at the band saw. The first is to make a hardboard template to simplify the layout. To do this, you can use the half-size pattern shown at right or you'll find a full-size pattern on our website.

Your other secret weapon is masking tape. As you cut the profiles, you begin to eliminate the flat surfaces needed for layout and stability on the following cuts. The solution is to save the cutoffs and tape them back in place. It's simple and it works.

THE RAILS. I guarantee that making the base rails will go a lot faster. The How-To box and drawings on the opposite page provide the basic details you'll need. And once the profiles on the rails are cut and smoothed, you can glue up the base frame.

BASE PANEL. Adding the base panel will complete the job. It's simply a piece of plywood with molded edging mitered around the front and both sides.

Once the panel is cut to size, you can miter the ¼"-thick edging to fit and glue it in place. It's easier to rout the bullnose profile with the edging already attached (detail 'b,' opposite page).

The top panel is screwed and glued to the base frame. But before doing this, I drilled the countersunk screw holes on the underside used to attach the base to the case. Once this is done, you can install the panel and then screw the base to the case.

How-To: Flared Legs

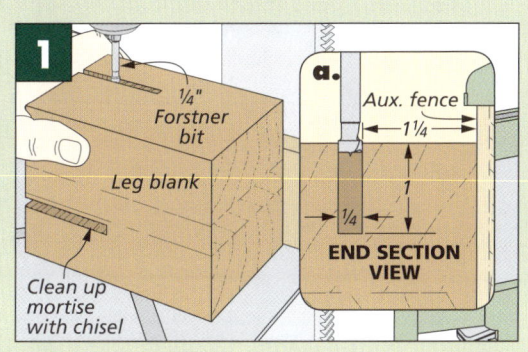

1 Mortises First. To accommodate the profiles, locate the mortises 1¼" from the outside faces. Drill out the waste, then square them with chisels.

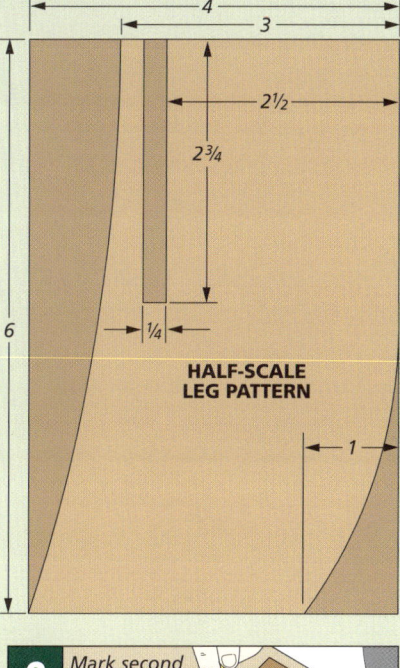

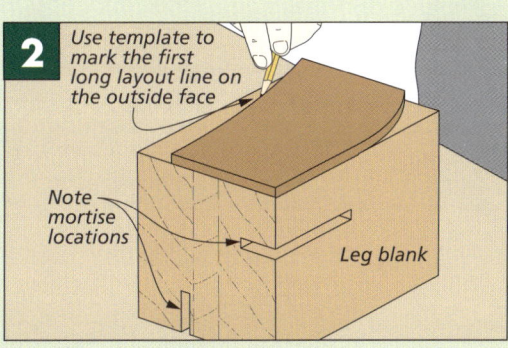

2 Outside Faces First. I wanted the profiles on the outside to look their best, so I laid out and cut these first. Mark one profile on the outside face.

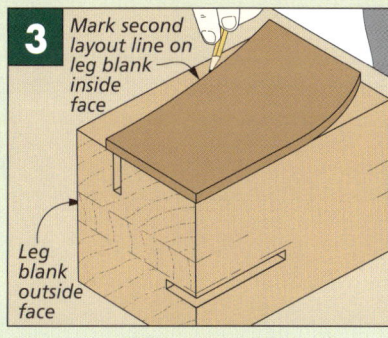

3 Second Profile. Then if you mark the second profile on the inside face, it won't be cut away during the first cut.

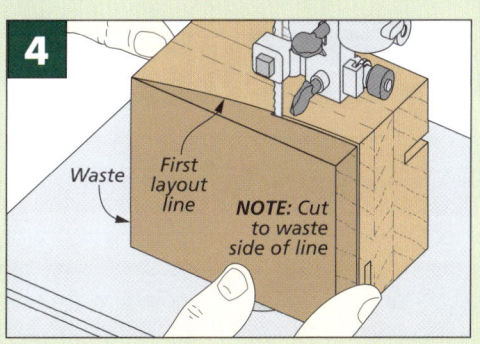

4 First Cut. Since the blank is still square, making the first cut is easy. To minimize cleanup, steer close to the outside of the layout line.

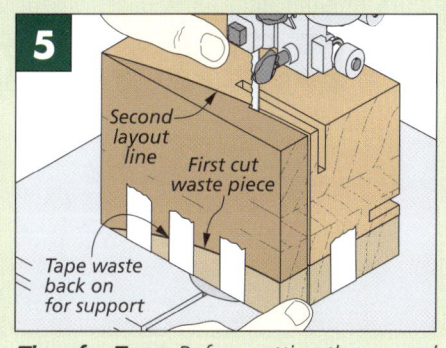

5 Time for Tape. Before cutting the second outside profile, you'll need to reattach the cut off piece with masking tape.

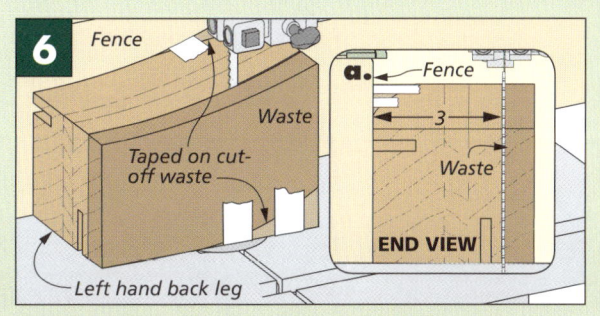

6 Trim Cut. The back legs have a profile cut on only one outside face. So after completing the three other cuts, you can trim 1" from the back face of each back leg.

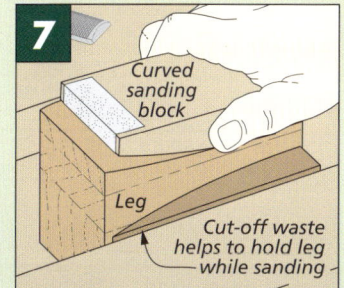

7 Sanding. Start sanding with 80-grit paper and work up to smooth the cut faces of the legs.

fitting the
DOORS, TOP, & SHELVES

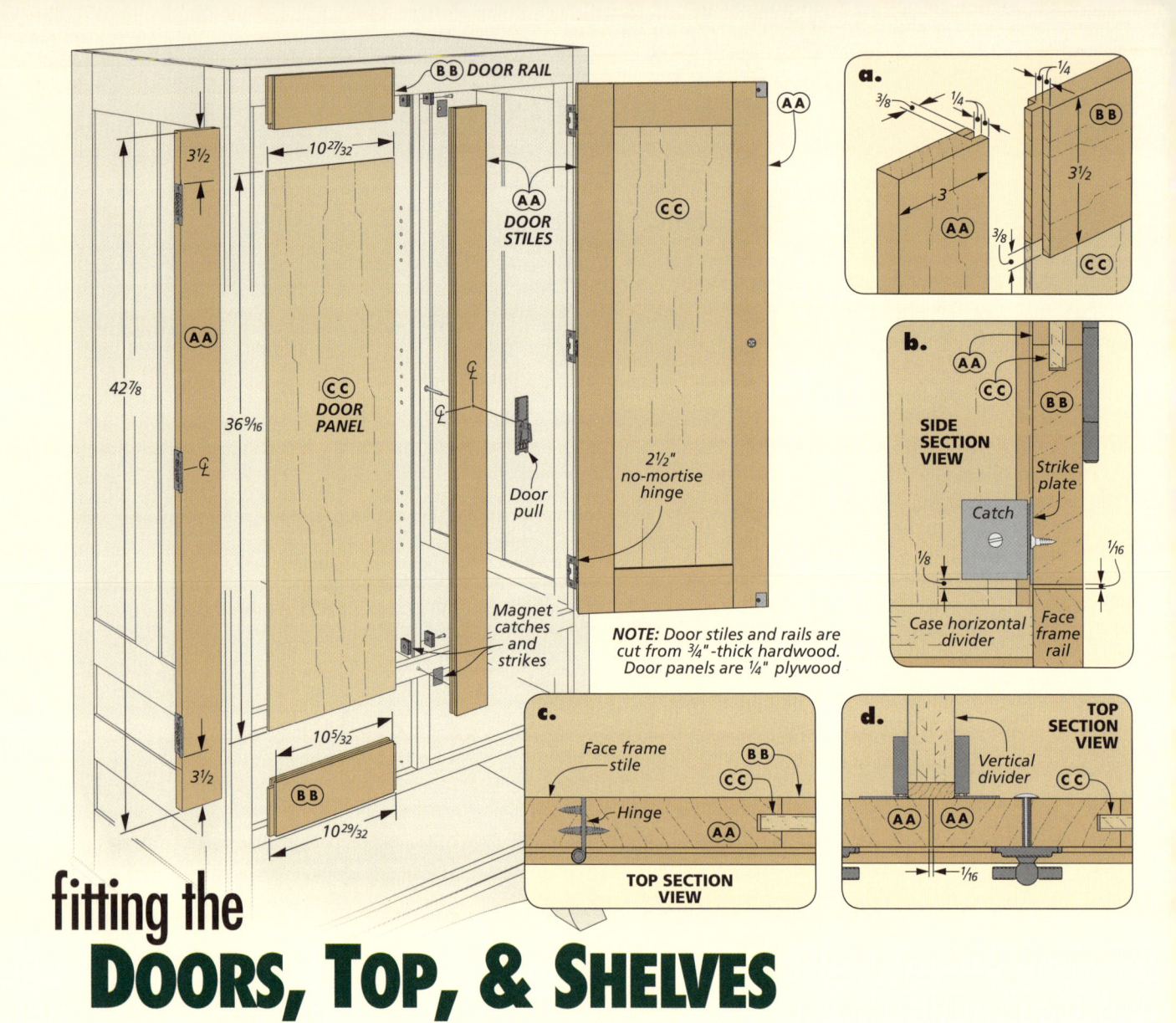

With the base in place, the armoire is really beginning to take shape. After the next few stages, starting with the addition of the doors, you'll see an even bigger change.

THE DOORS. Building the two frame and panel doors will seem pretty familiar. They're assembled with the same stub tenon and groove joints you used to assemble the side frames (detail 'a'). I won't go over this joinery again, but I will offer some advice you may find helpful.

I sized the doors to allow for a $1/16$" gap on all sides and between the doors. And since they're fairly large, you want to be pretty particular about stock selection when cutting your stiles and rails to size. Starting with straight, flat, and accurately dimensioned parts will give you a better shot at ending up with doors that fit well.

Likewise, once the joinery is completed and the panels cut to size, take extra care during the glueup. Be sure to double check for square. And to avoid ending up with a twisted door, make sure the assemblies lie perfectly flat while the glue dries.

How-To: Hinge Installation

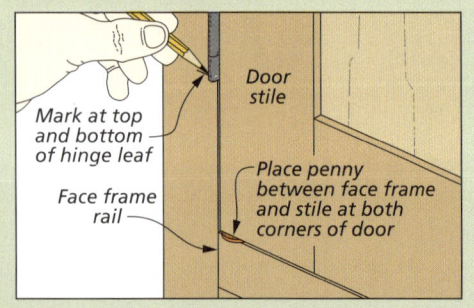

Mark. With the hinges attached to the doors and the doors in the openings, mark the hinge location on the face frame.

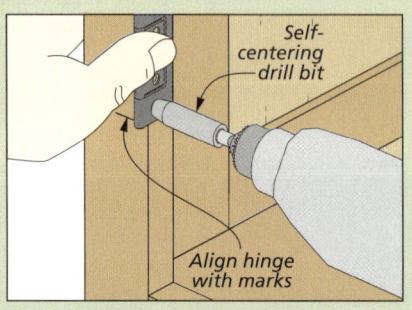

Pilot Holes. Next, I removed one of the hinges and used it as a template to drill pilot holes with a self-centering bit.

38   Woodsmith   No. 198

HINGES, CATCHES, & PULLS. Once the clamps come off, the doors can be installed on the case. No-mortise hinges make this a pretty quick task. A look at the box at the bottom of the opposite page will provide some help with this. Then after adding the pulls, I mounted a pair of magnetic catches for each door, as shown in the main drawing and details 'b' and 'd' on the opposite page.

THE CORNICE. Next, I finished up work on the top of the case. As you can see in detail 'a' at right, an overhanging top and a simple cove molding create a pleasing, traditional cornice effect.

The procedure for making the top is identical to that used for the base panel. I wrapped a plywood panel with a wider hardwood edging and then routed the same bullnose profile at the router table (How-To box below). When the panel is ready to go, you can screw it to the top of the case, flush at the back (detail 'd').

THE COVE. When it came time to add the cove, I took the easy route and used purchased molding. As you can see above, it's mitered around the front and sides. However, since I planned to paint the top panel and cove molding (and base) black, I decided to fit the molding now but wait until after it was painted to tack it in place.

SHELVES. Finishing up the interior of the upper compartment is your next focus. This starts by making a set of shelves to fill the left side. As you can see in the drawing above and detail 'c,' the three identical shelves consist of a plywood panel with thin hardwood edging glued to the front. This won't take you long.

CLOSET POLE. The right side of the upper compartment provides space to hang clothes. So here, you're going to install a closet pole near the top of the opening.

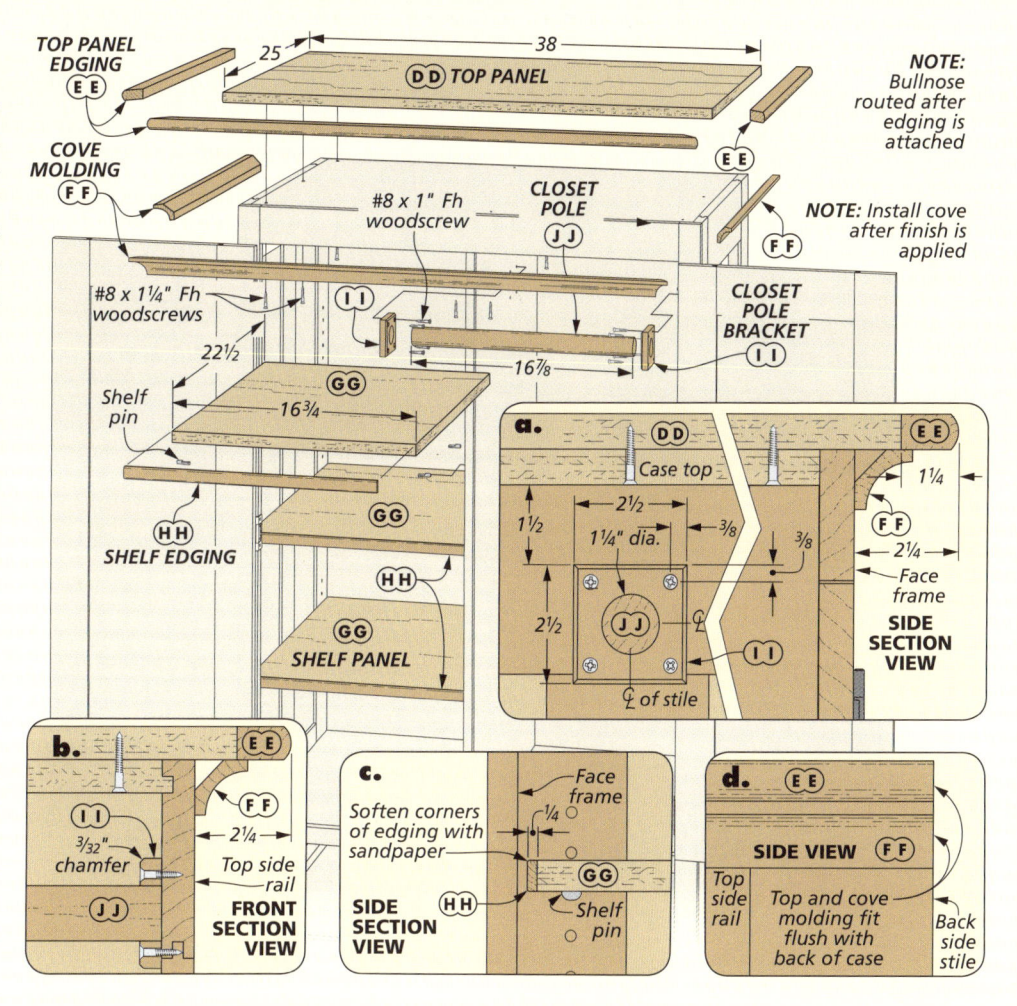

The pole (just a section of 1¼"-diameter dowel) is supported by shop-made brackets (detail 'a'). The How-To box below shows how I made them by drilling a hole through a square block and chamfering the edges.

After drilling countersunk screw holes, I positioned the brackets to drill pilot holes. Then I cut the pole to length and installed it and the brackets all at once.

How-To: Brackets & Bullnose

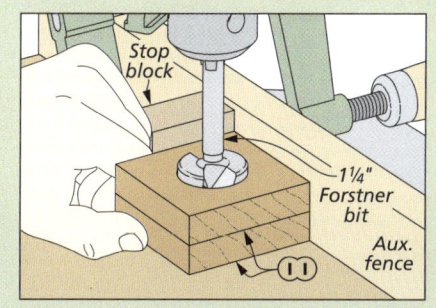

Holes First. I fastened the two bracket blocks together with double-sided tape and drilled both through holes at once.

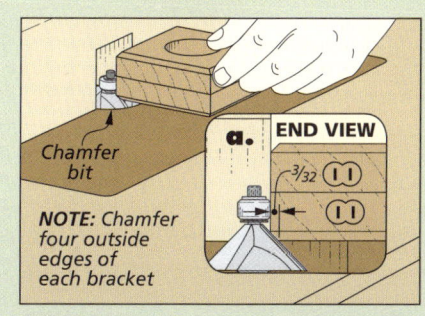

Chamfer Next. If you leave the blocks paired up while routing the chamfers, you'll have more to hold on to.

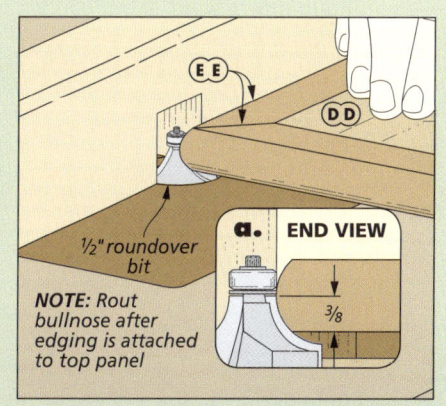

A Bullnose. With a roundover bit in the router table, make a pass from each face to produce a classic bullnose profile.

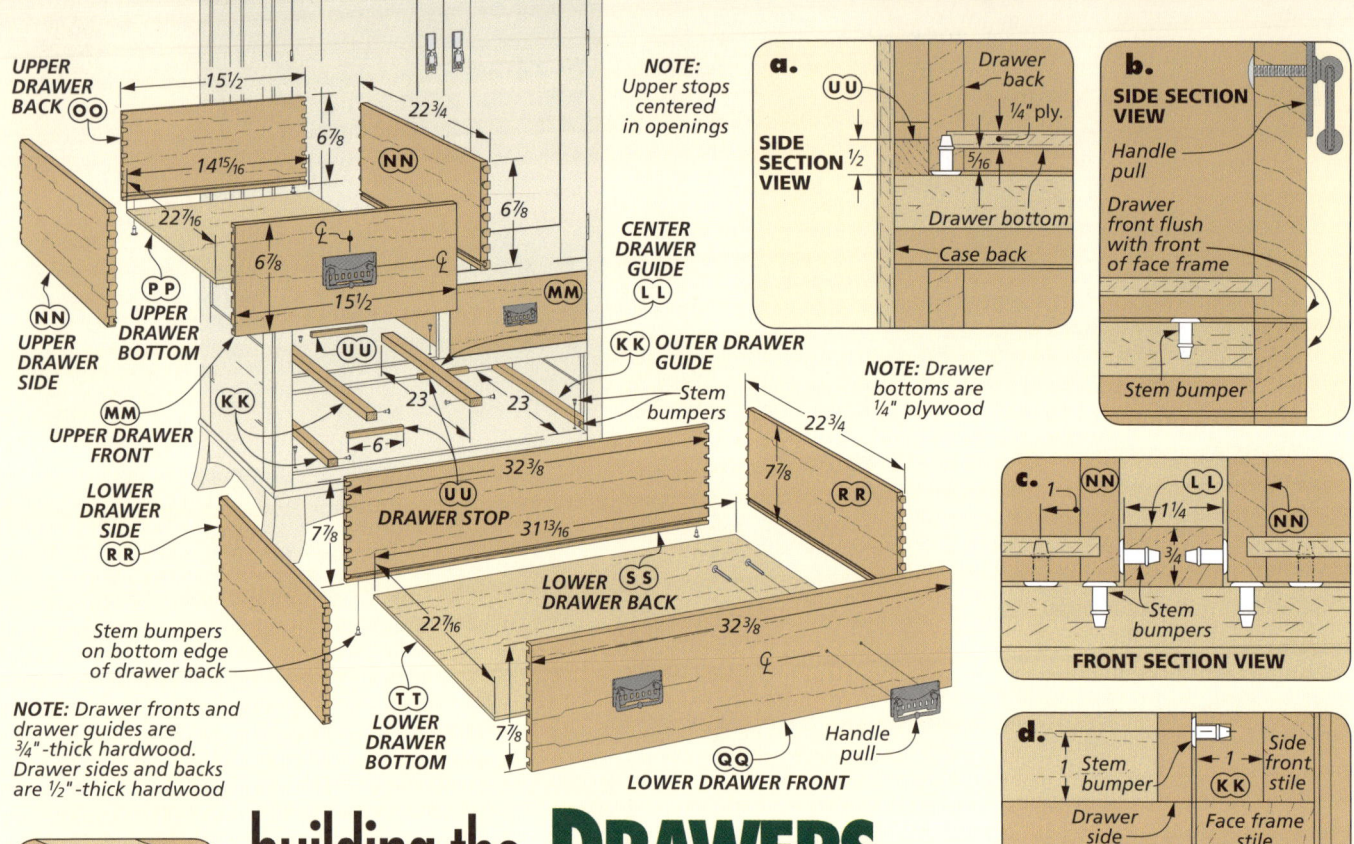

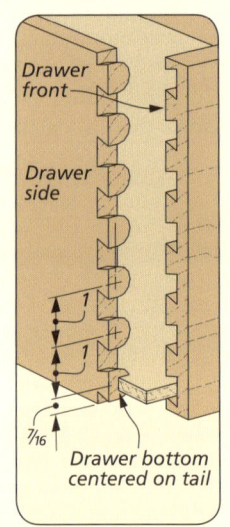

building the DRAWERS

You can see the light at the end of the tunnel. Building and installing the three drawers will bring the construction to an end.

GUIDES. Since the drawers don't use metal runners, the first thing I did was add a pair of guides to the openings (main drawing). A center guide positioned behind the dividing stile serves both upper drawers (detail 'c'). They should fit flush with the inside edges of the face frame stiles (detail 'd'). And don't forget to drill stem bumper holes before gluing them in place. (This is easier if you remove the case back.)

DOVETAILS. I took the traditional route and used half-blind dovetail joinery to build the drawers. But I also gave in to efficiency and used my dovetail jig to rout the joints. The only catch is that good results with a dovetail jig are not automatic. So if you need a refresher course on successfully building dovetailed drawers, check out the article on page 14.

THE OTHER DETAILS. Now let me go over the other important details. The drawer fronts are cut from ¾"-thick cherry, while the sides and backs are ½"-thick maple. And as usual, the bottoms are ¼" plywood. Like the doors, I sized the parts to create a ¹⁄₁₆" gap on all four sides. One more thing — the height of the drawers is based on cutting 7° dovetails with a 1" on-center spacing (margin drawing).

With the dovetail jig put back in its place, you can cut grooves for the bottoms (How-To box), cut the bottoms to size, and assemble the drawers. Before sliding the drawers into their openings for a test fit, I added pulls and stem bumpers to the bottom edges of the backs (detail 'c'). Finally, stops can be fit at the backs of the openings.

FINISH. While the armoire looks pretty impressive at this point, you don't get the full effect until the two-tone finish is applied. So it wasn't long before I started disassembling the pieces for paint and finish. But don't be in too big a hurry — the end result will certainly be worth the wait. **W**

How-To: Drawer Details

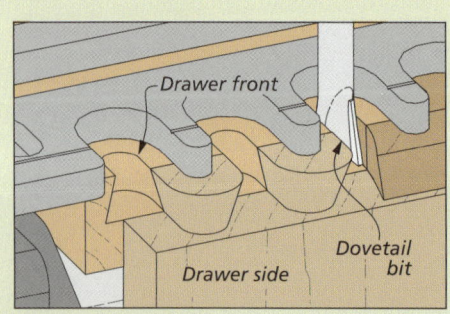

Attention to Detail. The keys to building drawers with machine-cut dovetails are simply careful setup and execution.

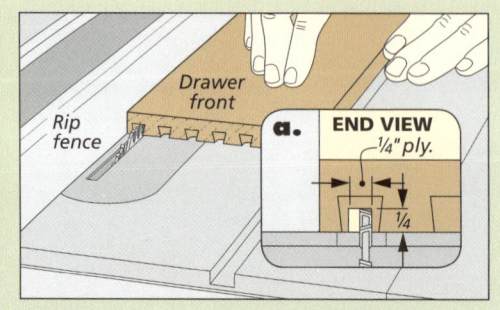

Grooves. To size the bottom grooves to the plywood, start with a single cut. Then tweak the rip fence setting until the fit is snug.

Materials & Supplies

A	Front Side Stiles (2)	3/4 x 2 3/4 - 64 1/2	FF	Cove Molding (1)	9/16 x 1 3/4 - 96 rgh.
B	Back Side Stiles (2)	3/4 x 3 1/2 - 64 1/2	GG	Shelf Panels (3)	3/4 ply. - 22 1/2 x 16 3/4
C	Bottom Side Rails (2)	3/4 x 5 - 17 3/4	HH	Shelf Edging (1)	3/4 x 1/4 - 60 rgh.
D	Middle Side Rails (4)	3/4 x 3 1/2 - 17 3/4	II	Closet Pole Brackets (2)	1/2 x 2 1/2 - 2 1/2
E	Top Side Rails (2)	3/4 x 4 1/2 - 17 3/4	JJ	Closet Pole (1)	1 1/4-dia. - 16 7/8
F	Center Side Stiles (2)	3/4 x 3 1/2 - 40 3/4	KK	Outer Drawer Guides (4)	3/4 x 1 - 23
G	Upper Side Panels (4)	1/4 ply. - 7 7/16 x 40 11/16	LL	Center Drawer Guide (1)	3/4 x 1 1/4 - 23
H	Lower Side Panels (4)	1/4 ply. - 17 11/16 x 4 11/16	MM	Upper Drawer Fronts (2)	3/4 x 6 7/8 - 15 1/2
I	Horizontal Dividers (4)	3/4 ply. - 23 x 35	NN	Upper Drawer Sides (4)	1/2 x 6 7/8 - 22 3/4
J	Vertical Divider (1)	3/4 ply. - 22 3/4 x 45 3/4	OO	Upper Drawer Backs (2)	1/2 x 6 7/8 - 15 1/2
K	Vertical Divider Edging (1)	3/4 x 1/4 - 45 3/4	PP	Upper Drawer Bottoms (2)	1/4 ply. - 22 7/16 x 14 15/16
L	Upper Drawer Kickers (3)	1/4 x 2 1/2 - 23	QQ	Lower Drawer Front (1)	3/4 x 7 7/8 - 32 3/8
M	Lower Drawer Kickers (2)	1/2 x 2 1/2 - 23	RR	Lower Drawer Sides (2)	1/2 x 7 7/8 - 22 3/4
N	Face Frame Stiles (2)	3/4 x 1 3/4 - 64 1/2	SS	Lower Drawer Back (1)	1/2 x 7 7/8 - 32 3/8
O	Face Frame Top Rail (1)	3/4 x 2 3/4 - 34	TT	Lower Drawer Bottom (1)	1/4 ply. - 22 7/16 x 31 13/16
P	Face Frame Lower Rails (3)	3/4 x 1 1/4 - 34	UU	Drawer Stops (4)	1/2 x 1/2 - 6
Q	Face Frame Dividing Stile (1)	3/4 x 1 1/4 - 8 1/2			
R	Case Back (1)	1/4 ply. - 35 1/2 x 64 1/2			
S	Side Base Fillers (2)	1/2 x 2 1/4 - 23	•	(3 pr.) 2 1/2" No-Mortise Hinges w/Screws	
T	Front/Back Base Fillers (2)	1/2 x 2 1/4 - 30	•	(2) Drop Pulls	
U	Front Legs (2)	4 x 4 - 6	•	(4) Handle Pulls	
V	Back Legs (2)	3 x 4 - 6	•	(12) 1/4" Shelf Pins	
W	Front/Back Base Rails (2)	3/4 x 3 - 32	•	(4) Low-Profile Magnetic Catches	
X	Side Base Rails (2)	3/4 x 3 - 20	•	(4) #6 x 5/8" Ph Woodscrews (for catches)	
Y	Base Panel (1)	3/4 ply. - 24 x 36	•	(18) Plastic Stem Bumpers	
Z	Base Panel Edging (1)	3/4 x 1/4 - 96 rgh.	•	(25) #4 x 3/4" Fh Woodscrews	
AA	Door Stiles (4)	3/4 x 3 - 42 7/8	•	(8) #8 x 1" Fh Woodscrews	
BB	Door Rails (4)	3/4 - 3 1/2 x 10 29/32	•	(10) #8 x 1 1/4" Fh Woodscrews	
CC	Door Panels (2)	1/4 ply. - 10 27/32 x 36 9/16	•	(6) #8 x 1 1/2" Fh Woodscrews	
DD	Top Panel (1)	3/4 ply. - 25 x 38	•	(10) #8 x 1 3/4" Fh Woodscrews	
EE	Top Panel Edging (1)	3/4 x 1 1/4 - 96 rgh.	•	(8) #8 x 2" Fh Woodscrews	

Cutting Diagram

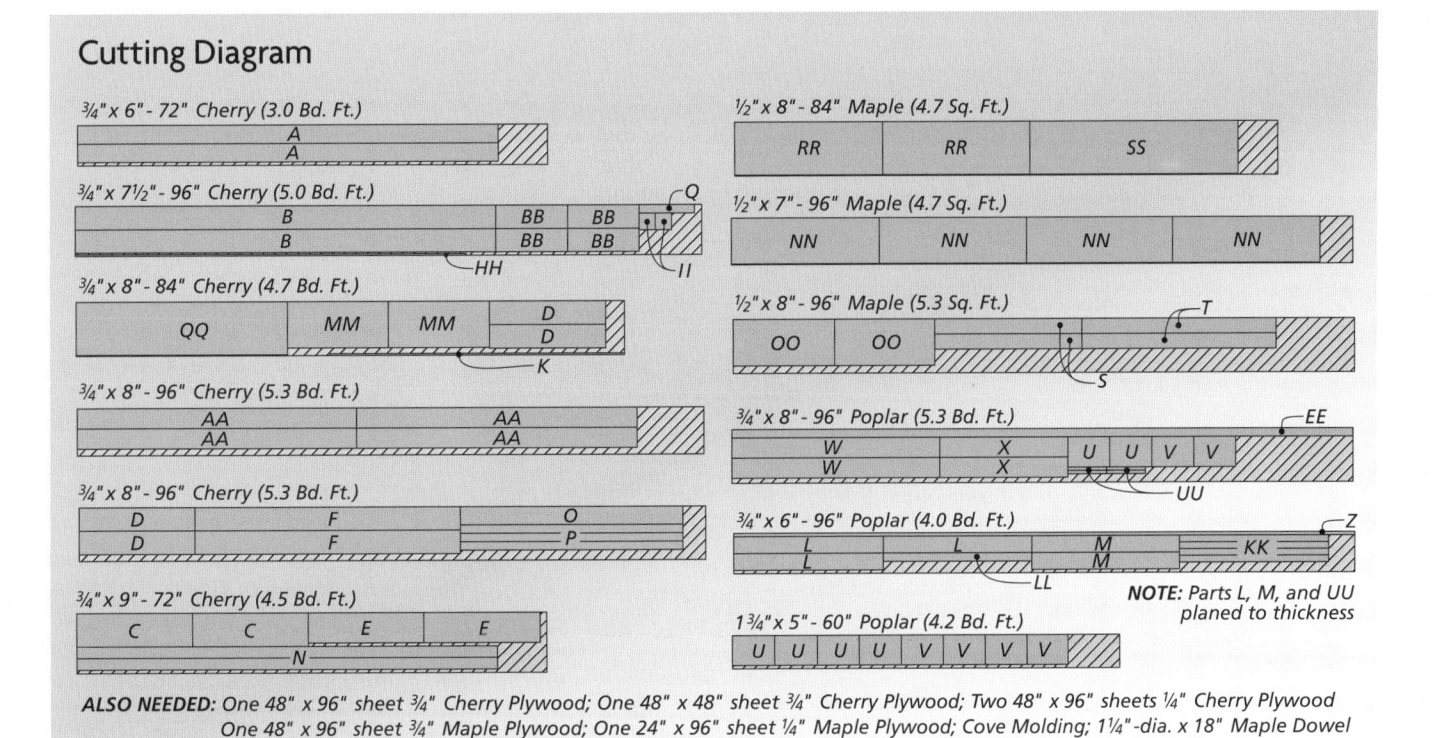

3/4" x 6" - 72" Cherry (3.0 Bd. Ft.)
3/4" x 7 1/2" - 96" Cherry (5.0 Bd. Ft.)
3/4" x 8" - 84" Cherry (4.7 Bd. Ft.)
3/4" x 8" - 96" Cherry (5.3 Bd. Ft.)
3/4" x 8" - 96" Cherry (5.3 Bd. Ft.)
3/4" x 9" - 72" Cherry (4.5 Bd. Ft.)

1/2" x 8" - 84" Maple (4.7 Sq. Ft.)
1/2" x 7" - 96" Maple (4.7 Sq. Ft.)
1/2" x 8" - 96" Maple (5.3 Sq. Ft.)
3/4" x 8" - 96" Poplar (5.3 Bd. Ft.)
3/4" x 6" - 96" Poplar (4.0 Bd. Ft.)
1 3/4" x 5" - 60" Poplar (4.2 Bd. Ft.)

NOTE: Parts L, M, and UU planed to thickness

ALSO NEEDED: One 48" x 96" sheet 3/4" Cherry Plywood; One 48" x 48" sheet 3/4" Cherry Plywood; Two 48" x 96" sheets 1/4" Cherry Plywood; One 48" x 96" sheet 3/4" Maple Plywood; One 24" x 96" sheet 1/4" Maple Plywood; Cove Molding; 1 1/4"-dia. x 18" Maple Dowel

techniques from our shop

tips for
Building From Plans

To get the best results from a woodworking plan, it pays to have a well-thought-out plan of your own for how to proceed.

Building a project from a set of plans can be a great experience. In theory, the plans have all the details worked out. But unless you work flawlessly and your stock doesn't expand or contract, there will likely be a few differences due to small deviations or other, unpredictable changes.

So beyond the standard advice like, "measure twice, cut once," here are a few more tips you can use while building a project from a plan. They're sure to help you successfully complete your projects and build your woodworking skills. They're also helpful even if the plan is your own.

GOOD HABITS
Success begins by developing good woodworking habits. Making these steps part of your routine can save both time and money.

ACCURATE TOOLS. The best results are only possible if the tools are accurate. That's why I try to always use the same tape measure for the entire project. Small differences between tapes can lead to errors. Another thing to check is whether your squares are actually square (far left photo). Few things can cause as many hard-to-fix problems as an out-of-square project part. Finally, using a steel rule to set up saw blades and router bits will improve accuracy. The near left photo shows you how.

Check your table saw, jointer, and other tools to make sure they're running true. With the fences squared and locked in, you can cut with confidence.

▲ To test the accuracy of a square, hold it against the edge of a board and draw a line. Then, flip it over and repeat. The lines should be parallel.

▲ A small metal rule is the perfect tool for setting the router table fence and bit height.

42   Woodsmith   No. 198

GETTING STARTED

After you've taken care of these common shop tasks, you're ready to dig into the plans. Here again, there's a logical flow for each phase of the project.

I like to photocopy the plan to keep it at hand while I work. I make notes on the copy and keep the original unmarked in case I need to revise it later.

READ EVERYTHING FIRST. Studying the entire plan before you begin can help you develop a strategy. This is a great time to make a few notes. Your goal here should be to understand the work flow and the details of each operation. Also, be sure to understand how to do each task. If you're going to change the plan, now is the time to work out the details of how changes impact the project.

INVENTORY. The next step is to make sure you have the tools (especially things like router bits) you need before you get started. This saves time.

HARDWARE. I also make sure to have the hardware on hand before I begin. Sometimes the hardware specified in the plan has been discontinued or sold out, making it necessary to find an alternative. Another thing to consider is that some specialty hardware might vary in size from the plan.

CUSTOMER SERVICE. Call or email the publisher of the plans before you begin. You can usually find the contact information at the beginning of the book or magazine. Asking about any updates and corrections up front can save you some grief down the road.

SELECT & PREPARE THE STOCK

At this point, you're ready to make a trip to the lumberyard. Once again, there are a few guidelines to help you out.

SELECTION. Look for straight stock (no twist) if possible. There's no need to fight twisted, bent, or crooked lumber. Also match the pieces for similar color.

EXTRA STOCK. Buying 20% extra stock for your projects may be the best advice I can give. This allows you to pick and choose the grain and color for every part and to work around any knots or other defects in the wood.

MILL THE STOCK. When you get the lumber home, let it sit for a few days to acclimate to your shop. Then joint and plane it to the dimensions required for the project. The photos at left show the correct sequence.

DON'T GET AHEAD OF YOURSELF. Even though the plan has dimensions for every part, it's not a good idea to cut all the parts to final size up front. A few small deviations in one section can mean that all the parts you make later will need to be adjusted.

That's why it pays to measure as you build (photo above). In most projects, the fit is more important than the exact measurement (within reason). For instance, if you cut your face frame pieces to $1\frac{7}{16}$" wide instead of $1\frac{1}{2}$", you can simply adjust the size of the drawer or door to accommodate the change.

SOME EXCEPTIONS. There are a few exceptions to this rule. For instance, don't be afraid to group similar operations to avoid extra blade changes or tool setups. A good example is ripping all the pieces to final width using the same fence setting for consistency.

▲ No matter what the plan says, measure the opening and build the door to fit.

▲ After finding the right lumber for your project, bring it home and let it acclimate for a few days. Then, prepare it for use by jointing one edge and one face, and plane it to final thickness.

BUILDING THE PROJECT

After you've prepared your tools and milled the stock, you're ready to get under way on sizing the parts for your project. This is where it pays to double check each operation and measurement.

MISTAKES. No matter how careful you are however, chances are a mistake or two will pop up from time to time. Sometimes you can cover your tracks, but sometimes only a new part will save the day.

Don't hesitate to make a new piece. This is why you milled extra stock. Many projects require lots of time and effort to build. You'll never regret going back and fixing a mistake now rather than living with it. (And even if you're the only one who notices, it can drive you crazy.) You can often use the "mistaken" piece to make a smaller part somewhere else.

PRACTICE. Of course, avoiding mistakes is still the best strategy. One way to do this when you try a new technique is to run through the entire procedure using an inexpensive test piece. For instance, if you've never shaped a cabriole leg, try your first one using a poplar blank (photo above). This way, if you make a mistake, you don't have to worry about replacing the expensive piece of cherry that matches the rest of your project perfectly.

Sometimes even inexpensive "two-by" lumber can be used, but avoid this for most joinery or carving operations. It simply machines too differently than hardwoods. That's why a handy supply of poplar is a great addition to the shop.

KNOW YOUR JIGS. Practice is great, but in woodworking, nothing beats a reliable jig. Jigs allow you to repeat operations by guiding a tool or the workpiece. They can be shop-made or commercially available, but they all take a certain degree of familiarity to work properly. It's up to you to understand how to build and use all of the jigs needed for a project.

There are many different ways and a variety of jigs to do any operation. The right way is the one you're comfortable with and gets consistent results. But I always keep some MDF in the shop in case I need to build a last-minute jig.

▲ Practicing a difficult cut, like a cabriole leg, on a piece of inexpensive wood can save you money. You can figure out all the tough parts of the cut without wasting expensive stock.

The same is true for $\frac{1}{4}$" hardboard. It makes great templates.

TRUST YOUR INSTINCT. Sometimes, in spite of all your preparation, you're confronted by a situation that just doesn't "feel right." When that happens, there's a good chance that your instinct is correct. If any technique or particular cut makes you feel a little shaky, take a break to think things through. The photos below show one example and an easy fix.

Read over the plan again, and double check any drawings and photos. Take a minute; then set up again. Make a dry run and look for the unsafe points in the operation. Make sure you have push blocks, featherboards, or any other safety gear necessary for the operation. Are you using the proper blade or bit? Are you getting tired and ready to stop for the day?

▲ If it doesn't feel right, it probably isn't. Accurately crosscutting a long workpiece can be difficult if you only have the stock miter gauge for support.

▲ A simple crosscut sled makes sizing workpieces a breeze. Providing support on both sides of the blade, the sled enables you to cut more accurately, exactly on your layout marks.

Sometimes, even a safe cut can be intimidating if you've never done it before. But no matter what, never ignore the little voice in your head. It's usually signaling a reliable warning.

HELP. If you get really stuck, don't be afraid to ask for help. Ask a fellow woodworker if you can't figure something out. Chances are there's a woodworking store or club in your area that can offer advice, too.

MORE NOTES. I like to use *Post-it* notes to help keep track of where I am in the process of building a project. This is especially helpful when you don't get into the shop every day. The notes serve as a reminder of what's next on the "to do" list. You can also use them to label project parts so you won't get them confused during the building process.

MAKING CHANGES. Another situation that may arise, is the need to modify a plan. It's not unusual to want to change the size or design of a piece of furniture to suit your particular surroundings.

If you modify a design, make sure you understand all the implications and adjustments you'll need. The law of unintended consequences can cause some frustrating mistakes unless you're very careful. It's often here where errors are made (for example, forgetting to make the shelves longer after you widened the case).

I find it helpful to make a detailed sketch of the proposed changes, including all dimensions. If you use design software, like *Google SketchUp*, then you have the perfect tool for planning and adjusting all the pieces. Once you've figured it out, make a note so you won't forget, like the one shown in the right photo.

FINISH: DECIDE EARLY. One of the most common places that woodworkers run into problems is the finishing process. It's true that finishing can be a challenge, but like every other aspect of building a project, it all comes down to good planning and execution. And there are a few things you can do to make it easier on yourself.

First, make your finishing decisions early on in the planning process. Consider what might be the best finish for a particular project. Do you need stain or just a clear finish? Do you need to fill the grain for a smooth finish? Would dye help bring out the figure? Will you apply it by hand or spray? These are just a few of the decisions you'll need to make before you finish the project.

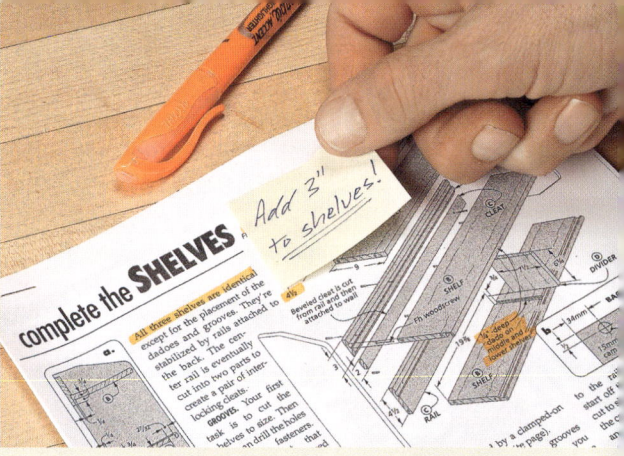

This is another opportunity to use some of that extra stock. Because it's a good color and grain match, you can experiment to create the perfect look.

Next, it's important to have plenty of supplies on hand before you begin. This includes brushes, solvents, and cleaning supplies.

Finally, you'll want to have a good area to finish. Somewhere away from the dust of the shop is best. But if that's not possible, then devote a few days to nothing but finishing. Keeping the dust out of the air will make a big difference in the end result. Often, finishing parts before assembly allows you do to a better job (box below).

Following these guidelines should give you a leg up on building from a plan. Now it's just a matter of finding a project you like and giving it a try. **W**

▲ When making changes to the project, it's a good idea to add notes to remind yourself of the details.

Time Saver: Prefinishing Project Parts

Finishing a project after it's assembled can be difficult and time-consuming. It's not too hard to brush or spray on the finish, but it can be a bear to keep the coat even and free of runs or drips. That's why I prefinish my project parts whenever possible.

Prefinishing allows you to apply a finish to the individual pieces before assembly. This means there are no nooks and crannies to reach into as you apply and wipe off stain or finish. You can easily see every surface of each piece and make sure you're getting the results you want.

The key is to keep finish off of or out of parts the will be glued together. The photo at right shows how painter's tape and foam insulation can be used to mask areas where you don't want finish.

You can also see an easy system for hanging the parts to dry. All you need to do is attach a hook in an inconspicuous place on each piece and then string a line to hang them on. I tie a knot about every 6" to provide a loop to hang the pieces. This prevents them from sliding around on the line. This system works great for many kinds of woodworking projects.

▲ A nylon line holds the prefinished workpieces while they dry. Masking prevents the finish from interfering with a good glue joint.

finishing room

the key to a
Winning Finish

With the right applicator, you can get a professional-looking finish. The trick is matching the tool to the finish.

Synthetic bristles are best for water-based finishes

Oil-based finishes go on smooth with natural (China) bristle brushes

We've all been there. Your project looks great. The joinery is perfect. You've scraped and sanded every square inch as smooth as glass. Now you're ready to apply the finish. But it's all too easy to goof up the finish and spoil a well-built project. Guaranteeing professional results relies largely on the type of applicator you use.

To help you choose the right brush, rag, or sponge for the job, I'll offer some basic guidelines. You should also take a look at the box at the bottom of the opposite page where you'll find some information on a different kind of finish applicator.

A brush is the most effective type of applicator for many finishes. They're made with either natural or synthetic bristles. Your choice depends on the type of finish you plan to use.

ALL NATURAL. China bristle brushes are made from natural animal hair (usually hog bristles). I use them to apply oil-based finishes like varnish, polyurethane, and alkyd paints. Hog bristles have natural split ends (splay) that leave fewer brush marks in the dried film than a synthetic brush. The splay also holds a lot of finish on the brush so you don't have to dip it so often.

Natural brushes aren't recommended for water-based finishes. They absorb water and the bristles get limp. For water-based finishes you'll want to use a synthetic bristle brush.

SYNTHETIC BRISTLES. When I apply a water-based finish like latex paint or clear polyacrylic, I always reach for a synthetic brush. Nylon is most common. The best of these brushes have artificially splayed ends so they too leave a smooth finish. Some nylon brushes are cut with a wedge at the bottom to further ensure a smooth finish.

DISPOSABLE BRUSHES. Of course, if you don't want to bother with cleanup, you can always use disposable applicators, either a brush or foam. Disposable brushes come with both natural and synthetic bristles. I use a throw-away brush for quick touchups or small parts that need finish before assembly, like wood drawer knobs. The downside is disposable brushes are thin and don't hold much finish, so it will take longer to apply finish to a large project.

FOAM BRUSHES. A disposable alternative to a bristle brush is a foam brush. They'll work for applying water-based finishes and some oil-based finishes. But they have a couple of drawbacks.

It's not a good idea to use them in shellac or lacquer, because the finish will dissolve the foam. Another problem I've encountered with sponge brushes is their tendency to generate bubbles in the finish. This happens especially when I scrape the excess finish on the edge of the can. The brush should just be dipped in the can and the excess allowed to run off before you move it to the surface of the project.

RAGS. To avoid bubbles and brush marks completely, you can use an absorbent rag to apply finish. While some finishes are made specifically to be wiped on, you can use a rag to wipe on any type of oil-based finish. I like to wipe on several coats with a rag. Each application will leave a thin, even layer that dries quickly.

For the best results use clean, cotton jersey or T-shirt rags. It's more absorbent than other fabric and it doesn't leave lint behind.

PAPER SHOP TOWELS. Another lint-free rag that's worth considering is a paper towel. You can use a shop towel made from paper to apply finish in the same way you'd use a cloth rag. Paper shop towels are made to hold together longer than kitchen paper towels and they're lint-free. They aren't as durable as cloth, so I just reach for a new one when they start to tear.

CLEANUP. It's always best to follow the manufacturer's recommendations for cleanup on specific finishes. But if you're unsure, mineral spirits will clean oil-based finishes and soap and water will remove water-based finishes from brushes. I thoroughly clean my good brushes and return them to the original package for drying and storage.

Occasionally I'll wash out a sponge brush or cloth rag a few times before I dispose of it. But before I throw it out, I always lay it flat to dry. This is especially important when you're using oil-based finishes which can ignite.

With these simple guidelines in mind, you'll have no worries when you're ready to put the finish on your next project. **W**

▲ For a bubble-free finish, avoid scraping excess finish on the rim of the can.

Disposable foam brushes are durable enough to wash and reuse

Lint-free paper towels work just as well as cloth

Cotton jersey rags work great for applying oil-based finishes

Worth a Look: Shur-Line Pad Applicators

You get the advantage of both a bristle brush and disposable foam in this pad applicator from *Shur-Line*. These applicators have a sponge base that holds the finish and short, synthetic bristles to lay down a smooth coat This means you'll get a smooth finish in less time with these applicators.

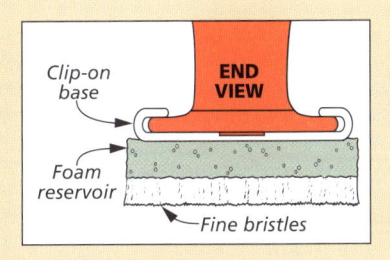

The trim pad (right photo) is small enough to apply finish in tight spaces. The pads are made in a variety of shapes to fit any surface, even corners (top photo).

Clip-on base
END VIEW
Foam reservoir
Fine bristles

Trim pad

Corner pad

details of craftsmanship

the secrets of a Face Frame

Adding a face frame to a cabinet serves more purposes than you might think. Here's what you need to know to build it right.

Almost all of the case projects we design and build incorporate a face frame. This is a fairly standard design feature and it seems like a pretty basic concept. The face frame simply creates the drawer and door openings.

But in reality, when working out the details and fine-tuning a design, you find that there's a lot more to it. Beyond providing a grid that frames and divides a cabinet, a face frame serves structural and functional, as well as aesthetic, purposes. So when designing, building, and installing a face frame, you need to consider several factors. Here I'll offer an overview of the points you need to think about.

THE BASICS. A face frame is simply a framework made up of stiles (vertical pieces) and rails (horizontal pieces) that's installed on the front of a case. The lower left drawing illustrates the most common configuration of the parts. The outer stiles usually run full height while the rails butt up to them. Any inner stiles that divide the frame butt up to the rails.

The face frame pieces are generally positioned over and attached to the sides and dividers of the case. But this isn't always the rule. Sometimes the rails or internal stiles are "free floating," attached only to other parts of the face frame. This allows you to subdivide the case into door and drawer openings without having to add internal case dividers.

STRENGTH. In most instances, a face frame serves several important structural purposes. When you build a case with an open front, you're creating a weak point in its structure. Installing a face frame can help overcome this. It adds an extra measure of rigidity against the racking forces that can distort the shape of the case. This is especially true with large case pieces such as the cherry armoire on page 30.

Face frame members also serve to reinforce the individual case

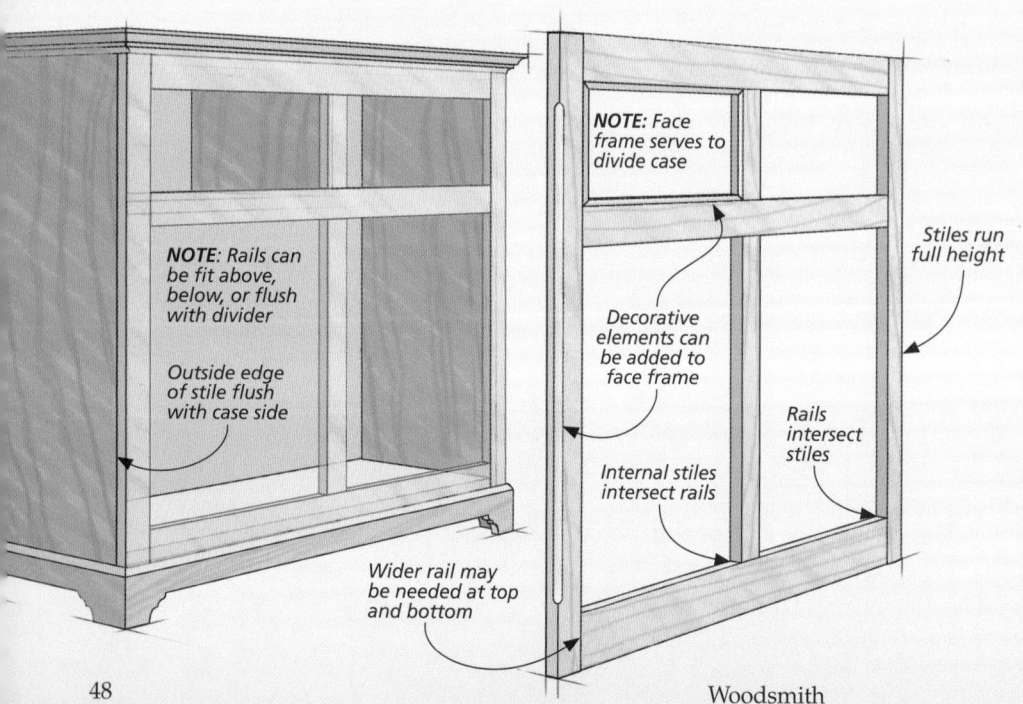

NOTE: Rails can be fit above, below, or flush with divider

Outside edge of stile flush with case side

NOTE: Face frame serves to divide case

Decorative elements can be added to face frame

Internal stiles intersect rails

Stiles run full height

Rails intersect stiles

Wider rail may be needed at top and bottom

parts — the sides and dividers. A stiff face frame stile glued to the long side of the cabinet will keep it from bowing and ensure that the openings stay consistent. Likewise, the face frame rails can help counteract any downward force exerted on the dividers.

FUNCTIONAL BENEFITS. A face frame also offers benefits in very simple ways. For one, it provides a place to mount hinges or catches for doors. And drawer guides or runners can also be mounted or hidden behind face frame parts.

Face frames can make building cases with plywood easier and more practical. The exposed edges of the plywood can simply be covered by the frame parts.

Sometimes structure, appearance, and function overlap in a face frame design. The lower right box shows a good example.

BETTER APPEARANCE. However, face frames are not installed for strictly utilitarian reasons. They can also be used to enhance the visual appeal of a cabinet.

Without a face frame, the front of a case can lack depth and "bulk." And doors and drawers may lack the spacial separation needed for the best aesthetic effect. A well-proportioned face frame can make the difference.

A face frame is also a place to add detail. A simple bead molding along inside edges can set off the doors or drawers. Or a chamfer routed on the edge of the outer stiles can act as a visual transition at the corners of the case.

PART SIZE. One of the first details to consider when building a face frame is how to size the parts. Most of our face frames are cut from ¾"-thick stock, however the width of the parts can vary quite a bit. This will affect both strength and appearance.

There is no firm standard for the width of face frame parts. The trick is to size the parts to meet your design considerations. My loose guideline would specify that stiles should be at least 1½" wide and rails 1¼".

Obviously, the width of the stiles and rails will affect both its structural and aesthetic effect.

Often, it's necessary to vary the width of the rails on a particular case. The upper and lower rails can be made wider to accommodate moldings that will be added to the case (lower drawing, opposite page). But, it's usually best to limit the width of the dividing rails in order preserve access to space within the case.

JOINERY. A face frame can be assembled in a number of different ways depending on what you need to achieve. Several of the joinery choices are shown in the drawings at right.

When maximum strength and racking resistance are the goals, the stiles and rails should be fastened together with a strong glue joint such as mortise and tenon or half-lap joinery.

A second tier of joinery options offers a tradeoff between strength and efficiency. Although not quite as rigid or long-lasting, pocket hole, dowel, or biscuit joints make up for this shortcoming by being fast and easy to create.

A small case may not need a rigid face frame. In this instance, I'll simply install the parts with butt joints alone. However, all the frame parts will need to be securely attached to case parts.

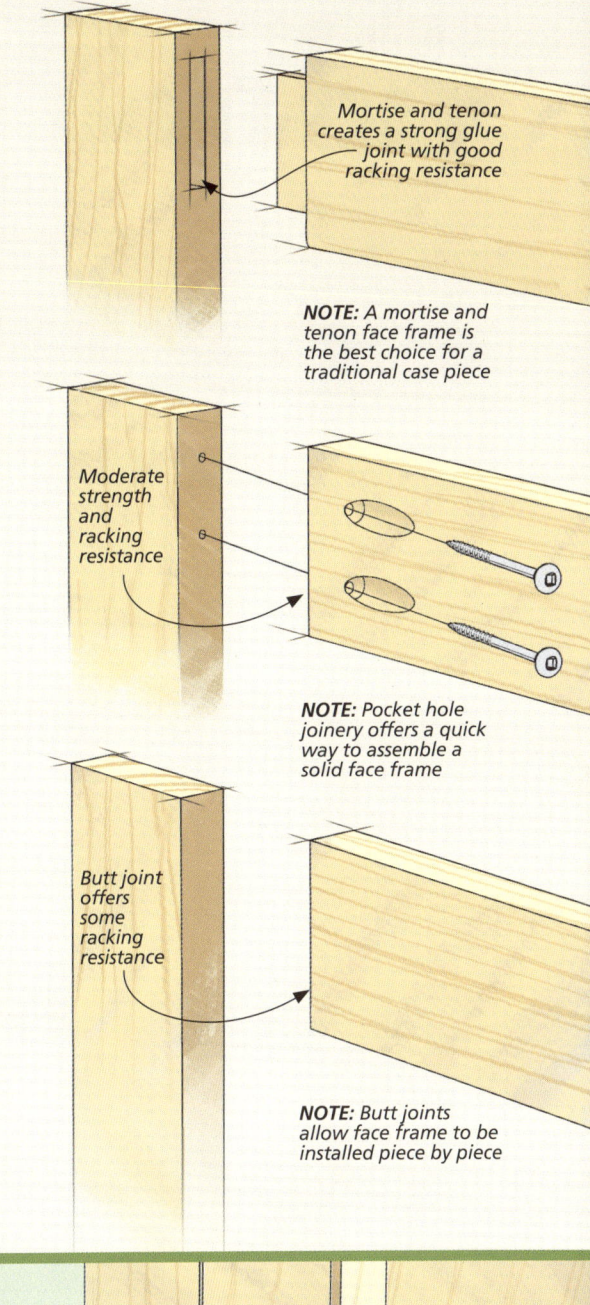

Mortise and tenon creates a strong glue joint with good racking resistance

NOTE: A mortise and tenon face frame is the best choice for a traditional case piece

Moderate strength and racking resistance

NOTE: Pocket hole joinery offers a quick way to assemble a solid face frame

Butt joint offers some racking resistance

NOTE: Butt joints allow face frame to be installed piece by piece

Triple Duty

Wide side stiles (4" to 5") are commonly found on some traditional styles of furniture such as Shaker or Early American. This design feature simplified the construction while serving multiple purposes.

The wide stiles can be attached to both the case sides and the dividers — stiffening the case while eliminating the need for face frame rails. And as you see at right, the bottom of the stile functions as a foot for the case. Finally, the wide stiles make a subtle and pleasing aesthetic statement.

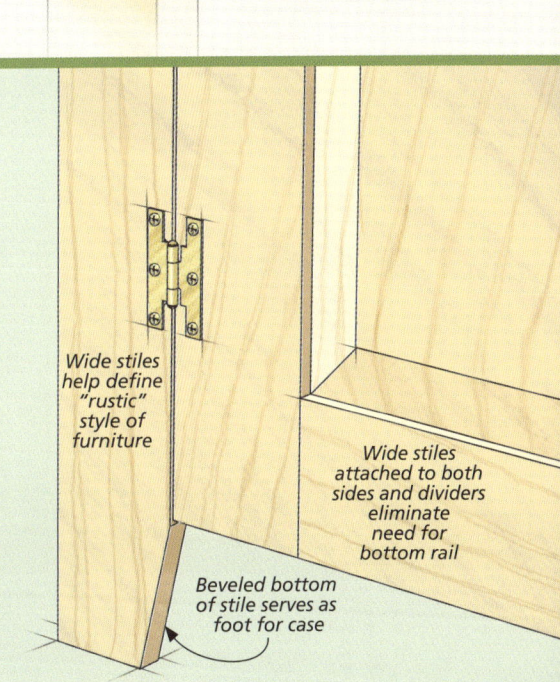

Wide stiles help define "rustic" style of furniture

Wide stiles attached to both sides and dividers eliminate need for bottom rail

Beveled bottom of stile serves as foot for case

installing a
FACE FRAME

Before you can start building your face frame, you have a couple more decisions to make. Both are in regard to its final installation on the case. First, you need to know how the individual parts of the frame will be positioned in relation to the case parts. And the final question is the method you're going to use to attach the frame to the case once it's constructed.

POSITIONING THE PARTS. When it comes to the alignment of the face frame pieces on the case, you have a few options that offer different advantages. The frame is almost always designed so that the outer stiles end up flush with the outside edge of the case sides. But rather than try to hit this fit dead-on, I like to make the stiles a bit extra-wide and then trim them flush after installation (drawing at right).

The drawings at left illustrate the different ways a rail can be fit to a divider. The most common is to place the rail flush with upper surface. This will give you the clean look you may want for a door opening or the flat surface you need for a drawer or shelf.

The only catch is that this requires very accurate assembly and installation of the face frame. This finicky work can be avoided by setting the rails either above or below the edge of the divider. A rail sitting proud can create a useful lip that helps contain items in the case. (The cherry armoire on page 30 features this handy trick.)

When doors are going to be added to an opening, you can place the rail about ¼" below the top surface so the edge of the divider can act as a ready-made stop. If you do this, the divider will have to be solid wood or plywood with an applied edging.

ATTACHING THE FRAME. The last step is to attach the frame to the case. You have two goals here — to align it on the case properly and then to hold it there solidly and permanently. The drawings across the bottom of the page show a few different examples.

One of the easiest ways to attach a face frame and my first choice is to simply glue it to the front of the case using lots of clamps. A tight glue joint between the face frame and either a solid wood or plywood case will form a very strong and permanent attachment. This basic method has proven itself over the years.

Mechanical fasteners such as nails or screws can take the place of the clamps during the glueup. The drawback to this assembly method is that you'll have to fill the nail holes or plug screw holes.

When you want to guarantee accurate alignment, you can add joinery between the face frame and case such as a rabbet or a tongue and groove joint. This will also add strength to the assembly, but on the downside, it adds another degree of difficulty to building and fitting the frame.

You can compromise and use biscuits or pocket screws to achieve the same end. But again, it's debatable whether this extra work is worth the payback.

I guess that there are two basic lessons here. The first is that adding a face frame to a case makes good sense. Second, there a lot of ways to get the job done.

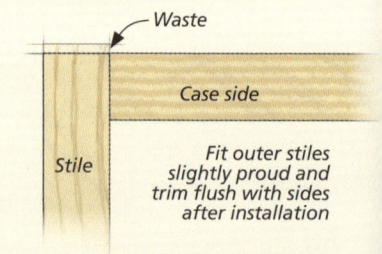

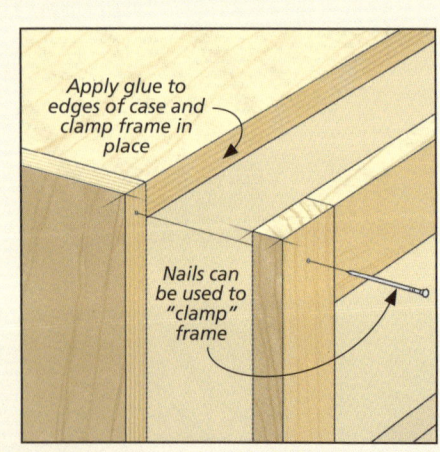

Glue alone is the easiest way to install a face frame. Nails can be added to "clamp" it in place while the glue dries.

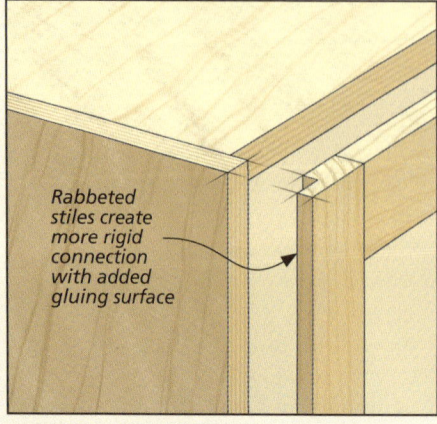

Rabbeting the stiles to fit the over the case sides helps with alignment and creates a stronger connection.

Biscuits can be fit between the face frame and case to help keep things aligned during assembly.

hardware & supplies
Sources

TABLE SAW BLADES
To get the most out of your table saw you need to use the right blades. The *Freud*, *Amana*, and *Forrest* blades shown in the article on page 8 can be found at several of the online retailers shown in the margin.

FIVE HAND TOOLS
Hand tools can be a great help to all your woodworking projects. For the article on page 10, I used a *Lie-Nielsen* 9$\frac{1}{2}$ block plane and medium shoulder plane. The card scrapers, *ryoba* saw, and chisels are available through *Rockler*, *Lee Valley* or other online woodworking sites.

FAST JOINT JIG
If you're looking for some unique joinery options, the *Fast Joint Precision Joinery System* might be just what you're looking for. Take a look at the article on page 12 to see what it can do. It's available through MLCS.

BENCH
I used a bowl & tray router bit to shape the bench seats. You can find this bit at *Woodcraft* (825834) or similar bits at several other online retailers.

An oil finish really brings out the beauty and depth of the wood (I used *General Finishes' Seal-a-Cell*). Then I sprayed two coats of lacquer.

CRAFTSMAN LAMP
Building the lamp on page 22 involves more than just woodworking. The good news is, the techniques for cutting and assembling stained glass aren't difficult. On top of that, there are a couple of online retailers listed in the margin that can supply everything you'll need to build the lamp.

For all the glass and associated supplies, you can go to *Glass Crafters*. The two types of glass are: *Kokomo Opal Orange* (K4-254D) and *Spectrum Light Orange, White Wispy* (S5-379.1). In addition to the glass, you'll need solid-core solder (C6040), flux (508), a roll of copper foil (4014), and black patina (530). Another supplier, *Warner Stained Glass* carries all the materials you need.

For the electrical parts, I turned to *MyLampParts.com*. The list of parts is pretty long, but not too expensive: 3-wire socket (SL19053LEV), porcelain base socket (SL19123P), 35W candelabra bulb (SL03224), $\frac{11}{16}$" brass neck (SL01117), brass coupling (SL00816), 3" brass nipple (SL04386), 4" brass nipple (SL04388), $\frac{1}{8}$" brass nut (SL02251), 18 ga. electrical cord (SL19715), harp (SL15207), and the harp bottoms (SL20640). The shade (ESK9554) came from *EveryLampShade.com*.

To finish the lamp, I used *Varathane Mission Oak* stain. Then, I wiped on a coat of *General Finishes' Seal-a-Cell* and followed up with two coats of sprayed lacquer.

ARMOIRE
The armoire featured on page 30 requires some hardware. I found the hinges (00H51.33), the door pulls (01A23.75), and the drawer pulls (01A23.73) all at *Lee Valley*. I ordered the shelf-support pins (22773), magnets (26534), and the drawer stem bumpers (28373) from *Rockler*.

The base and top of the armoire were painted black. The rest of the unit was stained with three parts *Zar* stain and one part *Woodkote Jel'd Stain* (both cherry). I sprayed the whole piece with lacquer. **W**

MAIL ORDER SOURCES

Project supplies may be ordered from the following companies:

Woodsmith Store
800-444-7527
Chisels, Finishing Supplies, Saws, Scrapers, Table Saw Blades

EveryLampShade.com
888-235-7978
Lamp Shade

Glass Crafters
800-422-4552
glasscrafters.biz
Stained Glass & Supplies

Lee Valley
800-871-8158
leevalley.com
Chisels, Door Pulls, Drawer Pulls, Hinges, Saws, Scrapers

Lie-Nielsen
800-327-2520
lie-nielsen.com
Block Plane, Shoulder Plane

MLCS
800-533-9298
mlcswoodworking.com
Fast Joint Precision Joinery System

MyLampParts.com
773-539-7910
Lamp Electrical Parts

Rockler
800-279-4441
rockler.com
Chisels, Finishing Supplies, Magnets, Saws, Scrapers, Shelf-support Pins, Stem Bumpers, Table Saw Blades

Warner Stained Glass
800-523-4242
warner-criv.com
Stained Glass & Supplies

Woodcraft
800-225-1153
woodcraft.com
Bowl & Tray Router Bit

Woodsmith SHOP DVDs

Get the 3-season set (seasons 4, 3, and 2) of the **Woodsmith Shop**! The set includes all the episodes plus CD-ROMs with bonus plans, articles, and videos. Order the the complete set and receive Season 1 free! Seasons 4, 3, or 2 are available individually ($29.95).

DVD Set: Seasons 4, 3, & 2..................... $79.85
Plus Season 1 Free!

Go to Woodsmith.com
or Call 1-800-444-7527 Today to Order Yours!

looking inside
Final Details

▲ *Entry Bench.* Whether you choose to build the painted version shown here or use a natural finish, the flowing lines of this bench are sure to please. You'll find complete plans on page 16.

▲ *Cherry Armoire.* With shelves, drawers, and an open compartment for hanging clothes, this armoire provides versatile storage options. Frame and panel construction and a two-tone finish give it an attractive appearance. Turn to page 30 for all the details you need to build it.

▲ *Craftsman-Style Lamp.* A three-position switch allows you to illuminate the upper and lower bulbs of this Craftsman-style lamp individually or together. But the stained glass panels in the base of the lamp are what really catch your eye. We'll walk you through the process for making them step by step. The experience begins on page 22.

Woodsmith

Volume 33 **INDEX**
Issues 193-198

A
air tools
    compressors, 197:10
    hand drill, 196:11
angle gauges, 193:12
angle jig, miter saw, 197:7
aprons
    Pack Rack Tool Apron, 197:13
armoire, cherry, 198:30

B
band saws
    circle-cutting jig, 194:28
    perfect cuts, 196:44
    table extension, 194:6
beading, 195:41
Beall Tool Company Tilt Box, 193:12
bed, modern four poster, 195:24
bench, classic entry, 198:16
Bench Cookie, 193:10
bench grippers, 193:10
benchtop, edge-grain, 193:40
bending, 197:32, 49
bent lamination, 197:48
bevel, tabletop edge, 193:49
bns, hardware, 195:6
blades, marking gauge, 194:17
blisters, oven mitts to prevent, 195:7
block planes, 198:11
Blumotion soft close hinges, 195:9
board jacks, 198:6
bookmark, parquetry, 197:16
box joints, 195:14, 17
boxes
    contoured, 194:22
    keepsake, 194:22
    mitered, 194:22
    parquetry, 197:16
brackets, towel holder, 193:37
brushes
    abrasive, 194:9
    for professional finish, 198:46
    Shur-Line pad applicators, 198:47
buffing wheel, orbital sander as, 198:7
bullnose edges, 193:36, 48
bun feet, 193:20

C
cabinet, cottage-style storage, 193:16
caddy, scraper, 198:5
camphor for rust-proofing, 193:7
cart, kitchen workstation, 193:32
CD/DVD storage cases for hardware
    storage, 195:6
chamfers, 193:30, 195:48
chisels, 198:11
circle-cutting jig, router table, 197:44
clamp blocks, notched, 196:33
clamps
    clothespins as, 195:7
    jig, 197:33
clothespin clamps, 195:7
coasters, 197:21
collets
    "third hand" for tightening, 194:7
compound miters, 195:7
construction goals, 196:48
cove edges, 193:49, 197:33
craft center, modular, 193:22

Craftsman-style projects
    folding table, 197:24
    stained glass lamp, 198:22
credenzas, 196:22
crosscutting
    sled stop, 193:5
    small parts, 197:15
cupboard, rustic step-back, 195:34
cutouts, large, 194:29

D
dadoes, centered, 198:34
design for successful construction, 196:48
DeWalt 611PK compact router, 194:10
disk sanders, 196:5
display cabinets
    curio, 196:34
    lights and lighting, 196:8
dock, drill, 197:5
doors
    glass, 194:18
    laminated, 197:41
    sliding, 194:18
dovetail jig, 198:12
dowel centers for aligning door magnets, 196:33
dowels
    chamfering, 193:30
    shop-made, 195:6, 197:45
drawers
    construction, 196:42
    dividers, 197:43
    flush fit, 198:7
    guides, 193:8, 9
    joinery, 193:27, 38, 198:14
    lining, 197:43
    temporary pulls, 196:6
Dremel abrasive brush, 194:9
drill press
    table extension, 196:6
    tool storage, 197:12
    vertical jig, 194:4
drilling jigs
    end, 194:28
    guide block, 196:33
    Wolfcraft drill guide, 195:12
drills
    cordless, 196:10, 197:5
    portable electric, 196:10, 197:5
drum sanders, 193:50
dyes, water-based, 197:46

E
edges
    beveled, 193:49
    bullnose, 193:36, 48
    cove, 193:49, 197:33
    drilling jig, 194:4
    ogee, 193:49
    routing, 193:14
    tabletop, 193:48
    thumbnail, 193:49
electricity
    lamp wiring, 198:27
entertainment center, contemporary, 194:30
Euro Handle-It, 194:12

F
face frames, 198:35, 48
Fast Joint Precision Joinery System, 198:12
fasteners, knock-down, 194:28
feet
    beveled, 195:33
    bun, 193:20
finger joints, 195:14, 17
finishes and finishing
    poplar, 196:46
    pre-finishing, 193:7, 198:45
    professional, 198:46
    supports for work, 194:7, 196:7, 198:5
    two-sided, 198:5
    water-based, 193:46
flap discs, 194:8
flapwheels, 194:8
Freud tools
    Box Joint Cutter, 195:15
    Premier Fusion saw blade, 198:9

G
glass
    panel doors, 193:26
    stained, 198:25
glue and gluing
    bottle tip improvement, 196:7
    box joints, 195:17
    disposable tray, 196:6
    laminations, 193:43
    pump bottle, 193:7
grips, oven mitts as, 195:7

H
hand tools, top five, 198:10
handles, interchangeable, 193:6
hardware
    see also hinges
    bins, 195:6
    installation templates, 194:12
    knock-down fasteners, 194:28
    nails, 195:33, 196:7
    screws, 197:7, 50
hinges
    Blumotion soft close, 195:9
    compact face frame, 195:8
    door, 195:8
    fall door, 195:8
    high-tech, 195:8
    hold-up, 195:9
    installing, 198:38
    lid-stay torsion, 195:8
    lipped door, 195:9
    no-mortise, 193:31, 195:9
    sewing machine, 197:31
hold-downs
    for large panels, 194:43

I
iGaging Angle Cube, 193:12
inlay boxes, 194:26
inserts, leveling, 195:5

J

jewelry chest, curved-door, 197:34
joinery
   box joints, 195:14, 17
   decorative, 198:12
   drawers, 193:27, 38, 198:14
   fast joint jig, 198:12
   key, 198:12
   locking rabbet, 193:38
   miter and spline, 194:29
   tongue and dado, 193:27
jointer jig for thin strips, 193:6

K

kerf, 197:49
key joinery, 198:12
kitchen projects
   coasters, 197:21
   towel holders, 193:37
   trays, 196:18, 197:23
   workcenter, 193:32

L

lamination
   chest doors, 197:41
   edge-grain top, 193:40
lamps, Craftsman-style, 198:22
lathe tool holder, 197:13
legs
   flared, 198:37
   notches, 193:31
lids
   lid-stay hinges, 195:8
   veneered, 194:26
lights, cabinet, 196:8
locking rabbet joinery, 193:38
lumber, mail-order, 195:44

M

magnetic tool holders, 197:13
marking gauges
   blade, 194:17
   shop-made, 194:14
Minifix knock-down fasteners, 194:28
mirrors
   remote control aid, 195:7
miter saws
   acute angle jigs, 197:7
   dust collection, 193:4
   leveling, 195:6
miters
   sanding, 198:4
   and spline joinery, 194:29
modular furniture, 193:22
mortises, square, 198:29

N

nail files as sanders, 198:6

O

orbital sanders as buffer, 198:7
outfeed devices
   band saw table extension, 194:6
   storage, 198:7
oven mitts for gripping, 195:7

P

Pack Rack Tool Apron, 197:13
paint and painting
   milk paint, 195:46, 47
painter's points, 193:5, 194:7
panels
   plywood, 194:42
   veneer, 196:14
parquetry, 197:16
Peachtree Woodworking Loc-Blocks, 193:10
pegboards, 195:5, 196:4
Perfect Mount for Drawers, 194:13
planers, benchtop vs. stationary, 195:50
plans, building from, 198:42
plywood
   panels, 194:42
   pre-finishing, 193:7
points, painter's, 193:5, 194:7
Porter-Cable 450PK compact router, 194:10
power cords, controlling, 197:6
protractors, digital, 193:13

R

remote control, shop vac, 196:7
ripping small parts, 197:14
Rockler tools
   Bench Cookie, 193:10
   JIG-IT, 194:12
   taper jig, 196:12
router tables
   benchtop, 195:10
   circle-cutting jig, 197:44
   edging on, 193:14
   fence bolt extensions, 196:5
   shop-made, 195:11
   tall fence, 194:5
routers and routing
   bit rack, 197:12
   circle jig, 197:44
   compact, 194:10
   Fast Joint Precision Joinery System, 198:12
   against a fence, 196:50
   frames, 196:50
   sculpted seat jig, 198:28
   stands, 197:4
   storage, 198:7
rust prevention
   camphor, 193:7
   talcum powder, 197:7
Ryoba saws, 198:11

S

sanders and sanding
   adjustable jig, 198:4
   belt cleaning, 194:7
   blocks, 195:7, 197:7
   disk sanders, 196:5
   drum sanders, 193:50
   nail files, 198:6
   profiles and contours, 194:8
   small stock, 193:7
sanding mops, 194:8
sandpaper
   reinforcing, 196:7
   sanding strips, 193:7
saw blades
   combination, 198:9
   crosscut, 198:9
   rip, 193:42
   table saw, 198:8
   thin kerf, 198:9
saws *see names of specific types of saws*
scrapers
   caddy, 198:5
   card, 198:10
   mini, 198:7
scratch stock, 194:48
scroll saw as sander, 193:7
seats, sculpted, 198:20, 28
serving tray, curved-handle, 196:18
sharpeners and sharpening
   cleaning stones, 194:7
   comparing grit, 193:45
   diamond plates, 193:44
   jig for skewed blades, 195:4
   Work Sharp, 197:6
shelf pin templates, 193:30, 198:29
shelf supports, sawtooth, 195:39
shop vacuum remote control, 196:7
shoulder planes, 194:44, 198:11
Shur-Line pad applicators, 198:47
sleds
   crosscut, 193:5
   tapering jig, 195:32
spray equipment, HVLP turbine system, 193:46
spray finishes, water-based, 193:46
squares and squaring, 194:7, 197:14
switches, remote control, 195:7

T

table saws
   auxiliary fence, 194:50
   rip fence, 194:50
   tapering jigs, 195:32, 196:12, 197:33
   wedges for compound miter jig, 195:7
   working with small parts, 197:14
tables
   Craftsman-style, 197:24
   folding, 197:24
templates
   hardware installation, 194:12
   shelf pin, 193:30, 198:29
   window, 196:32
tenons, wedged, 198:29
thumbnail edge, 193:49
tongue and dado drawer joinery, 193:27
tool stands
   pegboard-mounted, 196:4
   router, 197:4
tool storage
   magnetic, 197:13
   Pack Rack Tool Apron, 197:13
   router bit rack, 197:12
towel holder, 193:37
trays
   coaster, 197:23
   serving tray, curved-handle, 196:18

V

veneer
   box lid, 194:26
   large panel, 196:14

W

wall cabinet, curio
   curio, 196:34
wall shelf with sliding door, 194:18
wardrobe, cherry, 198:30
waxes, paste, 194:46
window opening, template for, 196:32
wine rack, 195:18
Wixey tools
   digital angle gauges, 193:12
   digital protractor, 193:13
Wolfcraft drill guide, 195:12
wood
   mahogany, 197:8
   poplar, 196:46
   rosewood, 194:14
Woodworker's Supply Wolf Bench Paws, 193:10